JAINA EPISTEMOLOGY
in Historical and Comparative Perspective

JAINA EPISTEMOLOGY

in Historical and Comparative Perspective

Critical Edition and English Translation
of Logical-Epistemological Treatises:
Nyāyâvatāra, *Nyāyâvatāra-vivṛti* and *Nyāyâvatāra-ṭippana*
with Introduction and Notes

PIOTR BALCEROWICZ

— Volume One —

MOTILAL BANARSIDASS PUBLISHERS
PRIVATE LIMITED • DELHI

Second Revised Edition: Delhi, 2008
First published by Franz Steiner Verlag, Stuttgart, 2001
in the series of Alt- und Neu- Indische Studien, Nos. 53, 1 & 53, 2

ISBN: 978-81-208-3346-3 (Vol. I)
ISBN: 978-81-208-3347-0 (Vol. II)
ISBN: 978-81-208-3345-6 (Set)

MOTILAL BANARSIDASS
41 U.A. Bungalow Road, Jawahar Nagar, Delhi 110 007
8 Mahalaxmi Chamber, 22 Bhulabhai Desai Road, Mumbai 400 026
203 Royapettah High Road, Mylapore, Chennai 600 004
236, 9th Main III Block, Jayanagar, Bangalore 560 011
Sanas Plaza, 1302 Baji Rao Road, Pune 411 002
8 Camac Street, Kolkata 700 017
Ashok Rajpath, Patna 800 004
Chowk, Varanasi 221 001

On the Dust Jacket:
Fragment of Page 30 of Manuscript B of the Nyāyâvatara-Vivṛti

Cover Design, Typeset by Piotr Balcerowicz

All diacritical fonts
as well as the Devanāgarī font,
including the [illegible] Devanāgarī
Sanskrit Keyboard Program,
used in the edition,
have been designed and developed
by Piotr Balcerowicz

PRINTED IN INDIA
By Jainendra Prakash Jain at Shri Jainendra Press,
A-45 Naraina, Phase-I, New Delhi 110 028
and Published by Narendra Prakash Jain for
Motilal Banarsidass Publishers Private Limited,
Bungalow Road, Delhi 110 007

Granted that I correctly understand what you mean,
if you assiduously pursue a subject of your studies,
you become more and more specialised,
and the subject gets narrower and narrower.
Then you know more and more
about less and less.
In the end,
you know everything
about nothing...

Malcom Egan
/Pacific, 9th March, 1995/

TABLE OF CONTENTS

— VOLUME ONE —

PREFACE TO THE INDIAN EDITION i

ACKNOWLEDGEMENTS iii

A NOTE TO THE EDITION AND ENGLISH TRANSLATION iv

INTRODUCTION . . . . . v–iv

Editions and translations of the *Nyāyâvatāra* and the commentaries xlii

Manuscripts and editions of the *Nyāyâvatāra* and of the commentaries used in the present edition xliii

ENGLISH TRANSLATION OF THE *NYĀYÂVATĀRA-VIVṚTI* 1

Nyāyâvatāra-vivṛti 0 (Introduction) 1
Nyāyâvatāra-vivṛti 1 9
Nyāyâvatāra-vivṛti 2 26
Nyāyâvatāra-vivṛti 3 29
Nyāyâvatāra-vivṛti 4 31
Nyāyâvatāra-vivṛti 5 38
Nyāyâvatāra-vivṛti 6 43
Nyāyâvatāra-vivṛti 7 47
Nyāyâvatāra-vivṛti 8 48
Nyāyâvatāra-vivṛti 9 50
Nyāyâvatāra-vivṛti 10 52
Nyāyâvatāra-vivṛti 11 53
Nyāyâvatāra-vivṛti 12 55
Nyāyâvatāra-vivṛti 13 55
Nyāyâvatāra-vivṛti 14 31
Nyāyâvatāra-vivṛti 15 59
Nyāyâvatāra-vivṛti 16 60
Nyāyâvatāra-vivṛti 17 61
Nyāyâvatāra-vivṛti 18 62
Nyāyâvatāra-vivṛti 19 64
Nyāyâvatāra-vivṛti 20 64
Nyāyâvatāra-vivṛti 21 65
Nyāyâvatāra-vivṛti 22 66
Nyāyâvatāra-vivṛti 23 67
Nyāyâvatāra-vivṛti 24 71
Nyāyâvatāra-vivṛti 25 74
Nyāyâvatāra-vivṛti 26 78
Nyāyâvatāra-vivṛti 27 79
Nyāyâvatāra-vivṛti 28 83
Nyāyâvatāra-vivṛti 29 84
Nyāyâvatāra-vivṛti 30 125
Nyāyâvatāra-vivṛti 31 126
Nyāyâvatāra-vivṛti 32 136

FOOTNOTES 138–317

TABLE OF CONTENTS

— VOLUME TWO —

SANSKRIT TEXT OF THE *NYĀYÂVATĀRA-VIVṚTI* 323–490

- *Nyāyâvatāra-vivṛti* 0 (Introduction) 323
- *Nyāyâvatāra-vivṛti* 1 333
- *Nyāyâvatāra-vivṛti* 2 353
- *Nyāyâvatāra-vivṛti* 3 356
- *Nyāyâvatāra-vivṛti* 4 358
- *Nyāyâvatāra-vivṛti* 5 367
- *Nyāyâvatāra-vivṛti* 6 373
- *Nyāyâvatāra-vivṛti* 7 379
- *Nyāyâvatāra-vivṛti* 8 380
- *Nyāyâvatāra-vivṛti* 9 382
- *Nyāyâvatāra-vivṛti* 10 384
- *Nyāyâvatāra-vivṛti* 11 386
- *Nyāyâvatāra-vivṛti* 12 388
- *Nyāyâvatāra-vivṛti* 13 389
- *Nyāyâvatāra-vivṛti* 14 358
- *Nyāyâvatāra-vivṛti* 15 394
- *Nyāyâvatāra-vivṛti* 16 395
- *Nyāyâvatāra-vivṛti* 17 396
- *Nyāyâvatāra-vivṛti* 18 398
- *Nyāyâvatāra-vivṛti* 19 400
- *Nyāyâvatāra-vivṛti* 20 401
- *Nyāyâvatāra-vivṛti* 21 403
- *Nyāyâvatāra-vivṛti* 22 404
- *Nyāyâvatāra-vivṛti* 23 405
- *Nyāyâvatāra-vivṛti* 24 409
- *Nyāyâvatāra-vivṛti* 25 413
- *Nyāyâvatāra-vivṛti* 26 418
- *Nyāyâvatāra-vivṛti* 27 420
- *Nyāyâvatāra-vivṛti* 28 424
- *Nyāyâvatāra-vivṛti* 29 425
- *Nyāyâvatāra-vivṛti* 30 475
- *Nyāyâvatāra-vivṛti* 31 477
- *Nyāyâvatāra-vivṛti* 32 489

INDEX OF SELECTED VOCABULARY TO THE SANSKRIT TEXT 491

INDEX OF QUOTATIONS FOUND IN THE *NYĀYÂVATĀRA-VIVṚTI* 511

INDEX OF MAXIMS (*NYĀYAS*) AND SAYINGS 513

INDEX OF SELECTED VOCABULARY TO THE INTRODUCTION AND ENGLISH TRANSLATION 514

INDEX LOCORUM 520

BIBLIOGRAPHY 527–548

- 1. Primary Sources 527
- 2. Secondary Sources 537

ABBREVIATIONS 546

PREFACE TO THE INDIAN EDITION

When Mr Narendra Prakash Jain of Motilal Banarsidass approached me with the suggestion to publish the book (which initially appeared in Franz Steiner Verlag, Stuttgart 2001 in the series of *Alt- und Neu-Indische Studien*, Nos. 53,1 & 53,2) in India, I greeted the idea with pleasure. I would like to express my thanks to the publishers for their efforts to make the book available also to the Indian reader.

In the present revised edition I have tried to remove some defects and misprints of the previous edition, although I am aware that probably there still remains regrettably certain number of misprints to be corrected. I have added two indices: (1) *Index of selected vocabulary and proper names to the Introduction and English Translation* and (2) *Index locorum*, which I hope should help the reader to orient in the contents of the book.

During the time which has elapsed since the first edition appeared, a few other papers have been written which throw, I hope, more light on the dating and authorship of *Nyāyâvatāra* and the relation of *Nyāyâvatāra* (NA) and the *Saṁmati-tarka-prakaraṇa* (STP), both being traditionally attributed to Siddhasena Divākara:

1. 'On the Date of the *Nyāyâvatāra*', in: Piotr Balcerowicz and Marek Mejor (eds.): *On the Understanding of Other Cultures. Proceedings of the International Conference on Sanskrit and Related Studies to Commemorate the Centenary of the Birth of Stanislaw Schayer (1899–1941). Warsaw University, Poland, October 7–10, 1999. Studia Indologiczne* [Warsaw] 7 (2000) 17–57. A revised version of the paper was reprinted in: *Essays in Indian Philosophy, Religion and Culture*, Ed. by Piotr Balcerowicz and Marek Mejor. Motilal Banarsidass, Delhi 2002.
2. 'Two Siddhasenas and the Authorship of the *Nyāyâvatāra* and the *Saṁmati-tarka-prakaraṇa*'. *Journal of Indian Philosophy* 29/3 (2001) 351–578.
3. 'On the Relationship of the *Nyāyâvatāra* and the *Saṁmati-tarka-prakaraṇa*', *Indologica Taurinensia* 29 (2005) 29–79? [in print].

In light of all the evidence presented in the above-mentioned papers I assume that the author of the *Nyāyâvatāra* is Siddhasena Mahāmati, who lived circa 710/720–770/780, and who is different from Siddhasena Divākara, the author of the *Saṁmati-tarka-prakaraṇa*, a work composed before Diṅnāga (c. 480–540).

In his review of the first edition of the present book, Sin FUJINAGA (*Saṁbhāṣā – Nagoya Studies in Indian Culture and Buddhism*, 23 (2003) 163–165) refers (p. 164) to my thesis that 'Siddhasena marks an important, widely known shift in Jaina epistemology, to interpret the directness of *pratyakṣa* in terms of sensory organs (*akṣa* = *indriya*)' (*vide infra*, p. xiv), and suggests that Akalaṅka may have been prior to Siddhasena on the following grounds: 'Akalaṅka refers to *akṣajñāna* in his *Pramāṇasaṁgraha* verse 4 and paraphrases the word with *cakṣurādijñāna* in the auto commentary on the verse. Cannot we say that Akalaṅka interpreted *akṣa* in *pratyakṣa* as *indriya* before Siddhasena?' However attractive the theory could be, it seems to lack unshakeable basis. As I have recently attempted to demonstrate in my paper: '*Pramāṇa*s and language. A Dispute between Diṅnāga, Dharmakīrti and Akalaṅka' (*JIPh* (2005) in print) not only did Akalaṅka know the work of Siddhasena Mahāmati, but he also tried to improve on some of Siddhasena's points, e.g. the character of perception, by explicitly applying in the *Laghīyas-traya* (LT 3–4) a new notion of clarity (*vaiśadya*), or lucidity (*spaṣṭatva*), which was introduced by Akalaṅka elsewhere, e.g. in the *Nyāya-viniścaya* (NVi 3.83) or the *Pramāṇa-saṅgraha* (PSa 1.2). However, it is indeed true that the careers of both Siddhasena Mahāmati and Akalaṅka Bhaṭṭa overlapped, although Siddhasena was probably slightly senior to Akalaṅka (c. 720–780), as it ensues from another paper mentioned above: 'On the Relationship of the *Nyāyâvatāra* and the *Saṁmati-tarka-prakaraṇa*', in which I offer relative chronology of some relevant thinkers as follows: Siddhasena Divākara (STP): 450–500 → Diṅnāga: 480–540 → Dharmakīrti: 600–660 → Pātrasvāmin: c. 660–720 → Uṁveka Bhaṭṭa: c. 700–750 → Siddhasena Mahāmati (NA): c. 720–780 (or: 710–770) → Prajñākaragupta: c. 800 → Haribhadra-sūri: c. 800. Besides, if one assumes, as Sin FUJINAGA proposes, that Siddhasena was posterior to Akalaṅka, it would be very difficult to account for the Siddhasena's verse (NA 4) which is quoted by Haribhadra-sūri, after all a junior contemporary of Akalaṅka, in his ṢDSa 56 (vide infra, xxxiii).

Likewise, while referring to my argument that '[5] The *pāda* C (*tad-vyāmoha-nivṛttiḥ*) of NA 3 ... recalls Dharmakīrti's statement found in $PV_{1,3}$ 1.7' (*vide infra*, p. xviii), Sin FUJINAGA (p. 165) draws our attention to 'Akalaṅka's statement in auto commentary on *Pramāṇasaṁgraha* 10ab: *vyāmohavicchedena pramāṇāntaravat*'. As a matter of fact, there is no doubt that both Siddhasena and Akalaṅka were directly influenced by Dharmakīrti's verse of $PV_{1,3}$ 1.7. Akalaṅka's indebtedness to Dharmakīrti is a well-known fact, see e.g. SHAH 1967; comp. also my paper: '*Pramāṇa*s and language. A Dispute between Diṅnāga, Dharmakīrti and Akalaṅka' (*JIPh* (2005) in print).

On the other hand, I see no reason to disagree with Sin FUJINAGA's suggestion that what is probably meant by the expression 'the experts in logic' (*nyāya-vid*)' in the context of intrinsic invariable concomitance (*antar-vyāpti*), who are mentioned in NA 20 (*vide infra*, xxiii) is indeed Samantabhadra: 'There is a possibility that with the word he (= Siddhasena—P.B.) implicitly refers to Samantabhadra. ... [Samantabhadra] uses syllogism without example or *dṛṣṭānta*. ... This is the first usage of the *antarvyāpti* in the history of Jaina philosophy'.

However, Despite Sin FUJINAGA's conviction that 'Samantabhadra is prior to Dharmakīrti', the issue is in fact not definitely decided. As I point out in my paper 'Dharmakīrti's criticism of Jaina *anekânta-vāda*', delivered at the Fourth International Dharmakīrti Conference, held recently in Vienna, August 23–27, 2005, there are two points that suggest that Samantabhadra was slightly posterior to, or contemporary with Dharmakīrti (and Kumārila Bhaṭṭa). One of them is the innovative use of the delimiting particle *eva* in the statements of modal description (*syād-vāda*) by Samantabhadra in his *Āpta-mīmāṁsā* (ĀMī 14–15), which is influenced by Dharmakīrti's PV 4.190–192. The other argument for Samantabhadra's posteriority is that ĀMī 11 is apparently a direct reply to Dharmakīrti's PV 3.40–41.

I hope that future research will help us decide on these issues.

Piotr Balcerowicz
Hamburg–Warszawa, Summer 2005

ACKNOWLEDGEMENTS

The present study was in the most part prepared during my stay in Hamburg between 1992–1996 when I was admitted to the Institut für Kultur und Geschichte Indiens und Tibets, Universität Hamburg, as a Ph.D. student. I am most grateful to the Deutscher Akademischer Austauschdienst for a scholarship of nearly two year duration that made my stay in Hamburg possible.

My very special thanks are proffered to Professor Albrecht Wezler, my supervisor, without whose help neither the inception nor the completion of the present study would have been possible. Over all the years spent in Hamburg at the Institut für Kultur und Geschichte Indiens und Tibets I have enormously profited from regular weekly sessions with Professor Wezler, during which we read the *Nyāyâvatāra-vivṛti*. Not only did I largely deepen my superficial knowledge of Sanskrit, but the contacts with him and his penetrating analyses were a source of numerous inspiring stimuli. It is only thanks to Professor Wezler's active support and direct help, that my stay in Hamburg was not abruptly brought to an untimely end, and I was able to complete my research. It was a great privilege for me to study in Hamburg under his the guidance. I am also greatly indebted to Professor Wezler for his help in procuring manuscripts of the *Nyāyâvatāra*, the *Nyāyâvatāra-vivṛti* and the *Nyāyâvatāra-ṭippana*, on which the present work is based.

I wish to express my gratitude to Muni Jambūvijaya who kindly provided a copy of the manuscripts from the Pāṭaṇa collection. I am also very grateful to Dr. Heinz Braun for his help in appropriating secondary literature from the library of the Seminar für Indologie und Buddhismuskunde in Göttingen. I would like to take this opportunity to thank Professor Lambert Schmithausen, Professor Ernst Steinkellner, Dr. Helmut Krasser and Professor M. A. Dhaky for their stimulating suggestions and valuable information. I am also very much obliged to Professor Marek Mejor for his encouragement and support, to Dr. Eli Franco for constructive discussions on selected Yogācāra, Vijñāna-vāda and Śūnya-vāda sections of the *Nyāyâvatāra-vivṛti*, and to Ms. Małgorzata Wielińska for her instructive remarks concerning intricacies of Sanskrit grammar and Pāṇini. Last but not least, I would like to thank Ms. Wanda Wyporska who helped me to polish my English.

A NOTE ON THE TRANSLITERATION

The system of transliteration of Sanskrit words adopted in this book follows the International Alphabet of Sanskrit Transliteration (IAST) and the transliteration system of ISO 15919, with some additional features.

The sign ⌜ ̥ ⌝ is used to mark vowel such as ⌜*ṛ*⌝, ⌜*ṝ*⌝ and ⌜*ḷ*⌝. The *anusvāra* is transliterated as ⌜*ṁ*⌝.

Additional convention has been adopted:

- to separate words with a space, e.g. *tathā ca* (not **tathāca*), *evam api* (not **evamapi*);
- to separate compounded words, when possible, with a hyphen, e.g. *syād-vāda* (not **syādvāda*), *Āpta-mīmāṁsā* (not **Āptamīmāṁsā*);
- to mark the *sandhi* with the circumflex (the caret) ⌜ ^ ⌝ within compounds, when hyphenation is not possible, e.g. *Śvetâmbara* (not **Śvetāmbara*), *Nyāyâvatāra* (not **Nyāyāvatāra*), *kāryôpacāra* (not * *kāryopacāra*), *salilâudana* (not *salilaudana*);
- to mark the *sandhi* with the circumflex (the caret) ⌜ ^ ⌝ outside compounded words, e.g. *bhavatîti* (*bhavati* + *iti*), *tathêdam* (*tathā* + *idam*), *tathâiva* (*tathā* + *eva*), *câivôpalabhyate* (not * *caivopalabhyate*).

A NOTE TO THE EDITION AND ENGLISH TRANSLATION

The punctuation and symbols used:

- square brackets ⌜ [ ] ⌝ contain my supplementation of the text (in the English translation);
- parentheses ⌜ ( ) ⌝ contain my additional explanations, a synonymical expression or the original technical term (in the English translation);
- full stop ⌜ . ⌝ in the Sanskrit transcription replaces the *daṇḍa* punctuation mark ⌜ | ⌝ instead of a usual slash ⌜ / ⌝;
- double slash ⌜//⌝ corresponds to the double *daṇḍa* punctuation mark ⌜ || ⌝ concluding a section;
- the signs ⌜ < > ⌝ in the Sanskrit text embrace the present editor's insertion (e.g. full stop), which is not present in the MSS or consulted editions;
- a single underline marks a proper name in the Sanskrit text, e.g. ⌜ devabhadra-sūri ⌝;
- double underline marks a work title in the Sanskrit text, e.g. ⌜ nyāyâvatāra-vivṛtiḥ ⌝;
- bolded style marks the *pratīka* or *sūtra* portion, e.g. ⌜ **pramāṇêty**-ādi anena ca ⌝.

C. – Causative

D. – Denominative

INTRODUCTION

Nyāyâvatāra, a work in thirty-two verses—and hence also called *Dvātriṁśikā*—ascribed by tradition to Siddhasena Divākara, opens indeed a new era in the history of Jaina epistemology. It is mostly in the realm of Jaina epistemic pursuits that the *Dvātriṁśikā* might claim the status of an innovative or prototypical work. When we, however, consider the development of logic and epistemology in India on a larger scale, the work seems to lose its flavour of originality and novelty.

Much has been written on the authorship of *Nyāyâvatāra*, on its alleged author Siddhasena Divākara and on the work itself.

The most comprehensive bibliographic survey of publications on Siddhasena Divākara is furnished by UPADHYE 1971. Thus, to avoid unnecessary repetition, I draw the reader's attention to his 'Introduction' (pp. xi–xxvii) and highly valuable 'Bibliographic Survey' (pp. *3–*72). To A. N. Upadhye's list, I would add a few more publications that have appeared since the review: (1) MOOKERJEE 1971, (2) DHAKY 1981–82, (3) GRANOFF 1989–1990, (4) DHAKY 1990, (5) DHAKY 1995 and (6) WAYMAN 1996.

There are two major—and mutually independent—problems related to the *Nyāyâvatāra* and its author. Firstly, can the work be accurately ascribed to a Siddhasena (Divākara?), the celebrated author of a series of *Dvatriṁśikās*, to a Siddhasena (Divākara?), the author of the *Sanmati-tarka-prakaraṇa* or to some other Siddhasena? A related problem concerns the date(s) of the author(s) of all these works. A second problem is the date of the *Nyāyâvatāra* itself, irrespective of its possible relation to other works ascribed to Siddhasena Divākara. On subsequent pages I would not venture to clarify the first question, both because of my inadequate knowledge of all the remaining works attributed to Siddhasena (Divākara) and because I am more concerned with the epistemic and logical tradition in India in general. Nor the historicity of Siddhasena Divākara and the accuracy of semi-biographical or legendary accounts about his career recorded in a series of *prabandhas* evokes much interest in me; besides, these are rather irrelevant to the text of *Nyāyâvatāra* and its relative chronology. Nonetheless, I shall try to establish the correlation of *Nyāyâvatāra* and other, mostly Buddhist, works.

There is a variance of opinions regarding the date of Siddhasena as the author of the *Nyāyâvatāra* and the date of the *Nyāyâvatāra*, and these fall in four groups: (1) Siddhasena was pre-Diṅnāgan[i], (2) Siddhasena flourished soon after Diṅnāga and

---

[i] (1) SUKHLAL (1945/a): 'He is associated with Vikrama of Ujjain; he belongs to the 5th–6th century of V.-era; and this Vikrama might have been either Chandragupta II, or his grandson Skandagupta.' [according to UPADHYE (1971:*19)]. (2) SUKHLAL (1945/b): '...so Siddhasena is earlier than Mallavādi and far earlier than Jinabhadra. So Siddhasena is to be assigned to the 5th century of the V. era. This is further confirmed by Pūjyapāda Devanandi, who, in the *vetteḥ Siddhasenasya*, refers to an opinion of Siddhasena actually illustrated by the form *vidrate* in the *Dvā.*, IX.22. Further Pūjyapāda quotes in his

before Dharmakīrti[ii], (3) Siddhasena belongs to a post-Dharmakīrtian tradition[iii], whereas (4) some hold that his date is still an open question[iv].

JACOBI (1926: iii) was the first to observe that 'To about the same time [i.e. Śaka-year 598 = 677 CE—P.B.] belongs Siddhasenadivākara whom Haribhadra quotes; for

---

Sarvārthasiddhi, VII,13, a line from the *Dvā.*, III.16. Any way, Siddhasena belongs to the 5th century of the Vikrama era either as a predecessor or senior contemporary of Pūjyapāda.' [according to UPADHYE (1971:*21)]. (3) H. R. KĀPADĪĀ (AJP, 'Introduction', Vol. II, pp. 98 ff.): [Siddhasena flourished before Haribhadra and Jinadāsa-gaṇin (*c.* 676 CE) at least 150 years, at the latest in the sixth century CE.]. (4) KRAUSE (1948) [Siddhasena flourished earlier than 450 CE.]. (5) Curiously early date in DAVE (1962): 'So Siddhasena is earlier than Mallavādi and the tradition puts him as a contemporary of Vikramāditya who flourished in 57 B.C.' [according to UPADHYE (1971:*53)]. 'Dharmakīrti is posterior to Siddhasena'. [according to UPADHYE (1971:*59)]. 'NA is considered to be earlier than the *Nyāyapraveśa* of Diṅnāga and the *Nyāyabindu* of Dharmakīrti.' [according to UPADHYE (1971:*64)]. (6) SUKHLAL–DOSHI (1963): 'Circumstances indicate that Siddhasena might have flourished 150–200 years earlier than Jinabhadra (609 CE). ... Siddhasena is earlier than Mallavādi (*c.* 457 CE). ... Thus Siddhasena belongs to the 4th or 5th century of the Vikrama era.' [according to UPADHYE (1971:*35)]. 'Siddhasena was the predecessor of these two (Bhāmaha and Dharmakīrti).' [according to UPADHYE (1971:*44)]; (7) about 450 CE according to WILLIAMS (1963: 19); (8) 500 CE according to MATILAL (1985: 241).

[ii] MALVANIA (NASV, 'Introduction', pp. 141 f.) ['There is nothing prohibitive to assign Siddhasena earlier than Dharmakīrti.', 'He has used the works of Diṅnāga in plenty'.]. See also QVARNSTRÖM (1999: 178) ['Thought tentative, these notices tend to place the *Nyāyāvatāra* in between Dignāga (A.D. 480–540) and Dharmakīrti (A.D. 530–600).'].

[iii] (1) JACOBI (1926), (2) VAIDYA (1928), (3) MUKTHAR (1948): '7) The *Nyāyāvatāra* is composed centuries later than the *Sanmati-sūtra*, because it shows the influence of Pātrasvāmi (later than Samantabhadra) as well as Dharmakīrti and Dharmottara.' [according to UPADHYE (1971:*30)]. (4) V.P. JOHRAPURKAR ('Introduction' to VTP, pp. 41 ff.) ['Haribhadra had written a commentary on the *Nyāyāvatāra* from which he has included a verse (No. 4) in his *Ṣaḍ-darśana-samuccaya* (No.56); so the *Nyāyāvatāra* was composed earlier than the 8th century. It takes the definition of the Āgama from the *Ratnakaraṇḍaka* and the definition *anyathānupapannatva* of the Hetu from Pātrakesari; therefore *Nyāyāvatāra* could not be assigned to earlier than 7th century.'].

[iv] UPADHYE (1971: xxv): Siddhasena as the author of most *Dvātriṁśikās* and the *Sanmati-tarka-prakaraṇa* "is earlier than Haribhadra (*c.* 750–800 A.D.), Jinadāsagaṇi Mahattara (A.D. 676) and Jinabhadra (*c.* 609 A.D.); and it is highly probable that he belonged to the Gupta period as a contemporary of Chandragupta (II) Vikramāditya (*c.* 376–414). Some other Siddhasena, alias Kumudacandra, composed the *Kalyāṇamandira* and *Cikura-dvātriṁśikā*; and the *Dvā.* No. 21, as accepted by all, is the composition of some other Siddhasena. For reasons noted above, the question of the date and authorship of the *Nyāyāvatāra* has to remain open for further investigation [emphasis—P.B.].'

he uses, no doubt Dharmakīrti[i], though he does not name him'. There are two points, according to him, that justify such a conclusion: (1) Siddhasena (NA 5) applies the term *abhrānta*—and Dharmakīrti was the first to use it in his definition of *pratyakṣa*, thus improving upon Diṅnāga's definition[v]—to both *pratyakṣa* and *anumāna*; (2) Siddhasena (NA 11[vi]) 'extends the distinction of *svārtha* and *parārtha*, which properly applies to *anumāna* only, to *pratyakṣa* also, ibidem 12f. Apparently, he thought to improve on Dharmakīrti by a wholesome generalisation of nice distinctions!' (JACOBI (1926: iii, n. 1)). VAIDYA (1928: xviii–xx) elaborates upon JACOBI's laconic remarks. (3) He further brings up one more important point: '...verses 6 and 7 above of Nyāyāvatāra unmistakably presuppose Dharmakīrti and the later phase of the Yogācāra school, as, without them, it is difficult for us to explain why Siddhasena Divākara is required to combat these views[vii] and emphatically declare:

> सकलप्रतिभासस्य भ्रान्तत्वासिद्धितः स्फुटम् ।
> प्रमाणं स्वान्यनिश्चायि द्वयसिद्धौ प्रसिध्यति ॥ ७ ॥" (p. xx).

On my part, I would only add that also NA 31 (*pramātā svânya-nirbhāsī*) must have been inspired by similar thoughts as NA 7.

The first argument is sound. Admittedly, the idea of *abhrāntatva* of perception was latent in pre-Dharmakīrti's literature (*vide infra*), but Dharmakīrti was the first to use the term in the context of *pramāṇa*.[viii] If we were to take this latency of *abhrāntatva*

---

[v] For their definitions see n. 244.

[vi] Not NA 12, as VAIDYA (1928: xviii, line 16) has it.

[vii] Vaidya refers to the verses quoted by him on pp. xix/xx as follows:

(1) सहोपलम्भनियमादभेदो नीलतद्धियोः ।
(2) भेदश्च भ्रान्तिविज्ञानैर्दृश्येतेन्दाविवाद्वये ॥ -प्रमाणवार्तिककारिका.
(3) अवेद्यवेदकाकारा यथा भ्रान्तैर्निरीक्ष्यते ।
(4) विभक्तलक्षणग्राह्यग्राहकारविप्लवा ॥
(5) तथा कृतव्यवस्थेयं केशादिज्ञानभेदवत् ।
(6) यदा तदा न संचोद्या ग्राह्यग्राहकलक्षणा ॥ -प्रमाणवार्तिककारिका.
(7) नान्योऽनुभाव्यो बुद्ध्यास्ति तस्या नानुभवोऽपरः ।
(8) ग्राह्यग्राहकवैधुर्यात्स्वयमेव प्रकाशते ॥ -प्रमाणविनिश्चय, I.
(9) अविभागोऽपि बुद्ध्यात्मा विपर्यासितदर्शनैः ।
(10) ग्राह्यग्राहकसंवित्तिभेदवानिव लक्ष्यते ॥ -प्रमाणविनिश्चय, I.

However, he does not give exact references. Line 1 is not found in PV_1, it is found instead in PVin I_1 55ab (p. 94, n. 4); line 2 = PV_1 2.389ab; lines 3–6 = PV_1 2.330cd–332ab = PVin I_1 39–40 (p. 88, n. 1); lines 7–8 = PVin I_1 38 (p. 86, n. 2) [Vetter has *svayam saiva (!) prakāśate* instead of **स्वयमेव प्रकाशते**]; lines 9–10 = PV_1 2.354 (not PVin.).

[viii] An interpretation of non-erroneousness (*abhrāntatva*) is offered by Dharmottara in $NBṬ_1$ 3.2 (p. 141.5–142.2): *abhrāntam artha-kriyā-kṣame vastu-rūpe 'viparyastam ucyate.*

as a serious counter-argument—which seems totally unconvincing to me—it would imply that Siddhasena chose the term *abhrānta* intuitively and applied it indiscriminately to both *pratyakṣa* and *anumāna*, as if he had adumbrated that Dharmakīrti would once qualify perception as a non-erroneous cognition and inference as erroneous. Coincidentally, his way of expression would tally with the actual term used by Dharmakīrti, who would follow him!

As regards the term *bhrānta* (*bhrānti*) itself, it is indeed attested in the pre-Dharmakīrtian literature, for instance in (1) MAVBh 1.4: *yasmān na tathâsya bhāvo yathā pratibhāsa utpadyate. na ca sarvathâbhāvo bhrānti-mātrasyôtpādāt*; (2) SacAcBh$_2$ 2: *tatra citta-bhrānty-abhrānti-vyavasthānataḥ: yac caturbhir viparyāsair viparyastam cittaṁ, tad bhrāntam ity ucyate. yat punaś caturbhir viparyāsair aviparyastaṁ, tad abhrāntaṁ ity ucyate. tatra yad bhrāntaṁ cittaṁ, tad acittam ity ucyate, prakṛti-bhraṣṭatayā <;> yathā hi loke bhavanti vaktāraḥ unmattakaṁ kṣipta-cittaṁ dṛṣṭvā "acitto 'yaṁ puruṣa-pudgalaḥ unmattaḥ kṣipta-citta" iti. tad anena paryāyeṇa yad bhrāntaṁ cittaṁ, tad acittikā bhūmiḥ. yat punar abhrāntaṁ, tat sacittikā.*; in (3) Comm. *ad* MSA 10.2: *bhrāntikā hīnā viparītâdhimokṣāt. abhrāntikā praśāntā*; MSA 11.13a: *tattvaṁ yas satataṁ dvayena rahitaṁ, bhrānteś ca saṁniśrayaḥ*, and Comm. *ad loc.*: *bhrānteḥ saṁniśrayaḥ paratatras tena tat-parikalpanāt*; MSA 11.15: *yathā mayā tathâbhūta-parikalpo nirucyate / yathā māyā-kṛtaṁ tad-vad dvaya-bhrāntir*

---

artha-kriyā-kṣamaṁ ca vastu-rūpaṁ sanniveśôpādhi-varṇâtmakam. tatra yan na bhrāmyati tad abhrāntam. Thus, there are two pivotal aspects of *abhrāntatva*, the lack of contrariety (*aviparyastatva*) and its reference to a thing capable of efficient action (*artha-kriyā-kṣama-vastu*). The first element, viz. the lack of contrariety, or correspondence to facts, may be taken to have been preconceived in the idea of *avyabhicāritva* in the non-Buddhist literature as early as NS 1.1.4 (*indriyârtha-sannikarṣôtpannaṁ jñānam avyapadeśyam avyabhicāri vyavasāyâtmakaṁ pratyakṣam*) and NBh *ad loc.* (*yad atasmin tad iti tad vyabhicāri, yat tu tasmin tad iti tad avyabhicāri pratyakṣam iti*). This tendency can be also observed in Jaina sources, e.g. in TBh 1.32 (p. 30.6, p. 31.1–2): *jñāna-viparyayo 'jñānam iti ... mithyā-darśana-parigrahād viparīta-grāhakatvam eteṣāṁ* (= *viparyayāṇām*). *tasmād ajñānāni bhavanti.*

However, the second element *artha-kriyā-samartha*, the capability to execute efficient action, is directly Dharmakīrti's innovation, see PV$_1$ 1:3:

pramāṇam avisaṁvādi jñānam artha-kriyā-sthitiḥ /
avisaṁvādanam śābde 'py abhiprāya-nivedanāt //

as well as PV$_1$ 2.3:

artha-kriyā-samarthaṁ yat tad atra paramārtha-sat /
anyat saṁvṛti-sat proktaṁ te sva-sāmānya-lakṣaṇe //

Cf. also HATTORI (1968: 14): 'The concept of "*artha-kriyā*" is unfamiliar to Dignāga, but it is an important criterion for the distinguishing of "*sva-lakṣaṇa*" from "*sāmānya-lakṣaṇa*" in Dharmakīrti's system of thought.', HATTORI (1968: 79 § 1.14) and FRANCO (1987: 445 n. 203), esp.: 'the concept of *arthakriyā* does not appear anywhere in Dignāga's writings'.

nirucyate // ; MSA 11.17 (*dvaya-bhrānti*); MSA 11.24–26: *bhrānter nimittam bhrāntiś ca rūpa-vijñāptir iṣyate / arūpiṇī ca vijñāptir abhāvāt syān na cêtarā // māyā-hasty-ākṛti-grāha-bhrānter dvayam udāhṛtam / dvayam tatra yathā nâsti dvayaṁ câivôpalabhyate // bimba-saṁkalikā-grāha-bhrānter dvayam udāhṛtam / dvayam tatra yathā nâsti dvayaṁ câivôpalabhyate //* ; Comm. *ad* MSA 11.27: *ye dharmā bhrānti-lakṣaṇā vipakṣa-svabhāvās te sad-asanto māyôpamāś ca*. In all these passages, however, the term *bhrānti* does not occur in the context of *pramāṇa*, still less of valid perception (*pratyakṣa*), in the first place.[ix] The term refers either to a general error based on the perceiving of subject–object duality in the world (*dvaya-bhrānti*), and is synonymous to *māyā* (in MSA), or to the nature of the cognised object (MAVBh 1.4). The latter rests on a rather subtle difference: erroneous is not the cognition as such (the emphasis on the inner, cognitive aspect, viz., erroneous correspondence of an act of cognition), but the way an object is constituted in the cognition (the emphasis on the 'outer', 'objective' side). In none of these texts where we come across the term *bhrānti* is the idea of cognitively valid procedures (*pramāṇa*) discussed; at the most, it points to an antithesis of a general, soteriologically relevant outlook of a person, viz., *citta-bhrānti / bhrāntaṁ cittaṁ / kṣipta-cittaṁ* (SacAcBh$_2$ 2). This is confirmed by the application of the past passive participle to people MSA 11.18 (*loko hy abhrāntaḥ*), as loci of *bhrānta-citta*. Besides, I do not think the reason, adduced for 'the erroneous consciousness' (*bhrāntaṁ cittaṁ*) in SacAcBh$_2$ 2, i.e. *prakṛti-bhraṣṭatayā*, would be at all relevant in the case of *pratyakṣa*: as a matter of fact, it is *abhrānti* which consists the nature of *pratyakṣa* for Dharmakīrti (and Siddhasena). In other words, the argument is that 'consciousness is erroneous (*bhrāntaṁ cittaṁ*), hence called "non-consciousness" (*acittam ity ucyate*), because it has lost (*sc*. is not faithful to) its nature;' if we apply the reason to *pratyakṣa*, we would clearly have a vicious circle: '*pratyakṣa* is non erroneous (*abhrānta*), because it has not lost its nature, and its nature is non-erroneousness (*abhrānti*).' I do claim that this kind of reasoning would at all be applicable to *pratyakṣa* (historically it is not); I employ it in order to show that the underpinning and ramifications of the notion of *(a)bhrānti* in the case of the pre-Dharmakīrtian texts and in the case of Dharmakīrti's definition are different. To sum up, none of the occurrences of the term *(a)bhrānta* in Yogācāra works seems to have been an inspiration for Siddhasena.

Whereas I completely agree with Jacobi–Vaidya's first argument, their second argument is not entirely convincing to me. Indeed, we cannot understand the idea of *svârtha-vākya* and *parârtha-vākya* (NA 10) and *svârtha-pratyakṣa* and *parârtha-pratyakṣa* (NA 11) without Diṅnāga's and Dharmakīrti's well-known division of *svârthânumāna* and *parârthânumāna*. It should suffice to remind the reader of NB 2.1–2: /1/ *anumānaṁ dvividhā. /2/ svârthaṁ parârthaṁ ca*. and of NB 3.1–2: /1/ *tri-rūpa-liṅgâkhyānaṁ parârthânumānam. /2/ kāraṇe kāryôpacārāt*.

[ix] On the other hand, Dharmakīrti's definition does go back to the usage of the term *bhrānta* in the Yogācāra school; his novelty was to mould it to the demands of his *pramāṇa* theory (we should remember about his idea that *anumāna* is *bhrānta* (cf. n. 307), which is a proper point of reference).

There can be no doubt, in my opinion, that the idea of *vākyasya parârthatvaṁ* necessarily presupposes the idea of *vākyasya svârthatvaṁ*, and that both these concepts—expressed in NA 10 ff.: *parârthaṁ mānam ākhyātaṁ vākyaṁ*—could only have been developed in the context of *svârtha-°* and *parârthânumāna*.

However, the idea of *svârtha-pratyakṣa* and *svârthânumāna* / *parârthânumāna*—central for Jacobi–Vaidya's reasoning—which is a prerequisite for Siddhasena to establish the thesis of *parârtha-pratyakṣa*, predates Dharmakīrti and is found also in the *saṅgraha-śloka* (*iti śāstrârtha-saṅgrahaḥ*) of *Nyāya-praveśa* of Diṅnāga's disciple, Śaṅkarasvāmin[x]:

sādhanaṁ dūṣaṇaṁ câiva sâbhāsaṁ para-saṁvide /
pratyakṣam anumānaṁ ca sâbhāsaṁ tv ātma-saṁvide //

Certainly it is not Śaṅkarasvāmin who developed the concept of *svârtha-°* and *parârthânumāna*. It was probably fathomed by Vasubandhu[xi], but terminologically conceived and worked out by Diṅnāga[xii], cf., e.g.: PS 2.1ab: *anumānaṁ dvividhā svârthaṁ tri-rūpāl liṅgato parârthânumānaṁ tu sva-dṛṣṭârtha-prakāśanam*; also PS 3.1ab, and PSV 2, K 109a.2–3 = V 27a.5 (*svârthânumāna*): *tshul gsum paḥi rtags las rjes su dpag paḥi don* (V: *rjes su dpag par bya baḥi don*) *mthoṅ ba gaṅ yin pa de ni raṅ gi don gyi rjes su dpag paḥo*.

There are, however, two other traits to be noticed in the aphorisms NA 10–11 that point, in my opinion, to Dharmakīrti as their source. The first of them is the idea of metaphorical transference (*upacāra*) used in a very similar context. Siddhasena speaks of the term 'inference for others' (*parârthaṁ mānam*)—which denotes, to be precise, the inferential cognition arisen in another person as a result of an argumentative procedure and/or debate—which is applied through metaphorical transference (*upacāra*) to a 'syllogistic' sentence (*vākyaṁ*), that is, as a matter of fact, merely a cause of such a cognition in another person. We come across the same idea in NB 3.1–2, and even the wording is to a certain extent similar (one should here take into account stylistic differences necessitated by the succinct *sūtra* style and versified *kārikās*). Below, both passages in question are given for the sake of convenience, relevant expressions being underlined:[xiii]

/NA 10/ *sva-niścayavad anyeṣāṁ niścayôtpādanaṁ budhaiḥ /*
parârthaṁ mānam ākhyātaṁ vākyaṁ tad-upacārataḥ //

NB 3.1–2: /1/ *tri-rūpa-liṅgâkhyānaṁ parârthânumānam*. /2/ *kāraṇe kāryôpacārāt*.

---

[x] As for a possible objection that the verse might be later, at least the commentator Haribhadra takes it to be a genuine part of the original work (NP$_1$, p. 9.12 ff.): ...*ity ādāv eva ślokaḥ*, etc.

[xi] Cf. FRAUWALLNER (1933: 476–477 [297–298]) and HATTORI (1968: 12, n. 60).

[xii] Cf. RANDLE (1926: 28–9), HATTORI (1968: 78, n. I.11) and Steinkellner's note 1, p. 21 in PVin II$_2$.

[xiii] In my analysis throughout I shall use, for the sake of brevity, underlining to mark corresponding phrases in NA and works of Dharmakīrti or of other authors.

Dharmottara's gloss confirms the interpretation: *kāraṇa* = *vacana* = *vākya*; *kārya* = [*parârtha*] *anumāna* = *parârtha-māna*.[xiv] Siddharṣi, whose comments are in a similar spirit, even quotes a verse, that establishes the relation between speech (*kāraṇa*) and resulting cognition (*kārya*)[xv]. The verse is so far untraced, but it refers most probably to another verse by Dharmakīrti, and—at any rate—to an idea expressed in PV_3 1.286[xvi]. Another striking feature is that the reference to the idea of the metaphorical transference (*upacāra*) occurs in both works (NA and NB) precisely at the moment of introducing the discussion of *parârtha-anumāna* and that this is the only occurrence of this idea in both works. Neither the term nor the idea as such is encountered at any other point.

Further, Vaidya's third point is rather weak, as well. He says: 'These verses [NA 6–7—P.B.] contain the favourite view of the Yogācāra School on the subject and the object (grāhya and grāhaka), which both they declare illusory. This view is dependent on the definition of pratyakṣa, and though its origin must be sought in Diṅnāga's works [emphasis—P.B.], the scholars who brought the idea to perfection are Dharmapāla and his pupil Dharmakīrti.' (p. xix). Indeed, we find the idea referred to by Vaidya in Diṅnāga's works, e.g. in his PS 1.10[xvii]:

Vasudhararakṣita/Seṅ-rgyal 15b.4:	Kanakavarman/Dad-paḥi śes-rab 96a.4–5:
gaṅ tshe snaṅ ba de gsal bya	*gaṅ ltar snaṅ ba de gṣal bya*
tshad ma daṅ deḥi ḥbras bu ni	*tshad ma daṅ deḥi ḥbras bu ni*
ḥdsin rnam rig pa de yi phyir	*ḥdsin rnam rig paḥo de yi phyir*
de gsum tha aad du ma byas	*de gsum tha dad du ma byas*

However, we do not find anything in NA 7[xviii] that would allude to either Diṅnāga's specific theory of triple division of *vijñāna* or to Dharmakīrti's ideas[xix]. What we do find instead is the realist's position that, at least: (1) acts of cognition are

---

[xiv] $NBṬ_1$ 3.2 (p. 41.11–13) = ($NBṬ_2$, p. 150.12–151.1): *tasmin kāraṇe vacane kāryasyânumānasyôpacāraḥ samāropaḥ kriyate. tataḥ samāropāt kāraṇaṁ vacanam anumāna-śabdenôcyate. aupacārikaṁ vacanam anumānaṁ, na mukhyam ity-arthaḥ.*

[xv] *vikalpa-yonayaḥ śabdā vikalpāḥ śabda-yonayaḥ /*
kārya-kāraṇatā teṣāṁ nârthaṁ śabdāḥ spṛśanty api //
See p. 226 of the translation.

[xvi] See n. 377.

[xvii] See HATTORI (1968: 107, n. 1.67):
yad-ābhāsaṁ prameyaṁ tat pramāṇa-phalate punaḥ /
grāhakâkāra-saṁvittī trayaṁ nâtaḥ pṛthak-kṛtam //
[*Vibhūti*, p. 221[1]: *grāhakâkāra-saṁ°* instead of *grāhakākāra-saṁ°*].

[xviii] *sakala-pratibhāsasya bhrāntatvâsiddhitaḥ sphuṭaṁ /*
pramāṇaṁ svânya-niścāyi dvaya-siddhau prasidhyati //

[xix] On the triple and fourfold division of *vijñāna* in the Yogācāra school see HATTORI (1968: 107, n. 1.67).

real, (2) acts of cognition happen to be true and accurate, (3) acts of cognition are self-validatory, (4) acts of cognition are accurate representations of external world, (5) the external world is real.

To have Diṅnāga's or Dharmakīrti's views criticised here we would need an explicit element of *sva-saṁvitti* (*sva-saṁvedana*) or *phala*. There are three possible expressions in NA 7 that might refer to *sva-saṁvitti* (and none to refer to *phala*): (A) *sphuṭaṁ*, (B) *svânya-niścāyi*, (C) *dvaya-siddhau*. (Ad A) The first of the list is highly improbable, for it never—to my knowledge—is used in Buddhist sources to refer to the idea of self-revelatory character of cognition (*sva-saṁvitti*). It is generally used to describe either the veracious, direct, non-inferential or the indubitable, etc., character of acts of cognition. It is explained by Siddharṣi accordingly by *suniścitatayā*. (Ad B) The second of these expressions (as a similar one in NA 31: *svânya-nirbhāsī*) mentions in fact only two aspects: the cognition (*sva*) and its counterpart—the object (*anya*). If *sva* were to mean *sva-saṁvitti*, the primary act of cognition would not be mentioned; if *anya* were taken to be *sva-saṁvitti*, the *bāhyârtha*, so fundamental for the realist, would not be mentioned. The expression is explained in NAV as *sva-para-prakāśakaṁ*, which does not bring anything new to our analysis. However, it is coupled in the NAV with the third expression. (Ad C) The third expression refers to duality, in the first place, and—like in the preceding case—it is highly problematic to take it to allude to Diṅnāga's theory of triple division of *vijñāna*. However, it is Siddharṣi's gloss on *dvaya-siddhau*: *svarūpârtha-lakṣaṇa-yugma-niṣpattau* that could be implicative of *sva-saṁvitti*: in it, *svarūpa* might refer to the self-revelatory character of cognition. It is especially suggestive in view of his statement in NAV 1 (gloss on *dvidhâivêti*, p. 25 of the translation): *sva-saṁvedanaṁ prati nikhila-jñānānām eka-rūpatayā sākṣāt-karaṇa-caturatvāt*. But even then, the third aspect of an act of cognition (apart from the act as such, an object), its self-revelatory character, is not explicitly mentioned here. As a matter of fact, Siddharṣi, so well conversant with Buddhist ideas, would not have wasted the availing opportunity to indicate the idea of *sva-saṁvitti* and to utilise it (as he does in several places, for instance in NAV 1, p. 25 ff., NAV 29, pp. 90 ff., 93 ff., NAV 31, etc.), if he had noticed any allusion to the Buddhist theories of triple or fourfold division of *vijñāna* in the aphorism of Siddhasena. In other words, there is nothing in Siddharṣi's gloss that might suggest that Siddharṣi had seen any point of convergence between the ideas expressed in NA 7 and certain concepts ascribable to Diṅnāga, as Vaidya would like it. To expel our doubts, he concludes, as a matter of fact, with *anyathā prameyâbhāve pramāṇâbhāvāt*, to show that no third element is implied.

In my opinion, NA 7 can be safely taken to disprove the doctrine of illusory character of worldly appearance propounded by the Buddhist idealist (Vijñāna-vādin), whose ideas directly influenced Diṅnāga and Dharmakīrti[xx]. The aphorism is clearly evocative of such ideas as those expressed in, e.g.:

(1) MAV 1.1, 3:

abhūta-parikalpo 'sti dvayaṁ tatra na vidyate /

[xx] Cf. HATTORI (1968: 106, n. 1.65).

śūnyatā vidyate tv atra tasyām api sa vidyate //
artha-sattvâtma-vijñāpti-pratibhāsaṁ prajāyate /
vijñānaṁ nâsti câsyârthas tad-abhāvāt tad apy sat //

(2) Triṁś 1, 29:
ātma-dharmôpacāro hi vividho yaḥ pravartate /
vijñāna-pariṇāme 'sau pariṇāmaḥ sa trividhā //
acitto 'nupalambho 'sau jñānaṁ lokôttaraṁ ca tat /
āśrayasya parāvṛttir dvidhā dauṣṭhulya-hānitaḥ //

(3) Viṁś 1ab:
vijñāpti-mātram evâitad asad-arthâvabhāsanāt /

(4) Viṁś 16 (to be coupled with NA 6–7):
pratyakṣa-buddhiḥ svapnâdau yathā sā ca yadā tadā /
na so 'rtho dṛśyate tasya pratyakṣatvaṁ kathaṁ matam //

As Siddharṣi expresses himself, if there is nothing to be cognised, there can be no cognition. Therefore, to establish the thesis of the existence of the external world is essential for the realist. Similarly, *mutatis mutandis*, it is crucial for the Buddhist idealist to deny the existence of external object. Furthermore, NA 7 fits quite well into the line of critics of the so-called 'Dreaming Argument'[xxi], that was commonly ascribed to the Buddhist and refuted, for instance, by Kumārila Bhaṭṭa[xxii], Uddyotakara Bhāradvāja[xxiii], Śaṅkara[xxiv] and by Siddharṣi-gaṇin[xxv].

Therefore, NA 7 is not a very useful indication to establish the date of the *Nyāyâvatāra*. However, there is a number of other conspicuous traits, that are instrumental in establishing the time of composition of the treatise quite convincingly as posterior to Dharmakīrti. To achieve this, I shall analyse several aphorisms of NA step by step in order to show Siddhasena's indebtedness to Dharmakīrti (especially to NB) in respect not only of certain 'loan' ideas but also, partially, of the dialectical

---

[xxi] In a typical formulation: 'The sensation in the waking state is erroneous, because it is a cognition, like the sensation in a dream' (*jāgrat-saṁvedanaṁ bhrāntaṁ, pratyayatvāt, svapna-saṁvedanavat*). See TABER (1994).

[xxii] MŚV$_4$ (*Nirālambana-vāda*) 23 (p. 159.7–8):
stambhâdi-pratyayo mithyā pratyayatvāt tathā hi yaḥ /
pratyayaḥ sa mṛṣā dṛṣṭaḥ svapnâdipratyayo yathā //

[xxiii] NV$_3$ on NBh 4.2.33: *ayam jāgrad-avasthôpalabdhānāṁ viṣayāṇāṁ citta-vyatirekiṇām asattve hetuḥ khyātiḥ svapnavad iti*.

[xxiv] BSŚBh 2.2.5.29 (p. 476.2–3): *yad uktaṁ bāhyârthâpalāpinā svapnâdivaj jāgarita-gocarā api stambhâdi-pratyayā vinâiva bāhyenârthena bhaveyuḥ pratyayatvâviśeṣād iti tad prativaktavyam*. Clearly, Śaṅkara criticises the Dreaming Argument from a different angle than the realists.

[xxv] The argument—in its typical wording—occurs in NAV 29 (the *Śūnya-vāda* section): *nirālambanāḥ sarve pratyayāḥ, pratyayatvāt, svapna-pratyayavad*.

structure of the text. Some of the following points are not entirely convincing, when taken singly. Their high number, on the other hand, could not have been a matter of mere coincidence.

[1] The opening line of NA 0 (*pramāṇa-vyutpādanârtham idam ārabhyate*) closely resembles the formulations of HB, p. 1*.5–6: *parokṣârtha-pratipatter anumānâśrayatvāt tad-vyutpādanârthaṁ saṅkṣepata idam ārabhyate*.

[2] Practically, the very first ideas expressed in the opening lines of NA and NB are very similar and have similar wording:

NA 1: *pramāṇaṁ* [...] *pratyakṣaṁ ca parokṣaṁ ca dvidhā*.

NB 1.1.2–3: *dvividham samyag-jñānam. pratyakṣam anumānaṁ ca*.

The differences are that (1) Siddhasena does not have *samyag-jñānam* (this expression is completely absent from NA), and (2) he has *parokṣa* instead of *anumāna*. The second difference is dictated by the Jaina demand to incorporate *śābda* / *āgama* (testimony, verbal cognition) in the *pramāṇas* (as a quasi-separate category, one of the two—alongside *anumāna*—primary sub-divisions of *parokṣa*). However, Siddhasena marks an important, widely known shift in Jaina epistemology, to interpret the directness of *pratyakṣa* in terms of sensory organs (*akṣa* = *indriya*), not—as it was customary—in terms of the cognitive subject (*akṣa* = *jīva* / *ātman*). The commentators are quite explicit about the interpretational shift, which diverts from the *Āgamic* tradition advocated, e.g. by Akalaṅka among many others.[xxvi]

Truly, a formulation similar to NA 1 is found also in PS_1 1.2ab: *pratyakṣam anumānaṁ ca pramāṇe* (Vasudhararakṣita/Seṅ-rgyal 13b.6: *mṅon sum daṅ ni rjes su dpag thsad ma*; Kanakavarman/Dad-paḥi śes-rab 94a.4: *mṅon sum daṅ·ni rjes su dpag tshad ma dag ni*) with the exception of the explicit (*sc.* with a numeral, not with the dual form °-*e* / *dag*) mention of 'twofold' (*dvividham* / *dvidhā* / *rnam pa gñis*), so Dharmakīrti is not the only potential source.

The question is what prompted Siddhasena to introduce this shift? Obviously, these were the demands of the general philosophic discourse in India to be up-to-date with and understood by such schools as Nyāya or Sāṁkhya. But I am deeply convinced that what was responsible for that shift to take the senses as the criterion of directness of *pratyakṣa* was, to a larger degree, Dharmakīrti's inspiration and his works (predominantly the *Nyāya-bindu*) as a groundwork for the *Nyāyâvatāra*. For what other reason would Siddhasena speak of the two-fold division of valid cognition

[xxvi] See n. 123 and NAV 1: ***pratyakṣaṁ*** *cêty-ādi*; *tatra siddhânta-prasiddha-pāramārthika-pratyakṣâpekṣayâkṣa-śabdo jīva-paryāyatayā prasiddhaḥ. iha tu vyāvahārika-pratyakṣa-prastāvād akṣa-dhvanir indriya-vacano gṛhyate. tataś câkṣaṁ pratigataṁ pratyakṣaṁ. yad indriyam āśrityôjjihīte 'rtha-sākṣāt-kāri jñānaṁ tat pratyakṣam ity arthaḥ. ... akṣebhyaḥ parato vartata iti parokṣam. akṣa-vyāpāra-nirapekṣaṁ mano-vyāpāreṇâsākṣād-artha-paricchedakaṁ yaj jñānaṁ tat parokṣam iti-bhāvaḥ*. (See p. 15 f. of the translation).

and justify it by referring to Dharmakīrtian ideas? And thereby we come to another element of NA 1 that resembles Dharmakīrti's formulations.

According to Siddhasena, the factor responsible for the division of cognitive acts into *pratyakṣa* and *parokṣa* is not the character of the 'cognising organ' (*akṣa*), either the sense organs (*indriya*) or the cognitive subject (*jīva*, *ātman*) as such. In his opinion, what is crucial in the categorisation of *pramāṇas* is the character of the object of cognition that determines the way the object of cognition is determined, or cognised. Clearly, in this revolutionary rearrangement he goes against the whole Jaina tradition. The expression he uses: *meya-viniścayāt* (NA 1d), can hardly be explicated without Dharmakīrti's formulations: *tasya viṣayaḥ svalakṣaṇam* (NB 1.1.12), *so 'numānasya viṣayaḥ* (NB 1.1.17) and *mānaṁ dvividhaṁ viṣaya-dvaividhyāt* (PV_3 2.1ab)[xxvii]. Even Siddharṣi in NAV 1 *ad loc.* (on *meya-viniścayād*)[xxviii] confirms that what is pivotal for the distinction is, in the first place, the character of extrinsic data apprehended by the cognitive subject, that determines the way of apprehension, irrespective of whether the 'cognising organ' are the senses or the soul. It is only in NA 4d that Siddhasena emphasises the way of cognising, or '[the manner of] grasping [an object]', for the first time: *grahaṇêkṣayā*. But even then, the tradition in the person of the commentator Siddharṣi takes the locution to refer to the existence and the nature of the cognoscible (see his detailed discussion in NAV 4 apropos of *grahaṇêkṣayā*, p. 31 f. of the translation).

If we compare what Diṅnāga has further to say on the two-fold division of *pramāṇa*, we discover that he does not mention the reason for the division explicitly, as Dharmakīrti and Siddhasena do, but he merely points to the parallelism of the two-fold *prameya*: PS_1 1.2bc: *lakṣaṇa-dvayam / prameyam...* (Vasudhararakṣita/Seṅ-rgyal 13b.6 = Kanakavarman/Dad-paḥi śes-rab 94a.5: *mtshan ñid gñis gṣal bya*). Clearly, one can easily understand the statement *lakṣaṇa-dvayaṁ prameyam* to be a reason adduced by the author for *pratyakṣam anumānaṁ ca pramāṇe* ('there are two cognitive criteria: perception and inference, [**because**] the cognoscible has two characteristics'), as the commentator himself does (*yasmāt* = Vasudhararakṣita/Seṅ-rgyal: *...phyir ṣe na*; Kanakavarman/Dad-paḥi śes-rab: *...gaṅ gi phyir*). However, neither the word 'because' (*yasmāt* / °*-tvāt*) nor any direct explanation ***why*** *pramāṇa* is two-fold is mentioned by Diṅnāga explicitly, as it is by Dharmakīrti in PV_3 2.1bc (*viṣaya-dvaividhyāt śakty-aśaktitaḥ / artha-kriyāyām...*). Moreover, Diṅnāga's elucidation of

---

[xxvii] Cf. also PV_3 2.63 (*anumāna-vicāraḥ*):

na pratyakṣa-parokṣābhyāṁ meyasyânyasya sambhavaḥ /
tasmāt prameya-dvitvena pramāṇa-dvitvam iṣyate //

[xxviii] *bahir-arthaṁ punar apekṣya kaścic cakṣurâdi-sāmagrī-bala-labdha-sattākaḥ svâvayava-vyāpinaṁ kālântara-sañcariṣṇuṁ sthagita-kṣaṇa-vivartam alakṣita-paramâṇu-pārimāṇḍalyaṁ sannihitaṁ viśada-nirbhāsaṁ sāmānyam ākāraṁ sākṣāt-kurvāṇaḥ prakāśaḥ prathate, tatra pratyakṣa-vyavahāraḥ pravartate. yaḥ punar liṅga-śabdâdi-dvāreṇa niyatâniyata-sāmānyâkārâvalokī parisphuṭatā-rahitaḥ khalv ātmano 'rtha-grahaṇa-pariṇāmaḥ samullasati sa parokṣatāṁ svī-karoti* (see p. 25 of the translation).

the two-fold character of *pramāṇa* (*lakṣaṇa-dvayaṁ prameyam*) differs completely in character from Siddhasena's explanation (*meya-viniścayāt*) and Dharmakīrti's (*viṣaya-dvaividhyāt śakty-aśaktitaḥ artha-kriyāyām*...), insofar as it is 'static' or 'taxonomic', viz., plainly juxtaposes two cases of double division (*pramāṇa—prameya*), whereas Siddhasena and Dharmakīrti offer 'intentional', i.e. actively directed to an object of cognition either by way of determining it (*viniścaya*, cognitive activity) or by any sort of efficient action (*artha-kriyā*).

[3] Apart from the noticeable similarity in wording between NA 1 and NB 1.1.2–3, there is another striking correspondence to be observed in the ideas expressed by Dharmakīrti and Siddhasena. Siddharṣi introduces NA 1 in the following way: *tatra tāval lakṣaṇa-saṁkhyā-vipratipattī nirācikīrṣur āha*. There is no doubt that Siddharṣi regarded NA 1 to aim at—beside enumerating subdivisions of *pramāṇa* (*pratyakṣaṁ ca parokṣaṁ ca dvidhā*...)—formulating its definition (*pramāṇaṁ sva-parâbhāsi jñānaṁ bādha-vivarjitam*). And, further, there can hardly be any doubt that a descriptive definition of *pramāṇa* is precisely what Siddhasena in NA 1ab does. In the aphorism, he does not only group all cognitively valid procedures under respective categories of 'direct' and 'indirect', which is a case of a typological definition that demarcates a notion by mentioning specimens to which the definition is applicable (ὁ διὰ τῶν γενῶν ὁρισμὸς), but he also attempts a real definition that describes the character and essential aspects or intrinsic characteristics of a thing (ὁ λέγων ἐξ ὧν ἔστιν ἐνυπαρχόντων [ὁρισμὸς]).[xxix] Clearly, these two definitions represent two diverse approaches and the latter is intellectually more sublime. Whereas we quite frequently find typological definitions of *pramāṇa* (viz., statements of its divisions) in Jaina literature, we do not, as a matter of fact, come across any attempt at a descriptive definition of *pramāṇa* of the second type in any works, both Jaina and non-Jaina, prior NA. Thus, the formulation of a descriptive definition of cognitive criterion seems definitely to be an advancement. And it would perhaps be surprising to find such an innovation in a work of generally secondary character that repeatedly borrows from other works (*vide infra*, esp. p. xxxviii), if NA had no predecessor. However, it is Dharmakīrti who must have inspired Siddhasena's descriptive definition. The opening verse (if we skip the first two introductory verses of obeisant nature) of the *Pramāṇa-siddhi* chapter, i.e. $PV_{1,3}$ 1.3—and subsequent verses up to $PV_{1,3}$ 1.7 are its elaboration—presents such a descriptive definition of *pramāṇa* that specifies its character and individual features. This section of PV is traditionally[xxx] assumed to offer

---

[xxix] Cf. Aristotelian twofold division in *MET.*998^b (p. 47.12–14): ἕτερος δ' ἔδται ὁ διὰ τῶν γενῶν ὁρισμὸς καὶ ὁ λέγων ἐξ ὧν ἔστιν ἐνυπαρχόντων.

[xxx] See: FRANCO (1997: 5961), esp.: 'Therefore, we can safely conclude that the definition of *pramāṇa* in general, unlike the definition of each *pramāṇa* in particular, was not undertaken by any Indian philosopher before Dharmakīrti's time. Consequently, there is no reason why one should expect Dharmakīrti to do so. During the time that separates Dharmakīrti from his commentators, some change in the philosophical requirements must have

the first comprehensive definition of *pramāṇa*. Clearly, for both Manorathanandin and Siddharṣi the passages of NA 1ab and PV$_{1,3}$ 1.3 respectively are cases of a *pramāṇa-lakṣaṇa*. Occasionally[xxxi], a doubt is raised whether Dharmakīrti's design was indeed a descriptive definition and that actually it was the subsequent Buddhist tradition of commentators where the idea of a comprehensive descriptive definition developed. Irrespective of whether one assumes that the formulation of PV$_{1,3}$ 1.3 was a genuine descriptive definition or that an idea of such a definition first originated with post-Dharmakīrtian commentators, both sides agree that such a descriptive definition did not exist before Dharmakīrti (*ergo* it is altogether absent from Diṅnāga, Śaṅkarasvāmin, etc.). Accordingly, since NA appears to present such a definition of a descriptive character, it must have been composed after Dharmakīrti and PV.[xxxii]

[4] Late Buddhist sources allegedly refer to NA 2, cf. QVARNSTRÖM (1999: 178): 'In the eighth-century commentary on Dharmakīrti's *Pramāṇavārttika* (II.5), Śākyabuddhi (or Śākyamati) quotes the second verse of *Nyāyāvatāra* and claims that this verse is the object of Dharmakīrti's critique', and refers to Chr. Lindtner's 'Marginalia to Dharmakīrti's Pramāṇaviniścaya'. *WZKSO* 28 (1984) 149–175, p. 163, n. 38. Surprisingly, NA 2, being a statement of *pūrva-pakṣa*, is the least suitable verse of the whole *Dvātriṁśikā* to serve as an object of anybody's critique. Thus, anyone referring to the verse with the purpose to refute it would have to be highly incompetent and incapable of noticing that the very verse is refuted by Siddhasena himself in NA 3! Therefore it could hardly be an 'object of Dharmakīrti's critique'. Furthermore, any reference to allegedly such a state of affairs would prove the source of such an information to be a highly unreliable one. Consequently, either Śākyabuddhi cannot have referred to NA 2 or his acquaintance with Jaina tradition would be liable to doubt.

As a matter of fact, NA 2 may plausibly be taken as a *prima facie* objection ('no purpose is known for stating the definition of cognitive criterion') against formulating a comprehensive definition of *pramāṇa* of descriptive character, inasmuch as '*cognitive criteria* (mind the plural!—P.B.) are well-known and everyday practice is accomplished by them'. Siddharṣi takes 'the definition of cognitive criterion' to be '[a statement] consisting in mentioning specific properties of cognitive criterion that

---

occurred that produced the expectation of a general definition of *pramāṇas*.' [p. 60]. Conf. also STEINKELLNER–KRASSER (1989: 3–5).

Cf., e.g. PVV$_1$ 1.3 (p. 2.17 ff.) = PVV$_3$ 1.3 (p. 3.17 ff.): *ayam ācāryo bṛhad-ācāryīya-pramāṇa-samuccaya-śāstre vārttikaṁ cikīrṣuḥ svataḥ-kṛta-bhagavan-namaskāraḥ tac-chāstrârambha-samaye tad-ācārya-kṛta-bhagavan-namaskāra-ślokaṁ vyākhyātu-kāmaḥ prathamaṁ pramāṇa-sāmānya-lakṣaṇam āha*... and PVV$_1$ 1.7–8 (p. 4.36 ff.) = PVV$_3$ (p. 8.6 ff.): *tad evam avisaṁvādanaṁ pramāṇa-lakṣaṇam uktam. idānīm anyad āha*...

[xxxi] See: FRANCO (1997: 54–62), e.g.: '...Dharmakīrti did not attempt a general definition of the *pramāṇas*, but only wanted to prove that the Buddha is a *pramāṇa*...' [p. 61].

[xxxii] I am indebted to Claus Oetke for drawing my attention to the above issue of PV 1.3–7 and its relevance to the problem of dating of NA.

are capable of distinguishing [it from that which has] another form,'[xxxiii] which is a very accurate explanation of descriptive definition. Interestingly enough, the reason adduced why such a definition is not necessary in the case of *pramāṇa* is *prasiddhāni pramāṇāni*, where the plural is expressly used. This would point to the more archaic kind of definition based on classification, that would define the notion of *pramāṇa* merely by specifying the *pramāṇa* 'inventory'. Thereby NA 2 supports our supposition that what Siddhasena really does is a descriptive definition of *pramāṇa*. Accordingly, NA 2 would rather be a record of the historical change and certain resistance against a new approach towards defining *pramāṇa*. This would also explain the role of the verse, that might seem unnecessary at first glance, in such a succinct work as NA is.

[5] The *pāda* C (*tad-vyāmoha-nivṛttiḥ*) of NA 3[xxxiv]—which is a rejoinder to the doubt raised in NA 2 whether it is 'purposeful to state the definition of cognitive criterion' (viz. whether the treatise, or the *Nyāyâvatāra* = *śāstra*, has a purpose), since 'cognitive criteria are well-known and everyday practice is accomplished by them'—recalls Dharmakīrti's statement found in $PV_{1,3}$ 1.7:

prāmāṇyaṁ vyavahāreṇa śāstraṁ moha-nivartanam /
ajñātârtha-prakāśo vā svarūpâdhigateḥ param //

A statement expressing a similar idea seems to be absent from PS.

[6] Corresponding to the sequence of topics discussed in NB (truly, it is a typical sequence not restricted to NB), as a next step Siddhasena in NA 5 makes his polemical statement and declares also inference to be 'non-erroneous because it is a cognitive criterion, just like perception.' (… *anumānaṁ, tad abhrāntaṁ pramāṇatvāt samakṣavat* …). The use of the term *abhrānta* as well as the polemical character directly points to NB_1 1.4: *tatra pratyakṣaṁ kalpanâpoḍham abhrāntam*. This issue, that was taken up by Jacobi and Vaidya, has been already discussed above p. vi ff. Dharmakīrti expressed such ideas that could have served both as a target and inspiration for Siddhasena also in PV_3 2.45–46 (*anumāna-vicāraḥ*):

ayathâbhiniveśena dvitīyā bhrāntir iṣyate /
gatiś cet para-rūpeṇa na ca bhrānteḥ pramāṇatā //
abhiprāyâvisaṁvādād api bhrānteḥ pramāṇatā /
gatir apy anyathā dṛṣṭā, pakṣaś câyaṁ kṛtôttaraḥ //

But this is not the only Dharmakīrtian trace to be found in NA 5. Inference is defined by Siddhasena to 'determine the *sādhya* on account of *liṅga*; *liṅga* (the inferential sign) is, in its turn, inseparably connected with the *sādhya*; the determining factor is here the relation of *avinâbhāva*: NA 5ac: *sādhyâvinâbhuno liṅgāt sādhya-*

[xxxiii] NAV 2 *ad loc.*: ***pramāṇa-lakṣaṇasyôktau*** *para-rūpa-vyāvartana-kṣamâsādhāraṇa-pramāṇa-dharma-kathana-rūpāyāṁ*.

[xxxiv] *prasiddhānāṁ pramāṇānāṁ lakṣaṇôktau prayojanam /*
tad-vyāmoha-nivṛttiḥ syād vyāmūḍha-manasām iha //

niścāyakaṁ smṛtam / anumānaṁ. This definition follows, in most—if not all—details, the ideas expressed by Dharmakīrti in PV_3 1.287:

anumānâśrayo liṅgam avinâbhāva-lakṣaṇam /
vyāpti-pradarśanād dhetoḥ sādhyenôktañ ca tat sphuṭam //

This striking correspondence does not only concern central elements in inference and their character as well as their mutual connection, but even the choice of vocabulary. The inseparable connection with the probandum as the defining characteristic of the probans reoccurs in NA 13: *sādhyâvinâbhuvo hetor*.[xxxv]

Furthermore, Siddhasena refers to his predecessors, or a certain tradition, by *smṛtam / anumānaṁ* ('inference is regarded traditionally to be…'). The rhetorical, as it were, question is whom else he might have had in mind, if such a definition of inference is not found— or at least we have no indication of it—in Jaina source prior to Siddhasena? One of possible answers would be he may have referred to the Yogācāra tradition, probably even to Dharmakīrti.

[7] NA 8 may have been influenced by Diṅnāga both in terms of vocabulary and notions. Its *pāda* D (*mānaṁ śābdaṁ prakīrtitam*) reminds of PS_2 5.1 (esp. *śābda*, *sgra las byuṅ ba*):

na pramāṇântaraṁ śābdam anumānāt tathā hi tat /
kṛtakatvâdivat svârtham anyâpohena bhāṣate // [xxxvi]

[8] In NA 13 Siddhasena takes a closer look at *parârthânumāna* and the conditions of its validity: *sādhyâvinâbhuvo hetor vaco yat pratipādakam / parârtham anumānaṁ tat pakṣâdi-vacanâtmakam //* The phrasing is reminiscent of NB 3.1: *tri-rupa-liṅgâkhyānaṁ parârthânumānam*. Clearly, the element of *tri-rūpa*—a criterion of validity of *anumāna* for the Dharmakīrtian tradition—is absent in NA, for this idea was not recognised by the Jainas. Instead, syntactically and semantically in the same position, we have the Jaina criterion of validity, viz. *sādhyâvinâbhuvaḥ*. Thus, NA 13 may be taken as Siddhasena's polemical reply to the Buddhist doctrine of *trairūpya*.

On the other hand, *pāda*s cd of NA 13 (…*anumānaṁ tat pakṣâdi-vacanâtmakam*) bear close resemblance to (1) NP_2 2 (=NP_1, p. 1.4–5): *tatra pakṣâdi-vacanāni sādhanam. pakṣa-hetu-dṛṣṭânta-vacanair hi prāśnikānām apratīto 'rthaḥ pratipādyata iti //* as well as to (2) the verse of NM 1: *pakṣâdi-vacanānîti sādhanam; tatra hi svayaṁ / sādhyatvenêpsitaḥ pakṣo viruddhârthânirākṛtaḥ //*, provided

---

[xxxv] Cf. also PV_3 3.31: *kārya-kāraṇa-bhāvād vā svabhāvād vā niyāmakāt / avinâbhāva-niyamo 'darśanān na na darśanāt //*, etc.

[xxxvi] *sgra las byuṅ ba rjes dpag las |*
tshad ma gźan min de ltar de |
byas sogs pa bźin du raṅ don la |
gźan sel bas ni rjod par byed |

The verse is quoted in TSaP *ad* TSa 1514 (p. 441.6–7), with a minor alteration (*anumānāt tathā hi saḥ* (*tat*) /).

G. Tucci's Sanskrit reconstruction is correct (cf. p. xx). However, this similarity is not decisive at all, inasmuch as all the quotations merely describe the widely known structure of any 'syllogistic' reasoning, that is composed of respective links, viz. members of proof formula.

[9] In the definition of *pakṣa*, NA 14ab: *sādhyâbhyupagamaḥ pakṣaḥ pratyakṣâdy-anirākṛtaḥ* /, we come across other formulations that bear obvious similarity especially to NB_2 3.37: *svarūpeṇâiva svayam iṣṭo 'nirākṛtaḥ pakṣa iti* (but also to NB_2 3.49–53). Dharmakīrti's *svarūpeṇa* stands for *sādhyatvena*, which is confirmed both by Dharmakīrti himself in the next two *sūtras* (NB_2 3.39–40: *svarūpeṇêti sādhyatvenêṣṭaḥ. svarūpeṇâivêti sādhyatvenâivêṣṭo na sādhyatvenâpi.*) as well as by Dharmottara ($NBṬ_2$ 3.37 *ad loc.*: *svarūpeṇâivêti sādhyatvenâiva.*). Dharmottara explains *anirākṛtaḥ* as *pratyakṣâdy-anirākṛtaḥ* ($NBṬ_2$ 3.37 *ad loc.*: *evaṁ-bhūtaḥ san pratyakṣâdy-anirākṛto yo 'rthaḥ sa pakṣa ity ucyate*), and—if we suppose that he expressed original ideas of Dharmakīrti (and I believe he did in this regard)—Siddhasena's formulations express almost the same idea as Dharmakīrti did in NB, barring Dharmakīrti's specific delimiting use of *eva* as well as *svayam*.

However, there can hardly be any doubt that the formulations of NA 14ab: *sādhyâbhyupagamaḥ pakṣaḥ pratyakṣâdy-anirākṛtaḥ* /, go back to $PV_{1,3}$ 4.86 (1: p. 378, 3: p. 390):

sādhyâbhyupagamaḥ pakṣa-lakṣaṇaṁ teṣv apakṣatā /
nirākṛte[xxxvii] *bādhanataḥ śeṣe 'lakṣaṇa-vṛttitaḥ* //

The idea itself goes back to Diṅnāga and his *Nyāya-mukha* (*svayaṁ sādhyatvenêpsitaḥ pakṣo viruddhârthânirākṛtaḥ*[xxxviii]), as it was pointed out by Manorathanandin in the *Vṛtti ad loc.* (PVV_1, p. 378.26 = PVV_3: p. 390.16). Another plausible source for NA 14 might be PS 3.2:

svarupeṇâiva nirdeśyaḥ svayam iṣṭo 'nirākṛtaḥ /
pratyakṣ*ârthânumānâpta-prasiddhena svadharmiṇi* // [xxxix]

Clearly, the word *ādi* of the phrase *pratyakṣâdi* of NA 14b m i g h t allude to the categories [*pratyakṣârtha*?], *anumāna*, *āpta*, *prasiddha* enumerated in Diṅnāga's

---

[xxxvii] Cf. Manorathanandin's *Vṛtti ad loc.*: *tathā ca teṣu śāstrêṣṭâdiṣu pañcasu vyāvartyeṣu mādhye nirākṛte pratyākṣâdi-bādhite bādhanato 'pakṣatā viruddhârthā.*

[xxxviii] Cf. also TUCCI's reconstruction of NM 1 on p. xx.

[xxxix] The above Sanskrit reconstruction of PS 3.2 follows FRAUWALLNER (1957/b: 885) and TILLEMANS (1997: 178, n. 2). Tibetan text reads as follows:

raṅ gi ṅo bo kho na[a] *bstan* |
bdag 'dod raṅ gi chos can la |
mṅon sum don daṅ rjes dpag daṅ |
yid ches grags pas ma bsal ba'o | |

[a] TILLEMANS 1997 reads *nar*.

PS 3.2 must have been in its turn the source for NB_2 3.37.

anirākṛtaḥ pratyakṣârthânumānâpta-prasiddhena, but it does not necessarily have to, since Siddharṣi (NAV 14 *ad loc.*: ***ādi***-*śabdād anumāna-sva-vacana-lokā gṛhyante*) takes *ādi* to stand for *anumāna-sva-vacana-loka*.

Another predecessor of Dharmakīrti in this regard was Śaṅkarasvāmin, see NP_2 2.1: *tatra pakṣaḥ prasiddho dharmī prasiddha-viśeṣaṇa-viśiṣṭatayā svayaṁ sādhyatvenêpsitaḥ*. ***pratyakṣâdy***-*viruddha iti vākya-śeṣaḥ*.

Out of all these possible sources, NA 14 has most in common with Dharmakīrti in terms of (1) exact wording (*sādhyâbhyupagamaḥ pakṣa...*), (2) replacement of Diṅnāgan *iṣṭa* with *abhyupagama*, (3) affinity in the explicit correlative *sādhya* (instead of Diṅnāgan *svarupeṇâiva nirdeśya*) to *abhyupagama* / *iṣṭa*.

[10] The description of *hetu* and its role in the inference for others (*parârthânumāna*) in NA 17 is not so conspicuously similar to NB in phrasing. Nevertheless, semantically both expositions are quite akin to each other. That in NA 17 we still deal with *parârthânumāna* is clear from the context itself, but also Siddharṣi leaves not doubt (NAV 17 *ad loc.*: ***parârthânumānasya*** *vacana-rūpatvād...*). Thus, in both cases we have 'the pronouncement of the logical reason' (*hetos ... prayogo*, NA) or 'the announcement of the inferential sign' (*liṅgâkhyānaṁ*, NB) as the principal element of the inference for others (*parârthânumāna*) and the idea that there is no difference in 'demonstrative force' between the two formulations of the logical reason:

NA 17: *hetos tathôpapattyā vā syāt prayogo 'nyathâpi vā / dvi-vidho 'nyatareṇâpi sādhya-siddhir bhaved iti //*

NB 3.1,3–7: /1/ *tri-rūpa-liṅgâkhyānaṁ* ***parârthânumānam***. /3/ *tad dvi-vidham*. /4/ *prayoga-bhedāt*. /5/ *sādharmya-vaidharmyavac cêti*. /6/ *nânayor arthataḥ kaścid bhedaḥ*. /7/ *anyatra prayoga-bhedāt*.

The idea expressed by Dharmakīrti goes back to his PV_1 3.16 and PVSV *ad loc.*[xl]

[xl] In PV_1 3.15 [p. 180] Dharmakīrti first recalls the triple character of *hetu* defined by Diṅnāga in *Nyāya-mukha*:

hetos triṣv api rūpeṣu niścayas tena varṇitaḥ /
asiddha-viparītârtha-vyabhicāri-vipakṣataḥ //

Then (PV_1 3.16ab) he states the reason for expressing the concomitance by way of dissimilarity (*vaidharmya-vacana*):

vyabhicāri-vipakṣeṇa vaidharmya-vacanaṁ ca yat /

only to quote Diṅnāga in $PVSV_1$ 3.16ab: *yad āha—eṣa tāvan nyāyo yad ubhayaṁ vaktavyaṁ viruddhânaikāntika-pratipakṣeṇa iti*. The rule is further explained by Dharmakīrti in PVSV as follows: *sādharmya-vācanaṁ viruddha-pratipakṣeṇa, vaidharmya-vācanam anaikāntika-pratipakṣeṇa*. Thereupon, in PV_1 3.16cd and PVSV *ad loc.*, he adds that :

yady adṛṣti-phalaṁ tac ca
yadi tena vipakṣe 'darśanaṁ khyāpyate
tad anukte 'pi gamyate //

[11] In NA 20 Siddhasena maintains that *dṛṣṭânta* is not an essential part of 'syllogistic' reasoning, inasmuch as the relation of invariable concomitance (*vyāpti*) suffices to prove the thesis. This is a continuation of the 'economical' trend in Indian logic—that starts with Vasubandhu and his *Vāda-vidhāna* and *Vāda-vidhi*[xli]—to limit the number of necessary members of the proof formula, to simplify the reasoning procedures and to make such procedures universally binding, without any need for further empirical justification than the premises themselves:[xlii]

NA 20: *antar-vyāptyâiva sādhyasya siddher bahir-udāhṛtiḥ / vyarthā syāt tad-asadbhāve 'py evaṁ nyāya-vido viduḥ //*

NB_2 3.121: *tri-rūpo hetur uktaḥ. tāvatā cârtha-pratītir iti na pṛthag dṛṣṭânto nāma sādhanâvayavaḥ kaścit. tena nâsya lakṣaṇaṁ pṛthag ucyate gatârthatvāt.*

Siddhasena was not so much innovative as it might seem at first glance, inasmuch as it is Dharmakīrti (NB_2 3.121) who had intuitively foreshadowed such an idea before him, when he had claimed that the example (*dṛṣṭânta*) is not a separate member of the proof (*sādhanâvayava*). It is much more natural and less surprising to find the direct continuation of the 'economical' trend, that had started with Vasubandhu, in the Yogâcāra tradition and Dharmakīrti's works, rather than in the Jaina tradition in the person of Siddhasena, where we do not find such an 'economic' tendency before Siddhasena. In my opinion, Siddhasena verbalised what had already been latent in Dharmakīrti's statement, even though Dharmakīrti himself had not been able to do without the example, which he had considered an integral part of the logical reason (*hetu*), indispensable to authenticate the general principle by taking recourse to its instantiations (relevant portions underlined):

NB_2 3.122: *hetoḥ sapakṣa eva sattvam asapakṣāc ca sarvato vyāvartī rūpam uktam abhedena. punar viśeṣeṇa kārya-svabhāvayor ukta-lakṣaṇayor janma-tan-mātrânubandhau darśanīyāv uktau. tac ca darśayatā—yatra dhūmas tatrâgnir, asaty agnau na kvacid dhūmo yathā mahānasêtarayor, yatra kṛtakatvaṁ tatrânityatvam, anityatvâbhāvo kṛtakatvâsambhavo yathā ghaṭâkāśayor—iti darśanīyam. na hy anyathā sapakṣa-vipakṣayoḥ sad-asattve yathôkta-prakāre śakye darśayitum. tat-kāryatā-niyamaḥ kārya-liṅgasya, svabhāva-liṅgasya ca svabhāvena vyāptiḥ. asmiṁś cârthe darśite eva dṛṣṭânto bhavati. etāvan-mātra-rūpatvāt tasyêti.*

Dharmakīrti expressed a similar idea already in his PV_3 3.27 (see also nn. 411, 520 below):

tad-bhāva-hetu-bhāvau hi dṛṣṭânte tad-avedinaḥ /
khyāpyete, viduṣāṁ vācyo hetur eva hi kevalaḥ //

Cf. also $PVSV_1$ 3.24–25 [p. 185]: *tasmāt svabhāva-pratibandhād eva hetuḥ sādhyaṁ gamayati. sa ca tad-bhāva-lakṣaṇas tad-utpatti-lakṣaṇo vā. sa evâvinâbhāvo dṛṣṭântābhyāṁ pradarśyate.*

[xli] Cf. FRAUWALLNER (1933) and FRAUWALLNER (1957/a).

[xlii] Cf. n. 393, 438.

Siddhasena, however, has to his credit that he clearly states the conditions of internal formal validity of the proof and dismisses the need to quote any instantiation: the proof is valid because the premisses are valid and the relation between them is universally binding.

What is puzzling is whom he might have had in mind when he speaks of 'the experts in logic' (*nyāya-vid*): ... *tad-asadbhāve 'py evaṁ nyāya-vido viduḥ*? Clearly, he refers to some tradition, not necessarily directly to his predecessor. In any case, both Dharmakīrti and Siddhasena differ from Diṅnāga in admitting that 'for scholars simply the logical reason alone is to be stated.'

[12] Siddhasena states explicitly five conditions that invalidate *pakṣa*—and adds that there are, in fact, several varieties of *pakṣâbhāsa*—in NA 21:

pratipādyasya yaḥ siddhaḥ pakṣâbhāso 'kṣa-liṅgataḥ /
loka-sva-vacanābhyāṁ ca bādhito 'nekadhā mataḥ //

These five *pakṣâbhāsas* are in concord with the list exemplified by Siddharṣi in NAV: (1) *pratipādya-siddha*, (2) *pratyakṣa-bādhita*, (3) *anumāna-bādhita*, (4) *loka-bādhita*, (5) *sva-vacana-bādhita*.

Having enumerated five varieties of *pakṣâbhāsa*, it would be redundant and pointless on Siddhasena's part to say by way of recapitulation in a succinct *kārikā* that these varieties are numerous: *anekadhā matah*, unless he had other varieties, not mentioned already by name, in mind. That being the case, he probably referred to other enumerations well-known from other sources.

In fact, Siddhasena's enumeration overlaps with Dharmakīrti's list of fallacies of the thesis, enumerated in NB_2 49–53: /49/ (2) *tatra pratyakṣa-nirākṛto yathā: aśrāvaṇaḥ śabda iti.* /50/ (3) *anumāna-nirākṛto yathā: nityaḥ śabda iti.* /51/ (4?) *pratīti-nirākṛto yathā: acandraḥ śaśîti.* /52/ (5) *sva-vacana-nirākṛto yathā: nânumānaṁ pramāṇam.* /53/ *iti catvāraḥ pakṣâbhāsā nirākṛtā bhavanti.* Interestingly, Dharmakīrti subsequently adds a few more conditions and the failure to meet them would render the *pakṣa* defective as well: NB_2 3.54: *evaṁ siddhasya, asiddhasyâpi sādhanatvenâbhimatasya, svayaṁ vādinā tadā sādhayitum aniṣṭasya, ukta-mātrasya nirākṛtasya ca viparyayeṇa sādhyaḥ. tenâiva sva-rūpeṇâbhimato vādina iṣṭo 'nirākṛtaḥ pakṣa iti pakṣa-lakṣaṇam anavadyaṁ darśitaṁ bhavati.* Thus, Siddhasena—by *anekadhā mataḥ*—may have referred to Dharmakīrti's catalogue of defective *pakṣas*. But not necessarily to Dharmakīrti's. He may have as well referred, e.g. to NP_2 3.1:

sādhayitum iṣṭo 'pi pratyakṣâdi-viruddhaḥ pakṣâbhāsaḥ, tad yathā: (1) *pratyakṣa-viruddhaḥ*, (2) *anumāna-viruddhaḥ*, (3) *āgama-viruddhaḥ*, (4) *loka-viruddhaḥ*, (5) *sva-vacana-viruddhaḥ*, (6) *aprasiddha-viśeṣaṇaḥ*, (7) *aprasiddha-viśeṣyaḥ*, (8) *aprasiddhôbhayaḥ*, (9) *prasiddha-sambandhaś cêti // tatra...*

In any case, NA 21 can in no way attest that Siddhasena was posterior or prior to Dharmakīrti. It merely points to certain similarities between Siddhasena's list and the

Buddhist tradition. Probably, it was the tradition of Śaṅkarasvāmin and Dharmakīrti that Siddhasena alluded to by *anekadhā mataḥ*.

[13] In Siddhasena's subsequent aphorism, we find further similarities with NB, though they are less of linguistic nature (similarities in formulations) but rather of methodological character. Analogously to the structure of NB, Siddhasena—after describing fallacious theses—proceeds to discuss fallacious logical reasons (*hetv-ābhāsa*). However, both the authors first look back to their previous definitions of a correct, not defective *hetu*:

NA 22: *anyathânupapannatvaṁ hetor lakṣaṇam īritam*[xliii] / *tad-apratīti-sandeha-viparyāsais tad-ābhatā* //

NB$_2$ 3.55–56: /55/ *tri-rūpa-liṅgâkhyānaṁ parârthânumānam ity uktam*[xliv]. *tatra trayāṇāṁ rūpāṇām ekasyâpi rūpasyânuktau sādhanâbhāsaḥ*. /56/ *uktāv apy asiddhau sandehe vā pratipādya-pratipādakayoḥ*.

Incidentally, it is the only case in both works that the authors first remind the reader/hearer of the definition of a correct member/term of the proof formula, and only then deal with its particular fallacies.

Likewise incidentally, both the authors first state general factors that invalidate a correct *hetu*, either singly or jointly, and subsequently enumerate resulting fallacies one by one. There are two such general invalidating factors for Dharmakīrti, viz. *asiddhi* and *sandeha* (NB 3.56,109): their various combinations (with regard to *trairūpya*) are responsible for particular varieties of *hetv-ābhāsa*. For Siddhasena, however, there are three—polemically, as it were—such factors: *tad-apratīti*, *sandeha* and *viparyāsa*; thus Dharmakīrti's *asiddhi* factor would seem to bifurcate into Siddhasena's *tad-apratīti* and *viparyāsa*. For instance, for Siddhasena the fallacies of NB 3.58 and 59[xlv] would be probably a case of *viparyāsa*, whereas the fallacy of NB 3.60[xlvi] should rather be considered a case of *tad-apratīti*. One could analyse all the remaining cases of fallacious *hetus* (ensuing from the combination of the factors *asiddhi* and *sandeha*) found in NB and map them onto the triple classification of Siddhasena in the same manner. Practically, it would mean to decide which of the *asiddhi* cases of Dharmakīrti would correspond to *tad-apratīti* cases of Siddhasena, and which to his *viparyāsa* cases. However, we do not have any explicit statement in

---

[xliii] Either in NA 5 (according to Siddharṣi) or in NA 17, see n. 447.

[xliv] NB 3.1: *tri-rūpa-liṅgâkhyānaṁ parârthânumānam*; cf. also NB$_2$ 2.5,11–12.

[xlv] NB$_2$ 3.57–9: /57/ *ekasya rūpasya dharmi-sambandhasyâsiddhau sandehe vâsiddho hetv-ābhāsaḥ*. /58/ *yathā*: *anityaḥ śabda iti sādhye cākṣuṣatvam ubhayâsiddham* [not proved for both parties]. /59/ *cetanās tarava iti sādhye sarva-tvag-apaharaṇe maraṇaṁ prativādy-asiddham, vijñānêndriyâyur-nirodha-lakṣaṇasya maraṇasyânenâbhyupagamāt, tasya ca taruṣv asambhavāt* [not proved for the opponent].

[xlvi] NB$_2$ 3.60: *acetanāḥ sukhâdaya iti sādhya utpattimattvam anityatvaṁ vā sāṁkhyasya svayaṁ vādino 'siddham* [not proved for the proponent himself].

the far too succinct NA, nor in NAV, that would provide us any algorithm of such a mapping, and the issue is open to our conjectures only.

Interestingly, in NP, for instance, to which NA might be thought to have occasionally referred to, we do not find any trait of such invalidating factors as *asiddhi* and *sandeha*, or anything similar.

[14] Also NA 23 and the classification of particular varieties of *hetv-ābhāsas* points to secondary sources of Siddhasena's ideas. There seem to be only two such potential sources, i.e. NB and NP:

NA 23: *asiddhas tv apratīto yo yo 'nyathâivôpapadyate / viruddho yo 'nyathâpy atra yukto 'naikāntikaḥ sa tu //*

NB_2 3.109: *evam eṣāṁ trayāṇāṁ rūpāṇām ekâikasya dvayor dvayor vā rūpayor asiddhau sandehe vā yathā-yogam asiddha-viruddhânaikāntikās trayo hetv-ābhāsāḥ.*

NP_2 3.2. *asiddhânaikāntika-viruddhā hetv-ābhāsāḥ //*

However, NB is a more probable source, inasmuch as the sequence of fallacies (*asiddha, viruddha, anaikāntika*) listed in NA is exactly the same as that of NB, not of NP, where the two last varieties are interchanged (*asiddha, anaikāntika, viruddha*).

What is striking is that Siddhasena has only three varieties of *hetv-ābhāsa*, like Dharmakīrti and Śaṅkarasvāmin, unlike Diṅnāga. Dharmakīrti outspokenly rejects Diṅnāga's subvariety, i.e. *viruddhâvyabhicārin*[xlvii]: NB_2 3.110: *viruddhâvyabhicāry api saṁśaya-hetur uktaḥ. sa iha kasmān nôktaḥ.* We do not find any polemical trait in NA, which could even suggest that Siddhasena adopted Dharmakīrti's criticism of *viruddhâvyabhicārin*. Apparently he subscribed to the criticism unhesitatingly.[xlviii]

[15] Both NA 24 and 25 reveal further similarities pointing to NB as its possible inspiration. One of them is the phraseological affinity as regards the use of *dṛṣṭânta-doṣa*, instead of *dṛṣṭântâbhāsa*, in both works. Both Siddhasena and Dharmakīrti use the expression *pakṣâbhāsa* as well as similarly *tad-ābha* and *hetv-ābhāsa*. However, both of them deviate from the general use of derivatives of *ā√bhās* to technically denote logical fallacies, when they refer to *dṛṣṭânta* by the term *doṣa*, and to *dṛṣṭânta* only:

[xlvii] Cf. also RANDLE (1926: 68–69, 79).

[xlviii] In may not be so irrelevant to note here in passing, that it might have been the discussion over the varieties of *hetv-ābhāsa* that eventually prompted Pārthasārathi Miśra to follow Dharmakīrti-Siddhasena classification, cf. p. 264.11 (ad MŚV.5.4.75): *samprati hetv-ābhāsān asiddhânaikāntika-viruddhān prapañcayan...*; whereas Kumārila distinguished *asiddha, sandigdha, viruddha* subtypes, see MŚV.5.4.75, p. 264: *saṁśayâdhī-viparyāyāḥ*: (1) threefold *asiddha* discussed in MŚV.5.4.76–83ab, (2) *sandigdha* and (3) *viruddha* discussed in MŚV.5.4.83cd–107 (e.g. in MŚV.5.4.83cd: *sandeha-viparītatva-hetū câtra nirākṛtau*), further (2) *sandigdha* spoken of again in MŚV.5.4.84b–96b and (3) *viruddha* in MŚV.5.4.96cd–107ab. Kumārila nowhere in the *Anumāna-pariccheda* section uses the term *anaikāntika* as a *hetv-ābhāsa*, throughout he has *sandigdha* instead.

NA 24: *sādharmyeṇâtra dṛṣṭânta-doṣā...*, NA 25: *vaidharmyeṇâtra dṛṣṭânta-doṣā...*
NB_2 3.123, 128–129: */123/ etenâiva dṛṣṭânta-doṣā api nirastā bhavanti. /128/ sādharmyeṇa dṛṣṭânta-doṣāḥ. /129/ vaidharmyeṇâpi: paramāṇuvat karmavad ākāśavad iti sādhyâdy-vyatirekiṇaḥ.*

Indeed, also Śaṅkarasvāmin has *dṛṣṭânta-doṣa* twice, but in a slightly different context, viz., that of refutation. Generally, when he discusses fallacious examples, he uses the standard term *dṛṣṭântâbhāsa*, e.g. NP_2 3.3: *dṛṣṭântâbhāso dvividhaḥ: sādharmyeṇa vaidharmyeṇa ca //* The only two occurences of *dṛṣṭânta-doṣa* are found in NP_2 6,7:

(6) *sādhana-doṣôdbhāvanāni dūṣaṇāni // sādhana-doṣo nyūnatvam. pakṣa-doṣaḥ pratyakṣâdi-viruddhatvam. hetu-doṣo 'siddhânaikāntika-viruddhatvam. dṛṣṭānta-doṣaḥ sādhana-dharmâdy-asiddhatvam. tasyôdbhāvanaṁ prāśnika-pratyāyanaṁ dūṣaṇam //*
(7) *abhūta-sādhana-doṣôdbhāvanāni dūṣaṇâbhāsāni // saṁpūrṇe sādhane nyūnatva-vacanam. aduṣṭa-pakṣe pakṣa-doṣa-vacanam. siddha-hetuke 'siddha-hetukaṁ vacanam. ekânta-hetuke 'nekânta-hetukaṁ vacanam. aviruddha-hetuke viruddha-hetukaṁ vacanam. aduṣṭa-dṛṣṭânte duṣṭa-dṛṣṭânta-doṣa-vacanam. etāni dūṣaṇâbhāsāni. na hy ebhiḥ para-pakṣo dūṣyate, niravadyatvāt tasya // ity uparamyate //*.

Conspicuously, *dṛṣṭânta-doṣa* occurs as exemplification of *dūṣaṇāni*, in the series of *sādhana-doṣa, pakṣa-doṣa, hetu-doṣa* and *dṛṣṭânta-doṣa*.[xlix] Another occurrence of *doṣa* (however, *pratijñā-doṣa*, not *dṛṣṭânta-doṣa*) in NP is attested in the concluding lines of NP_2 3.1, that summarise the discussion on *pakṣâbhāsa*: *eṣāṁ vacanāni dharma-svarūpa-nirākaraṇa-mukhena pratipādanâsaṁbhavataḥ sādhana-vaiphalyataś cêti pratijñā-doṣāḥ // uktāḥ pakṣâbhāsāḥ //*. Also here, the term *doṣa* has a more general meaning than the technical term *ābhāsa*, and the peculiarity of the usage of *pratijñā-doṣa* is confirmed by the closing *uktāḥ pakṣâbhāsāḥ*. The usage of *doṣa* in NP confirms the fact that in works preceding Diṅnāga, Dharmakīrti or Śaṅkarasvāmin—e.g. in NS, VS, NBh, PBh, etc.—*doṣa* is employed to denote general defects and is not used specifically as a *terminus technicus* in the sense of *ābhāsa*.

[16] There is a structural similarity to be observed: both Siddhasena (NA 24) and Dharmakīrti (NB_2 3.122–3) explicitly define fallacious examples by referring to the definition of a correct *hetu*. Accordingly, NB 3.122 recapitulates the definition of correct *hetu* as well as conditions of its validity. The successive statement of NB 3.123 (*etenâiva dṛṣṭânta-doṣā api nirastā bhavanti*; *vide supra* p. xxvi) shows that fallacious examples are refuted by referring to the correct definition of *hetu*, and all fallacies of the example share the same characteristic. Similarly, Siddhasena re-

[xlix] NP_2 6: *sādhana-doṣôdbhāvanāni dūṣaṇāni // sādhana-doṣo nyūnatvam. pakṣa-doṣaḥ pratyakṣâdi-viruddhatvam. hetu-doṣo 'siddhânaikāntika-viruddhatvam. dṛṣṭānta-doṣaḥ sādhana-dharmâdy-asiddhatvam. tasyôdbhāvanaṁ prāśnika-pratyāyanaṁ dūṣaṇam //*.

lates the deficiency of *dṛṣṭântâbhāsa*s to deficient logical reasons and, with *apalakṣaṇa-hetûtthāḥ*, he expresses the idea known from the work of Dharmakīrti.

[17] Strangely, in NA 24–25 Siddhasena refers to some tradition by *nyāya-vid-īritāḥ* as regards the classification of fallacious examples. However, there seems to have been no earlier (or contemporary) Jaina source he could have referred to. Thus, in default of any extant evidence attesting to a Jaina tradition which offered a typology of fallacious examples, one is prone to assume—unless we find any indication to the contrary—that, apparently, he must have referred to a general Indian tradition, where we do find such a typology of *sādharmya-°* and *vaidharmya-dṛṣṭântâbhāsa*s.

Besides, he also seems to have taken it for granted that the reader/hearer could easily determine what is meant by *sādhyâdi-vikalâdayaḥ* in NA 24. This task would naturally be quite easy for anyone who was acquainted with NB_2 3.124–125. At the same time, however, his elliptical formulation *sādhyâdi-vikalâdayaḥ* was, polemically as it were, unequivocal enough to rule out the three remaining varieties, viz., (A7) *ananvaya*, (A8) *apradarśitânvaya* and (A9) *viparītânvaya*, formulated by Dharmakīrti (NB_2 3.126–127), which could by no means have been hinted at by the formulations of NA 24.

Similarly, the sixfold classification of dissimilar *dṛṣṭântâbhāsas* systematised in NA 25 (*sādhya-sādhana-yugmānām anivṛtteś ca saṁśayāt*) closely corresponds to the first six fallacious examples of NB_2 3.129–132: (V1) *sādhyâvyatirekin*, (V2) *sādhanâvyatirekin*, (V3) *sādhya-sādhanâvyatirekin*, (V4) *sandigdha-sādhya-vyatireka*, (V5) *sandigdha-sādhana-vyatireka*, (V6) *sandigdha-sādhya-sādhana-vyatireka*. Seemingly, NA and NB are at variance as regards terminology, for Siddhasena's formulation: *sādhya-sādhana-yugmānām anivṛtteś ca saṁśayāt*, differs from Dharmakīrti's (V1)–(V6). In my opinion, however, *anivṛtteś* and *saṁśayāt* of NA 25 indicate rather plainly *°-vyāvṛtta* and *sandigdha-°* as the last and first elements of the compounds (V1)–(V3) and (V4)–(V6), respectively. Optionally, we could have (V1) **sādhyânivṛtta*, (V2) **sādhanânivṛtta*, (V3) **sādhya-sādhanânivṛtta*, (V4) **saṁśayita-sādhya*, (V5) **saṁśayita-sādhana*, (V6) **saṁśayita-sādhya-sādhana*, which is not different at all from the idea expressed in NB_2 3.129–132.

True, theoretically speaking, one could also interpret NA 25 to enforce the acceptance of only (1) *sādhyâvyatirekin*, (2) *sādhanâvyatirekin*, (3) *sādhya-sādhanâvyatirekin*—to use Dharmakīrti's terminology—and only one or more varieties out of (4) *sandigdha-sādhya-vyatireka*, (5) *sandigdha-sādhana-vyatireka*, (6) *sandigdha-sādhya-sādhana-vyatireka*, but not necessarily all of them. While *anivṛtteḥ* is unquestionably construed with *sādhya-sādhana-yugmānām*, the expression *saṁśayāt* might be conjectured to be taken separately, without any dependence on all elements of *sādhya-sādhana-yugmānām*. In this respect, attention should be drawn to an instance of different conceivable ways of construing an aphorism of NA by commentators which we encounter in the case of NA 8: *dṛṣṭêṣṭâvyāhatād vākyāt paramârthâbhidhāyinaḥ / tattva-grāhitayôtpannaṁ mānaṁ śābdaṁ prakīrtitam //* The aphorism is explained differently by the commentators, viz. (1) NAV *ad loc.*: ***dṛṣṭena** pramāṇâvalokitenê**ṣṭaḥ** pratipādayiṣito '**vyāhato** 'nirākṛtaḥ sāmarthyād* *artho yasmin vākye tat-tathā*; and (2) NAṬ ad loc.: ***dṛṣṭenêty-ādi***. *ayaṁ bhinnâdhikaraṇas tri-pado bahu-vrīhiḥ yadi vā iṣṭo 'vyāhato 'rtho yatra tad iṣṭâvyāhataṁ vākyam, tadanu dṛṣṭena pramāṇa-nirṇītena iṣṭâvyāhatam iti tat-puruṣaḥ.*[l] Definitely, such an unnatural interpretation—i.e. to take *anivṛtteś* to refer to all elements of the triad *sādhya-sādhana-yugmānām*, while limiting the scope of *saṁśayāt* to selected element(s) of the compound *sādhya-sādhana-yugmānām*—would be a mere guesswork, and one would rather, as a rule, construe *sādhya-sādhana-yugmānām* with both *anivṛtteś* and *saṁśayāt*, and obtain six varieties of dissimilar *dṛṣṭântâbhāsas*. One would not, in any case, obtain any further varieties mentioned by Dharmakīrti in NB_2 3.133–135: (V7) *avyatireka*, (V8) *apradarśita-vyatireka* and (V9) *viparīta-vyatireka*. Thus, Siddhasena apparently does not accept without reservation the Buddhist typology by rejecting (V7), (V8) and (V9).

As for another possible source of inspiration, also NP_2 3.3 distinguished—in accord with the prevalent tradition of those days—two general categories: similar and dissimilar fallacious examples (*dṛṣṭântâbhāso dvividhaḥ: sādharmyeṇa vaidharmyeṇa ca //*). However, a closer look at Śaṅkarasvāmin's varieties reveals essential differences, apart from the terminological ones. Accordingly, I see no way how the formulations of fallacies of examples based on similarity found in *Nyāya-praveśa*[li] could be interpreted to have influenced Siddhasena's *sādhyâdi-vikalâdayaḥ*. As regards *Nyāya-praveśa* on fallacies of examples based on dissimilarity[lii], the influence might have been restricted to (V1), (V2) and (V3) only.

[18] Also NA 26, where criticism / refutation (*dūṣaṇa*) and its fallacy (*dūṣaṇâbhāsa*) are discussed, might have partly been inspired by Dharmakīrti's NB_2 3.137–140. Thus, NA 26ac: *vādy-ukte sādhane prokta-doṣāṇām udbhāvanam / dūṣaṇaṁ*, reveals a certain similarity—in terms of both formulations and ideas—to the *dūṣaṇa*-section of NB_2 3.137–8: /137/ *dūṣaṇā nyūnatâdy-uktiḥ*. /138/ *ye pūrvaṁ nyūnatâdayaḥ sādhana-doṣā uktās teṣām udbhāvanaṁ dūṣaṇaṁ. tena parêṣṭârtha-siddhi-pratibandhāt*. Less conspicuous, though, is the remaining portion of the second hemistich of NA 26: *niravadye tu dūṣaṇâbhāsa-nāmakam //* The corresponding *dūṣaṇâbhāsa*-section of NB_2 3.139–140 reads: /139/ *dūṣaṇâbhāsāṣ tu jātayaḥ*. /140/ *abhūta-doṣôdbhāvanāni jāty-uttarāṇîti*. The reoccurring element *dūṣaṇâbhāsa* is not decisive at all, whereas Siddhasena's *niravadye* could be a vague echo of Dharmakīrti's *abhūta-doṣa*.

---

[l] Cf. BALCEROWICZ (1999/a: 4, n. 8).

[li] NP_2 3.3.1: *tatra sādharmyeṇa tāvad dṛṣṭântâbhāsaḥ pañca-prakāraḥ, tad yathā*: (1) *sādhana-dharmâsiddhaḥ*, (2) *sādhya-dharmâsiddhaḥ*, (3) *ubhaya-dharmâsiddhaḥ*, (4) *ananvayaḥ*, (5) *viparītânvayaś cêti // tatra*...

[lii] NP_2 3.3.2: *vaidharmyeṇâpi dṛṣṭântâbhāsaḥ pañca-prakāraḥ, tad yathā*: (1) *sādhyâvyāvṛttaḥ*, (2) *sādhanâvyāvṛttaḥ*, (3) *ubhayâvyāvṛttaḥ*, (4) *avyatirekaḥ*, (5) *viparīta-vyatirekaś cêti // tatra*...

As a matter of fact, NA 26cd (*niravadye tu dūṣaṇâbhāsa-nāmakam*) betrays more affinity to the closing section of NP_2 7: *abhūta-sādhana-doṣôdbhāvanāni dūṣaṇâbhāsāni // ... etāni dūṣaṇâbhāsāni. na hy ebhiḥ para-pakṣo dūṣyate, niravadyatvāt tasya // ity uparamyate //* It is this section, in all probability, that influenced both Dharmakīrti's NB_2 3.139–140 (*dūṣaṇâbhāsās tu jātayaḥ. abhūta-doṣôdbhāvanāni jāty-uttarāṇîti.*) and the portion of NA 26cd in question.

[19] The twenty-sixth aphorism (the exposition of *dūṣaṇa*) is the last section of the *Nyāyâvatāra*, where possible influences from Dharmakīrti's side—in terms of Siddhasena's direct use of Dharmakīrti vocabulary or his response to Dharmakīrti's ideas—are easily detectable. Strangely enough, the topic dealt with in NA 26 closely corresponds to the final issue discussed by Dharmakīrti in NB. Thus, the conspicuous absence of further possible Dharmakīrtian traces in NA—theoretically derivable from other works of Dharmakīrti— points, in my opinion, to the fact that Siddhasena—while composing NA—closely followed the structure and the contents of NB, up to NA 26.

In the remaining aphorisms (28–32) Siddhasena discusses issues peculiar to Jainism (viz. corollaries of *kevala-jñāna* and *syād-vāda*) and there could hardly have been any Buddhist influence to be noticed in any case: [27] the character of absolute cognition (*kevala-jñāna*); [28] the result of valid cognition in general; the results of absolute cognition (*kevala-jñāna*); the results of valid cognitive procedures other than *kevala-jñāna*; [29] the multiplex character of reality; the domain of cognitive acts; the domain of viewpoints (*naya*); [30] the character of viewpoints (*naya*); the description of the doctrine of seven-fold modal description (*syād-vāda*); [31] the character of the cognitive subject, the soul (*jīva*); [32] the eternal character of Jaina epistemology.

[20] The phrase *pramāṇa-phala* occurring in NA 28 is occasionally taken to be a proof of its dependence on Diṅnāga.[liii] It is commonly assumed that the phrase in question goes back to Diṅnāga, e.g. PS_1 1.8cd–10[liv]:

[liii] Cf., e.g. QVARNSTRÖM (1999: 178): 'Furthermore, the *Nyāyāvatāra* (28) uses the signature element of Dignāga, namely "pramāṇaphala"[61];' in his note 61, he further draws the reader's attention to the work of G. Dreyfus and Chr. Lindtner: 'The Yogācāra Philosophy of Dignāga and Dharmakīrti". *Studies in Central & East Asian Religions*. Vol. 2, Ed. by Per K. Sørensen et al. Copenhagen 1989, pp. 27–52.

[liv] For the Sanskrit text, see HATTORI (1968: 97, n. 1.55—107, n. 1.67). Tibetan text reads as follows:

Vasudhararakṣita/Seṅ-rgyal 15a.5–15b.4:	Kanakavarman/Dad-paḥi śes-rab 95b.5–96a.5:
bya daṅ bcas par rtogs paḥi phyir |	*bya daṅ bcas par rtogs paḥi phyir |*
tshad maḥi ḥbras bu ñid du ḥdod ||	*ḥbras bu ñid du yod tshad ma ||*
raṅ rig la yaṅ ḥdir ḥbras bu |	*yaṅ na raṅ rig ḥdir ḥbras bu |*
de yi ṅo bo las don ṅes |	*de yi ṅo bo las don ṅes |*
yul gyi snaṅ ba ḥdi ñid ḥdi |	*yul gyi snaṅ ba ñid de ḥdiḥi |*
tshad ma de yis ḥjal bar byed ||	*tshad ma de yis ḥjal bar bya ||*

savyāpāra-pratītitvāt pramāṇaṁ phalam eva sat //
sva-saṁvittiḥ phalaṁ vâtra tad-rūpo hy artha-niścayaḥ /
viṣayâkāratâivâsya pramāṇam tena mīyate //
yad-ābhāsaṁ prameyaṁ tat pramāṇa-phalate punaḥ /
grāhakâkāra-saṁvittī trayaṁ[lv] *nâtaḥ pṛthak-kṛtam //*

In these verses Diṅnāga asserts that the result of *pramāṇa* is *pramāṇa* itself, or introspective cognition which consists in the determining of an object (*sva-saṁvitti, artha-niścaya*). Precisely the same idea (*ātmânubhāva, artha-viniścaya*) is echoed in $PV_{1,3}$ 2.306–307ab,339:

tasmāt prameyâdhigateḥ sādhanaṁ meya-rūpatā /
sādhane 'nyatra tat-karma-sambandho na prasiddhyati //
sā ca tasyâtma-bhūtâiva tena nârthântaraṁ phalam /
yadā saviṣayaṁ jñānaṁ jñānâṁśe 'rtha-vyavasthiteḥ /
tadā ya ātmânubhāvaḥ sa evârtha-viniścayaḥ //

Generally, the idea is discussed at length by Dharmakīrti both in his PVin I_1 78.12–100.26 and in $PV_{1,3}$ 2.301–366,388–391. Accordingly, NA 28 might be taken to be a rejoinder of both Diṅnāga and Dharmakīrti, and there seems to nothing decisive to be found in NA 28 that would exclude any of the two authors.

On the other hand, any attempt to look for inspiration of NA 28 in works of either Diṅnāga or Dharmakīrti seems to me to be a result of misapprehension of the true import of the aphorism. In it, Siddhasena does not discuss the problem whether *pramāṇa-phala* can or cannot be equated with *pramāṇa* itself, which is the major concern of Diṅnāga and Dharmakīrti. What is intended in the verse are rather extra-epistemological issues of both soteriological (*kevala*) and mundane (*śeṣa*) character, viz. the result of *pramāṇa* is 'the cessation of nescience' (*ajñāna-vinivartana*), whereas the result of specific kinds of cognition is two-fold. The first category subsumes happiness and indifference (*sukhôpekṣe*) in the case of the perfect knowledge (*kevala*), being a prerequisite of liberation (*mokṣa*) and commonly taken by the Jainas to be tantamount to the destruction of nescience. Since it results from the destruction of *karman*[lvi] it is necessarily associated with innate happiness etc.[lvii] that are inhibited by *karman*. The other—pragmatic, as it were—category of results refers to 'the faculty of appropriation and avoidance' (*ādāna-hāna-dhī*) in case all the remaining kinds of (mundane) cognition. Consequently, what really the verse is reminiscent of is rather NBh 1.1.3: *yadā jñānaṁ tadā hānôpādanôpekṣā-buddhayaḥ phalam*, with all

gaṅ tshe snaṅ ba de gṣal bya |	*gaṅ ltar snaṅ ba de gṣal bya |*
tshad ma daṅ deḥi ḥbras bu ni |	*tshad ma daṅ deḥi ḥbras bu ni |*
ḥdsin rnam rig pa de yi phyir |	*ḥdsin rnam rig paḥo de yi phyir |*
de gsum tha dad du ma byas ||	*de gsum tha dad du ma byas | |*

[lv] NMa$_2$, p. 113.4 reads: *grāhakâkāra-saṁvittyos trayaṁ.*

[lvi] Cf. TS 10.1: *moha-kṣayāj jñāna-darśanâvaraṇântarāya-kṣayāc ca kevalam.*

[lvii] Cf., e.g. TBh 10.7 (p. 231 f.) v.23 ff.: *saṁsāra-viṣayâtītaṁ muktānām avyayaṁ sukham.*

the three elements of *hāna*, *upādana* / *ādāna* and *āpekṣā*, as a result (*phala*) of cognition (*jñāna*).

[21] Truly, the title *Nyāyâvatāra* is clearly reminiscent of Dharmakīrti's *Nyāya-bindu* (NA reflects its succinct character) as well as of Śaṅkarasvāmin's *Nyāya-praveśa* (≈ *avatāra*). Nonetheless, this could hardly be a convincing argument in favour of any inspiration.

What is important to remember is that there are numerous similarities, more and less conspicuous, and not all of them are decisive when taken alone. Some of these similarities indicated on the preceding pages may equally well point to a tradition or author prior to Dharmakīrti, e.g. to Diṅnāga or Śaṅkarasvāmin. Some of these similarities may be due to the general way of writing, of arranging a philosophical treatise, of structuring a philosophical discourse, etc. We should remember that both the *Nyāya-bindu* and the *Nyāyâvatāra* were primarily handbooks of logic and their purpose was predominantly didactic. However, the accumulation of evidence only enforces those of them that are quite conclusive and convincing. To sum up, my impression is that in all dubious cases, when both NP and NB seem relevant as possible sources of Siddhasena's ideas, Siddhasena probably took recourse to Dharmakīrti rather than to Śaṅkarasvāmin, inasmuch as in all those rare cases when there are clear similarities to be found between NA and NP, they are also traceable in NB. However, not all cases of similarities between NA and NB can be shown with regard to NA and NP. In other words, the development of certain ideas that had taken place in the period connecting Śaṅkarasvāmin and Dharmakīrti, was reflected in the contents of NA and some ideas still absent from NP, that were later either introduced or modified by Dharmakīrti, found their way into NA. Similarly, certain influences to be found in NA point both to Diṅnāga and to Dharmakīrti. However, Siddhasena seems to be acquainted with certain new developments or ideas that first developed with Dharmakīrti (not necessarily only in NB) and are not found in Diṅnāga's works.

Accordingly, depending on whether we follow the widely accepted dating of Dharmakīrti, viz. c. 600–660[lviii] or the results of latest research by KIMURA (1999) who assigns the years 550–620 for Dharmakīrti, we would have for the *terminus post quem* Siddhasena as the author of the *Nyāyâvatāra* circa 620 or 660, respectively.

There is still another factor to be taken account of, viz., the question of the defining characteristic of the logical reason (*hetu*) characterised as 'the fact of being otherwise inexplicable', or 'inexplicability otherwise' (*anyathânupapannatva*, *anyathânupapatti*) in NA 22: *anyathânupapannatvaṁ hetor lakṣaṇam īritam*. The author clearly refers to an earlier source and the idea did not originate with him in his NA. Independently, we find the idea reported and criticised by Śāntarakṣita in TSa_1 1364 ff. (p. 405 f.) in

---

[lviii] See: FRAUWALLNER (1961). Cf. also STEINKELLNER-MUCH (1995: 23).

the context of the validity of inference (*anumāna*).[lix] The most famous and relatively often quoted verse is TSa$_1$ 1369:

anyathânupapannatvaṁ yatra tatra trayeṇa kim /
nânyathânupapannatvaṁ yatra tatra[lx] *trayeṇa kim //*

Strangely enough, Śāntarakṣita in TSa interchanges the *pādas* ab with cd. The verse is also found in (1) TŚVA, p. 203 [the discussion of *anyathânupapatti* and the refutation of *tri-lakṣaṇa* is found there on pp. 198–217], (2) TBV, vol. II, p. 569.28–29, (3) PMĪ 2.1.9 § 33 (p. 45.17–18)[lxi].

Significantly enough, Śāntarakṣita TSa$_1$ 1364, p. 405.1) mentions Pātrasvāmin as the source of the idea: *anyathêty-ādinā pātrasvāmi-matam āśaṅkate...*, and the treatise in question is the lost *Tri-lakṣaṇa-kadarthana*[lxii] by Pātrasvāmin, identified occasionally with Pātrakesarin / Pātrakesarisvāmin = Vidyānanda. For obvious reasons this Pātrasvāmin cannot be Vidyānanda (*c.* 850), the author of the *Śloka-vārttika* on Umāsvāti's *Tattvârtha-sūtra*—as SUKHLAL–DOSHI (1928)[lxiii] and CHATTERJEE (1978: 331) would have it—but someone else who preceded Śāntarakṣita (*c.* 725–788)[lxiv], the teacher of Kamalaśīla.[lxv] Since the author of NA alludes to his predecessors and Śāntarakṣita mentions only Pātrasvāmin, it must have been the latter who

---

[lix] The relevant section is edited and translated in KUNST (1939: 11–53). See also PATHAK (1930–31) 71–83.

[lx] PMĪ misprints: *yatra*.

[lxi] Hemacandra's criticism against the Buddhist idea of *trairūpya* in PMĪ 2.1.9 § 33 (p. 45.1–16) closely follows the exposition of Pātrasvāmin's aphorisms quoted in TSa attesting to the authenticity of the quotation. Hemacandra, instead of the terms *anyathânupapatti*, uses the expression *avinâbhāva*, cf. PMĪ 2.1.9 (p. 43.34–35): *svârthaṁ sva-niścita-sādhyâvinâbhāvâika-lakṣaṇāt sādhanāt sādhya-jñānam.* The formulation *sādhyâvinâbhāvâika-lakṣaṇāt* resembles both Pātrasvāmin's *Tri-lakṣaṇa-kadarthana* (*tenâika-lakṣaṇo hetuḥ prādhānyād gamako 'stu naḥ* / = TSa 1379) as well as NA 5ac: *sādhyâvinâbhuno liṅgāt sādhya-niścāyakaṁ smṛtam / anumānaṁ.*

[lxii] A reference to the work is found in DHAKY (1995: 43), who refers to Jugal Kishor Mukhtar: 'Saṁmatisūtra aur Siddhasena' (Hindi), *Jaina Sāhitya aur Itihāsa par Viśada Prakāśa*, Calcutta 1956, pp. 538–543 [the work was not available to me].

[lxiii] Cf. UPADHYE (1971: *14–15), PATHAK (1930: *passim*) and PATHAK (1930–31: *passim*), who refers to him as Pātrakesari Vidyānanda or as Pātrakesarisvāmi.

[lxiv] Cf. STEINKELLNER-MUCH (1995: 56).

[lxv] Cf. BHATTACHARYYA (1926: ixvi–ixvii): 'In that case Pātrasvāmin must be an earlier author than both Śāntarakṣita and Vidyānanda, and he must have first propounded the theory that valid reason is that the existence of which cannot be maintained unless it is invariably concomitant with the major term... *cir.* 700 A.D.'.

was responsible for the idea of *anyathânupapannatva*.[lxvi] Had it been Siddhasena who introduced the idea, Śāntarakṣita would not, in all probability, have missed the opportunity to mention this. Certainly Pātrasvāmin is post-Diṅnagan, for his *Tri-lakṣaṇa-kadarthana* was conceived to refute the latter, but his dating is quite uncertain. It is surprising, nonetheless, that Śāntarakṣita seems nowhere to allude to the *Nyāyâvatāra* or its author. Consequently, the widespread opinion assuming that *Nyāyâvatāra* is the first Jaina treatise on epistemology per se loses its weight, inasmuch we can safely assume that Siddhasena had his predecessor in the person of Pātrasvāmin.

As regards the *terminus ante quem*, in view of the fact that the verse no. 4 of the *Nyāyâvatāra* is incorporated into ṢDSa as verse no. 56, it should be assigned to the date of Haribhadra-sūri. A supposition that it is ṢDSa 56 that was the source which NA 4 was borrowed from and that NA 4 is merely an interpolation seems inadmissible to me. NA 4 fits ideally the argumentative structure of the text: (1) NA 1 states the definition of *pramāṇa*, as well as the types and a general criterion of such a division, (2) NA 2 is polemical concerning the meaninglessness of formulating a definition for a well-known term/idea of *pramāṇa*, (3) NA 3 is a rejoinder to the objection, (4) NA 4 defines the two main divisions of *pramāṇa* along with a specific reason for such a division,[lxvii] (5) NA 5 opens a section dealing with erroneousness of *pramāṇas*, etc. The use of vocabulary in NA 4 is not unusual for NA. Coincidentally, two adjacent verses, viz. NA 4 and NA 5, are stylistically and structurally quite akin: *pāda* A/B: ⌜reason⌝ (*aparokṣatayā, sādhyâvinâbhuno liṅgāt*) + ⌜object + verbal derivative in the meaning of a present participle⌝ (*arthasya grāhakaṁ, sādhya-niścāyakaṁ*) + ... + *pāda* C: ⌜subject⌝ (*pratyakṣam, anumānaṁ*) ... Admittedly, the similarity is not a crucial argument in favour of the same authorship of the two verses, however, there is nothing that could speak against a common authorship. The argument gains on

---

[lxvi] Cf. MUKTHAR (1948) [according to UPADHYE (1971: *30)]: '7) The *Nyāyāvatāra* is composed centuries later than the *Sanmati-sūtra*, because it shows the influence of Pātrasvāmi (later than Samantabhadra) as well as Dharmakīrti and Dharmottara'; and V.P. JOHRAPURKAR ('Introduction' to VTP, pp. 41 ff.) quoted in n. iii above. See also DHAKY (1995: 42–3): '...the first foot of the *kārikā* 22 concerning the *hetu-lakṣaṇa* (character of probans) reflects sense-agreement, even partial verbal concordance with the verses from Pātrasvāmi's (Pātrakesari's) *Trilakṣaṇakadarthana* cited by the Buddhist scholiast Śāntarakṣita in his *Tattvasaṅgraha* (*c.* 2nd quarter of the 8th century A. D.) [32].' SHASTRI (1990: 31) is a bit more reserved and does not take for granted that Pātrasvāmin was anterior to Siddhasena: 'Nyāyāvatāra also defines hetu in the same manner'.

[lxvii] Both NA 1 and 4 go against the prevalent Jaina tradition to subsume cases of sensory cognition, inference and verbal testimony under *parokṣa*, whereas *pratyakṣa* was taken to denote extra-sensory and extra-mental acts of cognition (viz. *avadhi*, *manaḥ-paryāya* and *kevala*). For Siddhasena the criterion of directness (*akṣa*) was not the cognising subject, or the soul (*akṣa* = *jīva* = *ātman*), but—like in the general *pramāṇa* tradition—the senses (*akṣa* = *indriya*).

strength in view of the fact that Haribhadra-sūri quotes the verse no. 2 of NA in his *Aṣṭaka*[lxviii] and refers to its author as Mahāmati[lxix].

In view of the above, DHAKY's (1995: 44) claim[lxx]—to handle the discomfort that Haribhadra himself ascribes one of the verses to a Mahāmati[lxxi]—that both NA 2 and 4 were taken from lost *dvātriṁśikās* of Siddhasena Divākara is highly debatable to me. Not only NA 4 seems to represent an original *kārikā* of NA, but the same holds good in the case of *kārikā* 2. We could not make head or tail of NA 2 (the objection) if we did not have NA 1. Moreover, NA 3 (the rejoinder) would be pointless without NA 2. All the lost *dvātriṁśikās* of Siddhasena Divākara as a reference source in argumentation resemble rather a kind of *śaśa-viṣāṇa*. Naturally, as long as we do not have all *dvātriṁśikās* written by Siddhasena Divākara, we cannot, theoretically speaking, preclude the possibility that the verses indeed were taken from some lost *dvātriṁśikā*. But such an argumentation is not very constructive. I see no reason to doubt the authenticity of *kārikās* 2 and 4 as long as they form a consistent logical part of the *Nyāyâvatāra* as a whole and bear stylistic similarities to adjacent *kārikās*,[lxxii]

[lxviii] The work is not available to me. I am forced to rely here on Pt. Dalsukhbhai MALVANIA (1979: 287–288). Cf. also UPADHYE (1971: xxiv) and DHAKY (1995: 44).

[lxix] UPADHYE (1971: xxiv) is right to point out 'that Haribhadra, in his *Aṣṭaka*, quotes the *Nyāyāvatāra* 2, by referring to its author as Mahāmati. Elsewhere, however Haribhadra speaks plainly about the author of the *Sanmati* as Divākara and Śrutakevalin.' This enforces the supposition against the authorship of Siddhasena Divākara of NA.

[lxx] 'A formidable objection, however, to the above-postulated identification (Siddharṣi was the author of both NA and NAV—P.B.) as well as the period determination (ninth/tenth century for NA—P.B.) can be raised on the grounds of the ascription of a verse, which appears as the *kārikā* 2 of the *Nyāyāvatāra*, to Mahāmati (=Siddhasena Divākara) by Yākinisūnu Haribhadra sūri (active c. A. D. 745–785) in his *Aṣṭaka*[38]. And the *kārikā* 4 figures as a part of the *Ṣaḍdarśana-samuccaya* of the same Haribhadra sūri[39]. Since Haribhadra sūri ascribed the particular verse (*kārikā* 2) to Siddhasena Divākara, it must be so. However, this *kārikā* could be originally from some *dvātriṁśikā*, one of the lost 11 of Siddhasena Divākara, perhaps the *Pramāṇa-dvātriṁśikā*, from which Gandhahasti Siddhasena quotes in his *sa-bhāṣya-Tattvārthādhigama-sūtra-vṛtti*[40]. The *kārikā* 4 in the *Ṣaḍdarśana-samuccaya* may likewise have been taken from one of the unavailable *dvātriṁśikā* of Siddhasena Divākara. Alternatively, if that verse is Haribhadra's own, Siddharṣi must have borrowed it from the *Ṣaḍdarśana*. In any case, Haribhadra and Siddharṣi could have common sources from which they apparently may have drawn.'

[lxxi] It is debatable whether Mahāmati is Siddhasena Divākara, see n. lxix above.

[lxxii] I have dealt briefly with the style of NA 4 above. The same is even more true for NA 2 that is closely followed by NA 3 (the most conspicuous similarities underlined):

/2/ *prasiddhāni pramāṇāni vyavahāraś ca tat-kṛtaḥ* /
pramāṇa-lakṣaṇasyôktau jñāyate na prayojanam //
/3/ *prasiddhānāṁ pramāṇānāṁ lakṣaṇôktau prayojanam* /
tad-vyāmoha-nivṛttiḥ syād vyāmūḍha-manasām iha //

especially when the counter-arguments begin with 'perhaps' and are of merely could-or-may-have-been nature.

Further, the identification of Siddharṣi as the author of both NA and NAV, postulated by DHAKY, has very weak foundations. In the first place, there is ample evidence that Siddharṣi (the author of NAV) is not Siddhasena (the author of NA) and that the two texts were written by different authors, inasmuch as Siddharṣi refers to the author of NA explicitly, although not by name, but by the term *ācārya* or *sūtra-kṛt*, to cite a few cases only:[lxxiii]

[1] Introductory lines of NAV 3: /3/ *adhunâcāryo gṛhītas tāvakīno 'bhiprāyo 'smābhir iti paraṁ pratyāyayaṁs tan-matam anudrāvya tad evânumanyamānas tathâpi lakṣaṇôkteḥ sāphalyam āvedayann āha:...* (p. 29 of the English translation)

[2] The final sentence of NAV 3: *tad evaṁ pramāṇa-lakṣaṇaṁ sāmānyena pratipādya tad-gataṁ kucodyaṁ paryahāry ācāryeṇa.* (p. 30 of the English translation).

[3] NAV 13: *yad vâtyantâbhyāsena parikarmita-matitvāt tāvatâiva prastuta-prameyam avabudhyate, tadā hetu-pratipādanam eva kriyate, śeṣâbhidhānasya śrotṛ-saṁskārâkāritayā nairarthakyād ity-ādau hetu-pratipādanaṁ sūtra-kṛtā parârtham anumānam uktam* ('In this and similar [instances, the inference] which demonstrates the logical reason [alone] is called by the author of the manual 'the inference for others.'—p. 56 of the English translation).

[4] NAV 29: *ata evâcāryasya na tal-lakṣaṇâdi-svarūpa-kathane 'pi mahânādaraḥ* ('Precisely for this reason, [that is] no great insouciance [on the part] of the preceptor (*sc.* Siddhasena) even as regards the mention of the gist of its definition, etc.'—p. 97 of the English translation).

Additionally, in some cases, e.g. on NA 8[lxxiv], Siddharṣi does offer at least two different interpretations of a *kārikā*, or diverges from the contents of NA, e.g. in the case of NA 4d[lxxv].

[lxxiii] DHAKY (1995: 43) is so far right that indeed Siddharṣi nowhere mentions the author of *Nyāyâvatāra* by name: 'As noted in the beginning, Siddharṣi does not ascribe the *Nyāyāvatāra* to Siddhasena Divākara or to a different Siddhasena or for that matter to any other author.' However, he clearly misses the point when he further claims: 'Nor does he mention it as a composition of a *pūrvācārya*, *vṛddhācārya*, or some *cirantanācārya*. Also, in his verse by verse exposition, he nowhere uses qualificatory phrases such as *śāstrakāra*, *sūtrakāra*, *kārikākāra*, *ācārya*, etc. which may have denoted a second, an earlier revered personage, as the *kārikās'* author.'

[lxxiv] I discuss the problem briefly in BALCEROWICZ (1999/a: 4, n. 8).

[lxxv] Siddhasena emphasises the way of cognising, or '[the manner of] grasping [an object]', whereas Siddharṣi takes the expression to refer to the existence and the nature of the cognoscible. See p. xv above.

Thus, we can safely take the date-brackets for the *Nyāyâvatāra* to be firmly fixed after 620 CE (Dharmakīrti) and Pātrasvāmin and before *c.* 800 CE (Haribhadra-sūri).[lxxvi] As for the date of Haribhadra-sūri, JACOBI (1926: *Introduction*) assigns Haribhadra to *c.* 750, whereas UPADHYE (1971: xxv) to *c.* 750–800 CE and DHAKY (1995: 44) to *c.* 745–785. However, the *terminus post quem* for Haribhadra is Arcaṭa, since the latter is quoted in Haribhadra-sūri's NPV 9.15–19[lxxvii]. Arcaṭa, the teacher of Dharmottara, can be assigned to *c.* 730–790 or 720–780.[lxxviii]

As regards the name of the author of the *Nyāyâvatāra*, we are indeed in a quandary. Probably the earliest indication of his name is, as it has been mentioned above (p. xxxiv), Haribhadra-sūri who makes mention of him under the appellation 'Mahāmati'. The subsequent source from which we learn that NA was composed by a Siddhasena is NAVV of Śānti-sūri. The author of NA is explicitly identified there in at least four places: [1] NAVV 36 § 7 (p. 95.8): *śrīsiddhasena-ghaṭita-sphuṭa-gīḥśalākāṁ śuddhāṁ avāpya vimalaṁ vihitaṁ mayâitat //*, [2] NAVV 21 § 2 (p. 78.9–10): *evaṁ-rūpasya vadhaḥ tyāgaḥ siddhasenārkasyêty arthaḥ.*, [3] NAVV 53 § 2 (p. 107.18): *siddhasenasya sūtra-kartuḥ...*, [4] NAVV 1 § 11 (p. 13.14–15): *tat kiṁ svātantryeṇa? na ity āha — siddhasenārka-sūtritam iti. siddhasena eva jagaj-jantu-mano-moha-saṁtatitām asītamaḥ samūhâpoha-kāritvāt arka iva arkaḥ, tena sūtritam.* In the last reference Śānti-sūri is even more specific to give the full name of the author as well: Siddhasenārka. Indeed, Śānti-sūri speaks of Siddhasenārka, not of Siddhasena Divākara, as UPADHYE (1971: xxiv) would have it: 'iii) ... The earliest author, as far as I know, who specifies the name of Siddhasena Divākara as the author of the *Nyāyāvatāra* is Śānti-sūri of the 11th century A.D. or so.' Nevertheless, I would side with Upadhye in asserting that 'Arka' is just another name for 'Divākara'. Thus, I see absolutely no justification for the contention of DHAKY (1995: 49, n. 9), who—commenting on the clause: *siddhasena eva jagaj-jantu-mano-moha-saṁtati-tāmasītamaḥ-samūhâpoha-kāritvāt arka iva arkaḥ, tena sūtritam*—maintains that '"Arka" here is not in the sense of "Divākara" but "essence".' Clearly, *arka* here is an epithet of Siddhasena, who is compared to the sun (*arka iva*; *arka=divā-kara*), and by him (*tena*) the idea discussed before is composed in a *sūtra* form (*sūtritam*). If we took *arka* as Dhaky would like it, the whole clause could hardly be construable. All other references we encounter in the Jaina literature of this period are to Siddhasena Divākara as the author of other works, but

---

[lxxvi] Thus, I cannot but side with the opinion already expressed in VAIDYA (1928: xx): 'The *terminus a quo* would be the date of Dharmakīrti and the *terminus ad quem* that of Haribhadra'.

[lxxvii] Acc. to STEINKELLNER-MUCH (1995: 119) the original title found to the colophon is *Nyāya-praveśa-ṭīkā śiṣya-hitā.*

[lxxviii] See: STEINKELLNER-MUCH (1995: 64) and FRAUWALLNER (1961: 148).

none to him as the author of NA.[lxxix] In view of the extant evidence, the opinion of MUKTHAR (1948)[lxxx] still holds good that the author of the *Nyāyâvatāra* is apparently different from the author of the *Sanmati-tarka-prakaraṇa* and from the author of the twenty-one *dvātriṁśikās* ascribed to Siddhasena Divākara.

Strangely enough, the available colophons of NA and NAV contain no reference to the name of the author of NA. Since even the point is not clear whether the author of NA was a Siddhasena, not to mention the problem of deciding which Siddhasena he could have been,[lxxxi] I would—for the sake of convenience—suggest to tentatively call the author of the *Nyāyâvatāra* Siddhasena Mahāmati, after the specific identification of Haribhadra-sūri.

As far as the question whether NA is a *triṁśikā* or *dvātriṁśikā* is concerned, I see no structural reason to believe that NA was originally composed in 30 verses (like the famous *Triṁśikā-vijñapti-kārikā* of Vasubandhu). Both doubtful verses, viz. NA 4 and 9 fit well the general structure of the whole text. Especially NA 4 corresponds well to general wording of NA (*vide supra*). But also the wording of NA 9 partly follows the phraseology of the preceding verse:

> NA 8: *dṛṣṭêṣṭâvyāhatād vākyāt paramârthâbhidhāyinaḥ / tattva-grāhitayôtpannaṁ mānaṁ śābdaṁ prakīrtitam //*
> NA 9: *āptôpajñam anullaṅghyam adṛṣṭêṣṭa-virodhakam / tattvôpadeśa-kṛt sārvaṁ śāstraṁ kāpatha-ghaṭṭanam //*

[lxxix] Cf., e.g. [1] UPADHYE (1971: xiii): 'Haribhadra is one of the earlier authors to mention Siddhasena Divākara and his *Sanmati*. First, he calls him Śrutakevalin; and secondly, he tells us that his name was Divākara (p. *1). Then he has a pun on the name that he was like *Divākara*, sun, to the darkness of Duḥṣama-kāla.' [2] UPADHYE (1971: xvii): '...Pūjyapāda ...quotes Siddhasena's Stuti III.16 in his *Sarvārthasiddhi* (II.10; VII.13).' [3] H. R. KĀPADIĀ (AJP, 'Introduction', Vol. II, pp. 98 ff.): 'Haribhadra refers to Siddhasena in his *Sammaipayaraṇa*, in his *Anekāntajayapatākā* as well as in his *Paṁcavatthuya* (vv.1047–8), calling him Suyakevali. Jinadāsagaṇi (c. 676 A.D.) refers to him thrice in his *Nisīhavisehacuṇṇī*.' [4] DAVE (1962): 'So Siddhasena is earlier than Mallavādi and the tradition puts him as a contemporary of Vikramāditya who flourished in 57 B.C.' [according to UPADHYE (1971: *53)] and 'Akalaṅka and Vidyānanda quote the *Sanmati*.' [according to UPADHYE (1971: *59)].

[lxxx] 'The following points are clear: (1) The *Dvā.s* were not composed in the present order; (2) they are not of one and the same Siddhasena; (3) the *Nyāyāvatāra* is one of them; (4)... No indisputable evidence is brought forth for the common authorship of the *Dvā.s*, *Nyāyāvatāra* and *Sanmati*. ... There were thus three clear and distinct Siddhasenas: (1) the author of *Sanmati*; (2) the author of *Nyāyāvatāra*; (3) and another, the author of some *Dvā.s*.' [according to UPADHYE (1971: *28)].

[lxxxi] It is not established that Arka was indeed used by Śānti-sūri as a synonym of Divākara.

However, NA 9 may rise certain doubts as regards its authenticity, insofar as the verse agrees with *Ratna-karaṇḍaka* no. 9. Some believe that the verse originally belongs to *Ratna-karaṇḍaka*, e.g. Vidyadhara Pasusa JOHRAPURKAR ('Introduction' to VTP, pp. 41 ff.) ['It (=N.A.—P.B.) takes the definition of the Āgama from the *Ratnakaraṇḍaka* and the definition *anyathānupapannatva* of the Hetu from Pātrakesari...' Cf. also DHAKY (1995: 43): 'The opinion of the Digambara scholars, as a result, is sharply divided into two camps as regards the authorship of the *Ratnakaraṇḍaka*. My own view is that the style of the *Ratnakaraṇḍaka*, though, seeming not later than the seventh century A.D., does not correspond with that of Samantabhadra. (...) In any case, all aforenoted points considered, it clearly emerges that the author of the *Nyāyāvatāra* is posterior to the first half of the seventh century A. D.' Some scholars try to suspend their opinion, e.g. UPADHYE (1971: xxiv): '...iii) The *Nyāyāvatāra* Nos. 4 and 9, are common with the *Ṣaḍ-darśana-samuccaya* (No.56) and *Ratnakaraṇḍaka* (No.9). Here the question is not so much of chronological priority of one author over the other as that of genuineness of these verses in the respective texts based on MSS evidence and the context in discussion. If at all these are interpolations, the claim of the *Nyāyāvatāra* being a *Dvā.* gets shaken.' There is a group of scholars who believe that the verse originally belongs to NA, e.g. MALVANIA (in his 'Introduction' to NASV, pp. 141 ff.): ['Prof. Hiralal has proved that *Ratnakaraṇḍaka* is not of Samantabhadra; therefore there is no point in saying that Siddhasena is later than Samantabhadra.']. However, since NA antedates Haribhadra, the conclusion of Dhaky mentioned just now loses its weight.

The *Nyāyâvatāra* was definitely an achievement, being either the first or one of the first serious Jaina works on epistemology. Its author enters polemics with other, mostly the Buddhist, *pramāṇa* schools and endeavours to establish a Jaina tradition of its own. On the other hand, the work is rather secondary, in so far as it relies, for the most part, on the Buddhist legacy and has very little new ideas, genuinely of its own, to offer. But it is not surprising nor exceptional, for also Haribhadra subscribes to the Buddhist epistemological tradition by commenting on Śaṅkarasvāmin's *Nyāya-praveśa*, instead of choosing a Jaina work of, e.g. Samantabhadra or Pātrasvāmin.[lxxxii] Likewise, Siddhasena—by frequent mentioning of *nyāya-vid* etc.—signs up to the general Indian tradition of logic, not specifically to the Jaina tradition. On the other hand, opinions such as that of WAYMAN (1996: 4): 'Considering the *N. A.*'s standard in verses 21 and 22, we begin to wonder about the qualifications of the author to write on the topic of logic,' are not only unjust but also unjustified. If we were to put to doubt the qualifications of Siddhasena as a logician, we should also treat Dharmakīrti, Śaṅkarasvāmin, Diṅnāga, etc., according to the same standards, whose path Siddhasena followed. In any case, the role of NA is practically surpassed by Siddharṣi's commentary (*Nyāyâvatāra-vivṛti*) thereon. Perhaps the most important

[lxxxii] Cf. JACOBI (1926: *Introduction*) and UPADHYE (1971: *10): 'Haribhadra, however, instead of founding a logical school of the Jainas, induced them, by commenting on Diṅnāga, to study the original works of Buddhist Logicians.'

contribution of Siddhasena in the field of logic in general was a crucial step intended to simplify the logical structure of the proof by neglecting everything that was logically unnecessary and by reducing the number of members of the proof formula further on, along the lines pursued by Vasubandhu (his three-membered proof formula). This attempt, as I have mentioned above, was explicitly made in NA 20, namely that the role of example was merely "the recollection of the relation (*sc.* of the invariable concomitance)". The pronouncement of example was not necessary at all and the invariable concomitance was rather intrinsic to the logical reason instead of constituting, in a way, a part of the logical example that was supposed to demonstrate such a relation. In other words, the role to demonstrate the invariable concomitance was assigned to the logical reason alone, not to the example. Thus, conceiving of a proof formula as consisting of two stages only should be viewed as methodologically an important advancement in the history of Indian logic.[lxxxiii]

As for commentaries on the *Nyāyâvatāra*, the reader will find an account in VAIDYA (1928: xxi–xxii) and in scattered material in UPADHYE 1971: xi–xxvii, *3–*72) and there is nothing much to add.

Haribhadra is occasionally[lxxxiv] believed to have written a commentary on NA, but the only source mentioning the fact is a reference in a mediaeval catalogue of Jaina works. The reliability of that information is rather doubtful and I would side with VAIDYA (1928: xxi)[lxxxv] and take it to be a mistake, in so far as there is not other source available that would support Haribhadra's authorship of a commentary on NA.

The first extant—and probably the first ever written—commentary on the *Nyāyâvatāra* is *Nyāyâvatāra-vivṛti* by Siddharṣi, or Siddharṣi-gaṇin, also called Siddhavyākhyānika. Siddhavyākhyānika is the name recorded in all available colo-

[lxxxiii] See BALCEROWICZ 1999/a. I can hardly accept OETKE's (1994/a: 77–78) reservation: 'Vielmehr ermöglichen es uns die oben getroffenen Feststellungen (e.g. separate role ascribed to each of the five members of the proof formula—P.B.) zu erkennen, daß die Änderung von einem fünfgliederigen zu einem dreigliederigen Beweis vielleich als ein *Resultat* von Fortschritten entstanden ist, selber aber keinen Fortschritt repräsentiert.' and his general thesis: 'Eine rehabilitierung des fünfgiederigen Syllogismus' underlying OETKE 1994/a. In my opinion, behind the development (from Vasubandhu to Siddhasena) to reduce the number of the members of the proof formula there was an important tendency, first, to eliminate all unnecessary elements of any formal reasoning and, secondly, to emancipate formal schemata of reasoning from their empirical relativity and from the need of empirical instantiation.

[lxxxiv] E.g., V.P. JOHRAPURKAR's ('Introduction' to VTP, pp. 41) opinion quoted in n. iii above.

[lxxxv] 'The Jain Granthāvalī also mentions another commentary on the Nyāyāvatāra by Haribhadra, but this seems to be a mistake, based on a reference in the Bṛhaṭṭippanikā, a 15th century list of Jain works: न्यायावतारसूत्रं सिद्धसेनीयं तद्वृत्तिर्हारिभद्री. The book is not now found in the Patan Bhandars.'

phons of NAV (*kṛtir iyam ācārya-siddha-vyākhyānikasya tarka-prakaraṇa-vṛtter iti.*). This seems also to be the only genuine commentary on NA. Siddharṣi[lxxxvi] appears to phrase a pun on his name in the concluding verse of the colophon: (3) *nyāyâvatāra-vivṛtiṁ vividhāṁ vidhitsoḥ* ***siddhaḥ*** *śubho ya iha puṇya-cayas tato me / nityaṁ parârtha-karaṇôdyatam ā bhavântād bhūyāj jinêndra-mata-lampaṭam eva cetaḥ //*. He is generally accepted to have flourished at the turn of ninth and tenth centuries[lxxxvii]. He wrote a commentary *Heyôpādeyā* on *Upadeśa-mālā* as well as a compendium of didactic stories *Upamiti-bhava-prapañcā-kathā*. He is taken to have finished the latter work on 21st of May 906 CE (Vikrama Saṁvat 962)[lxxxviii]. He is also claimed to have been a cousin of the king-poet Māgha (*c.* 905 CE)[lxxxix]. In that case he would be prior to Māṇikyanandin[xc] which could be a reasonable clarification of the fact he seems not to have known the latter.

The significance of Siddharṣi's commentary *Nyāyâvatāra-vivṛti* and his erudition is often underestimated. He refers to most philosophical schools of his times (Sautrāntika, Yogâcāra, Śūnya-vāda, Saugata, Sāṁkhya, Mīmāṁsā, Naiyāyika-Vaiśeṣika, Cārvāka, Brahmâdvaita, etc.), and by name to authors such as Dharmottara, Arcaṭa, Kaṇabhakṣa, Akṣapāda Gautama, Kapila, Varṣagaṇya etc. Further, he either directly cites or avails himself this way or another of the following works: *Aṣṭādhyāyī* of Pāṇini, *Hetu-bindu-ṭīkā* of Arcaṭa Bhaṭṭa, *Mīmāṁsā-śloka-vārttika* of Kumārila Bhaṭṭa, *Nyāya-bindu-ṭīkā-ṭippaṇī* of Vinītadeva, *Nyāya-bhāṣya* of Vātsyāyana Pakṣilasvāmin, *Nyāya-praveśa* of Śaṅkarasvāmin, *Pramāṇa-samuccaya* of Diṅnāga, *Pramāṇa-vārttika* of Dharmakīrti, *Pramāṇa-vārttika-svôpajña-vṛtti* of Dharmakīrti, *Pramāṇa-viniścaya-ṭīkā* of Dharmottara, *Sāṁkhya-kārikā* of Īśvarakṛṣṇa, *Śloka-vārttika-vyākhyā-tātparya-ṭīkā* of Uṁveka Bhaṭṭa, *Tattvôpaplava-siṁha* of Jayarāśi, *Vāda-vidhi* of Vasubandhu, *Vaiśeṣika-sūtra* of Kaṇāda, *Yoga-sūtra*, *Yukti-dīpikā*. His commentary is widely quoted in Malliṣeṇa's SVM or Hemacandra's PMī. The latter work could even hardly be conceived without Siddharṣi's *Vivṛti*. He was responsible for the subsequent development of Jaina epistemological thought to a much larger degree than it has so far been recognised. However, he was

---

[lxxxvi] *ṛṣi* is apparently an appellation appended to his original name Siddha; cf. °*sūri*, °*vādin*, °*gaṇin*, etc.

[lxxxvii] Cf. e.g. SHASTRI (1990: 27), DHAKY (1995: 44): 'Siddharṣi flourished in the times as late as ninth and early tenth century A.D.'.

[lxxxviii] Cf. VAIDYA (1928: xxi) ('Siddharṣi is the author of the famous work Upamitibhavaprapañca Kathā and of a commentary called Heyopādeyā on the Upadeśamālā, a Prakrit work in verse of Dharmadāsa.'), A. B. Dhruva's 'Supplementary Notes' to SVM, p. 351.22–23 ('Siddharṣi, the author of Upamitibhava-Prapañcakathā, completed it in 906 AD') and CHATTERJEE (1978: 287).

[lxxxix] Cf. VIDYĀBHŪṢAṆA (1920: 147).

[xc] He flourished in the first decades of the tenth century. SHASTRI (1990: 41) assigns him to c. 900 CE. The dating accepted by Vidyābhūṣaṇa (1920: 188) *c.* 800 CE is unrealistic.

greatly influenced by the Buddhist thinkers, especially Dharmakīrti and Dharmottara. This commentary, viz. *Nyāyâvatāra-vivṛti*, is critically edited and rendered into English in the present publication.

Siddharṣi's *Nyāyâvatāra-vivṛti* was subsequently glossed by Devabhadra and his *Nyāyâvatāra-ṭippana*. Devabhadra-sūri of the Maladhārī gaccha (or in catalogues: Maladhārin Devabhadra-sūri) was a disciple of both Hemacandra Maladhārin Gandhavimukta and Śrīcandra (NPṬ), thus he must have lived about 1150[xci]. All available colophons mention the name of Deva-sūri, a pupil of Hemacandra / Hema-sūri. The gloss (*Ṭippana*) is of rather secondary philosophic value, but it is a useful source of quotations, thus attesting, that Devabhadra was well-acquainted with current philosophic discourse, though perhaps not an original and ingenious thinker himself. Larger parts of his *Nyāyâvatāra-ṭippana* are reproduced in the footnotes to the English translation of NAV. In many cases, Devabhadra's glosses hardly add anything new to the text of *Vivṛti*, hence I considered it unproductive to edit the whole text.

There is also quasi-commentary on the *Nyāyâvatāra*, i.e. *Nyāyâvatāra-sūtra-vārttika* of Śānti-sūri, who composed 57 kārikās, being inspired by certain ideas from the *Nyāyâvatāra*. Śānti-sūri wrote also an autocommentary thereon, viz. the *Nyāyâvatāra-sūtra-vārttika-vṛtti*.

And there is one more final remark to make. Throughout my text, whenever I happen to use such expressions as 'syllogism' or 'syllogistic' they are in quotation marks. Clearly, Indian *sādhana* or *pañcâvayava-vākya*, etc., is not Aristotelian syllogism,[xcii] and that is why the quotation marks are necessary. Why to use the term 'syllogism', 'syllogistic' or similar ones at all? I still think it is quite a handy expression, widely used even nowadays, that directly brings associations with formal procedures and structures of reasoning. Since I do not find any other concise expression that would convey similar ideas, I have decided to occasionally keep the term with the proviso of the quotes.[xciii] In general, however, the expressions 'proof formula' and 'based on / of the proof formula' is preferred to 'syllogism' and 'syllogistic'.

[xci] Cf. Vidyābhūṣaṇa (1920: 211), Vaidya (1928: xi-xxiii).

[xcii] The most notorious example of projecting Aristotelian ideas into Indian logic is perhaps VIDYĀBHŪṢAṆA (1920: 497 ff.).

[xciii] Apparently, OETKE 1994/a proceeds on the same assumption when he uses the term '*Syllogismus*' not only in the title *Vier Studien zum altindischen Syllogismus*, but throughout his book.

EDITIONS AND TRANSLATIONS OF THE *NYĀYÂVATĀRA* AND THE COMMENTARIES THEREON

Ānandasāgara-sūri (ed.): *Siddhasena Divākara's Aṣṭa-daśanī-dvātriṁśikā, with Nyāyâvatāra and San-mati-tarka*. Bhavnāgar 1908.

Satis Chandra Vidyābhūṣaṇa (ed.): *Nyāyāvatāra, The Earliest Jaina Work on Pure Logic*. Indian Research Society, *Research and Review* 1.2 (1908: 1–14). Reprinted as 'First edition': Indian Research Society, Calcutta 1909. Reprinted (First revised and re-arranged edition): BANERJEE (1981)].

Vitthal Śāstrī (ed.): *Nyāyâvatāra*, edited with Śānty-ācārya's *Jaina-tarka-vārttika*. In: *The Pandit* [Banaras] 36 (1914) and 39 (1917). [Reprinted: Banaras: 1917].

Satis Chandra Vidyābhūṣaṇa (ed.): *Nyāyâvatāra, The Earliest Jaina Work on Pure Logic*. Edited with extracts from Siddharṣi-gaṇin's *Vivṛti*. English translation and notes. Second edition: the Library of Jaina Literature, Sacred Books of the Jains, Arrah 1915. [Revised and reprinted: UPADHYE (1971)].

Sukhlalji (ed., Gujarati transl.): *Śrī-Siddhasena-Divākara-kṛtaḥ Nyāyâvatāraḥ*. Edited with Gujarati translation and notes. Ahmedabad 1926.

Bhagavāndās Harṣacandra (Harakhchand) (ed.): *Mahāvādi-śrī-Siddhasena-Divākara-praṇīta-Nyāyâvatāraḥ śrī-Rājaśekhara-sūri-viracita-Ṭippana-samalaṅkṛta-ācārya-Siddharṣi-viracita-Vivṛti-sahitaḥ*. Hemācāndrâcārya-Jaina-sabhā, Ahmedabad–Patan 1917.

Nemacandra Devacandra and Bhāgavandās (eds.): *Nyāyāvatāra*, edited with Rājaśekhara-sūri's [wrongly for: Devabhadra-sūri's] *Ṭippaṇī*. Patan 1917.

Ānandasāgara-sūri (ed.): *Siddhasena Divākara's Nyāyâvatāra*. Ahmedabad 1919.

Sukhlalji Saṅghvi (ed.): *Nyāyâvatāra*. Ahmedabad 1926.

P. L. Vaidya (ed.): *Nyāyāvatāra of Siddhasena-Divākara with The Vivṛti of Siddharṣigaṇi and with The Ṭippana of Devabhadra*. Shri Jain Shwetamber Conference, Bombay 1928. Reprinted in: *Vaishali Institute Research Bulletin* 1 [Vaishali] (1971) 1–95.

Dalsukh Malvania (ed.): *Nyāyâvatāra-sūtra-vārttika of Śrī Śānti Sūri critically and authentically edited in the original Sanskrit with an elaborate introduction, notes, indices etc. in Hindi* [with the *Vṛtti*]. Singhi Jain Śastra Śikshapitha 20, Bharatiya Vidya Bhavan, Bombay 1949.

Vijaya-mūrti Śāstrācārya (ed., Hindi transl.): *Ācārya-śrī-siddhasena-divākāra-viracitaḥ Nyāyāvatāraḥ, mūla aur śrī-siddharṣi-gaṇi-kī saṁskṛta-ṭīkā-kā hindī-bhāṣânuvād.* [With a Hindi paraphrase of Siddharṣi-gaṇin's commentary]. Bombay 1950. [Reprinted: Śrī Paramaśruta Prabhāvak Maṇḍal, Śrīmad Rājacandra Āśram, Āgas 1998].

A. N. Upadhye (ed.): *Siddhasena Divākara's Nyāyāvatāra (edited by the late S.C. Vidyabhusan with English Translation, Notes etc.) and with the Vivṛti of Siddharṣi as well as The Text of 21 Dvātriṁśikās and the Sammaï-suttam; Vinayavijaya's Nayakarṇikā edited by... with an Introduction, Bibliographic Review, Indices etc.*; Jaina Sāhitya Vikāsa Maṇḍala, Bombay 1971.

Satkari Mookerjee (ed., Eng. transl.): 'A critical and comparative study of Jain Logic and Epistemology on the basis of the *Nyāyâvatāra* of Siddhasena Divākara', *Vaishali Institute Research Bulletin* 1 [Vaishali] (1971) 1–143. [*Nyāyâvatāra*, edited and translated into English with extensive notes].

Satya Ranjan Banerjee (re-ed.): *Nyāyāvatāra, The Earliest Jaina Work on Pure Logic*. Edited and translated by Satis Chandra Vidyābhūṣaṇa. [Revised and re-arranged edition.] Indian Research Society, Calcutta 1909.' Sanskrit Book Depot, Calcutta 1981.

MANUSCRIPTS AND EDITIONS OF THE *NYĀYÂVATĀRA* AND OF THE COMMENTARIES USED IN THE PRESENT EDITION

The present edition of the *Nyāyâvatāra*, *Nyāyâvatāra-vivṛti* and *Nyāyâvatāra-ṭippana* is based on the following selection of manuscripts, see: PĀṬAṆA-CATALOGUE, Vol.1 Part I, p. 80 (made available to me by courtesy of Muni Jambūvijaya and Professor Dr. Albrecht Wezler):

	MS. No.	title	folio	author
A =	2448	*Nyāyâvatāra-vṛtti*	1–28	Siddhavyākhyānika
A =	2448	*Nyāyâvatāra-vṛtti-ṭippanaka*	28–41	Maladhārī Devabhadra-sūri
C =	2449	*Nyāyâvatāra-vṛtti-ṭippana*	22	Maladhārī Devabhadra-sūri
B =	6808	*Nyāyâvatāra-vivaraṇa*	33	Siddhavyākhyānika

Of much interest is Ms. A, the most fastidious of the three. It introduces additional a range of symbols:

[1] an *avagraha* in subscript 'ऽ' to mark *sandhi*, e.g. एकस्याऽनेक॰,
[2] an *avagraha* in superscript 'ऽ' as a word separator, e.g. प्रतिभासमानानामऽन्यथा,
[3] an *avagraha* in subscript along with a stroke 'ऽ' to separate words and to mark the elision of '*a*', e.g. ॰द्वारेणाऽसंजस॰ (*dvāreṇâsañjasa-°*, not **dvāreṇā-sañjasa-°*).

[4] As a rule, Ms. A inserts no marks within a compound, with the only exception of a comma-like hook in the subscript ',' to mark compound members beginning with *alpha-privativum*, e.g. दृष्टहान्य,दृष्ट° (*dṛṣṭa-hāny-adṛṣṭa-°*).

[5] Ms. A separates inflected words (viz., not members of a compound) with a stroke in superscript 'ˈ', e.g. °प्राप्तेस्तता° (consonant + consonant) as well as °तथाच (consonant + vowel) to distinguish *tathā ca* from **tathāca*.

In addition to the three manuscripts, I have availed myself of the following printed editions:

H = *Nyāyâvatāra* of Siddhasena Divākara; Ed. with Siddharṣi-gaṇin's *Vivṛti* and Devabhadra's *Ṭippana*, by Bhagavandas Harakhchand; Ahmedabad–Patan 1917;

V = *Nyāyâvatāra* of *Siddhasena Divākara*; Ed. with Siddharṣi-gaṇin's *Vivṛti* and Devabhadra's *Ṭippana*, by P. L. Vaidya, Shri Jain Shwetamber Conference, Bombay 1928; reprinted in *VIRB* No. 1, pp. 1–95, Vaishali 1971.

In my edition I mark even minor differences in MSS (e.g. irregular *sandhi*, punctuation, etc.), except for the following cases: I do not mark differences, that are either due to optional spelling (e.g. *kathaṁcit* versus *kathañcit*) or due to punctuation in the edited text (e.g.: *dṛṣṭam*, *ghaṭa-°* versus *dṛṣṭaṁ*, *ghaṭa-°*). I am convinced that even apparently insignificant differences in reading may be interesting for some students for, e.g. linguistic reasons.

Introduction to Logic
by Siddhasena Mahāmati, the Lion of Reasoning, with *The Commentary*[1] *on the 'Introduction to Logic'* by Siddharṣi-gaṇin accompanied by *the Gloss* by Devabhadra-sūri

[A TRANSLATION]

After homage to [Mahāvīra] Vardhamāna, who teaches the universal and the particular as inseparable, has been paid, 'the Commentary on the Introduction to Logic' is composed for the growth of the seed of memory[2].

[0.0] And the initial sentence of this ['Introduction to Logic' runs] as follows.

This [task] is undertaken[3] in order to teach cognitive criterion[4].

[0.1] [The commentary on the phrase] beginning with '**cognitive criterion**'. And [a Buddhist thinker] Dharmottara[5] maintains that—since it is unjustified to assume that a linguistic unit[6] [could possess any] cognitive validity[7] regarding an external object[8], inasmuch as the relation [between the speech element and the object, which can only be] characterised [both] by the relation of essential identity [of the speech element with the object] and by the relation of causality (*sc.* the origination of the speech element from the object)[9] is lacking[10]—students are incited to study (lit. hearing) by such [an initial sentence as 'In order to teach cognitive criterion,'] etc., [solely] due to the anticipation of success[11], which is induced by means of the indication of the subject-matter, etc. [But such an opinion] is not correct, for if the efficacy of speech element in revealing (*sc.* denoting) an object is not possible, how can this [speech element] be precise enough to indicate also the subject-matter, etc.? Besides, if that [initial sentence] had no cognitive validity, thoughtful people would not develop the anticipation of success on hearing this [initial sentence], for [otherwise] they would lose the status of being [thoughtful][12] and because [such an assumption would lead to] the undesired consequence no activity [would] cease even [when it turns out that it has initially been prompted] by wrong cognition[13]. Arcaṭa[14], however, says: 'That [initial sentence] does not encourage a hearer because it does not possess cognitive validity[15] and because the [thoughtful] people do not act on account of something that is no cognitive criterion[16], for otherwise [their] thoughtfulness would be impaired[17]. But rather the purpose [of the initial sentence] is to point out the unsoundness of the logical reasons brought forward by the opponent, who has turned up at the point of declaring the purpose of the treatise. For it is as follows: it is possible that someone holds the following position: "This [treatise] should not be undertaken because it is void of the subject-matter, etc., like examination of a crow's teeth, etc.". Thus, by such an utterance revealing that this [treatise] possesses that [subject-matter][18], the unsoundness of these logical reasons is pointed out.[19]' This [assumption of Arcaṭa] is even more incorrect because we regard [his reasoning]—[i.e.] if [the author] does not instigate [anyone to anything] by defining explicitly the subject-matter, etc., [of his treatise], because [he acts on the premise] that this [initial sentence] is not a cognitive criterion, then he [simply] speaks of the unsoundness of the arguments brought forward by the opponent—as void of logical congruity, because something which is [believed] not [to be] a cognitive criterion [must be] futile[20]; otherwise the inquiry into cognitive criterion [in general] would attain (*sc.* result in) purposelessness. Therefore, this [initial sentence] is a cognitive criterion and demonstrates an existing subject-matter, etc., [as well as] instigates thoughtful people; hence it is brought forward (*sc.* placed) to the beginning of the treatise.

[0.2] If [you argue:] 'Sincc there exists no relation [between the speech element and the object], how [can] this [initial sentence possess any] cognitive validity with regard to an object?,' [then your objection] is to be retorted [with a counter-question:] 'How [could] then this [cognitive validity be possible] likewise with regard to perception?' If [you reply]: '[The cognitive validity is possible] by the force of the relation [characterised by] the relationship of something-which-grasps and something-to-be-grasped,' we say that here, [i.e. in the case of the initial sentence,] as well [it is valid] due to the relationship between the denotatum and its denoter. If [you still argue]: 'How [could] this very [relationship between the denotatum and its denoter be possible?', your remonstrance] is to be retorted [with another counter-question:] 'How [could] then the relationship between the cogniser and the cognoscible [be possible] also in the case of perception?!' If [you reply]: '[The relationship between the cogniser and the cognoscible in the case of perception is possible both] on account of [1] the relation of causality [between the cognition and the object] and on account of [2] the relation of homology [viz. cognition's having the form of the object],' [we would, examining all the possibilities involved in order to refute your own thesis, ask:] [Ad 1] 'What is it, that [you] call the relation of causality [between the cognition and the object]?' If [you mean]: 'The relation of causality [is tantamount to] the production [of cognition] by this [object],' we [shall] argue that this [relation of causality] is difficult to demonstrate with regard to [the doctrine of] momentariness (lit. perishability at every moment). For it is as follows: there are three logical alternatives: a momentary perishable thing may produce its effect [1.1] in the moment [of its existence], [1.2] before or [1.3] subsequently.[21] [Ad 1.1] Among these [alternatives], the first alternative, to begin with, is not admissible, for no activity [can be executed] onto something existing in the same point of time; in the opposite case, a mutual cause-and-effect relationship of [entities] existing at the same moment [and which share their] moment [of existence with] all [other] things would be absurdly implied and, consequently, [it would follow that] the relationship between something-which-grasps and something-to-be-grasped is effected [jointly] by [all] these [entities existing at the same moment]—hence a nonsense would ensue. [Ad 1.2] If [it is admitted that a momentary perishable thing produces its effect] prior to its own moment, it not tenable, either, for something which itself does not yet exist, like the future Cakravartin Śaṅkha[22], etc., cannot become operative with regard to an effect existing in the past. [Ad 1.3] If you maintain that [a momentary perishable thing creates its effect posterior to its own moment, that is not any better, either, because something which has [already] been destroyed is incapable of producing [its] effect; otherwise the shriek of a dead peacock would be [possible]. [Ad 2] Does the relation of homology, [viz. cognition's having the form of the object, is] in its turn [based] [2.1] on the transference of the form of the object [onto the cognition] or [2.2] on the origination of cognition as something which is similar to this [object]? [Ad 2.1] If the first alternative [is maintained], it is not correct, [firstly,] because it would necessarily follow that the [cognised] object is bereft of its form, in as much as its form has been passed onto the cognition, [secondly,] because it would lead to the undesired consequence that one could not see objects larger than one's own body, [in as much as things of dimensions extending beyond those of one's own body could not be transferred onto it]; and, [thirdly,] because of the unwelcome consequence of misfortunes such as the swelling (splitting?) and flooding (submerging) of [one's own] head, etc.[23] [Ad 2.2] When the second [alternative is maintained], if it were indeed so [that the cognition originates as something which similar to the object], the [conclusion] reached [would be] that the determination of an object is on account of [its] similarity. And according to your doctrine, similarity is not something that really exists,[24] because [you] accept that things which are ultimately real are separate individual things that perish in a moment (*sc.* are momentary) and are characterised by infinitesimal atoms. If the grasping of an object was confined only to, [say,] a single dark-blue individual thing in a [single] moment[25], then—by the force of the similarity determined by conceptualisation arising in the point of time posterior to the [purely] non-conceptual distinct perception, whose existence (*sc.* of conceptualisation) is produced by the awakening of past impressions, that have been dormant from beginningless times[26]—determinate cognition of dark-blueness subsisting in crows, water-lilies, etc., that pervade the totality of time[27] would necessarily follow indiscriminately in any case, and, therefore, the relationship between something-which-grasps and something-to-be-grasped, which is fixed in every case, could in no way be possible. If [you argue]: 'Since [only a particular] shade of dark-blueness is ascertained [by the cognitive subject] by the force of seeing a [particular] dark-blue individual thing, which is situated in front of [the person] pointing [at it] with a finger tip, only this [particular shade of dark-blueness] is apprehended, [but] not past or future [dark-blueness] which subsists in water-lilies, crows, etc.,' then [we reply that] the conceptualisation [would thereby be] implied to be related to the individual thing because [in reality] one perceives an [individual] thing capable of efficient action that is delimited by its specific location and [its specific] circumstances. For it is as follows: the apprehension of this [object could either mean] [2.2.a] the conceptualisation of this [object] or [2.2.b] the direct grasping of this [object]. [Ad 2.2.a] To begin with [the first alternative], it is not the conceptualisation of this [object] because, according to your intention, the pertinence of conceptualisations does not [extend] to individual things. [For] it has been said [by Dharmakīrti]:

'Therefore, both speech elements and acts of knowledge jointly are taught to have as their province the exclusion of everything else and to have the universal as their domain because they are not possible with [reference to] an individual thing.'[28]

[0.3] If it were advocated [by you] that although conceptualisations [of objects] have as their domain the universal by their very nature[29], nevertheless a cogniser, who is perplexed because of the simultaneous occurrence of perception [of an object] and of conceptualisation [of the very same object], takes conceptualisation to be related to the individual thing—and it has been said [by Dharmakīrti] accordingly:

'A perplexed person, either due to simultaneous occurrence of conceptual and non-conceptual mental acts[30] or due to [their temporally] very close occurrence[31], takes these two for one [and the same act]'[32]

—so, is this [supposition] to be given credence to only because of [your] pledge, namely, [the supposition that the cognitive subject] apprehends an individual thing by conceptualisation due to confusion, but not [the supposition] that he perceives it directly by clear observation (*sc.* perception)? 'And in such a way [according to your supposition], perception, too, has as its domain [theoretically] all manifest particular entities, but due to the confusion [caused] by conceptualisation, [only] a proximate thing is observed!'—an opponent [of yours] drawing that inevitable conclusion would be difficult to repudiate. [Ad 2.2.b] If the apprehension [of an object is taken to mean] the direct grasping of this [object], then the fact that conceptualisation is related to an individual thing would be recognised (contended) by your own words. And in this way, in the pair of both alternatives (*sc.* [2.2.a] and [2.2.b]), the conceptualisation presents itself to be something whose existence is confined to an object capable of efficient action. And if you took a position: 'Conceptualisation resides in the interior of the mansion of (*sc.* pertains to) individual thing,' then, that being the case, [the conclusion that] the pertinence of linguistic unit, too, [extends] to this [object] would be difficult [for you] to negate because [linguistic unit] is a correlate of this [conceptualisation; and that is exactly] what your preceptor said: 'The very [same thing] is the province of speech elements which is [the province] of conceptualisations'[33]. And with the exception of conceptualisation, there is nothing else to establish similarity because perception is disposed towards grasping the individual thing which is different from the rest of the world. Thus, if the relation of homology, [viz., the cognition's having the form of the object, is taken to mean] the origination [of cognition] as something which is similar to this [object], then, according to the demonstrated argumentation, it has to be accepted that conceptualisation has as its domain a proximate thing[34]; and similarly, also a linguistic unit is proved to have this [proximate thing] for its province—thereby our goal is proved. The relation of homology, [viz., the cognition's having the form of the object,] is otherwise impossible because there is no other logical alternative. Consequently, the relation of causality [between cognition and its object] and the relation of homology, [viz., the cognition's having the form of the object,] are not possible as causes of the relationship between something-which-grasps and something-to-be-grasped.

[0.4] Or, let [us assume that the relation of causality and the relation of homology are possible [as causes of the relationship between something-which-grasps and something-to-be-grasped], but then you have to be asked [the following] by way of [examining different] alternatives: [viz.] are these two a cause of grasping [the object] separately or jointly? Accordingly, if the first proposition [is assumed], then one arrives [either at the contention—according to the relation of causality—that] the moment of potsherd [when a pot is broken] grasps (*sc.* incorporates) the final moment of the pot [when it was still existent] because [the potsherd] is produced from this [pot, and thus the pot would never cease to exist,] or [at the contention—according to the relation of homology—that] a reflection of the moon in water would grasp the [real] moon in the sky because [the reflection in water] has the form of this [real moon]. If the second [alternative is assumed], that being the case, it absurdly implies that the subsequent moment of the pot grasps (*sc.* incorporates) the previous moment, both because of the relation of causality and because of the relation of homology. If [you defend your position:] 'An object cannot grasp anything because it is insentient, but cognition can, since the relation of causality and the relation of homology are real[ly existent at the moment of cognition],' [you will be liable to the criticism:] now we know the following: also this [cognition (e.g. recollection)]—when the cognition to be brought about by mental activities characterised by past sensations that grasped similar objects [is concerned]—deviates from the definition[35] of something-which-grasps because [such a cognition] cannot grasp mental activity that occurred in the previous moment [of the object] which has produced [this cognition]. If [you still argue:] 'The phenomenon that the relation of causality and the relation of homology are the causes of grasping is complete (*sc.* intact), inasmuch as [the act of grasping due to the relation of causality and the relation of homology] is accompanied by the apprehension of this [object which produces the cognition]; [however,] that [apprehension of the object which produces the cognition] is not there in [the case of] mental activity [characterised by past sensations under discussion],' [we can ask] if this is an accompaniment by something that has a different domain? For it is as follows: your view is the following: 'Apprehension, that originates by the force of the awakening of past impressions, produces a conceptualisation of the universal that consists in something that is not a [really existing] object, [whereas] perception, the gaining of the existence of which is gained (*sc.* which comes into being) due to an external object [and] which has the form of this [external object], comprehends directly this very [object].' So, the accompaniment by past impressions [in the case of apprehension] does in no way contribute to the distinctive character of perception. Hence, this [accompaniment] that has been taught by you [to be] a cause of the relationship between something-which-grasps and something-to-be-grasped should be disregarded also in [the case of] perception because the more [closely] is it examined, the [quicker] it becomes shattered. Thus, just as it has been realised by you, too, that somehow or other—even though the [proper] definition of the relationship between something-which-grasps and something-to-be-grasped demonstrated [above] is lacking—perception is something-which-grasps and the object is something-to-be-grasped because [things] are seen (*sc.* experienced) in this manner[36], for otherwise [there would follow] the unwelcome consequence of the destruction of the entire everyday practice, in the same manner, you should recognise that the speech element is the denoter and the object is the denotatum, inasmuch as also in this case it would be tantamount—because of discarding empirical facts (lit. what is seen)—to the destruction of everyday practice.[37] If you [in order to undermine the validity of speech] argued in the following manner: 'For instance [people] who undertake an action on hearing a deceitful person's utterance, [such as]: 'There is a cart of molasses lumps turned upside down on the river bank! Run, run, kids!'[38] etc., fall victim to the wiles; hence all utterances [of that deceitful person] are under suspicion [for them],' then we [might—with the intention of casting doubt onto the cognitive validity of perception] take the following position: 'What the clear perception—when it reaches the path of rising (*sc.* when it occurs)—presents as water, [while] coming into contact with (lit. 'kissing') the disk of an intensely glittering mirage in a desert, is recognised as false; therefore all perception is liable to suspicion.' If [you maintain]: '[Indeed,] the cognition of water concerning mirages in the desert is not a cognitive criterion because it is subverted by a subsequent cognitive criterion that presents an object to the mind which is contrary [to the former illusion, but it is] not [the case with] the remaining true acts of cognition (lit. 'cognitions') of [such objects as] column, etc., because they are devoid of subversion,' then [we ask] whether this argument has been eaten by crows in the case of a linguistic unit, too[39]?! [There are both false and true statements, analogous to true and false acts of cognition], for we do not recognise the cognitive validity of all speech elements, only [the cognitive validity of statements] whose authors are firmly determined to be authoritative persons. So, we do not see any distinction between the perception and speech element as regards [the question of their] cognitive validity. But there could be the following distinction, [viz.] perception is a distinct representation that grasps a specific proximate object, because it is produced[40] by a particular causal complex [constituted by] eyes, etc.[41], whereas verbal knowledge is an indistinct representation that grasps both specific and non-specific (*sc.* universal) objects, because it lacks such causes (*sc.* the causal complex). This distinction does not, however, present any impairment to the cognitive validity; in the opposite case, the cognitive invalidity of inference would be absurdly implied as well, since this [inference] too grasps indistinct and non-specific objects. But, on the level of the ultimate truth, the transformation[42] in grasping proximate [and] distinct objects, [which takes place] by the force of the destruction-cum-subsidence of karmic veils, that concern (*sc.* obstruct) the causal complex [constituted by] eyes, etc., [in the case] of the living element substance[43], who pervades the three times (*sc.* is eternal) and who, although in its essential nature grasps all objects (*sc.* is omniscient)[44], is impeded by karmic veils, is called perception. On the other hand, the transformation [in the way] of grasping [both] specific and non-specific indistinct objects by the force of the destruction-cum-subsidence that concern (*sc.* obstruct) speech elements (*sc.* the verbal sphere) [in the case of the living element substance] is [called] verbal knowledge. Thus, neither the relation of causality nor the relation of homology have a factual bearing on perception, verbal knowledge or on any other [kind of] cognition. Therefore it is established that this initial sentence [above] demonstrates [three issues, namely] [1] an ultimately real subject-matter, [2] an [ultimately real] purpose and [3] an [ultimately real] relation (*sc.* relevance).

[0.5] Among these [three issues], [Ad 1] the subject-matter is that which is to be taught, and here [in the *Nyāyâvatāra*] this [subject-matter] is the cognitive criterion [mentioned at the very beginning of the initial sentence], inasmuch as only this [cognitive criterion] is to be taught by the treatise; [the author] indicates [precisely] this [subject-matter] by the part (*sc.* element of the compound) [of the initial sentence]: 'the cognitive criterion'. [Ad 2] The purpose is twofold: [that] of the student and [that] of the author. And again (*sc.* further) [this purpose] is twofold: immediate and separated [in time] (*sc.* eventual). [Among these four subdivisions], the immediate purpose of the student is [his] understanding, whose province is the cognitive criterion. [The immediate purpose] of the author, who is proficient, is the teaching [imparted] to the student, [and he is entitled to impart the teaching] because he is learned. Regarding these [three issues, the author] says [this][45]: 'is undertaken,' [thereby] indicating [his] own purpose, because this [initial sentence] is required [to be supplemented by] the pronoun 'by me'. The student's purpose, however, will be gained as something [the meaning of which is] comprised within this [act of teaching carried out by the author] by the very word aggregate [formed by] the verbal root √*pad* and the prefix *vyut°* ('to teach')—having the above in view, the author mentions specifically his own function by [using a derivative] ending with [a causative affix] *ṇic*[46] and, [therefore, says:] '**In order to teach the cognitive criterion**.' The purpose separated [in time] (*sc.* eventual) is twofold: worldly and pertinent to the ultimate truth. The worldly [purpose consists in] the avoidance of things which should be avoided, in the appropriation of things which are worth appropriating and in the indifference to things which deserve indifference[47]. The [purpose] pertinent to the ultimate truth [is] the attainment of [either] prosperity in the afterlife or of ultimate deliverance[48]. However, even though this [purpose separated in time (*sc.* eventual)] has not been mentioned explicitly, it is to be understood as implied by the very same statement [above referring to] this [immediate purpose,] because it is a result of the immediate purpose. [Ad 3] The relation (*sc.* relevance), in its turn, is characterised by the means and the goal. As for these two, the goal is the complete understanding of the meaning of the treatise, [whereas] the treatise [itself] is the means [to achieve it]. Therefore, even though the relation—viz., [the study of] this treatise should be undertaken by a person desirous of this [goal, viz. the complete understanding of the meaning of the treatise]—has not been [explicitly] mentioned by the [initial] sentence, it is understood from the context. Such is the intended purport [of the initial sentence].

[0.6] Presently, the meaning [according] to the 'letter'[49] is elucidated. As far as that is concerned, although there are those [other meanings that are] denoted by the speech element '*pramāṇa*' (cognitive criterion) [that are derivable] respectively [in conformity] with the grammatical formation [based both on] contributory factors [of an action][50], having the meaning of the agent, etc., and *nomina actionis*[51]—because the grammatical formation, following all the contributory factors [of an action] as well as *nomen actionis*, of the speech element '*pramāṇa*' can easily be explained, since [Pāṇini teaches] the rule: '[the primary suffixes denoted by the terms] *kṛtya* and *lyuṭ* [can be] variously [applied to the verbal root]'[52], [and explains this type of grammatical formation] also in other [rules][53]—namely, [such derivable notions of '*pramāṇa*' which] consist in the [1] cognitive subject[54], [2] object, [3] cognition, [4] efficient action, [5] totality of causes, [6] destruction-cum-subsidence and [7] action[55], nevertheless, here [in this treatise] only cognition has been made the subject, inasmuch as only this [cognition] is liable to examination because the examination of other [derivable notions of '*pramāṇa*' mentioned above] is preceded by that [examination of cognition] and is purposeless [without the notion of 'cognition']. For it is as follows: [Ad 1] it indeed [serves] no purpose to examine the cognitive subject, to begin with, because this [cognitive subject] is tantamount to erroneous and non-erroneous acts of cognition[56]. [Ad 2] It [serves no purpose to examine] the object, either, because it is the goal [to be cognised through cognition], inasmuch as it is understood only through the examination of cognition that represents the means [to ascertain it]. [Ad 4] It [serves no purpose to examine] efficient action because once this [object] is ascertained, the examination [of efficient action] is pointless. [Ad 5] It [serves no purpose to examine] the totality of causes, either, because before the origination of cognition the nature [of the totality of causes can] not [be] ascertained [and] after [the origination of cognition] the ascertainment of their pertinence or impertinence [to the origination of cognition] is a nonsense, because their nature is already determined[57]. [Ad 6] It [serves no purpose to examine] destruction-cum-subsidence, either, because this [destruction-cum-subsidence] has a form which can be deduced from the origination of cognition[58]. [Ad 7] It [serves no purpose to examine] the act of cognising in a valid way, either, because the propriety [of the act of cognising in a valid way itself] is established—inasmuch as this [act of cognising in a valid way] is to be proved by cognitive criterion—precisely by means of the compelling force of this [cognitive criterion]. Thus, that is the [real] intention [of the author]: although all these meanings of the speech element ['*pramāṇa*'], taken literally, are possible with regard to the real thing which is possessed of infinite qualities, nevertheless precisely that by which cognisers determine an object and undertake an action with desire [directed towards] a thing capable of efficient action is cognition [which]—although there [exists] the relation of essential identity [of cognition] with the cognitive subject, inasmuch as [cognitive subject] is the property-possessor (*sc*. the substratum of cognition)—is different [from the cognitive subject], because [cognition] is the property [of the cognitive subject][59], [and this cognition] is here called the cognitive criterion in the sense: 'that by means of which something is cognised in a valid way.' [The expression] '**to teach**' this [cognitive criterion means] revealing the [cognitive criterion's] intrinsic nature through [its] definition, etc.[60], as intended [by the author] himself, by rejecting [its] definition, etc., falsely conceived by the opponent. [As for the expression] '**in order to**' [accomplish] that, the speech element 'in order to' is a synonym of 'with the purpose of.' [The expression] '**this [task]**' reflects (*sc*. refers to) the body of the treatise that unfolds itself in the [author's] own mind as something consisting in the meaning; for the body of the treatise is two-fold: speech elements and meaning, because [the treatise]—although it will externally be revealed only as something that consists of speech elements—is internally clearly perceived as something the meaning of which is true[61]. [The expression] '**is undertaken**' is tantamount to 'is being performed through the composition of words, sentences and verses[62].'

[0.7] Further, in this world other [thinkers] are of a different opinion about the cognitive criterion as regards [its] definition, number, domain and result[63]. For it is as follows: as regards the definition, to begin with, the Buddhists [maintain] that 'the cognitive criterion is an unerring cognition'[64]. The Mīmāṁsaka [hold] that 'the cognitive criterion is that which comprehends a not [yet] comprehended object'[65]. The Naiyāyika and others [maintain] that 'the cognitive criterion is the cause of comprehension (cognition) of an object'[66]. Similarly as regards the number, the Buddhists [are of the opinion] that 'there are only two cognitive criteria: perception and inference.'[67] The Mīmāṁsaka [teach] that 'perception, inference, verbal testimony, analogy, presumption, absence [as negative proof] are cognitive criteria.' The Naiyāyika [contend] that 'perception, inference, verbal testimony, analogy are cognitive criteria.'[68] The Vaiśeṣika [take the stand] that 'perception, inference, verbal testimony are cognitive criteria.'[69] The Sāṁkhya also [accept] the same [three cognitive criteria][70]. The Cārvākas [believe] that 'perception is the only cognitive criterion.'[71] Likewise, as regards the domain, the Buddhists [are of the opinion] that 'the real domain of the cognitive criterion are individual things characterised by infinitesimal atoms detached from each other and perishing in a moment (*sc.* momentary)[72].'[73] The Mīmāṁsaka [take it to be] 'the real thing that consists in the universal and the particular[74].'[75] The Naiyāyika and the Vaiśeṣika [consider the domain of the cognitive criterion to be] 'the universal and the particular as [absolutely] separate from each other.'[76] The Sāṁkhya [are of the opinion] that [the domain of the cognitive criterion] is 'the universal[77] consisting in the triad of the constituents.'[78] The Cārvākas [maintain] that 'the scope of the cognitive criterion is the quaternary of gross elements.'[79] Similarly, [various thinkers] are of a different opinion as regards the result [of a cognitive criterion], too: The Buddhists [claim] that 'the result of the cognitive criterion is the comprehension of an object.'[80] The Mīmāṁsaka and others [are of the opinion] that 'in each and every case, first [comes] the cognitive criterion and then [its] result.'[81]

[1.0] In view of this [difference of opinion the author], desirous, to begin with, to rebut [those] misconceptions as regards [both] the definition and the number [of cognitive criteria], says:

> **/1/ The cognitive criterion is the cognition revealing itself and something else [different from it[82], and it is] free from subversion; [it is] two-fold: perception as well as indirect cognition, corresponding to [the way of] determination of the cognoscible.**

[1.1] Accordingly, in this [verse the author] rebuts the difference of opinion as regards the definition [of the cognitive criterion] by the first half [of the verse], whereas by the second half [of the verse he refutes] the difference of opinion as regards the number [of cognitive criteria]. And definition[83] is a specific property capable of distinguishing [a particular thing from all other things] that possess a different form. That by which a *definiendum* is defined, [i.e.] determined, as something distinguished from things that belong to a different class is called definition. And regarding that, there are two [groups of people] that should be apprised, namely [people who are] of a different opinion, whose discerning organs are devoted to their own doctrines [and who are] adherents of rival systems of thought[84] as well as [those who are] uncultivated, simple-minded people[85]. And therefore, whenever the definition is [meant] for [people who are] of a different opinion [in the first place], in every such case the relationship between the definition and the *definiendum* should be demonstrated in the following manner: 'That which is well-known to you as well as to us as **the cognitive criterion** should be regarded [by you] as **the cognition which reveals itself and something else [different from it] [and which is] free from subversion**'; [in other words,] having called to [their] minds the cognitive criterion as something [already] well-known, the fact that [the cognitive criterion] reveals itself and something else (different from it), etc., is introduced as something new (*sc.* still unknown to them). But when this definition is [meant] for [people] with uncultivated minds, then—since some kind of cognition which reveals itself and something else (different from it) [and which is] free from subversion is established for every creature[86], because otherwise [one would have to face] the undesired consequence of the destruction of everyday practice (*sc.* experience), [which is normally] fixed in each and every case—they are made understand[it] in the following way: 'You must understand that this very cognition [so] well-known to you—which grasps a specific object in a certain case, which reveals itself and something else (different from it), [and which is] free from subversion—is the cognitive criterion.' Also in this case [the same two procedures, namely] calling something [already] well-known to mind [and] introducing something new (*sc.* still unknown) should be applied [in order to apprise others].

[1.2] Now the meaning [according] to the 'letter'[87] [is elucidated]. In this [verse, the phrase] '**the cognitive criterion**' [is to be explained in the same] way as before. '**Itself**' means '[its] self', [i.e.] 'its intrinsic nature'; '**something else**' means 'an object'. Such whose character is to '**reveal**', [i.e.] to illuminate, both of them is of that kind (*sc.* revealing itself and something else). That by which reality is cognised, [i.e.] determined, is '**cognition**'. That by which something is subverted is '**subversion**'; it is tantamount to an activity of cognitive criterion which presents an object to the mind which is contrary [to the former illusion]. That cognition which is absolutely free[88] from, [i.e.] devoid of, this [subversion] is a cognitive criterion—such is the [syntactical] connection [between the elements of the verse].

[1.3] And here, [in the same verse,] by the [phrase] '**revealing itself and something else [different from it]**'[89]—since [as a rule] a qualification[90] functions with reference to a definition in relation to that which is to be excluded—are refuted [1] the Vijñāna-vādin[91], [i.e. a] particular [school of the] Buddhists, who maintain that cognition is only self-revealing, as well as [2] the Mīmāṁsaka, the Naiyāyika and others [who are of the opinion that cognition] reveals only something else (*sc.*

something different from it). [Ad 1] For if these [Vijñāna-vādins] argued: 'Since there is no external object, cognition is such the existence of which is confined to its own divisions'[92], [such an opinion would] not [be] correct because [it would lead to] the undesired consequence that, if there are no objects to be known, there is no cognition[93]. If you [the Vijñāna-vādin] say: 'All [cognition] is like that, [viz., it cognises only its own epiphenomena], since in the state of dreaming—even though there are no [real] objects [perceived]—cognition is seen [in form of] various representations[94] like a forest, a temple[95], etc.', that is not [right] because also this [cognition in the state of dreaming] is dependant[96] on the awakening—by the presence of the totality of causes such as drowsiness, etc.[97]—of subliminal impressions within the cognitive subject, [that have been] produced by seeing really existing objects present in the state of wakefulness; in the opposite case, there might [as well] occur an representation of a sixth gross element in addition to the five gross elements, which is never experienced.[98] Furthermore, you should be asked: 'How could one cognition [consist in] manifold transient occurrences of something white, yellow, etc.?' If [you answer]: '[That cognition is caused] by past impressions [brought about by] beginningless nescience,' then, also in that case, there arises an impeccable pair of [implausible] alternatives: [viz.,] either [1.1] that past impression differed from that cognition or [1.2] did not? [Ad 1.1] If [you answer]: 'It differed [from the cognition],' then—if it were indeed so [that it is different]—the cognitive criterion which grasps this [past impression] should be stated [explicitly by you], because there is no sensation of [a past impression][99] different from cognition, and [in such a case,] if there is a sensation of this [past impression] as [something] different from cognition, then there is a sensation also of an object which is different [from cognition], hence this [object] can hardly be rejected. If [you argue]: 'This [past impression] is inferred as something different only from such a cognition, which is defiled by the form of the cogniser and the cognoscible, as something which is the cause of that [cognition in the form of the cogniser and the cognoscible and] as something that solely consists in cognition,' [that] is not [correct] because one does not grasp (*sc.* there is no evidence of) any [causal[100]] relation with this [past impression] and because [it would lead to] the undesired consequence of discarding empirical facts (*sc.* what is experienced) and of falsely assuming fiction (*sc.* what is not experienced). Furthermore, [we can draw unwelcome consequences from such a way of arguing and conclude]: just like cognition, although [numerically] one, is multiform by the force of past impressions, [that are] different [from this cognition], in the same way also something insentient[101] [can] appear as something that consists in cognitive awareness merely by the force of these [past impressions]; hence, because of the contrariety (*sc.* entailment of something contrary), the object alone would become established, not cognition. [Ad 1.2] If [past impression] were not different [from that cognition], then—woe!—that would be nothing but cognition, not past impression, because this [past impression] is not be different from that [cognition], just like its intrinsic nature; so let [us] leave that alone[102]. [Ad 2] Now, if [the Mīmāṁsaka, the Naiyāyika, etc.,] took the position that [cognition] reveals [only] something else (different from it) because there is no self-revealing [of cognition], that [would be] incoherent, as well, because—if there is no self-revealing [of cognition]—[cognition] would be incapable of revealing something else (*sc.* its object). For a lamp is not[103] engaged in illuminating a pot, etc., without illuminating itself. And if the cognition, although [it] itself [remained] uncognised, [could] make [us] grasp the [object], then the cognition arisen in Devadatta would have Yajñadatta grasp it (*sc.* it would manifest itself to Yajñadatta), because there is no difference. And [there is still] something else, if the [cognition] were only revealing something else (i.e. its object), dependent on what [would] the difference [as regards being] distant, [being] nearby, etc., between objects that unfold themselves [to the mind] manifest itself[104]? If [you say:] '[The difference is] dependent on the body,' [that] is not [correct,] because also this [body] is not distinct [from other objects] in being something to be revealed[105]; therefore this [difference] is possible [only] when [a cognition] directed inwards[106] grasps an external object, not otherwise. If [you assume the following:] '[That something else] is grasped as being located inside [cognition] by further cognitive criterion, [such as] presumption, etc.,[107] [and] therefore the difference between [objects that are] distant, nearby, etc., will be justified with regard to that [further cognitive criterion],' [that] is not [correct] because also in that case [we face] the insurmountability of a pair of alternatives. For it is like that: does the further cognitive criterion [grasping] this [object] illuminate itself or illuminate something else? If [you answer]: '[The further cognitive criterion] illuminates itself,' then what is wrong with the first [cognitive criterion]!?[108] If [you contend as follows:] '[Another cognitive criterion] illuminates something else,' then [your position leads to the fallacy of] *regressus ad infinitum*, because also in that case this is all the same palaver. Hence it is established that cognition, precisely as [being something] revealing its intrinsic nature, is applied [for the epistemic purpose] as grasping an object.[109]

[1.4] What is refuted by the [word] '**cognition**,' however, is the cognitive validity of the [sense-object] contact which is falsely conceived to be a cognitive criterion by the Naiyāyika[110] and others. The intention [of the author] is as follows: Only that cognition is a cognitive criterion, on account of which cognisers—having determined an object capable of executing efficient action, such as bathing, drinking, plunging [in water], etc.—immediately undertake an action, not the [sense-object] contact [itself], which is insentient, because there is no immediate decision [in the case of the sense-object contact]. If [you assume the following]: 'Because [the sense-object contact] is caused by comprehension of an object, it is a cognitive criterion,' then immediately the limited number of cognitive criteria is shattered because [such a standpoint would] entail that also the body, etc., would be cognitive criteria, inasmuch as they are the causes of this [comprehension of an object], too; so let [us] leave that alone[111].

[1.5] By the [phrase] '**free from subversion**,' however, [the author] disproves such a cognition [1] that is—[in the case] of [people for whom] the beam of light, etc., [entering their] eyes [is] obscured by ophthalmological disorder[112], etc.—a representation, [for instance,] of two moons suspended in the sky, etc., and [2] [such a cognition] that is—[in the case] of [people] whose minds err due to faulty reasoning—a representation, [for instance,] of the world as [either] perishing in the moment (*sc.* momentary), [or] as absolutely [consisting in] the universal or absolutely in the particular, [or] created by a supreme being, etc., [and such faulty cognitions have their] origin in listening to [these people's] own respective doctrines; [the author disproves any such act of cognition] because it is washed away (*sc.* subverted)[113] by a subsequent cognitive criterion that makes one know an object opposite to this [erroneous cognition]. Yet, by the mention of the prefix '*vi*-°' meaning distinction, as one should realise[114], it has been taught to the effect that the cognitive awareness apprehending yellowness in [place of] a white shell, which ensues [in] those whose faculty of sight [is] suppressed by various [afflictions like] jaundice and purblindness[115]—even though it is not subverted by the cogniser's own perception when this defect persists all the time, nevertheless, since it is subverted by other people's perception which grasps the whiteness of this shell [in question]—is no cognitive criterion.

[1.6] On the other hand, by the whole definition [the author] has refuted what others have taught, namely [such definitions of cognitive criterion] like [1] 'the cognitive criterion is that which comprehends a not [yet] comprehended object' [upheld by the Mīmāṁsaka][116], [2] 'the cognitive criterion is an unerring [cognition]' [maintained by the Buddhists][117], [3] 'the cognitive criterion is the cause of comprehension (*sc.* cognition) of an object' [advocated, e.g. by the Naiyāyika][118], etc. [Ad 1] For it is as follows: [one can ask] what is called the phenomenon of being something which comprehends a not [yet] comprehended object? If [you reply]: 'That which comprehends an object not [yet] comprehended by another cognition is cognitive criterion,' then does this another cognition belong to somebody else or to [the cogniser] himself? [1.1] If it belongs to somebody else, that is not correct, [firstly,] because [that would lead to] the undesired consequence of the cognitive invalidity of acts of cognition of all ordinary people, since [they] cognise objects cognised [already], inasmuch as the domain of an omniscient person's cognition [encompasses] all objects and, [secondly] because it is possible that other people's perception can grasp the [same] object. [1.2] If it belongs to [the cogniser] himself, then also in that case there are eight [equally implausible] alternatives, namely, is this object to be comprehended [1.2.1] a substance or [1.2.2] a mode? Or [is it] [1.2.3] a mode qualified by a substance or [1.2.4] a substance qualified by a mode? Or, perhaps, [is it] [1.2.5] the universal or [1.2.6] the particular? Or [1.2.7] the particular qualified by the universal or [1.2.8] the universal qualified by the particular? Among these [alternatives], [Ad 1.2.1] if you accept the first one, that is not correct because there is no uncognised division of eternity and of oneness [in the case] of a substance[119]. [Ad 1.2.2] If [you accept] the second [alternative], that is not tenable, either, because any qualification of the mode which has been destroyed in the instant of the production of past sensations would be purposeless, inasmuch as it is impossible [for it] to wait as long as the time of the origin of another sensation [comes]. [Ad 1.2.3] Or [if you accept] the third [alternative], that is not any better, either, because it does not pass [the test of] the two alternatives. For this mode qualified by substance, [being] uncognised, is either cognised by a cognition [1.2.3.a] existing at the same point of time or [1.2.3.b] by [a cognition] existing at some different point of time. [Ad 1.2.3.a] [It is certainly] not [cognised by the cognition] existing at the same point of time, to begin with, because of the futility of [such] qualification, inasmuch as that [cognition existing at the same point] is not possible. For there is no possibility that one cogniser—at the same time—[could] have two sensations [which have as their respective] province one mode embraced by the substance, because [we do] not experience anything like that and because that would lead to the undesired consequence of cognitive invalidity [of such a pair of sensations[120]], inasmuch as [each of them] would mutually cognise an object [already] cognised [by its correlative]. [Ad 1.2.3.b] Neither is [it cognised by the cognition] existing at some different point of time because the mode which is being grasped [at the present moment] cannot leap into the different point of time, inasmuch as it is related only to the present moment, which is detached from previous and subsequent moments. [Ad 1.2.4] With the same [argumentation one can] also contravene the alternative of a substance qualified by a mode because it is based on one and the same productive-supportive principle[121]. [Ad 1.2.5] If [you accept the alternative that the object to be comprehended is] the universal, that [is] incoherent as well, because—since the entirety [of the universal] is grasped, inasmuch as it is one, by the first cognition—[such an alternative would lead] to the undesired consequence of cognitive invalidity of [all] subsequent acts of cognition cognising the universal, inasmuch [their] domain [would be] an object [already] cognised. [Ad 1.2.6] If [you accept the alternative that the object to be cognised is] the particular, then it has to be discussed whether it is [1.2.6.a] permanent or [1.2.6.b] impermanent. [Ad 1.2.6.a] If [you say] that [the particular] is permanent, then, that being the case, [we have] the unwelcome consequence—since the totality [of the particular] is grasped only by the first sensation—of the cognitive invalidity of [all] subsequent [sensations (*sc.* acts of cognition)] that have [that particular] as their province, inasmuch as [their] domain [would be already] cognised. [Ad 1.2.6.b] If [you say] that [the particular] is impermanent, [then such an alternative] is disproved by the [above] criticism [referring to] the mode. [Ad 1.2.7] If [you accept the alternative that the object to be cognised is] the particular qualified by the universal, [then we can ask:] what does it mean that this [particular] is qualified? [Does it mean] [1.2.7.a] the relation of essential identity or [1.2.7.b] nothing but the proximity to the [particular]? [Ad 1.2.7.a] If [you say that] the relation of essential identity [is here meant, then]—since, like [in the case of] the universal [discussed in § 1.2.5 above], this [particular qualified by the universal] is grasped by the first cognition, for otherwise [there would be] the impairment of the relation of essential identity—the cognitive invalidity of other acts of cognition that have the [particular] as their province would absurdly be implied. [Ad 1.2.7.b] However, when the alternative concerning the proximity to the [particular is considered], there follows the criticism, [as if] clinging at the back [of such an argumentation], brought forward against the pair [consisting] of [these complementary] alternatives, [i.e. separately against the particular and separately against the universal], because both of them, [i.e. the qualified particular and the universal qualifier, have] mutually disconnected forms. [Ad 1.2.8] When, on the other hand, the alternative [asserting] that [the object to be cognised is] the universal qualified by the particular [is considered], the very same [argumentation] has to be applied the other way round. Therefore—since [the Mīmāṁsaka's assertion that cognitive criterion is] a cognition which comprehends a not [yet] comprehended object can in no way bear the weight of burden of examination—it is established that [the definition of cognitive criterion formulated by the Mīmāṁsaka] is not a [proper] definition. [Ad 2] Now the phenomenon of being an unerring[122] [cognition, that is maintained to be the proper *definiens* of cognitive criterion by the Buddhists,] is examined. So, do you speak of the cognitive validity of cognition as [2.1] the attainment of an indicated object or as [2.2] that which shows an object amenable to the attainment or as [2.3] that of which the province is unwavering? [Ad 2.1] If the first alternative [is meant], it is not correct because that would bring the consequence that the sensation brought about by an entity just about to become extinguished, like a bubble on water, etc., is not a cognitive criterion, inasmuch as this [object] would be destroyed in the moment of [its] attainment. [Ad 2.2] If the second alternative [is meant], it is not tenable, either, because of the unwelcome consequence that the cognition, which has as its domain planets, constellations and other [celestial bodies] abiding at places unsuited for attainment (*sc.* beyond reach), would become invalid, inasmuch as these [celestial bodies, etc.], being indeed situated in unusual places, are not amenable to the attainment (*sc.* cannot be reached). [Ad 2.3] If the third alternative [is considered], in this case, too, how can you know that the province [of an act of cognition] is unwavering? If [you reply]: '[We know it] because the province of this [cognition] is not revoked by another cognition,' this is exactly what has been taught by us; why does it look repellent to you? For—save the cognition revealing itself and something else [which is different from it and which is] free from subversion—we do not observe that one cognition revokes the province of another [cognition]. So, you have accepted, as a logical consequence, that only this [cognition, as defined in NA 1ab,] is the cognitive criterion. [Ad 3] Also this [third alleged definition,] viz. 'the cognitive criterion is the cause of the comprehension (*sc.* cognition) of an object,' does not stand the examination, because [it would lead] to the undesired consequence that also the body, sense-organs, etc.—inasmuch as they are causes of this [comprehension as well]—[would be] valid [as cognitive criteria]. If [you claim]: '[Only] the immediate cause of the comprehension of an object is cognitive criterion, not the body, etc.,' so [we shall retort] that only the cognition that manifests itself and something else [different from it and that is] void of subversion is cognitive criterion, not the [sense-object] contact, etc., because the determination of the object [can] not take place even when this [sense-object contact is] present. Hence, only this [definition formulated by us in NA 1] is a tenable (*sc.* proper) definition of cognitive criterion.

[1.7] Now, [the author] states the number these [cognitive criteria when he says]: '**perception**', etc. Concerning that, the linguistic unit 'perceiving organ'—with regard to ultimately real perception well-known from the Canon[123]—is well-known as a synonym of the living element. Here [in this verse], however, the linguistic unit 'perceiving organ' is used—since [we] are dealing [here] with the conventional perception—as an utterance [denoting] the senses. And, therefore, that which has gone towards 'the perceiving organ' is perception[124]. The meaning is as follows: such a cognition perceiving directly an object which commences resorting to the senses is perception. And that is the factor [accountable for the etymological] origination of the speech element 'perception', but not the factor [accountable for its] usage. For this [speech element] formed grammatically in such a manner indicates a particular cognition that grasps directly something-to-be-grasped because [this speech element] has grown (*sc.* is traditionally used) precisely in this [meaning]; like the speech element '*go*', [denoting in fact 'a cow'], even though formed grammatically as [connoting] the action of waking[125], refers to a particular physique possessed of a neck hump, etc., either walking or not walking, because [this speech element] is well-known only in this [meaning, and] it [does] not [refer] to people, etc., even though [they are] furnished with the action of walking, because of the contrary[126]. And, therefore, what it amounts to is the following: that which is a sensation of the intrinsic nature [of an object in the case] of acts of omniscience is perception, as well, because direct perception of the intrinsic nature [of an object] which is to-be-grasped is present also in [case] of these [acts of omniscience].[127] That which operates aloof from the perceiving organs, [i.e. the senses][128], is indirect cognition. The intent is as follows: the cognition which determines an object indirectly by the operation of the mind, independent of the operation of the perceiving organs (*sc.* the senses) is the indirect cognition.

[1.8] The two speech elements '**and**'[129] indicate that both perception and indirect cognition are on an equal footing. Thereby, as a result, what some [thinkers] have promulgated has been controverted, namely, 'perception is superior to all cognitive criteria', etc.[130], because there is no difference between both of them regarding [their] cognitive validity, inasmuch as a particular distinct or indistinct representation, even though it is there, is not a requisite for (*sc.* criterion of) superiority. If [you maintain the following]: '[Perception is superior to the indirect cognition because] the indirect cognition is born later, [hence it is inferior,] inasmuch as perception precedes [it],' that is not absolutely true, because it is an empirical fact that [a person is] known [to be] alive or dead—even though there is no (lit., 'there might be the harm of') perception that [could] perceive directly the living element (*sc.* soul)—due to presence or absence, [respectively,] of [such] characteristic marks of the living element [like] breathing-in and breathing-out, etc., that are concluded with [the help of the relation of] the inexplicability otherwise[131] in all cases; otherwise [that would lead to] the undesired consequence that no everyday practice [would] take place among people. If perception were conjectured to be superior, on account of [the argument that] in certain cases the indirect cognition proceeds by the force of the relation which has [first been grasped by perception, [then] the superiority of the indirect cognition would follow immediately on account of [the argument that] it is [also] an empirical fact that [1] a perception the province of which is a deer [that is observed] due to a sudden movement of the neck[132] by the force of the speech element (*sc.* expression): 'Look! A deer is running!' etc., [or] similarly [2] [a perception] the domain of which is a forest or a temple, etc.[133] [that are recognised] either due to the recollection [of the forest or the temple, etc.,] as such or due to grasping the linguistic convention [relating the word 'temple' and the object *temple*] as such with curiosity, etc., to see objects not seen before, is preceded by the indirect cognition [in both cases].[134]

[1.9] [Now we comment upon the expression] **'two-fold'**. On account of the maxim that 'every sentence functions with a restriction'[135]—[which holds true] because otherwise, inasmuch as no [expression could] indicate [some] specific [fixed] meaning, [it would lead to] the undesired consequence [that it would be] purposeless to utter this [expression in question], since it is incorrect [to admit] an activity [that takes place] without expectancy, [e.g. in the case of uttering this expression that would turn out to be purposeless and without the expectation that it is effective,] for [the expression in question] would not be possessed of aptitude to revoke that which has contrary form—[the author] rules out, by [setting] the restriction, viz. 'there are only two [cognitive criteria],' any other number contrary [to (*sc.* different from) the number 'two' that is] falsely conceived by opponents because the propriety of that [number larger or smaller than two] is subverted.

[1.10] For it is like that, [the opinion of the materialists] that perception is the only one cognitive criterion is untrue because—if there were no indirect cognition—it would be unjustified to assume that this [perception] itself is a cognitive criterion. For he[136]—having comprehended [some] individual acts of perception as undeviating, inasmuch as [they] make one reach a thing capable of efficient action, and [having comprehended some] other [individual acts of perception] as deviating, inasmuch as [they] are contrary to that[137]—afterwards again at some other point of time, he would insist that individual acts of perception of this sort and opposite are, [respectively,] cognitive criteria and the opposite[138]. Consequently, perception—[being] void of the reflection of the previous and of the subsequent [and being such] the existence of which is confined to grasping an object [situated] in front [before the cogniser]—is not capable of apprehending the similarity, [that constitutes] the foundation of cognitive validity (*sc.* the status of cognitive criterion), between individual acts of perception existing at previous and subsequent points of time. And, [as a result,] he is not able to demonstrate the cognitive validity of individual acts of perception to [his] opponent, even though they are the domain of his own awareness. Therefore, another cognitive criterion—consisting in inference [and] comprised within the indirect cognition—has to, by necessity, be accepted, [firstly, as something that] makes one know the cognitive validity of individual acts of perception of the present moment by means of the similarity with [other] individual acts of perception as they have [previously] been made and, [secondly, as something that] demonstrates [that cognitive validity] to the opponent[139]. And [such a materialist], telling that perception is the only cognitive criterion [which is at his disposal] in order to convince an opponent, [and] there is no other [cognitive criterion than that], indicates his own insanity because of the following argumentation: since one [can] not perceive directly other [people]'s mental operations with [the help] of perception, the cognitive validity of the indirect cognition in order to ascertain of a particular cognitive awareness [of another person] from seeing (*sc.* experiencing) [his] particular acts, declarations and gestures, inevitably results. [He] is not in a position to corroborate [his] negation of [the existence of] heaven, the moral deterministic principle[140], deities, etc., with [the help] of perception because this [perception] has only proximate [objects] as its province. Our mind is bewildered, for how can he persist in the following incongruity: he neither attains the Cārvākahood of a strident donkey[141] by [simple] negation of these [points of dispute without any justification] nor does he want any other cognitive criterion in order to negate these [points of dispute]?! Furthermore, [if one rejects any additional cognitive criterion,] it should be stated how this very perception in its turn appropriates cognitive validity, because it adopts positive concomitance and negative concomitance regarding an entity that is being grasped[142]. For it is like that, if you say: 'This [perception] emerges by the force of an entity the causal complex of which is complete;[143] when that [causal complex] is absent, [perception] does not arise for the cogniser,[144] even though he has the pair of wide-open eyes,' then [we can reply that] it is exactly the same also in the case of the indirect cognition: this [indirect cognition], too, comes forth due to the efficacy of an external object, [firstly,] because it originates by means of a inferential sign or of a speech element which are related to this [external object to be proved, for] otherwise [it would lead to] the undesired consequence of the fallacy of the indirect cognition, and, [secondly,] because it is unjustified to assume that the cognitive validity (*sc.* the status of cognitive criterion) of the ultimate indirect cognition—when this [indirect cognition happens once to be] false—is impaired[145], [for] otherwise—since likewise [one act of] perception which is apt to see a pair of moons suspended in the firmament [and which] is recognised to be false—all acts of clear perception, even though they were considered to be true, would attain the status of falsehood. Hence, it is established that—since the indirect cognition, which is [indeed] a cognitive criterion, can never originate without the existence of an entity which is being grasped—[the indirect cognition] inevitably ascends to the prominent rank of cognitive criterion, just like perception[146].

[1.11] Similarly, whatever any other number of cognitive criteria in addition to [these] two taught [above] were asserted by other [thinkers], also with reference to this [number higher than two], that [kind of cognition] which appropriates cognitive validity, when being analysed, just like [1] analogy and [2] presumption, should be included in these very two [categories of] perception and the indirect cognition. [3] That, on the other hand, which—when being examined, just like absence [as negative proof] falsely conceived by the Mīmāṁsaka—does not ascend to the [status of] cognitive validity, [serves] no purpose for us, be it excluded [from] or be it included [in these two categories, viz. perception and indirect cognition] because it is nothing real[147]; hence it should be ignored[148].

[1.12] [Ad 1] If you ask: 'How is it possible that analogy is a cognitive criterion?', it is replied: [it is possible] for such a sensation—which arises in [the case of] a man who, first, [knows] the distinctive character of the physique of a cow that is comprehended by the clear perception, in whom the subliminal impression is left by hearing the sentence: '*gayal* is like a cow'[149] [and] who is [afterwards] roaming in a forest, [secondly,] which is preceded by a distinct perception the province of which is a particular physique of a *gayal*, [thirdly,] which has its birth that is produced [jointly] by a previous operation of perception the domain of which is a physique of a cow and by a subsequent [operation of perception the domain of which is a physique of] a *gayal*, [fourthly,] which refers either to a physique qualified by similarity or to similarity qualified by [two or more] physiques [in the following manner, respectively:] 'this is similar to that' or 'there is similarity between the two'—is analogy. Just like the propounders of this [analogy] have said:

> 'Hence, what is seen may be for analogy [either] the cognoscible distinguished by similarity or similarity linked to this [apprehended object].'[150]

[1.13] And therefore—since, [firstly,] the two acts of perception, [namely] the former and the subsequent, whose existence is confined to grasping a physique of a cow and of a *gayal*, [respectively, situated] in front [before the cogniser,] since, [secondly, they are] void of the reflection of the previous and of the subsequent[151], since, [thirdly, they are] void of the description by speech elements, inasmuch as they observe clearly—analogy, which is subsequent to these [two acts of perception][152], which is undeviating, which is conducive to everyday practice [and] which ascertains similarity [between objects apprehended by these two acts of perception], is a cognitive criterion, inasmuch as it reveals itself and something else [different from it] and because it is free from subversion. If [you claim]: 'No other similarity in addition to (*sc.* except for) the physiques of the previous and the subsequent is comprehended,' what is [then] this comprehension (*sc.* cognition) [that grasps similarity according to you], if perception is that by which the similarity is not comprehended? If similarity—since it is the domain of analogy—does not occur in perception, what is wrong with it? For it is not possible to say that this [analogy] has no domain, [only] because its domain[153] does not occur in another cognition, [i.e. in perception]; in the opposite case, it would necessarily follow that perception has no domain, only because a manifest particular entity[154]—inasmuch as it is to be grasped by perception [only]—does not occur in analogy, either. Therefore, in the same way as perception is a cognitive criterion with reference to its own province, so is the case with analogy, as well. For it is not correct to exhibit arbitrary partiality towards one of two [alternatives] that unfold themselves [to the mind with equal right][155], if there is no [real] distinction [between them]. Through this[156] the cognitive validity of other unerring particular [varieties of] the indirect cognition, [e.g.] [1] the cognition of recognition, [2] reminiscence, [3] induction, should be considered as [already] explained because they adhere to (*sc.* follow) one and the same productive-supportive principle[157]. [Ad 1] For it is as follows: [the process of recognition can be illustrated in the following manner:] first, the perception of an object leaves a subliminal impression in the cognitive subject; due to the perception of [an object of] this sort this subliminal impression awakes; [when] awakened, [the subliminal impression] generates the cognition of recognition—that has the former object as its province—[characterised] by the description: 'This is precisely the same [object]' or 'it belongs to the same class,' because this [recognition] lays the foundation to the dyad of homogeneity[158] subdivided into diachronic and synchronic[159] [and] because this [recognition] does not arise [in the case] of [a person in whom] the perception, the domain of which [should be] the former[ly observed] object, has not taken place. [Ad 2] Similarly, precisely this subliminal impression, awakened by the perception of an object of this sort or by the afterthought[160], etc., gives rise to recollection (*sc.* reminiscence) characterised by the non-loss of the [previously] experienced thing,[161] inasmuch as recollection is inexplicable [in the case] of a man [who has] not seen the object [before].[162] [Ad 3] Induction[163]—which is disposed towards grasping the relation of the inferential sign, that is characterised by the inexplicability otherwise[164], with the probandum that cannot be sensed by perception or by inference—will be, in its turn, declared [to be] another cognitive criterion[165].

[1.14] [Ad 2] However, taking into account that [people] conclude from fire, etc., another object, which is additional to the domain of previous perception [and] undeviating, [namely, that fire] is possessed of the power of burning, etc., inasmuch as such entities as blisters, etc., that constitute the domain of perception, etc., are otherwise inexplicable[166], presumption[167] [too] appropriates undeniably cognitive validity, because it satisfies its definition[168]. In the same way, it should be corroborated that also any other sensation—that produces an addition (*sc.* a conclusion additional) to the domain of perception [and] which is conducive to everyday practice, inasmuch as it is without expectancy[169]—is a cognitive criterion because [such a sensation] reveals itself and something else [different from it] and is free from subversion, for instance, the sensation (cognition) of the number of those [steps] that arises in the point of time posterior to seeing the [sequence of] previous and subsequent steps of a stair-case. And all these [sub-varieties] are included in the indirect cognition because they are apt to [produce] a sensation of the object under discussion by the means of perception of another object which is otherwise inexplicable. On the other hand, if another cognitive criterion were falsely conceived on account of a certain [insignificant] distinction, the limited number of cognitive criteria would be shattered because one would reach infinity, in view of [the fact that] cognitive operation is diverse, due to the diversity of [various stages of] destruction-cum-subsidence of [the *karman*] veiling [cognition and perception][170]. Now [an objection is raised by the opponent]: 'If it is indeed so, how will this very dyad of the indirect cognition, which is being taught [by you to consist] in the difference between inference and verbal knowledge, be explicable at all, for also in this case it is not difficult to demonstrate that the cognition the origin of which are utterances imparted by an authoritative person, being otherwise inexplicable [without] the object, is [also] included in inference? And, therefore, there remains one inference only; [and] only that is [denoted] by the speech element "the indirect cognition".' If that is said, it endures right, for scholars are insouciant as far as phraseology is concerned. It is [indeed] true, but [still] the following is maintained: even though verbal knowledge can be included in inference by a certain procedure, nevertheless some [thinkers] are of a different opinion regarding this [verbal knowledge]; hence, the cognitive validity (*sc.* the status of a separate cognitive criterion) of this [verbal knowledge,] after it has been gouged out[171], should be corroborated[172]. And it is not possible to speak of [*x* (here: verbal knowledge) as being] distinct from *y* (here: inference) [if *x*] has not been made separate; hence, this [verbal knowledge] is specified separately[173]. And thereby, the following is apprehended: even though it is also possible to include some other particular [varieties] of indirect cognition, too, into inference, [nevertheless] with regard to whichever [variety of cognitive criterion] there is an [actual] difference of opinion among opponents, the cognitive validity of each and every of them should be communicated, by specifying a distinct rule, after each and every [variety of cognitive criterion] has been singled out from the indirect cognition. And what this amounts to is the following: similarly, the definition of induction, etc., which has been formulated by preceptors in other philosophic systems is nothing but proper.[174]

[1.15] [Ad 3] 'How then it is possible that absence [as negative proof], falsely conceived by the Mīmāṁsaka, is not a cognitive criterion?' [To this objection] we reply: because it has no domain. For it is like that, perception alone, which—by means of affirmation and preclusion[175]—possesses the capacity to determine the fact[176] as follows: 'this is the surface of the ground, there is no pot, etc., [there],' inasmuch as there is no [other] object to be grasped in addition to this [perceived real thing], refutes [absence as negative proof], that is falsely conceived [to be] another cognitive criterion. So why should we bother [about absence as negative proof], all the more so as this [perception] is well-known to every creature as grasping the real thing that consists in [both] existing and non-existing [aspects][177]? If [the Mīmāṁsaka] sometime took the position: 'Perception seizes the existent aspect alone, inasmuch as [perception] originates by means of sense and because this [sense] is operative only with regard to the existent aspect; but the cognition of non-existence[178] emerges as [a purely] mental [phenomenon], independent of the operation of perceiving organs, in [some later] point of time posterior to grasping the real thing [in question], in the presence of the recollection of the negatum[179] [of the real thing in question]. For it has been said:

> /1/ Certainly, the following idea: "[the thing] is not [there]," is not brought about[180] by [any] sense, for a sense has the connection only with the existent aspect because it is capable [of that alone].[181]
>
> /2/ After the presence of the real thing has [once] been grasped[182] and after the negatum [of the real thing] has been [later] recollected, the cognition of non-existence is born as [a purely] mental [phenomenon] independent of perceiving organs.'[183]

[1.16] Regarding this [objection of the Mīmāṁsaka, we] reply [with the following question]: is then the non-existent aspect different or not different from the existent aspect? If [the Mīmāṁsaka replies]: '[It is] not different,' [then we ask again:] how is it possible that [the non-existent aspect] is not grasped? [The non-existent aspect should be grasped together with the existent aspect] because [the non-existent aspect] is indeed not different from the existent aspect, just like the intrinsic nature of that [non-existent aspect]. If [the Mīmāṁsaka, on the other hand, claims]: 'It is different,' then [to say] that the surface of the ground is grasped by the first perception as detached (*sc.* free)[184] from the absence of the pot, etc., implies that the pot, etc., is [indeed] grasped [on the surface of the ground] because non-grasping of the absence of this [pot] is invariably coequal with grasping its existence[185]. And, thus, also absence [as negative proof][186] operating subsequently would not be in a position to rule them [i.e. such objects like a pot, etc.,] out; otherwise perception—since it would grasp something unmingled as mingled[187]—would repeatedly prove erroneous. Furthermore, your intention is that the absence of an object [in a given place] is proved by the cognitive criterion [in the form of] absence [as negative proof] because there is no [other] cognitive criterion [that could grasp the absence of an object], on account of the following utterance:

/1/ 'With regard to which form of the real thing the quintuplet of cognitive criteria[188] is not born in order [to acquire] the cognition of the existence of the real thing, to this [form of the real thing] the cognitive criterion [in the form of] absence [as negative proof] is [applicable].'[189]

[1.17] [But] that is not correct because how could the absence of a cognitive criterion be grasped? If [you reply]: '[The absence of a cognitive criterion is grasped] on account of the absence of [any] another cognitive criterion which could grasp this [cognitive criterion assumed to be absent],' [there follows] *regressus ad infinitum*: [only] when the absence of that [another cognitive criterion,] too, is grasped, the absence of another cognitive criterion which could grasp that [cognitive criterion assumed to be absent] can be grasped. If you, [the Mīmāṁsaka,] maintained: 'On account of the absence of the object [the absence] of the cognitive criterion [is recognised (*sc.* inferred)], and on account of the absence of the cognitive criterion the absence of the object is recognised (*sc.* inferred),' then the following *circulus vitiosus* could hardly be avoided because of the circuit: as long as the absence of an object is not grasped, the absence of the cognitive criterion is not proved, and the absence of the object will be proved from the absence of the cognitive criterion. If you took the position 'Like [in the case of] the senses, the absence of the cognitive criterion, even though [the absence] itself is not known, will make one know the absence of the object,' that is not correct because this [absence of a cognitive criterion], inasmuch as it is hollow, is characterised by the deprivation of all powers, whereas [any] sense, inasmuch as it is contrary to that (*sc.* is not hollow), is capable of bringing about cognition. Therefore, perception possesses in this way the capability to grasp real things that are fixed in each and every case [to be located on] the surface of the ground, etc.[190], [even] when [actually this very perception] seizes the fact that this [surface of the ground] is deprived of any other real thing, [which is] the negatum, like the pot, etc., [and which] is different from this [surface of the ground], not otherwise, because—if there were no exclusion of [everything else belonging to] a different class—it would not be correct [to speak] of this very [surface of the ground] as established in each and every case, inasmuch as [that would lead to] the undesired consequence of grasping [this surface of the ground] as [something that is] mingled with everything else (*sc.* together with all other things that are not there and that belong to a different class). Hence, it is established that, inasmuch as [absence as negative proof] has no province, because there is no additional [object] to be grasped [by it], what the opponents falsely conceived to be a cognitive criterion called absence [as negative proof] is not a cognitive criterion[191].

[1.18] Even though this [cognitive criterion] is [specified by the author] as **'two-fold'**, by indicating the specific dichotomy [with] the following [words]: **'both perception as well as the indirect cognition**,' [the author] casts off the dichotomy, namely perception and inference, falsely conceived by the Buddhist, because, [taking] their intention [into account], that [dichotomy of cognitive criteria conceived by the Buddhist] is not justified. For their intention is as follows: only inference—the birth of which is produced by the triad of logical reasons (probans), constituted by [1] the effect, [2] the identity and [3] the non-comprehension[192], which are marked by the relation characterised [both] by the relation of essential identity and by the relation of causality[193]—is a cognitive criterion additional to perception, not verbal knowledge, induction, etc., because [the latter varieties] lack [that two-fold] relation. But that [intention] is not correct, because there [would be] no means of grasping the absence (*sc.* non-existence) of another cognitive criterion additional to perception and inference [at the Buddhist's disposal][194]. [1] There is no [way to] ascertain the absence (*sc.* non-existence) of another cognitive criterion through perception, to begin with, because [that would lead to] a contradiction [that] this [perception] grasps absence, inasmuch as [it has] the individual thing [as its] province. [2.a,b] Nor [can the non-existence of another cognitive criterion be ascertained] through the inference from the effect or through the inference from the essential nature, because they both prove [only] the real thing. [2.c] Neither [can the non-existence be ascertained] through [the inference] from the non-comprehension, because [that leads to] a contradiction [that] also this [non-comprehension] proves the absolute absence (*sc.* absolute non-existence). For this [non-comprehension] is described as four-fold in accordance with [its] main divisions, namely: [1] the comprehension of the contrary, [2] the comprehension of the contrary effect, [3] the non-comprehension of the cause and [4] the non-comprehension of the essential nature.[195] [Ad 1] The absolute absence (*sc.* absolute non-existence) of any other cognitive criterion cannot [be ascertained] through [the sub-variety of inference known to be based on] the comprehension of the contrary, to begin with, because [the comprehension of the contrary can only] prove the absence of the opposite[196] [which is to-be-negated, e.g. cold sensation,] by means of the contrary, [e.g. the fire], which is perceptible by its nature[197], inasmuch as it [offers] a proof of the absence of the negatum only in a proximate place. [Ad 2] By the same [argument], also [the sub-variety of inference known to be based on] the comprehension of the contrary effect should be explained, because it, too, proves the absence [of something, e.g. of cold sensation,] by means of effectuating the presence [of a thing, e.g. smoke,] that stands in contradiction to that [which is] to-be-negated, [e.g. to the cold sensation]. [Ad 3] Also [the sub-variety of inference known to be based on] the non-comprehension of the cause, [e.g. of fire,] proves the absence only of the effect, [e.g. the absence of smoke,] about which (*sc.* the effect) there is no doubt that it is in this particular place [at a given point of time], not everywhere [or in the same place at all times],[198] because [the absence of the cause, e.g. fire, everywhere or in the same place at all times] is not proved itself. [Ad 4] Also [the sub-variety of inference known to be based on] the non-comprehension of the essential nature [of an entity, e.g. of a pot, that is perceptible by its own nature], consisting in the comprehension (cognition) of an entity [e.g. surface of the ground,] that is a correlative [of the pot] in one cognition, discloses the absence of [its] counterpart, [viz. of its negatum like a pot, etc.,] only in the same place, [e.g. on the ground].[199] Consequently, the preclusion of another cognitive criterion as well would be [possible] in some cases, [but] not always. Therefore, it is not possible [for inference] to subvert [the existence of] another (additional) cognitive criterion.

[1.19] Consequently, [given the Buddhist intention, one immediately raises] a query as to where perception and inference [get their] cognitive validity from? [1] [Certainly it is] not [possible] due to perception, because, even though being existent [itself], it resembles[200] something non-existent, inasmuch as it is non-conceptual. However, the conceptualisation that immediately follows this [perception][201] does not plunge in the middle of the ocean of (*sc.* does not apprehend) individual things, [because it deals with general concepts]. How, therefore, could [the conceptualisation] that does not reside there [in 'the ocean of individual things'] determine their[202] intrinsic nature? And [to speak of] the determination of cognitive validity [of perception or of inference] on account of this [conceptualisation,] which is not a cognitive criterion [itself, is] a demonstration of rigid inanity in your case. [2] If [you, the Buddhist, defend your position by saying]: 'The determination of the cognitive validity [of perception and inference can be accomplished] through inference,' [that is] not [correct either,] because also this [inference] plunges outside the individual thing, [viz. it pertains to general ideas]. If [you argue]: 'Through this [inference] the exclusion of cognitive invalidity [of alleged cognitive criteria] is proved,' [that is] not [correct either], because exclusion is not separate from the excluded; in the opposite case, it would immediately follow that inference resembles[203] dancing in the dark, because [it would] have no province [of its own]. Furthermore, [we may ask:] is the [further] inference determining the cognitive validity of this [inference itself] a cognitive criterion or not? It is not something that is not a cognitive criterion, to begin with, because then it is incorrect [to assume any] cognitive validity [at all] on account of such an [inference].[204] It is not a cognitive criterion either, because [there is] nothing to prove the cognitive validity of this [inference which determines the cognitive validity of perception and inference][205]. For this [cognitive validity of inference which determines the cognitive validity of perception and inference] cannot be proved through perception, because [the latter] is futile, inasmuch as it is void of conceptualisation, as it has [just][206] been pointed out. But if this [cognitive validity of inference which determines the cognitive validity of perception and inference could] be proved through [still another] inference, there would abide again a pair of alternatives circumscribed precisely as above[207], [and there would follow] *regressus ad infinitum*, namely [we would have to] conjecture [still another] inference [in order] to prove the cognitive validity of this [another inference that has been conceived to prove the cognitive validity of inference which determines the cognitive validity of perception and inference] as well. Furthermore, inference could function [only] for [a person who has] grasped the relation. The relation, [in its turn,] is something-to-be-grasped the domain of which are three times and perception is not capable of observing this [relation], because [perception is something] the existence of which is confined to grasping the present moment, that, by its form, is detached from previous and subsequent moments, [and] because also the conceptualisation that exists at the point of time posterior to this [perception][208] is accepted—in accordance with the intention of the conventional truth—to be related to this [present moment]. If [you claim]: '[The relation] will be grasped through inference,' well, also this [inference] could function [only as being] preceded by the relation [it is supposed to prove, and thus we arrive at the fallacy of] *regressus ad infinitum*, namely [the result is] all the same palaver also with regard to grasping this [relation]. Therefore, since there is no other logical alternative, anybody postulating inference should [also] accept inductive reasoning, which is disposed towards grasping that relation, the domain of which are three times [and] which is undeviating. And thus, since the dichotomy of these [two cognitive criteria, i.e. perception and inference,] under discussion is demolished, there is also another unerring cognition of such a kind which has to be [accepted as] a cognitive criterion,[209] so enough of this groundless belief. If, on the other hand, [somebody] wanted [to maintain that] inference [is] produced by the logical reason which is otherwise inexplicable [without] the object to be proved, then this very dichotomy, namely perception and inference, would indeed be possible, because it is possible [then] to include [all] cognition, different from perception, in its totality into inference [and] because—without any other object [that is] otherwise inexplicable—there [remains] no [other] knowledge whose province is the object of the indirect cognition.

[1.20] Presently, the ground for the circumscription under consideration is stated precisely by a part of the aphorism [NA 1] in a different manner: **'corresponding to [the way of] determination of the cognoscible'** and [this ground]—following the maxim of a crow's eyeball[210]—should also be related there [in the aphorism] with [the expression] **'two-fold'**. Hence this is the [intended] meaning: precisely these two varieties [are distinguished] corresponding to [the way of] determination, [i.e.] corresponding to [the way of] ascertainment of the intrinsic nature, of the cognoscible, [i.e.] of the object to-be-grasped; namely there are only two cognitive criteria as described [above]—no less and no more. With regard to that, this is the intention [of the author]: as for self-cognition there is no difference between all kinds of cognition at all, because [each of them is] apt to perceive directly [itself], inasmuch as [they all have] one form. Referring to the external object, however, certain revelation, the existence of which is gained by the force of the causal complex [constituted by] eyes, etc., unfolds itself [to the mind as] perceiving directly the universal form [which] pervades [its] own parts (*sc.* which constitutes one whole), [which is] prone to continue in another point of time (*sc.* which is not momentary), the momentary transient occurrences of which are concealed (*sc.* which does not change continually), the spherical form of infinitesimal atoms of which is unobservable, [which is] proximate [enough to be apprehended and which is available to] clear observation—with regard to such an [object] proceeds the process of perception. On the other hand, [only] such a transformation [in the way] of the grasping of an object which ensues [in the case] of the cognitive subject, as one should realise, by means of logical reasons, speech elements, etc., as [that which] recognises a universal form, [that is both] specific and non-specific[211] [and as that which is] devoid of transparency [characteristic of perception] appropriates the status of the indirect cognition. And except for these two varieties, we [can] see no [other] noetic activity [that could be regarded] another variety [of cognitive criterion]; and since we do not see [any further variety], we cannot permit of any false assumption of [still] another cognitive criterion; and we have no regard for [a person] denying one amidst these two [varieties of cognitive criterion that] unfold themselves [to the mind], because there is no difference, [viz. someone who recognises only one cognitive criterion out of these two is as much mistaken as the one who admits more cognitive criteria than these two]. Therefore, it is established that only such a dichotomy [as characterised above] should be accepted.

[2.0] Presently[212], merely by having a look only at the aphorism[213] [above, i.e. NA 1,] about what has heretofore been taught by us [who] explain [matters], [people] endowed with lucid minds could understand [this], namely that this definition here of cognitive criterion [presented in this work NA 1], which is capable of removing disorientation of [people who are] of a different opinion as well as of the uncultivated ones. The weak-minded, however, will not apprehend [the teaching] so easily; that is why [the author]—even though being desirous of teaching the evident result of stating [explicitly] the definition of cognitive criterion with the wish for their benefit—presents, to begin with, the *prima facie* position to be refuted, so that those [weak-minded] could be aware of (*sc.* understand) [the teaching] completely[214] [when it is combined] with the *prima facie* position to be refuted, and says:

/2/ Cognitive criteria are well-known and everyday practice is accomplished by them; [therefore] no purpose is known for stating the definition of cognitive criterion.

[2.1] [Presently, the *prima facie* position to be refuted is stated].Here [it should be pointed out that any] utterance has to be considered by the [person] articulating [it], who speaks after deliberation, namely: 'does this utterance of mine [I am just expressing] leave any subliminal impression in the hearer[215] or not?' In the opposite case, his status of [a person] acting in a reflected [manner] is lost. If [the person articulating an utterance resolves that his] utterance leaves a subliminal impression in the hearer, then he utters [the utterance]; otherwise the contrary [takes place: he remains silent]. The [above] sentence (*sc.* the first aphorism) defining cognitive criterion, however– since it conveys the meaning prevalent from beginningless [times] among all people—leaves no subliminal impression in the hearer, because it has been said [that cognitive criteria] are '**well-known**', [i.e.] are prevalent, which means

[they] are not to be proved presently. **'Cognitive criteria'**, [means] perception, etc.: the plural[216] [has been used] with regard to divisions comprised within the indirect cognition with the purpose of demonstrating that even the universal [cognitive criterion] differs somehow as far as the difference among individual [varieties of cognitive criterion] is concerned[217]. For it is as follows: that cognitive criterion, [mentioned in the first aphorism in the singular,] possesses a singularity [based on] individual [varieties] not intended [here]; on the other hand, while being delimited by [its] delimitation to individual [varieties, the singular cognitive criterion] adopts the following plurality: 'perception, inference and verbal knowledge [are] cognitive criteria,' because [cognitive criterion] has a form [both] different and non-different from individuals. For it is as follows: in the cognition [of the kind]: 'there is a tree in the distance,' [acquired] through a speech element or via eyes and other [senses], only the common property [of] 'tree-ness' manifests itself, with no regard to a particular [tree belonging to a species] like *Grislea Tomentosa* (or *Anogeissus Latifolia*?), *Accacia Catechu*, *Butea Frondosa*, etc. Consequently, this [common property of 'tree-ness'] is different from those [individuals], because it is represented in cognition as a form which is separate from [all] these [individuals], just like a pot, etc. But in the moment of seeing a particular [tree belonging to a species] like *Grislea Tomentosa* (or *Anogeissus Latifolia*?), *Accacia Catechu*, *Butea Frondosa*, etc., that [becomes] discernible, this [common property of 'tree-ness'] is no [longer there]. Since it appears as a redundant form [in view of those particular trees, this common property of 'tree-ness'] is not different [from them], because it is sensed as non-separate from them, like their intrinsic nature. If [someone claims]: 'The really existing form of the universal is not at all different from the particulars, because only this [particular] is capable of efficient action like burning, cooking, etc.; [the universal] as something different [from the particulars], however, is nothing real because it is based[218] on knowledge characterised by conceptual construction,' [is] not [right], because it is impossible to deny one of the two appearing [aspects]. Otherwise, there would be no [means of] invalidating the words[219] of people who express even [the following idea]: 'Only [the universal] as something different [from particulars] is existent by its own nature, whereas the other one (*sc.* the universal as identical with the particulars) is shown through knowledge characterised by conceptual construction.' Yet, the non-distinction concerning the execution of efficient action [in both cases]—even though the form is different [in the case of the universal and of the particular]—is not difficult to demonstrate, because also this [universal, which is different from the particular,] is able to be conducive [both] to common everyday practice and to cognition. And [further on] we shall proclaim that efficient action is not the characteristic of the real thing[220]; therefore the element expressing the plural is [used] in order to show that in all cases the universal and the particular are both different and non-different. Therefore, [let us] leave [the plurality of] cognitive criteria alone.

[2.2] The syntactical relation [in the aphorism] is as follows: **'and'** it is well-known that **'everyday practice is accomplished by them.'** The speech element **'and'** has the meaning of the speech element 'also'. What is thereby meant is the following: the opponent, even though he has [in fact] the intention [to say the following]: 'That which is the purpose [of] the examination of cognitive criteria is also everyday practice, like drinking water, protection from cold, etc., which is prevalent from beginningless [times]; hence, to state [explicitly] the definition of cognitive criterion is purposeless,' expressed himself—[propelled] by a desire to avoid impoliteness—in a different manner: '**[Therefore] "no purpose"**, [i.e.] no result of this[221], **"is known"**, [i.e.] is determined by us, **"for stating the definition of cognitive criterion"**, [i.e.] for [a statement] consisting in mentioning specific properties of cognitive criterion that are capable of distinguishing [it from what has] another form, because the argument of yours, [the Jaina,] is of excessive subtlety!' In the above manner [our opponent] questions ironically [the alleged purpose for stating the definition of cognitive criterion] and pulls [our] leg. Furthermore, [the opponent considers the following] pair of alternatives: 'Is the definition of cognitive criterion stated [explicitly] either [1] as undetermined or [2] as determined by its intrinsic nature?'[222] [Ad 1] To begin with [the first alternative], it is [certainly] not [the case that the definition] is undetermined, because it is unjustified to [formulate] a definition [which is] undetermined; [because that would be] like a lunatic's mumble. [Ad 2] If [one admits that the definition] is determined, then [it should be decided] whether it is [determined] [2.1] on account of something which is not a cognitive criterion or [2.2] on account of a cognitive criterion? [Ad 2.1] It is [certainly] not [determined] on account of something which is not a cognitive criterion, to begin with, because it is unjustified to assume that something which is not a cognitive criterion determines [anything]. If, alternatively, it were agreed upon that also something which is not a cognitive criterion determines [anything], then the inquiry into cognitive criterion would be shattered, because [such a position would] entail nonsense, inasmuch as [it would entail] the acceptance to determine [certain things] also on account of something which is not a cognitive criterion. [Ad 2.2] If [it were supposed that the definition of cognitive criterion is determined] on account of a cognitive criterion, then [one has to face still another dilemma]: [2.2.1] is [this cognitive criterion determining the definition of cognitive criterion itself] undefined or [2.2.2] does [this cognitive criterion determining the definition of cognitive criterion] fall under a definition? [Ad 2.2.1] If the determining cognitive criterion is [itself] undefined, then stating [explicitly] the definition of all cognitive criteria is purposeless, inasmuch as the determination of the meaning [of cognitive criterion] is [attempted to be] established by the very preclusion of this [determining cognitive criterion][223], as [in the case of] the cognitive criterion determining the definition [of cognitive criterion] intended by you. [Ad 2.2.2] If [the determining cognitive criterion] falls under a definition, then also in this case there follows a pair of sub-alternatives [like] an unimpeded stream: is the definition of this [determining cognitive criterion] [2.2.2.A] determined or [2.2.2.B] undetermined? [Ad 2.2.2.B] [The second alternative is not correct because] a definition [that is itself] undetermined, to begin with, does not define a *definiendum*. [Ad 2.2.2.A] [If it] indeed determined, [then the question arises: is it determined] [2.2.2.A.a] on account of a cognitive criterion or [2.2.2.A.b] on account of something which is not a cognitive criterion? [Ad 2.2.2.A.b] Since it is incorrect to determine [anything] on account of something which is not a cognitive criterion, then [Ad 2.2.2.A.a] [the first alternative, namely the definition of the determining cognitive criterion is determined] 'on account of a cognitive criterion' should be [further] discussed. [2.2.2.A.a.α] [Thus,] likewise is this [cognitive criterion that determines the definition of the determining cognitive criterion] undefined or [2.2.2.A.a.β] is it accompanied by a definition? [Ad 2.2.2.A.a.α] If [we assume that the determining cognitive criterion is] undefined, what is wrong if the initial [undefined cognitive criterion] grasps the meaning [of cognitive criterion, that has been discussed in § 2.2.1]? [Ad 2.2.2.A.a.β] If it is accompanied by a definition, [one has to consider still another pair of alternatives]: is its definition [i] determined or [ii] not determined? [In this manner the examination of] that [definition accompanying the cognitive criterion that determines the definition of the cognitive criterion determining the definition] cannot but go round in circles [leading to *regressus ad infinitum*][224]. So, there is no means of stating [explicitly] the definition of cognitive criterion; therefore [the statement] **'cognitive criteria are well-known'** should be sanctioned.

[3.0] Now[225], the preceptor makes the opponent know the following: 'we have understood your intention,' pursues the [opponent's] opinion, thinks further on precisely along its lines, but still acknowledges the effectiveness of stating the definition [of cognitive criterion, and] says:

> **/3/ The purpose for stating the definition of cognitive criteria, [although they are] well-known, should be the eradication of disorientation concerning that [definition of cognitive criterion] in the case of the disoriented-minded here.**

[3.1] The following has been [explicitly] stated by you, namely: '"**Cognitive criteria are well-known**" [as it has been pointed out already in NA 2]; therefore it remains [to be supplemented] what "**the purpose**", [i.e.] the result, "**for stating the definition**" of these [cognitive criteria], [i.e.] for [a statement] the province of which to mention specific properties of these [cognitive criteria], is, [if you claim there is any purpose]?' Accordingly, that is not correct, because, although cognitive criteria are well-known to every creature—because otherwise [one would have to face] the undesired consequence of the destruction of the entire everyday practice [which is] accomplished by [the means of] these [cognitive criteria], and if this [everyday practice were] destroyed, [that would] entail [that one would] discard empirical facts (*sc.* what is experienced), etc.—nevertheless some [people] whose discerning organ [is] obstructed by immense confusion are not aware of [that], even though they experience the intrinsic nature of these [cognitive criteria]. Therefore—since we see them [and] our minds are filled with compassion for these [people][226]—[our] mind proceeds towards stating [explicitly] the definition of cognitive criterion, so that [eventually] we remove their disorientation by means of presenting the definition of cognitive criterion corresponding to the state of affairs. So, the following is the purpose [of stating the definition of cognitive criteria]: [so that there] **'should be the eradication of disorientation concerning that [definition of cognitive criterion].'**

[Now we solve the compound: 'there] **should be**,' [i.e.] there should take place, that '**eradication of**' this [disorientation]; it means, through the ascertainment of the correct[227] definition [there should take place] the removal of this [disorientation. What kind of disorientation?]—disorientation concerning that, [i.e.] concerning the definition of cognitive criterion, [in the case] of those who accept the contrary (*sc.* incorrect definition), [disorientation which, on the one hand,] is characterised by a cognitive error [in the case] of philosophers lacking in discrimination between cognitive criterion and something which is not a cognitive criterion and, on the other hand, [disorientation] which consists in the non-apprehension [in the case] of simple-minded common people. To [the question] 'Whose [disorientation]?' [we] reply: of those, whose '**mind**', [i.e.] discerning organ, is '**disoriented**', [i.e.] affected by contrary (*sc.* false) comprehension, [i.e.] is sunken in thoughtlessness. '**Here**' means in this world—such is the intended purport [of the aphorism]. Had there from beginningless been times nobody at all who were disoriented with regard to the [supposedly] well-known definition of cognitive criterion, then what you have claimed before, namely 'stating [explicitly] the definition of cognitive criterion is purposeless,' would indeed be proper. But this is not the case, because [one can] see [people who are] disoriented as regards this [definition of cognitive criterion]. Consequently, it has to be realised that even the criticism which was advanced [by you above], namely 'Is a definition of cognitive criterion stated [explicitly] as undetermined or as determined, etc.'[228], does not create any subversion for us, because it is entirely based on[229] [an argument] in which that to-be-proved is [taken to be already] proved.[230] If [you argue as follows]: 'This [criticism] as regards revealing the definition of cognitive criterion applies also to the disoriented-minded [people],' [your contention is] not [right], because what is proved in [the author's] self-cognition is [subsequently] revealed by [his] utterance, inasmuch as this [the process of] revealing operates only with regard to removing the disorientation [of other people]. Just like someone who, while actually seeing the empty surface of the ground, cannot recognise the absence of a pot, etc., by perception due to the disorientation caused by defective perception, may be censured [for his misjudgement]: 'There is no pot here, because it is not comprehended, even though [all] causes [necessary for its] comprehension are complete[ly there],' for the absence [of the pot] there [on the ground] is proved by perception, [and his] disorientation may be eradicated by [such an] utterance, in the same way the scholars should see [this case] here, too. [Consequently,] it is established that the definition of this [cognitive criterion] is determined by perception, because this [perception] has a form of decision, whereas utterance is engaged in the revocation of the superimposition of the contrary (*sc.* of something false). Thus, [as regards the definition] the preceptor—having taught in the above manner[231] the definition of cognitive criterion in general—avoided the defective criticism directed against him.[232]

[4.0] Now[233], these two individual [varieties] of cognitive criterion, defined as perception and the indirect cognition, were mentioned before [in NA 1] by the [author] desirous of rebutting the difference of opinion regarding the number with reference only to cognitive criterion [as such][234]; some [thinkers, however,] are of a different opinion regarding the definition of these very two [varieties of cognitive criterion]. Hence, also the definition of these two should be taught--[having this in view, the author,] desirous of stating [explicitly] the definition of perception, to begin with, says:

/4/ Such a cognition that grasps an object not-indirectly is perception; the other one should be known as the indirect cognition, as far as [the manner of] grasping [an object] is considered.[235]

[4.1] In this [aphorism, the word] '**perception**' is [used as] the element expressing the *definiendum*. [The expression:] '**a cognition that grasps an object not-indirectly**' is [used as] the element expressing the *definiens*. 'Indirect' [means] 'beyond the domain of the perceiving organ'; [that which is] 'different from that' is '**not-indirect**'; the state of that [means] such a manner [and the whole expression stands in the aphorism] in the instrumental case[236]; it is tantamount to 'perceiving directly.' 'That which is understood[237]' is '**object**'—the essence[238] [of which is] 'that which is ascertained'; or 'that which is striven after' is '**object**'—which is tantamount to 'that which is desired by those who aim at efficient action like burning, cooking, etc.' The syntactical connection is as follows: '**such a**' cognition, [i.e. a cognition] only of such a kind—inasmuch as it consists in decision—'**that grasps**' this [object, i.e.] that determines directly this [object,] is perception. Regarding this [perception], what the followers of Sāṁkhya have promulgated, namely 'perception is the operation of [sense-organs, such as] the ear, etc.,'[239] is ruled out by [mentioning the manner of] grasping [the object] through cognition, because, inasmuch as [sense-organs, such as] the ear, etc., are modifications of the primordial matter, it is unjustified to assume that their operation—since, [consequently, the operation of sense-organs] being characterised by activity is insentient—constitutes perception. If [the operation of sense-organs constituted] perception, inasmuch as [they are considered to be] the causes of determination of an object, that would result in [the contention that] also the activity of the totality of such insentient causes like light, etc., would be perception, because there is no difference [between sense-organs and other causes of perception, inasmuch as all of them are insentient].

[4.2] [Recapitulation of the Yogācāra's position and their criticism.] Since the phrase '**as far as [the manner of] grasping [an object] is considered**' will be taught [later in the same aphorism] as depending on [the expression] '**that grasps an object**,' now [the author] refutes those[240] who declare all cognition with no exception [to be] lacking in seizing [even] a jot of an object, also [if] the object is external, for just as the inner sensation is engaged in grasping its own divisions, in the same manner [it cognises] also an external [object]; in the opposite case, other personal series of cognition[241] [experienced by other people]—just like the [external] object—would be shattered as well, inasmuch as [such a position] entails nothing but the falsification of the inference [that proves the existence] of these [other personal series (*sc.* other people)] by the example of dream,[242] because only one's own consciousness shows itself in each and every case [and nothing else].[243] And, consequently, the relation between cognitive criteria and the cognoscible, [the relation] between that-to-be-demonstrated and that-which-demonstrates, [the relation] between effect and cause, etc., would perish, because [such a position would] entail the annihilation of the operation of cognition of both the moments [that are] previous and subsequent to this [cognition] itself, with the exception of its own [moment]. If [you, the Yogācāra, argue as follows]: 'You can progress favourably (*sc.* successfully) by proving the reality of non-dualistic consciousness,' that [opinion of yours] could be [right], if there were nothing unfavourable (*sc.* contradictory) [that speaks]—by way of [demonstrating] the destruction of the entire everyday practice [which can be] deduced with [the help of] cognitive criteria—against your false assumption of the non-dualistic reality, [that is] left (deposited) [in consciousness] on account of past impressions [based on] defective doctrines and [that is] unperceived. So, without an [external] object there is no origination of cognition, which is a cognitive criterion [with respect] to external [phenomena], because [that would lead to] the undesired consequence [that such a cognition is] uncaused.

[4.3] [Recapitulation of the Yogācāra-Sautrāntika conception and their criticism.] Besides, [the expression] **'that which grasps'** should be considered [to mean] 'that which determines,' because it is unjustified to assume that an object is grasped, if it is not determined. Consequently, what the Buddhists have taught, namely: 'Perception is [1] free from conceptual construction and [2] non-erroneous,'[244] turns out to be controverted, because it is void of logical congruity. [Ad 1] For it is as follows: these [Buddhists try to] chase away[245] logical incongruities [involved] when perception is [assumed to be] non-conceptual. As they say, this [perception] arises due to the efficacy of an object[246], because it grasps an object [that is] proximate [and that is] capable of efficient action. And no linguistic units are [to be found] in an object, because [linguistic units] are produced[247] by other causes different from causes of this [object]; and therefore this [object,] having occurred close [to the perceiver] produces—while generating a sensation the domain of which is this [very object itself]—the likeness of its own form [within the cogniser]. So, it is not correct [to maintain that] there is an association with speech elements in the consciousness grasping this [object][248]. Furthermore, if this [object bringing about a sensation]—even though [in the moment when] the object which brings about [a sensation] is used—could not be grasped immediately, but also if the sensation produced by the recollection [of that object] remained [dormant] waiting until the connection with the linguistic unit denoting this [object is established]—then the final blow to [the process of] grasping an object would be given. For it [would be] like this: without seeing a given object, one cannot recollect the linguistic unit—[which] denotes this [particular object]—the linguistic convention [governing the usage of which (*sc.* the linguistic unit) is] grasped with regard (*sc.* grasped as being related) to this [particular object], because there is no means [for its reminiscence otherwise]; and without recollecting [the linguistic unit], one cannot connect [the linguistic unit] with the object which is in front [before the cogniser], inasmuch as it is impossible to connect these two [with each other, viz.

the linguistic unit with the object,] without the awakening of reminiscence; and without connecting [the linguistic unit with the object]—according to your intention—one cannot see [the object]![249] In such a way, blindness results from foolishness[250]. And if one considered cognition, even though it is produced by the senses, to be defiled by a conceptualisation, then—if there takes place a manifestation of another conceptualisation, like the conceptualisation of some kingdom of fancy, etc.—also this [cognition] would disappear; but that is not the case, [first], because the sensation produced by eyes, the domain of which is a proximate physique of a cow, does not disappear even when [another] conceptualisation whose province is, [say], a horse, etc., is produced, and, [secondly], because it is established that even [a person who] has got rid of all conceptualisation [experiences] a perception whose province is a discernible, proximate object. So, one does not experience [any] cognition [that is] produced by perceiving organs (*sc.* by senses) [to be] associated with speech elements.[251] Such is [the exposition of the Buddhist's standpoint.]

[4.4] As for this [misconception of the Buddhist], it is controverted [by us]. What has been said [before], to begin with—namely that perception is devoid of linguistic units, because it comes into existence due to the efficacy of an object, in which there are no speech elements[252]—is not correct, for it is not possible to claim that [perception] is destitute of speech designation simply by stating that it is produced by an object not associated with speech elements; otherwise [one would have to admit that] this [perception] is also insentient because it is produced by an object which [itself] is insentient. If you say that [this perception] is not insentient because it is accompanied by mental activity consisting in cognitive awareness, then, if that were indeed the case, also [this perception] would be accompanied by speech designation [anyway], because of [its] connection with mental activity, [which on its part] is associated with speech designation. Furthermore, how can separate (*sc.* individual) infinitesimal atoms—that bring about cognition, the province of [which they are] themselves, by means of rendering their own form [to this cognition]—unfold there [in that cognition] a form, which does not exist in them, [which] pervades [its] own parts (*sc.* which is one whole) [and which is] prone to continue in another point of time (*sc.* which is not momentary)? If [you say] that it is due to confusion[253], [that contention of yours is] not [right][254], not only [because] that which occurs is [located] in the object at the present moment, because also a gross form, even though it is not there [in the object consisting basically of infinitesimal atoms,] occurs [in cognition]. Similarly, [that is the case with] speech element, too; [for] what harm would it do if something unknown in the object would occur in the cognition grasping this [object]? Besides, what has been said in [the above passage] beginning with [the words]: 'if [this object bringing about a sensation]—even though [in the moment when] the object [which brings about a sensation] is used—[could not be grasped immediately, but also if the sensation] produced by the recollection [of that object] remained [dormant] waiting [until the connection with the linguistic unit denoting this object is established]'[255] up to [the words]: 'blindness results'[256], the same [applies] to your thesis, as well. For it is as follows: even if the non-conceptual cognition, [which is] produced by the senses [and] whose province is an individual thing, is present, so long there [can be] no determinate cognition of an object [in the form:] 'it is this [object]' or 'is it not this [object]', as long as a pair of conceptualisations is not resolved[257] by means of confirmation and negation, [and such a state of affairs is] in accordance with the following utterance: 'Precisely with regard to which aspect a conceptualisation is produced, with regard to that [aspect] only that [conceptualisation] is a cognitive criterion'[258], because [otherwise] the non-conceptual [perception], even though it were existent, would resemble[259] something non-existent with regard to everyday practice. Besides, this conceptualisation ought to arise only in [a person] recollecting a universal speech designation that emerges in the moment of [grasping] the linguistic convention; and how could the seed (*sc.* subliminal impression being the cause) of recollection of the universal speech designation awake? If [you reply]: '[It awakes] due to the perception of an [object] of this sort,' well, [then we make the following objection:] also this perception does not go beyond (*sc.* is limited to) the object because it is non-conceptual [as well]; so, how could the seed of the conceptualisation, whose province is the universal, be awakened? That notwithstanding, you [evince] contumacy [in claiming] that the object would not produce understanding, whose essence is the decision [pertaining to] the universal. Consequently, [it follows that,] like an object [itself], perception whose province is this [object]—since [perception] is void of decision—does not awaken the seed of recollection, whose domain is the universal speech designation; that [seed of recollection], when not awaken, does produce recollection; recollection, when not produced, cannot establish the connection with the speech element; the speech element, when unconnected, does not determine the object; the object, when, undetermined, does not enter into everyday practice; [the same object], when it has not entered into everyday practice, is not distinguished from something invisible; [the same object], when not distinguished [from something invisible], indicates the blindness of the cogniser. Because of that [reason], we do not consider [the following contention] absolutely improper: just as the non-conceptual perception, even though it itself—since it is does not determine [anything] whatsoever—is unknown, having generated a conceptualisation by means of the awakening past impressions, expresses its own activity, whose province are some aspects, in the same manner, also the object—when it itself cannot but be unknown, because such is its essential nature, inasmuch as it has penetrated into the causal complex [constituted by] eyes, etc.—should originate—by means of the awakening a subliminal impression of itself, [and such a subliminal impression] whose province is the universal speech designation, that emerges in the moment of [grasping] the linguistic convention—a sensation, whose province is [the object] itself [and such a sensation] which is associated with speech designation. And this cognitive awareness [of the object that is produced by the senses[260] and] accompanied by a conceptualisation does not resemble[261] the conceptualisation of some kingdom of fancy, etc., because [the former] is produced by the causal complex [constituted by] eyes, etc., whereas the latter one (*sc.* a conceptualisation of a kingdom of fancy) has [its] origin in the mind only. Therefore, how could it disappear when another conceptualisation manifests itself? [Clearly, no conceptualisation of an object produced by the senses can disappear when another conceptualisation manifests itself] because only mental conceptualisation disappears due to another conceptualisation, whereas this [conceptualisation of an object that is produced by the senses] is activated inevitably due to the efficacy of [its] causes. By this [fact] also the following [argument] is disproved, namely 'This [conceptualisation produced by the senses[262]] would not become manifest in the state of [a person who] has got rid of all conceptualisations,' because this [conceptualisation produced by the senses] cannot be got rid of [simply] at the wish of the cogniser, inasmuch as his efficacy [in getting rid of a conceptualisation] is explicable only with regard to getting rid of [a purely] mental conceptualisation. And the above [rejoinder] has been given an account of[263] by us who demonstrate that the thesis [asserting that] perception is absolutely non-conceptual is even worse than the thesis [asserting] that perception is associated with speech elements.

[4.5] On the level of the ultimate truth[264], however, [any] direct manifestation of a speech element in perception is not accepted because this [perception] is apt to perceive directly an object by clear decision. In fact, only that [perception] is called conceptual that refers to an entity—like a column, etc.—which is proximate, which is discernible, which pervades its own parts, which is prone to continue in another point of time, whose momentary transient occurrences are concealed (*sc.* which does not change), the spherical form of infinitesimal atoms of which is unobservable, whose form is both similar and dissimilar with other entities, which has a universal form [composed] of its infinitesimal atoms; [here, perception is called conceptual] either in order to negate [the idea]—falsely conceived by others—of the non-conceptual perception disposed towards grasping the individual thing characterised by separate infinitesimal atoms perishing in a moment, or in order to show that [perception is a cognition] whose domain is capable of being somehow associated with speech designation. And what this amounts to is the following: in this manner, when an object becomes the domain of perception, all verbal processes with no exception, that [consist in] grasping the relationship between the denotatum and the denoter, etc., [and] whose province is this [object], are possible, when taken literally. If [you say the following]: 'If, on the other hand, perception were not a representation capable of being associated with speech elements, what would be the defect thereof?'[265], [then we have] the undesired consequence of destruction of the entire everyday practice, because the conceptualisation could not be generated. For it is as follows: [neither] a perception which is free from decision, even though it is endowed with [corresponding] absolute potential, [and] which leaves the seed of reminiscence, nor a perception of [another object] of this sort [as the one perceived before], that arises in the point of time posterior to that [previous perception], is able—although the potential of past impression and repeated practice [is there]—to accomplish the awakening of this [seed of reminiscence (*sc.* subliminal impression)], on account of which[266] everyday practice should operate by the origination of the conceptualisation of the universal, because this [everyday practice] is never seen, at any time, [to operate] with regard to momentariness, etc., even though [such ideas like momentariness, etc., may be] accepted as something that is experienced by the non-conceptual perception. Therefore, with regard to whichever aspect of an object [some] posterior operation of everyday practice [take places], with regard to the same [aspect] a previous determining sensation has to be accepted, otherwise everyday practice would perish with regard to all aspects, just like [in the example of] the aspect of momentariness, etc. So, [to express it metaphorically], freedom from conceptual construction [in the case] of perception never experiences the phenomenon of [itself] turning into the domain of awareness of the cogniser whatsoever[267]. And it is hard to believe that this [perception remains] unknown, because of too far-reaching consequence; consequently [the expression 'is free from conceptual construction'[268]] is not a proper *definiens* [of 'perception'].

[4.6] [Ad 2] Also 'non-erroneousness' [as a part of the Buddhist definition above[269]] is not possible [as a *definiens*] either, because—according to your intention—a sensation grasping a persistent, gross object has the form of something contrary [to the real thing characterised by invisible and momentary infinitesimal atoms], whereas [that real thing consisting in atoms] contrary to that [form of the sensation grasping a persistent, gross object] does not appear even in the time of dreaming. So, if non-erroneousness [is taken to mean that perception] grasps an object [in the manner] corresponding to the state of affairs, then it is not possible at all, because separate infinitesimal atoms perishing in a moment, [of which objects are composed], are never represented [in perception] at all and because these [infinitesimal atoms] are ultimately real. If [you claim] that—in accordance with the intention of the conventional truth—that [cognition] is intended as non-erroneous which does not make one err with regard to that which is this [particular] individual thing, like a pot, etc., capable of efficient action, then [we can reply that] the phrase 'free from conceptual construction' should be ruled out, because now in this case [non-erroneousness] is not compatible with this[270] [property of being free from conceptual construction], inasmuch as an individual thing, like a pot, etc., that has entered into everyday practice [can be] grasped only by determination [that is in its turn characterised by conceptual construction]; otherwise, [i.e. if the object were not grasped by determination[271]], everyday practice would not operate, because also what is experienced does not go beyond (*sc.* does not differ from) what is not [directly] experienced[272]. Therefore, it is established as only tenable that perception has the nature of decision [characterised by conceptual construction].

[4.7] On the other hand, by the following [expression] '**not-indirectly**' [the author] avoids [the mendacity] of perception [as] being mingled with characteristics of the indirect cognition, because this [perception] consists in grasping an object, inasmuch as [it] perceives [the object] directly[273]. By [the word] '**such**', [that functions] with a restriction on account of the maxim taught earlier[274], however, [the author]—by indicating [a particular] cognition accompanied by a series of qualifications—disproves [the possibility that some other variety of cognition] conforming to definitions falsely conceived by others is perception. And in this manner, what has been said [by proponents of rival systems]—namely [1] 'Perception is cognition [that is] produced by the contact of an object with a sense organ, [that is] non-verbal, [that is] unerring, whose nature is decision'[275] as well as [2] 'Perception is the birth of cognition when the contact of a person's senses with a [really] existing [thing takes place],'[276] etc.—turns out to be deemed incorrect, because the existence of something previously not manifested [at any time] is subverted by cognitive criterion, inasmuch as [that would lead to] the undesired consequence that also absolutely non-existent [things], such as a hare's horn, etc., [could] originate, [i.e. could come into existence, as in the case of perception, as defined by the Naiyāyika and the Mīmāṁsaka]. Therefore, [to prevent such an undesired conclusion one has to accept that] this [perception] should unfold—inasmuch as [perception] consists in transformation [in the way] of grasping an object directly—only an existing [thing][277] as [something] that has the own form [of perception][278] on account of the presence of the totality of causes that effect the distinctive character [of that particular object]; and, consequently, the qualifications 'produced' and 'birth' [occurring in the first and the second definition, respectively,] could not be possible. If you argue that this [perception] is nothing but indicative of an object of such a kind (*sc.* an existing thing), then, that being the case, there is no discord [between us;] so let [us] leave that alone[279].

[4.8] Now, [the author] describes the definition of the indirect cognition [and says]: **'the other one'**, etc. The cognition that grasps an object not-indirectly has been called perception; the other cognition [different] from that, which grasps an object indirectly **'should be known'**, [i.e.] should be ascertained, [to be] the indirect cognition. [The author] says: **'as far as [the manner of] grasping [an object] is considered'** [in order to] demonstrate that also this [indirect cognition] is nothing but perception with regard to self-cognition; it receives the designation of 'the indirect cognition,' however, with regard to the external object.[280] Here [in the aphorism, the manner of] grasping is called [the manner of] operating externally on account of advancing outwards, because otherwise [such a] qualification [would be] purposeless. [The expression 'as far as the manner of grasping is considered' means] 'with regard to this [manner of grasping,' and the whole expression stands in the aphorism] in the instrumental case: it is tantamount to [saying] 'recognising [its] external activity.' So, the meaning is as follows: even though [the cognition] is perception in itself, nevertheless it is called the indirect cognition because it is engaged in grasping the external province (*sc.* object)—inasmuch as it perceives [its objects] indirectly—by means of inferential signs, speech elements, etc. And this [indirect cognition] possesses the property of producing [a result, i.e. a conclusive cognition,] on account of the awareness of another object which is otherwise inexplicable [without] the object which one wants to cognise. Such [is the general definition of the indirect cognition]. Although [the indirect cognition] has one form due to the presence of the general definition, it is—in order to revoke the difference of opinion—divided into two [subtypes], namely inference and verbal knowledge, because even nowadays others, [i.e. opponents of rival systems], do not recognise that speech element is otherwise inexplicable [without the corresponding] object and [because] it is not possible to speak of [*x* (here: inference and verbal knowledge) as being] distinct from *y* (here: the indirect cognition) [if *x*] has not been made separate; hence the specification by division.[281]

[5.0] As for these [divisions of the indirect criterion, the author]— desirous of stating [explicitly,] to begin with, the definition of inference—says:

/5/ Inference is regarded traditionally to determine the probandum on account of the inferential sign, which is inseparably connected with the probandum[282]. It is non-erroneous because it is a cognitive criterion, just like perception.

[5.1] In this case too[283], '**inference**' is [used as] an element expressing the *definiendum*, because it is to be called to mind as [something] well-known. [The expression:] '**to determine the probandum on account of the inferential sign, which is inseparably connected with the probandum**' is [used as] an element expressing the *definiens*, because it is to be introduced as something [yet] unknown. Also here[284] the mention of the meaning of the speech element 'inference' should be considered respectively [in conformity] with the grammatical formation based on contributory factors [of an action], such as agent, etc., just like [in the case of] the speech element 'cognitive criterion.' And therefore, also in this case such a cognition—by which an object, like fire, etc., that is the inferendum[285], is cognised in a valid way, [i.e.] determined, in consequence of, [i.e.] subsequently to, the time when the inferential sign is grasped and when the relation with the inferential sign, which is characterised by the property of being inseparably connected with the probandum, is recollected—is called inference.[286] [As a reply to the question:] 'What is this [inference] like?', [the author] says: [it is] '**to determine the probandum**'; the probandum means the inferendum, because the probandum (lit. something to-be-proved) is either that which deserves proof[287] or that which can be proved[288]; determining this [probandum] is tantamount to ascertaining its intrinsic nature. [As a reply to the question:] 'On account of what is it possible?' [the author] says: '**on account of the inferential sign**'; that by which an object is marked or understood is an inferential sign, [i.e.] the logical reason; [and it is possible to determine the probandum] on account of that [inferential sign. As a reply to the question:] 'On account of [the inferential sign] of what kind [is it possible to determine the probandum]?' [the author] says: [on account of the inferential sign] '**which is inseparably connected with the probandum**'; unconnected is that which exists separately; that which is different from it is that which is inseparably connected; that which is inseparably connected together with the probandum is that which is inseparably connected with the probandum; the meaning is as follows: that which does not exist without the probandum; the cognition [that] '**is regarded traditionally,**' [i.e. that] is intended by the logicians to determine the probandum on account of this [inferential sign of such a kind] is inference—the above [sequence shows] the syntactical relation [in the aphorism]. In this [aphorism, the author]—by the [expression]: '**to determine the probandum on account of the inferential sign**'—wards off the idea that inference is mingled with the characteristics of perception or of the verbal knowledge. By the [expression]: '**inseparably connected with**

the probandum' [the author] argues for the rejection of the definition of the inferential sign imparted by others.

[5.2] And, consequently, what others (*sc.* Diṅnāga) have taught, namely—[1] there are only three inferential signs marked by the triad consisting in the characteristics of [a] the inherence of a property in the locus, of [b] positive concomitance and of [c] negative concomitance: [α] non-comprehension, [β] identity and [γ] effect[289]; hence it has been said [by one of them]:

> '[a] The presence in the inferendum as well as [b] [the presence] in its coequal, [c] non-existence in the non-existent, [i.e. in a thing belonging to a different class (*sc.* heterologue)—these are the three characteristics of logical reason]; three logical reasons are called [α] non-comprehension, [β] [the thing] itself and [γ] effect, [and each of these three logical reasons concerns] the determined [thing] (*sc.* inferential sign)'[290];

also [2] what some others [,viz. Kaṇāda, have said], viz. 'The discipline [based on] the inferential sign (*sc.* inference) has the form: "[a] this is its effect, [b] this is its cause, [c] this is its connected [attribute], [d] this is its inherent [property] and [e] this stands in contradiction with [that]"[291]';[292] likewise, [the following standpoint]: [3] '[Inference is threefold:] â priori, ā posteriori and commonly seen'[293], and so forth—[all] these [opinions] should be considered to be a childish twaddle, as it were, because in all of these [cases] it is nothing but the property of being inseparably connected with the probandum that leads to the comprehension [of the inferendum], whereas [Ad 1] anything that is devoid of this [property of being inseparably connected with the probandum], even though it is characterised by the triplet of characteristics [of the logical reason], does not lead to the comprehension [of the inferendum], because, in the opposite case, [that would lead to] the undesired consequence that also [such invalid logical reason]s like 'being his son,' etc.,[294] would lead to the comprehension [of the inferendum], just like the respective circumscription, [i.e. just like the limited triplet of characteristics the logical reason leads to the false comprehension of the inferendum]. If [you argue in the following manner]: 'The triplet of characteristics [of the logical reason] is a [proper] definition, and not just anything, hence it is free from any undesired consequence,' [it is] not [right], because it is nothing but the property of being inseparably connected with the probandum that throws light, [i.e. allows to draw a valid conclusion], by circumscription.[295] If [you agree]: '[It is indeed] that [inferential sign inseparably connected with the probandum that throws light],' [then] what is the use of requirement of the triplet of characteristics [of the logical reason]? Certainly, that being the case, the triplet of characteristics of the logical reason is useless] because this [inferential sign inseparably connected with the probandum] alone leads to the comprehension [of the inferendum]. [Ad 1.a] For it is as follows: we do infer, even without [the characteristics of] the inherence of a property in the locus, like in the following [examples]: [i] from [the reflection of] the moon in the water [we infer] the moon in the sky, [ii] from the rise of the constellation of the Pleiads [we infer] the rise of the *Rohiṇī* constellation, [iii] from one blossoming mango-tree [in the proper season we infer] that all mango-trees are blossoming, [iv] from the rise of the moon, [we infer] the opening of clusters of *kumuda* white water lilies[296], [v] from a tree [we infer its] shadow, etc. If [you further argue]: 'It is only possible that in these cases the time, etc., are the property-possessor, [hence] in these cases the inherence of the inferential sign in the locus is grasped,' [that position] is not [right], because [that would have] too far-reaching consequences, inasmuch as in this manner [one would have to meet] the unwelcome consequence that also the blackness of a crow, etc., leads to the comprehension regarding the probandum, viz. the impermanence of speech element, for also in this case it is possible to conceive the world, etc., as the property-possessor. [Ad 1.b] Similarly, it is possible—inasmuch as [the inference is based on] a correct logical reason—to corroborate the following [reasoning,] even though it is lacking in positive concomitance[297], namely: 'Speech element (sound) is impermanent because it is audible'; hence, positive concomitance is not the characteristic of the logical reason, either. For it is as follows: precisely according to your intention the whole of existence is embraced by impermanence; consequently, how could the property of being audible, that is a property of existence, [and therefore impermanent], occur in the heterologue, without impermanence[298]? [Certainly, it could not] because that would entail that [the heterologue] lacking this [impermanence] is devoid of its essential nature, inasmuch as existence freed from impermanence is impossible, [according to you]. [Ad 1.c] Thereby also the following [reasoning]—namely 'The living body is endowed with the soul because it possesses vital forces, etc., because if it were not endowed with the soul [that would lead to] the undesired consequence that is lacking these [vital forces], etc., just like a pot, etc.'—is explained [as the one] leading to the comprehension [of the inferendum], because also here [the relation of] being otherwise inexplicable [without] the object to be proved is present, whereas [both] the inherence of a property in the locus and positive concomitance [can] not be demonstrated [in this case], inasmuch as they are not characteristics [of the logical reason].[299]

[5.3] [Ad 2.a,b] Similarly, also such a circumscription [effected] by the triad of inferential signs consisting in effect, identity and non-comprehension, as they say, that is reduced to the following [idea]—the existence of the relation characterised [both] by the relation of essential identity and by the relation of causality[300] is [possible] without exception with regard to all these [three kinds of inferential signs]—is not correct either, because one can see that a [perceptible] form, etc., even though it is lacking in the pair of relations under consideration, leads to the comprehension [of the inferendum] like taste, etc. [Ad 2.d] If the Vaiśeṣika maintained 'It is inadmissible that this [logical reason] should lead to the comprehension [of the inferendum] on account of [both] the relation of essential identity and the relation of causality, [because, as a matter of fact, the logical reason] will [lead to the comprehension of the inferendum] on account of inherence; nevertheless, [the relation of] being otherwise inexplicable is by no means the characteristic of the logical reason,' he should be turned down in another manner. For he has to be questioned in accordance with two alternatives: is inherence [2.d.1] different [from inherent properties] or

[2.d.2] not different from inherent [properties]? [Ad 2.d.1] If [inherence] is not different, then there [remain] inherent [properties] only, [and] there is no inherence, because [the latter] is not different from these [inherent properties], just like their intrinsic nature. [Ad 2.d.2] If [you say] that [inherence] is different [from inherent properties], then [you should say] how [inherence] might occur[301] in these [inherent properties]: [2.d.2.a] in its totality or [2.d.2.b] [piece] by piece? [Ad 2.d.2.a] So, if [inherence occurs] in its totality, that is not correct because [that would lead to] the undesired consequence of the plurality of inherence, inasmuch as [such a thesis] would entail that this [inherence] would be complete regarding [each and every] single inherent [property]. [Ad 2.d.2.b] If [inherence is supposed to occur piece] by piece, that is not tenable either, because—in view of the undesired consequence [that inherence would] have divisions—it would impair [the Vaiśeṣika thesis that inherence] has no parts and because [inherence] would fall to the criticism [based on the same alternative of inherence occurring] [2.d.2.b.1] in its totality or [2.d.2.b.2] [piece] by piece with regard to [its] occurrence in its divisions, as well. [Ad 2.d.2.b.1] Also here, in the case of the thesis of [inherence occurring in its divisions] in its totality [the result] is only plurality [of inherence] as circumscribed above; [Ad 2.d.2.b.2] whereas in the case of the thesis of [inherence occurring in its divisions piece] by piece [the result is the fallacy of] *regressus ad infinitum* in view of the undesired consequence of [inherence having still] further divisions. So, one should not hold out any hopes that [the logical reason] leads to the comprehension [of the inferendum] by the force of inherence, because this [inherence] has a bad footing altogether in this matter. [Ad 2.c] By the same [argument the thesis that] also a connected [attribute] leads to the comprehension [of the inferendum] is censured because it [is open to] similar criticism. [Ad 2.c] Also the [fact that the thing] standing in contradiction (e.g. fire)[302] leads to the comprehension of the absence of the contrary (e.g. cold sensation) indicates nothing but [the fact that the thing standing in contradiction (e.g. fire) is in the relation of] being otherwise inexplicable, because it is unjustified to assume that [the thing standing in contradiction may]—without this [relation of being otherwise inexplicable]—lead to the comprehension [of the inferendum].

[5.4] [Ad 3] In this manner, any other characteristic of inferential sign as well, falsely conceived by opponents, which is a requisite (*sc.* criterion) for an [inferential sign] leading to the comprehension [of the inferendum], does not deviate from (*sc.* can be reduced to) [the relation of] being otherwise inexplicable, because [a fallacious logical reason] that is legitimate (*sc.* explicable) also without the probandum lacks [the capacity to] lead to the comprehension [of the inferendum, inasmuch as it is explicable in a different manner, too]. Consequently, it is established that [any other variety of the inferential sign falsely conceived by opponents] should be included in this very pervader (*sc.* the relation of being otherwise inexplicable) which is the [true] characteristic of an inferential sign, whereas what is contrary [to the relation of being otherwise inexplicable] should be refuted.

[5.5] Thus, having taught the definition of inference in the above manner[303], now [the author will refute] what has been announced by the disciples of Śuddhodana's son, [i.e. by the Buddhist], namely: 'Inference is erroneous because, firstly, it represents the universal, and because, [secondly,] that [universal] is not possible—inasmuch as it is done away with by two alternatives of difference and non-difference with regard to an external individual thing[304], and because, [thirdly,] this [individual thing] is apprehended by that [inference] as having the form if of that [universal], and because, [fourthly,] without this [individual thing inference] grasping that [universal] is characterised by error. Furthermore, inference [possesses] the status of cognitive criterion because [the status of cognitive criterion] is acquired by the force of an external individual thing in succession. For it is as follows: without an object there exists no inferential sign based on the relation characterised [both] by the relation of essential identity and by the relation of causality[305], without this [inferential sign] there is no cognition whose province is this [object], without the cognition of this [object] there is no recollection of the relation concluded before, if there is no recollection of this [relation], there [can be] no inference; hence, it is agreed that [inference is] a cognitive criterion, even though it is erroneous, because it is undeviating with regard to [its] object.[306] It has been said: "The comprehension (*sc.* inference) of that [real individual thing] regarding something that is not that [real individual thing], although it [constitutes] an error, is a valid cognition (*sc.* cognitive criterion) on account of the relation [to the real individual thing]"[307].' [The author]—in order to do away with this [opinion]—says '**It is non-erroneous**', etc. '**It**' [means] inference; 'erroneous' is that which makes one err, [i.e.] which is contrary to its own domain; what is different from that is '**non-erroneous**', which is tantamount to 'that which grasps a object that is not contrary.' This [phrase '**It is non-erroneous**'] is the thesis [of the proof formula proving the validity of inference]. That by which an object is cognised in a valid way corresponding to the state of affairs, [i.e. that by which the object] is determined, is cognitive criterion, the state of it [means] such a character, [so] because of that[308], [i.e. '**because it is a cognitive criterion**']. This [phrase] is the logical reason [of the proof formula]. What is conjoined with perceiving organs is perception; in the same manner as that [is the meaning of the phrase] '**just like perception**' [that introduces] an example [of the proof formula]. So, this [part of the verse] that revokes [the idea that] inference is erroneous is a [proof formula] with complete members because the two [other traditionally accepted parts of the five-membered proof formula, i.e.] application and conclusion, are implied precisely by the demonstration of the triad of members [of a proof formula]: [In this proof formula] cognitive criterion [as the repetition of the logical reason in the conclusion] is [already] indicated [explicitly,] but the pronouncement (*sc.* application) [of this proof formula] can be demonstrated in the following manner: '[The thesis:] inference is non-erroneous; [the logical reason:] because it is a cognitive criterion; [the demonstration of the invariable concomitance together with the example:] in this world, whatever is a cognitive criterion is non-erroneous, just like perception; [the application:] and similarly, inference is accepted by you to be a cognitive criterion; [the conclusion:] therefore, [inference] is non-erroneous, inasmuch as it is a cognitive criterion'—this is what has to be recognised. Among these [Buddhists], the realist, to begin with, is not able to demonstrate the lack of probandum in the example characterised by perception, because precisely he himself accepts perception as non-erroneous. The propounder of the theory of the universal emptiness, however, inasmuch as he denies [the existence of] everything, is entirely incapable [of proving anything] with regard to the process [based on] cognitive criterion and the cognoscible, hence, [if we] take him (*sc.* his convictions) into consideration, the defects [revealed by] our proof cannot be avoided [by him], because—inasmuch as [he is someone whose] thesis is subverted by his own utterances—it is not [possible] to establish his theory. For it is as follows: [he has to resolve] whether the utterance demonstrating the non-existence of everything [itself] exists or does not exist. If [he says that] it exists then [this is tantamount to] the abandonment of [his own] thesis. If [he replies that] it does not exist, then the existence of everything is established, because there [remains] nothing [more] that could negate [the existence of everything].

[6.0] A Vijñāna-vādin[309], however, subscribes to [the view that] sensation, that lacks in the form of the cognoscible and of the cogniser, that is beyond the domain of all conceptualisation [and] is non-conceptual, can be cognised by a distinct and ultimately real self-cognition, [and] who asserts that all cognition with no exception, which originated by the force of past impressions that were dormant from beginningless times, that is defiled by the form of something-to-be-grasped and something-which-grasps [and] that unfolds the external [object], is contrary [to the truth] (*sc.* false). [He] might take a position that the example under consideration [in NA 5], characterised by perception, is void of the probandum. Hence, in order to denounce his opinion, [the author] says [the following]:

/6/ Neither is perception erroneous, because it is determined to be a cognitive criterion, since [to say:] 'a cognitive criterion is erroneous' is a contradictory utterance.

[6.1] What is happening is your mind—namely: 'Not only inference is erroneous, but also perception, that has been mentioned by you as an example, is likewise nothing but erroneous on account of the utterance: "every [cognition] is erroneous with regard to the objective substratum"[310]'—is not [right]. [If you ask:] 'Why?,' [the author] says: **'because it is determined to be a cognitive criterion,'** which means: 'because it is ascertained to [have] the status of a cognitive criterion.'

[6.2] [The author]—having suspected [that there might be] room for [a doubt expressed in the following] utterance of a non-partisan bystander: 'And now, if the opponent were of the opinion that cognitive validity (*sc.* the status of cognitive criterion[311]) is inexplicable otherwise than being non-erroneous, how could he then, while accepting that [cognitive validity], hold out for this difference of opinion regarding erroneousness [of perception and inference]?'—has distinguished cognitive validity from this [erroneousness] by the proof of contradiction between [the idea of] erroneousness and [the idea of] cognitive validity and says **'erroneous'**, etc., [in order] to demonstrate that this [cognitive validity] is under the sway of (*sc.* is inferable from) the asserted non-erroneousness, inasmuch as there is no other defence [for the opponent]. And likewise, '[To say:] "**A cognitive criterion**", [i.e.] the cause of the determination of something-to-be-grasped, is "**erroneous**", [i.e.] contrary,'[312] [means that] '**this utterance**', [i.e.] a linguistic unit conveying a meaning of such a kind, is '**contradictory**', because it is the inception of (*sc.* entails) a meaning [in which] the antecedent and the subsequent [elements of the above linguistic unit] are [mutually] contradicted.

[6.3] And now [the Vijñāna-vādin opponent might argue in the following manner.] 'This [utterance] is not contradictory at all. For it as follows. We argue—[in order to] justify the empirical truth[313] [given credence to] by people[314] with a practical intention of a [person] who does not know the ultimate truth—that both perception and inference, whose existence is produced by the awakening of very firm past impressions, are cognitive criteria, because—inasmuch as [both of them] make one reach the object shown [by them] with this [practical] intention—both of them are unerring.[315] However, [perception and inference,] whose birth is brought about by the disposition of feeble past impressions, are not cognitive criteria because—precisely with the same [practical] intention—they are deceptive with regard to the object shown [by them]. Therefore, on the other hand—since all representation, which produces a false image of the external [object and] which is criticised for [its] defilement with the form of something-to-be-grasped and something-which-grasps, has a form contrary to the non-dualistic sensation on the level of the ultimate truth—we state explicitly, with the intention of a person who reflects upon the truth, that [perception and inference] are erroneous because the representation concerning the external [object], inasmuch as it is incapable of [standing] the examination of the [external] object [that is supposed] to be grasped by this [representation], has a falsified form. For it is as follows: the object could either [1] consist in the whole or [2] consist in parts, because there is no other logical alternative. [Ad 1] [The object as] the whole, to begin with, does not stand the examination, because it is unjustified to assume [it as] the whole if it is deprived of its parts and because an alternative that this [whole] occurs (*sc.* resides) in these [parts] is inexplicable. For it is as follows: either this [whole] occurs in these [parts] [1.a] [piece] by piece or [1.b] in its totality. [Ad 1.a] [The whole] does not [occur in its parts piece] by piece, to begin with, because it has no parts itself. If one assumed some other divisions [of the whole] by reason of the occurrence [of the whole] in parts (*sc.* to enable the whole to reside in its parts), [one would have to face] the undesired consequence [impelling us to] assume some other divisions [of the whole] also [to enable its] occurrence in these [divisions]—and in this manner [the result would be the fallacy of] *regressus ad infinitum*. [Ad 1.b] [The whole] does not [occur (*sc.* reside) in its parts] in its totality, either, because [it would lead to] the undesired consequence of the plurality of the [numerically one] whole, inasmuch as its form [would already be] complete with reference to each and every [its] part. If [our opponent puts forward an rejoinder, namely] 'In the case of a thesis [assuming] the difference [between the whole and its parts] that is a defect, [but] in the case of a thesis [assuming] the non-difference [between the whole and its parts] there is no [defect],'[316] that is not [correct, for] also in this case there may either be exclusively the whole or exclusively the parts, because they are not different from each other, just like [two things that have] mutually the same nature. Furthermore, in the case of accepting [the thesis] that the whole pervades all [its] parts, then—on every act of seeing the red colour and flapping, etc., of one scrap belonging to a piece of cloth, etc.—acts of seeing the red colour and flapping, etc., [that belong to] the entire [piece of cloth] could be difficult to negate[317], because it is unjustified to attribute contrary properties, like red and non-red, etc., to one [and the same thing]. [Ad 2] An object consisting in parts cannot pass through the domain of examination (*sc.* is inadmissible), either, because it would be controverted precisely by the same criticism [as directed above against] this [whole], inasmuch as members, such as hands, feet, the head, the neck, etc., would [assume] the form of the whole with regard to their own parts. If [our opponent retorted:] 'It is explicable that infinitesimal atoms have parts, [even though they] have no divisions,' that is not [correct], because that would entail that they too have six divisions [each] due to the relation with the hexade of the cardinal points, inasmuch as they cannot be situated in any other way. And, therefore, since [cognitive awareness] is deprived of a [real external] object, the form of something-to-be-grasped which anticipates this [real external object] is false; since this [form of something-to-be-grasped] is false, also the form of something-which-grasps does not reproduce the [real] situation, because it is unjustified to assume something-which-grasps, if there is nothing-to-be-grasped.[318] The actuality of the intrinsic nature of that [something-which-grasps] depends exclusively on that [something-to-be-grasped] and when the forms of something-to-be-grasped and of something-which-grasps are annihilated, there remains [only] the form of cognitive awareness, because this [cognitive awareness] has the undeviating form in all instances; hence, this [cognitive awareness] alone is ultimately real.[319]' [The above was the exposition of the Vijñāna-vādin's standpoint.]

[6.4] As for this [misconception of the Vijñāna-vādin], it is controverted [by us]. What has been said, namely 'The non-dualistic sensation (*sc.* consciousness) is ultimately real, whereas [the sensation] that occurs [as having] the form of something-to-be-grasped and something-which-grasps is unreal,' is not proper, because there is no cognitive criterion [to prove it]. For it is as follows: a sensation, that unfolds itself through [affections like] joy, distress, etc., and through transformations [consisting in] grasping an object accompanied by several properties, like persistence, grossness, etc., is comprehended as manifold both externally and internally. On the other hand, such a cognition that is described by you as distinct from (*sc.* lacking in) the form of the cognoscible and the cogniser never experiences the phenomenon of [itself] turning into the domain of awareness of anybody whatsoever[320], because a non-dualistic representation is not experienced even in the state of dreaming. Besides, also those [people] who, even though they reflect upon the truth, determine their own intention without a cognitive criterion do not become people whose utterances are to be taken into consideration by the thoughtful [persons]; otherwise someone who says: 'Brahman, even though being one, unconscious [and] imperishable, unfolds itself—due to nescience—as manifold, conscious [and] exposed to perishability in a moment (*sc.* momentary),' would be irrevocable. Also the criticism which has been advanced with the thought to revoke [the existence of] an external object by means of the whole and [its] parts—since it is like swearing of a prostitute, who is disposed towards deceiving, in front of [somebody] who sees the act of spitting out into (in the middle of?) the meal[321], inasmuch as the body of this [criticism] is crushed with a pestle of representations, that are known to all creatures and that unfold themselves [both] externally and internally—does not appeal to the minds of wise people, either, because if representations [gained through] perception are denied, the alternatives [based on] defective reasoning [underlying the criticism]—inasmuch as [this criticism] is rooted in these [representations gained through perception]—cannot be established. Furthermore, also the criticism [based on the occurrence of a sensation] in its totality or [piece] by piece, etc., [as characterised by] difference or non-difference, etc., with regard to the occurrence of the sensation [that itself is numerically] one [but appears] in manifold forms, e.g. white or not white, etc.,[322] is just the same, hence it is not a [proper] criticism. If [you argue as follows]: 'Since [a representation consisting in] manifold transient occurrences is false, there is no issue of difference or non-difference between the ultimately real sensation and this [false representation],' well then, in this manner the *circulus vitiosus* presents itself as unanswerable. For it is as follows: if the falsehood of this [manifold representation] is established, then the non-dualistic sensation is established and—as a logical consequence—if this [non-dualistic sensation] is established, then [the result is] the falsehood of this [manifold representation]. And [there is still] something else, just like a sensation occurring in one [present] moment, even though it is non-dualistic, experiences the relation (*sc.* is linked) to both the previous and the subsequent moments[323], similarly what would be improper if infinitesimal atoms, even though they have no divisions, entered into an association with the divisions of the [six] cardinal points or with other infinitesimal atoms? Further, the criticism concerning the alternative of absolute separateness (*sc.* difference) or absolute non-separateness (*sc.* non-difference) of the whole and [its] parts does not create any subversion for our opinion, either, because these [both, viz. the whole and its parts,] are accepted as such the difference between which should be displayed with the intention that their forms are not detached from each other, for it is impossible to deny both of them (*sc.* the whole and its parts), inasmuch as they appear [both] externally and internally exactly in this manner, [i.e. not absolutely different from each other]. Thereby, [your] pointing out the contradiction [of properties like] red and non-red, flapping and non-flapping, etc., [in one piece of cloth], is contravened as well, because there is no contradiction with regard to an object well-known through a cognitive criterion, since only [a thing] subverted by a cognitive criterion is contradictory and since it is unjustified to assume that the alternatives [based on] defective reasoning—inasmuch as these [alternatives], when [cognitive validity of] perception is denied, have no basis—can subvert anything, for [they] cannot be established when that [perception] is demolished; and since all properties [exist] by reason of [their] different occurrences[324], the contradiction produced as something contrary to this [one object] is instantly cast off far away.[325] Furthermore, the intention of negating [supposedly] erroneous attribution of [supposedly] contrary properties to an external object [in the case] of somebody who accepts [that] the very sensation itself consists [either] in perception or non-perception, conceptual or non-conceptual [cognition], in erroneous or non-erroneous [cognition], etc., depending on the ultimate truth or on the practical convention [respectively], indicates nothing but inanity [of such a person]. So, it is established that it is in no way possible that cognitive criterion [might be] erroneous, because [such a position would lead to] the undesired consequence of the dissolution of the intrinsic nature [of cognitive criterion].

[6.5] And now [another objection is raised by the Yogācāra opponent]: 'Cognition (*sc.* cognitive criterion) is erroneous, inasmuch as the object shown by it is false, not on account of the intrinsic nature [of this cognition]; and in the instant of the production of this [cognition], the restriction [delimiting the realm of real things] by the following discrimination 'this is a false object, whereas that is a non-false (*sc.* real) object' is not possible for anybody, either, because both what is considered to be erroneousness and what is considered to be non-erroneousness are revealed as having one and the same form of this [cognition]. And when [false objects] are seen, [e.g.] a pair of moons, etc., that—even though they move onto the path of (*sc.* are perceived by) the clear perception—ascend to falsehood (*sc.* are proven false), then there [remains] nothing but mistrust because the doubt concerning false objects (*sc.* the suspicion that the perceived objects are false) has not been excluded, also with regard to all [other] representations considered [to depict] true objects. And the attainment of the object of these [representations] as well as other [purposeful activities[326] involving the object of these representations] cannot be assumed [to be] the ground for revoking the suspicion[327], because it is established that objects are false in the state of dreaming despite the presence of those [purposeful activities, like the attainment of the object in the state of dreaming]. If [you maintain]: "This [cognition in the state of dreaming[328] is proved to grasp] a non-true object on account of the occurrence of a subverting cognition [later in the waking state]," that is not [correct] because it is unjustified to assume that this [subverting cognition[329] in the waking state] can subvert [anything in the state of dreaming], inasmuch as it is confined to its own domain, [viz. to the world in the waking state]. Otherwise, Devadatta's knowledge grasping something blue would result in the subversion of [his] knowledge of something yellow, that occurred before. Besides, every representation is similar[330], inasmuch as it is established that there is no [cognition] subverting [them]. Therefore, this must be an error [consisting in] a cognition [that is] erroneous and non-erroneous because—inasmuch as there would be no discrimination[331]—everything [would turn out to be] false objects.'

[7.0] With regard to this [objection the author] says [the following]:

/7/ Since it is incorrect to assume erroneousness of all representation, cognitive criterion, which is patent [and] which determines itself and something different [from it], proves to be correct with regard to establishing the dyad.

[7.1] What is maintained is the following: even someone, [say, a Yogācāra][332], who asserts that all sensation is erroneous[333], has to accept the non-erroneousness of [the reasoning] proving that [assumption of his][334] because [a contrary position would lead to] the undesired consequence that—since, if that [reasoning] were erroneous[335], [all] things demonstrated by this [reasoning] would be false—all knowledge would be non-erroneous; for otherwise it would be unjustified to assume the erroneousness of [all] this [sensation]. And in this manner any other [sensation] belonging to this class, as well, would be non-erroneous, and therefore '**since it is incorrect to assume erroneousness,**' [i.e.] inasmuch as there is no verification to the contrary, '**of all representation,**' [i.e.] of every sensation, that '**which is patent [and] which determines itself and something different [from it],**' [i.e.] that which—inasmuch as it is firmly determined—reveals itself and something else [than itself], that is '**cognitive criterion**'. The above [sequence shows] the syntactical relation [in the aphorism]. And that [cognitive criterion] '**proves to be correct,**' [i.e.] is positively verified, '**with regard to establishing the dyad,**' [i.e.] with regard to positive verification of the pair characterised by the intrinsic nature [of cognitive criterion] and by the object [of cognitive criterion]; otherwise if there were nothing cognoscible, there would be no cognitive criterion. Consequently, a person accepting cognitive criterion has to accept also the object [of cognitive criterion]—such is the intention [of the author].

[8.0] Thus, having taught the definition of the inference for oneself in the above manner[336] and having revoked the difference of opinion (sc. misconceptions) concerning erroneousness [of the inference for oneself] among [scholars] dealing with that [inference for oneself, the author] states forthwith the definition of the verbal knowledge, to begin with, inasmuch as a little has to be said about the very definition of the inference for others[337], that has not been taught [yet].

> **/8/ The cognitive criterion—arisen as grasping reality[338] due to a [momentous] sentence, which is accepted as what is experienced, and which is not contradicted[339] [as well as] which communicates the ultimate truth—is declared [to be] the verbal knowledge.**

[8.1] Here too[340], '**the verbal knowledge**' is the *definiendum*, because it is to be called to mind. [The whole expression] beginning with '**which is accepted as what is experienced, and which is not contradicted**' is the *definiens*[341], because it is to be introduced [as something [yet] unknown. [There are more than one possible solutions of the compound in question.[342] The first one is the following:] 'momentous sentence whose meaning is accepted as what is experienced, and which is not contradicted,' [i.e.] in which [momentous] sentence the meaning—due to its efficacy—is '**accepted,**' [i.e.] desired to be demonstrated, as '**what is experienced,**' [i.e.] as what is seen by [means of] a cognitive criterion, [and which is] '**not contradicted,**' [i.e.] which is not revoked; that [momentous sentence] is such. That is tantamount to: 'such whose meaning is determined through a cognitive criterion [and] which is not subverted'; '**due to**'[343] [such a sentence arises the cognitive criterion]. '**The meaning**'[344], [i.e.] what is to be taught, is '**ultimate**', [i.e.] non-fictitious (authentic), [viz.] something which is useful to people or something possible to be carried out; [such a sentence] whose character is to communicate this [ultimate meaning (truth)] is that **'which communicates the ultimate truth'**; that means: that which demonstrates the distinguished meaning. Such a **'cognitive criterion'** that—due to that [momentous sentence]—has **'arisen as grasping reality,'** [i.e.] which has gained its essence (*sc.* it has come into existence) as having the character [disposed] to catching the meaning to be demonstrated by the [momentous] sentence under consideration, **'is declared [to be],'** [i.e.] has been described by former preceptors as, **'the verbal knowledge'**. The above [sequence shows] the syntactical relation [in the aphorism]. Here [in the aphorism, the author]—by the following [expression:] **'accepted as what is experienced, and which is not contradicted'**—refutes [the idea that] utterances of heterodox thinkers and remarks of [both] common people and deceivers [might also be classified as] the verbal knowledge, because [they are] subverted by cognitive criteria. By the [phrase] **'due to a [momentous] sentence,'** however, [the author]—while demonstrating [the idea] that only a [momentous] sentence, inasmuch as it demonstrates the specific meaning, can communicate the ultimate truth—states that the verbal knowledge is not [possible] due to ordinary word[s]. By the following [expression, namely:] **'which communicates the ultimate truth'** [the author] rebuts [the supposition] that a cognition, which has its origin in utterances [consisting in] instructions about antipyretic remedies, [in instructions] of carpenters, [in instructions] about crest-jewels and ornaments, etc.[345]—inasmuch as [such instructions are] fruitless [in a wider context]—[may be] a cognitive criterion.[346] However, by the [phrase] **'arisen as grasping reality,'** however, [the author] wards off [the conjecture that a cognition] which—even though it has thus arisen (*sc.* as grasping the reality) due to a [momentous] sentence—is manifested due to hearer's defect, [e.g. due to defective hearing, acoustic obstacles, etc.], [might be] the verbal knowledge, inasmuch as it is apt to grasp an object contrary [to reality], etc. By the [word] **'the cognitive criterion'** (*māna*)—inasmuch as the meaning of the prefix *pra* is therein included[347]—[the author] rules out the opponent's intention that the verbal knowledge is not a cognitive criterion[348], because—if this [verbal knowledge] were not a cognitive criterion—[that would lead to] the undesired consequence of the disintegration of the inference for others, inasmuch as this [inference for others] consists in utterances. If [the opponent argues]: 'Since [the inference for others] is indicative of the three-membered logical reason[349], it is a cognitive criterion [only] metaphorically, not in reality,' that is not [correct] because it would be unjustified to assume that something which is not a cognitive criterion [can be] indicative [of anything]. And now [another objection is raised by the opponent]: 'If this [verbal knowledge] were a cognitive criterion with regard to the demonstration of the logical reason [to another person], then the looking out for (*sc.* the need of) another cognitive criterion (*sc.* inference) corroborating the logical reason would be shattered, inasmuch as the intrinsic nature of that [logical reason could be] determined by this [verbal knowledge] alone[350], because if [the logical reason], in its turn, [were] well-known through one cognitive criterion (*sc.* the verbal knowledge), [the existence of] another criterion (*sc.* inference) [would be] purposeless.' [But] that is not [the case] because [that would lead to] the undesired consequence of the cognitive invalidity of the perception, falsely conceived by you [to be free from conceptual construction][351], as well. Because of the looking out for (*sc.* the need of) the conceptualisation concerning the object shown by this [perception], it would immediately follow that only this [conceptualisation] is a cognitive criterion. If [you riposte]: 'This [conceptualisation] expresses only the object grasped by this [perception],' then the same argumentation [is applied against your thesis], namely another cognitive criterion corroborates the logical reason that is [in its turn] demonstrated by speech elements.

[9.0] And the verbal knowledge turns out to be twofold, namely commonplace and produced by an authoritative treatise. As for this [twofold division], this common definition of both these two [varieties] has been demonstrated [in NA 8]. On the other hand, the corroboration of the commonplace [verbal knowledge]— whose origin are utterances of [people] who are not deceitful—has been introduced as something new (*sc.* still unknown) here [in this work] precisely while speaking of (*sc.* dealing with) the initial sentence[352], whereas [the corroboration of the verbal knowledge] produced by an authoritative treatise has to be introduced as something new (*sc.* still unknown); hence [the author] demonstrates by what sort of an authoritative treatise [the verbal knowledge,] that experiences cognitive validity (*sc.* is a cognitive criterion), is produced.[353]

> **/9/ Authoritative treatise is that which has been discerned by an authoritative person, which is not negligible, which does not contradict what is accepted or what is experienced, which gives the instruction about reality, which is for everybody [and] which obliterates errant paths.**

[9.1] That which instructs, [i.e.] edifies, [i.e.] makes one grasp the reality[354] [consisting in] living elements, lifeless elements, etc., or that by which one is edified is '**authoritative treatise**.' [In order to answer the question] 'What is it like?', [the author] states its distinctive features. '**An authoritative person**' is somebody who has annihilated completely the conglomeration of defects such as passion and other [affections]; '**that which has been discerned**' by this [authoritative person means] that which has been comprehended [by authoritative person] in the beginning. By this [remark the author] states the exclusion of [the idea of] the divine origin [of authoritative treatises], because this [idea of the divine origin of authoritative treatises] is subverted by cognitive criteria, inasmuch as—if there is no activity of man—there is no comprehension of utterances (*sc.* no utterance can take place), and even if there is a comprehension (*sc.* even if an utterance does take place), there is no ascertainment of its meaning; for if one resorts to man in order to determine the meaning of these [utterances, that leads to] the undesired consequence [classifiable under] the maxim of the elephant's bath[355], because—inasmuch as [man] is defiled by passion and other [affections]—[his] operation to recount [their] meaning [is] futile. If effects of [any authoritative treatise] itself[356] are [accepted to be] established[357] on account of carrying out[358] [injunctions of the authoritative treatise] by this [man], why is man not accepted [by you] also in order to [account for] the composition [of authoritative treatise], because there is no difference, [i.e. in either case the human factor is equally indispensable]? So, with the exception of the utterance of [a person who is] free from defects, there is no other operation referring to invisible thing[s], such as the next world, etc.,[359] that [seems] proper to thoughtful [people]; so, precisely that [operation which furnishes the proof of the existence of invisible things] is authoritative treatise, inasmuch as it is explicable to take the meaning of [its] words literally; so let [us] leave that alone[360].

[9.2] Further on, that which is neglected, which is approached with violence, which is attacked by others is negligible; that which is different from it is **'that which is not negligible'**—that is tantamount to that which surpasses all utterances. Further on, [let us explain the compound: 'which contradicts what is accepted or what is experienced,' of which there are two possible solutions. The first possibility is the following:] that in which there is a contradiction between **'what is accepted,'** [i.e.] what is to be taught by this [authoritative treatise][361], with **'what is experienced,'** [i.e.] with that which is determined by cognitive criterion is exactly such ['which contains a contradiction between what is accepted and what is experienced']. Alternatively, [there is] **'what is experienced'** by a cognitive criterion, [and there is] **'what is accepted'** by another (*sc.* subsequent to the act of cognition) utterance; that which contradicts these two [is that 'which contradicts what is accepted or what is experienced'], because it communicates a meaning contrary to them; that which is different from it is that **'which does not contradict what is accepted or what is experienced'** [or, alternatively: **'which does not contain a contradiction between what is accepted and what is experienced'**], which means: that which communicates a meaning free from subversion.[362]

[9.3] Heretofore, [i.e. by this part of the verse], the fulfilment of the objectives [assigned to authoritative treatise] with regard to itself[363] has been described. Now, [the author] states the fulfilment of the objectives [assigned to authoritative treatise] with regard to others, inasmuch as [such purposes as] the instruction about reality, etc., are for the sake of others. **'Reality'**[364] are the entities (*sc.* ontological categories) such as the living element, etc., because [reality] is determined by cognitive criteria [to consist in these entities (*sc.* ontological categories)]; **'the instruction'** about these [entities (*sc.* ontological categories) means] revealing [their] intrinsic nature or, alternatively, the means of their rescue, etc.[365]. That which effectuates this [instruction] is that **'which gives the instruction about reality**[366].' Further on, [the expression] that **'which is for everybody'** [means] beneficial for everyone, because [authoritative treatise] is for all people, inasmuch as it ensures [for them] the final beatitude through the instruction, which is the means of rescue for creatures. Thereby it has been declared that this [authoritative treatise] fulfils the objectives [assigned to it] with regard to others.

[9.4] Now [the author] states the fact that [authoritative treatise] eliminates the misfortune of nobody else but opponents. **'Errant paths'** [means] evil paths, [i.e.] heterodox systems of thought[367]; that **'which obliterates'** these [errant paths means] that which overthrows [or] that which revokes [heterodox systems of thought]; the meaning [of the expression 'that which obliterates errant paths'] is as follows: that which ruins defective opinions leading all people astray. The verbal knowledge produced on account of exactly such an authoritative treatise, not on account of any other [treatises], is a cognitive criterion, because these [works other than authoritative treatise described here] deceive [people].

[10.0] Now, the definition of the inference for others should be taught; and [the author]—while tackling this [inference for others] in [the context of] perception[368], because [both perception and the inference for others] are based on one and the same productive-supportive principle[369]—states [its definition] in general:

> **/10/ A sentence which brings about the determination for others—just the way [it brings about] the determination for oneself—is called by the learned the cognitive criterion for others because of the metaphorical transference of this [cognitive criterion onto the sentence][370].**

[10.1] Here [in the aphorism] '**the cognitive criterion for others**' is the *definiendum*; [the whole expression] '**just the way [it brings about] the determination for oneself**' is the *definiens*. '**Oneself**' [means] the cognitive subject; '**the determination**' for this [cognitive subject means] the comprehension of the cognoscible [on the part of the cognitive subject]; '**just the way** [it (*sc.* a sentence) brings about]'[371] that [determination for the cognitive subject, in the same way a sentence] '**brings about the determination,**' [i.e.] manifests the cognition discerning the cognoscible, '**to others,**' [i.e.] to [people] to be taught. The meaning is as follows: just like the ascertainment of an object [is brought about through the sentence] for the cognitive subject, in the same way [the sentence] produces the ascertainment [of an object] for other [people]. [Such a sentence] '**is called,**' [i.e.] is declared [to be], '**by the learned,**' [i.e.] by scholars, '**the cognitive criterion,**' [i.e.] that by which [an object] is cognised in a valid way, '**for others,**' [i.e.] that by which an objective, [i.e.] purpose, [is accomplished] for the sake of other [people].

[10.2] And now [in order to controvert the objection]: 'If bringing about the determination [of an object in others] is the cognitive criterion for others, then also a cognition, which is applied in order to make others know [a particular object, cognised previously by the cognitive subject], becomes [wrongly a cognitive criterion] for others,' [the author] says: a sentence is for others, not a cognition, because this [sentence] alone [executes its] activity immediately and because its sole purpose is for others[372], whereas the other one, [i.e. cognition], is separated (*sc.* detached)[373] and because it is efficacious [both] for oneself (*sc.* cognitive subject) and for another [person]. [In order to answer the following question]: 'How could a statement, which does not consist in cognition, be a cognitive criterion?,' [the author] says: '**because of the metaphorical transference of this [cognitive criterion onto the sentence].**' [The compound is to be solved as follows:] '**of this,**' [i.e.] of cognition, '**the metaphorical transference,**' [i.e. the act of] grasping of [an object]—although it consists in non-*x*—as [an object] consisting in *x*, inasmuch as [the object consisting in non-*x*] is a constitutive element of *x*; [the compound is in the ablative:] because of that [metaphorical transference of this [cognitive criterion onto the sentence]. What this amounts to is the following: also such an utterance that will arise [later] as a cognition subsisting in (*sc.* belonging to) [people] to be taught—because [this utterance] is the immediate (*sc.* direct) cause [of the subsequent cognition in other people]—is called metaphorically a cognitive criterion. As for this [issue of efficacy for others], it is indeed accepted by opponents that inference is for others, [but they] do not recognise that perception [can be for others, too][374]. As they say, this [perception] grasps an individual thing that is void of penetration through speech elements[375]; hence the domain of this [perception] cannot be demonstrated to others. And perception, that is able to grasp [only] individual things, will not emerge for another [person] on account of speech element[s], because speech element[s]—inasmuch as [they themselves] are brought about by a conceptualisation—bring about a conceptualisation also in another [person]. So, it has been said [accordingly]:

> 'Speech elements have [their] inception[376] in conceptualisations; acts of conceptualisation have [their] inception in speech elements; they are cause and effect [for each other]; speech elements do not even touch [the actual] object.'[377]

[11.0] Besides, [the author]—having availed himself of the following inference: 'perception is non-conceptual, hence it is not produced[378] by speech elements' as an example—states the following in order to prove that also perception is for others:

> **/11/ Because of revealing well-known objects through perception [as well as] through inference, [and] because these two are means for another [person], both of them are for others.**

[11.1] '**Because of revealing well-known objects**,' [i.e.] because of conveying the cognoscible [things] discerned by oneself, '**through perception**' and '**through inference**' alike, '**both of them**,' [i.e.] perception and inference, '**are for others**,' [i.e. they serve their] purpose for [people] to be taught, inasmuch as [both perception and inference have] equal causes—the intention is that not only inference alone [is for others]. Besides, these two speech elements [supplied] here [in the commentary]—since they are not heard and since their meaning is comprehended—[viz.,] 'and [...] alike'[379], which are expressed implicitly, have to be [clearly] demonstrated. And the following is the intention of [the author] who asserts that objects discerned [by oneself] can be conveyed through perception: what the opponent maintains, namely 'The domain [of perception] cannot be demonstrated to others,' is not correct, because—since perception, excluding the non-conceptual perception, has been proved just a while ago to have the form of decision[380]—the domain [of perception], inasmuch as it can be comprehended through conceptualisation, can be somehow demonstrated through speech elements. So, just the way an object discerned through inference, [when] it assumes the form of utterance while being demonstrated to another [person, becomes] the inference for others, similarly [an object] discerned through perception as well [becomes] the perception for others, because [the way of] conveying [the discerned object] to another [person] is equal [in both cases], whereas the act of utterance alone [constitutes] the difference. For it is as follows: [a person] conveying [an object] discerned through inference enunciates an utterance in the following manner: '[1] There is fire here, [2] because there is smoke; [3a] wherever there is smoke, there is fire, like in the oven, etc.; or by [applying an example] based on dissimilarity, [one can reason in a negative way:] [3b] if there is no fire, there no smoke at all, just like in a water reservoir, etc.; [4] and thus, this is smoke; [5] therefore—because [there is] this smoke [here,] there is fire here'[381], because it is possible to demonstrate that exactly such is [the state of affairs either] to a [person] who does not know the relation or to a [person] who has forgotten the relation. If the relation is, however, recollected [then the inference consists of only two members], as follows: '[1] There is fire here, [2] because it is explicable due to [the occurrence of] smoke'; [alternatively,] by [applying an example] based on dissimilarity, [one reasons in a negative way:] '[1] There is fire here, [2] because [the occurrence of] smoke would be otherwise inexplicable.'[382] On the other hand, [a person] demonstrating [an object] discerned through perception, says thus: 'Look, the king is going!' And therefore, since on account of the twofold utterance, [viz. inference-bound and perception-bound,] there originates an awareness whose province is [either] the inferendum or the object of perception, [respectively,] for [the person] to be taught, who is familiar with the complete causal complex, that is why both of them are for others; hence, [the author] says:[383] **'because these two are means for another [person],'** which means the following: because—with regard to the awareness of [the person] to be taught—these two [perception and inference constitute] the cause of revealing the object determined by perception and inference, that are both located in (*sc.* belong to) [the person] who is teaching.[384] And thereby[385] [the author] characterises the cause of the metaphorical transference mentioned in the previous verse.

[11.2] What has been said [by Buddhist opponents], namely: 'The origination of perception for another [person cannot take place] on account of a speech element because this [speech element][386] produces a conceptualisation, for perception—inasmuch as it has individual things for its province—is non-conceptual,' is not proper because there is no contradiction [in the fact that] this [perception], which has the object consisting [both] in the universal and the particular as its province [and] which assumes the form of [conceptual] ascertainment, can be—inasmuch as somehow [it shares] one [and the same] province [with speech elements][387]—brought about by a speech element, and because it has been corroborated just before[388] that [perception] is of this kind, [i.e. perception, save the non-conceptual variety of perception, has the form of decision and grasps the universal and in the particular]. If [the opponent argues]: 'This [perception] arises on account of the causal complex [constituted by] eyes, etc., not because of a speech element,' [we reply that] also inference originates for the cogniser, who has not forgotten the relation, because of the logical reason that has been determined by perception, not because of a speech element; consequently also the efficacy for others [in the case of inference] would be shattered. If [the opponent further maintains]: 'In that case [of inference], the utterance [as the instrument of inference] is for others on account of the mention of the efficacious logical reason [corroborating the probandum],' we say that also in this case [of perception, the utterance as the instrument of perception is for others] on account of the demonstration of an object amenable to perception. So, there is no comprehension of any (*sc.* we see no) distinction concerning the efficacy for others between perception and the indirect cognition[389]; hence the [Buddhist] arbitrary partiality towards the thesis denying the perception for others] has to be abandoned.

[12.0] Thus, having taught in the above manner[390] that both of these two [perception as well as inference] are for others, [now the author] states their intrinsic nature:

> **/12/ And such an utterance that demonstrates an object recognised through perception is called perception, because it is the external sign for the representation.**

[12.1] The syntactical relation [in the aphorism] is as follows: **'such an utterance' 'that demonstrates an object recognised through perception,'** [i.e.] that is apt to mention the domain of the cognition which perceives directly, '**is called perception**.' By the speech element 'and', since it has several meanings, [the author] demonstrates the following [idea]: '**and**' this [utterance] is perception when articulated as something which consists in nothing but perception[391]; however, when articulated by the means of inference towards a [person who is] of a different opinion [in order to prove a thesis], it [becomes] nothing but inference.[392] [In order to answer the following objection]: 'How could an utterance possibly be a perception?!' [the author] furnishes [the rationale]: '**because it is the external sign for the representation**,' which means that [an utterance] is called metaphorically [perception] because it is the cause of revealing [an object] through perception to a [person] to be taught.

[13.0] [Presently, the author] describes inference:

> **/13/ Such an utterance that demonstrates the logical reason as inseparably connected with the probandum is the inference for others, whose essence are propositions, like the thesis[393], etc.[394]**

[13.1] That which conveys, [or] discloses, an object is the logical reason; '**such an utterance' 'that demonstrates,'** [i.e.] that displays, this [logical reason] '**as inseparably connected with the probandum**,' which has been described before[395], is—since it is the cause of revealing inference [to other people]—'**the inference for others**.' [In order to answer the question]: 'What is this [inference for others] like?,' [the author] says: such [members of the proof formula] like the logical reason, example, application, conclusion, etc., that have as their beginning this thesis, whose definition will be taught later [in NA 14], are these [elements of the compound denoted by 'thesis, etc.']; '**propositions, like** these [expressions' means] statements demonstrating these [expressions]; that whose essence, [i.e.] whose intrinsic nature is [constituted by] exactly these [members of the proof formula] is such an [utterance] '**whose essence are propositions, like the thesis, etc.**'.

[13.2] And now [an ironical objection] is raised [by the opponent]: '[We encounter here a highly remarkable] congruity of speech[396], wherein the antecedent and the subsequent are [mutually] contradicted, on the part of [the author] who—having [first explicitly] stated that an utterance which demonstrates the logical reason is the inference for others—expresses [the idea that inference for others is] such **whose essence are propositions like the thesis, etc.**!' [But] that is not [the case]; in the above manner, [the author] maintains that there is not [only] one variety of the inference for others, but also [that the cognoscible object] should be conveyed meticulously [to another person] in such a way so that the awareness of the cognoscible comes about easily [on the part] of the other person. For this [purpose], there is the ten-membered proof as the means of demonstration [of the cognoscible object], namely: the five [members of the proof formula], like the thesis, etc., and their clearances.[397] In this case [of reasoning based on the proof formula, when [either] [1] a [person] to be taught is someone who has determined the thesis due to the way of arguing alone[398], who has not forgotten the cognitive criterion grasping the invariable connection which can be [now] recollected by an example[399] and who is capable—inasmuch as he is endowed with a cultivated mind—of supplementing [the proof formula] with remaining members, or else, when [2] [he]—inasmuch as his mind has been [appropriately] prepared[400] by an infinitely repeated practice—cognises the cognoscible [object] under discussion just like that [without effort], then the demonstration of the logical reason alone is carried out (*sc.* it suffices to mention solely the logical reason) because the explicit statement of the remaining [members of the proof formula]—inasmuch as they have the form of subliminal impressions in the hearer—is purposeless. In this and similar [instances, the inference] which demonstrates the logical reason [alone] is called by the author of the manual 'the inference for others.' When, however, the [person] to be taught had no ascertainment of the thesis even presently, then a specification of the logical reason all of a sudden[401] would cast an invisible hammer, [i.e. it would be destructive]; hence, also the thesis is pointed out. Similarly, if someone cannot recollect the cognitive criterion grasping the invariable connection, also an example should be described because otherwise the efficacy of the logical reason cannot be ascertained [by him]. Although the cognitive criterion underlying the example has been recollected, the application is demonstrated to somebody who does not know how to connect [the thesis, the invariable connection and the logical reason with each other]. In the very same manner, the conclusion is stated for someone who has the expectancy [to hear the conclusion of the proof formula], because otherwise the object which is evidently under discussion could not be proved [for him]. Likewise, with regard to whichever [member of the proof formula, like] the thesis, etc., there [arises] a difference of opinion concerning their intrinsic nature, with regard to that [particular member of the proof formula] the clearance of this [member of the proof formula] should be carried out by [means of] cognitive criterion because, in the opposite case, they could establish neither the probandum nor themselves. And, [consequently,] all these [ten elements] are the members of the proof, because they are the means of [inducing] knowledge of the [person] to be taught.

[13.3] And now [another objection is raised by the opponent]: '[A sentence] which brings about the determination for others—just the way [it brings about] the determination for oneself—is said [in NA 10] to be the inference for others. This sequence, however, [of members of the proof formula that characterise the inference for others], is not experienced in the time of [drawing] the inference for oneself because a [person] who knows the relation establishes the knowledge of the probandum merely on seeing the logical reason, for the cogniser, having [first] delimited the thesis, neither finds out the logical reason on account of that [thesis] nor contrives [remaining members of the proof formula, like] an example, etc., because [his] knowledge does not originate in such a manner. Furthermore, on account of [both] positive and negative concomitance the efficacy of logical reason alone is inferred, not [the efficacy] of the thesis and other [members of the proof formula], because also without them the probandum can be proved, inasmuch as if one assumed that they are the components of the proof in the very same way [as the logical reason is, that would lead to] the undesired consequence of [the fallacy of] *regressus ad infinitum*. And if the efficacy of those [remaining members of the proof formula] were [possible], then—inasmuch as one could ascertain the probandum on account of the sole specification of the thesis and nothing else—the logical reason would attain purposelessness (*sc.* become purposeless) as well as remaining members [of the proof formula would prove purposeless], for their efficacy could be established in this manner, [viz. on account of sole specification of the thesis], not otherwise. Therefore, only that which reveals the probandum independently of other [components, and] nothing else, is the logical reason [which constitutes] the proof (*sc.* is the means of accomplishing the epistemological aim), not the thesis and other [members of the proof formula].'

[13.4] Regarding this [objection, we] riposte [as follows]. What has been said [in NA 10], namely: '[A sentence] which brings about the determination for others—just the way [it brings about] the determination for oneself—is said to be the inference for others, etc.,' has been said correctly, but you simply do not understand its meaning, because by [the expression] 'just the way' the coequality only with regard to determination is stated explicitly. Similarity in everything, however, is not intended; otherwise, that would absurdly imply that—since in [the case of] the inference for oneself the probandum is cognised without uttering any linguistic unit—the determination [of the probandum] in another [person] (*sc.* the inference for others) could be brought about without uttering this [linguistic unit]. And that is not the case, because the demonstration [of the probandum] to another [person] is impossible without uttering a speech element; if speech elements are admitted for the purpose of this [demonstration of the probandum to another person (*sc.* the inference for others)], then each and every such a [factor] without which the demonstration [of the probandum] to another [person] is impossible should be accepted, because of one and the same productive-supportive principle[402]. And it is not possible to demonstrate [the probandum to] a particular [person] to be taught without the thesis, etc., either, because this [particular person to be taught]—inasmuch as he is lacking in the knowledge of the object-to-be-proved of these [remaining members of proof formula that constitutes] the domain of the logical reason, etc.—has the expectancy [to hear the thesis, the example, etc.].[403] Furthermore, if there were no cognitive awareness of an object which one wants to cognise, one would remain absolutely unaware [of anything, viz. nothing could be conveyed to him]; hence, in order to arouse the cognitive awareness of this [object which one wants to cognise], the thesis and other [members of proof formula] should be shown. Therefore, also these [remaining members of proof formula] should be [accepted as] the components of the proof. What has been said [by the opponent], namely: 'No proof is [possible] without adopting [the principles of both] positive and negative concomitance, because also the probandum is proved solely on account of the logical reason,' is not proper because—since in certain cases the cognoscible object can also proved solely on account of an utterance, [e.g.] in the form 'There is fire here' or similar, [pronounced] by a person whose non-deceitfulness has been determined—[that would lead to] the undesired consequence that also the logical reason does not prove [anything in certain cases]. [The opponent may add:] '[But also that would lead to the undesired consequence] that even without this [logical reason] the probandum can be proved.' And that is [indeed] proper, because [the opinion] that utterance[s] of a [person] who is not deceitful possess the cognitive validity has proved to be correct just a while ago [in NA 9]. What has been said [by the opponent], namely: 'If the efficacy of these [other members of the proof formula] were [possible], then—inasmuch as one could cognise the probandum on account of the thesis alone—the logical reason would be purposeless,' is even more improper [than his previous assumption that no proof is possible without positive and negative concomitance] because also in your thesis it is the same, inasmuch as also in that case, [i.e. if the logical reason alone possessed the efficacy], one could ascertain the probandum on account of the specification of the efficacious logical reason alone [and there would be no need of other members of the proof formula], for otherwise [it would be] unjustified to assume the efficacy [of the logical reason]. Who could prevent [two other members of the proof formula, viz.] the corroboration of this very [logical reason] by a cognitive criterion following immediately and then the use (*sc.* application)[404] of a property-possessor [in the case] of the thesis [presented] to a [person] who has grasped the invariable concomitance in all cases, from becoming purposeless?[405] If [the opponent defends his position and says]: 'Without them, [i.e. without the corroboration of the logical reason and its application], the efficacy of the logical reason is not ascertained, hence they are purposeful,' [then we can reply that] it is not possible to demonstrate [the probandum to] a particular [person] to be taught without the thesis, etc., either. Consequently, it is not difficult to demonstrate that also these [other members of proof formula] are purposeful; hence [the opponent's] attack has to be abandoned. Therefore, just like the logical reason, also the thesis and other [members of proof formula constitute] the proof (*sc.* are the means of accomplishing the epistemological aim) because the logical reason—inasmuch as, with reference to certain [objects] to-be-demonstrated, it is dependent on these [members of the proof formula]—is not established to be independent, either. So, having taken into consideration everything that [has been mentioned above, it cannot be denied] that this [inference for others] is such '**whose essence are propositions, like the thesis, etc.**'.

[14.0] Thus, having come, in the above manner[406], to speak of the thesis and other [members of the proof formula] as far as their purpose (*sc.* function) is concerned, [the author] states, to begin with, the definition of the thesis:

/14/ The thesis is the acceptance of the probandum;[407] [it] is not revoked by perception, etc.[408]; the pronouncement of it has to be made here as showing the domain of the logical reason.

[14.1] That which is [further] developed[409] is the thesis, the intent is: that which is expressly manifested. [In order to answer the question:] 'What is it like?,' [the author] says: [the thesis is] **'the acceptance'**, [i.e.] admitting, **'of the probandum,'** [i.e.] of the inferendum; that means: holding a thesis in front of questioners, etc. [With the intention that the following doubt] 'Is it only the acceptance?' [should be cleared away by the negative reply] 'no', [the author] says: [the thesis] **'is not revoked by perception, etc.' 'Perception'** is the sensation perceiving directly [an object]. On account of the speech element **'etc.'** inference, one's own utterances and opinion prevalent among people are comprised[410] [as factors sufficient to create the revocation in the case of a faulty thesis]. The thesis is **'not revoked'**, [i.e.] not subverted by them—such is the syntactical relation. [The thesis can be] for instance: 'everything has a multiplex nature' or 'there exists an omniscient person,' etc. And to somebody who might maintain the following: 'That [thesis] has simply to be accepted; it is not, however, to be stated explicitly by an utterance in the time of [presenting] the inference for others'[411], [the author] replies: **'the pronouncement'**, [i.e.] the explicit statement **'of it'**, [i.e.] of the thesis, **'has to be made'**, [i.e.] has to be introduced [as something yet unknown], **'here'**, [i.e.] at the point of [drawing] the inference for others. [In order to clear up the doubt]: 'What [does the pronouncement of it have to be made] for?', [the author] says: **'as showing the domain' 'of the logical reason'**, which has been [in its turn] described before[412]; that means—on account of the utterance 'generally, all [statements (*ukti*?)] are seen with reference to the instrumental causes and logical reasons'[413] and because the expressing element has action as its main [import][414]—'because [the pronouncement of the thesis] displays the province [of the logical reason].' The intention here is the following: for not in every case the logical reason is specified to a disputant who has determined the thesis—due to the way of arguing alone[415]—in such a way that the elegance of the beard comes in front, but in certain cases [and] sometimes [it can be specified].[416]

[15.0] Subsequently, if a [person] to be taught has not known the object of the thesis until now, then—if, all of a sudden, the logical reason were mentioned—the defect characterised by an error would occur due to the disorientation as to the [actual] province [of the logical reason]; hence [the author] says:

/15/ Otherwise, for a [person] to be apprised, who is confused regarding the domain of the logical reason intended by the proponent, the logical reason might appear to be suspected[417] of being contradictory, just like...

[15.1] **'Otherwise'** means 'when—referring to [a thing] contrary to what has been stated—the pronouncement of the thesis is not made.' The meaning is as follows: **'intended'**, [i.e.] considered, **'by the proponent'**, [i.e.] by someone who brings forward the specification of the logical reason; and that is **'the domain of the logical reason'**—[such is the solution of the compound] **'the domain of the logical reason intended by the proponent'**; and **'for such a [person] to be apprised'**, [i.e.] for the disputant, whose character is confused, or wobbles regarding that [matter], the logical reason **'might appear to be suspected of being contradictory'**, [i.e.] could occur as sullied by the doubt regarding the contradiction [contained in it]. And therefore, also regarding the logical reason that is [in fact] correct, one could—due to the disorientation [in the form] 'This [logical reason] occurs only in the heterologue'—express the criticism [accusing the logical reason] of being contradictory. Due to the specification of the thesis, however, this defect would not occur [in the case] of someone who has determined the domain of the logical reason—[and] such is the intention [of the author]. Exactly this meaning [is what the author illustrates] with a lucid example [and] says: **'just like...'** [Such] is the purpose of the specification of that [thesis].

> **/16/ ...for a person watching an archer's skill, the archer who hits without the specific mention of the target [is endowed with both] skill and its opposite[418].**

[16.1] Just like skill and incompetence of an archer shooting an arrow—without the specific mention of the target—appear both together as contrary to a person watching that [display of archery, viz.] both skill [appears] as incompetence as well as incompetence [appears] as skill, in the same manner skill and incompetence of the proponent specifying—without the specific mention of the thesis—the logical reason, that are characterised by the efficacy or inefficacy [respectively] in proving the probandum intended by [the proponent] himself, appear both together as contrary to questioners, opponents, etc. Such is the intended meaning. The meaning [according] to the 'letter', however, [is as follows: the one who] walks with a bow is **'an archer'**; his **'skill'** is characterised by the dexterity at hitting the target; since viewers are curious[419] about that [skill], only that [skill] is mentioned, otherwise also incompetence should be demonstrated as well. 'Just like' **'for a person watching** that [skill of an archer],' [i.e.] for a man whose character (*sc.* current concern) is to watch that [skill of an archer], '**[the archer] who hits**,' meaning: [the archer] who somehow or other discharges an arrow, '**the archer** [who hits] **without the specific mention of the target**,' [i.e.] a bowman [who hits] without any specific mention of the butt, **[is endowed with both] 'skill and its opposite**,' [i.e.] skill and incompetence, [that] become 'suspected of being contradictory,'[420] in the same manner [skill and incompetence] of the proponent [become suspected of being contradictory to questioners, opponents, etc.], too. Such is the meaning. Therefore, it is established that the arrow, which is the logical reason, may be pronounced first after the target, which is the thesis, has been specifically mentioned by the archer, who is the disputant, to the opponent to whom the object of that [logical reason is] unknown.

[17.0] Presently, there is an occasion [to formulate] the definition of the logical reason and this [definition] should be demonstrated, like in the inference for oneself, without distinction[421]. The pronouncement [of the logical reason] is, however, not demonstrated in the case of that [inference for oneself], because the inference for oneself consists in cognitive awareness, whereas here [in the case of the inference for others] it should be demonstrated, because the inference for others consists in utterances. Thus, [the author] demonstrates this [pronouncement of the logical reason]:

/17/ The pronouncement of the logical reason may be either by [its] explicability in this way or exactly otherwise; it is twofold, since the probandum may be proved precisely in either way.

[17.1] Indeed, while dealing with the inference for oneself[422] it has been determined—by way of banning other definitions imparted by opponents—that the [only] one definition [of the logical reason] is [such a definition] alone [that states] the non-occurrence of the logical reason, in its totality, in what is different from the probandum. Also in the case of the inference for others this very definition has to be revealed (*sc.* stated), but the formulation of a proposition functions in certain cases[423] somehow or other; [the author]—having the above intention—states its twofold character: '**the pronouncement of the logical reason may be [...] twofold**'—such is the syntactical relation. [In order to meet the query:] 'How [is it possible]?' he says: '**[its] explicability**'[424], [i.e.] the fact of [its] being present only '**in this way**', [i.e.] only [in the case] of presence of the probandum; '**by**' [indicates that the whole expression stands in the instrumental case in the aphorism, thus we have] '**by [its] explicability in this way**.' [One can see this principle] for instance [in the following proof formula]: 'There is fire here, because the smoke is explicable only in this way.' By this [abridged expression] '**or exactly otherwise**' [the author]—due to metaphorical transference of a word aggregate onto [its] part—indicates the inexplicability otherwise [of the logical reason].[425] '**Or**' [the pronouncement of the logical reason may be by its] inexplicability, [i.e.] the fact of [its] being nothing but absent, '**otherwise**', [i.e.] in the case of the preclusion of the probandum; 'by' [indicates that the whole expression is used in the instrumental case, viz.] the pronouncement of the logical reason may be by [its] inexplicability otherwise. For instance: 'There is fire here, because the smoke is otherwise inexplicable.' And in order to instruct someone who might maintain: 'Both of these two together have to be pronounced with regard to one [and the same] probandum,'[426] [the author] says: '**precisely in either way**,' [i.e.] by the pronouncement of [its] explicability in this way or by the pronouncement of [its] inexplicability otherwise, '**the probandum**', [i.e.] the object which one intends to demonstrate, '**may be proved**', [i.e.] may be verified [positively, i.e.] may arise in the awareness of a [person] to be taught. '**Since**' [means] because. Therefore, both of these two [propositions] do not have to be pronounced together, because [only] the formulation of a [particular] proposition bifurcates into the very dyad of pronouncements, but not the object [which one intends to prove]. Furthermore, the result of [either] pronouncement is the proof of the probandum. If this [probandum] is proved just by one [of these two ways of pronouncement], the pronouncement of the other one would only evince the ineptitude of the speaker, because it is purposeless. Such is the intention [of the author].

[18.0] Now, there is an occasion [to formulate] the definition of the example. Likewise, this [example] is twofold: based on similarity and based on dissimilarity. [The author,] having made the example based on similarity the subject [of discussion], states [the following]:

> **/18/ Such [a statement] in which the invariable concomitance between the probandum and the probans is determined in the best possible way because of the recollection of the relation is known as the example based on similarity.**

[18.1] [Such a statement] in which '**the extent between**', [i.e.] the delimitation of, two '**experienced**' [things, i.e.] of the probandum and the probans recognised within the context (from the circumstances), which is based on the determinate cognition of the relationship between the probandum and the probans by [means of] positive concomitance or by [means of] negative concomitance, [takes place] is '**the example.**' That which has the same property is 'based on similarity'; its state (*sc.* the *abstractum* derived from it) is the fact of being based on similarity; 'based on' [indicates that the term is used in the instrumental case, hence] '**based on similarity**'; [thus, we have the expression: '**the example based on similarity.**' In order to answer the question:] 'What is this [example based on similarity] like?', [the author] says: '**the probandum**' consists in an object one intends to know; '**the probans**' is the logical reason which leads to the comprehension of this [probandum]. '**Such [a statement] in which,**' [i.e.] in whichever [particular statement] '**the invariable concomitance**' between these two, [namely] '**between the probandum and the probans**'—which has such a form [that can be paraphrased] in the following manner: 'without that [invariable concomitance] this [particular thing] does not occur'[427]—'**is determined in the best possible way,**' [i.e.] is perfectly ascertained, is the example based on similarity. [This kind of an example based on similarity is exemplified] for instance [in the following proof formula]: 'There is fire here, because the smoke is explicable only in this way; just like in the oven, etc.' Subsequently, [having in mind] that this [example] does not have to be pronounced for the disputant who has not forgotten the invariable connection, [the author] says: '**because of the recollection of the relation,**' [wherein] the ablative is used in the place of the gerund[428], [i.e.] having taken account of the recollection of the relation, which has been grasped previously and [has been afterwards] forgotten; this [example] '**is known as,**' [i.e.] intended, by logicians, not in any other case. For when a [person] to be taught does not know the relation characterised by the property [on the part of the probans] of being inseparably connected with the probandum even now, then he should be made grasp the relation by [means of] a cognitive criterion, not merely by an example, for just by seeing [two things] together in some cases it is not proved that one [of them] does not occur without the other one in all cases, because [that would have] too far-reaching consequences.[429] And if the invariable connection, which has been grasped [before], is being recollected, then simply the logical reason has to be shown; since an object which one wants to cognise is proved by that much only, an example does not have to be stated, because it is purposeless. But when the relation—even though it has been grasped [before]—has somehow been forgotten, then an example is mentioned with the purpose of its recollection, [i.e. in order to remind the opponent of the invariable concomitance].

[18.2] And now [an objection is raised by the opponent]: 'How is the ascertainment of the relation as pervading (*sc.* invariably valid in) the three times and all places [possible]?[430] Neither is perception, to begin with, even though it has the nature of ascertainment, capable of observing the relation between the probandum and the probans, which is prone to continue in another place and time, because it operates as a clear apprehension with regard to the proximate object [only]. Nor is the ascertainment of this [relation possible] due to a speech element, because of the undesired consequence that this [speech element]—inasmuch as it consists in the instruction of another [person]—cannot [constitute] the inference for oneself[431], for in [the case of] this [inference for oneself] no instruction of another [person takes place, consequently] if this [speech element] were absent, the relation could not be proved; if that [relation] were not proved, then the inference could not be established. If the relation were grasped by inference, there would necessarily follow an endless *regressus ad infinitum*, because inference is, in its turn, even though it grasps the relation, dependent on grasping [still] another relation.' To this [objection we] reply: in the case of those who have a wrong predilection [to the idea] that there are only two cognitive criteria, viz. perception and inference, it is their fault, not ours, for [we] accept still another cognitive criterion (*sc.* inductive reasoning, *vitarka*)—which arises in the point of time posterior to [either] perception or non-comprehension that grasp [either] positive concomitance or negative concomitance [respectively], which is undeviating and whose domain pervades the three times[432], which is based on the sensuous cognition[433] [and] which is technically called induction[434]—as grasping the relation, because if this [induction] were not accepted, that would lead to the undesired consequence of the ruin of empirical fact[s] and everyday practice[435], and in the case of their ruin any examination would become purposeless. Here in this treatise, [i.e. in the *Nyāyâvatāra*], however, induction is not shown separately (*sc.* dealt with as separate) from inference, because this [treatise] has been undertaken for the advantage of [human] beings who delight in concise [form]; the verbal knowledge, on the other hand, was corroborated (*sc.* tackled) as separate because it is conducive to the inference for others in this very [treatise]. So let us leave that alone.[436]

[19.0] Now, [the author], showing the example based on dissimilarity, states [the following]:

/19/ But such an example—in which, when the probandum is absent, the non-existence of the probans as well is predicated—is thus regarded traditionally [to be] based on dissimilarity.

[19.1] That which has a dissimilar property is 'based on dissimilarity'; its state (*sc.* the *abstractum* derived from it) is the fact of being based on dissimilarity; 'based on' [indicates that the term is used in the instrumental case, hence] 'the example **based on dissimilarity**.' [In order to answer the question:] 'What is this [example based on dissimilarity] like?', [the author] says: '**when the probandum**,' [i.e.] when that which is to be comprehended, '**is absent**' [i.e.] is non-existent. The speech element '**but**' has the meaning of the restriction [to a particular case]; it stands in a different position [in the sentence than usual due to metrical reasons] and it should be taken here in the sense 'only' referring to '**the non-existence**' '**of the probans as well**,' [i.e.] 'of that which leads to the comprehension.' In such a particular '**example in which**' [the non-existence of the probans] '**is predicated**,' [i.e.] is demonstrated, becomes [the example] '**based on dissimilarity**'—because on account of the speech element '**thus**' the relation is recollected.

[20.0] [The author] relates that [question of the two-fold example] also to the present issue. Having suspected [that there might be] a room for an opponent's following utterance: 'Since the pronouncement of this very [example]—when the relation is being recollected—is unjustified as well, for what reason is the example pronounced only for the disputant who has forgotten the relation, [and] not in any other case?', [the author] says:

/20/ Since the probandum is proved only by the intrinsic invariable concomitance,[437] an exemplification from outside would be pointless[438]; experts in logic have recognised that also in its absence [this is] such.

[20.1] Surely, 'in any other case'[439] [may mean that the example] should be pronounced either [1] when the relation is being recollected or [2] when [the relation] has not been grasped. [Ad 1] If the first alternative [is meant], then it is not proper. If a [person] to be taught recollects the logical reason as inseparably connected with the probandum in all cases, how could he then—having [re]cognised this [logical reason] in the thesis—not understand the probandum? And consequently, '**an intrinsic**', [i.e.] within the locus, '**invariable concomitance**', [i.e.] the fact that the probans is under the sway of probandum[440], is [what is known as] '**the intrinsic invariable concomitance**.' Inasmuch as only through this [intrinsic invariable concomitance] '**the probandum**', [i.e.] that which is to be comprehended, '**is proved**', [i.e.] is known, '**an exemplification**'—that refers to the property-possessor (*sc.* subject) of the example [and] consists in the demonstration of an invariable concomitance—[which is taken] '**from outside**', [i.e.] concerns something other than the property-possessor (*sc.* subject) in question, is '**pointless**', [i.e.] purposeless, because there is no object to be conveyed by this [exemplification]. [Ad 2] Refuting also [a supposition that] the second alternative is not defective, [the author] says: '**also in its absence [this is] such**', [which means] that also if there is no intrinsic invariable concomitance, because the relation is not grasped, [this is] 'such', [i.e.] an exemplification from outside is nothing but pointless. For by seeing [two things] together in some cases it is not proved that [these two things] are seen together in all cases, because one [can] see deviations [from this rule]. Therefore, the invariable connection should be proved by a cognitive criterion to a [person] to be taught, who has not grasped the relation. **'Experts in logic'**, [i.e.] specialists in logic, **'have recognised'** [i.e.] they know, that when this [invariable connection] has been proved, an exemplification by [adducing] an example is ineffective, inasmuch as the probandum is [already] proved by this [invariable concomitance]. And even though the definition of the remaining members [of a proof formula] characterised by application, conclusion and the five clearances have not been taught directly here in this treatise, inasmuch as this [treatise] aims at the advantage of [human] beings who delight in concise [form], nevertheless [respective definition] can be deduced by the learned from this very triad of the members of the proof formula demonstrated [above], because there are [eventually] three kinds of discourse as regards the [number of] members of the proof formula, viz. lower, intermediate and superior. Out of them, the lower one is a mere demonstration of the logical reason; the intermediate one is a proclamation of two or more [but not all] members of the proof formula; the superior [discourse] is the mention of complete ten members of the proof formula. Regarding these [varieties of the discourse], by the direct mention of the intermediate [discourse] here [in this treatise the author] indicates both the lower and the superior [varieties of the discourse] by implication, because their presence can be proved by cognitive criterion.

[21.0] After the definition of the thesis and other [members of the proof formula] have been taught in the above manner, now the fallacies[441] of the thesis, of the logical reason and of the example, that are opposed to them, [i.e. to the thesis and other members of the proof formula][442], should be taught, so that—when the cognition which should be avoided is [demonstrated]—[a cognition] which is worth appropriating [can] be recognised more distinctly. Out if these [fallacies, the author] states fallacies of the thesis, to begin with, that are opposed to the [proper] definition of the thesis:

/21/ The fallacy of the thesis is what is [already] proved for a [person] to be taught, [what] is subverted by the perceiving organ and by the inferential sign[443] as well as by the opinion prevalent among people and by one's own utterances; it is known [to be] manifold.

[21.1] [That which] looks like a thesis, because it is brought forward in place of the thesis and because it does not produce an effect [which should be] this [thesis], is **'the fallacy of the thesis.'**[444] It is **'known [to be]' 'manifold,'** [i.e. it is known] to have several varieties—such is the syntactical relation. [In order to answer the question:] 'How [is the fallacy of the thesis manifold]?', [the author] says: [1] that particular [thesis] **'which is [already] proved for,'** [i.e.] which has actually constituted itself in the awareness of, **'a [person] to be taught,'** [i.e.] a disputant, is a fallacy of the thesis, because only the probandum (*sc.* what still requires proof) [constitutes] the thesis, inasmuch as something which has already been proved is unfit for proving, [i.e. to prove something which has [already] been proved is tantamount to the fallacy of *petitio principii*], because [that would have] too far-reaching consequences.[445] Further on, that which **'is subverted,'** [i.e.] ruled out, '[2] **by the perceiving organ and** [3] **by the inferential sign,'** [i.e.] by [either] perception or by the logical reason, '[4] **as well as by the opinion prevalent among people and** [5] **by one's own utterances,'** is the fallacy of the thesis. Out of these [varieties of the fallacy of the thesis], [Ad 1] [the thesis] that is [already] proved for a [person] to be taught is, for instance, the following: 'Pot is material' [for everybody], or 'Everything is momentary' for the Buddhist, etc. [Ad 2] [The thesis] that is subverted by perception is, for instance, the following: 'Individual things have no divisions' or 'the universal and the particular are mutually [absolutely] separate.' [Ad 3] [The thesis] that is subverted by inference is, for instance, the following: 'There is no[body who is an] omniscient person.' [Ad 4] [The thesis] that is subverted by the opinion prevalent among people is, for instance, the following: 'One's [own] mother is accessible [as a sexual partner].' [Ad 5] [The thesis] that is subverted by one's own utterances is, for instance, the following: 'All entities are not existent.'

[22.0] Presently, [the author]—reminding [the hearer] of the definition of the logical reason—states fallacies of the logical reason, which are opposed to that [very logical reason]:

> **/22/ The definition of the logical reason has been proclaimed [to be] the inexplicability otherwise; the fact that [the logical reason is] fallacious is due to non-discernment, doubt and cognitive error concerning it.**

[22.1] **'The definition of the logical reason,'** which consists in [outlining] specific properties [of the logical reason], **'has been proclaimed,'** [i.e.] has been disclosed, or [properly] demonstrated, since there are several meanings (*sc.* interpretations) [of the term 'the logical reason'][446], while dealing with the inference for oneself[447], **'[to be] the inexplicability otherwise.'** [The conditions when fallacies] of this [logical reason occur are]: [1] '**non-discernment**' of it, [i.e.] non-apprehension [of the logical reason]; [2] '**doubt**' concerning it, [i.e.] the fact of wobbling[448] [with regard to the logical reason, and] [3] '**cognitive error**' concerning it, [i.e.] the ascertainment of contrariety [regarding the logical reason]. [This triad forms] a *dvandva*-compound: non-discernment and doubt and cognitive error. Afterwards, then, [they form] jointly a *tat-puruṣa*-compound: by these [three, i.e.] **'by non-discernment, doubt and cognitive error concerning it.' 'The fact that [the logical reason is] fallacious'** [means its] looking like—or semblance of—[something] like this, i.e. of [something] like a correct logical reason; such that is like [that,] [i.e.] possesses the semblance, [means] such that resembles that; its state [means] the fact of being such; [that] is the fact of being the fallacy of the logical reason—such is the meaning.[449]

[23.0] Now, [the author] demonstrates that which becomes a [particular] fallacy of the logical reason bearing a particular name on account of its respective characteristic:[450]

/23/ Unproved is that which is not discerned; on the other hand, that which is explicable only otherwise is contrary; however, that which is proper here also otherwise is inconclusive.[451]

[23.1] [1] Such a particular [logical reason] '**which is not discerned**,' [i.e.] which has not become the domain of cognition, or is not determined, is the fallacy of the logical reason called '**unproved**'. The speech element '**on the other hand**' points out the division of the very triad. [2] '**On the other hand**,' that '**which is explicable**,' [i.e.] is possible '**only otherwise**,' [i.e.] exclusively without the probandum, which is tantamount to [saying that it is possible] 'only in the heterologue,' [bears] the designation of '**contrary**'. [3] However, that which is '**proper**,' [i.e.] justified, '**also otherwise**,' [i.e.] also as being contrary to the probandum—[whereby what is really meant] by the speech element '**also**' [is: 'proper] also [inn the case] of the probandum'—'**here**', [i.e.] in a given case, should be known [to be a fallacy] technically called '**inconclusive**'. As for these [fallacies], one should ascertain that all these logical reasons, with no exception, that are specified by disciples of Kaṇāda, Akṣapāda, the Buddha, etc., whose understanding stands in contradiction to the [theory of] multiplexity [of reality] well-known to every creature and determined by cognitive criteria—namely [logical reasons in the following reasoning and similar cases]: [α] Speech element (sound) is impermanent in the absolute sense or [β] [speech element (sound) is] permanent [in the absolute sense], because it is existent, because it is endowed with origination, because it is produced, because it is being recognised, etc.'[452]—secure the status of being [1] unproved, [2] contrary or [3] inconclusive according to the intention (*sc.* in compliance with what ultimately intended by these scholars).

[23.2] [Ad 1] For it is as follows: [Ad 1.α] in case [when speech element (sound) is assumed to be] impermanent in the absolute sense[453], to begin with, all these logical reasons [enumerated above], with no exception, are u n p r o v e d , [firstly], because—like visibility[454]—they are not existent in [the case of] a linguistic unit (sound)[455], for they are—inasmuch as they exclude the non-existent, etc.—fabricated by false empirical truth[456], whereas on the level of the ultimate truth—inasmuch as it is entailed that one [thing has] several forms—the theory of multiplexity of reality is entailed, and, [secondly], because [these logical reasons], whose existence is formed by conceptual construction, are—inasmuch as they are deprived of all powers—devoid of their essential nature. Nevertheless, when they are [assumed to be] the probantia, also the probandum [they want to prove] is devoid of its essential nature; consequently, a donkey's horn results in proving a hare's horn—such is the splendid use of the probandum and the probans! If [you, the Buddhist, rise the following objection]: 'All this entire use of inference and the inferendum by [means of] the argumentation [based on] property and property-possessor, that constitutes itself in the [organ of] understanding, does not require existence or non-existence of an external [thing]; hence it is not a defect,' then we shall retort that [in such a case when existence or non-existence of an external thing is not required] also visibility—after having been projected on speech element by the [organ of] understanding [and thus] being called the logical reason—should not be pointed out as the unproved [logical reason], because there is no difference. If [you adduce the following argument]: '[Only] by the exclusion of invisibility, visibility can be projected [on speech element] by the [organ of] understanding, not this way or other; and this [exclusion of invisibility[457]] is not [found] in [the case of] speech element because this [speech element] can be grasped without eyes, hence that is not a defect,' [then we shall ask you]: What is it that is called the exclusion of invisibility: is it [1.1] the amorphous (*sc.* without any object) exclusion as such or [1.2] the excluded individual thing or [1.3] the excluding understanding that—although immersed in its divisions (*sc.* is confined to itself)—drifts (*sc.* appears) as consisting in grasping external real things? If [you retort]: 'You are desirous of advancing a criticism—by means of the alternatives of difference and non-difference—in case where there is no further property of the real thing!'[458]; [then we ask]: what kind of talk is this [to maintain] that this [exclusion of invisibility] is not [found] in [the case of] speech element? For, in this way, [to say] that a sky lotus is not [found] there [in a linguistic unit (sound)] would absurdly imply that it is not possible to conceive [the logical reasons] like existence, etc., [enumerated above in the case of a linguistic unit (sound)], either. Furthermore, in your doctrine these properties of the probans, [that are of conceptual nature], even though they occur in the property-possessor, do not ascend to awareness (*sc.* cannot be cognised) because [according to you] perception—inasmuch as it lacks conceptualisation—is void of ascertainment of properties, for the understanding [consisting in] conceptualisation—which arises in the point of time posterior to that [perception] [and] which is produced[459] by the awakening of past impression—does not penetrate the external individual thing, inasmuch as its body is confined to grasping its own divisions (*sc.* the awareness grasps nothing but its own epiphenomena); and, consequently, all [these properties of the probans]—since they are not discerned—[turn out to be] unproved.

[23.3] [Ad 1.β] Also in the case [when a linguistic unit (sound) is assumed to be] permanent in the absolute sense, then—since the properties of the probans [admitted by the Naiyāyika-Vaiśeṣika and the Advaita-vedāntin] themselves, that are either [maintained by the Naiyāyika-Vaiśeṣika to be] absolutely different from the substratum or [maintained by the Advaita-vedāntin to be] ultimately unreal[460], [can] not be known by [means of] cognitive criterion—[all these logical reasons] should be regarded as u n p r o v e d , because one cannot deny that all properties are non-detached from [their] substratum, [and] are ultimately real, inasmuch as they are well-known [as such] through cognitive criteria such as perception, etc.[461]

[23.4] [Ad 2] Similarly, the properties of all the probantia can be deduced to be c o n t r a r y in [the case of] both these theses [α and β], as well, because—inasmuch as their essential nature is interrelated in a multiplex way—they are disposed to prove this [multiplex character of reality]. And we shall teach that in the subsequent [section][462].

[23.5] [Ad 3] In this way, all these logical reasons with no exception, when being mentioned specifically with regard to both these theses [α and β], appropriate an inconclusive character, [i.e. they turn out to be inconclusive], because they do not escape from their mutual (*sc.* corresponding) contrary [alternative][463], inasmuch as one can demonstrate [the same property] with regard to the heterologue, as well, by specifying (*sc.* applying) the same rule[464].

[23.6] [Ad 3.α] For it is as follows: the [Buddhist] propounder of the theory of impermanence adduces the following proof to the propounder of the theory of permanence, [i.e. to the Naiyāyika-Vaiśeṣika and to the Advaita-vedāntin]. 'Everything is momentary, because it is existent. [This proof formula is true, firstly], because [otherwise] there would be a contradiction concerning efficient action in [the case of] a non-momentary (*sc.* permanent) [object, when efficient action is considered to be executed either] [3.α.1] consecutively or [3.α.2] simultaneously and [secondly], because the fact that efficient action is executed is the characteristic of the being. Efficient action, when done away with on account of that [contradiction entailed by its execution consecutively or simultaneously], would do away with the existence (the being) which is embraced by it—such is the proof of momentariness. [A permanent object could not execute any efficient action, either consecutively or simultaneously.] [Ad 3.α.1] For a permanent (non-momentary) object cannot operate with reference to efficient action consecutively, because the operation with regard to a subsequent action [is possible only] by means of the termination of the essential nature [of the object] producing the previous efficient action; otherwise [one would have to face] the undesired consequence of non-cessation of [the essential nature of the object] producing the previous efficient action. And when the essential nature [of the object producing the previous efficient action meets its] dissolution (*sc.* terminates), then permanence vanishes because the phenomenon of not preserving the same condition is the characteristic of something impermanent. If [the proponent of permanence, viz. the Naiyāyika-Vaiśeṣika, comes up with the following argument:] "Likewise, a permanent [object]—awaiting an object which should occur consecutively as an auxiliary cause—remained first [inactive]; afterwards, it would, having met this [auxiliary cause], consecutively produce an effect", it is not [correct] because an auxiliary cause is ineffective with regard to a permanent [object, that despite the action of the auxiliary cause remains unaltered], inasmuch as—when that ineffective [auxiliary cause], too, were looking out for [its own auxiliary cause]—that would lead to the undesired consequence of [the fallacy of] *regressus ad infinitum*. [Ad 3.α.2] A permanent (non-momentary) object does not execute efficient action simultaneously, either, because it is contradicted by perception. For nobody observes that all actions commence at the same point of time. Or [let us suppose that a permanent (non-momentary) object] could execute [efficient action simultaneously], nevertheless, what presents itself inevitably is—inasmuch as all actions [of the permanent object] are complete in the very first moment—the impermanence [of the permanent object, which becomes in such case] inactive in the second and subsequent moments, because it is contradictory to be active or inactive in [the case of] one [and the same thing].[465,466]

[23.7] [Ad 3.β] On the other hand, a propounder of the theory of permanence, [e.g. the Naiyāyika-Vaiśeṣika,] adduces the following proof. 'Everything is permanent, because it is existent. [This proof formula is true, firstly], because [otherwise] there would be a contradiction concerning efficient action with regard to a momentary (*sc.* impermanent) [object] [3.β.1] in the time of [its] existence and [3.β.2] in the time of [its] non-existence. Existence (*sc.* entity), which is characterised by that [momentariness], does not hold on to the circumstances (*sc.* does not secure any real foundation?)[467]; [however], when exonerated from that [momentary character]—inasmuch as there is no other defence [for the opponent]—[existence (*sc.* entity)] proves [its] permanence. For it is as follows: a momentary object may either [3.β.1] produce [its] effect existing [in the same moment] or [3.β.2] [produce its effect] not existing [in the same moment], because there is no other logical alternative.[468] [Ad 3.β.1] The first alternative, to begin with, is not [correct], because it is unjustified to assume that [a momentary object] operates with regard to [something] occurring in the same instant and because of the too far-reaching consequences, inasmuch as one would arrive at a mutual cause-and-effect relationship of all entities (*sc.* all entities would be simultaneously causes of each other). [Ad 3.β.2] The second alternative does pass through the ordeal [of examination], either, because something non-existent lacks the power to produce an effect; otherwise also a hare's horn and other [non-existent things] would be able to produce an effect, because there is no difference, [viz. in both cases we deal with non-existent entities].'[469]

[23.8] Thus, whichever logical reasons [are applied] in the above manner[470] to both these [theses, viz. (α) impermanence and (β) permanence of speech element taken] in the absolute sense, none of them can escape [their] contrary [thesis], inasmuch as the same logical reasoning [is applicable to the contrary thesis], and these [logical reasons] bring about intellectual blindness of simple-minded people, inasmuch as [what is] not [properly] examined is pleasant [to them]. Hence [in the manner demonstrated above by means of two kinds or argumentation based on the same logical reason, the fallacious logical reasons of] the i n c o n c l u s i v e [type] do not escape [their] contrary [thesis][471,472] because all properties of the real thing are in fact interrelated in a multiplex way. Consequently, it is established that all such [varieties], with no exception, that are [proper] logical reasons, cannot be explicable without a multiplex [object]—in this way, [proper logical reasons] are capable of demonstrating nothing but this [multiplex object]; whereas these [seeming logical reasons], that are specified by perplexed-minded people in order to prove the heterologue (*sc.* simplistic object, *ekânta*), win—according to the intention (*sc.* in compliance with what ultimately intended by these scholars)—the status of being [1] unproved, [2] contrary or [3] inconclusive.

[24.0] Thus, [the author]—having demonstrated the fallacies of the logical reason in the above manner[473]—states the fallacies of the example, which are opposed to the definition of the [proper] example:

/24/ Defects of the example, here based on similarity, have been proclaimed by the experts in logic [as such that] rise from logical reasons of inapplicable definition and [that] lack the probandum, etc., and so forth.

[24.1] That in which the probans is intended to be demonstrated as being under the sway of the probandum[474] is '**similarity**', [which is used in the instrumental case in the aphorism in the sense of]: '**based on**'; '**here**' [means] in a given case; '**defects**' are those that can be criticised (*sc.* are liable to criticism); '**defects of the example**' [can be decomposed as] defects that are nothing but examples, whose meaning is 'fallacies of the example.' '**Proclaimed by the experts in logic**' [means] asserted by the scholars. '**The probandum**'[means] that to-be-comprehended; on account of the speech element '**etc.**' the probans as well as both these, [viz., to lack the probandum and the probans jointly], are included; to '**lack**' them, [viz. the probandum, the probans or the probandum and the probans together, means] to be void of them. On account of the speech element '**and so forth**' the properties of doubtful probandum, of [doubtful] probans and of both [doubtful probandum and probans jointly] are grasped (*sc.* referred to). [In order to answer the question:] 'What are these [defects] like?', [the author] says: those from which the [proper] definition is detached are such (*sc.* 'of inapplicable definition'); and these [that are of such a kind] are these '**logical reasons**'; those that '**rise from**' these [logical reasons], viz. are generated by [these logical reasons], are '**[such defects that] rise from logical reasons of inapplicable definition.**' And this is a general qualification [shared by all varieties of the fallacious example], inasmuch as [some] fallacies of the example—even though the logical reason is correct—are explicable [as such] on account of the speaker's defects, for instance: 'the speech element (sound) is [both] permanent and impermanent, because it is audible, l i k e a p o t ', etc. [Thus, the six varieties of the fallacy of the example are as follows: [1] the fallacious example based on similarity, lacking the probandum, [2] the fallacious example based on similarity, lacking the probans, [3] the fallacious example based on similarity, lacking both the probandum and the probans, [4] the fallacious example based on similarity, of doubtful probandum, [5] the fallacious example based on similarity, of doubtful probans, [6] the fallacious example based on similarity, both of doubtful probandum and of doubtful probans.]

[24.2] [Ad 1] Among [the six varieties of the fallacies of the example based on similarity, the example] lacking the probandum is for instance: 'Inference is erroneous, because it is a cognitive criterion, l i k e p e r c e p t i o n . ' [This example is fallacious] because perception lacks erroneousness. Since—if this [perception] were erroneous, that would lead the undesired consequence of the destruction of the entire everyday practice, and if it the destruction [took place], there would be no cognitive criterion and no cognoscible—nothing [could] be proved by anybody; consequently [a thesis assuming the erroneousness of perception] would inevitably result in dumbness of the propounder of the theory of erroneousness [of perception].[475] [Ad 2] [The example] lacking the probans is for instance: 'The sensation of a person in the waking state is erroneous, because it is a cognitive criterion, like the sensation in dream.'[476] [This example is fallacious] because the sensation in dream is subverted—inasmuch as it lacks the status of cognitive criterion—by the occurrence of the cognition of a person in the waking state, which is opposite to this [sensation in dream].[477] [Ad 3] [The example] lacking both, [i.e. lacking the probandum as well as probans], is for instance: 'There is no omniscient person (*sc.* omniscient person is non-existent), because he is not comprehended through perception, etc., like a pot.' [This example is fallacious] because, [firstly], a pot is existent and, [secondly], it is comprehended through perception, etc.[478].[479] [Ad 4] [The example] in which the property of the probandum is doubtful is for instance: 'This [particular person] is dispassionate, because he is mortal, like a man in the street.' [This example is fallacious] because the quality of being dispassionate is doubtful in [the case of] a man in the street, inasmuch as there is no ascertainment of that [quality of being dispassionate] in [the case of] a man in the street, either, for particular mental properties can be comprehended by means of inferential signs like particular declarations, etc.[480].[481] [Ad 5] [The example] in which the property of the probans is doubtful is for instance: 'This man is mortal, because he is passionate, like a man in the street.' [This example is fallacious] because in [the case of] a man in the street it is doubtful whether he is passionate, inasmuch as it is equally possible, as well, that he is dispassionate.[482] [Ad 6] [The example] in which the property of both [the probandum and the probans] is doubtful is for instance: 'This [particular person] is not omniscient, because he is passionate, like a man in the street.' [This example is fallacious] because in [the case of] a man in the street they both, [i.e. the probandum and the probans], are doubtful on account of the argumentation indicated [above][483].[484]

[24.3] And now [a doubt is raised]: 'Some [thinkers] have taught an additional triad of fallacies of the example, as well, namely [7] [the fallacious example] without positive concomitance, [8] [the fallacious example] with unindicated positive concomitance and [9] [the fallacious example] with inverted positive concomitance[485]. [Ad 7] Out of these [three additional varieties of the fallacies of the example, the example] without positive concomitance is for instance: 'This person in question is passionate, because he is a speaker (*sc.* he talks), like any selected[486] person.'[487] Even though endowment with passions, etc., and being a speaker (*sc.* being capable to talk) are perceived as the properties of the probandum and of the probans in, as they say, any selected person, nevertheless this example is without positive concomitance, inasmuch as the invariable concomitance in the form: 'whoever is a speaker (*sc.* talks) is passionate' is not established. [Ad 8] Similarly, [the example] with unindicated positive concomitance is for instance: 'The speech element (sound) is impermanent, because it is produced, like a pot'[488]. In this case, even though positive concomitance is real, nevertheless it has not been revealed *expressis verbis* by the speaker, hence [it is] an example with unindicated positive concomitance. [Ad 9] [The example] with inverted positive concomitance is for instance: 'The speech element (sound) is impermanent, because it is produced'[489]; since—after the logical reason has thus [explicitly] been stated—invariable concomitance is demonstrated in an inverted manner, viz. 'whatever is impermanent is produced, like a pot,' [instead of: 'whatever is produced is impermanent'], [this is an example] with inverted positive concomitance, for in the pronouncement of [the example] based on similarity the probans should be shown as being under the sway of the probandum; whereas in this case—inasmuch as the reverse is shown—[the invariable concomitance] is inverted. So, why have you not taught that [additional triad of fallacies of the example based on similarity]?'

[24.4] Regarding this [objection, we] riposte that [we have not taught those additional varieties] in order to make [others] know that this explicit statement of the triad of the fallacies of the example has not been properly reflected upon by the opponents. For it as follows:[490] [Ad 7.a] [the example] without positive concomitance, to begin with, is not in a position to become a fallacy of the example. For if the invariable concomitance between the probandum and the probans could be demonstrated by the force of an example, then [the example] without positive concomitance would be [indeed] a fallacy of the example, because it would not produce its effect, [viz. it would not demonstrate the invariable concomitance between the probandum and the probans]. But when it is established that an exemplification by [adducing] an example serves the purpose of producing a recollection, whose domain is a cognitive criterion grasping the relation that has occurred before, then the characteristic of being without positive concomitance is not the defect of example, but of the logical reason itself, because the invariable connection has not been determined by cognitive criterion until now; and if there is no invariable connection, then positive concomitance is not proved [either]. And the defect of the logical reason should not be taught in [the case of] (*sc.* should not be blamed on) the example, because that would have too far-reaching consequences. Similarly, both [Ad 8.a] [the example] with unindicated positive concomitance and [Ad 9.a] [the example] with inverted positive concomitance do not secure the status of the fallacy of the logical reason, because not indicating positive concomitance as well as indicating positive concomitance as inverted are the defects [on the part] of the speaker. If the demonstration of fallacies of the logical reason [were carried out] by taking into account the defects of this [speaker] as well, the limited number of those [fallacies] would be shattered, because defects of the speaker [can be] infinite.[491] Also when [some fallacies of the example] are defects [on the part] of the speaker, one [simply] requires the proficiency of this [speaker] in [the case of] the inference for others. And if [the opponent argues]: 'If [the character of these two varieties is] specified in the above manner, then these two [fallacies] do not prove an object which one wants to cognise [anyway]; hence these two are [indeed] the fallacies of the example,' then we shall retort that, [following the line of your argumentation], also the incapability of [proper] articulation, etc., should be taught to be the fallacies of the example. For it is as follows: without the capability of [proper] articulation it is not possible to convey anything to another [person], either, because if one does not hear phonemes distinctly, one cannot ascertain their meaning as something evident. So let us leave that alone[492].

[25.0] Thus, [the author]—having demonstrated the fallacies of the example based on similarity in the above manner[493]—states [the fallacies of the example] based on dissimilarity:

/25/ Defects of the example, here based on dissimilarity, have been proclaimed by the experts in logic [to arise] from non-exclusion of the probandum, of the probans and of their combination and from the [liability to] suspicion [regarding their presence].

[25.1] That in which the absence of the probandum is intended to be demonstrated, while the invariable concomitance is absent in the probans, is **'dissimilarity'**, [which is used in the instrumental case in the aphorism in sense of: 'based on'; **'dissimilarity'** is used in] the imparted sense[494]: **'defects of the example, here based on'** this [similarity], **'have been proclaimed by the experts in logic [to arise].'** [These defects arise] **'from the non-exclusion,'** [i.e.] from lack of exclusion, **'of the probandum, of the probans and of their combination,'** [i.e.] of that-to-be-comprehended, of that-which-leads-to-the-comprehension and of both of them, and—inasmuch as the speech element **'and'** is pronounced (*sc.* used) [in a] separated (*sc.* untypical) [place in the aphorism][495]—**'from the [liability to] suspicion,'** which means: 'and from doubt concerning [their] exclusion.' Thus, on account of that, six fallacies of the example are indicated, namely: [1] [the fallacious example based on dissimilarity] lacking negative concomitance with the probandum, [2] [the fallacious example based on dissimilarity] lacking negative concomitance with the probans, [3] [the fallacious example based on dissimilarity] lacking negative concomitance both with the probandum and with the probans as well as [4] [the fallacious example based on dissimilarity] in which negative concomitance with the probandum is doubtful, [5] [the fallacious example based on dissimilarity] in which negative concomitance with the probans is doubtful, [6] [the fallacious example based on dissimilarity] in which negative concomitance both with the probandum and with the probans is doubtful.[496]

[25.2] [Ad 1] Among [the six varieties of the fallacies of the example based on dissimilarity, the example] lacking negative concomitance with the probandum is for instance [in the proof formula already mentioned]: 'Inference is erroneous, because it is a cognitive criterion.' Here the example based on dissimilarity [can be formulated in the following manner]: 'Whatever is non-erroneous, however, is not a cognitive criterion, f o r i n s t a n c e : c o g n i t i o n i n d r e a m '[497]. [This is an instance of an example] lacking negative concomitance with the probandum, inasmuch as erroneousness is not excluded from cognition in dream, [viz. cognition in dream can be erroneous].[498] [Ad 2] [The example] lacking negative concomitance with the probans is for instance [in the proof formula already mentioned]: 'Perception is non-conceptual[499], because it is a cognitive criterion.' Here the example based on dissimilarity [can be formulated in the following manner]: 'Whatever is accompanied by a conceptualisation, however, is not a cognitive criterion, for instance: inference.' [This is an instance of an example] lacking negative concomitance with the probans, inasmuch as the cognitive validity (*sc.* the status of cognitive criterion) is not excluded from inference, [viz. inference is indeed a cognitive criterion].[500] [Ad 3] [The example] lacking negative concomitance with both, [viz. with the probans and the probandum], is for instance [in the proof formula already mentioned]: 'The speech element is [both] permanent and impermanent, because it is existent.' Here the example based on dissimilarity [can be formulated in the following manner]: 'Whatever is not [both] permanent and impermanent, however, is not existent, for instance: a pot.' [This is an example] lacking negative concomitance with both [the probandum and the probans], inasmuch as both of them do not but occur in (*sc.* are not excluded from) the pot, [viz. a pot is both permanent and impermanent as well as existent].[501][502] Similarly, [Ad 4] [the example] in which negative concomitance with the probandum is doubtful is for instance [in the proof formula already mentioned]: 'Kapila and other [thinkers of his kind] are neither omniscient nor authoritative persons, because they do not teach the four noble truths.' Here the example based on dissimilarity [can be formulated in the following manner]: 'Whoever were either an omniscient or an authoritative person, however, he would teach the four noble truths, for instance: Śuddhodana's son (*sc.* the Buddha).'[503] Or else, [one could say as well that] this is [the first variety of fallacious example] lacking negative concomitance with the probandum, because—inasmuch as the four noble truths characterised by the suffering, [its] origin, the path [leading to its cessation and its] cessation[504] are subverted by cognitive criteria[505]—an advocate of these [four noble truths] is explicable [only] as a non-omniscient and a non-authoritative person. Simply, [the above fallacious example] has been specified as such [an example in which negative concomitance with the probandum is doubtful] because to [people] lacking the recognition of the efficacy of cognitive criteria that revoke these [four noble truths][506] it appears as [the fallacious example] in which negative concomitance with the probandum is doubtful. For it is as follows: even though Śuddhodana's son (the Buddha) taught the four noble truths, nevertheless his omniscience and his authority are not proved, because there is no proof that teaching the four noble truths is otherwise inexplicable except together with these two, [i.e. omniscience and authority][507], inasmuch as it is [equally] possible that a cunning person of an adroit mind, who acts with an intention of cheating others, although he is neither omniscient nor authoritative, can impart teaching of that kind. Therefore, non-occurrence of the probandum characterised by non-omniscience and by lack of authority is doubtful in [the case of] Śuddhodana's son (the Buddha); hence [this instance is called an example] in which negative concomitance with the probandum is doubtful.[508] [Ad 5] [The example] in which negative concomitance with the probans is doubtful is for instance [in the proof formula]: 'A particular person in question is untrustworthy, because he is endowed with passion, etc.' Here the example based on dissimilarity [can be formulated in the following manner]: 'Whoever is trustworthy, however, is not endowed with passion, etc., for instance: the Bud-d h a .' Even though the Buddha's trustworthiness ascends to the interior of the mansion of correctness (*sc.* is established beyond any doubt) to [people] whose discerning organ is devoted to his doctrine, nevertheless the absence of the endowment with passion, etc., [in the case of the Buddha] experiences [itself as] moving into the domain of doubt[509], because there is no cognitive criterion that [can] demonstrate this [absence of passion in his case]. Hence, [this is the fallacious example] in which negative concomitance with the probans is doubtful because of the [liability to] suspicion regarding the non-occurrence of the endowment with passion, etc., in the case of the Buddha.[510] [Ad 6] [The example] in which negative concomitance with [both] the probandum and the probans is doubtful is for instance [in the proof formula]: 'Kapila and other [thinkers of his kind] are not dispassionate, because—inasmuch as [their] consciousness is not filled with compassion—they have not offered any bits of their own flesh even to the abodes of compassion (*sc.* to hungry beings who deserved compassion).' Here the example based on dissimilarity [can be formulated in the following manner]: 'Those, however, who are dispassionate, inasmuch as their consciousness is filled with compassion, offered bits of their own flesh to the abodes of compassion (*sc.* to hungry beings who deserved compassion), f o r i n s t a n c e : B o d h i s a t t v a s .' Here the non-occurrence of the properties of both the probandum and the probans in the case of Bodhisattvas is doubtful. Because of lack of any cognitive criterion that [could] demonstrate that (*sc.* that passions, etc., are excluded in the case of Bodhisattvas), it is not known whether those [Bodhisattvas] are endowed with passion, etc., or whether they are dispassionate; similarly, [it is not known] whether they have offered bits of their own flesh to those worthy of sympathy, or not. Hence, [this is the fallacious example] in which negative concomitance with [both] the probandum and the probans is doubtful.[511]

[25.3] Other [thinkers], inasmuch as they are [such a kind of people] who speak without deliberation[512], have demonstrated three additional fallacies of the example, as well, namely: [7] [the fallacious example] without negative concomitance, [8] [the fallacious example] with unindicated negative concomitance and [9] [the fallacious example] with inverted negative concomitance. These [three additional varieties of the fallacious example]—inasmuch as they are improper—cannot be demonstrated (*sc.* accepted) by us. For it is as follows: [Ad 7] [the fallacious example] without negative concomitance is demonstrated by them in the following manner: '"A particular person in question is not dispassionate, because he is a speaker (*sc.* talks)." Here the example based on dissimilarity [can be formulated in the following manner]: 'Whoever is dispassionate, however, is not a speaker (*sc.* does not talk), f o r i n - s t a n c e : a b i t o f s t o n e .' Even though both [the probandum and the probans] do not occur in (are excluded from) a bit of stone, as they say, nevertheless [this example] is without negative concomitance, because negative concomitance is not proved as the invariable concomitance.'[513] [Ad 7.a] It is improper to say so, because if there were no negative concomitance, then that would be the defect of the logical reason. For if negative concomitance could be demonstrated by the force of the example alone, then [an example] lacking the efficacy of this kind, [viz. incapable of demonstrating negative concomitance], would be justified as the fallacy of this [example], but that is not the case, because the example is mentioned in order to produce a recollection the domain of which is a cognitive criterion—disposed towards grasping the relation [between the probandum, the probans and the logical reason]—that occurred previously. For [the example] is not established without a cognitive criterion that grasps the invariable connection [in the form]: 'If [at least] in one case, when *y* is absent, *x* is not seen, then *x* does not occur, when *y* is absent,' because that would have too far-reaching consequences. Therefore, that is the defect of the logical reason, alone, whose invariable connection is not proved, not [the defect] of the example. Similarly, it is improper to teach either [the fallacious example] with unindicated negative concomitance or [the fallacious example] with inverted negative concomitance, because these are the defects of the speaker. For it is as follows: [Ad 8] [the fallacious example] with unindicated negative concomitance was taught by those [other thinkers] for instance [in the proof formula]: '"Speech element (sound) is impermanent[514], because it is produced, l i k e s p a c e ." Here, [in this reasoning based on the proof formula], negative concomitance—even though it is present—is not pointed by the speaker *expressis verbis*, hence the defectiveness [of this variety of the example].'[515] [Ad 9] [The fallacious example] with inverted negative concomitance, on the other hand, is expressed [by those thinkers] for instance [in the proof formula]: '"Speech element (sound) is impermanent, because it is produced." Here the example based on dissimilarity [can be formulated in the following manner]: "Whatever is not produced is permanent, f o r i n s t a n c e : s p a c e ." [516] Here [the example is] with inverted negative concomitance, because [it] indicates negative concomitance inversely. For in the pronouncement of [an example based on] dissimilarity the absence of the probandum should be demonstrated as being under the sway of (*sc.* encompassed by) the absence of the probans[517], and this is not the case here, because the absence of the probans is explicitly stated as being pervaded (*sc.* encompassed) by the absence of the probandum.'[518] ·

[25.4] [Ad 8.a] Not indicating negative concomitance as well as [Ad 9.a] indicating negative concomitance inversely is not the defect of the real thing, but of the [person] communicating [the proof formula and the example], who lacks the proficiency in expressing himself. Furthermore, yours is that view—namely: inasmuch as, in the time of the inference for oneself, one knows the probandum himself merely by seeing the logical reason, also at the point of the inference for others, only the demonstration of the logical reason should be carried out[519]—on account of the following utterance: '[…] since for scholars simply the logical reason alone is to be stated'[520] [pronounced by you] whose description of all fallacies of the example, as well—inasmuch as the probandum intended to be proved can be proved by specifying the logical reason alone [in the form of] nothing more than: 'because it is produced'—demonstrates [your] aptitude for formulations in which antecedent and subsequent statements are contradicted [by each other]. Let us leave therefore these two [fallacious examples (8) and (9)] alone, because the example is not accepted as a part of the probans[521]. If you argue in the following manner: 'If [someone does] not [possess] the complete understanding of the negative and positive concomitance, these two (*sc.* negative concomitance and positive concomitance) cannot be shown to a [person] to be taught without an example, hence an example has to be [explicitly] stated in order to demonstrate negative concomitance and positive concomitance; and therefore [all] those [examples] which do not produce their effect are fallacies of that [example],' that is an outcry of a [person] caught by his throat; nevertheless, the two [fallacious examples, viz.] with unindicated negative concomitance and with inverted negative concomitance, are not real fallacies of the example, but rise from the defects of the speaker; hence it is not correct to state them explicitly [as separate fallacious examples], because a person of this kind, [viz. lacking the rhetoric proficiency], who is devoid of efficacy in revealing existing real things [and] who obstructed by rigid inanity, is not entitled to [participate in] a debate, neither is [such a person] competent to discuss with scholars, inasmuch as he is fit for the primary school where the alphabet is taught.

[26.0] Thus, what has been said [by the author] by way of commenting upon the inference for others in the above manner[522], namely 'this [inference for others is such] whose essence are propositions like the thesis, etc.'[523], is generally completed [now], inasmuch as the thesis, the logical reason and the example alongside with their fallacies have been demonstrated. But only due to dismissal of [any] criticism expressed by opponents alone [can] this [inference for others] win propriety. With this [idea in mind, the author]— desirous of stating [explicitly the definition of] the criticism alongside with its fallacy at this point—says [the following]:

> **/26/ Criticism is [the act of] pointing out the defects, taught previously, in a proof enunciated by the propounder; but [an alleged criticism] with regard to an unobjectionable [proof] bears the name of the fallacy of criticism.**[524]

[26.1] '**A propounder**', [i.e. someone] whose character is to propound, [viz. someone] who conveys [a thesis]; [defects] '**enunciated**', [i.e.] brought forward by him, in what? '**in proof**'; that by which the inferendum is proved, [i.e.] ascends to the awareness of the [person] to be taught, is proof. And [the author] has previously[525] demonstrated that it has several forms—namely: in certain cases there is one logical reason alone, in certain cases the thesis and the logical reason, in certain cases the thesis, the logical reason and the example, in certain cases exactly these [three members] alongside with the application, in certain cases [these four] alongside with the conclusion, in certain cases [these five] with augmentation by every respective clearance—because in certain cases a [person] to be taught can be made know [something] this way or other and because the means of demonstrating [something] to that [person constitutes] the proof. With reference to this [proof] here, since it is not possible to criticise a correct proof, inasmuch as efficacy of that [criticism] is explicable only with regard to the fallacy of the proof, the fallacy of the proof itself [remains] unrecognised [as such] in the state before the occurrence of criticism, [i.e. as long as criticism is not expressed, and] is referred to in general by the term 'proof'. '**The [act of] pointing out,**' [i.e. the act of] revealing in front of questioners, '**the defects, taught**

previously,' [contained] in this [proof,] that are characterised by the specification of the thesis revoked by perception, etc.[526], of the unproved logical reason, etc.[527], of the example lacking the probandum, etc.[528] an so forth, should be known as criticism, namely that by which the proof is criticised, [i.e.] is inferred as a distortion [of a correct proof] characterised by the lack of [efficacy in] conveying the probandum intended by [the opponent] himself.

[26.2] Now, [the author] states the fallacy of this [criticism]: such [a proof] from which [something] objectionable, [i.e.] failure, [that is to say,] defectiveness characterised by defects of the thesis, etc., is departed, inasmuch as [the proof] is pronounced correctly, is **'unobjectionable'**; [it is mentioned in the aphorisms in the locative case]: **'in'**, [and] is used in the sense: **'in a proof'** enunciated by the propounder. Nevertheless, that [act of] pointing out non-existent (*sc.* unreal) defects[529] which is of destructible internal structure, [done] out of enmity--inasmuch as it is specified in the place of [correct] criticism, inasmuch as it does not produce the effect of that [correct criticism and] inasmuch as [the act of] pointing out defects in a correct proof is [nothing but] twaddle—[falsely] looks like [proper] criticism hence it is **'the fallacy of criticism'**[530]. That whose **'name'**, [i.e.] denotation, is that very [fallacy of criticism] is that whose [nature] is such, [i.e. that which 'bears the name of the fallacy of criticism']. The pointing out of defects of corrupt words, [defects of] rhetoric ornamentation[531], etc.—even though the probandum has [already] been proved, inasmuch as an efficacious proof has been specified—**'bears the name of the fallacy of criticism'**, as well. By the speech element **'but'**, that has the adversative meaning[532], [the author] demonstrates that the objective of undertaking a debate is to prove the real thing[533], because that [i.e. the fact that the debate aims at proving the real thing,] is established,[534] for—inasmuch as corrupt words, etc., are not under discussion (*sc.* taken account of)—revealing of defects by means of these [corrupt words, etc.,] consists in an incoherent twaddle; in the opposite case—inasmuch as the refutation [adduced] by the opponent [could be] established by that much only[535]—the endeavour to search for an efficacious proof would be shattered, because it would have no purpose.

[27.0] Thus, [the author], having [already] demonstrated in the above manner[536] the definition of the conventional cognitive criterion, subdivided into [such] divisions [like] perception, indirect cognition, [inference] for oneself, [inference] for others, etc., now—in order to demolish the opinion of those, who do not accept the absolute cognition, which is ultimate, which can be gained through the cessation of all [karmic] veils [and] whose domain is [constituted by] completely all objects—[being] desirous of stating [explicitly] the definition of that [absolute cognition], says [the following]:

/27/ That whose essence is freed from all veils[537], which shines as [something] absolute is perception representing constantly the essences of all objects[538][539].

[27.1] **'All'** [means] every[thing]; that which veils or by which [something] is veiled is **'veil'**, which means: karmic matter obfuscating the intrinsic nature of that [everything]. And **'all'** that veil means **'all veils.'**[540] That whose **'essence'**, [i.e. whose] intrinsic nature, is **'freed from'** those [veils, i.e.] devoid of those [veils], is that whose [nature] is such [as described, namely 'that whose essence is freed from all veils']. For this very reason, **'absolute'** [means] unaccompanied [by anything], because—inasmuch as destruction-cum-subsidence of [karmic] veils is nothing but manifold—cognitive awareness operates as multiform, whereas—when [karmic] veils in their totality are shattered—this [cognitive awareness] alters [and becomes] nothing but uniform due to lack of causes of obstruction. Hence that **'which shines'** independent of other [kinds of] cognition—which means: unfolds itself, [i.e.] radiates unconditionally[541]—is perception on the level of the ultimate truth. Thus, [the author]—having [heretofore] described this [absolute cognition] by means of [its] causes, [viz.] as **'that whose essence is freed from all veils'** as well as according to [its] intrinsic nature by [the clause] **'which shines as [something] absolute'**—now he describes [the absolute cognition] by the means of [its] effects, [and] states [the following]. [The compound] **'representing constantly the essences of all objects'** [is to be solved as]: **'representing constantly'**, [i.e.] revealing incessantly, **'the essences of all objects'**, [i.e.] the intrinsic natures of each and every real thing. That by which something is represented is **'representation'**, which is tantamount to cognition intended [to be] qualified by difference of the cognitive subject as consisting in a property. And this [cognition] is ultimate, inasmuch as the meaning of the speech element ['perception'] is explicable as taken literally. For it is as follows: the speech element 'perceiving organ' is synonymous to living element; and consequently that which operates with regard to the living element is perception[542], with regard to which a direct activity of a cognitive subject [takes place]. The conventional [perception], however, is on the level of the ultimate truth—inasmuch as [it] is produced[543] by the activity of a cognitive subject that is separated (*sc.* mediated) by the senses—nothing but an indirect cognition, just like the cognition of fire [inferred] from smoke, because there is no difference [concerning the fact of] obscuring [in both cases].[544]

[27.2] And now [an objection is raised by the opponent]: '*Definiens*, being not [yet] well-known, is introduced as something new, after *definiendum*, which [itself] is well-known, has been called to mind—this principle [is followed] in all cases. When *definiendum*, however, were not well-known, then *definiens*, when being stated [explicitly], would become destitute of [its] domain, like the *definiens* "flowers" [with regard to the unknown *definiendum*:] "a cluster of sky lotuses"[545]. So what is the intention of [the author] who states [explicitly] the *definiens* without vindicating [beforehand] this [absolute cognition] in accordance with its intrinsic nature?' Regarding this [objection, we] riposte as follows: for all those whose discerning organs are filled with wrong self-conceit, who are of a different opinion regarding that [absolute cognition], even though [the absolute cognition] is well-known through cognitive criteria, [the author] demonstrates hereby—inasmuch as these are [people whose] minds are blinded in their thoughts—that [the absolute cognition] has to be concluded [as real].[546] If [these people question]: 'What cognitive criterion demonstrates this [absolute cognition]?,' we reply [adducing] these two [following proof formulae].

[27.3] [Proof formula no.1] '[1. the thesis:] the clear perception, whose domain is the range of all real things, is possible,[547] [2. the logical reason:] inasmuch as the inference whose domain are [all] these [things] can be drawn; [3. the invariable concomitance accompanied by the example:] in this world, for any *x*, if inference, whose domain is *x*, is drawn, perception grasping *x* reaches somehow the path of rising (*sc.* occurs), like [the inference as well as the perception] of fire, [viz. fire can be inferred as well as perceived]; [4. the application:] and inference is [indeed] drawn, whose province are all objects; [5. the conclusion:] hence, there must be also a clear perception, that recognises these [all objects].' If [those people ask]: 'What is [this] inference, whose province are all objects, [that] is drawn?', likewise we reply the following: '[1. the thesis:] In this world, everything whatever exists, experiences [a] continued existence, [b] rise and [c] termination[548], [2. the logical reason:] because it is the real thing; [3. the invariable concomitance accompanied by the example:] whatever is the real thing, is embraced by [a] continuity, [b] birth and [c] disintegration, for instance: snapping one's fingers with regard [a] to the act (or sound?) of snapping one's fingers, [b] to the act of bending [and flicking one's fingers] and [c] to the act of straightening [one's fingers]; [4. the application:] and the real thing is [indeed] that which exists; [5. the conclusion:] therefore that [real thing] has to be ascertained as being under the sway of (*sc.* encompassed by) the triad under discussion, [viz. as undergoing continuity, origination and termination].' This very inference of the multiplex [reality], whose domain are all objects, becomes the clear perception because—when all [karmic] veils have ceased due to the culmination of repeated practice of cognition and [of repeated practice] of action[549]—there are no [more] causes obstructing [cognition]. And when the cogniser, even though inference has been drawn, does not become active (*sc.* omniscient), inasmuch as [his cognitive activity] has no object, a deviation [from the above inference proving the absolute cognition]—consisting in the impossibility of perception whose domain is the inferendum—should not be put forward as an objection, because the possibility [of such a perception grasping the inferendum is first] intended as the probandum [in the thesis: 'the clear perception, whose domain is the range of all real things, is possible']. There is no deviation concerning the possibility *per se*, either, because all inferentia are pervaded (*sc.* encompassed), inasmuch as [such an absolute] perception is possibly existent.

[27.4] [Proof formula no.2] Or, we [can] draw inference in another manner: '[1. the thesis:] the cognitive subject is such whose complete purification is possible, [2. the logical reason:] because the means for [his] purification exists; [3. the invariable concomitance accompanied by the example:] in this world, whatever is such the means for the purification [of which] exists is [also] such the complete purification of which is possibly existent[550], like a particular gem for the purification of which the means exists, [namely] prolonged calcination in a clay furnace[551] with the alkali, etc.; [4. the application:] and indeed the cognitive subject is such for whose purification the means exists, [namely] repeated practice of cognition, etc.[552]; [5. the conclusion:] hence [the cognitive subject is] such whose complete purification is possibly existent.' And the cognitive subject, [when] completely purified, is called the absolute, because there is no difference at all[553] between cognition and cogniser[554]. If [an objection is raised]: 'How could repeated practice of cognition, etc., possibly be a cause of purification?', we say: [repeated practice of cognition, etc., can be a cause of purification] because it consists in counteractive measures[555] [directed] against impurities of [karmic] veils. If [another objection is raised]: 'How could it possibly be concluded that it consists in the counteractive measures?', [we reply]: because it is precisely your view[556]. For it is as follows: every moment it is seen [as an empirical fact] that the annihilation of [karmic] veils [takes place] on account of repeated practice of cognition, etc., because one experiences cognitive awareness, etc., which is the effect of this [repeated practice of cognition, etc., and] which [becomes] gradually more and more distinct; when, however, its culmination [is reached], then complete destruction [of karmic veils] should take place—we take such a position. On account of that, what some [thinkers][557] have taught—namely 'The sensation of all objects is taught to be the domain of a sixth cognitive criterion called absence [as negative proof], since it goes beyond the domain of the quintuplet of cognitive criteria beginning with perception [up to presumption]'—is not proper because the possibility of this [cognition grasping all objects can be] demonstrated by inference, inasmuch absence [as negative proof] is not proved to operate with regard to the quintuplet of cognitive criteria[558]. Furthermore, how could you ascertain the following: 'The quintuplet of cognitive criteria does not function as having as its domain that [cognition of all objects]?' [Can you deny the possibility of omniscience] [1] by the invariable concomitance [limited to] a specific place and time or [2] by ascending to all places and times? [Ad 1] If the first alternative [is assumed], then just the way the quintuplet of cognitive criteria—negating the domain which is that [particular pot]—proves the absence of the pot, etc., in a certain place, in the same way that [quintuplet of cognitive criteria]—negating also the domain which is the sensation of all real things—could prove the absence [of the sensation of all real things] delimited by a specific location and [specific] circumstances, but not everywhere. And consequently, that [sensation of all objects] would be difficult to negate, like the pot, etc. [Ad 2] If the second alternative [is maintained], it is not possible at all, for [only a person] perceiving directly sensations of the lot of people occurring in all places and times is entitled to express himself in that manner, namely 'There is no sensation of all objects anywhere,' [but] not you because [you] do not accept the possibility [of existence] of such a person. In the opposite case, precisely such a [person] who—having determined [the facts himself]—stated [explicitly the denial of the possibility of an omniscient person] in this manner, indeed such a [person] would be someone who has insight into the cognition pervading the range of all real things. Hence, the sensation whose domain are all objects is proved. So let [us] leave this alone[559].

[28.0] Thus, as regards the province (*sc.* the topic for our discussion) [which is] cognitive criterion, having [first] revoked in the above manner[560] the difference of opinions as regards the definition and number[561] now [the author]—without revoking [for the time being] the difference of opinions as regards the domain [of cognitive criteria[562]], whose turn has come, because [this question] needs to be discussed at length—[being] desirous of rebutting the difference of opinions as regards the effect [of cognitive criteria], to begin with, says [the following]:[563]

/28/ The direct result of cognitive criterion is the cessation (*sc.* removal) of nescience; [the result] of the absolute [cognition] is [both] happiness and indifference; [the result] of the remaining [ones] is the faculty of appropriation and avoidance[564].

[28.1] Surely, **'the result of cognitive criterion'** is twofold, [namely] direct and indirect, which means: immediate and separated [in time] (*sc.* eventual). Out of these two [results], **'direct'** is [such a] **'result of cognitive criterion'** [which is] **'the cessation,'** [i.e.] effecting absolutely disintegration, of **'nescience'**, [i.e.] non-apprehension, [or] non-determination of the cognoscible, because this [cognitive criterion] operates by means of demolishing nescience. And because this [nescience] leads astray the cogniser, inasmuch as it is the root of all misfortune, it is proper beyond any doubt that the disappearance of this [nescience] is the purpose [of cognitive criteria]. And this immediate purpose—inasmuch as all acts of cognition have one form—is taught in general (*sc.* once for all varieties cognitive criteria). On the other hand, [the author] describes the purpose separated [in time] (*sc.* eventual) individually: [the result] **'of the absolute [cognition]'**, [i.e.] of an omniscient person's cognition, is **'happiness'**, [i.e.] an experience of highest joy beyond corporeal happiness[565] [as well as] **'indifference'**, [i.e.] abiding in a state of equanimity because, although one experiences all objects directly, there is no wish to appropriate or to avoid—which means that these two, [viz.] **'[both] indifference and happiness'** [constitute] the result [of the absolute cognition]. That **'faculty of appropriation and avoidance'**, [namely] **'the faculty'**, [i.e.] the knowledge, of these two, [viz.] 'of appropriation and avoidance'—[wherein] **'appropriation'** [means] to grasp [and] **'avoidance'** [means] to evade—is tantamount to the result **'of the remaining [ones]'**, [i.e.] of [every] cognitive criterion of ordinary people [which is] different from that [absolute cognition]. And therefore, such a desire to appropriate [things] worth appropriating, like [spiritual qualities, e.g.] correct conation, etc.[566], and [material things, e.g.] garlands, sandal wood, etc., as well as such a desire to avoid [things] that should be avoided, like wrong conation, etc., and [material things, e.g.] poison, thorns, etc., should be proved through cognitive criterion, because [these two desires] could not be proved by something which is not a cognitive criterion, inasmuch as it is unjustified to assume that [people] whose actions are preceded by deliberation undertake [an action] on account of that [something which is not a cognitive criterion]. The above is what [the aphorism] amounts to.

[29.0] Now, [the author] rebuts the difference of opinions as regards the domain [of cognitive criterion]:

/29/ The real thing, whose essence is multiplex, [forms] the domain of all acts of awareness; an object qualified by [only] one facet is known as the province of the viewpoint.

[29.1] The one **'whose essences'**, viz. [whose] intrinsic natures, [consist in] '**multi**-[ple]', [i.e. in] many aspects or properties—[wherein 'divisions or properties' paraphrase the suffix] **'°-plex'**—is such **'whose essence is multiplex.'** What is that [thing whose essence is multiplex]? [It is] **'the real thing'**, which is [both] external and internal, [and] **'[forms] the domain'**, [i.e. forms] the province, **'of all acts of awareness'**, [i.e.] of each and every act of cognisance[567]. By this [part of the verse, the author] demonstrates the exclusion (*sc.* impossibility) of a stream of sensations without a multiplex [object][568], because even erroneous sensations operate as being capable of illuminating a multiplex [object]; yet it is agreed that they are no cognitive criteria, inasmuch as they are misleading with regard to certain aspects [of reality]. Thus, the following is the intention [of the author]: [some people maintain]: 'Even if the sensation as such cannot operate without a multiplex [object], then a cognitive criterion, that constitutes a particular [variety] of this [sensation], will operate [only] with regard to one facet [of the object]'—[all] that palaver is such the occasion for which is cast off far away, [viz. such a reasoning is groundless]; nevertheless many people whose discerning organs are possessed with beginningless wrong predilection [and] whose [organs of] understanding are deceived by erroneous views are of a different opinion as regards this [question of a multiplex object]. In view of the above, cognitive criterion is [explicitly] stated to prove [that] the domain of all cognitive criteria is a multiplex [object. The proof formula proving the thesis that the object of cognition is the multiplex object can be drawn as follows]:[569] '[1. the thesis:] in this world, whatever is a cognitive criterion, it [also] grasps the real thing that is accompanied by multiple properties not detached from each other[570]; [2. the logical reason:] because this [multiplex object] alone is represented in that [cognitive criterion]; [3. the invariable concomitance accompanied by the example:] in this world, [if an object] *x* occurs in [a cognitive criterion (cognition)] *y*, this [object] *x* alone should be accepted as the domain of this [cognitive criterion (cognition)] *y*; thus, [for instance]:[571] just the way a [scarlet] China rose flower is being represented as roseate in perception having its origin in flawless[572] eyesight, exactly as such (*sc.* as a roseate object) it is accepted as the domain of that [cognitive criterion]; [4. the application:] and [similarly] the real thing, both external and internal, endowed with a form that is under the sway of multiplex essential natures not separate from each other[573], unfolds itself in all cognitive criteria; [5. the conclusion:] hence, this [multiplex object] alone is the domain of those [all cognitive criteria].'[574]

[29.2] And the defect of being unproved, etc.[575], [in the case] of this logical reason[576] can not be demonstrated by disciples of Kaṇāda and Akṣapāda, to begin with, who are propounders of the relationship between the property-possessor and [its] properties, that are mutually disconnected[577], because without accepting that [multiplex object] the real thing intended by them would not [secure any real] position[578]. For it is as follows: how could many properties occur in one [and the same] property-possessor, [if their] constitution [is] different from this [property-possessor]? [Obviously, being absolutely different from the property-possessor, properties could not occur in it] because [that would lead to] the undesired consequence that these [properties] would occur[579] everywhere, inasmuch as there is no differentiation regarding the difference [between properties and their property-possessor and the difference between properties and every other thing]. If [you, the Naiyāyika-Vaiśeṣika, assume]: '[The properties] do not occur anywhere else because of their inherence in that very [property-possessor],' well, [we shall reply then that] if this inherence, in its turn, subsists even without [assuming] the relationship between something-to-be-supported and something-which-supports, then that would absurdly imply [their presence] indiscriminately everywhere, because there is no difference concerning the absence of this [relationship between something-to-be-supported and something-which-supports]. If [you concede the point to us]: 'There is indeed the relationship between something-to-be-supported and something-which-supports,' woe! then you are vanquished, inasmuch as something-which-supports multiple [properties] turns out to have a multiple essential nature, because if [something-which-supports] is deprived of that [multiple essential nature], it would not be the case that there is something that supports multiple [properties]. For, by this very essential nature by which [the property-possessor, whose multiplexity is denied,] supports one [property, it can] not [support] a second [property], because this [essential nature of the property-possessor] is employed for that very [particular property] alone, inasmuch as the essential nature that [may] support a second [property] originates [only] by means of bringing that [first essential nature] to the termination; in the other case, [the property-possessor] would remain as supporting only one [property], because there is [only] one essential nature of that [property-possessor]. If [you reply:] '[The property-possessor] supports [its properties] through [its] different endowments, not through [its] different essential natures; hence it is not multiplex,' then [you] should tell [us] how these [different endowments] occur in this [property-possessor]? If [your] riposte [is]: 'These different endowments occur in the property-possessor] by inherence,' then how [is it at all possible]—without the relationship between something-to-be-supported and something-which-supports—that this [inherence], in its turn, [does] not [operate] everywhere? In this way, [there immediately] follows the foregoing criticism—[as if] clinging at the back [of such an argumentation of yours]. If, on the other hand, the relationship between something-to-be-supported and something-which-supports is accepted in its turn, then—again on account of the logical reasoning demonstrated [above that proves that the property-possessor] has a multiplex essential nature—the very same [foregoing criticism] comes back with reference to the false assumption [regarding] endowments as different from something-which-supports [these] endowments (*sc.* from their property-possessor). So, there is no escape from the multiplex [property-possessor], even if properties are falsely assumed as [absolutely] different [from the property-possessor]. Thereupon, it is better to accept, having avoided enmity [against the theory of the multiplexity of reality] at the very outset, that the real thing is possessed of multiple properties. What is the use of conjecturing, indeed out of place (unreasonably), the [absolute] difference [between the property-possessor and its properties] which itself [involves] trouble?! Furthermore, if one accepts multiplex [property-possessor], the advantage is the following: in [the case of related pairs, e.g.] the connected [attribute] and connection, the inherent [property] and inherence, the quality and quality-bearer, the part and the whole, the manifest particular entity and the universal, etc., [when the elements of the each pair are taken] as [absolutely] separate from each other, [1] such a net of criticism which falls with reference to the issue of occurrence of [such related substrata like] connection, inherence, quality-bearer, the whole, the universal, etc., with regard to [their relata like] the connected [attribute], the inherent [property], the quality, the part, the particular, etc., [respectively][580], also turns out to be [easily] avoided, because this [criticism] is explicable (*sc.*) only in [the case of] the absolute difference [between property-possessor and its properties, whereas] [2] this [criticism] is not established in [the case of] a multiplex [property-possessor]. [Ad 1] For it is as follows: [such related substrata like] connection, etc., can be conceived by means of alternatives [to be], as one should realise, different from [their relata like] the connected [attribute], etc.—namely[581], how do these [related substrata] in these [relata]? Do [they occur] [1.1] [piece] by piece or [1.2] in their totality? [Ad 1.1] If [they are assumed to occur with regard to their relata piece] by piece, that is not proper because [1.1.1] these [related substrata like connection, etc.][582] are accepted to have no parts. [1.1.2] Even when [these related substrata were assumed that] to have parts, then [1.1.2.1] if [these related substrata] were not different from these parts, on account of that [having parts] the multiplex [object] would be entailed, because one [thing would] turn out to have multiple parts. [1.1.2.2] If [these related substrata] were different [from these parts, you] should tell [us]: how [these related substrata] occur with regard to these [parts] in their turn? [Do these related substrata occur with regard to their parts] [1.1.2.2.a] [piece] by piece or [1.1.2.2.b] in their totality? [Ad 1.1.2.2.a] If the alternative [is assumed that these related substrata occur with regard to their parts piece] by piece, the very same [criticism][583] comes back, hence [the fallacy of] *regressus ad infinitum* [results]. [Ad 1.2 = Ad 1.1.2.2.b] If [these related substrata are assumed to occur with regard to their parts/relata] in their totality, that [assumption] is not any better, either, because [that would lead to] the undesired consequence of the plurality of [these related substrata like] connection, etc., inasmuch as they would be [already] complete in every individual case (*sc.* with regard to each and every particular part / relatum). [Ad 2] On the other hand, [these related substrata like] connection, etc., as non-different from these [relata], are not exposed to [any of these destructive] alternatives.[584] If [you argue]: 'Even if [one assumed] the alternative of the non-difference [between the related substrata and their relata,] there would [either] be [the related substrata like] connection, etc., and nothing else, or [their relata like] the connected [attribute], etc., and nothing else,' [we reply:] no, [there would not,] because this [non-difference between the related substrata and their relata] is not accepted as absolute either. Rather, all these [related substrata and their relata], with no exception, are accepted as such the intrinsic natures of which are mutually not disjoined [but] the difference [between which] can be displayed according to the intention (*sc.* if one wishes to)[585] because they, being of that kind, are capable of revoking the amassment of criticism generated by alternatives of defective reasoning, inasmuch as they are represented precisely as being of this kind in all unsubverted representations (*sc.* acts of cognition), for, otherwise, if [the related substrata and their relata] were [falsely] assumed to be manifested as representations differently, [one would] arrive—by means of discarding empirical facts (*sc.* what is experienced) and of falsely assuming fiction (*sc.* what is not experienced)[586]—at nonsense; and thus [such false theories] like the monistic doctrine of the absolute or the theory of the universal emptiness, etc., would attain correctness (*sc.* prove correct), because there is no difference [regarding the principle of discarding empirical facts and of falsely assuming fiction].

[29.3] By the same [argumentation], also the disciples of Kapila, [viz. the propounders of Sāṁkhya], who are desirous of stating [explicitly] the defect of being unproved, etc., [in the case] of this logical reason[587], are brought to speechlessness. For it is as follows: how could they—who [themselves] define explicitly one internal sensation as such whose form is under the sway of (*sc.* reflects) infinite properties and transient occurrences such as various [emotions like] joy, distress, etc., and [who define explicitly] an external object like a pot, etc., as such whose body is resting upon multiple essential natures such as new, old, etc., or roundness, being made of earth, etc.—venture to recount [something] that is contrary to that [multiplex object]?! If [you, the Sāṁkhya, argue in the following manner]: 'Only the single substance consisting of the primordial matter and the supreme being is really existing; whereas [any] transient occurrence producing an error of modes is ultimately unreal,' [we reply]: no, [that is not true], because it is not possible to deny—without arbitrary partiality (*sc.* unless you evince arbitrary partiality)—one of both of them (*sc.* substance and modes) that appear in all cognitive criteria, that are not subverted [and] that [serve as] the foundation to all everyday practice. If that were the case, [viz. if it were possible to draw a line of distinction between substance and modes and designate them either as real or unreal], it would be difficult to preclude [a person], who is arbitrarily partial towards modes, [from] drawing [such an] undesired conclusion: 'Only transient occurrence is really existing, whereas substance is false.' If you took the following position: 'Substance is real, inasmuch as its form is invariable in all cases (*sc.* it never alters in time or space), whereas modes are variable (*sc.* they change in time and space), hence they are unreal,' [we would say:] that is not proper. Namely because one cannot teach the following: 'Substance endures in all cases, inasmuch as it consists in non-difference, but modes are isolated, inasmuch as they consist in difference;[588] nevertheless, this [substance] is real, [whereas] the other ones (*sc.* modes) are false,' for on account of [saying] that much only: '[the] blue [thing] does not possess yellow form,' [one can] not [maintain] that this [blue thing] is unreal, because that would have too far-reaching consequences, inasmuch as everything would turn out to be false, for [every thing] comes into being by avoiding the form of other [things]. If you adduce [the following two] proofs: '[1. the thesis:] modes are nothing but substance, [2. the logical reason:] because they are not different from this [substance]; [3. the example:] just like its intrinsic nature,' or '[1. the thesis:] modes do not exist as different from substance; [2. the logical reason:] because they are devoid of their essential nature; [3. the example:] just like a [non-existent] sky flower,' if that were the case, who could ward off [the likelihood of] someone else adducing [the following two] proofs: '[1. the thesis:] substance is nothing but modes; [2. the logical reason:] because it is not different from these [modes]; [3. the example:] just like their intrinsic nature,' or '[1. the thesis:] substance does not exist as different from modes; [2. the logical reason:] because it is devoid of modes; [3. the example:] just like a sky lotus'?! Thus, one comprehends (*sc.* observes) no difference whatsoever with regard to both these alternatives.[589] Hence, precisely the way the real thing appears (*sc.* is represented) in all cognitive criteria as something which is possessed of infinite modes occurring concurrently and consecutively[590], exactly as such [it] has to be accepted. And in such a way it has been established that—since there is no other [thing than the multiplex object]—'this [multiplex object] alone is the domain of these [cognitive criteria]'[591].

[29.4] Similarly, among the followers of the Buddha's teaching as well, the Sautrāntika[592], to begin with, cannot demonstrate that this logical reason[593] is unproved, because—without acceptance of this [multiplex object]—the foundations of their own doctrine are inexplicable. For it is as follows: one external cause, to begin with, is acknowledged to produce multiple effects, inasmuch as it falls within (*sc.* is included in) various causal complexes; for instance: [one visible] form simultaneously produces a moment posterior to itself as well as the cognition plunging in it (*sc.* apprehending this form), etc.[594] And if [it were indeed] the fact [that an external cause]—which occurs in one moment [and] which indeed experiences difference on account of the difference of [various] causal complexes—produces various effects in different places, then, if that were the case, the criticism brought forward [by the Sautrāntika] against the thesis about the permanence [of things and in support of his doctrine of momentariness][595] would fall onto his own head (*sc.* it would turn back against the Sautrāntika himself), because [that would lead to] the undesired consequence that also this [cause]—in exactly the same manner[596] [as in the case of the thesis about the permanence criticised by the Sautrāntika]—would not be different, even though it would execute effects [that belong to] different points of time. And thus, the acceptance of the difference between individual things, whose forms perish in a moment (*sc.* that are momentary), etc., due to the difference in [their] representation would, in such a way, [prove to] be bereft of any foundation (*sc.* justification), because that would lead to the unwelcome consequence that for substance, although it possesses unchangeability, there would be no contradiction—inasmuch as it is comprised (*sc.* included) in the totality of various causes—in [its] producing [various] effects characterised by the appearance of [different] new and old modes, etc., [as well as by the appearance of various] forms, tastes, smells, [sensations of] touch[597]. Furthermore, this [Sautrāntika]—[even] while observing directly one [and the same] form, which pervades its own parts (*sc.* which is homogeneous) [and] which is prone to continue in another point of time (*sc.* appears permanent)—should argue for individual things [to be] characterised by infinitesimal atoms perishing in a moment, not otherwise, because—in accordance with [his] intention—the appearance of these [individual things] is not apprehended even in the state of dreaming. And while declaring—due to the revocation of [the essential] difference [of the observable thing] from what is not observable—that the observable [thing] is identical with (*sc.* stands in the relation of essential identity to) these [individual things that are invisible, he himself] corroborates the multiplex appearance of [an object] by [his own] words! For it is as follows: an individual thing—although its spherical form [composed of] infinitesimal atoms is unobservable [and] its [every] transient occurrence is momentary—demonstrates its intrinsic nature as something whose essence is persistent, gross, etc.; otherwise, [i.e. if an individual thing could not visibly manifest itself], it would immediately follow that the whole world is deeply asleep [without images], because—if that [individual thing could] not be revealed [as persistent, gross, etc.—that would lead to] the undesired consequence that also another cognitive criterion (*sc.* inference) that communicates the individual thing as something absolutely different [from the visible object we perceive]—could not operate. Analogously, how could the appearance of the multiplex [object seem] incorrect to a [person] who accepts [any] internal sensation—[consisting in] the representation [that is both] directed outwards and directed inwards, [that is both] accompanied by the conceptual and non-conceptual [aspects], [that is both] erroneous and non-erroneous, etc.,[598] with regard to the intrinsic nature of an object—[to be] one!? Likewise, how could a [person]—who permits of [any] sensation, tinted with[599] [various] forms consigned [to that sensation] by the multitude of objects abiding in diverse places, to be] one, although there is the difference (*sc.* plurality) in forms [that are represented in that sensation, and their plurality has to be accepted] because otherwise a determinate cognition [apprehending various] objects, [for instance] something white, something not white, etc., [that] appear simultaneously, would be inexplicable—consider, by the force of multiple transient occurrences of [such emotions like] joy, distress, etc., taking place in different instants, the difference of these [transient occurrences] in the absolute sense? [Obviously, he cannot consistently hold such a position], because [these both, i.e. sensations of the external object and introspective sensations (emotions), are] based on one and the same productive-supportive principle[600]. If [the Sautrāntika argues in the following manner]: 'There is the oneness of forms located within the awareness [that] occur simultaneously, [but] not [the oneness] of [such emotions like] joy, etc., because [emotions] are contrary to these [forms that enter the cognition][601],' [we shall reply:] no, [that is not true] because [such an assumption would lead to] the undesired consequence that there would be no difference among [external] objects to be established by the efficacy of these [apprehended forms][602], due to the fact that—inasmuch as these [forms] would be one—the cognition concerning [a multitude of objects such as] something white, something yellow, etc., would be non-distinguished (*sc.* undifferentiated) because of having the form of nothing but cognitive awareness[603]. Thus—since the individual thing has been established through cognitive criteria in the above manner[604] to have [both] one and multiplex form [both] externally and internally[605], because otherwise it would be unjustified to assume the foundations of the views accepted by these [Sautrāntikas]—the

[Sautrāntika] realist is not in a position to disprove the revelation of the multiplex [object in the cognition].

[29.5] Analogously, the rope of [arguments establishing] the revelation of the multiplex [object] inevitably ensnares also [a person] who has accepted the teaching of the Yogācāra[-Vijñāna-vāda school][606], because [the Yogācāra] accedes to [the fact] that cognition, although being one, unfolds itself as having the multiple form of the cogniser and the cognoscible. If [the Yogācāra Buddhist argues in the following manner]: '[One has to accept] the oneness of this [cognition], because of one and the same productive-supportive principle[607],' [we shall reply:] no, [that is not true] because [such assumption would lead to] the undesired consequence of oneness of all personal series (*sc.* people) who simultaneously [undergo] rise and disintegration [and] cognise [the same object] concurrently. If [the Yogācāra Buddhist comes up with the following thesis]: 'Since multiplexity is shown by the empirical truth[608], that [argument presents] no impairment to [the idea of] ultimately real oneness that is perceived directly through self-cognition[609],' [we shall reply:] no, [it is not true] because of the unwelcome consequence that the teaching of the propounder of the absolute[610] (*sc.* Advaita-vedāntin) [could] not negated, [either], because it is not difficult for that [Advaita-vedāntin], too, to demonstrate the following: the absolute—although it is one, without gradation (*sc.* changeless), endowed with consciousness [and] perceived directly through self-cognition—is observed, by the force of the beginningless nescience, as manifold, as endowed with gradation (*sc.* changing), as [both] conscious and unconscious [and] as extra-sensory and not extra-sensory, just like the distinct [pure mental] sensation in the form of something-to-be-grasped and something-which-grasps [that is] conceived by you. Or, let the appearance of the multiplex [object] be erroneous, nevertheless it is not observed that the sensation (*sc.* consciousness) is non-dualistic, because if it were observed [to be non-dualistic] then all creatures would immediately attain liberation in this very moment.[611] Yet, this [sensation (*sc.* consciousness)] is somehow observed [to be multiplex]; because in the opposite case [that would lead to] the undesired consequence of the destruction of the entire everyday practice like in the state of deep sleep [with no images]. Therefore, inasmuch as [the sensation] is [sometimes] observed and [sometimes] unobserved, it is hardly possible to d ıy the multiplex representation [in the case] of sensation, although [the sensation is] one. Hence, the [Yogācāra-]Vijñāna-vādin, too, should remain silent[612] regarding the presentation of [evidence demonstrating] this logical reason to be unproved.

[29.6] [As regards the thesis] of the propounder of the theory of the universal emptiness (*sc.* Śūnya-vādin):[613] 'The revelation of the multiplex [object] is unproved, because nothing exists,'[614] [we claim:] no, [that is not true]; it is also not possible for that [Śūnya-vādin][615]—if [both] cognitive criteria and the cognoscible [are supposed by him to be] non-existent—to communicate the non-existence of everything;[616] otherwise there would be no [means for the Śūnya-vādin to] invalidate the words[617] of the [Sāṁkhya] opponent[618], either, who expresses [an opposite idea that is] not [proved by] cognitive criteria such as [the following thesis of the Sāṁkhya]:

'everything exists everywhere';[619] if these [cognitive criteria and the cognoscible] were accepted[620] [that would be tantamount to] the impairment of the [very] acceptance [of his own doctrine].[621] Consequently, both of them, [viz. cognitive criteria and the cognoscible,] are revealed as multiplex, like [any object] shown [in the cognition], hence the logical reason [in question] is not unproved. Even if [there appears] a sensation, while coming into contact with the complex of a mirage in a desert, in which water is manifested, you will not doubt that this [manifestation of water]—inasmuch as it is not accepted as a [real] domain [of our cognition]—is inconclusive[622], because this [manifestation of water] is erroneous, for [solely] the non-erroneous revelation [can be] the cause for the acceptance of this [object represented in the sensation as really existent[623]]. If you argue: 'Also this [non-erroneous revelation] is [in reality] erroneous, because it is subverted by the cognitive awareness of [a thing] perishing in a moment (*sc.* momentary), viz. of infinitesimal atoms detached from each other,' that is not proper, because [then the following dilemma arises]: is the cognitive awareness of these [infinitesimal atoms] [1] the comprehension (*sc.* perception) *per se* or [2] the ascertainment (*sc.* conceptual process) *per se*. [Ad 1] If the first alternative [were adopted], then inference would be shattered, because [inference] would be void of its domain, due to the fact that, [firstly], one would accept—out of fear of contradiction[624]—that real things are by all means grasped by the non-conceptual, distinct perception, which is [in our case] nothing but the content of the first alternative[625], and, [secondly,] if [the real thing can] be apprehended by [one] cognitive criterion (*sc.* perception), another cognitive criterion (*sc.* inference) is purposeless, inasmuch as [otherwise, when cognitive criteria were admitted to overlap], one would arrive at the [fallacy of] *regressus ad infinitum*. [Ad 2] If the second [alternative were accepted], then, if that were the case, all non-conceptual [perception] would attain the status of cognitive invalidity. Besides, the ascertainment (*sc.* conceptual process) does not subvert the revelation of the multiplex [object]; on the contrary, [the ascertainment] corroborates [it], because it show itself precisely as such (*sc.* as multiplex) both externally and internally. If[626] you maintained the following: 'If indeed the real thing is by all means grasped, [then] precisely with regard to this very aspect—concerning which the non-conceptual [perception] gives rise to a subsequent decision accomplishing everyday practice—[this non-conceptual perception] ascends to the [status of] cognitive validity, not with regard to any other [aspect],' then, if that were the case, it would immediately follow that only such an ascertainment (*sc.* conceptual process) could secure cognitive validity, immediately after which a person, [urged] by a desire for a thing capable of efficient action, undertakes [an action], not the non-conceptual [perception]; just like the [sense-object] contact, etc., [which is not a cognitive criterion], even though [the sense-object] produces this [ascertainment].[627] If [you argue in the following manner]: 'It is the non-conceptual [perception] which is the cognitive criterion, because it comprehends a not [yet] comprehended object,[628] not the decisive cognition, because that [decisive cognition] is a conceptualisation,' [we reply]: no, [that is not true], because [that would lead to] the undesired consequence that also the inferential cognition would be invalid like this [decisive cognition, because the inferential cognition is also conceptual]. And the inferential cognition is not marked by distinction (*sc.* is not exceptional) by virtue of being apt to revoke a contrary (*sc.* false) form [of, say, a mirage in a desert], because also the determining cognition is able to obliterate that [contrary (*sc.* false) form], inasmuch as it does not operate with regard to the province not [based on] projection [of an object onto the mind].[629] If [you defend your position as follows]: 'The distinction [that makes the inferential cognition exceptional]—inasmuch as [the inferential cognition] is produced by the triple-formed inferential sign—proves that the inferential cognition is a cognitive criterion,' then we can see your immaturity, for the origination [of the inferential cognition] from direct experience [forms] a grave offence against the determining cognition.[630] Furthermore, just like the non-conceptual [perception], although unobservable [and] disposed towards grasping the individual thing distinguished from everything [else], generates the conceptualisation whose province is [merely] a certain aspect [of the thing and not of other objects], in the same manner nothing but the object, inasmuch as it has entered into contact with sense-organs, light, etc., may produce a direct clear conceptualisation whose province is a certain aspect of its own. In view of the above, [one may wonder]: what is [the use] of assuming a non-conceptual [perception] that resembles[631] a nipple [hanging] from the neck of a she-goat, [viz. something inefficacious and useless]?! If, [in order to refute the multiplexity of reality, you aver]: 'So many [divergent] aspects stand in contradiction [to each other] in [the case of numerically one] external object,' [we question you in order to point out the falsehood and arbitrariness of your thesis:] is it [then] an ordinance of kings that [several faculties such as] the potential, the lack of potential, etc.[632] do not stand in contradiction [to each other] even in [the case of numerically] one perception?! Therefore, even you do not, in any case and anywhere, observe a perception observing an individual thing characterised by infinitesimal atoms perishing in a moment (*sc.* momentary);[633] you simply do not—inasmuch as the discerning organ is tinged with that [individual thing] itself—recognise the non-existence of that [individual thing]. The ascertainment, which pervades its own parts [and] which advances to another point of time, unfolds itself as revealing one [both] external and internal object as well as the cognitive awareness [of that object]; it is not, however, subverted by alternatives of defective reasoning that are without basis; hence [ascertainment] is not erroneous. Furthermore, someone who declares that this [ascertainment] is erroneous uproots the foundations of all cognitive criteria and [all] cognoscible. For it is as follows: precisely that [sensation][634] which is a cognitive criterion with regard to existence, to possessing a form of cognitive awareness, to experiencing happiness, etc., is not a cognitive criterion[635] with regard to the fact of perishing in a moment (*sc.* momentariness), to the fact of being furnished with the power of attaining heaven, etc.; similarly, precisely that real thing which is the cognoscible, inasmuch as its form is [say] blue, quadrangular, erected, etc., is not the cognoscible, inasmuch as [its] transient occurrences, etc., [fall to] the moment of the median segment [of its existence][636], etc.; similarly, precisely that [sensation] which—either as conceptual [cognition] with regard to an external object or as the perception in a dream[637]—is erroneous, is non-erroneous with regard to its own intrinsic nature; similarly, also that [sensation] of two moons, which is false regarding the duality [of the moons], is not false regarding [their] whiteness, [their] movement in a specific place, etc.[638]—[such are instances of] ascertainment [that clearly point out its multiplex nature]. But if you, being afraid of contradiction, denied this [revelation of the multiplex object][639], could you abide by your own intention, having [eventually] accepted [both] cognitive criterion and the cognoscible as absolutely divergent?! Our mind is [filled] with curiosity [regarding that].

[29.7] If the Vijñāna-vādin, having accepted that the revelation of non-duality is indistinctive, took a position that cognitive awareness which possesses [the property of] manifoldness is erroneous, because [cognitive awareness] is subverted by this [non-duality of consciousness, we would object:] that is not proper because [that would lead to] the undesired consequence of discarding empirical facts (*sc.* what is experienced) and of falsely assuming fiction (*sc.* what is not experienced) and because non-conceptual perception, that is indistinctive, has been disproved just a while ago[640]. However, [the Vijñāna-vādin may argue] 'Logical reasoning could subvert the manifold cognitive awareness. For it is as follows: since it is impossible to effect the discrimination between erroneous and non-erroneous sensations, whereas awareness *per se* [remains] undeviating in all cases, [therefore] the non-dualistic sensation revokes the manifold representation of [something] white, of [something] not white, etc., which appears as furnished with multifarious [properties and] the existence of which is shown by the empirical truth produced by past impressions, which have been dormant from beginningless times.' As for this [misconception of the Vijñāna-vādin], we controvert it [as follows]. Would this cognitive awareness whose form is multiplex [1] differ from the non-dualistic sensation or [2] not? [Ad 1] And what [would follow] from this, if [the multiplex cognitive awareness] differed from that [non-dualistic sensation]; how could this [multiplex cognitive awareness], being different [from the non-dualistic sensation], make one infer this non-dualistic sensation, if it is not seen that [the multiplex cognitive awareness] is the result of this [non-dualistic sensation][641]? [Ad 2] If, on the other hand, [one assumed] the alternative of [its] not being different [from the non-dualistic sensation], how could [the multiplex cognitive awareness]—which is multi[plex and] which unfolds itself as identical with (*sc.* standing in the relation of essential identity to) [numerically] one sensation—not demolish non-duality?! If you say the following: 'This [multiplex cognitive awareness][642], which is [marked by] outwards-directed[643] defilement with forms [of external object such as] white, non-white, etc., is—inasmuch as [the multiplex cognitive awareness] is false, because it is shown by the empirical truth—inexplicable by means of [any of the two] alternatives [analysing it as] different or as non-different from the really existing (*sc.* non-dualistic) cognitive awareness,' then, if that were the case, a [hypothetical] opponent [of yours] who claims the following: 'Cognitive awareness is ultimately unreal, because it is shown by nescience, whereas the existence of objects constitutes the truth, because it is invariable in all cases,' would be difficult to negate. If [you argue:] 'Since it is unjustified to assume an insentient [thing] to reveal itself, sensation (*sc.* awareness) is true, not the object,' then we [accordingly] assert: since [numerically] one [sensation] does not have the appearance of multiple [reality], [therefore] the multiplex [cognitive awareness] is true, not non-dual [sensation].[644] If [you reply]: 'Also [this] diverse representation of non-duality is not contradictory in view of the empirical truth,' [then] it would not be too difficult to anticipate the following cunning riposte of a [hypothetical] opponent [of yours], as well: 'It is not contradictory [to assert]—by the force of the beginningless nescience—that also an insentient [thing] reveals itself as consciousness.' Furthermore, since—in view of the fact that consciousness as such, which is defiled by diverse forms, possesses the efficacy of [the relation of] the inexplicability otherwise[645]—this [multiplex consciousness defiled by diverse forms] is proved, [hence] this [hypothetical opponent of the Vijñāna-vādin] could prove the non-dualistic sensation as unproved, for otherwise no proof could be drawn, inasmuch as it would be bereft of [any] foundation. And consequently, someone who proves—on account of [only] one aspect of an object cognised as persistent, gross, etc.—the essential identity of [a series of] momentary modes of disconnected infinitesimal atoms, is not in a position to disprove that propounder of the theory of multiplexity of reality,[646] because the logical reasoning is equal with regard to both of these [alternatives]. Furthermore, the intention of yours (*sc.* of the Vijñāna-vādin) is this: 'Even such a [cognition] which [consists in] this ascertainment of multiple forms [such as something] white, yellow, etc., has a non-dualistic form with regard to self-cognition.' And just the way all cognition is—out of fear of [the fallacy of] *regressus ad infinitum*—accepted [by you] to be self-revealing, similarly all determination should be accepted [by you] to be self-determining, otherwise the defect of *regressus ad infinitum* would necessarily follow in that case and [individual] acts of determination would have to determine [their] intrinsic nature completely, not [piece] by piece, because 'how could such a form which is not determined by [individual] acts of determination [become] their province?'[647]—in such a way, [it has been shown that] this very twaddle of yours is self-abortive. And consequently, if the intrinsic nature, [that is] non-dualistic [and] perishing in a moment (*sc.* momentary), were grasped by these [individual acts of determination], then the mundane world could not arise from the very beginning, because nothing contrary [to that non-duality (*sc.* nothing multiplex)] could be superimposed[648]. Hence, [the Vijñāna-vādin who cherishes] the belief [that the mundane world] is not liberated would [prove himself to] be merely someone [whose reasoning is] void of logical congruity. And [certainly, the state of affairs] is not like that, because the [phenomenon of] coming into being is well-known to every creature. Thus, it is established that this revelation of substance and modes, that are mutually not detached [from each other], is not erroneous, because there is no other cognitive criterion that could present an object that is contrary to that [revelation of substance and its modes as interrelated] to the mind.

[29.8] If propounder of the theory of the universal emptiness (*sc.* Śūnya-vādin), however, declared that this [revelation of substance and its modes as interrelated] is erroneous by the force of the inference drawn in accordance with the opponent's intention[649], namely: 'All acts of cognition are void of the objective substratum, because [they are] acts of cognition, like a cognition in dream,' then an inference contrary [to the former inference] should be presented against him: 'All acts of cognition have the objective substratum, because [they are] acts of cognition, like a cognition of a person in the waking state.' If he pointed out that [our] example lacks the probandum[650], then this [defect of lacking the probandum] should be shown also in his example. If he, however, did not let [the matter] rest [and] announced: 'It is accepted [also] by you that the cognition in dream is void of the objective substratum,' then he should be questioned according to [the following] alternatives: is our acceptance [1] a cognitive criterion for you or [2] not cognitive criterion [for you]? [Ad 1] If [our acceptance] is a cognitive criterion [for you], then why do you—just the way you [administer] the corroboration of the example by the force of this [acceptance that the cognition in dream is void of the objective substratum]—not administer the corroboration of the object which is the domain of the cognition of a person in the waking state, as well? What does this maxim of the semi-senile woman [supposed to mean]?![651] [Ad 2] If [our acceptance] is not a cognitive criterion [for you], then, that being the case, another cognitive criterion proving that the cognition in dream is void of the objective substratum has to be sought for; what is the use of clinging to grass this way or another?![652] Also as regards that another cognitive criterion [proving that the cognition in dream is void of the objective substratum], there arises an impeccable pair of [implausible] sub-alternatives: [2.1] is that [another cognitive criterion] void of the objective substratum or [2.2] does it have the objective substratum? [Ad 2.1] If [you say that another cognitive criterion] is void of the objective substratum, then [you are] no [longer] in a position to assert that another cognition is void of the objective substratum, because [that another cognitive criterion] has no domain [and cannot prove anything]. [Ad 2.2] If [you say that another cognitive criterion] has the objective substratum, then: woe! you are vanquished, because [your thesis initially] asserted: 'All acts of cognition are void of the objective substratum,' is impaired because this very [alternative 2.2 accepted by you, i.e. 'that another cognitive criterion proving the assertion: "the cognition in dream is void of the objective substratum," has the objective substratum,'] is the deviation [from your initial thesis: 'all acts of cognition are void of the objective substratum']. In the above manner, the cunning [Śūnya-vādin] should be turned down with a counter-cunning expedient. Thus, [it has been proved that] this [logical reason of ours] is not inconclusive.

[29.9] The[653] doubt concerning the contrary character [of our logical reason] is, in its turn, simply inapplicable[654] because, as regards the object revealed by cognitive criteria, there is no discord among propounders of all philosophical schools in accepting it that way, [viz. that the object is revealed by cognitive criteria in a multiplex way]. By virtue of this[655], the [attempt]s [of our opponents at] criticism—generated by wrong conceptualisations without basis—[that impute the defects of liability to] suspicion, [of] contradiction, [of] *regressus ad infinitum*, [of] pertinence to disparate loci, [of] impossibility, etc., [to our logical reason], cannot survive because [their] head has been crushed by a thump of a hammer[656] [constituted by] the representation [of multiplex objects in cognition]. Therefore, this logical reason defined as 'the representation in such a manner' (*sc.* as multiplex), being freed from the defects of being unproved, etc., makes opponents accept the fact that the domain of cognitive criterion is the multiplex [object]—so, enough of [any further] detailed [discussion]. Hence, it is established that **'the real thing, whose essence is multiplex, [forms] the domain of all acts of awareness,'** 'because this [multiplex object] alone is represented in that [cognitive criterion].'[657]

[29.10] Thus[658], this domain of cognitive criteria was demonstrated in conformity to the intention of the cogniser who analyses the operation of cognitive criteria corresponding to the state of affairs. But then, of what sort is this [object] a viewpoint expresses? Since there is room for teaching [this issue now, the author] says: **'one'**, etc. That which leads to—[i.e.] which makes one reach [or] which elevates to consciousness—the real thing, [although it is in reality] possessed of infinite properties, as qualified by [only] one property intended by this [viewpoint] itself, is **'the viewpoint'**; that means: the reflection which arises in the point of time posterior to the operation of cognitive criterion. Its **'province'**, [i.e. the viewpoint's] domain, is **'known'**, [viz.] is intended, as **'an object'**, [viz.] a cognoscible form, [that is] **'qualified'**, [i.e. made] different from other forms, **'by [only] one facet'** [i.e.] by a characteristic such as the property of impermanence, etc., because it has been established in accordance with the following intention of ours: 'cognitive criterion grasps only an object of exactly such a kind [viz. possessed of infinite properties].'

[29.11] Alternatively[659], [the author]—having revoked the four-fold difference of opinion concerning the cognitive criterion as regards [its] definition, number, domain and result [already in previous sections][660]—says: **'one'**, etc., [in order to] describe the domain of the viewpoint here in this very [place]. And now [an objection is raised by the opponent]: 'The announcement [made] by the initial sentence was to teach cognitive criterion alone [as the sole objective of this treatise]; so why is this domain of the viewpoint, [although it is] not [the point] under discussion, being taught here [in this treatise]?' That is true, [but what] is [really] meant is the following: the viewpoint does not go very far (*sc.* is not completely different) from cognitive criterion; [but] rather it constitutes, as a matter of fact, a component of that [cognitive criterion] because cognitive criterion is produced by the aggregate of viewpoints;[661] hence, when the announcement to teach that [cognitive criterion as the sole objective of this treatise was made in the initial sentence], also this [viewpoint] was in fact grasped (*sc.* comprised) by virtue of the maxim: 'Something which is incorporated in *x* is grasped by [the very act of] grasping *x*'—consequently, this [viewpoint] cannot but be under discussion[662].

[29.12] Also here, [in this alternative exposition of the hemistich], the meaning of words is the same; simply there is a difference in the meaning of the sentence. For it is as follows: in this [hemistich,] the following combination [of elements is possible]. **'The province of the viewpoint is known'** to logicians [to be] **'an object qualified by [only] one facet.'** And now [an objection is raised by the opponent]: 'If every single domain of the viewpoint is being taught, even though [the viewpoint] falls within (*sc.* is comprised under the concept of) cognitive criterion, then—like [in the case of] cognitive criterion—also the difference of opinion concerning this [viewpoint] as regards [its] definition, etc.[663] should be revoked.' That is true, nonetheless, the process of the viewpoint is not well-known to propounders of other schools, hence—since there is no[thing that could be the] subject [of such a controversy among various schools]—there is no difference of opinion regarding this [viewpoint] whatsoever. Besides, those [propounders of other schools] could not be taught the truth (reality) by means of this [viewpoint], because cognitive criterion alone is operative as regards teaching the truth, whereas the viewpoint, inasmuch as it is related to [only] one facet [of the reality], lacks the efficacy to teach that [truth (reality)]. Precisely for this reason, [that is] no great insouciance [on the part] of the preceptor (*sc.* Siddhasena) even as regards the mention of the gist of its definition, etc.[664] However, [the author]—while emphatically assigning the domain [of the viewpoint] to the inadmissible sphere[665]—teaches [it] explicitly[666]: it does not befit the slow-witted [opponents,] who cleave to their own doctrines[667], [to yield to] the contumacy characterised by the predilection to corroborate [only] one facet [of the real thing], although the real thing is recognised by cognitive criteria as multiplex in its essence. Such [is one plausible reply to the opponent's objection]. Alternatively, [we can say that] by this very mention of the domain [of the viewpoint, the author] indicates—inasmuch as [the very mention of the domain has the] implicative [power]—the definition, etc. (*sc.* number and result), [of the viewpoint] to [opponents] who cleave to their own doctrines. Among these, the [general] definition is as follows: 'The reflection of one facet of an object recognised by cognitive criterion is the viewpoint,' because this [general definition] pertains to all particular viewpoints and because it is capable of distinguishing [among viewpoints of] different forms. According to the number, however, [viewpoints are] infinite, because the real thing is endowed with infinite properties and because [various] outlooks confined to [one] property[668] of this [real thing] are viewpoints.[669] Nevertheless[670], ancient preceptors taught that there are seven viewpoints, by means of assuming seven outlooks that collect together all [possible viewpoints],[671] namely 'there are [following] viewpoints: comprehensive, collective, empirical, direct, verbal, etymological and factual'[672]. Therefore, also we have described them exactly [in the same way].

[29.13] [In order to answer the opponent's objection]: 'How could possibly these [seven vie1wpoints] collect together all outlooks?,' [it] is said: outlook, to begin with, may operate[673] [either] [A] by means of object or [B] by means of speech element, because there is no other logical alternative; furthermore, object [may] consist in the universal or [it may] consist in the particular; speech element, in its turn, [may function] according to the usage and according to the grammatical formation; the grammatical formation, in its turn, may be effected by virtue of a factor [constituted by] the universal or effected by virtue of a factor existing in its point of time, [viz. in the point of time when the grammatical formation is reflected upon]. [Ad A] Among [all] these [possible varieties], all those particular outlooks of the cogniser, with no exception, which are disposed to describe an object are included in the first quadruple of [object-bound] viewpoints. And out of these [four object-bound varieties], [1] the comprehensive [viewpoint] consists in an aggregate of such [outlooks] that consider [jointly] the universal and the particular as being disconnected from each other.[674] [2] The collective [viewpoint], in its turn, is produced[675] out of an amassment of such [outlooks] that affirm solely the universal. [3] The empirical [viewpoint], on the other hand, is produced out of a complex of such [outlooks] that intend an entity, like a pot, etc.—[when it] enters into[676] people's everyday practice—in the case of which [both] the universal and the particular, being of philosophical pertinence, are disregarded. [4] The direct [viewpoint], on the other hand, is combined out of a conglomerate of such [outlooks that] maintain that particulars, perishing in a moment (*sc.* momentary) [and] characterised by infinitesimal atoms, are real. [Ad B. Three speech-bound viewpoints are described.] Similarly, [5] the verbal [viewpoint] is established by a collection of such [outlooks that] affirm that the usage of speech elements [complies] with the linguistic convention.[677] [6] Further, the etymological [viewpoint] is produced out of the multitude of such [outlooks] that affirm that the usage of a linguistic units [complies] with the grammatical formation, and not otherwise. [7] The factual [viewpoint], however, as one should realise, is combined out of a conglomeration of [outlooks that] maintain that speech elements function by taking account of the factor [responsible] for the grammatical formation [and] existing in the present point of time, not otherwise.[678] Thus, it has been established in the above manner[679] that these [seven viewpoints listed above] collect together all [possible] outlooks, because there is not any other alternative referring to[680] the real thing that does not count among this septuplet of the viewpoints.

[29.14] Presently, we describe [every] opinion out of all these [seven viewpoints enumerated above] individually[681]. [Ad A] Among them, [Ad 1] the comprehensive [viewpoint[682] is explained in the following manner]. Comprehending is comprehension, which means discernment. Determined comprehension is the comprehensive discrimination, [that is to say] grasping of multifarious real things, and precisely that is [the comprehensive viewpoint] on account of the rule concerning the affix *aṇ*, that preserves the original meaning [unchanged, and referring] to the grammatical set of patterns of '*prajñā* (understanding), etc.'[683]. Alternatively, [one can explain the derivative meaning of the comprehensive viewpoint as follows:] those which are comprehended discriminatively, i.e. which are discerned in a specific manner, are comprehensible objects; such an outlook which has its existence in these[684] [objects and] which consists in the discriminative discernment is the comprehensive [viewpoint]. Indeed, this [comprehensive viewpoint] intends [1] the highest universal consisting in existence and [2] [lower] intermediate universals, [viz.] substantiality, qualitativeness and the state of being an object of an action, furthermore, [it intends] [3] ultimate particulars consisting in [specific] forms not common to all, as well as [4] intermediate particulars, capable of being distinguished from particulars that have] other form by [the cognition of] recurrent continuity[685, 686] because [these particulars] are in their intrinsic nature absolutely detached from the universal.[687] For, it is like this: as they say, acts of determinate cognition [grasping] entities are located in the awareness, and there is no appearance of the particular in the consciousness grasping the universal because this [universal] is grasped by a reflection of one [and the same] form that endures [unchanged], inasmuch as it is unjustified to assume that [consciousness could] grasp the universal in another way. No universal manifests itself in the sensation which is able to grasp the particular, either, inasmuch as such [a sensation] operates as grasping an entity delimited by its particular location and [by its particular] circumstances, because it is unjustified to assume a sensation of the particular in another way. And, these two, [i.e.] the universal and the particular, both being represented as being different from each other, can not somehow intermingle because that would have too far-reaching consequences, inasmuch as essences[688] of all objects, even though they have [mutually] different representations [in consciousness, would] turn out to be one. And [the propounder of the Nyāya-Vaiśeṣika school] adduces the following proof: '[1. the thesis:] the universal and the particular are disjoined from each other, [2. the logical reason:] because they are comprehended separately; [3. the demonstration of the invariable concomitance accompanied by the example:] in this world, whatever substances[689] are comprehended separately, they are disjoined from each other; for instance: Devadatta and Yajñadatta; [4. the application:] and [indeed] the universal and the particular are comprehended separately; [4. the conclusion:] hence, they are disjoined from each other.' If [the opponent raises an objection against the Nyāya-Vaiśeṣika thesis]: 'There is no comprehension of the particular as separate from the universal,' [the Naiyāyika-Vaiśeṣika asks]: 'Then one should say how the comprehension of this [particular is at all possible]?' If [the opponent says]: '[There is a comprehension] of [the particular as] pervaded by the universal,' [the Naiyāyika-Vaiśeṣika replies]: 'Then this is no [longer] the comprehension of the particular, because through this [comprehension] also the universal is grasped; and therefore the cogniser could—since the particular is not grasped as separate by this cognitive awareness—neither pronounce [any] linguistic unit that expresses this [particular] nor accomplish [any] everyday practice that can be established by virtue of this [particular]. And that is [obviously] not the case because it is an empirical fact that both an explicit statement about, as well as everyday practice with regard to the particular are pronounced/accomplished. Therefore, someone who postulates the particular and who accomplishes everyday practice with regard to this [particular] has to accept that the cognitive awareness grasping this [particular] is separate [from the cognition grasping the universal]. Similarly, if the universal, in its turn, did not appear as having a separate form in the cognition grasping this [universal], then in the very same manner [as it was case of the particular]—since the particular, as well, would be seized by the sensation considered to have this [universal as its] domain—one should speak of the destruction of [any endeavour either to pronounce] an explicit statement about, or to accomplish everyday practice with regard to the universal, inasmuch as both of them, [viz. an explicit statement about, as well as everyday practice with regard to the universal], are rooted in the cognitive awareness that grasps the universal as separate [from the particular], because—if these two were not located in this [cognitive awareness grasping the universal as separate]—that would entail the non-existence of both of them. And, it is not proper to accept either the universal or the particular alone, having ruled out either the particular or the universal alone [respectively][690], because there is no difference between [these two], inasmuch as both of them are represented in the cognition grasping them. Therefore, one is compelled to admit that both of these two, [viz. the universal and the particular], are mutually disconnected.' Such is [the gist of] the comprehensive [viewpoint].[691]

[29.15] [Ad 2] Now, the view of the collective [viewpoint] is described.[692] In this case, the collective [viewpoint] is that which] collects together, [i.e.] it takes the world as consisting in the universal, by means of completely ruling out the particular. For this[693] [view] expresses [the following idea]. Particulars could either be falsely conceived [1] as such whose form differs from the universal consisting in the being or [2] as such whose form does not differ [from this universal], because there is no other logical alternative. Out of these two, [Ad 1] if the first alternative [were assumed], then these [particulars] would appropriate the state of being (*sc.* they would become) devoid of their essential nature, because [they would be] separated from the being, just like a sky lotus, etc. [Ad 2] If the second alternative [is adopted, which is the true one], then [they] result in (*sc.* become) the being alone. For it is as follows: [the following proof formula is supposed by the Monist and the Sāṁkhya, etc., to prove the second alternative]: '[1. the thesis:] the particulars are the being alone; [2. the logical reason:] because [they] are not different from this [being]; [3. the demonstration of the invariable concomitance accompanied by the example:] in this world, if x is not different from y, then x is nothing but y; for instance: the intrinsic nature of the being itself; [4. the application:] and [indeed] the particulars are not different [from the being]; [5. the conclusion:] hence they consist in nothing but in this [being].' And now [the following objection may be raised against the Monist and the Sāṁkhya, etc.]: 'If reality is nothing but the being alone, then—since that [being] is not distinct from everything (*sc.* is identical with all things)—all these everyday practices, well known to every creature, that can be established by virtue of particular real things, such as column, elephant, pitcher, lotus, etc., would reach [their] disintegration (*sc.* would cease to exist) without exception; hence also the particulars have to be accepted as causes of everyday practices.' [To the above objection the Monist and the Sāṁkhya, etc. retorts:] 'That is not [true], because everyday practice is accomplished by the force of beginningless nescience, inasmuch as there is no connection between the reality determined by cognitive criteria [operating] on the level of the ultimate truth [and] this [everyday practice]. Furthermore, in particular the insistence on the particulars should be given up, because there is no cognitive criterion that establishes the particulars. For it is as follows: the particulars consist in difference; and no cognitive criterion at all plunges into (*sc.* cognises) the difference. For perception, to begin with, the existence of which is produced by the being, is able to perceive directly only that [being], not the non-being, [firstly,] because that [non-being]—inasmuch as it has a form deprived of all powers—[can effect] no activity with regard to bringing about this (*sc.* perception), and, [secondly], because—if [it were possible to] perceive directly [an object which] does not bring about [perception]—[that would lead to] the undesired consequence of perceiving directly everything. And thus, because there would be no distinction, any perceiver would be all-perceiving. And that (undesired consequence) is not accepted by you; hence that [perception] has to be accepted as grasping the being alone. And since that being is not distinguished everywhere, therefore that [being] can be grasped by this [perception] precisely in this manner. However, the conceptualisation which arises in the point of time posterior to this [perception,] which has the following form: "This is a pot, not a piece of cloth, etc.," [and] which occasions everyday practice, is not a cognitive criterion, because it is rooted in nescience. So the ascertainment of the particulars [can] not [take place] on account of perception. [The particulars can] not [be cognised] on account of inference and other [cognitive criteria], either, because the set of all the remaining cognitive criteria is undeniably rooted in perception.[694] Therefore, only the universal is the ultimate truth, and not the particulars.' Such is [the gist of] the collective [viewpoint].[695]

[29.16] [Ad 3] Presently, the opinion of (according to) the empirical [viewpoint] is taught. In this case, the empirical [viewpoint is explained] as practical use, or as such an outlook with which [something] is used practically by common people. This [view], in its turn, expresses [the following idea]. Let the real thing be exactly just the way people take [it]; what is [the use] of this indigestible rice flour cake [in the form] of assuming the real thing [which is both] invisible and cannot be used practically? And cognitive criterion is observed to favour precisely what enters the path of people's everyday practice (*sc.* what is used practically by people), not anything else. For the universal—with no beginning nor end, [numerically] one, considered by the collective [viewpoint]—[does] not [constitute] the scope of a cognitive criterion, because there is no such experience and because [that would lead to] the undesired consequence that all [people] would be all-perceiving. The particulars—[which are] characterised by infinitesimal atoms [and which are] perishing in a moment (*sc.* momentary)—[do] not [constitute] the domain of cognitive criterion, either, because [they do] not occur in that manner. Therefore only that [which is] not subverted by opinions prevalent among people[696], [which is] well-known due to cognitive criterion, [which] possesses grossness lasting for some time, [which is] capable of executing efficient action such as fetching water, etc., [and which] consists in the real thing, like a pot, etc., must be ultimately real. On the other hand, the recognition of the modes of that [real thing] occurring in the previous and posterior points of time is not better [than the recognition of the universal], because the stream of cognitive criteria does not [occur] with regard to them[697] and because it is not possible to carry out the examination [concerning these past and future modes of an object] without a cognitive criterion. Moreover, because they are indeed nothing real[698], what is [the use] of the recognition of the domain [constituted] by these [past and future modes]? For it is as follows: transient occurrences of a substance, [which] take place in the previous and posterior points of time, or the particulars, [which are] characterised by infinitesimal atoms [that] perish in a moment (*sc.* are momentary), can never effect people's everyday practice; so these [transient occurrences] do not constitute the real thing, because only [entities that are] conducive to people's everyday practice are real things. Such is [the gist of] the empirical [viewpoint][699 700].

[29.17] [Ad 4] Presently, the outlook of the direct [viewpoint] is spoken of. In this case, the direct [viewpoint is explained as follows]: [it] draws out, [i.e.] plainly demonstrates—directly, [i.e.] in a straight manner, [or] not crookedly, [viz.] by evading past and future bends[701] [of the real thing]—the form of the real thing, whose transient occurrence [falls to] the present moment. For it is as follows: the outlook of this [direct viewpoint is as follows]: since the past [has already been] destroyed [and] since the gaining of the essence has not been gained [in the case] of the future (*sc.* because the future has not yet come into existence)—on account of which [both the past and the future] forms are deprived of all powers, as [something that is] not distinguishable from [such an unreal things like] a donkey's horn, etc.—therefore [both the past and the future] are not capable of executing efficient action. And it is the real thing that is capable of executing efficient action. Since [these two] do not have that capability of executing efficient action], both [the past and the future] are no real thing. And, on the other hand, since the form of the real thing, which is embraced by the present moment, is engaged in all [purposeful activities, only this [real thing] is existent on the level of the ultimate truth. And moreover, this [real thing] has to be accepted to have no divisions, because [to suppose] that it pervades [its own] divisions is void of logical congruity, inasmuch as it is unjustified to assume that one [thing]—without having multiple essential natures—pervades its own parts [that are] multiple. If [an opponent says]: "Let [the real thing] have multiple essential natures," [The Buddhist retorts]: "That is not [true], because it is attacked by a tiger of contradiction. For it is as follows: if the essential nature is one, how could it be multiple? If it is multiple, how could it be one? [It is impossible], because one and multiple abide by avoiding each other. Therefore—since infinitesimal atoms alone, which are immersed in their intrinsic nature [and which] have somehow assumed a complex form by means of getting together with each other, are expedient to activities [aiming at] all effects—only these [infinitesimal atoms] are individual thing[s]; [it is] not [something] retaining grossness [that is] ultimately real. Furthermore, the determination of an object [is accomplished] on account of cognitive criterion; but a cognitive criterion can in no way operate with regard to grasping the pervasion (*sc.* extension) in space and time, because all cognitive criteria consist in the revelation of the present. [1] For it is as follows: perception, to begin with, whose existence is gained due to the quadruplet of causes characterised by [perceptible] form [of an object], light, mental operations and the eyes, occurs only in the present moment, because past and future moments are not proximate (*sc.* not within reach). And therefore, that [perception] is capable of perceiving directly a [visible] form of the real thing, [a form which is] related to the moment of that [perception], not a previous or a posterior [form], because [past and future moments] are in fact not proximate (*sc.* not within reach). If, however, a form that occurred in the previous moment could be seized, even though [it is now] destroyed, then an endless series [of past or future] moments would be cognised in this [perception], because there is no difference concerning the fact of being destroyed. And, that being the case, it would necessarily follow that perception grasps, by addition, a beginningless series of [former] births. The same [argumentation] is applicable to grasping future moments, too. And that [sort of undesired consequences] is not accepted; therefore this [perception] has to be accepted only as being able to grasp the present moment." And now [the following objection against the Buddhist may be raised]: "If perception could recognise that essences[702] of objects are perishable in a moment (*sc.* momentary), then this [momentariness]—when represented [in cognition as patently] as blueness [of a perceived object]—would not become the domain of the difference of opinion; hence, common people's everyday practice would operate as having this [momentariness as its] province. But that is not [the case], because everyday practice proceeds by means of persistence." As for this [objection against momentariness], it is controverted [by the Buddhist as follows]: "Even though they perceive [momentariness] directly, ignorant [people], whose minds are deceived by [incessant] origination of various subsequent similar [individual things that are responsible for the impression of one persistent object], do not apprehend the evanescence within a moment (*sc.* momentariness), and—because of the efficacy of the wrong conceptualisation produced by the awakening of past impression prevalent from beginningless times—they accomplish everyday practice [based on] the persistence [which is] contrary [to the momentary reality] (*sc.* false). Therefore, this [falsely conceived everyday practice based on the persistence] is not the offence [on the part] of perception, but only [on the part] of cognisers (*sc.* it is not perception to blame, but cognisers). Thus, even a massive form is simply displayed by a wrong conceptualisation that exists on the back of (*sc.* follows) perception, because it is unjustified to assume that this [massive form] is represented in a distinct perception. For nothing but members [of the body], such as hands, feet, the head, the neck, etc., which are separate from each other, appear in this [perception], not a form pervading [them] (*sc.* the form of the whole). And these [members of the body], in their turn, do not appear as pervading their own parts because their own divisions, too, are represented as having forms that are mutually disconnected, as long as nothing but infinitesimal atoms unfold themselves [to perception], because the pervading form [of the whole] is not liable to examination. The above has been taught adequately enough [in order to controvert the above objection]. [2] There no [way to] prove [the existence of] a persistent and gross real thing through inference, either, for inference could proceed [only after] it has met (*sc.* recognised) the relation grasped [already] by perception; and when that [perception] is demonstrated to possess the aptitude to grasp separate divisions [which are] perishable in a moment (*sc.* momentary), then also inference, which has its roots in the connection with this [perception], determines successively nothing but the domain of that [perception], because this [inference]—inasmuch as the form represented in this [inference, viz. the universal,[703]] is false—possesses cognitive validity (*sc.* is a cognitive criterion) only by means of determining that [individual thing][704]."[705] And now [another objection is raised against the Buddhist]: "[Such cognitive faculties like] recollection, recognition, etc., are not explicable without a persistent and gross real thing because [such] wholes like man, etc., are recollected and recognised, for—if [a persistent and gross real thing] has not been perceived before—there is no [cognitive faculty like recollection, recognition, etc.]." [The Buddhist defends his position]: "That is not [true], because it is unjustified to assume the cognitive validity of these [cognitive faculties like recollection, recognition, etc.], inasmuch as they are generated by the awakening of false past impressions. Furthermore, also these [cognitive faculties like recollection, recognition, etc.,] themselves appear only in the present moment, but by the force of a blunder[706], they take their very own nature for a form of a past object produced by past impressions and project a non-existent massive (gross) form on that [own form]. So, [there] is no [way to] prove [the existence of] the real thing pervading [its own parts] by means of any of these [cognitive faculties like recollection, recognition, etc.], either. Therefore—since cognitive criteria do not get down to a form pervading [its own parts]—on the level of the ultimate truth, [there exist] only infinitesimal atoms [that are] disjoined from each other.' Such is [the gist of] the direct [viewpoint].[707]

[29.18] So, this is the opinion of (according to) [object-bound] viewpoints, [which are] adroit at describing the intrinsic nature of objects, [as it] has been described [above]. [Ad B] Now, [the opinion of (according to) viewpoints], which are apt to examine speech elements, is described. With regard to them, this is the common intention [shared] by all three [speech-bound viewpoints, i.e.] verbal, etc., namely: it is only speech element [that constitutes] the ultimate truth, not [external] object, because that [object] is not different from this [speech element]. If [an opponent objects]: 'Since [speech element and object] are established as real things separately, how can [one claim that] there is no difference [between speech element and object]?', [a grammarian replies]: 'We say: on account of cognitive criterion. For it is as follows: [the following proof formula proves our thesis]: "[1. the thesis:] object is not, [by any means,] different from speech element;[708] [2. the logical reason:] because that [object] is cognised, when that [speech element] is cognised; [3. the demonstration of the invariable concomitance accompanied by the example:] in this world, if x is cognised when y is cognised, then x turns out to be not different from y; for instance: the intrinsic nature of that very [speech element], when the speech element is cognised; [4. the application:] and [indeed] object is cognised when speech element is cognised;[709] [5. the conclusion:] hence that [object] is not different from this [speech element]".' If [another objection is raised]: 'Since there [arises] no cognition of a pot [in the case] of a person who has not grasped the linguistic convention [governing the usage of a speech element][710], even when [he] hears the speech element "pot", [object must be] different [from the speech element],' [a grammarian replies]: 'So, in this way, the fact that poison is in its essence lethal does not occur [in the case] of (*sc.* poison does not kill) a person who does not know this [lethality of poison]; hence, this [lethality] would result in [its being] different (*sc.* separated) from this [poison]. And that is [obviously] not the case, because—inasmuch as there is no distinction regarding the difference in these two cases, [viz. in the case of the relation between the speech element "pot" and the object "pot", on the one hand, and in the case of the relation between poison and its lethality, on the other]—[that would] entail that also poison is not lethal, like a bit of molasses, etc., and because the contact with something which is different has already been controverted before[711]. So, it is not so that [in the case] of the real thing [situation presents itself] in a different manner due to the fault of a non-discerning cogniser (*sc.* a person who does not know the linguistic convention), because otherwise—since a blind man cannot see the [perceptible] form [of an object]—also the non-existence of this [object] should be recognised.' If [one objects]: 'Such objects [which] occur as [things] without designation are proved to [have the status of] real things separately from speech element,' [a grammarian argues]: '[That is] not [right] because there are no objects without designation; simply, some [objects] are referred to by speech elements [pertaining to] the particular, some [other objects are referred to] by linguistic units [pertaining to] the universal—there would only be that much difference. Alternatively, linguistic units [pertaining to] the particular are not denoters of all objects, hence there is no cognitive criterion concerning (*sc.* which could establish) these [particular objects without designation]. And further—by the force of the [following] cognitive criterion (*sc.* inference): "all objects (denotata)[712] have [corresponding] denoters [that convey] them as existing [things], because they are objects (denotata), like the object (denotatum) «pot»"—all [objects], inasmuch as they have [corresponding] denoters [that convey] them, are proved not to be separate from speech elements due to the logical reasoning exposed above. Consequently, on the level of the ultimate truth there is no [external] object in addition to speech elements, whereas metaphorically, [object] is used practically by common people, who do not reflect upon the ultimate truth. Also this object, either the metaphorical one or the one having speech element as its essence, should be held to be momentary (lit. perishable at every moment), because phonemes are known to be annihilated after a moment (*sc.* to be momentary) and because of the totality of logical reasoning (*sc.* argumentation) demonstrated [above in the case of] the direct [viewpoint].'

[29.19] Presently, [every] outlook out of all these [three speech-bound viewpoints] is spoken of individually. [Ad 5] Among them, the verbal [viewpoint] intends, as they say, by the force of understanding, one object (denotatum)[713] for all such linguistic units, like 'Indra', 'Śakra', 'Purandara', etc., that are used—in accordance with the usage—to denote a specific object (denotatum). Exactly in such a way the non-difference of object (denotatum) from speech element is demonstrated, in the very same way either oneness or non-oneness of that [object / denotatum in the case of such linguistic units] has to be demonstrated. And speech elements that are synonyms, like 'Indra', 'Śakra', 'Purandara'[714], etc., are never understood as denoting different objects, because they always in all cases originate a reflection of one [and the same] form, for it is empirical fact that—inasmuch as the operation [of synonymous speech elements] is infallible[715]—everyday practice [proceeds] in exactly that manner. Therefore, speech elements that are synonyms have only one object (denotatum) [as their province]. Such is [the gist of] the verbal [viewpoint], because—in consonance with the etymological explanation, viz. '[the verbal viewpoint is] such an outlook by which an object (denotatum) is verbalised or articulated'—linguistic units that are synonyms are pronounced exclusively with the outlook (intention) to demonstrate [only] one object (denotatum).[716]

[29.20] [Ad 6] Presently, the opinion of (according to) the etymological [viewpoint] is described. In this case, the etymological [viewpoint is explained] as such an intention concerning the usage of speech elements that ascends altogether, [i.e.] 'by way of singularity,' towards, [i.e.] which leaps up to (*sc.* seeks) the factor [accountable] for the grammatical formation [of given words].[717] For this [etymological viewpoint] considers an object (denotatum) of speech elements that are synonyms only as individually distinct. For instance, Indra ('possessed of sovereign authority') [is called as such] because of sovereign authority; on the level of the ultimate truth, the denotatum of the word 'Indra' is divine supremacy; however, [the word 'Indra'] is used metaphorically to denote an object possessed of this [divine supremacy]. Or [one could say that] nobody is possessed of this [divine supremacy] because no speech elements—inasmuch as [they] demonstrate objects (denotata) which are separate from each other—are proved to operate by [way of] the relationship between the substratum and the substratum-bound [property]. Similarly, Śakra ('possessed of might') [is called as such] because of might; Purandara ('destroyer of strongholds') [is called as such] because of destroying of strongholds—by these and other [examples] one [can] demonstrate that all speech elements have different objects (denotata). And one [can] adduce a proof [in support of that, namely [the following proof formula]: '[1. the thesis:] speech elements that are synonyms have different objects (denotata); [2. the logical reason:] because they have the factor [accountable] for their grammatical formation individually (*sc.* in every individual case) distinct; [3. the demonstration of the invariable concomitance accompanied by the example:] in this world, whatever [speech elements] have the factor [accountable] for their grammatical formation individually distinct, they have [also] different objects (denotata), [for instance such] speech elements like 'Indra', 'pot', 'man' have different meanings; [4. the application:] and indeed [such linguistic units] that have the factor [accountable] for their grammatical formation individually (*sc.* in every individual case) distinct are speech elements that are synonyms; [5. the conclusion:] hence they have different objects (denotata).' [The assumption], however, that one [can] demonstrate that [synonyms] denote one object (denotatum) by the force of understanding which is not reflected upon, is not proper, because that would have too far-reaching consequences. For it is as follows: if the very understanding void of logical congruity is taken recourse to, then—since [several trees growing in a thicket, like] the *Nimb* tree (*Azadirachta Indica*), the Kadamba tree (*Nauclea Cadamba*), the fig tree (*Ficus Religiosa*), *Feronia Elephantum*, etc., with their trunks clustered together, [while being seen] in a very dim light in a very distant place, although [they are] different [from each other], are cognised as possessing a form of one tree—these [several trees growing in a thicket] would have to be accepted as only one tree. And that is not [the case], because—inasmuch as the former [false] understanding is subverted by the occurrence of a cognition opposite [to the former one] which grasps the intrinsic natures of these [trees] as [something] different—these [trees] are accepted to be nothing but separate. So, there are no linguistic units which denote one [and the same external] object (denotatum), [there is], however, the usage regarding [linguistic units] whose meaning has not [properly] been reflected upon. Such is [the gist of] the etymological [viewpoint].[718]

[29.21] [Ad 7] Presently, the outlook of (according to) the factual [viewpoint] is demonstrated [whose literal meaning is 'thus arisen']. In this case, the speech element 'thus' denotes manner; and therefore, the speech element [which is] grammatically formed 'thus', [i.e.] in such a way, [viz.] that which has 'arisen' [in such a way, i.e.] which has assumed this manner, is [the speech element] 'thus arisen' (*sc.* the factual viewpoint).[719] Also [such an] outlook whose main [import] is to corroborate this [speech element 'thus arisen'] is the factual [viewpoint], because this [speech element 'thus arisen' constitutes] the province [of the factual viewpoint][720] and because [the outlook] characterised by [this particular] province (*sc.* 'thus arisen') is designated by the speech element [which constitutes its] province. For [when] this speech element *x* is formed grammatically (derived) with regard to an object (denotatum) *y*, [then] that object (denotatum) *y* [constitutes] the factor [accountable] for grammatical formation [of this speech element *x*; and the factual viewpoint] intends this speech element *x* as such that is being used to denote [that external object (denotatum) *y*], only then when that [external object (denotatum) *y* really] happens (*sc.* enters particular practice), not as the universal (*sc.* in general). Just like a pot is called ['pot' when it is] indeed accompanied by particular movements, [when] lifted up onto the head of a woman, etc., in the moment of fetching water, etc., [and] nothing else [can be called 'pot'], because [everything else] is void of the factor [accountable] for the grammatical formation of the speech element 'pot', like 'a piece of cloth.' If [the following objection is raised]: '[The speech element "pot"] is uttered indeed as the universal (*sc.* in general) [where we] have taken account of past or future movement[s],' [a grammarian conforming to the factual viewpoint may reply:] '[It is] not [right] because both these [past or future movements]—inasmuch as [they] have [already] been destroyed or [have] not yet arisen, [respectively]—resemble a hare's horn[721]. Nevertheless, if speech element functioned by means of the [universal][722] (*sc.* in general), it would have to be used to denote everything, because there is no difference[723]. Furthermore, if the speech element "pot" were pronounced with regard to past or future movement[s], even though it is not possessed of [these past or future] movements, [then] it would be difficult to negate that this [speech element "pot" should] be used to denote also potsherd[724], a clod of clay, etc., because there is no difference. Therefore, only in such a moment, when there exists the factor [accountable for] the grammatical formation [of the speech element "*x*"] in a full-fledged form, the object (denotatum of the word) *x* can be denoted by the speech element "*x*".' Such is [the gist of] the factual [viewpoint].[725]

[29.22] Thus, the knowledge grasping an object endowed with multiple properties[726] in the above manner[727] is cognitive criterion; whereas the reflection acquired by its means[728] that is disposed to corroborate an object related to [only] one property and that occurs by means of appropriating, ruling out or avoiding [all other] remaining properties is viewpoint. And it is of infinite divisions because of the infinity of properties [it may emphasise]. Nevertheless, it has been exposed in the above manner to be seven-fold by means of assuming [seven] outlooks that collect together all [possible viewpoints].[729] And[730] only such a reflection which functions as [a reflection] that in its essence [sets] the restriction [limiting its own domain to only one] property intended by itself [and which accomplishes that] by means of ruling out [all] the remaining properties receives the denotation 'defective viewpoint,' for these [afore-mentioned] assertions of opponents, as one should realise, have their existence originated by the force of these [defective viewpoints]. For it is as follows: [1] the Naiyāyika and the Vaiśeṣika are the followers of the doctrine [rooted in] the comprehensive viewpoint; [2] all monistic theories with no exception as well as the Sāṁkhya doctrine proceed [taking recourse to] the collective outlook (*sc.* viewpoint); [3] the doctrine of the Cārvākas generally adheres to the empirical viewpoint; [4] the Buddhists with [their] minds[731] proceed [taking recourse to] the direct outlook (*sc.* viewpoint); [5–7] the grammarians, etc.[732] cling to opinions of (according to) the verbal and other [remaining] viewpoints, [viz. the etymological and the factual]. If you express [your doubt] in the following way: 'How can these [opinions of opponents] that—by means of [setting] a restriction [regarding their domains]—corroborate their respective objects [and] that revoke [any object which is] contrary to this (*sc.* their respective objects) possibly acquire the status of (*sc.* turn out to be) defective viewpoints?,' with reference to that [the following explanation] is given. [These opinions of opponents become defective viewpoints] because, [when they] function in such a manner, they have no domain, [and] it is unjustified to assume that [an opinion] having no domain [constitutes] a [proper] viewpoint. For it is as follows: that outlook which leads to, [i.e.] which makes one reach an object qualified by a certain aspect, is viewpoint;[733] but [an outlook that] proceeds by means of keeping out (disproving) [all the] remaining properties from the [only one] property intended by itself does not lead to anything, because defective outlooks which aver the denial of that [multiplexity]—inasmuch as they are subverted by the [multiplex] representation [of any object in cognition]—are false, for such a real thing which is embraced by (*sc.* endowed with) [only] one property, [and as such it is represented by defective outlooks,] is impossible, inasmuch as this [real thing] is represented [in cognition both] externally and internally as such whose essential nature is accompanied by multiple properties[734] [735].

[29.23] For it as follows. [Ad 1] The comprehensive viewpoint, to begin with, which should demonstrate the universal and the particular as disjoined from each other[736] is not proper, because both of them are never represented [in cognition] in such a manner. What has been taught [above]—namely, that there is no representation of the particular in which the universal can be grasped by a reflection of one [and the same] form that endures [unchanged], and that there is no ascertainment of the universal in which the particular can be grasped by a reflection delimited by particular location and [by particular] circumstances [of a perceived individual thing][737]—is merely an utterance [and nothing] else, because without all particular [trees] like *Grislea Tomentosa* (or *Anogeissus Latifolia*?), *Accacia Catechu*, *Butea Frondosa*, etc., there would be no representation [in cognition] of the universal tree-ness, etc. If [the proponent of the Nyāya-Vaiśeṣika claims]: 'Even though the particulars are not grasped because [they are] in a distance, simply nothing but this [tree-ness] manifests itself,' [we shall retort: that is] not [correct] because also in such cases (*sc.* when the particulars are not perceived directly because of the distance) [there is] the representation of the particulars that have been interiorised (*sc.* comprised) [in the universal], for without these [particulars][738] [the universal] would [assume] a form of a hare's horn (*sc.* would be non-existent).[739] In this manner, also the particulars do not occur as absolutely different from the universal because they are grasped only as being immersed in this [universal]; in the opposite case, the entities as [something] separate from existence[740] [would] appropriate a character of being devoid of their essential nature. Likewise, there would be no trees, etc., [if they were] different also[741] from [their respective] universals like tree-ness, etc., because their intrinsic nature is established, inasmuch as they are based on the non-difference from that [respective universal]. Therefore, it is taught that the very same sensation [in which] the particularity is made subordinate[742] [and in which] one [common] form is made the main [import] grasps the universal, whereas [the very same sensation in which] the sameness is disregarded[743] [and] diversity is [made] dominant grasps the particular[744], because sameness and diversity are existent in all objects as [something] somehow [both] different and not different from each other, inasmuch as the representation of such a kind [would be] inexplicable if they were not [somehow both different and not different from each other]. By [the force of] this [argument], what has been expressed [by you above[745]], viz. 'And, these two, [i.e.] the universal and the particular, both being represented as being different from each other, can not intermingle somehow,' etc., has to be accepted as controverted because there is no representation [of them] as different [from each other]. Also the whole everyday practice can only be effected [with regard to] the universal and the particular, which are somehow mutually not detached, by means of the main [import] and the subordinate [level], for neither the universal [alone] can be employed in such actions like milking, carrying [commodities], etc.,[746] because only the particulars are employed in these [actions],[747] nor the particulars alone accomplish these [actions] because these [particulars] void of [the universal] cow-ness would lack the efficacy to accomplish these [actions], inasmuch as they would not be distinguished from tress, etc.[748] Furthermore, [we may ask you the following question]: if there is an absolute difference between the universal and the particular, why does a person instigated to cut a [universal] tree[749] cuts[750] a [given] *Butea Frondosa* tree, [which is but] a particular [specimen] of that [universal tree-ness]? If [the Naiyāyika and the Vaiśeṣika reply]: 'Because that [universal] inheres in these [particulars][751],' [we say: that is] not [correct] because, [firstly,] there is no cognitive criterion which could grasp the inherence, [and] even if there were, it would be incapable of bringing about the knowledge of non-separation of (*sc.* relation between) both [the universal tree-ness and the particular tree] which are disjoined [from each other], inasmuch as this [inherence], too, is different [from both the universal tree-ness and the particular tree,] and because, [secondly, such an assumption would lead to] the undesired consequence that this [act of cutting] would be accomplished with regard to all [trees], inasmuch as [inherence] is common to [all] other entities [as well] and is permanent, one [and] all-pervading. On the other hand, what you have expressed, namely: 'If the universal were perceived as related to the particulars or the particular [were comprehended] as pervaded by the universal, then this whole everyday practice, [which is] characterised by [both] efficient action with regard to and denoting the universals and particulars [that are] different [from each other], would—inasmuch as both of these [universals and particulars would be] on no occasion comprehended as different—meet [its] disintegration, because the discrimination (*sc.* cognition) of these [two] is impossible to be actualised in the oscillating manner (*sc.* by moving to and fro between the two extremes, viz. the universals and particulars),'[752] is improper, too, because even though the universals and the particulars are in all cases comprehended as not different from each other, nevertheless, precisely such a [thing] a cogniser aims at is the universal[753], or, having made the particulars the main [import, the universal] makes one pronounce a linguistic unit or [makes one] accomplish efficient action with reference to these [particulars], because, on the one hand, the activity [accomplished] with regard to these [particulars takes places] by way of subordinating the other one (*sc.* the universal), [and] because, on the other hand, the other one (*sc.* the universal) that lacks these [particulars] could on no occasion be employed, inasmuch as it would resemble a hare's horn. Moreover, if the universal were absolutely different from the particulars, the [following] series of hammer [blows] of criticism falling on [the opponent's] head—[that is executed] by means [1] of alternatives regarding the occurrence, [2] of the comprehension, [3] of the relation with the new particular, etc.—would be difficult to withstand.[754] For it is as follows: [1] how would that [universal] occur in these [particulars]: [1.1] in its totality or [1.2] [piece] by piece? [Ad 1.1] In the case of the alternative [assuming that the universal would occur] in its totality, the undesired consequence of the plurality of the universals [would follow], inasmuch as [the universal would already] be complete with regard to each and every particular. And that [consequence] is not accepted because it would impair the accepted [thesis asserting] the oneness [of the universal][755]. [Ad 1.2] If , on the other hand, [the universal] occurred [in the particulars piece] by piece, so and so many particulars [would] absurdly imply so and so many divisions of that [universal];[756] and that is not [the case], because the universal has no parts. Even if [the universal] has parts, however, [one should posit the dilemma]: are these [parts] [1.2.1] non-different or [1.2.2] different[757] [from the universal as a whole]? [Ad 1.2.1] If [its parts are] non-different [from the universal as a whole], then why are the particulars not accepted as non-different [from the universal as a whole], because there is no difference [between the parts and the particulars regarding their relation to the universal]? [Ad 1.2.2] In [the case of] the alternative [assuming the] difference [of the universal and its parts], on the other hand, [there arises another question, namely] how would [the universal] occur in all these [parts], in their turn: [1.2.2.A] in its totality or [1.2.2.B] [piece] by piece? In such a way, this very criticism enters the unreachable limit (*sc. regressus ad infinitum*), so [one has to conclude that] the occurrence of [the universal] as absolutely different [from these particulars] is not possible. [2] Furthermore, if [numerically] one universal could occur in all particulars as possessed of the difference (*sc.* as different from them), then [one is confronted with the dilemma:] is that [universal] [2.1] comprehended in the point of time of the comprehension of [only] one particular or [2.2] not? [Ad 2.1] If the first alternative [is considered], it would immediately follow that—since that [universal] is [numerically] one, it is comprehended in every [particular and] inasmuch as it is established that, when that which is pervaded (*sc.* the particulars) is not grasped, the pervader (*sc.* the universal) is not grasped—all these particulars which are pervaded by that [universal] would be grasped. And that is not [obviously the case] because only the particular which is in front [of the cogniser] is directly perceived, inasmuch as [all] the remaining particulars are not present. [To conclude,] that [universal] is comprehended only as being related to the proximate particular. If [the opponent argues]: '[It is so] because only this [proximate particular] manifests momentarily that [universal, whereas] the remaining [particulars] are absent in that [universal],' [we dissent:] no, [it is not correct]. That [universal]—since it is unjustified to assume that [the universal,] whose essential nature is [numerically] one [and indivisible,] is momentarily manifested bit by bit—is momentarily manifested in the proximate particular alone and the form of this [universal]—since no other essential nature [but that of the universal] is present in every [particular]—is accommodated in all particulars; hence who could ward off [the consequence] that [all of] these [particulars] are seen [in the point of time of the comprehension of one particular][758]? [Ad 2.2] If the second alternative [is postulated], that being the case, if [the universal] were not comprehended in the instant of the comprehension of one particular, then [the universal] would not be comprehended in the point of time of the comprehension of remaining particulars, either, because there is no difference. Hence, nothing but the non-existence of this [universal] should be taught, because it alone would not be comprehended. Even if [the universal] were comprehended [in the point of time of the comprehension of remaining particulars], that would entail that the continued existence of its essential nature consists in the particulars. [3] Likewise, how could that [universal] whose existence has been determined by old particulars experience (*sc.* enter into)—when a new particular arises—the relation with this [new particular]? [3.1] That [universal which is established] by other (*sc.* former) particulars, to begin with, is not in a position to reach to the location of (*sc.* cannot enter into a relation with) the particular which is about to arise,[759] because [it is] destitute of any action[760]. [3.2] It could not be [already] present in that very [particular which is about to arise], either, because—before the rise of the particular—that [universal] cannot be comprehended in the location of that [new particular]. [3.3] [The universal can] not arise together with the [new] particular itself, either, because it is permanent, and because it is a contradiction [to say] that [something] permanent originates. [Ad 3.1] If that [universal] were stated [explicitly by the opponent]—with the desire to avoid this fault, [viz. the undesired consequence that the universal determined by old particulars never enters into any relation with a new particular]—to be possessed of action, also then [one would face the following dilemma]: would [the universal determined by old particulars] access the location of the new particular either [3.1.1] by giving up [all] the previous manifest particular entities (*sc.* particulars)[761] or [3.1.2] by not [giving up all the previous particulars]? [Ad 3.1.1] The first alternative, to begin with, is not [plausible] because [it would lead to] the undesired consequence that the old manifest particular entities (*sc.* particulars)—inasmuch as they would lack the universal—would be deprived both of the cognition and of linguistic units by which the relation with that [particular which is about to arise] can be established;[762] and that is not [the case], because—even when various subsequent particulars [still] arise—it is an empirical fact that this [cognition and linguistic units] refer to past manifest particular entities (*sc.* previous particulars). [Ad 3.1.2] If the second alternative [is considered], it is incoherent, too, because [Ad 3.1.2.A] [the universal which] has no parts—as long as [it] has not given up [all] the previous manifest particular entities (*sc.* particulars)—[can] not approach the manifest particular entity (*sc.* the particular) which is about to arise. [Ad 3.1.2.B] On the other hand, since the alternative [assuming the universal] possessed of parts has already been controverted before[763], it is not any better to avoid [the undesired consequence ensuing from the assumption of the universal which has no parts] by means of accepting that [the universal possesses parts]. [4] And [there is still something] else,[764] if entities (*sc.* particulars encompassed by their respective universal) are similar on account of the relation with the universal which is different [from them], not on account of their intrinsic nature, then [the following question arises:] are these entities [4.1] existent before [entering into] the relation with existence[765] or [4.2] non-existent. [Ad 4.1] If [they were] existent [before entering into the relation with existence, their] relation with existence [would be] purposeless; otherwise the *regressus ad infinitum* would absurdly be implied, because the relation with [still] another existence again [and again could] not be prevented. [Ad 4.2] If [they were] non-existent [before entering into the relation with existence, it] would result in the fact that also absolutely non-existent [things like] sky lotus, etc., would consist in existence (*sc.* would become existent) on account of the relation with existence. [5] In the same manner, all this [argumentation which has just been applied to the case of the highest universal consisting in existence] has to be taught with regard (*sc.* applied) also to [lower intermediate universals, like] substantiality, qualitativeness, the state of being an object of an action, cow-ness, etc., because [they are] based on one and the same productive-supportive principle[766]. Hence, [both] the universal and the particular are in no way possible as absolutely different from each other. Due to this very [reason], the outlook which is disposed to corroborate them [as absolutely different from each other and] which disproves the relation of essential identity between them—inasmuch as [it is] void of [any] objective substratum—ascends to (*sc.* acquires) the designation of the defective comprehensive viewpoint, for [only such an outlook] which corroborates the difference between the universal and the particular by merely putting aside [the question of] their identity is the comprehensive viewpoint [proper], because both of them, [viz., the universal and the particulars], although [they are] different [from each other], are somehow (*sc.* not absolutely) present in the real thing, inasmuch as, in the opposite case, [i.e. if they were identical][767], it would be impossible to demonstrate [them] in such a manner, [i.e. as different][768], even if one had the wish to express [that difference], (1) because the relationship between the main [import] and the subordinate [level] is related by (located in) duality, [and] (2) because—if the identity [of the universal and the particulars] were absolute—[it would lead to] the undesired consequence that also the intention asserting that [difference[769] of the universal and the particulars would be] void of [its] domain. Therefore, it is established that these two, [i.e. the universal and the particulars], are somehow truly [both] different and not different from each other; [such a viewpoint], however, which corroborates [only] one of these [two, i.e. either the universal or the particular], appropriates the status of a defective viewpoint, because [it is] void of [any] objective substratum.

[29.24] [Ad 2] Similarly, the collective [viewpoint] too, [inasmuch as] it corroborates the universal as the [only] one [thing] by means of disproving the particulars completely, is a defective viewpoint because this [collective viewpoint can have the status of a correct] viewpoint only by means of putting [the question of the particular] aside, for the universal lacking the particular is impossible. For it is as follows: first, what has been taught [by you]—namely: 'If the first alternative [were assumed], then these [particulars would] be devoid of their essential nature, because [they would be] devoid of existence. If the second alternative [were adopted, which is the true one], there would be the being alone, because [the particulars would] not [be] different from [the universal, viz. from the being], like its intrinsic nature'[770]—is not proper, because such an alternative is possible also [in the case] of the propounder of the particulars.[771] For it as follows: 'Is the universal [1] different or [2] not different from the particulars? [Ad 1] If [it were assumed to be] different, then [there would be] no universal, because [the universal]—inasmuch as it would be determined as their intrinsic nature—would consist in the particulars. [Ad 2] If [it were assumed to be] not different, then [there would be] no universal, either, just because [the universal would] not be different [from the particulars], [for it would be] like their intrinsic nature.' Similarly, that what has been expressed [by you]—namely: 'Everyday practice [based on] the particulars is accomplished by the force of beginningless nescience, [hence] the universal is [the only] really existing [thing]'[772]—is nothing but merely an [unwarranted] utterance, because [it] is void of logical congruity, inasmuch as there would be no [means of] invalidating the words[773] of the propounder of the particulars, either, who expresses the following [opinion]: 'It is the universal that is shown by the beginningless nescience, whereas the particulars are ultimately real.' However, what has [explicitly] been stated by [you who] teach the non-existence of any cognitive criterion [that is capable of] grasping the particulars—namely: 'Perception, whose existence is produced by the being, perceives directly only that [being], not the non-being, because that [non-being] does not bring about [perception], etc.'[774]—is even more improper because what close friend of yours has proclaimed [the following inaccurate revelation to you], viz. 'It is the being alone that generates perception; but the non-being [can] certainly not'? If [you attempt to vindicate your position]: '[The fact that perception, produced by the being, grasps directly only it, can be established] by [the force of] the totality of logical reasoning[775] that demonstrates the absence of [any] activity of the non-being,' [all we can say is that] you have been deceived by a fool![776] [You are wrong,] because the absence of [any] activity of this [non-being] is not proved, inasmuch as the real thing that consists in [both] the existing and the non-existing [aspects][777] is operative with regard to all actions, for there is no contradiction in [assuming] an activity of the non-being [that is] determined as identical with (*sc.* standing in the relation of essential identity to) the being. If [you object]: 'How is the relation of essential identity of the being and the non-being [possible]? [Obviously it is not possible], because of the contradiction!,' [we retort: that is] not [right,] because there [can be] no contradiction regarding [something] well-known through cognitive criteria. For it is as follows: the essence of an entity, [say] a pot, etc., is existent by its intrinsic nature, not at all by the nature of a piece of cloth, etc.; hence [it consists] in [its] essence in [both] the being and the non-being. If, however, [the entity] were not somehow in [its] essence the non-being, then it [would] become in [its] nature everything (*sc.* it would assume the nature of everything), inasmuch as its being [would subsist] also as consisting in a piece of cloth, etc. If [you, while thinking further on along these lines, draw the following conclusion]: 'That is correct; therefore for this very [reason], the annihilation of manifestation of [any] difference [between the universal and the particular] is proved,' [we shall retort:] it would only [then] be [proved], if also the heart of the propounder of the theory of the universal emptiness (Śūnya-vādin) were not filled with satisfaction because of the absolute absence (non-existence) of [all entities like] a piece of cloth, etc., [viz. if the consequence of your position would not lead to the absolute denial of all entities, which the Śūnya-vādin propounds]. For [according to the Śūnya-vādin] it is like that: 'A pot is experienced as distinct from a piece of cloth, etc., and [the pot's] not being a piece of cloth does not experience the relation of essential identity with [the pot's] being [a piece of cloth, etc.]; therefore this [pot] consists in nothing but in the non-being. In such a manner also [such entities like] piece of cloth [become non-existent] with regard to each other. Thus, [we] arrive at the universal emptiness.' [Our position is, however, as follows]: therefore, [in order to avoid such a consequence, it has to be admitted that] the real thing—which possesses its intrinsic nature [and] which is in fact distinguished from other forms[778]—[can] be applied[779] in all actions. Thus, there is activity of nothing but [the real thing,] which consists in [both] the being and the non-being, because retaining one's own intrinsic nature is the being and being distinguished from other forms is the non-being. In a similar manner, [the real thing] is applied in [the act of] bringing about the perception, whose domain is [constituted by] this [real thing] itself, and, hence, this [perception] may perceive directly only the form of this [real thing which consists in both the being and the non-being][780]. Hence, perception operates precisely with regard to the real thing, which is confined by its intrinsic nature[781] [and] which is distinguished from other forms[782], because [perception] is produced by this [real thing, and perception does] not [operate] with regard to the being only, because it is unjustified to assume that this [real thing]—inasmuch as it is not determined by is intrinsic nature [alone]—produces [perception] as [the] only [factor]. And it is stated that object is not something-to-be-grasped, because it produces [cognition], neither is cognition something-which-grasps, because it is produced [by the object], inasmuch as [such an assumption would have] too far-reaching consequences. But rather [it has to be agreed upon that] cognition, whose existence is gained due to the cessation, etc., of [karmic] veils[783], grasps [an object] because of transformation [in the way] of grasping, whereas the object is grasped [by the cognition] because of [its] presence [in front of the cogniser], etc.; and this [object] is cognised only as [something] whose form [both] endures [as being itself] and is distinguished [from all other things]. On account of that, [the object] has to be accepted as being of such nature (*sc.* as consisting in the being and the non-being), not as consisting exclusively in the universal. If [the opponent objects] the above[784] as follows: 'How [is it at all possible] that both the existent and the non-existent aspects abide in [numerically] one [object]?', we reply: because of the relation of essential identity [between them]. Now, [the objection may be raised by the opponent]: 'If [the existent and the non-existent aspects] were identical, it would result either in the being alone or in the non-being alone, because, [they are supposed to be] mutually non-different, like [two things that have] mutually the [same] intrinsic nature. So, it is not proved that the real thing consists in both [existent and non-existent aspects].' That is not [correct] because essential identity is a relation and [every] relation is located in two [related things]; without these [two relata], what with what would the relation [relate]? [A relation without two relata could not obviously be possible], because it would have no domain. Therefore, [on the one hand], these two existent and non-existent aspects—inasmuch as they consist in [being] the property-possessor—are non-different (*sc.* identical) because the real thing (*sc.* the property-possessor) which consists in [both] existent and non-existent [aspects] is one [and the same]; on the other hand, [these] two [existent and non-existent aspects, when] intended as [something] consisting in properties, experience difference (*sc.* are different), because [they] exist as their [respective] intrinsic nature [and] because [they] do not exist as other forms[785]. Thus, when (*sc.* since) perception, which grasps multifarious real things, has been proved in the above manner[786] to be the foremost [one] among all cognitive criteria, also [all] the remaining cognitive criteria—inasmuch as they follow this [perception]—establish their own [respective] domain only as [something] multifarious. Consequently, [such] a defective outlook which denies that [multifarious object and] which determines the universal alone appropriates the designation of the defective collective viewpoint, because [only such a viewpoint which] determines the universal precisely with regard to the particulars is the collective viewpoint [proper].

[29.25] [Ad 3] Similarly, also the empirical [viewpoint]—which, [on the one hand,] denies the intrinsic nature of the real thing, well-known through cognitive criteria, [and which, on the other hand,] corroborates [the real thing] as [something that] follows (*sc.* is in accordance) the path of people's everyday practice [but] is void of logical congruity [and is] satisfactory for [people] who do not reflect upon [reality]—takes upon itself the status of (*sc.* becomes) a defective viewpoint, because even [such a viewpoint which merely] accomplishes people's everyday practice [can] not be determined with reference to [something] which is not accepted as the other one, [i.e. as the real thing well-known through cognitive criteria]. For it is as follows: such a [real thing,] like a pot, etc., which lasts for some time, which possesses grossness, which is instrumental to people's everyday practice [and] which is intended by you as really existing, is not accidental, but rather [it is] combined of permanent infinitesimal atoms; in the opposite case, [it would lead to] the undesired consequence that [the real thing] would [either] exist always or [it would never] exist, inasmuch as it would be causeless. If [you object:]: 'These infinitesimal atoms do not appear [in cognition] as such, [viz. as something existent],' [we retort: that is] not [right]; for this very reason, they are proved by inference[787]. If, however, all that, with no exception, which does not manifest itself directly in the clear perception could be denied, then, woe! in this case [quite] a lot should be denied because—inasmuch as also [in the case] of [any] real thing, such as a pot, etc., solely the surface situated in the segment on this side (*sc.* on the side of the perceiver) is represented [directly in cognition]—[it would lead to] the undesired consequence of denying inner and other (*sc.* not directly perceived by the cognitive subject) segments, etc., [of a perceived object]. And thus, also the fact that [the real thing] is instrumental to people's everyday practice would be shattered, because [the existence of] the real thing [can] not be proved by this much only, [viz. the portion of the surface situated on the side of the perceiver directly observed by him]. If [one can furnish] proof of a complete (*sc.* forming one whole) real thing, that is capable of being [an object] of everyday practice, by the force of inference in this (*sc.* above) case, then accordingly, one should demonstrate a proof of infinitesimal atoms [endowed with] past and future modes, too, because there is no difference. For it is as follows: just like these [real things], that are complete (*sc.* form one whole) [and] are capable of [being objects of] that [everyday practice], are proved by the proof of the inner segments, etc., (*sc.* and the portion of the surface that is not accessible to the perceiver) [of a perceived object]—although merely the outer surface [of the object] is represented [directly in cognition]—because no real things at all are present in everyday practice as this much only (*sc.* as merely the portion of the surface situated on the side of the perceiver directly observed by him), in the very same manner, these [real things], although they are perceived as [something that] lasts for some time and has massive form, should be proved as [things] whose bodies are determined by the relation of essential identity (*sc.* as being identical) with beginningless and infinite (eternal) infinitesimal atoms, because—if these [infinitesimal atoms] were not [existent], either, [like in the case of invisible segments]—these [real things would be] inexplicable. For it is as follows: the present mode[788], to begin with, [that] enters into everyday practice [and is] amenable to perception [turns out to be] uncaused, if past modes are not accepted; and the defect of such [a reasoning] has [already] been discussed[789]. When, however, [another] immediately [antecedent] mode bringing about this [present mode] is accepted, a mode producing this [earlier mode] should also be accepted—in this manner, a beginningless series of modes should possess correctness (*sc.* prove correct). Similarly, the ultimate (*sc.* present) mode of the real thing that enters into everyday practice—inasmuch as it does not bring about [any] other (*sc.* subsequent) mode—presents itself inevitably as nothing real, because precisely according to your logic [this ultimate (*sc.* present) mode] lacks [the capacity] to execute efficient action. However, since [the present mode] brings about this [another (*sc.* subsequent) mode], also this [another (*sc.* subsequent) mode] brings about [further] subsequent mode—in this way [as above demonstrated], the infinite continual chain of modes is explicable. Similarly, also [a thing] possessed of a massive form, being perceived directly by the clear perception, is not explicable without ultimate parts, that [in their turn] have no [further] spatial units (*sc.* are not further divisible), because members [of the body], such as hands, feet, etc., consist—inasmuch as [the whole can] be divided [into its parts] bit by bit—in the whole, for also their parts are combined of further [minor] parts. It is infinitesimal atoms alone [that constitute] ultimate (*sc.* further indivisible) parts, that—on the level of the ultimate truth—are causes of [things] possessed of a massive (*sc.* perceptible) form. Without them, however, this [thing possessed of a massive form] either would in all cases be observed as [something] accidental or [would be observed] in no case [at all], because there would be no difference. Thereby, also what has been stated, namely: 'Cognitive criterion is that which favours the real thing as [something that] enters people's everyday practice (*sc.* what is used practically by people), not [that which favours] something else,'[790] has to be accepted as [already] disproved, because—inasmuch as [any] perceived object is, in fact, otherwise inexplicable—that [fact that objects are possessed of ultimate parts and modes] is established. On the other hand, what has been stated [by the opponent], viz. 'What is [the use] of the recognition of these past and future modes and infinitesimal atoms, etc., because—inasmuch as they are not conducive to people's everyday practice they are nothing real,'[791] and so forth, is improper because [any] real thing that [exists] present[ly] would—due to indifference [of somebody towards the thing in a given moment]—attain the status of [being] something unreal, inasmuch as [it would] not [be] conducive [to people's everyday practice at that given moment], for nothing can be conducive (*sc.* serviceable) to all people [all the time].[792] If something is [admitted to be] the real thing, because of [its] being conducive (*sc.* serviceable) [for somebody], this [conduciveness] is necessarily possible for all these [people], because it is the domain of the cognition, etc., of omniscient [people]. So let [us] leave that alone[793]. Thus, an empirical [viewpoint], since it denies the object cognised through cognitive criteria in the above manner[794], is a defective viewpoint, because [only such a viewpoint] that corroborates the real thing [that] adheres to everyday practice—inasmuch as it puts aside this [false object]—is the empirical viewpoint [proper].

[29.26] [Ad 4] Now, also the direct [viewpoint], that expresses—by denying what is perceived—the intrinsic nature, never perceived though, of the real thing characterised by infinitesimal atoms which perish in a moment (*sc.* momentary) as ultimately true, ascends to the status of (*sc.* becomes) defective viewpoint, because a reflection that [could] corroborate the real thing [as it is] intended by [the direct viewpoint] itself does not arise, inasmuch as [such a reflection would be] without basis, if [any] perceived persistent and gross object were denied. For it is as follows: [first] observing directly a form, which pervades its parts [and] is prone to continue in another point of time, [the Buddhist opponent] would later—by [availing himself of] acts of conceptualisation [based on] defective reasoning[795]—discriminate, namely: this form that is being perceived as persistent and gross is, as one should realise, not possible. And it is not possible to subvert—by [means of] acts of conceptualisation [based on] defective reasoning that display something what is not perceived in accordance with [your argumentation above]: 'because the pervading form [of the whole] is not liable to examination' and so forth[796]—something what is perceived, inasmuch as [it would lead to] the undesired consequence of mistrusting everything. If you took the following position: 'Just as a former error [of taking] a rope, in a place [characterised by] a very dim light, [for] a snake is [later] subverted by conceptualisation that—[as it] emerges—effects the ascertainment of that [fact that the perceived object is a rope], similarly, also this perception of a persistent and gross [form is later subverted] by [means of] a reflection (*sc.* mental process) that vindicates [the ultimate existence of] infinitesimal atoms that perish in a moment (*sc.* momentary).[797] What is here [in this reasoning] improper?!' [we would retort:] it is not [the case,] because the representation of the rope alone is capable of obliterating the error [of seeing] a snake [in place of a rope] that occurred before and because it is impossible to negate [the representation of a snake] even by [means of] a hundred acts of conceptualisation[798], if this [representation of the rope] is not there. If [you defend your position as follows]: 'Even in this case—since the past and the future are not proximate (*sc.* not within reach), inasmuch as [they have already been] destroyed or [have] not [yet] arisen [respectively] and since [objects having] gross parts, [when] being analysed by means of [their] difference or non-difference [from their own parts], do not abide in their own parts—only infinitesimal atoms which perish in a moment (*sc.* are momentary) appear [in cognition]; and, therefore, it is the very representation (*sc.* mental process) [in the cognition that] subverts the perception of the persistent and gross [object],' so [we shall retort:] since it is inexplicable that the representation [of an object] can be comprehended through an instruction, everyday practice should function exactly in such a manner (*sc.* with regard to momentary infinitesimal atoms). If [you object:] '[Everyday practice] does not function [with regard to momentary infinitesimal atoms] because of the blunder [caused by] a subsequent false conceptualisation (*sc.* an idea of a persistent and gross object),' [that is] not [correct] because this [kind of a] riposte is caused by a blunder[799] also in other [situations]. For it is as follows: who could ward off [the situation when] a cunning [person—in accordance] with your argumentation—asserts: 'Although a shell, etc., is represented [in cognition] as white, it is [in reality] seen as blue by perception; [but] because of the blunder [caused] the subsequent false conceptualisation, [it] appears [to be] white'? So, it is not possible to carry out the denial of what is perceived; hence [the existence of] the real thing [as something] persistent and gross is established, because only this [real thing as persistent and gross] is perceived [and] because the other one (*sc.* momentary infinitesimal atom) can be inferred [as something] that is proved by means of perception [grasping] this [persistent and gross real thing], inasmuch as also that [momentary infinitesimal atom] is not established if this [persistent and gross real thing] is not accepted. Thereby [your] teaching that the real thing [as something] persistent and gross is deprived of efficient action[800] is contravened, too, because it is an empirical fact that only [the real thing as being] exactly of this kind (*sc.* persistent and gross) is operative in all activities and because [the infinitesimal atom which] perishes in a moment (*sc.* momentary) is precluded from [any] activity, according to what has formerly been voiced [by us]: 'Could at all the essence of an object that is perishable in a moment (*sc.* momentary) produce its effect [1.1] in the moment [of its existence], [1.2] before or [1.3] subsequently? And so forth'[801]. Furthermore, since every real thing is cognised as [something] whose form endures [in itself] as well as is distinguished [from other things] together with [its general characteristics such as the universal] existence, [the universal] man-hood, consciousness, etc., and with [its modes such as being] a child, [being] an adolescent, [being] an adult, [being] an old man, joy, distress, etc., [it is established that the real thing] consists in substance and modes, because [its] non-difference [with other similar objects] is [tantamount to its] substance, [whereas its] difference [from other objects] is [tantamount to the fact that it] consists in modes.[802] And, consequently, your teaching—by means of [the argument based on] the absence of past and future moments—that only the present moment has [the capacity] to execute efficient action does not present any subversion to us because [any] substance, only when embraced by the present mode (*sc.* only in its present manifestation), inasmuch as modes exist consecutively, is apt to execute efficient action. Not only this [substance] pervades the three times, [but] also the perceiving person—inasmuch as [he] consists in substance—is exactly of such a kind (*sc.* exists in the past, present and future). And, therefore, this [substance] only as [something] persistent, due to accumulating these [past, present and future] forms by means of ruling out (*sc.* neglecting) momentary modes, is applied in all activities—that [is the idea that] enters the path of cognition (*sc.* becomes known), because also persistent existence is really existing [and] because momentary modes, even though they are present, [can] not be grasped, for the cognition of ordinary people—inasmuch as [it] depends on the destruction-cum-subsidence of [karmic] veils—has as its province [merely] a certain aspect. If, however, the knowledge of substance—inasmuch as it is acquired by the force of perceiving a series of modes—were conceived unreal, then one should say whether the antecedent mode [passes]—at the rise of the subsequent mode—with succession or without succession, because there is no other logical alternative. If [it passed] with succession, substance should be called another synonym [for mode]; whereas, if [it passed] without succession, [there would follow] the undesired consequence that the subsequent mode would not arise because it would be without cause. Thus, efficient action [can] not be established without the real thing which consists in both, [viz. in modes and substance]. And efficient action is not the characteristic of the real thing, either, because final moments of sound, lightning, light, etc., would—inasmuch as [they would] not initiate another moment—attain the status of [being] something unreal, because, on the other hand, if [their final moment] were something unreal, also [their] last but one moment could not be operative with regard to the real thing—[and] further on in such a manner up to, by addition, all moments of the real thing. If the fact that something, even though [it does] not initiate another moment, produces the cognition the domain of which is [that very thing] itself, were falsely conceived to be efficient action, then, if that were the case, also a series of modes existing in the past would secure the status of the real thing, because [the series of past modes] becomes the domain of the [supernatural] cognition of a yogin. Hence, efficient action is not the characteristic of the real thing[803]; on the contrary, [the true characteristic of the real thing is] its being furnished with origination, annihilation and permanence,[804] because it is determined [as such] by cognitive criteria. If [you object:] 'Origination and annihilation stand in contradiction to permanence,' [we ask]: how is this contradiction [established]? Is it [established] on account of a cognitive criterion or on account of something that is not a cognitive criterion? The first alternative, to begin with, is not [the case], because all cognitive criteria have [already] been proved to be capable of illuminating the real thing of this kind, both internally and externally.[805] The second [alternative] is not [feasible], either, because something that is not a cognitive criterion is ineffective. Thereby, the criticism [directed against the idea of] grossness [of the real thing] is disproved, as well, because it is refuted by [the above argument referring to] the representation [of the real thing], for the pointing out the contradiction by denying this [grossness of the real thing] is nothing but a twaddle, inasmuch as it is without basis. What has next been claimed [by you]—namely that all cognitive criteria grasp the real thing which is related to them, inasmuch as they consist in the revelation of the present[806]—is not proper, for they are not established to be exclusively related to the present moment in the absolute sense, because—inasmuch as they are somehow non-different from the cognitive subject and this [cognitive subject] pervades the three times—they also abide as consisting in this [being the pervader of the three times]. And, therefore, since the cognitive subject consists in transformations in [the way of] grasping objects, all cognitive criteria are operative only with regard to the real thing that is subject to transformation, not with regard to [the real thing that is] momentary. And, even though one grasps the real thing that occurs in a past or future moment, there is no undesired consequence of grasping a beginningless and infinite series of births,[807] because [the faculty of grasping a beginningless and infinite series of births] depends on the cessation of [karmic] veils, inasmuch as this [cessation of karmic veils constitutes] the inner cause of manifesting [things in] consciousness in conformity with the ultimate truth, whereas something-to-be-grasped, etc., are external elements. However, the [alleged] undesired consequence of grasping a beginningless and infinite series of moments of the [whole] range of all real things, when the complete annihilation of [karmic] veils is [attained], presents no subversion for us, because [this is exactly what] is accepted [by us]. So, when, on the other hand, a partial destruction-cum-subsidence of [karmic] veils [takes place], the operation of cognitive awareness follows this [partial destruction-cum-subsidence of karmic veils]. Because of that, acts of cognition of ordinary people operate with regard to a gross real thing, lasting for some time, not completely (*sc.* not with regard to every thing). And these [acts of cognition of ordinary people] are not false, because even the [particular] aspect which can be grasped by them exists in the real thing, inasmuch as everyday practice is established by that much only, [viz. omniscience is not indispensable]. What has been stated [by you]: 'Ignorant [people]—since they are deceived by several originations of [various] similar [momentary things]—do not apprehend momentariness, even though they grasp [it directly], and they accomplish everyday practice [based on] the persistence [of the real thing] by the force of wrong conceptualisation,'[808] is not proper because according to your intention there is no [thing like] similarity,[809] [and] if this [similarity] does not exist, the origination of the error considered [by you] to be brought about by this [similarity] is impossible, inasmuch as it is without the seed (*sc.* cause). Accordingly, also the superimposition of persistence onto certain things is logically correct only [in the case] of a [person who] has grasped a persistent [object], not otherwise, just like the superimposition of a snake, when [in fact] a rope is seen in a place [characterised by] a very dim light, [in the case] of a [person who] has seen a snake. And [you claim that] persistence never experiences the phenomenon of [itself] turning into the domain of awareness of yours (*sc.* is not cognised by you); so [we can ask]: how is [then] the superimposition of this [persistence]—even though it is seen by perception—onto each [and every] real thing, that is every moment associated with rise and termination, [at all possible]?! Therefore, the real thing becomes the domain [of cognition] through all cognitive criteria, that are of importance in practical life, as something whose momentary transient occurrences are ruled out (*sc.* neglected) [and] in which the fact that it is differentiated into infinitesimal atoms is not [directly] observable. Thus, the outlook that determines invisible infinitesimal atoms which perish in a moment (*sc.* are momentary) by means of ruling out (*sc.* neglecting) this [persistence] receives the denotation of a defective direct viewpoint, because [such an outlook alone] which demonstrates these [momentary invisible infinitesimal atoms] only by putting aside this [persistence] is the [direct] viewpoint [proper].

[29.27] [Ad 5-7] Similarly, also the verbal [viewpoint] and the remaining [two, the etymological and the factual viewpoints—inasmuch as] they corroborate complete[810] non-difference of an object from the speech element—are defective viewpoints because the logical reason that is brought forward in order to corroborate this [non-difference and that is] characterised by the fact that 'when that [speech element] is cognised, [the object] is cognised,' is inconclusive. For it as follows[811]: it is not absolutely true [to say]: 'if *x* is cognised when *y* is cognised, then *x* is necessarily non-different from (*sc.* identical with) *y*,' because fire, etc., although being different, is cognised, by the force of the relation characterised by [its] being otherwise inexplicable, when smoke is cognised. In the similar way, also speech element, since it is the denoter, will convey an object (its denotatum)[812], even though [the latter] is different [from speech element], because the non-difference (*sc.* identity) [of the speech element and the object (denotatum)] is subverted by perception, etc., for [the object (denotatum)] is experienced [as different] from the speech element by nothing but the discrimination. And when this logical reason[813] is proved to be inconclusive, then also the proof of the non-difference [of object (denotatum)] with speech element is cast off far away by means of a proof of the fact that all objects (denotata) have [corresponding] denoters [that convey] them.[814] And no cognitive criterion grasps the invariable connection in the following case, either: 'whatever is an object, it must have a [corresponding] denoter [that conveys it],' because this [invariable connection can] not be established merely on account of the example of a pot, etc., and because it is established that [certain] momentary or indescribable transient occurrences of a substance[815] are inexpressible, inasmuch as it is impossible to express [them], if there are no means of grasping the linguistic convention [relating them and the linguistic units denoting them]. The assertion, on the other hand, that also those [objects] are perishable in a moment (*sc.* momentary) is to be refuted [in the same way] like [in the above case of] the direct viewpoint[816]. Thus, [these three viewpoints] that determine [a particular object] intended by [each of] them depending in fact on [a respective] individual opinion [expressed by a given viewpoint]—[inasmuch as] they rule out [an external] object [as denotatum] of the speech element that is contrary to that [object intended by each of these viewpoints]—appropriate a character of a defective viewpoint. For that much [only] is determined by cognitive criteria, by way of confirmation, namely[817]: 'speech element is a denoter of an object (denotatum).' There is, however, no[thing like] the following [binding] circumscription, viz.: 'this [particular speech element] is a denoter of this [particular object (denotatum)] only, not of any other [object],' because—inasmuch as [possible] conventions, etc., [depending on] place, time, people, etc.,[818] are manifold—all speech elements are explicable as denoting various objects (denotata) by means of [their] various capabilities, for [speech elements are] observed to demonstrate various objects (denotata) [and objects] have infinite properties, whereas [there is] no contradiction [in the assumption that] objects (denotata)—precisely because [they possess] infinite properties—can be denoted by various speech elements, for it is an empirical fact that [verbal] communication [proceeds] due to [the fact that] there is no discord[819] [that it is] exactly like this, inasmuch as [there would follow] the undesired consequence of the disintegration of this [verbal communication] if these [facts] were not accepted.[820] Hence, all linguistic units are [theoretically] denoters of all objects (denotata), inasmuch as [they] are capable [of that]; however, depending on partial destruction-cum-subsidence [of karmic veils], they somehow produce the understanding concerning [only] certain [objects (denotata)]. And therefore, [Ad 5] they are used to denote certain [objects (denotata)] in accordance with the usage [when] the factors [accountable for their] grammatical formation [are] disregarded; [Ad 6] [they are used to denote] certain [other objects (denotata)] depending on the grammatical formation [based on] the universal; [Ad 7] [they are used to denote] certain [other objects (denotata)] depending on the factors [accountable for their] grammatical formation that occur at their [point of] time (*sc.* when the speech elements are uttered). On these grounds, the insistence on a circumscribed object (denotatum) referring to those [objects (denotata)] can not be enjoined by a rational person (*sc.* someone who relies on cognitive criteria). Consequently, when these [viewpoints like] the verbal [viewpoint], etc., demonstrate an object (denotatum) [denoted by a particular] speech element, which is intended by a respective [viewpoint], putting aside (*sc.* neglecting) [the fact that] the object (denotatum) and [respective] speech elements are intended by (*sc.* point to) each other, then they are [proper] viewpoints, because also this [object (denotatum)] exists in (*sc.* is related to) these [speech elements]. [When] used, however, to denote [a particular object (denotatum)], by [way of] mutual subversion [of the object (denotatum) or the respective speech element], they share the status of [opinions that] have the form of defective viewpoints because they are void of the objective substratum.

[29.28] And now [an objection is raised by the opponent]: 'If outlooks, which are solely devoted to corroborating one single property respectively [and] which lead to ruling out [all] the remaining properties, are demonstrated [to have] the status of a defective viewpoint, then [any other] utterance, as well, that is used to denote [a particular object (denotatum)] by means of mentioning [only] one property and that leads to disproving [all] the remaining properties, inasmuch as [it functions] with a restriction[821], results in [being] (*sc.* turns out to be) false. And therefore, only the utterance which displays the real thing as possessed of infinite properties—since it demonstrates [its] object (denotatum) corresponding to the state of affairs—is true. Yet utterances [are] not used to denote [their objects (denotata)] in such a manner because it is an empirical fact that in the [verbal] communication speech elements are pronounced as related [to their objects (denotata)] by the demonstration of one single property, like "this pot is a white shape," for it is impossible to state all properties simultaneously, even though [speech elements] denoting these [properties are theoretically] infinite. And these utterances, although they display [only] one single property, cannot be called false because [that would lead to] the undesired consequence of the destruction of the entire verbal communication, inasmuch as if these [utterances] were false, the practice [of the verbal communication] based on them could not be established.' As regards this [objection of the opponent, the following reply] is given. In this world, to begin with, people who demonstrate the real thing are two-fold: [1] common people and [2] people who reflect upon the truth. [Ad 1] Among these [two categories], common people, to begin with, designate—at the time of the [verbal] communication—an object, that is well known by perception, etc., in a neutral manner because they have [a particular aspect of the object as their] purpose, namely: 'a blue water-lily' [or] 'a fragrant lotus', but they do not care about grasping (*sc.* approving of) or revoking other properties subsisting in the property-possessor (*sc.* water-lily, lotus) of this [particular property (*sc.* blue, fragrant)], because they do not have [other properties as their] purpose, for any [verbal] communication in question is completed (*sc.* carried out) by that much only. And [such] utterances [predicating] of this [property in question] are not false, inasmuch as other remaining properties are not disproved [by them], because only [such utterances] that lead to disproving [all] the remaining properties are false. If [the opponent objects:] 'Since it is established—because of the maxim 'all utterances function with a restriction'[822]—that also [these utterances] lead to ruling out [all] the remaining properties, then also these [utterances] result in falsehood according to your logic,' [that is] not [correct] because the restriction is operative with regard to excluding merely the possible non-existence[823] of this [particular property]; for instance, to a person standing at the door, etc., [leading] into a hall filled with many people, with his mind wobbling: 'Is there possibly Devadatta here or is [he] not?,' someone states [explicitly], say: 'Devadatta is [here].' Even though it is understood that in this case the two words brought forward (*sc.* 'Devadatta is [here]') [function] with the restriction, for otherwise [one would have to face] the undesired consequence that it would be purposeless to utter them, nevertheless the restriction excludes merely his possible non-existence [in this place], [it does] not [exclude] other people. It does not [exclude his] non-existence (*sc.* not being) as another form, either, because the sentence under discussion is pronounced[824] with the intention of excluding that (*sc.* merely his possible non-existence)[825], inasmuch as [any] linguistic unit has the efficacy to demonstrate its own object (denotatum) only depending on the intention, etc.[826], of the person who pronounces [this sentence]. But [that does] not [imply that] the relation characterised by the relationship between the denotatum and the denoter is purposeless because, if this [relation between the denotatum and the denoter were] not [there], it would be impossible to make use even of the form [of a particular word or a sentence] merely by the intention of the person who pronounces [the word or the sentence]. And we do not take a position that the utterance which demonstrates the real thing only as furnished with [its] all properties [alone] is true, because [the result] would be that [utterances] that display the real thing as embraced by (*sc.* endowed with) one [single] property are false. [But] rather [we maintain] that [any utterance] demonstrating an object, which is possibly there[827], is true; and [indeed any selected] properties that have become the domain of [particular] utterances, while [all] the remaining properties have not been disproved, are possibly there. Hence, [any utterance] that demonstrates that [selected single possibly existent property] is necessarily true. But when adherents of rival systems of thought, whose minds are attached to opinions of (according to) defective viewpoints, pronounce that [utterance] with the restriction merely [having] the intention of revoking other properties subsisting in the property-possessor of that [particular property expressed by a given utterance]—like, for instance: 'the real thing is either exclusively impermanent or exclusively permanent', etc.—then who could ward off [the consequence of such an utterance] assuming the status of falsehood (*sc.* becoming false), inasmuch as it would be void of the objective substratum? [Ad 2] People who reflect upon the truth, on the other hand—while demonstrating the real thing, that is established by [means of] cognitive criteria like perception, etc., that is in its essence multiplex—may demonstrate [the real thing] in two ways, namely: by [means of] an incomplete account or by [means of] a complete account.[828] Out of these [two alternatives], the incomplete account is subject to a [respective] viewpoint, [whereas] the complete account is reliant upon cognitive criterion. For it is as follows: when [they], being desirous of demonstrating a particular property in a neutral manner due to the fact that they have [a particular aspect of the object as their] purpose, pronounce a statement with the thought indifferent to either affirming or revoking [all] the remaining properties, then also people who reflect upon the truth, like common people, communicate [this particular property or object] as [something having] imprecise form [in the cognition], namely: 'the living element is the agent, the cogniser, the experiencing subject'[829]. Hence, [such a statement]—inasmuch as it does not demonstrate the whole real thing—is called the incomplete account, which means that it merely shows [selected] properties that are possibly there in consonance with the opinion of (*sc.* according to) a [respective] viewpoint. But when they intend to demonstrate [the real thing] by reflecting upon the operation of cognitive criteria completely, then [people who reflect upon the truth] demonstrate [the real thing] by a phrase [which functions] with the restriction and [which is] appended with the speech element (viz. the modal functor) 'in a certain sense,' [being] synonymous to [the expression] 'somehow', that is indicative of all properties [of a particular real thing] which are admitted to [be either] secondary or main, like [the phrase] 'the living element, in a certain sense, indeed exists'[830] and similar ones. Hence, this [statement] is called the complete account because it displays the real thing [in question, which, firstly,] is endowed with infinite properties that are indicated by and interiorised in (*sc.* comprised by) the speech element (viz. the modal functor) 'in a certain sense', [secondly,] the being itself of which is made the main [import] by [both] the speech element (*sc.* substantive) 'the living element' and the verb (*sc.* 'exists') that are explicitly brought forward, [and, thirdly,] the possible non-existence of which is excluded by the restriction (*sc.* 'indeed'); [in other words, the complete account] is tantamount to recounting (*sc.* portraying) the complete object as it is recognised by through cognitive criteria. That [idea] has been expressed [in the following aphorism]:

> 'This cognitive approach to a particular cognoscible [thing] may consist in viewpoints and cognitive criteria. Among these two [categories], cognitive criterion should be known to grasp completely (or: a complete thing), whereas viewpoint [should be known] to grasp incompletely (or: an incomplete thing).'[831]

[29.29] What this amounts to is the following: whatever the propounder of the doctrine of [seven-fold] modal description, who is conversant with [both] viewpoints and cognitive criteria, predicates of with the intention of demonstrating the intrinsic nature of the real thing—while taking into consideration [both] the complete and the incomplete accounts—that is true, because the domain [of his predications] are possibly existent objects. However, whatever propounders [of simplistic theories interpreting reality] in the absolute sense, who cling to opinions of (according to) a [respective] defective viewpoint, argue is false, because the province [of their predications] are possibly non-existent objects.

[30.0] Presently, [the author]—reinforcing precisely this [multiplex] object, [as it has been described in NA 29, and] demonstrating the following [idea]: 'also the aphorisms in the Canon that proceed [by following] every individual opinion of (according to) one [single] viewpoint do not communicate the complete object; on the contrary, [only] that[832] which proceeds [by following] an outlook that [is formed as] an aggregate of [all] these [individual viewpoints] proclaims (*sc.* conveys) an object [in] a full-fledged [form]'—states [the following]:

> **/30/ Since viewpoints are active in the course of testimony [as] being related to one [aspect[833]], [testimony] determining the complete object is called the testimony [based on] the doctrine of [seven-fold] modal description.**

[30.1] In this world testimony is three-fold, namely [1] wrong testimony, [2] testimony [based on a particular] viewpoint and [3] testimony [based on] the doctrine of the [seven-fold] modal description. Regarding this, that which has been heard is testimony, [viz.] oral tradition. [Ad 1] Testimony which is wrong, [viz.] false, is wrong testimony. And this [wrong testimony] proceeds [by following] an outlook of (according to) a [particular] defective viewpoint [and] is related to [heterodox] thinkers because it is without domain. [Ad 2] Similarly, testimony [acquired] by [means of respective] viewpoints, which are [its] causes, is testimony [based on a particular] viewpoint; and this [testimony based on respective particular viewpoints] is comprised within the oral tradition of the venerable ones (Arhants) itself [and] is based on an outlook of (according to) one viewpoint, for instance: 'when a hellish being has originated at [a given] moment, it perishes [immediately],' etc., because even momentariness is possibly existent (contained) in this [hellish being] according to direct viewpoint.[834] [Ad 3] Similarly, the [technique of] propounding that is furnished with [the modal functor] 'in a certain sense', that indicates all other infinite properties different from the property, which is mentioned specifically, [and that has a form of] a proposition [expressing explicitly only] the intended property is the doctrine of the [seven-fold] modal description; a testimony whose essence is that [doctrine] is the testimony [based on] the doctrine of the [seven-fold] modal description. If [a question] is asked: 'What is it like?', [the author] says [in reply]: '**complete**' [means] full-fledged; and this [complete thing] is that '**object**'; '**[testimony] determining**' this [complete object] is called in such a way because [it] is a cause of the ascertainment of this [complete object]. That means that [this testimony] demonstrates in its turn[835] the intrinsic nature of the real thing as a whole in conformity with the ultimate truth, because—inasmuch as it consists in the verbal level—determination has the form of cognitive awareness. [In order to counter the objection]: 'Why does then the testimony [based on a particular] viewpoint not become [a testimony] determining the complete object?', [the author] says: since '**viewpoints**', [i.e.] the comprehensive and other [viewpoints], '**are active**', [viz.] operate, '**in the course of testimony**,' [i.e.] in the path of the oral tradition, '**[as] being related to one [aspect]**,' [viz. as being] confined to grasping [only] one property, this [testimony based on a particular viewpoint] that is based on one single outlook [respectively can] not determine the complete object because their aggregate alone determines the complete object. Such is the [author's] intention [expressed in the above aphorism].

[31.0] Thus, having taught the intrinsic nature[s] of viewpoints and cognitive criteria in the above manner[836], now [the author]— desirous of stating [explicitly] the cogniser who pervades completely all viewpoints and [completely all] cognitive criteria, inasmuch as these [viewpoints and cognitive criteria] abide in this [cogniser] due to the relation of essential identity—says:

/31/ The cogniser[837] is the observer of himself and of something different, the agent, the experiencing subject, is subject to change, is well-established by self-cognition[838], is the living element [and is someone] whose essence is not of earth, etc.

[31.1] With regard to this [issue of the cogniser], '**the living element**' [is so called] because of [his] living in the three times, which means [that he is] the bearer of vital forces, [i.e.] the cognitive subject. [He is]—because he cognises in a valid way—the cogniser, [i.e.] determiner of the cognoscible. [As a reply to the question:] 'What is [he] like?', [the author] says: [the one] whose character is to observe, [i.e.] to illuminate, '**himself and something different**,' [i.e.] his self and something else [different from him], is '**the observer of himself and of something different**' [which] is tantamount to [someone who] reveals his intrinsic nature and [his] object. Similarly, [someone] who acts is the '**agent**'; [someone] who experiences is '**the experiencing subject**.' Alteration [or] going through various modes [means] '**change**', [i.e.] transformation; [the one] who possesses this [change] '**is subject to change**.' That by which the '**self**', [viz.] the cognitive subject is sensed (*sc.* cognised) is '**self-cognition**'; [the one] who is correctly established, [viz.] determined or known, by this [self-cognition] '**is well-established by self-cognition**.' Those whose [enumeration] begins [with] '**earth**', [i.e.] the earth element, are '**earth and other [gross elements]**.' On account of the speech element '**etc.**' [other gross elements, such as] water, fire, air [and] ether, are comprised. [The one] whose '**essence**', [i.e. whose] intrinsic nature, does not exist [as..., is] '**[someone] whose essence is not [...]**.' Is it [meant] with regard to his intrinsic nature? No, [it is meant with regard to gross elements like earth, etc., namely: the one] whose essence is not of [gross elements like] earth, etc., [is] '**[someone] whose essence is not of earth, etc.**,' which means [someone] who does not [have] the intrinsic nature of earth, etc.

[31.2] By the [expression] '**the cogniser is the living element**' in the above [aphorism, the author] rebuts those [Buddhist] propounders of the theory of momentary annihilation (*sc.* of momentariness) who do not accept the ultimately real cogniser, [but who], on the contrary, maintain [the cogniser to be] ultimately unreal, fabricated by wrong conceptualisation, [to be such] whose existence is produced by past impressions prevalent from beginningless time [that are] awakened by the force of the experience of a series of moments of consciousness; [he rebuts them] because [the idea of] annihilation in a moment (*sc.* momentariness) has been negated just a while ago[839], inasmuch as the real thing which is subject to transformation [both] external[ly] and internal[ly] has been proven [to exist].

[31.3] And now [an objection is raised by the Buddhist opponent.] '[Things like] pot, etc., to begin with, are empirically seen to undergo extinction; and [the question arises] whether the extinction could be effected by the totality of causes, like a club, etc., either [in case] [1] of such [things] whose essential nature is non-evanescent (*sc.* permanent) or [2] of such [things] whose essential nature is evanescent? [Ad 1] If the first alternative [is assumed], it is not proper because it is impossible to dissolve essential nature [which is believed to be permanent], inasmuch as this [essential nature] is of a fixed (*sc.* unchanging) form, otherwise it would be unjustified to assume [the existence of an unchanging] essential nature. [Ad 2] If you say: "The essential nature, which evolves by the force of its own causes, of the [object that undergoes extinction] is exactly of such a kind (*sc.* evanescent), namely it will perish after having met a cause of [its] extinction," then [the question], nevertheless, [remains] whether the presence of the cause of its extinction [2.1] is fortuitous or [2.2] is indeed produced[840] by the essential nature of this [object which undergoes extinction]. [Ad 2.1] If the first alternative [is assumed], then the presence of this [cause of the extinction of the object in question] is not necessary, [firstly,] because [this cause of the extinction of the object in question], even though it is present, may disappear due to the occurrence of a casual condition opposite [to it, secondly,] because also [auxiliary] causes that effectuate the presence of this [cause of extinction of the object in question] depend on the totality of causes that effectuate their own presence, [thirdly,] because also [these auxiliary causes that effect the occurrence of this cause of extinction of the object in question], even though they are present, may disappear due to [the occurrence of] their counterpart (*sc.* a casual condition opposite to them) and, [fourthly,] because these [very causes] are fortuitous. And therefore, no [object like] a pot, etc., whatsoever, [which stands in a relation to] a series of causes (*sc.* causal complex) of its own extinction that are [in fact] not present, could even perish. And this [consequence] is not accepted because everything which has been produced [stands in] non-discord with (*sc.* is liable to) extinction. [Ad 2.2] If the second alternative [is considered], then, if that were the case, the causes of the extinction [of the object in question] will be present also afterwards by the force of this [very object in question, i.e. they will endure as long as the object exists]; hence [it follows that the causes of the extinction of the object in question] must be present only in the first moment [of the existence of the object in question]; also in this manner [we are forced to conclude that] the object is nothing but momentary. If [you maintain the following]: "[The object] is produced by its own cause alone, as constituted by the following [principle]: this [object] will effectuate the presence of the cause of its own extinction after a fixed [period of] time," [we object:] no, [it is not correct]; also in this way the perishability in a moment (*sc.* momentariness) is ascertained. For it is as follows: that [particular object in question] has been created—let us assume—by its own cause as such [a thing] whose essential nature is capable of effectuating the presence of the cause of its own extinction after a year; and [now we may posit a question:] [1] is this essential nature [of the object existent] in the second moment after the moment of its origination or [2] not? [Ad 1] If it is [existent], then, that being the case, a [whole] year should be established (*sc.* measured out) again [and again] by this [essential nature]. In this way, if that very essential nature of this [object is existent] also in the last but one moment of whichever (*sc.* the given) year, then continued existence [of the essential nature of the object in question] would reach (*sc.* extend to) the subsequent next year, as well, and then [the object in question] would be[come something] existing immutably for infinite aeons[841] because [its] essential nature that exists immutably (*sc.* continues) for a year [would] not be dissolved. [Ad 2] If you say that this essential nature [of the object in question] is not [existent] in the second moment [after the moment of its origination], then woe! nothing but momentariness presents itself [as a consequence], because the phenomenon of not preserving the same condition [turns out to be] the characteristic of this [object in question][842]. Furthermore, [the following dilemma has to be solved]: would the cause of the extinction effect the extinction of an entity as [1] [something] different [from the entity] or as [2] [something] non-different [from it]. [Ad 1] If effecting [the extinction] as [something] different [from the entity to be destroyed were admitted], nothing could be effected [in this way], and therefore, the entity would experience the phenomenon of [its] preserving the same condition (*sc.* it could never be destroyed). If [you reply]:

"The relation between these two [viz. between the entity and its extinction] is effected," it is not [correct] because [any] relation different from the relation of essential identity [with the cause] and from the relation of causality (*sc.* origination from the cause) is negated (*sc.* cannot be admitted); and any of these two [kinds of] relation is not possible with regard to these [two, viz. between the entity and its extinction][843], either, [firstly,] because [as far as the relation of essential identity is concerned] it is unjustified to assume the relation of essential identity with [something which is] different, [secondly,] because [as far as the relation of causality is concerned] that which has been produced by] another cause and [has] arisen afterwards lacks the relation of causality [with the main cause in question][844]. Thus, the extinction cannot be effected [as something] different [from the entity to be destroyed]. [Ad 2] If, on the other hand, effecting [the extinction] as [something] non-different [from (*sc.* identical with) the entity to be destroyed were admitted], then [the consequence] arrived at [would be] as follows: the cause of extinction effects nothing but this entity itself because [the extinction being] non-different [from the entity] is characterised by this [entity]. And this [entity] cannot be effected [by its extinction] because [the entity can be] made exclusively by its own cause. Besides, if effecting (*sc.* producing) this [entity by the cause of its extinction were admitted], then nothing but the perpetuity of this [entity] would [result], not its disintegration. Hence, [to sum up the above discussion], the extinction of such [things] whose essential nature is non-evanescent (*sc.* permanent), [on the one hand], is not possible to be effected subsequently [in the future] in any way whatsoever; [the extinction of such things] whose essential nature is evanescent, [on the other], takes place—inasmuch as they evolve by the force of their own causes—every moment even before [and is] not dependant on [any] other cause, because [their] essential nature has a fixed form [as something evanescent]; therefore, momentary annihilation (*sc.* momentariness) breathes even now (*sc.* is always present).'[845] Such [may be the objection of a Buddhist propounder of momentariness].

[31.4] Regarding this [objection, we] riposte [as follows]. This is [basically] true,[846] nonetheless, why could [1] continued existence and [2] origination not be recognised [by you] to take place at every moment exactly in the same way as extinction is recognised by you—inasmuch as it is unjustified to assume a cause of extinction—to take place every moment, because also the causes of these [two, when] being examined, [turn out] to be impossible. [1] For it is as follows: [one should solve the dilemma] whether entities as such could be established, to begin with, by a cause of continued existence as [1.1] having a non-persistent essential nature or [1.2] having a persistent essential nature? [Ad 1.1] The first alternative, to begin with, does not pass through the ordeal [of examination] because it is impossible to assume the essential nature in a different manner, inasmuch as this [essential nature] has a fixed form in every case [as something permanent], like the essential nature of consciousness or [the essential nature of something] unconscious, for otherwise, [one would have to] abandon the idea of essential nature. [Ad 1.2] If the second alternative [is assumed], in its turn, then of what use is the cause of continued existence [in the case of entities that] as such have a persistent essential nature? If [an objection is raised]: 'Continued existence is by no means accepted; that is why this [argumentation of yours] is nothing but a reproach that cannot be accepted,' woe! then you are vanquished, for in this manner entities could not remain [existent] even for a single moment. If [the Buddhist opponent ripostes]: '[Indeed, all entities, being momentary, exist only for a single moment, because their continued existence] is, as a matter of fact, accepted to exist for a moment,' then we say that this [continued existence] cannot be effected even by a hundred of causes [in the case of entities whose] essential nature has no continued existence [at all,] because if [their] essential nature had no continued existence[847], in its turn, the operation of the cause [of continued existence] would be purposeless. [The consequence of such a reasoning is that,] being without a cause, [continued existence has to] exist all the time [and momentariness is impossible]—thus, the final blow has been given to momentary annihilation (*sc.* momentariness). [2] Likewise, [one has to answer the question,] as well, whether the cause of originating could accomplish the origination [2.1] [of an entity] whose essential nature is that [origination] or [2.2] [of an entity] whose essential nature is not that [origination]? [Ad 2.1] The first alternative, to begin with, cannot be logically correct, for the cause which is engaged in bringing about [something] that itself is endowed with origination grinds ground flour [that is already ground, or] whitens a shell [that is already while] (*sc.* uselessly accomplishes a task that has already been accomplished), because—even though that [cause of originating] were not [there—the entity could] originate, inasmuch as it is capable [of originating] by itself. [Ad 2.2] The second alternative cannot be admitted, either, because it is impossible for [an entity which] itself is not endowed with the property of origination to be brought about; otherwise, also [such non-existent things], like a hare's horn, etc., could possess the prominent rank of [real entities that] can be brought about because there is no difference [between the origination of real entities and the origination of non-existent things from this point of view]. And, consequently, there would be no absolutely non-existent [thing] at all. Thus, [the following conclusion] inevitably possesses correctness (*sc.* is established without doubt): just like extinction [of entities], inasmuch as it is without a cause, takes place every moment, exactly in the very same manner—according to the logical reasoning shown [above]—continued existence and origination as well [have to be accepted to take place every moment]; hence, every real thing that is produced must be accepted as [being] under the sway of the triad, [viz. the origination, continued existence and extinction]. That being the case, the following [statement] inevitably possesses correctness (*sc.* proves correct): the cogniser, that is [something] ultimately real, is likewise the living element, that undeniably possesses continuity due to [his] animateness, consciousness, substantiality, etc., is [at the same time] endowed with the properties of origination and annihilation [both] due to [such emotions like] joy, distress, etc., as well as due to [his] transformations [consisting in] grasping various objects.

[31.5] And now [an objection is raised by an impartial witness watching the Buddhist-Jaina debate.][848] 'If it is proved by you that origination, annihilation and continued existence—inasmuch as [they] are without a cause—exist all the time, then how [is it possible that] this operation of the totality of their causes, which is—as one should realise—well-known through cognitive criteria like perception, etc., may be inferred by positive concomitance and negative concomitance? And it is not possible to deny this [totality of causes of origination, of annihilation and of continued existence]! For it is as follows: when the operation of the group of causes (*sc.* causal complex), like a potter, etc., [takes place, objects like] a pot, etc., are perceived; and when this [operation of the causal complex of origination] is absent, these [objects] are not observed. Hence, it is said that [these objects] are produced by that [causal complex contributing to origination]. Also continued existence [takes places] before the presence (*sc.* emergence) of causes of extinction simply by its own force. Similarly, extinction, as well, is cognised as experiencing the existence or the non-existence [respectively] of the presence (*sc.* emergence) or of the non-presence (*sc.* absence) of [such causes of extinction like] a hammer, etc.,[849] [i.e. is cognised] as [being] effected by that [causai complex contributing to extinction]; [anyway, extinction] is not without a cause! So, how is it possible [to persevere in] this [conviction, namely that origination, annihilation and continued existence are without a cause]?'

[31.6] Regarding this [doubt, a reply] is stated. We do not ward off (*sc.* deny) the operation of causes completely, [but] rather [we maintain that] causes of [any] substance, which [in its turn] unfolds itself as [something] whose essence is origination, annihilation and continued existence, experience their operation (*sc.* become active) with regard to effecting the particular (*sc.* an individual manifestation) of that [substance], [1] because it is an empirical fact that these [three factors, viz. origination, annihilation and continued existence,] are in compliance with positive concomitance and negative concomitance [in relation] to this [substance] alone, [not with the particular], and [2] because, if the perceived [phenomena] were denied, we would be inactive, inasmuch as [one can be] arbitrarily partial towards [a particular conviction, viz. maintain a particular opinion, on account of] the dyad characterised by [Ad 2] cognition and [Ad 1] logical congruity. Simply, we admit neither [Ad 1] logical congruity lacking cognition nor [Ad 2] cognition destitute of logical congruity, because this [cognition]—inasmuch as it would [have] a possibly non-existent[850] object as its domain—would be void of the objective substratum.[851] So let [us] leave that alone[852]

[31.7] By the following [expression] **'the observer of himself and of something different'** [the author]—like [in the case of] the qualification of cognitive criterion: 'revealing itself and something else [different from it],' that has been taught previously[853]—disproves the Mīmāṁsaka, who are propounders of indirect [character of any] knowledge [and deny the possibility of self-cognition], as well as the Yogācāra, who are propounders of the sole [existence] of cognition [and reject the existence of the external world; and there is no need to repeat his arguments] because there is no difference between this [case] and the argumentation presented [previously][854], inasmuch as somehow there is no difference between cognition and cogniser[855]

[31.8] By the double qualification, viz. **'the agent, the experiencing subject,'** [the author] denounces the opinion of the Sāṁkhya, for the intimation [implied] emphatically [in the verse is that] 'the agent is also the experiencing subject,' because [any] experience is inexplicable [in the case] of an [individual] who is not an agent, inasmuch as only someone capable of executing the action of experiencing [can be] the experiencing subject[856]. Well, [the Sāṁkhya opponent may defend his position presenting the following argument:] 'Like the apparition of redness, etc., in a crystal [is possible] due to the presence of a [scarlet] China rose flower, etc., the apparition of the experience of happiness, suffering and other [mental states accessible only to introspection] is logically correct also [in the case] of an [individual] who is not an agent[857] due to the contiguity of the primordial matter. For it is as follows: the supreme being is designated [as the spectator] experiencing—simply due to the presence [of the primordial matter]—objects that consist in happiness, suffering and other [mental states accessible only to introspection, and are] transferred onto (*sc.* reflected in) the intellect, which has the form of a mirror [reflecting multifarious] modifications of the primordial matter; [such is the state of affairs] according to the following utterance: "the supreme being becomes conscious of an object [when it is] apprehended in the intellect".[858] '[859] [His reasoning is] not [correct] because, without [assuming] that somehow [the supreme being] is endowed with action, [the fact of experiencing various mental states like happiness, suffering, etc.,] as taking place in a different manner [than through self-cognition] is inexplicable, even though [there is] the contiguity of the primordial matter, according to the following argumentation: since [the supreme being whose] antecedent form has not [yet] been dissolved is unfit [to apprehend a new] apparition, and inasmuch as [the supreme being], when the dissolution of that [antecedent form takes place], gets in the possession a successive form by way of giving up [its] former form, it entails the [fact that the supreme being] is endowed with action. Even in the [above] example of the crystal, redness which—in the presence of a [scarlet] China rose flower, etc.—is not manifested in [things like] a non-translucent stone[860], etc., whereas it is manifested in this [crystal][861], indicates such a (*sc.* action-bound) transformation of this [crystal]; otherwise [redness] would not become manifest—just like in a non-translucent stone—in that [crystal], either. Thus, the idea that an [individual] who is not an agent [can be] the experiencing subject is not explicable.

[31.9] By the following [expression:] '**is subject to change**,' however, [the author] refutes [the notion of] the cogniser as absolutely permanent and not subject to transformation, who is falsely conceived [as such] by the Naiyāyika and the Vaiśeṣika, etc., because a transformation [in the way] of grasping an object is inexplicable [in the case] of [a cogniser that is possessed of] a completely unwavering form. If [the Naiyāyika-Vaiśeṣika opponent objects:] '[The cogniser], although being absolutely permanent, cognises in a valid way because of the inherence of different [acts of] cognition [in him],' [then we say: that is] not [correct] because, [first, the concept of] inherence has already been disproved above[862] and because, [secondly,] any other relation with a separate [entity] is inexplicable, except for [the relation of] being otherwise inexplicable[863]. And this [relation of being otherwise inexplicable] is not possible in [the case of] a cognition separate [from the cogniser], either, because there is no cognitive criterion [that could] grasp this [difference of the cogniser and the cognition] and because the [introspective] experience of the non-difference [of the cogniser and the cognition] subverts this [difference][864]. Furthermore, if [an act of] cognition inheres in a [particular] cognitive subject by the force of inherence, then, since [both] cognitive subjects and [the relation of] inherence are [supposed to be both] omnipresent and singular, why does [this act of cognition] not inhere in all cognitive subjects, because there is no difference [between the case of cognition inhering in a particular cognitive subject and the case of the same cognition inhering in all cognitive subjects]? And similarly, also Yajñadatta and others could cognise the reality (*sc.* essence) of an object via Devadatta's cognition. And [there is still] something else, [viz.] some who says the following: '[the cognitive subject, being] previously a non-cogniser—[who] persists invariably as [being] precisely of such a kind in the previous state as [he is] in the very instant of the rise of consciousness (*sc.* cognition)—[becomes] subsequently the cogniser,'[865] demonstrates, as one should realise, insanity on his part, nothing else. So, let [us] leave that alone[866].

[31.10] By the latter half [of the verse,] however, [the author—while] demonstrating that the living element [is] different from gross elements [and] can be grasped by the perception [in the form of] self-cognition—rules out the view of the Cārvāka, because[867] [their view leads to] the undesired consequence that experience of [various introspective] transient occurrences [like] joy, distress, etc., [that assume] the form of cognitive awareness, which is [in its turn] different from these [gross elements, would] not be [possible] if [the living element] were not different from gross elements insentient in their essence (*sc.* by nature). And now [an objection is raised by the Cārvāka opponent]: 'Nothing but gross elements, transformed into the corporeal form, bring consciousness, [that is] different from them, into being[868]. And this [consciousness] persists invariably in (*sc.* has as its substratum) these [gross elements,] that have been transformed into a transformation of such a kind (*sc.* transformed into consciousness). When, however, this [transformation of gross elements into consciousness] does not [continue any longer], it disintegrates into these [gross elements] alone. Consequently, it is not established that the living element departs to the next world, even though [he is] experienced as different from these [gross elements], because empirical facts (*sc.* what is experienced) and everyday practice[869] are explicable by this much only[870].' [To the above objection of the Cārvāka we retort:] it is not [true], for the following dyad, to begin with, is observed to experience [mutual] connection: the body consisting in the five gross elements and consciousness. Out of these two together, the body is experienced by the cognitive awareness as [something] insentient through [its] form directed outwards (*sc.* outwardly accessible) by way of having a form of an [external] object, whereas consciousness is perceived directly as perception [in the form of] self-cognition through [its] form directed inwards (*sc.* inwardly accessible)[871]. For this very [reason], the thesis of the non-difference [between the living element and the five gross elements] cannot but be doubted[872], because it is revoked by the representation [of the body and of consciousness in the cognition]. On the other hand, since [the body and consciousness] are revealed [in cognition] as different [from each other], if it is falsely conceived by you that gross elements alone bring consciousness into being, then we regard the following logically more correct: 'Consciousness alone, having reached the place of origination after coming into being (*sc.* in the next existence), would bring about the body that produces the error of gross elements; then again, [consciousness], desirous of moving to next existence, would abandon [its body]; that [body] governed by this [consciousness] would perform movements of walking, etc.; however, disconnected from this [consciousness, the body would be] like a piece of wood; hence, the body is produced by the living element alone, [whereas] this [living element] is, in its turn, not produced by that [body],' because [to assume] the living element endowed with consciousness is legitimate—inasmuch as it is possessed of action—with regard to roaming from one existence (*sc.* birth) to another and to bringing about various bodies. If [you object]: 'It is not observed by perception that the living element enters the place of origination after coming into being (*sc.* in the next existence),' then [we reply:] gross elements are not apprehended to bring consciousness into being by means of retaining the corporeal form either—it is the same principle. If [you maintain:] 'On account of the [relation of] inexplicability otherwise [characterised as follows]: "consciousness is observed when gross elements are indeed transformed into the corporeal form, [but] not in any other case," [consciousness] is concluded to be produced by that [transformation of gross elements into the corporeal form][873],' then accordingly we demonstrate the following: consciousness is not comprehended in the state of a dead [person], even though [gross elements] possess a corporeal form; alternatively—precisely on account of the [relation of] inexplicability otherwise [characterised as follows]: 'transformation into the corporeal form, inasmuch as it [takes place] occasionally, is dependent on some other cause [then gross elements]'—consciousness, being capable of bringing about this [transformation into the corporeal form][874], is related to the living element who has entered next existence. Furthermore, [to say] that the living element, to begin with, proceeds in order to bring about the body due to the relation of the karmic matter and consciousness[875], cannot but be logically correct, whereas [the dilemma presents itself:] being of what sort would gross elements[876] proceed in [order to] produce consciousness: as [1] conscious or [2] unconscious? [Ad 1] If the first alternative [is assumed], then a pair of sub-alternatives arises: is that consciousness [1.1] different from these [conscious gross elements] or [1.2] not different? [Ad 1.1] If [consciousness] is different from [conscious gross elements], then—like in [the case of] the human body—also in [the case of] these[877] [conscious gross elements, consciousness], even though it occurs together with gross elements, makes [us] infer a cause which is the cognitive subject that is different from gross elements—the proof of the living element is circumscribed (*sc.* is demonstrated) precisely in this way[878]. [Ad 1.2] If [consciousness] is not different from [conscious gross elements], then, that being the case, [the numerical] oneness of all gross elements is absurdly implied because they are not different from [numerically] one consciousness, like the essential nature. If [you claim:] 'Gross elements are not different from their own respective consciousnesses, hence that [consequence] is not a defect,' [we reply: that is] not [correct] because [that would lead to] the undesired consequence that also in the human body produced by these [gross elements] there would be five consciousnesses produced by these [gross elements]. If [you defend your position:] 'Although [being] five, these [consciousnesses, related to five gross elements respectively, produce]—having got together (*sc.* jointly)—a large human consciousness, like numerous sesame seeds produce [numerically one] pot of sesame oil,' then [the question arises]: is that human consciousness [1.2.1] nothing but their connection or [1.2.2] something else indeed brought about by them? [Ad 1.2.1] If the first alternative [is considered], it is not proper because a connection of [five] consciousnesses, inasmuch as they do not intermingle with each other, [entails] contradiction; in the opposite case, numerous human consciousnesses, having got together (*sc.* jointly), would initiate a very large consciousness. [Ad 1.2.2] If the second alternative [is assumed], also in that case [the question arises]: [1.2.2.1] is there any association between them [and their product] or [1.2.2.2] is there none? [Ad 1.2.2.1] If [you assume that] there is some association between them [and the produced consciousness], that is not proper because that would entail that [their product] would consist in five consciousnesses produced by them, precisely like before, [and that would be tantamount to the fallacy of the *regressus ad infinitum*]. [Ad 1.2.2.2] If there is no [association between them and their product], it is not tenable, either, because a [possibility of a product] brought about without any association is subverted by cognitive criteria. Thus, conscious gross elements are not in a position to become participants in the activity of giving rise to consciousness. [Ad 2] Unconscious [gross elements can] not [produce consciousness], either, because [to assume that] these [unconscious gross elements], being absolutely different [from consciousness, lead to] the origination of consciousness [entails] contradiction; in the opposite case, gravel, etc., could give rise to sesame oil, etc. Furthermore, consciousness could either be [2.1] effected by nothing but an aggregate of these [gross elements] or [2.2] effected[879] by their distinguished transformation.[880] [Ad 2.1] The first assumption, to being with, is not [correct] because consciousness is not comprehended even in the accumulation of earth, water, fire, air and ether. [Ad 2.2] If the second assumption [is analysed] in its turn, it should be stated [by you] what this distinguished character is? If [you say:] '[This distinguished character is] the transformation into the corporeal form,' then why does this [transformation] not take place all the time? If [you reply:] '[The transformation does not take place all the time] due to its dependence on some other cause,' then we infer: this another cause is consciousness of the living element who has reached another existence because this [consciousness belonging to the living element] alone is the material cause equivalent to the consciousness effected by the transformation into the corporeal form, inasmuch as without this [consciousness belonging to the living element], in the state of dead [person]—although the transformation [of gross elements] into the corporeal form takes place—movements of walking, etc., are not comprehended due to the absence of this [consciousness belonging to the living element]. Thus, consciousness in not produced by the transformation [of gross elements] into the corporeal form; on the contrary, it is the [transformation of gross elements into the corporeal form] itself that is produced by that [consciousness]—this is what we consider logically correct. If [you contend the following:] 'There is no other cognitive criterion except perception and it is not apprehended by this [perception] that consciousness goes or does not go to the next world, etc.; hence, gross elements, precisely as they are perceived, have to be assumed as the cause of this [consciousness],'[881] [that is] not [correct] because just a while ago [in NA 1] [additional] cognitive criteria have been proved by means of disproving perception as the only one [cognitive criterion]; and, thus, numerous [illustrations of] inference may be drawn that prove that the living element advances to the next world. For instance: '[1. the thesis:] the desire for the first breast (*sc.* suckling) [in the case] of a male baby born on that day is preceded by a previous desire, [2. the logical reason:] because [it is] a desire; [3. the example:] like the desire for the breast (*sc.* suckling) on the second and next days.' Thus, the same inference that makes [us] infer that the desire for the first breast (*sc.* suckling) is preceded by another desire implies through presumption[882] that the living element departs to the next world, because there is no other (*sc.* previous) desire at his birth.[883] In the above manner also other [instances of inference] can be mentioned by way of exemplification, so let [us] leave that alone[884].

[31.11] Thus, it is established that the living element—who is the revealer of himself and something else [different from him, who is] the agent, [who is] the experiencing subject, [who is] of [both] permanent and impermanent essence, [who is] different from gross elements, [who is possessed of] his own infinite modes and [of infinite] transient occurrences that exist from beginningless [times] and for infinite (endless) times [and are] inferred from his own certain modes perceived directly [through self-cognition, who is] determined by cognitive criteria [and who is] ultimately real—is the cogniser who pervades all viewpoints and [all] cognitive criteria.

[32.0] Presently, [the author]—summarising the purpose of the treatise by the concluding aphorism—says:

/32/ These foundations[885] of cognitive criteria, etc., in [their] essence with no beginning nor end, even though [they are] well-known to all [people] absorbed in everyday life, are declared [here].

[32.1] '**Cognitive criteria**', [means] 'perception, etc. (*sc.* indirect cognition)'; on account of the speech element '**etc.**' viewpoints are included; the '**foundations** of these [cognitive criteria and viewpoints' means] the demarcated area constituted by definition, etc.[886], fixed in every case [of respective cognitive criteria and viewpoints]; they are '**these**' [foundations that] '**are declared [here]**' with [their] firmly established stand stated immediately afterwards—such is the syntactical relation. [As a reply to the question:] 'What are [these foundations] like?', [the author] says: '**beginning**' [means] origin, '**end**' [means] the close; that which has neither beginning nor end is this [essence]; those[887] which have such an essence, [i.e. such an] intrinsic nature, are [foundations that are] '**in [their] essence with no beginning nor end.**' '**Even though [they are] well-known to,**' [i.e.] although [they are] prevalent among, '**all [people] absorbed in everyday life,**' [i.e.] all [people] engaged in everyday practice, subdivided into [such] divisions [like] common people, thinkers, etc., because—if they were not well-known—[that would lead to] the undesired consequence of the destruction of the whole everyday practice and, if the destruction of this [everyday practice took place], no determination of any truth at all would be [possible], inasmuch as the [process of] examination [could] not be established. [These foundations] **'are declared [here],'** [i.e.] are put into words, in order—as it is understood—to remove the disorientation of the uncultivated [people] or [people who are] of a different opinion, because—due to heavy karmic veils, defective conation and past impressions—certain [people suffer from] the presence of disorientation consisting in non-apprehension and cognitive error as regards the object [of their cognition], even though it is well-known through cognitive criteria, and the compassionate undertake [some actions] in order to obliterate this [disorientation of such people], if there is a [corresponding] efficacy.

/1/ [Valid] reason[s]—having avoided the deer [who are] heterodox thinkers who have resorted to viewpoints, who have no other shelter [and] who are fleeing with agitated eyes moving to and fro in panic [caused by] highly terrifying roar of the lion of the doctrine of the [seven-fold] modal description—are with the Jina; [hence] resort to him!

/2/ This pious reverence (*sc.* the present treatise) to the Lord has openly been formulated by me in order to recount [certain] aspects of His teaching; [these are] not idea[s] of my own. Therefore, if anything turned out imperfect here [in my work] due to [my] confusion, let the perfect ones, who take compassion on me, purify (*sc.* correct) it.

/3/ [If there is] any auspicious increase of merit that has been effected by [me] wishing to accomplish the manifold commentary on the 'Introduction to Logic,' thanks to it let my mind, solely devoted to the teaching of the Lord Jina, be permanently zealous to realise the highest goal up to the end of [my] existence.

Thus ends
The Commentary on the 'Introduction to Logic'.

This is the work of the preceptor Siddhavyākhyānika (*sc.* Siddharṣi) [commenting] on the gloss on the treatise about reasoning [titled *Introduction to Logic*].

FOOTNOTES

[1] The appellation *ṭīkā* occurring in the prefatory line of the commentary (*nyāyâvatāraḥ śrī-Devabhadra-gaṇi-kṛta-ṭippana-saṁvalita-śrī-Siddharṣi-gaṇi-kṛta-ṭīkā-sahitaḥ*) is but a common noun and the real title of the work is *Nyāyâvatāra-vivṛti*, not *Ṭīkā*, since the title occurs in the first *śloka* of Siddharṣi's commentary as well as in the colophon: ***Nyāyâvatāra-vivṛtiḥ*** *samāptā*. Moreover, the apparent play on words *Vivṛti* and *vṛdhaye* in the first *śloka* of the NAV may also testify against the title *Ṭīkā*. Besides, the title is confirmed also by Devabhadra-gaṇin in his subcommentary, who annotates the aphorism: ***tasya*** (=*Nyāyâvatārasya*) ***vivṛtiḥ*** *vivaraṇaṁ kriyate iti saṁbandhaḥ* and concludes his work with the verse: ***Nyāyâvatāra-vivṛtau*** *viṣamaṁ vibhajya*, etc.

[2] That is to say, *Nyāyâvatāra* is 'the seed of memory' which is to undergo the process of its growth, i.e. its elaboration and exemplification, in the form of the commentary. The remark points to the didactic role of Siddhasena's aphorisms, which seem not have been meant to form an entirely autonomous treatise but were rather a kind of register of the most important topics, or a handy device for a preceptor in the teaching process. That would explain the apparent redundancy of some aphorisms as well as certain minute inconsistencies. They become, however, understandable only in the case of imparting knowledge to students; to cite some instances, (1) NA 2—as a *pūrva-pakṣa*—states uselessness of providing any definition of a cognitive criterion, since it is a well-known notion, whereas NA 3 partly contradicts that by giving a reason why it should nevertheless be taught; in this way NA 32 becomes redundant; in a systematic and highly condensed lecture a single occurrence of a *pūrva-pakṣa* would rather be unusual, unless the treatise bore a polemical character, which is not the case here; (2) partial repetition of the contents of NA 13 in NA 22; (3) NA 1 and 7 (the nature of cognitive criterion is repeated, although in a slightly different context; true, it was necessitated by the peculiar dialectical structure of the argumentation); (4) to the didactic character points an unexpected allegory, superfluous in the case of a systematic exposition of a doctrine: NA 16 (a simile of an archer); (5) the self-revelatory and object-revelatory aspect in NA 1 (*pramāṇaṁ sva-parâbhāsi jñānaṁ*) and NA 31 (*pramātā svânya-nirbhāsī*); the redundancy at this point is observed by Siddharṣi in 31.7: ***svânya-nirbhāsîty****-anena prāg-ukta-sva-parâbhāsi-pramāṇa-viśeṣaṇavan*...

The symbolism of seed as a general basis of growth is widely encountered in literature, also in Jaina works, e.g. in ĀA 21:

dharmād avāpta-vibhavo dharmaṁ pratipālya bhogam anubhavatu /
bījād avāpta-dhānyaḥ kṛṣīvalās tasya bījam iva //

—'The person who in consequence of piety has acquired prosperity may have enjoyments while preserving piety, like the peasant who gets corn from the seed, but (preserves) the seed of that corn.' [translated by Rai Bahadur J.L. Jain]. Cf. also Vijñāna-vāda literature (e.g. Triṁś).

[3] Cf. similar formulation, for instance, in the opening line of HB (p. 1*.5–6): *parokṣârtha-pratipatter anumānâśrayatvāt tad-vyutpādanârthaṁ saṅkṣepata idam ārabhyate.*

[4] For several reasons given below, I have decided to render *pramāṇa* consistently as 'cognitive criterion'. Since, in conversations with some of my colleagues, my proposal has been met with various objections or lack of understanding, I feel obliged to justify my choice in more than just two lines.

Firstly, the term 'cognitive criterion', or—to be precise—its semi-equivalents like 'criterion of truth', 'Wahrheitskriterium', etc., have been widely used in a similar sense in divergent streams of European philosophical reflection, to cite but a few examples: (1) *norma veritatis* in Spinoza's *Ethices*, *Pars II* ad *Propos. 43*, p. 116: 'Deinde quid idea vera clarius et certius dari potest, quod norma sit veritatis? Sane sicut lux seipsam et tenebras manifestat, sic veritas norma sui, et falsi eii. ... quod veritas sui sit norma'; (2) *Kriterium der Wahrheit* in KANT's KRV (1781: 58 = 1787: 83 = Akad. Ausg.: 79 = 1995: 106); (3) likewise, the senses as the source of sensory cognition may be taken, when critically examined, a criterion of truth, cf. HUME (1913: 160, the section: 'Of the Academical or Sceptical Philosophy'): '... the senses alone are not implicitly dependent on; but ... we must correct their evidence by reason, and by considerations, derived from the nature of the medium, the distance of the object, and the disposition of the organ, in order to render them, within their sphere, the proper *criteria* of truth and falsehood'; that the idea of *criteria* is implicit in sensations, reason, etc., can also be seen in HUME (1913: 19, the section: 'Of the Different Species of Philosophy'); (4) *Erkenntnismaßstab* in MAX SCHELER's *Probleme der Religion*, (Band V, 1954: p. 288) and his *Phänomenologie und Erkenntistheorie* (Band X, 1957: 380 ff., esp. 398–410), where he discusses *Erkenntnismaßstäbe* in the context of *Denkverfahren* and *Schauverfahren*, *Urteil / reine, formlose Anschauung*, etc.; (5) *Kriterium für die Richtigkeit* in WITTGENSTEIN (1984: § 258 as well as pp. 176–177 ff.); (6) *Gültigkeitskriterium* in CARNAP (1935: 163 ff.) = *criterion of validity* in CARNAP (1937: 98–102, § 34a); (7) *criterion of the material adequacy* in the context of the definition of truth and cognition in TARSKI (1944: 343 ff. § 4; 351 ff. § 10) and *criterion of truth* in TARSKI (1944: 363–4) and in (1969, § 2 'Proof'), (8) *kryterium* (criterion) in BOCHEŃSKI (1986: 139–141), used with reference to validity of cognition and acceptability of a paradigm. What is even more relevant in this context is the opinion of Aristotle who distinguishes ἐπιστήμη (rational, discursive, dianoetic, scientific knowledge) and αἴσθησις (sensory, intuitive cognition or faculty) and—describing them as μέτρον (a measure, norm or criterion)—relates these two kinds of cognition/cognising directly to the idea of validity and cognitive norm, cf. *MET*.1053b (p. 197.31–33): καὶ τὴν ἐπιστήμην δὲ μέτρον τῶν πραγμάτων λέγομεν καὶ τὴν αἴσθησις διὰ το αὐτό, ὅτι γνωρίζομέν τι αὐταῖς, ἐπεὶ μετροῦνται μᾶλλον ἢ μετροῦσιν ('Accordingly, we call cognition the measure of thing[s], and perception, likewise, [is called] the same, because we can know something through them; but, in fact, they are rather measured (*sc.* subject to measure) than [they] measure [things].').

Thirdly, admittedly the rendering *source of valid cognition*, *means of acquiring certain knowledge*, etc., closely relates to similar Occidental classifications of cognitive faculties, or sources of cognition ('Fountains of Knowledge'), that divide them mainly into intuitive cognition derived from sensory experience and abstractive cognition relying upon mental faculties; e.g. (1) cf. Aristotle's *Post.An.*81b,87b (αἴσθησις–ἐπιστήμη); (2) cf. OCKHAM's 'Prologue' to the *Ordinatio*, Q. i., N *sqq.* (p. 18): 'Ostendam, quod intellectus noster, etiam pro statu isto, respectu eiusdem obiecti sub aedem ratione potest habere duas notitias incomplexas specie distinctas, quarum una potest dici intuitiva et alia abstractiva' ('First, I intend to show that our intellect, even in this life, can have two specifically distinct kinds of non-complex knowledge even when it is concerned with the same object under the same aspect. The one may be called intuitive, the other abstractive cognition.'); and (p. 24): 'Et ideo, sicut secondum *Philosophum* i^{0} *Metaphysicae* et ii^{0} *Posteriorium* scientia istorum sensibilium quae accipitur per experientiam, de qua ipse loquitur, incipit a sensu, id est a notitia intuitiva sensitiva istorum sensibilium, ita universaliter notitia scientifica istorum pure intelligibilium accepta per experientiam incipit a notitia intuitiva intellectiva istorum intelligibilium.' ('And therefore, just as the knowledge of sensible facts that is obtained from experience (as the Philosopher says in the first book of the *Metaphysics* and in the second book of the *Posterior Analitics*) begins with the senses, i.e. from a sense-intuition of these sensible facts, so in general the scientific knowledge of these purely intelligible facts of experience begins with an intellective intuition of these intelligible facts.'); (3) cf. LOCKE (1975: 104.22–26; Book II, Ch. I, § 2): 'Our Observation employ'd either about *external, sensible Objects*; *or about the internal Operations of our Minds, perceived and reflected on by our selves, is that, which supplies our Understandings with all the materials of thinking*. These two are the Fountains of Knowledge, from whence all the *Ideas* we have, or can naturally have, do spring'; LOCKE (1975: 105.6–10; Book II, Ch. I, § 3): '… they (= senses—P.B.) from external Objects convey into the mind what produces there those *Perceptions*. This great Source, of most of the *Ideas* we have, depending wholly upon sense, and derived by them to the Understanding, I call *SENSATION*'; LOCKE (1975: 105.11–30; Book II, Ch. I, § 4): 'Secondly, the other Fountain, from which Experience furnisheth the Understanding with Ides, is the *Perception of the Operations of our own Minds* within us …; and such are, *Perception*, *Thinking*, *Doubting*, *Believing*, *Reasoning*, *Knowing*, *Willing*, and all the different actings of our own Minds … But as I call the other *Sensation*, so I call this *REFLECTION* … By *REFLECTION* then, in the following part of this Discourse, I would be understood to mean, that notice which the Mind takes of its own Operations, and the manner of them, by reason whereof, there come to be *idea* of these Operations in the understanding. These two, I say, *viz.*, External, Material things, as the Objects of *SENSATION*; and the Operations of our own Minds within, as the Objects of

REFLECTION, are, to me, the only Originals, from whence all our *Ideas* take their beginning'; (4) cf. RUSSELL (1917: 152–167) and his distinction of 'knowledge by acquaintance' and 'knowledge by description', which he further relates directly to pairs 'universal–particular', 'abstract–concrete', 'concept–percept' (p. 155) respectively (the juxtaposition is highly evocative of the Buddhist distinction *parokṣa–pratyakṣa* and *sāmānya-viśeṣa*!).

Perhaps, an interpretation of 'criterion' as a means of cognising the truth or of verifying the truth—that bifurcates into sensory cognition and mental cognition—closest to the notion of *pramāṇa*, is found in Diogenes' account on the Sceptic philosophy in his Περὶ Βίων καὶ γνωμῶν... DIOGENES LAERTIOS, while discussing Pyrrho's system and views of the Skeptics, first enumerates their crucial ideas regarding the possibility of knowing the truth: (90) Ἀνῄρουν δ' οὗτοι καὶ πᾶσαν ἀπόδειξιν καὶ κ ρ ι τ ή ρ ι ο ν καὶ σημεῖον καὶ αἴτιον καὶ κίνησιν καὶ μάθησιν καὶ γένεσιν καὶ τὸ φύσει τι εἶ ναι ἀγαθὸν ἢ κακόν · [pp. 248.54–249.3] ('[The Skeptics] reject every proof and c r i t e r i o n , as well as sign (*sc.* argument) and cause, likewise motion and study, and creation, along with [a conviction that] something can be either good or bad by nature.'). Subsequently, he discusses every item one by one: (1) proof (ἀπόδειξιν) in 90/91 (πᾶσα γὰρ ἀπόδειξιν..., p. 249.3–20), (2) criterion (κριτήριον) in 92–95 (τοὺσ δ' οἰομένους..., pp. 249.20–250.9), (3) sign (σημεῖον) in 96 (Σημεῖον τ' οὐχ..., pp. 250.9–23), up to 'the conviction that something can be either good or bad by nature' in § 101 (Φύσει τε μὴ εἶναι ἀγαθὸν ἢ κακόν ... ἄγνωστον οὖν τὸ φύσει ἀγαθόν. '...[objective] goodness by nature is not cognisable', p. 251.12–24). What is important here is that in the second section—which is devoted to 'criterion' (κριτήριον)—Diogenes states explicitly what he understands under the 'criteria': εἰ δ' ἔνιά ἐστιν ἀληθῆ, τίνι διακριτέον; οὔτε γὰρ αἰσθήσει τὰ κατ' αἴσθησιν, πάντων ἴσων αὐτῇ φαινομένων, οὔτε νοήσει διὰ τὴν αὐτὴν αὐτίαν. [92, p. 249.29–32] ('If, therefore, only some things are [supposed to be] true, [whereas others are believed to be false], what is the way to judge critically? Not t h r o u g h t h e s e n s e s , if [the thing] is accessible to the senses, inasmuch as every thing is equally true [to the senses], nor w i t h t h e i n t e l l e c t due to the same cause.'). Thus, according to Diogenes, the Skeptics distinguished two c r i t e r i a t o k n o w t h e t r u t h , divided into the senses (αἴσθησις; *sc.* 'sensory perception') and the mind (νόησις; 'mental perception'). Furthermore, Diogenes cites the standpoint of the Skeptics as to conceivable varieties of criteria of knowing the truth: πρὸς τῷ καὶ διαφωνεῖσθαι τὸ κριτήριον, τῶν μὲν τὸν ἄνθρωπον κριτήριον εἶναι λεγόντων, τῶν δὲ τὰς αἰσθήσεις, ἄλλωον τὸν λόγον, ἐνίων τὴν καταληπτικὴν φαντασίαν. [p. 250.5–8] ('And further, opinions differ as to what a c r i t e r i o n is; some regard the man as the c r i t e r i o n , others—the senses, still others—the mind, cataleptic fantasy.'). Subsequent lines suggest that 'the man' (ἄνθρωπος) would be not very far from the idea of testimony (*śabda*), inasmuch the veracity of his words are at stake. To sum up, the term κριτήριον—at least in the above context—connotes precisely both the means of cognising and a method of verification (criterion of truth), either sensory (perceptual) or mental (rational, inferential). Thus, is very akin to the idea of *pramāṇa*.

Secondly, *criterion of truth* or *cognitive criterion* is far more compact and precise an expression than, say, *the means of valid cognition*, *means of acquiring certain knowledge*, *source of valid cognition*, etc. However, in order not to equate the idea of *pramāṇa* with the terminology established within the European philosophic tradition and to avoid the danger of reading European ideas directly into Indian philosophy, I prefer to the rendering of 'cognitive criterion', instead of 'criterion of truth'.

It should also be remembered that sometimes (e.g. Locke) sensation/intuitive cognition and reflection/abstractive cognition were not understood to be false cognitive acts, or fallacies. Thus, to render *pramāṇa* as 'means of [valid] cognition' would not be very far from the meaning of 'sensation' / 'intuitive cognition' and 'reflection' / 'abstractive cognition', etc. However, to understand *pramāṇa* in terms of a mere source of knowledge would be too reductive.

Accordingly, and fourthly, the rendering *source of valid cognition*, *means of acquiring certain knowledge*, or similar, proves extremely problematic in Jinistic and Buddhist contexts, unlike the Naiyāyika and the Bhāṭṭa, where the causal ('means') and resultant ('cognition') aspects of '*pramāṇa*' are equated, cf., e.g. NAṬ 4 (ad *indriyârtha-sannikarṣêty-ādi*): *jñānaṁ tu pratyakṣa-pramāṇa-phalam, hānôpādānâdi-buddhy-apekṣayā tu tad api jñānaṁ pramāṇam eva*; and PSV 1 ad 1.8cd (Vasudhararakṣita/Seṅ-rgyal: 15a.5–7; Kanakavarman/Dad-paḥi śes-rab [K] 95b.6–7): *ḥdi la phyi rol pa rnams kyi bźin du tshad ma las ḥbras bu don gźan du ḥgyur ba ni med kyi, ḥbras bur gyur baḥi śes pa de ñid yul gyi rnam pa can du skyes pa daṅ, bya ba daṅ bcas par rtogs pa de ñe bar blaṅs nas tshad ma ñid du ḥdogs pa ste, bya ba med par yaṅ*[a] *yin no. dper na ḥbras bu rgyu daṅ rjes su mthun par skyes pa la rgyuḥi gzugs ḥdzin źes brjod do. bya ba med par yaṅ yin*[a] *pa de bźin du ḥdir yaṅ yin no*. Obviously, in both the passages just quoted, *pramāṇa* can in no way be 'source' or 'means of acquiring'. [[a] HATTORI's conjectures.]

Fifthly, the rendering 'criterion' perfectly conveys also the aspect of 'measure; correct measurement; norm, standard', etc., denoted by the root √*mā*. That the term *pramāṇa* may convey precisely such a meaning is corroborated for instance by a passage in NS 2.1.16: *prameyā* (or: *prameyatā*) *ca tulā-prāmāṇyavat*, and in NBh 2.1.16: *gurutva-parimāṇa-jñāna-sādhanaṁ tulā pramāṇam. jñāna-viṣayo guru-dravyaṁ suvarṇâdi prameyam.*—'The balance, that is an instrument to know and measure weight [of a given object], is a criterion. The province of cognition, or weighty substance [such as] gold, etc., is that (lit.) which is to be measured.'

Sixthly, as for an hypothetical objection that validity is not incorporated in the term *cognitive criterion*, the argument is not sound, inasmuch as the term *criterion* itself contains the element of validity, being itself a kind of *measure* or *procedure* that ensures valid results. In other words, the validity of cognitive measures, or cognitive procedures, or the validity of the ensuing cognition itself, generally connoted by '*pramāṇa*', is entailed in the term 'criterion'. Thereby the idea of 'valid means / source of cognition' is covered by the expression *cognitive criterion*.

Seventhly, despite various interpretations of the term *criterion of truth*, or *Wahrheitskriterium*, encountered in the broad spectrum of occidental philosophical works, they all pertain to the notion of validity and reliability of our knowledge or epistemic measures. Generally, the *criterion* of an entity is a particular property by which that entity is recognised. In the case of cognition such a property is a special procedure that ensures validity to ensuing knowledge, that comprises certain decision procedure and a method leading to desired results. Accordingly, the criterion with reference to cognition and its veracity allows us to decide whether the cognitive measures are valid and consistent. Similarly, in Indian philosophic tradition, generally speaking, such ideas as validity and reliability of cognition and valid procedural epistemic measures, etc., are incorporated in the notion of *pramāṇa*. A *pramāṇa* is not merely a way of cognising things, but a *critical* strategy or procedure that leads to reliable epistemic results, .e.g. to cite a common Indian example, apprehending an image of water in the desert would not be considered an instance of *pramāṇa* (*pratyakṣa*), inasmuch as it would subsequently be invalidated by further cognitive acts (the Mīmāṁsaka case of *svataḥ-prāmāṇya* of *pratyakṣa* would need a separate treatment). Such an act of cognition or cognition itself (and I lay aside the question of Naiyāyika distinction or identity of *pramāṇa* and *pramiti*) must implicitly fulfil additional criteria of validity. The Jaina epistemology, for instance, recognises the notion of *pramāṇa* (cf., TS 1.9–10: *mati-śrutâvadhi-manaḥ paryāya-kevalāni jñānam. tat pramāṇe.*) that is clearly distinguished from the notion of *ajñāna*, or *apramāṇa* (cf. TS 1.32: *mati-śrutâvadhayo viparyāyaś ca*), which as a rule takes recourse to *similar* epistemic measures, but due to certain procedural factors, generally speaking, is deemed invalid, hence does not acquire the status of validity. Hence, an European equivalent should cover also the verificative aspect of *pramāṇa*; indeed, the notion of verification is incorporated in the term 'cognitive criterion'. In addition, we encounter quite an exceptional usage of the term in Mīmāṁsā, where '*pramāṇa*' looses its strictly epistemic reference in favour of ethical and salvific implications, and is rather applied in the sense of a *normative principle*, cf., e.g. the epitome of Mīmāṁsā in MŚV$_1$ 5.2. (*Nirālambana-vādâdhikaraṇa*).1–5 (pp. 155–165). But even in that case, *pramāṇa* retains its character of a *criterion* of ethical and pragmatic evaluation of individual acts within social, ritual and individual context.

By way of summing up, the term '*pramāṇa*'—as HIRIYANNA (1994: 68–69) and MATILAL (1971: 35) rightly pointed out—involves the cognitive side and probative side of noetic processes, i.e. it emphasises dual character of cognitive procedures and cognition: causal factor (in terms of giving rise to a particular cognitive episode) and evidential aspect (in terms of giving verification or providing justification for adopting a particular cognitive episode as a valid piece of knowledge). These two sides are not entailed by usual renderings, such as *the means of valid cognition*, *means of acquiring certain knowledge*, *source of valid cognition*, etc They are, however, directly implicated by 'cognitive criterion'. The rendering of *criterion* in the context of *pramāṇa* occurs sporadically with other authors, cf. MATILAL (1971: 21–22),

FRANCO (1983/I: *passim*). Likewise, SCHAYER (1933b: 93): 'Erkenntnisnorm,' and SCHAYER (1933c: 123): 'norma poznawcza' (= cognitive norm).

[5] See $PVSV_1$ 3.24–25 [p. 185]: *tasmāt svabhāva-pratibandhād eva hetuḥ sādhyaṁ gamayati. sa ca tad-bhāva-lakṣaṇas tad-utpatti-lakṣaṇo vā. sa evâvinâbhāvo dṛṣṭântābhyāṁ pradarśyate.* Cf. also Dharmottara on NB_1 2.23 (*vastutas tādātmyāt tad-utpatteś ca*) in $NBṬ_1$ 2.23: ***vastuta*** *ity-ādi. sa sādhyo 'rtha ātmā svabhāvo yasya tat tad-ātma*[a]. *tasya bhāvas tādātmyam.*—[NB_1 2.23]: 'In reality [there are only two relations between words and their denotation, namely] the relation of essential identity [of the word with the object] and the origination [of the word] from the object'; [$NBṬ_1$ 2.23]: '[The aphorism beginning with the words] "In reality", etc., [has the following meaning]. "That" is the thing to-be-established (proved); the essence, or intrinsic nature, of that [thing] is its essence. The relation with (the state of) "that" is the identity [of the word with the object].' Cf. also NB_1 3.31: *sa* [= *svabhāva-pratibandhaś*] *ca dvi-prakāraḥ sarvasya: tādātmya-lakṣaṇas tad-utpatti-lakṣaṇaś cêty uktam.*—'All [relations are] two-fold, since it has been said [that they are either] characterised by the relation of essential identity or by the relation of causality (*sc.* the origination of the word from the object).' The question whether the relation of essential identity and the relation of causality are to be taken separately or jointly is examined below, p. 5 ff. See also $PVSV_4$ 1.25: *tasmāt svabhāva-pratibandhād eva hetuḥ sādhyaṁ gamayati. sa ca tad-bhāva-lakṣaṇas tad-utpatti-lakṣaṇo vā. sa evâvinābhāvo dṛṣṭāntābhyāṁ pradarśyate.*—'Therefore, solely because of the invariable connection of essential nature [between the probans and the probandum], [the occurrence of] the logical reason discloses (*sc.* makes one infer) the probandum. And this [invariable connection] is either characterised by the relation of causality or characterised by the relation of essential identity. This inseparable connection as such is indicated by both [kinds of] example, [i.e. based on similarity and based on dissimilarity].' Cf. PVin I_1 46.17–22 (p. 112).

[a] After C, D Mss. of DhPr 2.22 instead of *tadātmā*.

[6] Since the semantic field of the synonymous terms *śabda* and *dhvani* is far too broad to be rendered by one term, I have resolved to use, in most cases, their English equivalents 'speech element' and 'linguistic unit' respectively; thereby such notions like 'word', 'statement', 'utterance', 'particle', 'phoneme', etc., are connoted.

[7] In most cases I render *prāmāṇya* and *pramāṇatā* by 'cognitive validity'. Alas, the immediate association with the term *pramāṇa* is in such cases lost in the translation.

[8] Cf. HBṬ, p. 2.10–11: *na ca prayojana-vākyasya prāmāṇyam asti, śabdānāṁ bahir arthe pratibandhâbhāvāt.*—'And the [initial] statement declaring the purpose [of the treatise] has no validity, because of the absence of connection between words and the external object.'

[9] Cf., e.g. NB_1 3.33: *sa ca dvi-prakāraḥ sarvasya* [*pratibandhasya*]: *tādātmya-lakṣaṇas tad-utpatti-lakṣaṇaś cêty uktam.*

[10] In all probability, Siddharṣi refers to the opinion of Dharmottara contained in PVinṬ$_1$ Dse. 4b1–5a2: ཅི་སྟེ་རང་རྒྱུད་བརྟགས་པའི་རྒྱུ་ཡིན་པས་ཀུན་ལས་བཏུས་པས་བཤད་པར་བྱེད་པ་རྣམ་པར་ངེས་པ་བརྩམ་པར་བྱ་བ་ཉིད་ཀྱི་དགོས་པོ་ཅི་ཞིག་ཡིན། ཚིག་ཚད་མ་མ་ཡིན་པས་དགོས་པ་བསྟན་ཀྱང་བསྟན་བཅོས་ཉན་པ་ཉིད་ལས་ངེས་པར་བྱ་བ་མ་ཡིན་ནམ། འདིར་དགོས་པ་སྟོན་པའི་ངག་གིས་ཅི་ཞིག་བྱ་ཞེ་ན། བདེན་ཏེ་དེ་ལྟར་ན་ཡང་ཚིག་ལས་རྟོགས་པ་དང་། ལྡན་པ་རྣམས་ཐེ་ཚོམ་སྐྱེ་ཞིང་། དེས་ན་དོན་དུ་གཉེར་ལ། དེ་ལས་ཀྱང་འཇུག་པར་འགྱུར་བའི་ཕྱིར་རོ།། བརྗོད་པར་བྱ་བ་ལ་སོགས་པའི་ངག་མེད་ན་ནི་འདི་ཡི་བརྗོད་པར་བྱ་བ་ནི་བྱ་རོག་གི་སོ་བརྟན་པ་བཞིན་དུ་འབྲས་བུ་མེད་པར་དོགས་པའམ། མཐའ་ཡས་ཀྱི་གཙུག་གི་ནད་ཐམས་ཅད་སེལ་བའི་རིན་པོ་ཆེའི་རྒྱན་གྱི་མན་ངག་བཞིན་དུ་ཡོད་ཀྱང་སྒྲུབ་པར་མི་ནུས་པའམ། མ་བག་མར་ལེན་པའི་མན་ངག་བཞིན་དུ་འདི་ཉན་བའི་དགོས་པ་ནི་མངོན་པར་འདོད་པ་མ་ཡིན་ནོ་ཞེས་དགོས་པའམ། བསྟན་བཅོས་མཉན་པ་དེ་བས་ཀྱང་དགོས་པ་དེ་འགྲུབ་པའི་ཐབས་སླ་བ་གཞན་ཡོད་དོ་ཞེས་དོན་མེད་པའི་ཐེ་ཚོམ་གང་ཡང་རུང་བས་ཀྱང་དོན་དུ་གཉེར་བར་མི་འགྱུར་ཏེ། དེས་ན་མཉན་པ་ལ་འཇུག་པར་མི་འགྱུར་རོ།། འབྲེལ་པ་ལ་སོགས་པ་བརྗོད་ན་ནི་དོན་ལ་ཐེ་ཚོམ་བྱ་བ་རིགས་ཏེ། བསྟན་བཅོས་བྱེད་པ་བསྟན་པཅོས་ཀྱི་དང་པོར་བརྗོད་པར་བྱ་བ་ལ་སོགས་པ་ཕིན་ཅི་ལོག་ཏུ་སྟོན་པ་ལ་དགོས་པ་ཅུང་ཟད་ཀྱང་མེད་པའི་ཕྱིར་རོ།། དེའི་ཕྱིར་དགོས་པའི་ངག་བཀོད་པ་ཡིན་ནོ།། འཆད་པ་པོ་རྣམས་ནི་བརྩིབ་ལ་སོགས་པའི་དོན་དུ་ལོགས་པར་སྟོན་སྲིད་ཀྱི། བསྟན་བཅོས་བྱེད་པ་ནི་མ་ཡིན་ནོ།། དེའི་ཕྱིར་འཇིག་པའི་ཡན་ལག་ཏུ་དོན་དུ་འགྱུར་བ་ཉིད་ཀྱི་ཐེ་ཚོམ་བསྐྱེད་པའི་ཕྱིར། ཕན་པ་དང་ཞེས་བྱ་བ་ལ་སོགས་པས་དང་པོར་བརྗོད་པར་བྱ་བ་ལ་སོགས་པའི་ངག་གསུངས་སོ།། ངག་འདིས་ཀྱང་བརྗོད་པར་བྱ་བའི་དགོས་པ་ཉིད་སྟོན་ཏོ།། ངག་གི་རང་བཞིན་འདི་ཐམས་ཙད་ནི་སྒྲའི་ལུས་དང་དོན་གྱི་ལུས་སོ།། དེ་ལ་སྒྲའི་ཆ་ནི་དོན་རྟོགས་པ་ཡིན་པས། འག་འཞིག་ཏུ་ཡང་འབྲས་བུ་མེད་པ་མ་ཡིན་པར་རང་ཉིད་ཀྱིས་འགྱུར་རོ།། དོན་གྱི་ཆ་ལ་ནི་དོན་དང་མི་ལྡན་པ་ཉིད་མཐོང་ལ། དེ་ལྟ་བུའི་དོན་ཀྱང་བརྩམ་པར་བྱ་མ་ཡིན་ཏེ། རྟོག་པ་དང་ལྡན་པའི་རྩོམ་པ་ཐམས་ཅད་ནི་དགོས་པ་ཁྱབ་པའི་ཕྱིར་དང་། སྐྱེས་བུའི་དོན་ལ་ཉེ་བར་མཁོ་བའི་དོན་ཀྱང་མེད་པའི་ཕྱིར་རོ།། དེའི་ཕྱིར་བསྟན་བཅོས་བརྩམས་པ་འབྲས་བུ་དང་བཅས་པ་སྟོན་པར་བྱེད་པས། བརྗོད་པར་བྱ་བའི་དགོས་པ་ཉིད་བཤད་པར་བྱ་བ་ཡིན་ནོ།།

For the refutation of any possible relation between a verbal statement and the external object, which is of major importance to the following discussion of the validity of testimony (*śruta* = *śabda* = *āgama*), see also Dharmakīrti's PV$_3$ 3.92 (*svârthânumāna-pariccheda*):

śabdāḥ saṅketitaṁ prāhur vyavahārāya sa smṛtaḥ /
tadā svalakṣaṇaṁ nâsti saṅketas tena tatra na //

—'Speech elements express a convention-bound meaning/object. This [convention-bound meaning/object] is thought [to be of relevance] for everyday practice. Then, [a convention-bound object] is not the individual thing [that is used at the time of everyday practice.] Therefore, the linguistic convention regarding this [individual thing] is not [proper].'

On Dharmakīrti's analysis of lack of relation between words and particulars comp. SHAH (1967: 124–140). Here, I shall only quote BTBh 1 (p. 17.29 ff.), that briefly recapitulates Dharmakīrti's arguments: ***śabdôpamānârthâpatty-abhāvānāṁ pramāṇântaratva-nirasanam***. *śābdaṁ ca jñānaṁ bāhyârthâvisaṁvādakatvena pramāṇam eṣṭavyam. avisaṁvādakatvaṁ ca sambandham antareṇa na saṁgacchate. na ca śabdānāṁ bāhyârthena saha kaścit sambandho 'sti. tathā hi: śabdârthaḥ* *sambandho bhavan tādātmyaṁ tadutpattir vā bhavet. tatra na tāvat tādātmyaṁ śabdârthayoṛ atyanta-bhedena pratibhāsanāt. tādātmyaṁ hy ekatvam abhidhīyate. bhinna-pratibhāsayor apy ekatve svīkriyamāṇe gavâśvâdīnām py ekatva-prasaṅgaḥ. nâpi tad-utpattiḥ. anvaya-vyatirekâbhāvāt.*—'[A gloss on:] "Refutation of verbal knowledge, analogy, presumption and absence [as negative proof]." Verbal knowledge (*sc.* knowledge derived from words or testimony) could be accepted as a cognitive criterion, inasmuch as it would not stand in contradiction to the external object, and non-contradictoriness is not possible without a relation. However, there does not exist any relation whatsoever between words and the external object. For it is as follows: the relation between words and the object, if there were any, would have to be either the relation of essential identity or the relation of causality. Out of these two, the relation of essential identity, to begin with, is not [the case], because words and objects appear as absolutely different (i.e. they are mentally apprehended as absolutely different); [hence, the relation of essential identity is not possible], because the relation of essential identity is, as a matter of fact, called selfsameness. If selfsameness of two [things], having different representation though, were agreed upon, [that would lead to] the undesired consequence that a cow and a horse, etc., would be selfsame. The relation of causality is not [the case], either, because there is neither causal continuity nor causal discontinuity [between words and objects].'

[11] *artha-saṁśaya*—which literally means 'doubt with regard to the purpose[fullness of an action]'—is an anticipation of success or a presupposition that an action to be undertaken is likely to bring prosperity and success; cf. NBṬ$_1$ 1.1 (p. 2.18–19): *artha-saṁśayo 'pi hi pravṛtty-aṅgaṁ prekṣāvatāṁ anartha-saṁśayo nivṛtty-aṅgam.*—'Anticipation of success is indeed a requisite for the activity for thoughtful people, [whereas its opposite, i.e.] anticipation (*sc.* apprehension) of misfortune (i.e. anxiety that an action may bring misfortune) is the requisite for (*sc.* basis of) the suspension [of activity]'.

[12] It is so, inasmuch as thoughtfulness entails accomplishing an efficient action only in the case of an undertaking that is very likely to be beneficial and to bring success and, therefore, initial assumptions should have their validity. Cf. also HB, p. 3*.1–2: *artha-kriyârthī hi sarvaḥ pramāṇam apramāṇam vânveṣate prekṣavān.*

[13] In other words, given mere anticipation of success (*artha-saṁśaya*)—while misleading, or wrong cognition being the only means to assess the situation—any action must inevitably lead to failure. At this point, however, without any participation of a rational criterion evaluating accuracy of initial presumptions (*pramāṇa*) the action goes on, instead of being terminated. To wit, fiasco will not teach a lesson, if there is only a blind wish for success.

[14] Cf. HBṬ, p. 1–3, wherein we find his criticism predominantly of the Mīmāṁsaka, cf. MŚV$_1$ 1.12. The passage in question is not a proper citation; it is, apparently, a brief review of Arcaṭa's arguments. It is not improbable, however, that the passage comes from a work of Arcaṭa which is nowadays lost, namely from his *Pramāṇa-*

dvitva-siddhi, mentioned by the author himself in HBṬ, p. 189.2. The identical passage occurs also in NPV, p. 1.13 ff., but whether it has been taken directly from the other lost work of Arcaṭa, or borrowed *in extenso* from Siddharṣi, cannot be decided yet.

[15] HBṬ, p. 2.10–11: *na ca prayojana-vākyasya prāmāṇyam asti, śabdānāṁ bahir-arthe pratibandhâbhāvāt.*—'And the [initial] statement declaring the purpose [of the treatise] has no validity, because there is no connection between words and the external object'.

[16] I.e., without any valid justification of an action to be undertaken. Cf. HBṬ, p. 2.8: *yogyam etad vivakṣitaṁ kāryaṁ nipādayitum.*—'[Only] that action which is purposeful is warranted to be performed'.

[17] HBṬ, p. 2.5–6: *anyathā hy aniścitôpāyānām upeyârthināṁ pravṛttau prekṣāvattâiva hīyeta.*—'For otherwise, the very thoughtfulness—[in the case] of those, who aim at a goal, but have no determined means [to attain the goal]—with reference to [their] activity would be abandoned.'

[18] *asya tadvattā = prakaraṇasya abhidheyâdivattā.*

[19] Cf. HBṬ, 2,27 ff., p. 3.2–3: *yat prayojana-rahitaṁ vākyam, tad-artho vā, na tat prekṣāvatā 'rabhyate kartuṁ pratipādayitum va. tad yathā daśa-dāḍimâdi-vākyaṁ*[a] *kāka-danta-parīkṣā*[b] *ca. niṣprayojanaṁ cêdaṁ prakaraṇaṁ tad-artho vā iti vyāpakânupalabdhyā pratyavatiṣṭhamāṇasya tad-asiddhatôdbhāvanârtham ādau prayojana-vākyôpanyāsaḥ.*—'[An opponent might argue]: "If either a statement is void of purpose or its contents [is void of purpose], then a thoughtful person does not undertake to act with regard to this [treatise] or to teach [its contents. It is] like a statement about ten pomegranates, etc.,[a] and like an investigation of crow's teeth[b], and that means this treatise has no purpose [at all] or its contents [has no purpose]". In order to point to the unsoundness of these [arguments of an antagonist,] who opposes in the above manner by [demonstrating that] the pervader (*sc.* the property of being purposeful and meaningfulness of the present treatise, which is to be proved) is not comprehended [in the case of our treatise], the statement [revealing] the purpose [of the treatise] is specified (placed) in the very beginning.' A Similar passage is found in NPV (introduction) s. 9.13–18: ... *adhikṛta-śāstrasya prayojanâdi-pradarśanena prekṣāvatāṁ pravṛtty-artham iti. śāstrârtha-kathana-kālôpasthita-para-sambhāvyamānânupanyāsa-hetu-nirākaraṇârthaṁ ca nyāya-praveśakâkhyaṁ śāstram ārabhyata ity ukte sambhavaty evaṁ-vādī paraḥ—nârabdhavyam idam prayojana-rahitatvāt, unmattaka-vākyavat; tathā nirabhidheyatvāt kāka-danta-parīkṣāvat*[b]*, tathâsambaddhatvāt, daśa dāḍimāni*[a] *ṣaḍ apūpāḥ kuṇḍam ajājinaṁ palala-piṇḍaṁ sara kīṭikêty-ādi-vakyatvat*. See also DNC, p. 881.1–2.

[a] For the ambiguous expression *daśa-dāḍimâdi-vākyaṁ* cf. NAVV 56 § 2, p. 113.6: *anarthakam ca tad vacaś ca daśa-dāḍimâdi-vākyavat.*—'And that is meaningless speech, just like the statement about ten pomegranates'; and PALV 1: *nanu sambandhâbhidheya-śakyânuṣṭhānasyêṣṭa-prayojanavanti śāstrāṇi bhavanti.*

tatrâsya prakaraṇasya yāvad abhidheyaṁ sambandho vā nâbhidhiyate na tāvad asyôpādeyatvaṁ bhavitum arhati. eṣa vandhyā-suto yātîty-ādi-vākyavac ca daśa-dāḍimâdi-vākyavac ca.—'There are indeed treatises that have a purpose accepted for carrying out effectively [both their] relevance and subject-matter. In their [case], as long as relevance or subject-matter of such a [given] work is not stated explicitly, one is not in a position to pursue such [a work]. It is [then] like a [self-contradictory] statement: "a son of a barren woman is coming," etc., as well as like a statement about ten pomegranates, etc.' The maxim serves for Haribhadra in NPV (introductory part) p. 9.16–17 as an illustration of an incoherent speech, being one of alleged arguments—beside aforementioned lack of purpose and of the subject-matter—raised against undertaking the treatise by an hypothetical opponent: *tathâsambaddhatvāt daśa-dāḍimāni ṣaḍ apūpāḥ kuṇḍam ajājinaṁ palala-piṇḍaṁ sara kīṭikêty-ādi-vakyatvat.*—'Similarly [this treatise should not be undertaken] because it is incoherent, just like the [following] statement: "ten pomegranates, six cakes of flour, a bowl cumin seed, a lump of sesame, creep worm!", etc.' The expression occurs also in NAVV 55 § 2, p. 113.6: *anarthakaṁ ca tad-vacanaś ca daśa dāḍimâdi-vākyavat. Locus classicus* is MBh_1 1.1.3 apropos of *vṛddhir ādaic* [*vārttikā* 2, *ad* Pāṇ 1.1.1 (3 *āhṇika*), vol. I, p. 38.3–6]: *loke hy arthavanti cânarthakāni ca vākyāni dṛśyante. arthavanti tāvat devadatta gām abhyāja śuklaṁ daṇḍena devadatta gām abhyāja kṛṣṇam iti. anarthavanti daśa dāḍimāni ṣaḍ apūpāḥ kuṇḍam ajâjinaṁ palala-piṇḍaḥ adharôrukam etat-kumāryāḥ sphaiya-kṛtasya pitā pratiśīna iti.*—'For in this world, both meaningful and meaningless sentences are seen. Meaningful [sentences], to begin with, are [for instance]: "Devadatta, drive a white cow with a stick!" [or] "Devadatta, drive a black cow with a stick!". Meaningless [sentences], in their turn, are [for instance instances like the following incoherent series of words]: "ten pomegranates six cakes a bowl of goat skin a lump of grounded sesame a petticoat (?) of this girl the father of the opulent one liquefied".' Talking of instances of incoherent statements, I would like to draw the reader's attention to a failed rendering of the above passage found in DASGUPTA (1991: 151): 'Meaningless sentences are as follows: "ten pomegranates, the six cakes, the feet goat skin, lump of flesh, petticoat of this girl, the father of the abundantly made this limb".' The same division into meaningful and meaningless statements occurs in $ŚBh_1$ 1.1.5.5 (vol. I, p. 14.16–18): *laukikāni vacanāny upapannârthāny anupapannârthāni ca dṛśyante. yathā — 'devadatta! gām abhyāja' ity evam ādīni, 'daśa dāḍimāni ṣaḍ apūpāḥ' ity evam ādīni.* It is referred to by other Jaina authors, e.g. by Mallavādin in DNC, vol. III, p. 881.1–2: *daśa dāḍimānîty-ādi-vākyavat.*

[b] The maxim of an investigation of a crow's teeth (*kāka-danta-parīkṣā*), viz., of something non-existent, is here—as well as in the above quotation of HBṬ, p. 3.2–3—a stock illustration of purposelessness (*prayojana-virahitatva*), and not an instance of lack of subject-matter (*nirabhidheyatva*) as in the case of Haribhadra's NPV (introduction) p. 9.15–16, where the purposelessness is illustrated by a statement of a lunatic: *nârabdhavyaṁ idaṁ prayojana-rahitatvāt unmattaka-vākyavat. tathā nirabhidheyatvāt kāka-danta-parīkṣāvat.*—'This [treatise] should not be undertaken,

because it is void of purpose, like a statement of a lunatic. Similarly, [it should not be undertaken], because it is empty of the subject-matter, like an investigation of a crow's teeth.'

For both the expressions *daśa-dāḍimâdi-vākyaṁ* and *kāka-danta-parīkṣā*—as instances of the lack of serviceability, incoherence, impertinence and ineffectiveness—see also PV_1 3.124 and n. 345 below.

[20] The sense of Siddharṣi's argument is as follows: if we admit that the prefatory sentence has no validity of its own, therefore, all arguments it contains are also invalid, *ergo*, the refutation of the opponent it supposedly expresses is—by definition—futile. Siddharṣi attempts to show the self-abortive character of Arcaṭa's argumentation, that may— being so reformulated—exhibit some resemblance to a version of the Epimenides' paradox (*sc.* the Liar's antinomy: *Ego dico falsum*): 'This initial sentence is invalid.' (lit. 'I'm expressing falsehood').

[21] Cf. similar argument below, NAV 23: *tathā hi: kṣaṇiko 'rthaḥ sad vā kāryaṁ kuryāt, asad vā, gaty-antarâbhāvāt ...* (p. 70 of the translation).

[22] The mention of this Cakravartin, being an example of a future agent, the existence of whose is now unverifiable though, is not restricted to the Jaina literature only; cf. BTBh 1 on *abhāva* (p. 20.21): *nâpi jñāna-mātram [abhāvaḥ], deśa-kāla-svabhāva-viprakṛṣṭasyâpi sumeru-śaṅkha-cakravarti-piśācâder api jñāna-mātrā abhāva-pramāṇād abhāva-prasaṅgāt.* The author of the translation, Dr. B. N. Singh, fails to understand the passage, however, since he translates it: '... objects inaccessible in time and space like demons residing in *Sumeru Śaṁkha* (an island) ...'! I have failed, however, to find any more detailed account of the Cakravartin Śaṅkha in the narrative and mythological literature, neither Jaina nor Hindu.

[23] Would it mean that the cognitive subject's head would swell or be full, etc., of cognised objects, that have transferred their forms onto the cognition (mind), viz., if the objects kept transferring their forms onto the cognition (mind) seated in the skull, the head would be filled with them to the maximum, and would perhaps, eventually, burst or break? Or would it imply that the head would be split, inundated, or befallen by other misfortunes, that are being perceived, viz., when one perceives and act of splitting something, his or her head would be directly affected by this act of splitting? I believe both arguments would fit equally well, but I am not quite sure which is the real import of the phrase *śiraḥ-sphoṭana-plāvanâdy-anartha-prasakteś ca.*

[24] See p. 121 of the English translation.

[25] Polemical passage with Arcaṭa's HBṬ, p. 35.22–27: *punar apy anubhavôttara-kāla-bhāvino nīla-vikalpasya prāmāṇyam apanetum upacaya-hetum āha—"tato 'pi" yathôktād vikalpād na kevalaṁ nīla-svalakṣaṇânubhavād "vastuny eva" svalakṣaṇa eva "tad-adhyavasāyena" svalakṣaṇâdhyavasāyena anyathā tatra pravṛtty-ayogāt "puruṣasya pravṛtteḥ" adhigate svalakṣaṇe tat-sāmarthya-janmā vikalpo na*

pramāṇam iti sambandhaḥ. pūrvam anadhigata-vastu-rūpânadhigater aprāmāṇyam uktam.

[26] Compare the solution of the compound in NAṬ *ad loc.*: ***anādîty-ādi***. *anādi-kālād ālīnā sambaddhā yā vāsanā tasyāḥ prabodhas tena sampāditā sattā yasya sa câsau, nirvikalpakaṁ vyavasāya-śūnyaṁ viviktaṁ*[a] *sphuṭaṁ yad darśanaṁ pratyakṣaṁ tad uttara-kālaṁ bhavana-śīlo vikalpaś ca tena vyavasthāpitaṁ yat sādṛśaṁ tasya vaśaḥ sāmarthyam. yad uktaṁ: 'āyattatāyām āyatte*[b] *prabhutve*[c] *ca vaśaṁ viduḥ' tasmāt.*— '[We comment on the phrase]: "From beginningless times, etc.". Awakening of past impressions that were dormant, i.e. inactive, since beginningless times. That [conceptualisation] the existence of which has been brought about by this [awakening]. Non-conceptual, [i.e.] devoid of decision, and distinct, [i.e.] patent, perception, [i.e.] direct percei·ing. And conceptualisation comes into existence in the moment following this perception. [On] account (lit. capability) [of, i.e. due to] the efficacy [of], such a similarity that is determined by this [conceptualisation]. As it has been said: "They understand «capability« in [the sense of] reliance upon or in [the sense of] having power over [something that is] reliant"; [thus,] because of this [capability (*sc.* on account of).'

[a] A: *vyaktaṁ*.

[b] A marks with its system of notation: *āyattatāyā mâyatte*.

[c] A=V; H: *prabhatve*; C: *prasuttve*.

[27] I.e., immediate determinate cognition of dark-blueness of all things in all past, present and future moments.

[28] $PV_{1,3}$ 2.134. Worth noticing is the reading *manasor* instead of *manaso* attested in available editions. This supports Miyasaka's conjecture to read *manasor* (PV_6), cf. FRANCO (1997: 80, n. 35) and FRANCO's reservation to accept it: '[35] Miyasaka conjectures *manasor* on the basis of the Tibetan translation: *rtog bcas rtog pa med pa'i yid*. Even if the conjecture is accepted…'.

[29] *tattvatas* = *vikalpatvatas*, due to their being conceptualisations.

[30] However PV, as comprised within PVṬ and PVBh, reads originally *manaso yugapad-°*, instead of *manasor yugapad-°*. That being the case, the translation would run as follows: 'due to simultaneous occurrence of conceptual and non-conceptual [phenomena/activities] of the mind …'

[31] Cf. PVV_1 2.133: *laghu-vṛtter* = *śīghra-vṛtter* ('rapid [subsequent] occurrence'); that is to say, because they take place one after the other in hardly discernible intervals. Devabhadra-gaṇin comments in NAṬ *ad loc.*: ***laghu-vṛtter vêti***. *athavā*[a] *yathā bhavato laghu-vṛtteḥ*[b] *śākhā-candrâdi*[c]*-viṣaya-sannidhau na krameṇa grahaṇâdhyavasāyas tathā mamâpi nirvikalpaka-samanantaraṁ jhagity eva vikalpôtpādāt tayor*[c] *aikya-vyavasāyaḥ, na punas*[d] *tattvatas tayor aikyam. viśeṣatas tv etat-kārikârtho bauddhâlaṅkārâder avaseyaḥ.*—'[A gloss on:] "very close occurrence". Or, just like you, in [the case of] proximity of [two] things like the bough and

the moon[e], etc., have no apprehension of grasping [these two] consecutively due to [their] very close occurrence, similarly, also mine is the decision that these two [conceptual and non-conceptual mental acts] are one [and the same] due to the rise of conceptualisation [taking place] at once without delay immediately after the non-conceptual [perception], whereas these two are in reality not one [and the same]. The meaning of this strophe in particular should be ascertained on account of *Bauddhâlaṁkāra*, etc.' By *Bauddhâlaṁkāra* (or *Vārtikâlaṁkāra*) Devabhadra-sūri refers explicitly to PVBh on PV 2.133, comp. esp. PVBh_1, p. 241.22–24: *kathaṁ tarhi krameṇa grahaṇaṁ na bhavati. yugapad-viṣaya-sannidhānena eva. nahi varṇa-vikalpa-kāle pratyakṣârtho na sannihitaḥ. yathā ca bhavato laghu-vṛtter viṣaya-sannidhānena krameṇa grahaṇâdhyavasāyas tathā grahaṇam api mamêty-aviśeṣaḥ.*

[a] A=C; H,V omit *athavā*.
[b] C: °-*vṛtte* / .
[c] C: *vikalpôtpādat tayor*.
[d] A: *punaḥ*.

[e] It is an application of the maxim of 'the moon on the bough' (*śākhā-candrâdi-nyāya*), that speaks of two things that are, in reality, distant and separate, but make the impression of being contiguous due to their appearance.

[32] PV_3 2.133.

[33] It is a quotation from Dharmottara's AP: རྣམ་པར་རྟོག་པ་རྣམས་ཀྱི་ཡུལ་གང་ཡིན་པ་དེ་སྒྲའི་དོན་ཡིན་ནོ།། It resembles Dharmakīrti's statement from his auto-commentary to his PV 3.184 (PV_1, p. 264.27; PV_3, p. 92.2–3): *sa hi eva śabdānāṁ na viṣayo yo na vitarkāṇām*. Cf. FRAUWALLNER (1937).

[34] In order to avoid plethoric formulation, I replace 'object', i.e. my usual rendering of *artha*, by 'thing' in the above sentence.

[35] *lakṣaṇa* conveys both meanings: 'definition' and 'a characteristic; a characteristic [feature]'; they are practically, however, inseparable from each other. Cf. n. 83. I shall translate the term depending on context.

[36] I.e., 'because this is the way we experience the facts'; it is hard to find a better self-description of the Jinistic realist-empirical position!

[37] Evidently, *atrâpi* is to be construed with *vyavahārôcchedasya samānatvāt* and relates—by way of pointing out the analogy—the above logical reason with the preceding undesired consequence, viz., *nikhila-vyavahārôccheda-prasaṅgād*, whereas *dṛṣṭa-hāner* must be understood as a sub-reason for *atrâpi* ... *vyavahārôcchedasya samānatvāt*. Therefore, *ca* of Mss. A and B must be taken as an unnecessary addition.

[38] Cf. PA 6.51–53: *rāga-dveṣa-mohâkrānta-puruṣa-vacanāj jātam āgamâbhāsam. yathā nadyās tīre modaka-rāśayaḥ santi dhāvadhvaṁ māṇavakāḥ. aṅguly-agre hasti-yūtha-śatam āste iti ca.*—'Fallacious oral tradition is produced by utterances of a person exposed to passion, enmity and confusion, for instance: "There are heaps of sweetmeats on the river bank! Run, run, boys!" Or like: "A hundred herd of elephants sits on the tip of the finger.' This goes back to the problem of the veracity of testi-

mony, discussed, e.g., in ŚB 1.1.2 (p. 4.10 ff.): *nanv atathā-bhūtam apy arthaṁ brūyac codanā. yathā yat kiñcana laukikaṁ vacanam: "ndyās tīre phalāni santi" iti. tat tathyam api bhavati, vitatham api bhavatîti.*

[39] I.e., 'Why do you not admit this argument in the case of sound, too?' Namely, a false statement is subverted by a subsequent true statement, whereas there remain statements that are true because they are free from subversion.

[40] See n. 675.

[41] However, cf. PALV 2.11 (18.18): *sāmāgrī dravya-kṣetra-kāla-bhāva-lakṣaṇā.*—'The causal complex is characterised by the substance (*sc.* an entity), place, time and existence.' For the idea of the causal complex (*hetu-sāmagrī*) see VETTER (1964: 18–20, § 2a).

[42] For similar usage of the word *pariṇāma* cf. TBh 2.19: *upayogo praṇidhānam āyogas tad-bhāvaḥ pariṇāma ity arthaḥ.*—'Cognitive faculties mean [in other words] attention, noetic activity, essential nature, transformation.'

[43] I.e., the type of substance [which is] a living element, or soul. Living elements (*jīva*) and four 'entities' (*ajīva-kāya*) subdivided into the principle of motion (*dharma*), the principle of rest (*adharma*), the space (*ākāśa*) and the matter (*pudgala*) make up five substances (*dravya*); cf. TS 5.1–2. Some Jainas, mostly the Digambaras, recognise a sixth substance, viz., time (*kāla*); cf. TS 5.38, SSi 5.39. I render the term *jīva* as a 'living element', instead of traditional 'living being' or 'soul', for several reasons, the first of them being the intention of preserving the original sense of the original Sanskrit term, derived from √*jīv* 'to live, to remain alive', and its relation to *jīva*, denoting 'a living being, animal, creature', synonymous to *prāṇa*, etc. Secondly, I do so in order to emphasise its substantial and spatial character as *res extensa*, like the four elements or the afore-mentioned five substances (*dravya*) and unlike the term 'soul', which in its turn, could too easily be associated with the occidental idea of a non-extensive soul, or Descartes' *res cogitans*. Thirdly, in my opinion the established rendering 'living being' can too directly be confused with a specimen of the fauna. Last but not least, I intend to retain the terminological difference between *jīva* and *āṭman* in my translation.

[44] Cf. TS 2.8.

[45] The construction of the original sentence seems faulty; it is either extremely elliptical or some elements are missing. If the latter is the case, it is probable, that originally, instead of *darśayann ārabhyate*, the text reads: *darśayann āhârabhyate*, wherein the aspirate '*h*' disappeared, as it was hardly discernible when pronounced due to its devocalisation; though this assumption seems less tenable in my opinion. The proposed emendation is partly (depending on the interpretation of the element *āha*, that may be taken to belong the NAṬ) supported by the NAṬ *ad loc.*: *nanu pramāṇa-vyutpādanârtham idam ārabhyata*[a] *ity ukte*[b] *prayojana-mātraṁ*[c] *darśitaṁ nâtmana iti ced, āhârabhyata ity*[d] *asya mayêti-pada-savyapekṣatvād iti.*

[a] H,V: *ārabhyate.* [b] C: *ākte.* [c] C: *prayojanaṁ mātraṁ.*
[d] A: *cet / āha // ārabhyate ity*; C: *cet // āha // ārabhyate ity*; H,V: *cet, āha—* ***ārabhyate ity.***

[46] See Pāṇ 1.3.74; 3.1.21,25. This is what Siddharṣi means: both the purpose of the student ('understanding', *vyutpatti*) and of the author ('[giving] instruction', *vyutpādana*) are derivatives of the verbal root *pad* prefixed by *vy-ut*; the latter is, however, a causative derivative formed with the affix *ṇic* (hence 'instruction = the cause of somebody's understanding').

[47] Cf. YS 2.16 ff. and NBh on NS 1.1.1: *heyaṁ tasya nirvartakam hānam ātyantikam tasyôpāyo 'dhigantavya ity etāni catvāry artha-pādāni samyag buddhvā niḥśreyasam adhigacchati.*—'"What should be avoided, what brings it about, absolute avoidance [of the former and] the means [to accomplish] this [avoidance]—[which] should be realised"—having understood these four beneficial statements properly, one attains the ultimate.' For the interpretation of *artha-padāni* and *adhigantavya*, cf. WEZLER (1984: 325 ff.).

[48] Cf. NAṬ *ad loc.*: ***abhyudaya***[a]***-niḥśreyasâvāptir iti.*** *abhyudayo 'pavarga-prāpter arvāg*[b] *deva-loka-sukula-lābhâdikaṁ sāṁsārikaṁ kalyāṇam; niścitaṁ kevala-paramânanda-mayatvāc* ***chreyaḥ***[c] *kalyāṇaṁ samāsânte* ***ati*** *niḥśreyasaṁ muktis tayoḥ prāptiḥ.*[d] *yady api cêhâbhyudaya-sāmanya-grahaṇena*[e] *tad-viśeṣa-svarūpasya niḥśreyasasyâpi grahaḥ siddhas,*[f] *tathâpi go-balīvarda*[g]*-nyāyenôbhayor*[h] *abhidhānam iti.*—'[The gloss on]: "the attainment of [either] afterlife prosperity or of ultimate deliverance." Afterlife prosperity [is] mundane happiness [such as] the acquisition of [the rebirth in one of] heavens or [in] a noble family, etc., before the emancipation. [The expression "ultimate deliverance" can be dissolved into "ultimate" (*niḥ*) and "fortune" (*śreyas*) as follows:] positively, the fortune, inasmuch as it consists in the absolute supreme beatitude, is happiness; ["ultimate" means] utmost (*ati*) [and comes] at the end of compound; [thus, we have the compound word] "ultimate deliverance", [i.e.] liberation. ["The attainment" means] the acquisition of these two. And even though by grasping (*sc.* mentioning) the general [idea] of afterlife prosperity, the inclusion of ultimate deliverance is effected as well, which is in [its] intrinsic nature a particular [variety] of this [afterlife prosperity], nevertheless, both of them are stated explicitly following the maxim of "the cattle and bulls"[h].' Such a twofold formulation of the purpose and goal of the existence, bifurcated into mundane prosperity and final emancipation, were to meet conflicting demands of both the lay and ecclesiastic communities; cf., e.g. VSU_1 1.1.2: *yato 'bhyudaya-niḥśreyasa-siddhiḥ sadharmaḥ.*

[a] C: *abhyuyada-°.* [b] A: *arvāk*; C: *avāk.*
[c] A,C,H,V: *°-mayatvāt śreyaḥ.* [d] A,C: *prāptir.*
[e] C: *°-grahaṇo na.* [f] H,V: *siddhaḥ, .*
[g] A,C: *°-valīvardda-°*; H: *°-balīvardda-°.*

[h] The maxim of 'the cattle and bulls' (*go-balīvarda-nyāya*) justifies the redundant or pleonastic explicit mention of a subcategory in one breath with the main class, in order to single out or emphasise the former, which is actually included in the latter and does not necessarily have to be named, e.g. 'the cattle and bulls.' Thus, in accordance with the maxim, nothing would be wrong with the politically incorrect conjunction 'the humans and women.'

[49] It is, of course, a pan on the English usage of the word 'letter' in such locutions as 'to the letter', 'keeping to the letter of the law / an agreement' and similar ones, and on the word *akṣara* itself, not infrequently taken erroneously to stand for 'letter.' We should, of course, keep in mind that *akṣara* refers not to a graphical, written symbol, or a unit of an alphabet, but refers to the uttered level of language and denotes sound of speech, or minimum unit of distinctive vocal feature, i.e. phoneme. On misunderstandings related to, and on misinterpretations of, terms *akṣara*, *varṇa* and °*-kāra*, in the linguistic context, that are occasionally translated wrongly as 'letter', as well as on certain socio-anthropological implications of such cases of misapprehension of the true meaning, cf. WEZLER 1994.

[50] *Kāraka*s—or factors contributing to an accomplishment of an action, divided into six categories and fundamental to Pāṇinian system of derivation—relate semantics and the notion of grammatical cases. They express a particular relation of a noun to an action usually expressed by means of a particular grammatical case; they should not be confused with grammatical cases as such. Their enumeration and rules of derivation are listed in Pāṇ 1.4. For details and discussion of their character cf., e.g. HARTMANN (1955: 176–8), STAAL (1969: 506–9), CARDONA (1976: 215–21, § III.1.5.5c.1) and MATILAL (1990: 40–48). Cf. an analogous analysis of the word *anumāna* in accordance with the sequence of the *kāraka*s in NAV 5: *atrâpy anumāna-śabdasya kartr-ādi-kāraka-vyutpatti-krameṇârtha-kathanaṁ pramāṇa-śabdavad draṣṭavyam* (p. 38 of the translation). The term *pramāṇa* is said to be, relying strictly on the interpretation of its grammatical formation, pregnant with a range of meanings that emphasise various aspects of a cognitive act: as *karman*, *bhāva*, *kartṛ*, etc., discussed below. Another instance of applying grammatical terminology and the idea of *kāraka*s to epistemic analysis can be found in MŚV$_1$ 5.2. (*Nirālambana-vādâdhikaraṇa*).41–44 (pp. 162–163).

[51] *Bhāva* is an abstract, impersonal notion denoted by a verb and expressed by a noun, *nomen actionis*. This is the fundamental notion of the verbal root, from which *pramāṇa* is derived (≅ *pramiti*).

[52] Pāṇ 3.3.113 (H gives a wrong reference to Pā.3.4.113 instead). This *sūtra* sets up a rule that enables forming verbal derivations other than those of *nomina actionis* (*bhāva*) and the passive form (*karman*). A reference to Pāṇ 3.3 and to the suffix *lyuṭ*—though not always to Pāṇ 3.3.113, but, e.g. to Pāṇ 3.3.117—is found also in other works, e.g. in YDī$_2$, p. 67.6–7 (on SKā 4d): *karaṇa-sādhano lyuṭ*. The reference

in YDī was probably inspired by NBh$_{1}$ 1.1.3 (p. 18.3–4): *pramīyate 'nenêti karaṇârthâbhidhāno hi pramāṇa-śabdaḥ*.

[53] Despite P. L. Vaidya's note in his edition indicating Pān.3.3.130, *anyatrâpi* seems, however, to refer here generally to the whole section on the factors [contributing to an accomplishment of an action] (*kārakas*) described in Pāṇ 1.4.23 ff. and no particular *sūtra* is intended here, for the only relevant aphorisms beginning with *anya°* are the three instances listed below. These, however, refer only to particular *kṛt* affixes: (1) Pāṇ 3.2.75: *anyebho 'pi dṛśyante* refers only to the *maniN*, *KvaniP* and *vaniP* affixes, (2) Pāṇ 3.2.101: *anyeṣv api dṛśyate* refers only to the *Ḍá* affix, (3) Pāṇ 3.3.130: *anyebhyo 'pi dṛśyate* refers only to *yuC* affix.

[54] *ātman* = *jīva* (soul).

[55] I.e., the general idea expressed by the verb; in our case it is tantamount to *pramiti*, or the act of cognising in a valid way. Those various notions enumerated above overlap with the six factors [of an action] (*kārakas*) and with corresponding ideas of grammatical cases along with the notion of *nomen actionis* (*bhāva*): (1) cognitive subject (*ātman*) corresponds to the nominative case to denote the agent (*kārtṛ*), (2) object (*artha*)—the accusative case to denote object (*karman*), (3) cognition (*jñāna*)—the instrumental case to denote instrument (*karaṇa*), (4) efficient action (*artha-kriyā*)—the dative to denote the intended goal of an action (*sampradāna*), (5) totality of causes (*kāraṇa-kalāpa*)—the ablative (and instrumental) to denote the point of departure (*apādāna*), (6) destruction-cum-subsidence (*kṣayôpaśama*)—the locative to denote the locus (*adhikaraṇa*), (7) action (*kriyā*)—*nomen actionis* (*bhāva*).

[56] Lit. cognitions (*jñānāni*). The Jainas admit that cognition, being one of two basic cognitive qualities, besides perception/conation (*darśana*), is an inherent attribute of the cognitive subject, i.e. of the living element (*jīva*); cf. TS 2.8: *upayogo lakṣaṇam*—'Cognitive faculties [are] distinctive qualities [of a living element],' TBh 1.3: *jñāna-darśana-upayoga-svâbhāvyāt.*—'because its (i.e. living element's) essential nature [is characterised by] its cognitive faculties, such as cognition and perception/conation.' Cf. also TS 2.8,9,18,19; 5.44, etc., and TBh 1.8,31, etc. On *upayoga* (Pkt. *uvaöga*) cf. SCHUBRING (1962: 153 ff., 170 ff.). By implication, if we know the types of cognition and conation a living element is presently endowed with we can thereby identify his/her ontological status. Those non-erring and erroneous types of cognition apparently refer to two related typologies. The first one is the differentiation into *jñāna* and *ajñāna* (nescience); cf. TBh 1.32: *ajñānāni ... matyajñānaṁ śrutâjñānaṁ vibhāṅga-jñānam iti*—'the kinds of nescience [are as follows] sensuous nescience, scriptural nescience and deceptive cognition' (cf. also TS 2.9), whereas the second typology is represented by the concept of the fourteen stages of the spiritual progress (*guṇa-sthāna*); *vide* SSi 1.8 and 9.1; cf. also GLASENAPP (1942: 75–92). For instance, the first and lowest stage in the spiritual development of a liv-

ing element (*sc.* soul) is a wrong believer (*mithyā-dṛṣṭi*), characterised by a minimal degree of the correct conation (*samyag-darśana*) and by dormant cognitive faculties.

[57] I.e., it is nonsensical to debate *post factum* on the subject and whether potential causes could be relevant for a particular event or not, inasmuch as they are already known from the results.

[58] The Jainas assert certain parallelism between a particular type of knowledge and karmic states of the living element. There are altogether five of them to be distinguished, though only the first three karmic states have some relevance to the mentioned parallelism, for they depict the degree of loosening the contact between the living element and the karmic matter, that veils it, and as such they are concurrent with the gradual emergence of the correct cognition (*samyag-jñāna*, cf. TS 1.1 ff.), which is itself anteceded by the advent of predilection for truth (*samyaktva*; see TSṬ 2.3: *tattva-rucih samyaktvam*; *samyaktva* ≅ *samyag-darśana*, cf., TS 1.2). They are, listed (in TS 2.1–6) in order of steady decrease in binding influence of *v*, viz., (1) the state of subsidence (*aupaśamika-bhāva*), (2) the state of subsidence-cum-destruction (*kṣayâupaśamika-bhāva*), i.e. the state of partial subsidence and partial destruction, (2) and the state of total destruction (*kṣaya-bhāva*) of *karman*. Predilection for truth dawns already in the first state, but it is only in the second and third states that it awakens valid cognition. On this see GLASENAPP (1942: 40–43).

[59] This passage emphasises the instrumental notion (*karaṇa-kāraka*) derivable from the cognitive criterion.

[60] I.e., by stating definition, number, domain and result of cognitive criterion, cf. n. 9 and n. 63.

[61] *tattvârtha*; or: 'the meaning [of which corresponds to] reality.' The expression *tattvârtha* appears, to my mind, to be used deliberately in an ambiguous meaning and may connote far more than plain 'a true meaning', or 'a meaning that corresponds to reality', or simply 'truth.' This intended equivocality of the phrase, which has a history of its own within Jainism (cf. the title of Umāvāmin's work: *Tattvârtha-sūtra*), is testified, for instance, in TS 1.2: *tattvârtha-śraddhānaṁ samyag-darśanam* ('The right belief is the conviction [regarding] the objects as ontological categories') as well as in the explanation offered in its two commentaries that underscore this amphiboly: (1) in TBh 1.2: *tattvānām arthānāṁ śraddhānaṁ tattvena vârthānāṁ śraddhānaṁ tat samyag-darśanam* ('The right belief is the conviction [regarding] the objects as ontological categories or the conviction [regarding] the objects according to the reality') and (2) in SSi 1.2: *artha-śraddhānam iti cet sarvârtha-grahaṇa-prasaṅgaḥ. tattva-śraddhānam iti ced bhāva-mātra-prasaṅgaḥ; sattā-dravyatva-guṇatva-karmatvâdi tattvam iti kaiś cit kalpyata iti. tattvam ekatvam vā sarvâikya-grahaṇa-prasaṅgaḥ; puruṣa evêdam sarvam ity-ādi kaiścit kalpyata iti. tasmād avyabhicārârtham ubhayor upādānam.*—'If [we interpreted] "the conviction [regarding] the objects", it would lead to the undesired consequence [consisting in] encompassing all objects. [On the other hand,] if [the statement ran as follows:] "the

conviction [regarding] the ontological categories", it would lead to the undesired consequence [of referring] only [to] the being; inasmuch as some [thinkers, viz., the Naiyāyika-Vaiśeṣika,] assume that existence, substantiality, qualitativeness, motion, etc., are ontological categories (or reals). Alternatively, ontological category (or reality) [could be taken] as oneness, [which might lead to] the undesired consequence of taking everything to be one, inasmuch as some [thinkers] assume that *puruṣa* himself is each and every thing, etc. Therefore, both [terms] are mentioned in order to ward off [any possible] deviation [from truth].'

The seemingly irrelevant context of the cited passage as well as its supposed reference to the sphere of faith are only due to dissimilar connotations the European notion of *belief* is heavily loaded with. It should, however, be borne in mind that semantically Jinistic *darśana* as *belief* or *faith* is very far from the meaning it usually connotes in the Judeo-Christian tradition, and neither should the term be misunderstood nor its epistemic compass underestimated. Certain aspects of *darśana* can be much better represented by the term *conation*. We may clearly see from TBh 1.2 that the right belief is not void of its cognitive relevance. On the contrary, unquestionable and exact—i.e. 'according to the true state of affairs' or 'positive' (TBh 1.2: *bhavato niścitam*)—cognition (*jñāna*) of ontological categories (*tattva*) is naturally assumed the ultimate constituent of the right belief, the verity of which is accordingly asserted to be testified by its 'accordance with reality' (*tattvena*). The individual, subjective experience of certainty inherent in the right belief in Jainism appears to have firmer grounds than a problematic irrational sanction granted by some religious authority, the latter being an idiosyncratic feature of the Judeo-Christian religiosity. The belief is described as the ascertainment of what is evident (TBh 1.2: *ta eva câthârthās teṣāṁ śraddhānaṁ eṣu pratyakṣâvadhāraṇam*) and these objects of the right belief are known to constitute either seven (TS 1.4) or nine (Uttarā 28.14) ontological categories, inclusive of merit (*puṇya*) and demerit (*pāpa*), which are of purely ethical relevance. It follows, henceforth, that some constructive cognitive effort is intended to be present on the part of the cognising subject, and that *darśana*, or conation, does not merely indicate uncritical trust but it occupies an important place in the epistemological context as well. The supposition of equivocality hidden in the phrase *tattvârtha* is further confirmed by the fact that *Nyāyâvatāra* itself (NA 8, 9) refers also to ontological categories and, implicitly—in the opinion of Siddharṣi—it is not restricted to logical questions; cf. Siddharṣigaṇin's introductory verse referring to 'teaching the universal and the particular' (p. 1). Moreover, both locutions (*tattva* and *artha*) characterise reality, cf. especially NAV 9: *tattvaṁ jīvâdayaḥ padârthāḥ*—'reality are entities (*sc.* ontological categories) such as the living element etc.' (p. 51 of the English translation). Cf. also note 338.

[62] Cf. NAṬ *ad loc.*: ***padêty-ādi***. *padaṁ prasiddham, vākyaṁ viśiṣṭa-pada-samudāyaḥ.*[a] *yad āha*:

> *padānāṁ*[b] *saṁhatir vākyaṁ*[c] *sâpekṣāṇāṁ parasparam /*
> *sâkhyātāḥ kalpanās tatra paścāt santu yathā-yatham //*[†]

ślokaś[d] *chando-mātram.*[e] *ādi-grahaṇāt pratyakṣânumāna-prakaraṇâdi-grahaḥ.*

[a] A,C: *samudāyo.* [b] C: *pādānāṁ.* [c] A: *vākyaṁ* / . [d] C: *ślokas.*
[e] C: °*-mātraṁ.* [†] I have failed to identify the source of the quotation.

[63] The definition and the number of cognitive criteria are discussed in NA 1, their domain in NA 29 and their result in NA 28. They are summarised in NA 32.

[64] PV_3 1.3:

pramāṇam avisaṁvādi jñānam artha-kriyā-sthitiḥ /
avisaṁvādanam śābde 'py abhiprāya-nivedanāt //

Cf. also $NBṬ_1$, p. 2.5 (= $PVinṬ_2$ 5.2–3): *avisaṁvādakaṁ jñānaṁ samyag-jñānam.* 'Unerring' means 'correct', as it is explained in PVṬ. 4.16: *avisaṁvādakatvaṁ samyaktvaṁ vivakṣitam iti darśayati* (cf. DhPr 17.10 f). For the refutation of this definition cf. p. 13 ff. of the English translation.

[65] The idea of comprehending a not yet comprehended object as a criterion of validity of cognition apparently goes back to $ŚBh_1$ 1.1.5: *autpattikas tu śabdasyârthena sambandhas tasya jñānam upadeśo 'vyatirekaś câ̲r̲t̲h̲e̲'̲n̲u̲p̲a̲l̲a̲b̲d̲h̲e̲ t̲a̲t̲ p̲r̲a̲m̲ā̲ṇ̲a̲m̲ bādarāyaṇasyânapekṣatvāt.* Pārthasārathi commenting on this *sūtra* formulates a definition of *pramāṇa* in ŚDī, p. 45: *kāraṇa-doṣa-bādhaka-jñāna-rahitam agṛhīta-grāhi-jñānaṁ pramāṇam.*

A reference to this concept is found in TSop 13, p. 281.19–23: *yad api kumārilâdibhir uktam. yadîndriya-jñāna-gṛhītam arthaṁ gṛhṇāti mānasam. tadā gṛhīta-grāhitvād asyâprāmāṇyam. athêndriya-jñānâgṛhītam arthaṁ gṛhṇāti. tadā cândha-badhirâdy-abhāva-doṣa-prasaṅga iti.* However, as Tucci writes (p. 281, n. 6), 'Source [is] unknown.' Comp. also TUS_1 2.2, p. 146.1–3 (TUS_2, p. 22.18): *anye tv anadhigatârthâdhigantṛtvena pramāṇa-lakṣaṇam abhidadhati. te tv ayukta-vādino draṣṭavyāḥ.* On the above Bhāṭṭa-Mīmāṁsaka's definition of cognitive criterion see FRANCO (1987: 390, n. 135), who likewise fails to identify the exact source, apart from a reference to $MŚV_1$ 5 (Vṛtti-kāra).11ab, which comes closest to the quotation in question:

sarvasya 'nupalabdhe 'rthe prāmāṇyam smṛtir anyathā /

We find two relevant citations referring to Mīmāṁsā works in the *Nyāya-kośa* under the entry '*pramāṇam*': [p. 553:] *athavā anadhigatârthakânubhava-kāraṇatvam. tac ca gṛhīta-grāhītarânubhava-kāraṇam iti mīmāṁsakā āhuḥ* (*ku*° *ṭī*° 3), (Śrīkaṇṭha's [=Śitikaṇṭha's] *Tarka-prakāśa* [=*Śiti-kaṇṭhī*] *khaṇḍa* 4, p. 9). [p. 554:] *anadhigatârtha-gantṛ pramāṇam iti bhaṭṭa-mīmāṁsakā āhuḥ* (Śrīkṛṣṇa Dhūrjaṭī Dīkṣīta's *Sidhânta-candôdaya* 1, p. 20; saṁ. 1942), (*ku*° *ṭī*° 4/5). Alas, the editors fail to mention in any place what treatise *ku*° *ṭī*° might stand for. Could it be a reference to K̲u̲m̲ārila's *Ṭup-ṭ̲īkā* or to K̲u̲m̲ārila's *Bṛhaṭ-ṭ̲īkā*, or perhaps to Umbeka's *Tātparya-ṭ̲īkā* on K̲u̲marila's *Śloka-vārttika*?

In *Nyāya-dīpikā* § 25 (pp. 18–19) we find a reference to still another Mīmāṁsaka definition found in Pārthasārathi's *Śāstra-dīpikā*, an independent commentary on *Śābara-bhāṣya*: *anadhigata-tathā-bhūtârtha-niścayakaṁ pramāṇa* [*Śāstra-dī*° p. 123] *iti bhāṭṭāḥ*. Alas, the editor of the ND does not mention the edition of *Śāstra-dīpikā* he is referring to.

Surprisingly enough, the idea of cognitive criterion grasping a yet uncognised object alone can be found also among Jaina thinkers themselves; one of its proponents was Māṇikyanandin, who enunciated it at the very outset of its treatise, see PA 1.1: *svâpūrvârtha-vyavasāyâtmakaṁ jñānaṁ pramāṇam.*—'Cognitive criterion is cognition the nature of which is the decision regarding [the cognition] itself and an object previously not [cognised].' This standpoint was expressly criticised, having first been recapitulated as a *pūrva-pakṣa*, later on by Hemacandra in PMī § 14 on 1.1.3–4 (p. 4): *nanu ca paricchinnam arthaṁ paricchindatā pramāṇena piṣṭaṁ piṣṭaṁ syāt.*[a] *tathā ca gṛhīta-grāhiṇāṁ dhārā-vāhi-jñānānām api prāmāṇya-prasaṅgaḥ. tato 'pūrvârtha-nirṇaya ity astu lakṣaṇam; yathâhuḥ—svâpūrvârtha-vyavasāyâtmakaṁ jñānaṁ pramāṇam iti, tatrâpūrvârtha-vijñānam iti ca. tatrâha*: [1.1.4] ***grahīṣyamāṇa-grāhiṇa iva gṛhīta-grāhiṇo 'pi nâprāmāṇyam.***—'And now [an objection is raised by the opponent]: "[To apprehend] by a cognitive criterion that determines an object [already] determined would be to grind ground flour (*sc.* to uselessly accomplish an already accomplished task). And subsequently [there would ensue] the unwelcome consequence that also acts of cognition that grasp an [object already] grasped, which flow [in a series in the mind like] a stream of water, [would have] the status of a cognitive criterion. Therefore, let the [proper] definition [of cognitive criterion] be «the determination of an object previously not [cognised].» Just as it has been promulgated: «Cognitive criterion is cognition the nature of which is the decision regarding [the cognition] itself and an object previously not [cognised]» and «[Cognitive criterion is] the discernment of an object previously not [present] in this [cognitive criterion]»." With regard to this [opinion, we] say: [1.1.4] Just like the [cognition] grasping an [object] that will be grasped [in the future], also the [cognition] grasping an [object already] grasped does not lack the status of a cognitive criterion.'

For the Jaina refutation of such an idea and of the Mīmāṁsaka definition in NAV, see p. 13 ff. of the present translation. Comprehension of a not yet comprehended object (*pramāṇasya anadhigatârthâdhigantṛtva*) constituted a part of the Buddhist definition of the cognitive criterion, as well; cf. NAV 29: *nirvikalpakam anadhigatârthâdhigantṛtvāt pramāṇaṁ* (p.91 of the translation) and n. 628.

[a] The quotation, slightly altered though, is found as early as in Jayantabhaṭṭa's NMa_2 (1. *āhnika*) Vol. II, p. 45.14–15: *adhigatam arthaṁ adhigamayatā pramāṇena piṣṭaṁ piṣṭaṁ syād iti*.

[66] NBh 2.1.11 (Dvārikādās Śāstrī: p. 99.11; Jayanārāyaṇa Tarkapañcānana: p. 57.3): *upalabdhi-hetuś ca pramāṇam*. See also NBh 2.1.15: *upalabdhi-sādhanaṁ pramāṇam*, NBh 2.1.16: *buddhir upalabdhi-sādhanatvāt pramāṇam*, etc. For the refutation of this definition cf. p. 13 ff. of the English translation.

[67] Cf. NB_1 2–3: *dvividhaṁ samyag-jñānam: pratyakṣam anumanaṁ ca*; NP_2 4: *ātma-pratyāyanârthaṁ tu pratyakṣam anumānaṁ ca dve eva pramāṇe*; etc.

[68] Cf. ND 1.3, wherein testimony (*śabda*) and inference (*anumāna*) are interchanged.

[69] In VS the material is scattered and no systematic enumeration of cognitive criteria is to be found. Thus, perception is discussed in VS_2 4.1.6–14, 9.13–17, whereas inference is described in VS_2 3.1.8–9, 9.18. The third cognitive criterion, the verbal knowledge, is treated as a special kind of inference, nonetheless, it finds its separate place: VS_1 9.19: *etena śābdaṁ vyākhyātam.*—'By this [exposition of inference, also] the verbal knowledge is explained', VSU_1 3.2.8: *tasmād āgamikam.*—'Therefore, [the soul] is established by the scriptures'; cf. also FADDEGON (1918: 284–310). In his commentary to VS_1 9.19 (that corresponds to VSU 9.2.3 according to the numbering in other editions), Śaṅkara Miśra states that all other cognitive criteria, except for perception and inference, can be included into inference, VSU 9.2.3 (p. 397): *pramāṇântarāṇi laiṅgike 'ntar-bhāvayituṁ prakaraṇântaram ārabhate.*

[70] Cf. YS 1.7 and SKā 4: *dṛṣṭam anumānam āpta-vacanam ... trividhaṁ pramāṇam.*

[71] Cf. ṢDSa 84d (p. 306): *mānaṁ tv akṣa-jam eva hi* / and TSaP 1860 (p. 520): *na ca pratyakṣād anya-pramāṇam asti.*

[72] The verb *vi-nir√luṭh* as such is not attested by any dictionary or lexicographic work available to me. For the analysis of the verbal roots √*luṇṭh* 'to rob', √*luṭ* 'to roll, wallow' and √*luṭh* 'to strike, beat against', augmented either with the prefix *nir-* or *vi-*, cf. B. N. MISRA p. 38–47. Its derivative *vinirluṭhita* (or *vinirluṇṭhita*) occurs, however, in NAV quite frequently (see *infra*). Siddharṣi-gaṇin explains its meaning by a series of synonymous expressions in NAV 29: *parasparâvinirluṭhita* (not detached from the other) = *parasparâvibhakta* (not separate from each other) = *na itarêtara-viśakalita* (not mutually disconnected). It is explained in NAṬ 1 (H: p. 33, V: p. 22): ***vinirluṭhitam*** *rahitam* (see n.184). The expression is not so uncommon, as it might seem at first glance, for we find it, for instance, also in SVM 7.14–16, p. 32: *tayā vṛttyā samavāya-sambandhena tayor dharma-dharmiṇor avinirluṇṭhitatve 'pi dharma-dharmi-vyapadeśa iṣyate.* Cf. A. B. Dhruva's corresponding note on p. 80 in SVM: '*vinirluṇṭhita* = separate.'

We come across the past participle of *luṭhita* ('bound') in a verse quoted in TRD § 79 on $ṢDSa_1$ 11 (p. 3–4), probably, from PVin (identified by the editor, Mahendra Kumar Jain, as PrVā.2.327: *Pramāṇa-vārtikâlaṁkāra*, ed. Jāyasavāl Research Institute, Paṭnā):

bāhyo na vidyate hy artho yathā bālair vikalpyate /
vāsanā-luṭhitaṁ cittam arthâbhāse pravartate // —

—'For an external object does not exist, as it is falsely conceived by the ignorant; [It is] consciousness b o u n d with past impressions [that] functions as a false image of an [external] object.'

[73] Cf. $PVinṬ_2$ 7,10–12: *dvividho hi viṣayaḥ pramāṇasya, grāhyaś ca yad ākāram utpadyate prāpaṇīyaś ca yam adhyavasyati*, as quoted in $NBṬ_2$ 1.12 (p. 71.1f) and $PVinṬ_2$ 8.1–2: ... *prāmāṇyaṁ vastu-viṣayaṁ dvayoḥ* (cf. Steinkellner's respective

n. 30, p. 77–8). However, the domain of cognitive criterion is described occasionally in a different, viz., non-epistemological manner, e.g. in HB as quoted in HBṬ, p. 28.8: *artha-kriyā-sādhana-viṣayam eva pramāṇam nêtarad iti.*

[74] I.e., class-representative and specimen-specific.

[75] Cf. NRĀ on MŚV$_1$ 4 (*Pratyakṣa-sūtra*) 119: *yā tv iyaṁ gr̥hyamāṇasya dvy-ātmakatvâkhyā sā lakṣaṇâkhyā gr̥hyamāṇasya vastuno lakṣaṇam ākhyāyate sāmānya-viśeṣâtmakaṁ tad vastv iti.*

[76] Cf. VSV 1.2.3: *bhinneṣu piṇḍeṣv anuvartamānāṁ "gaur gauḥ" iti buddhim apekṣya ebhya eva ca parasparato vyāvartamānām "ayam asmād anyaḥ" iti tad anuvr̥tti-buddhy-apekṣaṁ sāmānyaṁ vyāvr̥tti-buddhy-apekṣo viśeṣa iti.*

[77] *Sāmānya* = *vaiśva-rūpya*, the world. See YDī$_2$ *ad* SKā 9, p. 109.15: *viśvâtmakānāṁ sattva-rajas-tamasām...* See also YDī$_2$ *ad* SKā 15d, p. 154.10–11: *viśeṣasya sāmānya-pūrvakatvād iti yo 'rthas tad uktaṁ bhavati* ***avibhāgād vaiśva-rūpyasyêti.***

[78] Cf. SKā$_1$ 9 (= LARSON (1979) / SKā$_4$ 11):

> *tri-guṇam aviveki viṣayaḥ sāmāyam acetanaṁ prasava-dharmi /*
> *vyaktaṁ tathā pradhānaṁ tad-viparītas tathā ca pumān //*

and YDī$_1$ on SKā 13, p. 62.24 ff.: *āha—aviveky-ādir idānīṁ guṇaḥ katham pratipattavya iti? ucyate:* ***avivekyâdiḥ siddhas traiguṇyāt.*** *yat tri-guṇaṁ tad viveki viṣayaḥ sāmānyam acetanaṁ prasavadharmîti katham avagamyata iti cet* ***tad-viparyayâbhāvāt.*** *yasmād guṇa-viparyayaḥ kṣetrajñā. tatra viṣayatvam acetanatvaṁ prasadharmitvaṁ ca na bhavatîti purastāt pratipādayiṣyamaḥ.*

[79] Cf. TSaP 1860 (p. 520): *idaṁ ca mahā-bhūta-catuṣṭayaṁ pratyakṣa-saṁsiddham. na câitad-vyatirekeṇânya-tattvam asti pratyakṣa-siddhaṁ.*

[80] Cf. PVin I$_1$ 260b p. 78.12–13: | *yaṅ tshad ma 'di'i 'bras bu gaṅ yin* | *gźal bya rtogs pa'o* || (**tad-pramāṇa-phalaṁ kiṁ ca? prameyâdhigatiḥ.*). As it is well-known, the Buddhist equate *pramāṇa* with cognition; cf. PS 1.8cd: *savyāpāra-pratītatvāt pramāṇaṁ phalam eva sat* and PSV 1 *ad loc.* (Vasudhararakṣita/Seṅ-rgyal 15a.5–7; Kanakavarman /Dad-paḥi śes-rab [K] 95b.6–7): འདི་ལ་ཕྱི་རོལ་པ་རྣམས་ཀྱི་བཞིན་དུ་ཚད་མ་ལས་འབྲས་བུ་དོན་གཞན་དུ་འགྱུར་བ་ནི་མེད་ཀྱི། འབྲས་བུར་གྱུར་པའི་ཤེས་པ་དེ་ཉིད་ཡུལ་གྱི་རྣམ་པ་ཅན་དུ་སྐྱེས་པ་དང་། བྱ་བ་དང་བཅས་པར་རྟོགས་པ་དེ་ཉེ་བར་བླངས་ནས་ཚད་མ་ཉིད་དུ་འདོགས་པ་སྟེ། བྱ་བ་མེད་པར་ཡང་ཡིན་ནོ།། དཔེར་ན་འབྲས་བུ་རྒྱུ་དང་རྗེས་སུ་མ།—
—'Regarding this [relation between cognitive criterion and its result], the result [of cognitive criterion, i.e. the cognition itself,] is not accepted as being different from cognitive criterion, as the realists (*bāhyârtha-vādin*) [believe]. This cognition, which is the result [of cognitive criterion], originates as having the form of its (*sc.* of the object) province and is accepted to be endowed with the [cognitive] activity (*savyāpāra*). Hence, [this cognition] is called cognitive criterion by metaphorical transference, even though the [cognitive] activity is absent (*vyāpārâbhāve 'pi*). For

instance, it is said (*ity abhidhīyate*) that the result assumes the form of its cause (*kāraṇa-rūpa-gṛhīta*), when it occurs by way of similarity with the cause, even though the process [of assuming the form of the cause] is not there. Analogous (*evam api*) is [the case] with that [cognition as the result of cognitive criterion].' Cf. also NB_I 1.18–21: *tad eva ca pratyakṣaṁ jñānaṁ pramāṇa-phalam. artha-pratīti-rūpatvāt. artha-sārūpyam asya pramāṇam. tad-vaśād artha-pratīti-siddher iti*, as well as $NBṬ_I$ 1.21: *na câtra janya-janaka-bhāva-nibandhanaḥ sādhya-sādhana-bhāvo, yenâikasmin vastuni virodhaḥ syāt; api tu vyavasthāpya-vyapasthāpaka-bhāvena. tata ekasya vastunaḥ kiñcid rūpaṁ pramāṇaṁ kiñcid pramāṇa-phalaṁ na virudhyate.* Comp. also HATTORI (1968: 97–100, nn. 1.55–57). Surprisingly, *arthâdhigatiḥ pramāṇa-phalam* is quoted in BTBh 26.29 (*pramāṇa-phala-vyavasthā*) = $BTBh_3$ § 8 (p. 61), where it is ascribed to Dharmakīrti: *yathôktam: artha-sārūpyam asya pramāṇam, arthâdhigatiḥ pramāṇa-phalam iti.* Indeed, *artha-sārūpyam asya pramāṇam* is NB 1.20, but the phrase *arthâdhigatiḥ pramāṇa-phalam* as such is nowhere found in NB.

[81] I.e., they maintain that cognitive criterion precedes and differs from cognition, that is result of the former. The Mīmāṁsakas, e.g. Kumārila Bhaṭṭa, opposed the idea of equating the resulting cognition with cognitive criterion as a means to acquire it, by pointing out the absurdity of identifying the instrument with the goal accomplished by its means; cf. $MŚV_I$ 4.74–75 (p. 113):

viṣayâikatvam icchaṁs tu yaḥ pramāṇaṁ phalaṁ vadet /
sādhya-sādhanayor bhedo laukikas tena bādhitaḥ //
chedane khadira-prāpte palāśe na chidā yathā /
tathâiva paraśor loke chidayā saha nâikatā//

—'However, if somebody, wishing [to preserve] the oneness of the province, called cognitive criterion a result, then the commonplace difference between that-to-be-established and means-to-establish would be subverted. Just like—when an act of cutting is executed with regard to an acacia tree—a *Butea Frondosa* tree is not cut [by this very act], in the very same way an axe is not one with the [act of] cutting.'

'The others' designated in NAV are, for instance, the Naiyāyikas. Vātsyāyana Pakṣilasvāmin in his introduction to NBh 1.1.1 lists the well-known four factors contributing to the resulting cognition, which are different from cognitive criterion: *tatra yasyêpsā-jihāsā-prayuktasya pravṛttiḥ sa pramātā, sa yenârthaṁ pramiṇoti tat pramāṇam, yo 'rthaḥ pramīyate tat prameyam, yad artha-vijñānaṁ sā pramitiḥ.* The act of cognising and the cognitive result are repeatedly distinguished from each other, either explicitly, e.g. in NBh 1.1.1: *pramāṇato 'rtha-pratipattiḥ …*; *pramāṇair artha-parīkṣaṇam …*; *pramāṇam antareṇa nârtha-pratipattiḥ*, or implicitly, by means of formulating a recursive definition[a], e.g. in NBh 1.1.9: *bhoga-sādhanânīndriyāṇi*; *bhoktavyā indriyârthāḥ*; *bhogo buddhiḥ*.

However, also the Jaina were not unanimous regarding the selfsameness of cognitive criterion and the resulting cognition, and perhaps it is those among Jaina thinkers who opposed the idea of equating both notions that should be comprised under the above expression 'and others' as well. For instance, Akalaṅka, commenting on

Tattvârtha-sūtra, says in TRV, p. 56.12–14: *loke pramāṇāt phalam arthântara-bhūtam upalabhyate. tad yathā: chetṛ-chettavya-chedana-sannidhāne dvaidhī-bhāvaḥ phalam. na ca tathā sva-saṁvedanam arthântara-bhūtam asti. tasmād asya phalatvaṁ nôpapadyate.*—'In this world, through cognitive criterion a result is obtained, which is [some]thing different [than the cognitive criterion itself]. For it is as follows: when [the three factors, viz.,] the agent of cutting, the object to be cut and the act of cutting are present, [there occurs] a result that has a secondary (*sc.* distinct) status [different than these three factors]. And, similarly, self-cognition [being a resulting representation of an object] is [some]thing different [then the cognitive criterion]. Therefore, this [cognitive criterion] is not explicable as a result (*sc.* resulting cognition).'

[a] For the notion of recursive definition see BOCHENSKI (1954: 92), who owes this concept to KOTARBINSKI (1929: 478).

[82] As MALVANIA (1979: 287) pointed out, there is some correspondence between the above expression and Samantabhadra's *Bṛhat-svayambhū-stotra* 63. Cf. also DHAKY (1990: 7)= DHAKY (1995: 42): 'the first phrase of the opening verse of the *Nyāyāvatāra* (*Pramāṇam svaparābhāsi*) ... shows correspondence with the wording of the strophe of the verse 63 of the *Bṛhat-svayambhū-stotra* of Samantabhadra[30] (*c.* A. D. 600) to which Malvaniya has hinted[31].' SvSt 63 reads as follows:

parasparêkṣânvaya-bheda-liṅgataḥ prasiddha-sāmānya-viśeṣayos tava /
samagratâsti sva-parâvabhāsakaṁ yathā pramāṇaṁ bhuvi buddhi-lakṣaṇam //

In this place, I would like to point very briefly to a striking similarity of this view to the opinion expressed in NS 2.1.19: *na, pradīpa-prakāśavat tat-(=pramāṇa)-siddheḥ*—'No, [cognitive criteria do not need any cognitive meta-criterion, i.e. an additional cognitive criterion, that would prove their validity], because they (cognitive criteria) are established in the same way as the light of a lamp (which reveals both itself and its object).' This opinion is referred to by Nāgārjuna in VīVy 33, who—while refuting (in VīVy 31–33) early Naiyāyika position (cf. NS 2.1.8–20, Mādhyamika-Naiyāyika controversy over cognitive criteria) concerning the way in which the validity of cognitive criteria can be proved—recapitulates Gautama's position: *pramāṇāny eva svâtmānaṁ parâtmāṇaṁ ca prasādhayanti* ('cognitive criteria themselves demonstrate their own essence as well as the essence of the other (*sc.* their objects)'), and quotes an unidentified, clearly Naiyāyika verse, that corresponds to NS 2.1.19:

dyotayati svâtmānaṁ yathā hutāśas tathā parâtmānam /
sva-parâtmānāv evaṁ prasādhyanti pramāṇānîti //

—'Fire illuminates its own essence as well as the essence of the other (*sc.* something different from it); in the same way cognitive criteria demonstrate themselves and the other.' Vātsyāyana understands NS.2.1.19 differently, though, strictly in accordance with the established Nyāya tradition, that cognition reveals only its object (*parâbhāsin*): *yathā pradīpa-prakāśaḥ pratyakṣâṅgatvāt dṛśya-darśane pramāṇaṁ, sa ca pratyakṣântareṇa cakṣuḥ sannikarṣeṇa gṛhyate.*—'Just like the light of a lamp which, [on the one hand], is a cognitive criterion in the case of seeing something visible, because it is an expedient of [visual] perception; [but on the other], it is grasped by a different [visual] perception, [namely] through the contact with eyes.' In other words, light illuminates other objects; however, when it is perceived, it becomes an object of cognition for another kind of perception. With such an interpretation, the Nyāya principle of non-cognisablility of cognition by itself is in this case retained. Nevertheless, Nāgārjuna's recapitulation of evidently Akṣapāda Gautama's own opinion may point to an earlier strand of the Nyāya tradition and be an attestation of a change within the Nyāya school that might have taken place after Gautama and before Vātsyāyana, as far as the self-revealing character of *pramāṇa* is concerned. This supposition, however, would necessitate further research.

[83] The term *lakṣaṇa* seems to be far too comprehensive as to be rendered systematically by one and the same term: it denotes a characteristic, a distinguishing feature, or a defining property (for instance, in a phrase *grāhya-grāhaka-bhāva-lakṣaṇa*), as well as definition (e.g. in the preceding section on various misconceptions regarding cognitive criterion upheld by opponent philosophers, p. 9 ff.). Both connotations of '*lakṣaṇa*' seem to be mingled due to certain parallelism and the term itself is used ambiguously. Indeed, '*lakṣaṇa*' connotes a specific feature on the physical level, where it refers to a particular physical thing, a property or a phenomenon, hence it is a c h a r a c t e r i s t i c. On the other hand, on the level of conscious reflection and verbal expression, it is a property that distinguishes a given notion or conceptualisation from other notions, hence it is a d e f i n i t i o n. Cf. n. 35. For an analysis of the semantic field of the term see MATILAL (1985: 164–202, §§ 2.8–9).

[84] *tīrtha* lit. 'a ford.' Sometimes the meaning of *tīrtha* is very close to 'religion', and *tīrthântarīya* comes very close to 'adherent of another religion', 'non-believer', 'heretic.' Above, however, *tīrtha* clearly refers to various systems of thought, including also the Cārvākas, the materialists. That is why I have decided to preserve a less restrictive rendering 'adherent of rival systems of thought.' The term is explained, referring to the Jaina religion, in NAṬ *ad loc.*: ***tīrthântarīyêty-ādi****. tīryate bhavâbdhir anenêti tīrthaṁ dvādaśâṅgaṁ tad-ādhāro vā saṁghaḥ.*[a] *tasmād anyat tīrthântaraṁ*[b], *tatra bhavās tīrthântarīyāḥ.*—'That with the help of which the ocean of birth is forded through is the ford consisting of the twelve Limbs (=the Jaina Canon) or the community recognising that [Canon]. What is different from this [ford] is another ford; those who have their existence in this [other ford] are adherents of another religion (*sc.* heretics).' This elucidation clearly points to two crucial aspects of any religion: (1) an established body of tenets handed down through tradition, including soteriology, eschatology, etc., as means of salvation, viz., the doctrine incorporated in the body of twelve main canonical scriptures (*dvādaśâṅga*), and (2) the religious community (*saṅgha*) of believers who place confidence in the doctrine of the Canon (*tad-ādhāra*). The third component (i.e. religious practice) of religion understood as the classical triad doctrine–practice–community[c], that apparently is missing here ex-

plicitly, is indirectly implied in this definition in the doctrinal aspect, for the Canon contains an enormous number of prescriptions, rules and practices to be conscientiously carried out by both ascetic and lay followers. Cf. a similar definition where all the tree elements are present in VABh 1380/1026: *titthaṁ ti puvvaṁ bhaṇiyaṁ saṁgho jo nāṇa caraṇa saṁghāö.* [d]—'The "ford" [means] the propounded Ancient text (= the Jaina Canon), the community, knowledge, conduct with regard to the community.'[c] For details cf. BALCEROWICZ 1997.

[a] A,C: *saṁghas.* [b] H,V: *anya-tīrthântaraṁ.*

[c] For the (at least) three crucial aspects involved in any definition of religion, i.e. (1) the doctrine as the theoretical expression of religious intuitions and *Weltanaschauung*, (2) the religious practice or the cult as its practical expression and (3) the community as its social materialisation, including both collective and individual aspect, see MALINOWSKI (1911: 67), DURKHEIM (1912: *livre* 1, I § 3), WACH (1944: Ch. II *passim*) and BALCEROWICZ (1997: 197–200).

[d] I do not intend to enter upon a philological discussion regarding the reading of Prakrit passages as such, which in its linguistic layer is not univocal and allows for more grammatical interpretations, e.g. alternatively, "The 'ford' [means] the propounded Ancient text (= the Jaina Canon) [and] the community which consists of knowledge and conduct." (*titthaṁ ti puvvaṁ bhaṇiyaṁ saṁgho jo nāṇa-caraṇa-saṁghāö*). Whatever the final solution of the Prakrit text (either compounded or not) and its syntax, and whether *saṁghāö* is Sanskrit *saṅghātaḥ* ('compounded, consisting of') or an Ablative of *saṁgha* (**saṅghāt-tas* = *saṅghāt*, *saṅghatas*), the most essential elements of the sentence relevant here are clear.

[85] In other words, the first group comprises those who are aware of the conception of cognitive criterion, but whose misconceptions are to be corrected, and to the other group belong those, to whom the notion must be first explained, inasmuch as they are not aware of its existence or its meaning.

[86] We must not lose sight of the fact that into the category of the living element the Jaina include not only men or animals but also plants, minerals, etc. The taxonomy is listed, for instance, in TS 2.10–14, where all living elements are divided into the liberated and the mundane (TS 2.10). The latter are further subdivided (TS 2.12) into those capable of motion, i.e. fire, wind, living beings possessed of two and more sense-organs (TS 2.14), and into those incapable of motion, i.e. earth, water, plants (TS 2.13). This classification overlaps with the division into living elements possessed of mind and those without mind (TS 2.11; 2.25 ff.).

[87] See n.49.

[88] *viśeṣeṇa varjitam* ('absolutely free') is the explication of the prefix *vi-* (absolutely) in *vivarjitam* ('free') of the verse in question.

[89] Cf. NAV 31 on *svânya-nirbhāsin*, p. 131 ff. of the English translation.

[90] In this particular case, the qualification of cognitive criterion, being the *definiendum*, is the factor 'revealing itself and something else (different from it)' (*sva-para-bhāsin*) and it excludes all other (false) views.

[91] Clearly what is referred to is the Vijñāna-vādin/Yogācāra's theory of *vijñāna-mātratā*, or *viñjāpti-mātratā*; cf. ĀP 6:

yad antar-jñeya-rūpaṁ tu bahirvad abhāsate /
so 'rtho vijñāna-rūpatvāt tat-pratyayatayâpi ca //—

—'That which appears as an external [thing] but assumes the form of an internal cognoscible [thing] is the [real] object, because it consists in consciousness and is the casual condition of that [consciousness].'

Comp. also ĀPVṛ 1: *jñānena svarūpam eva nirdhāryate tad-ākāratayā jāyamānatvāt.*—'Cognition ascertains only its own form, because [the own form of an object] arises as [something that] has the form of this [cognition].' Vasubandhu in his commentary on Viṁś$_{I}$ 12 says: *tasyâsiddhau* (i.e. *paramāṇor asiddau*) *rūpâdīnāṁ cakṣurâdi-viṣayatvam asiddham iti siddhaṁ vijñapti-mātraṁ bhavati.*—'Since this [atom] is not proved [to be existent,] visual forms, etc., as the [respective] province of eyes and other [sense-organs] are not proved [to be existent]; therefore, the sole [existence of] the contents of consciousness turns out to be established.'

[92] That is to say, cognition grasps its own epiphenomena. Cf. Viṁś$_{I}$ 1,9:

vijñapti-mātram evâitad asad-arthâvabhāsanāt /
yathā taimirikasyâsat-keśa-candrâdi-darśanam //
yataḥ sva-bījād vijñaptir yad-ābhāsā pravartate /
dvividhâyatanatvena te tasyā munir abravīt // —

—'[All] this [that exists] is solely the contents of consciousness, because it is the appearance of non-existent objects, just like perception of non-existent [things such as] hair, moon, etc., [in the case] of [a person] suffering from ophthalmological disorder. Of these two—viz., of the own seed, from which the contents of consciousness proceeds, and of what [it is] a false image of—spoke the Buddha as the two-fold basis [of consciousness].' Cf. also Triṁś$_{I}$ 25,28:

dharmāṇāṁ paramârthaś ca sa yatas tathatâpi[a] *saḥ /*
sarva-kālaṁ tathā-bhāvāt sâiva vijñapti-mātratā //
yadā tv ālambanaṁ jñānaṁ[b] *nâivopalabhate tadā /*
sthitaṁ vijñāna-mātratve grāhyâbhāve tad-agrahāt //

—'And this [three-fold essential nature] is the ultimate truth (*sc.* nature) of constituents of reality, because this is "suchness" (i.e. Absolute Reality)[a], inasmuch as it endures [unchanged] as such all the time; this very ["suchness" (i.e. Absolute Reality)] is the sole existence of the contents of consciousness. When, however, consciousness comprehends no objective substratum at all, then [consciousness] is established in its sole existence as consciousness, because—when there is nothing-to-be-grasped—there is no comprehension of that [thing-to-be-grasped].' Cf. also ADhS 1.1.23:

sarva-bījakam ālaya-vijñānaṁ, as well as a refutation of external objects in Chapter 23 (*bahir-artha-parīkṣā*) in TSa_I 2001–2033, esp. TSa_I 2032:

saṁvedanam idaṁ sarvaṁ na cârthântara-gocaram /
saṁvedana-svabhāvatvāt svâtma-saṁvedanaṁ yathā //—

—'Everything with no exception is consciousness and there is no domain [of consciousness which could be] some other [external thing], because the essential nature [of everything] is consciousness, just like consciousness of its own self.'

[a] *tathatā*, variously translated as 'this-ness', 'that-ness','thusness', 'True Reality', 'true nature underlying all things,' etc., is the absolute, or ultimate reality; compare, for instance, the meaning of the term in BoBh, p. 28.7–12: *tasmāt sā parama-śūnyatâdhimokṣa-bhāvanā bodhisattvasya śikṣā-mārga-saṅgṛhīto mahān upāya ity ucyate yad uta tathāgata-jñānâdhigamāya. sa khalu bodhisattvas tena dūrânupraviṣṭena dharma-nairātmya-jñānena nirabhilāpya-svabhāvatāṁ sarva-dharmāṇāṁ yathā-bhūtaṁ viditvā na kiñcid vikalpayati nânyatra vastu-mātraṁ gṛhṇāti tathatā-mātram. na câsyâivaṁ bhavati vastu-mātraṁ vā etat tathatā-mātraṁ cêti* [Nalinaksha Dutt misprints: *câiti*]. Cf. also ROSPATT (1995: 71–76 [= § 2.3.1], 212 [= § 3.4]).

[b] S. Lévi (p. 43.10) clearly misreads the manuscripts: *yadā tv ālambanaṁ vijñānaṁ*... See the MSS.A(5a 5b) in Mimaki–Tachikawa–Yuyama's *Vasubandhu* p. 5/6. Jacobi (1932: 60 n. 188) is clearly misled by Lévi, but his conjecture is wrong: 'Lies ālambam metri causa für ālambanam, wie in V.5 auch wirklich geschrieben ist.'

[93] This inevitable objection was well-known to the Vijñāna-vādin. Another objection—much akin to the one above, though, but of more specific nature—was raised by Vasubandhu himself in $Vi\dot{m}\acute{s}_I$ 2 [Sanskrit text reconstructed by S. Lévi], and was afterwards refuted:

yadi vijñaptir anarthā niyamo deśa-kālayoḥ /
santānasyâniyamaś ca yuktā kṛtya-kṛiyā na ca // —

—'If the contents of consciousness were without object, [there would be] no circumscription to [a given] place and time and [there would be] no circumscription to personal series (*sc.* person) [i.e. no object could be cognised by more people than one], and no efficient action with regard to objects amenable to activity [would be] logically correct (*sc.* possible).'

Comp. also the argument, commencing with different assumptions, against solipsism that was put forward by Dharmakīrti in NB_I 2.49: *pramāṇa-nivṛttāv apy arthâbhāvâsiddher iti.*—'Because it is improper [to infer] that things cease to exist even on cessation of cognitive criterion,' and was subsequently commented by Dharmottara: *na ca pramāṇaṁ prameyasya kāraṇaṁ nâpi vyāpakam. ataḥ pramāṇayor nivṛttāv apy arthasya prameyasya nivṛttir na sidhyati. ... yat punaḥ pramāṇa-sattayā prameya-sattā sidhyati tad yuktam. prameya-kāryaṁ hi pramāṇam.*—'And cognitive criterion is neither a cause of the cognoscible nor invariably concomitant [with it]. Therefore, the cessation of a cognoscible object, even when both cognitive criteria (i.e. perception and inference) cease, is not admissible. ... On the other hand, it is logically correct, when existence of the cognoscible is proved through the existence of cognitive criterion, since cognitive criterion is the result of the cognoscible.'

[94] For *pratibhāsa* see NASV 13: *dūrâsannâdi-bhedena pratibhāsaṁ bhinatti yat / tat pratyakṣaṁ parokṣaṁ tu tato 'nyad vastu kīrtitam*; NB 1.5: *abhilāpa-saṁsarga-yogya-pratibhāsa-pratītiḥ kalpanā* ('conceptual construction is an awareness of a representation capable of association with speech'); DhPr, p. 50.6 (on. NBṬ 1.5): *pratibhāsasya jñānâkārasya niyamaḥ*; etc., ('[there is] the circumscription of the representation having the form of cognition: ...'), PVinṬ$_2$ 7,11–12, etc.; cf. also STEINKELLNER–KRASSER (1989: 77, 80, 89–90): 'das Erscheinungsbild' (*pratibhāsa*). See also 'representation' and 'objectified representation' in SCHMITHAUSEN (1987: 384–5, n. 628a) as well as 'appearance' in MATILAL (1985: 215–228). To a certain degree, the subjective appearance of an external thing, be it real or unreal, or its representation within the mind, may resemble εἴδωλα of Democritus, or inner impressions or facsimiles of external things presented within the senses.

[95] The possibility of a *karmadhāraya*-compound, viz., 'a forest temple, etc.', is ruled out by a subsequent Devabhadra-gaṇin's gloss on the expression: *tathā smaraṇāt...* below, who understands the phrase as a *dvandva*-compound: *vana-viṣayaṁ deva-kula-viṣayaṁ vā*. Cf. similar case on p. 16 and n.133.

[96] Or perhaps 'sees ... the awakening of subliminal impressions,' if we admit the reading of H,V and Ms. A (°-*vyapekṣatvāt*).

[97] Ms. A has a marginal note: 'drowsiness, weak sleep, etc.' (°-*middha-manda-nidrâdi*-°).

[98] I.e., otherwise there would be no reason why there should not occur an illusory sixth gross element in a state of dreaming, if entities that are never experienced could occur in our cognition.

[99] *jñāna-vyatiriktāyāḥ* must be a qualifier of *vāsanā* on account of the gender.

[100] Cf. NAṬ 1 *ad loc.*: ***tayêty-ādi***. *tayā vāsanayā saha vedya-vedakâkāra-kaluṣa-jñānasya kārya-kāraṇa-bhāva-lakṣaṇa-sambandha-grahaṇâbhāvāt; tad-abhāvaś ca bhavad-abhiprāyeṇa*[a] *pūrvâpara-kṣaṇa-varti-jñāna-vyatiriktasya grāhakasyâtmano*[b] *'sattvāt.*—'[A gloss on]: "with this". Because [we] grasp no r e l a t i o n , that [can be] c h a r a c t e r i s e d b y t h e c a u s e - a n d - e f f e c t d e p e n d - e n c e , of the cognition defiled by the form of the cogniser and the cognoscible "with this" past impression. And this [relation] does not exist, because according to your intention there is no cognitive subject (soul) that [would] grasp [an object] who is different from the [series of acts of] cognition occurring in previous and subsequent moments.'

[a] C: *abhiprāyeṇa* / . [b] A: °-*vyatirikta-grāhakasyâtmano*.

[101] I interpret here *jaḍa* against Devabhadra-gaṇin's explanation, who comments: '"also the insentient" [means] also the cognition which has an unconscious form' (NAṬ 1 *ad loc.*: ***jaḍam apîti*** *acid-rūpam*[a] *api jñānam*), firstly, because *jaḍa* has already been used in the sense of an insentient object (*jaḍatvād arthasya na grāhakatvam api tu jñānasya tad-utpatti-tad-ākāratayoḥ satyor iti cet*) and, secondly, because of the ensuing conclusion: 'only the object would become established...' (*artha eva siddhim āskanded, na jñānam*).

[a] A: *acit rūpam*; C: *acid arūpam*.

[102] *āstāṁ tāvat*; lit. 'let it be so', 'so enough of it', 'let's leave it as it is', meaning: 'and that is it'; viz., one could discuss the particular topic further on, but since we have already proved our thesis, there in no point to debate the issue further on.

[103] Cf. NAṬ *ad loc.*: ***nahîti***. *yad uktam*:

dīpavan nôpapadyeta bāhya-vastu-prakāśanam /
anātma-vedane jñāne jagad-āndhyaṁ prasajyate // [†]

—'Like [in the case of] a lamp, revealing of an external real thing [only] is not explicable; if the knowledge were bereft of consciousness of its own self, it would absurdly imply blindness of the world.'

[†] I have failed to identify the source of the quotation.

[104] I.e., what would constitute the distinction between the cognitive subject and cognised objects?

[105] I.e., because also this body is revealed in the same manner as any other external object that is different from cognition.

[106] NAṬ explains: 'that cognition which has a form that illuminates its interior' (*antaḥ-prakāśaka ākāro yasya jñānasya*...). The term *antar-mukha* is a correlate of *bahir-mukha*, both of them occurring in NAV 29: *tathântaḥ-saṁvedanam artha-svarūpâpekṣayā bahir-mukhântar-mukha-savikalpâvikalpa-bhrāntâbhrāntâdi-pratibhāsam ekam abhyupayataḥ katham anekântâvabhāso 'siddhaḥ syāt?* (pp. 89 of the translation) and in NAV 31: *tatrâpi śarīraṁ bahir-mukhâkāreṇa bodhenârtha-rūpatayā jaḍam anubhūyate, cetanā punar antar-mukhâkāreṇa sva-saṁvedana-pratyakṣeṇa sākṣāt-kriyate* ... (pp. 133 of the translation). For the expressions *bahir-mukha* and *antar-mukha*, see n.598.

[107] Cf. NAṬ *ad loc.*: ***arthâpatty-ādinêti***. ... *yad uktam*:

nânyathêhârtha-sadbhāvo dṛṣṭaḥ sann upapadyate /
jñānaṁ cen nêty ataḥ paścāt pramāṇam iti kalpyate // [†] ...

[†] I have failed to identify the source of the quotation.

[108] Lit. 'What is the harm of the first?', viz.: 'Why do you reject the idea of a cognition revealing itself and something else?' The word *kṣūṇa* seems to be a re-sanskritised Prakrit substantive *khūṇa*, derived from Skt. √*kṣud* 'trample upon, crush'

and *kṣuṇṇa* 'shattered, broken to pieces', and Prakrit variant reading *khuṇṇa* / *khūṇa*. However, comp. √*khuḍ* classified—unconvincingly, in my opinion—as a *deśya* word in SHRIYAN (1969: 217, § 896): '√***khuḍ*** — "to chop off", "to cut off": ... [Compare √*khuṭṭ*– = *tuḍ*–, "to break". (H. 4 116, Tr. 3 1 62); cf. *kuṭṭa*– = *truṭitam*, "broken" (D. 2 74); cf. √*khuṭṭ* in Bh. and √*khuṁṭ*– in NC. in the same sense; cf. M. *khuṭṇe* = "to crop or pluck, to be arrested in progress"; cf. Hi. *kõṭnā* = 'to nip.'...]."

[109] The phrase *svarūpam avabhāsayad eva jñānam* restates the idea of *svâbhāsin* whereas that of *parâbhāsin* is expressed by *artha-grāhaṇāya vyāpriyate*.

[110] Cf. NS 1.1.4: *indriyârtha-sannikarṣôtpannaṁ jñānam avyapadeśyam avyabhicāri vyavasāyâtmakaṁ pratyakṣam*.—'The cognition which is produced by the contact of an object with a [corresponding] sense organ, [which is] non-verbal, [which is] unerring, the nature of which is the decision [regarding the nature of the object], is perception.' It is intriguing, however, to find a similar expression with regard to sensuous cognition (*mati-jñāna*), or perception, in Umāsvāti's TBh 1.11: *indriyârtha-sannikarṣa-nimittatvāt* ('because [the sensuous cognition] is occasioned by the contact of sense organs with their respective objects'). A similar concept, as an underlying postulate, is encountered once more in the characterisation of subvarieties of sensuous cognition (*mati-jñāna*) and testimony (*śruta-jñāna*), in TBh 1.14: *tatrêndriya-nimittaṁ sparśanâdīnāṁ pañcānāṁ sparśâdiṣu pañcasv eva sva-viṣayeṣu. anindriya-nimittaṁ mano-vṛtti ogha-jñānaṁ ca*. Instrumental in solving the dilemma to what extent the sense-object contact can be relevant for the cognitive validity of cognition in the Jainas' opinion is the discussion in PMī 1 §§ 107–109, p. 26, where Hemacandra criticises only later exponents of the Nyāya school, namely Trilocana and his disciple Vacaspāti Miśra, who consider the first part of NS 1.1.4 (*indriyârtha-sannikarṣôtpannaṁ jñānam*) to be the definition proper of perception, the series of predicates being merely an elaboration, and interpret the *sūtra* by inserting the ellipsis *yataḥ*: /§ 107/ *naiyāyikās tu*: "*indriyârtha-sannikarṣôtpannaṁ jñānam avyapadeśyam avyabhicāri vyavasāyâtmakaṁ pratyakṣam*" *iti pratyakṣa-lakṣaṇam ācakṣate. atra ca pūrvâcārya-kṛta-vyākhyā-vaimukhyena saṁkhyâvadbhis trilocana-vacaspāti-pramukhair ayam arthaḥ samarthito yathā*—"*indriyârtha-sannikarṣôtpannaṁ jñānam avyabhicāri pratyakṣam*" *ity eva pratyakṣa-lakṣaṇam. yataḥ-śabdâdhyāhāreṇa ca yat-tador*[a] *nityâbhisambandhād ukta-viśeṣaṇa-viśiṣṭaṁ jñānaṁ yato bhavati tat tathā-vidha-jñāna-sādhanaṁ jñāna-rūpam ajñāna-rūpaṁ vā pratyakṣaṁ pramāṇaṁ iti. asya ca phala-bhūtasya jñānasya dvayī gatir avikalpaṁ savikalpaṁ ca. tayor ubhayor api pramāṇa-rūpatvam abhidhātuṁ vibhāga-vacanam etad*: "*avyapadeśyaṁ vyavasāyâtmakam*" *iti*. /§ 108/ *tatrôbhaya-rūpasyâpi jñānasya prāmāṇyam upekṣya yataḥ-śabdâdhyāhāra-kleśenâjñāna-rūpasya sannikarṣâdeḥ prāmāṇya-samarthanam ayuktam. katham hy ajñāna-rūpāḥ sannikarṣâdayo 'rtha-paricchittau sādhakatamā bhavanti vyabhicārāt, saty apîndriyârtha-sannikarṣe 'rthôpalabdher abhāvāt. jñāne saty eva bhāvāt, sādhakatamaṁ hi karaṇam avyavahita-phalaṁ ca tad iti*. /§ 109/ *sannikarṣo 'pi yadi yogyatâtiriktaḥ saṁyogâdi-sambandhas tarhi sa cakṣuṣo 'rthena saha nâsty aprāpya-kāritvāt*[b] *tasya. dṛśyate hi*

kācâbhra-sphaṭikâdi-vyavahitasyâpy arthasya cakṣuṣôpalabdhiḥ. atha prāpya-kāri cakṣuḥ karaṇatvād vāsyâdivad iti brūṣe, tarhy ayas-kāntâkarṣaṇôpalena lohâsannikṛṣṭena vyabhicāraḥ. na ca saṁyukta-saṁyogâdiḥ sannikarṣas tatra kalpayituṁ śakyate, atiprasaṅgād iti.—'/§ 107/ On the other hand, the propounders of Nyāya argue for the following definition of perception: "The cognition which is produced by the contact of an object with a [corresponding] sense organ, [which is] non-verbal, [which is] unerring, the nature of which is the decision [regarding the nature of the object], is perception". And with regard to this [definition], the following meaning was corroborated by numerous [scholars] headed by Trilocana and Vacaspāti [Miśra] by way of opposition against the explanation propounded by former preceptors, namely, the definition of perception is exclusively as follows: "The unerring cognition which is produced by the contact of an object with a [corresponding] sense organ, is perception." And on account of supplying the speech element "because of"—inasmuch as [the relative pronoun] "which" and [the demonstrative pronoun] "that" [stand] in permanent relation—[they interpret the aphorism NS.1.1.4 in the following manner]: "**that** because of **which** the cognition qualified by the aforesaid qualifications comes into existence is a means of such a cognition, [and this means has] the form of cognition or the form of something else than cognition, [this means is] perception, [which in its turn has the status of] a cognitive criterion." Further, this cognition, being a result, has two operative modes: non-conceptual and accompanied by conceptualisation. In order to state [explicitly] that both of these [operative modes] with no exception have the form of cognitive criterion, there is the following mention of the typology [of perception]: "[perception which is] non-verbal [and perception] the nature of which is the decision [regarding the nature of the object]." /§ 108/ The [attempt] to corroborate the cognitive validity of the [sense-object] contact, [believed] to consist in cognition, through pains of supplying the speech element "because of"—while expecting cognitive validity from the cognition that has the form of both of these [operative modes, viz., of cognition itself and of something else than the cognition]—is not proper. For how can [phenomena like] the [sense-object] contact, etc., that have the form of something else than cognition, be efficient enough in determination of an object? [Of course, they cannot,] because of discrepancy [between your assumption and the facts], inasmuch as—even if there is a sense-object contact—there is no comprehension of an object. Accordingly, since [the comprehension of an object] takes places only when there is cognition, [therefore] what is efficient enough, [i.e. something that is] conducive [to producing the comprehension of an object] and [something which brings] immediate results, is that cognition. /§ 109/ Also, if the [sense-object] contact is [said to be merely] a relation, like connection, etc., in addition to the capability [of the senses], even then such a [relation, like connection, etc.,] with an object is not [possible] for the eye, because the latter operates [without coming into contact with the object] to-be-reached. For the comprehension of an object through the eye is empirically observed, even [when the object] is separated by [transparent obstacles such as] glass, mica, crystal (lens), etc. If you claim that the eye operates [by coming directly into contact with the object] to-be-reached, because it is an instrument, like an axe, etc., then [we can reply that] there is discrepancy [of your assumption] with [the fact of] attracting [iron] by lodestone without [lodestone] entering into a contact with iron. And it is not possible to conceive a [sense-object] contact [like] the connection [of the eye] with an [object] connected [with it], etc., because of too far-reaching consequence.'

The passages of Vacaspāti Miśra referred to by Hemacandra above are, e.g. NVTṬ 1.1.4.3, p. 133.9–13 and similar: ***vyavasāyâtmaka-padaṁ*** *sākṣāt savikalpakasya vācakaṁ, tathā hi vyavasāyo viniścayo vikalpa ity anarthântaram. sa eva ātmā rūpaṁ yasya tat savikalpakaṁ pratyakṣam. tad etad atisphuṭatvāt śiṣyair gamyata evêti bhāṣya-vārttika-kārābhyām avyākhyātam api asmabhiḥ ...*

[a] The Mookerjee-Tatia's edition reads *yattadonityâbhisambandhād*.

[b] This well-known issue of the peculiar operation of the organ of sight by coming into contact with the object to-be-reached (*prāpya-kāritvu*) by means of ocular rays of light (*cakṣū-raśmi*)—upheld by the Naiyāyika and described in NS_1 3.1.32,43 = NS_2 3.1.32,42: *raśmy-artha-sannikarśa-viśeṣāt tad-grahaṇam*; *naktaṁ-cara-nayana-raśmi-darśanāc ca.*)—and especially the refutation of this idea (found in Jayarāśi's TUS_1 1.4 (p. 136 ff.), is mentioned, e.g. by FRANCO (1987: 381–383, nn. 124,125).

[111] Cf. n. 102.

[112] I.e., *timira*. I have failed to identify this eye disease, which is a widely quoted standard example of an ocular morbid affliction and well known by its name. However, cf. FRANCO (1987: 446, n. 203), who does not quote any source: '... *timira* sickness gets its name from the fact that it causes the crystalline lens to become opaque.'

[113] Cf. NAṬ 1 *ad loc*.: ***plāvitatvād iti***. *bādhitatvāt*.

[114] The word *khalu* emphasises the fact that the expressed idea is well determined and there is no place for any doubt or debate left; cf. NKa [26], p. 47.5: *khalu-śabdo niścaye.*—'The speech element "as one should realise" [is used] in [the sense of] "determination".' Cf. n. 686.

[115] *avalepa*; most probably a kind of eye disease; M.W. has '***avalipta***, (=*api-ripta*) blind (?)' and '***apiripta***, "smeared over," i.e. grown blind.'

[116] Cf. p. 9.

[117] Cf. p. 9 and n. 64.

[118] Cf. p. 9.

[119] I.e., since substance in itself forms one unity, both spatially and temporarily, therefore, knowing its part is tantamount to cognising it in its entirety.

[120] *prāmāṇya* must refer here to *saṁvedana-dvaya* from the preceding line; the author apparently equates here *saṁvedana* with *jñāna*.

[121] Lit. 'because it has the same acquisition and maintenance.' Cf. n.600.

[122] Cf. E.g. PV_1 1.3 (see also n. 64).

[123] See PSā 1.36 (p. 83.1–2):

tamhā ṇāṇaṁ jīvo ṇeyaṁ davvaṁ tihā samakkhādaṁ /
davvaṁ ti puṇo ādā paraṁ ca pariṇāma-saṁbaddhaṁ //

Devabhadra-sūri cites in this place, as a matter of reference, the following verses, which he wrongly ascribes to Bhadrabāhu, NAṬ 1 *ad loc.*: ***siddhânta-prasiddhêty-ādi***. *tathā ca bhagavān bhadrabāhuḥ*:

/1/ *jīvo akkho*[a] *taṁ paï jaṁ*[a] *vaṭṭaï taṁ tu hoï paccakkhaṁ /*
paraü[c] *puṇa akkhassa*[d] *vaṭṭantaṁ*[e] *hoï pārokkhaṁ*[f] //
/2/ *kesiṁci iṁdiyāïṁ akkhāïṁ tad-uvaladdhi*[g] *paccakkhaṁ /*
taṁ tu na jujjaï jamhā aggāhagam[h] *iṁdiyaṁ visaë*[i] // †
/3/ *navi iṁdiyāïṁ uvaladdhimaṁti vigaësu*[j] *visaya-saṁbharaṇā /*
jaha geha-gavakkhāïṁ[k] *jo aṇusariyā sa uvaladdhā*[l] //
/4/ *dhūma-nimittaṁ nāṇaṁ aggiṁmi liṁgiyaṁ*[m] *jahā hoï /*
taha iṁdayāïṁ liṁgaṁ taṁ nāṇaṁ[n] *liṁgiyaṁ*[o] *na kahaṁ* //—

—'/1/ That with regard to which the living element, i.e. the perceiving organ, operates is, however, perception [and] indirect cognition is what is active, in its turn, as different from the perceiving organ. /2/ For some [thinkers] the senses are the perceiving organs [and] the comprehension with their help is perception. But that [standpoint] is not justified, because a sense cannot grasp [anything] if there is [only] an object [and no living element present that would grasp the object]. /3/ Nor the senses are capable of comprehension if [their objects] are gone, either, [even though] a reminiscence of an object [is possible in its absence], like, for instance, a round window of a house which is [merely] remembered is [in fact] comprehended. /4/ Just like the cognition which is occasioned by smoke arrives at (*sc.* concludes the existence of) the fire by inference (*laiṅgikam*, lit. "based, relying upon the inferential sign"), in the same way the senses are the inferential sign; isn't [then] such a cognition of inferential character (*laiṅgikam*, lit. "based upon the inferential sign")?!'

Devabhadra-sūri's gloss further reads on: *laukikā apy akṣa-śabdena jīvam āhuḥ. yad āha gauḍaḥ*[p] ‡: *jñānâtma-cakra-śakaṭe pāśaka*[r]*-vyavahārayoḥ /*
tuṣe karṣe pumān akṣaṁ tucche sauvarcalêndriye //
bibhītaka[s]*-dyūta-cakranâbhigatâvayaveṣv api. puṁsîti /*

idam iha siddhānta-rahasyam:

egaṁteṇa parokkhaṁ liṅgiyam ohāïyaṁ ca paccakkhaṁ /
iṁdiya-maṇo-bhavaṁ jaṁ taṁ saṁvavahāra-paccakkhaṁ // §

atra 'ohāïyaṁ' iti[t] *avadhi-manaḥ-paryaya*[u]*-kevala-rūpaṁ jñāna-trayam*.

[a] C: *akho*. [b] C: *jha*. [c] H,V: *paraö*.
[d] A,C: *akkhassā*. [e] A: *vaṭṭanto*. [f] A: *pārokkho*.
[g] A,C: °*-ubaladdhi*. [h] A: *ajāhagam*. [i] C: *bisaë*.

[j] C: *visaësu.* [k] C: °-*vakkhāiṁ.* [l] C: *aṇusariyāü sa valaddhā.*
[m] C: *aggi-liṁgiyaṁ.* [n] C: *tan ṇāṇaṁ.* [o] C: *liṁgiāṁ.*
[p] C: *goḍaḥ.* [r] C: °-*pīśaka*-°. [s] A: °-*vibhītaka*-°.
[t] A: *ohāïyaṁ ti.* [u] A,C: °- *paryava*-°.

[†] The above verses 1 and 2, even though they bear conspicuous similarity to, are not identical with—as P. L. Vaidya suggested on p. 104 (V. edition of NA)—VABh 89–91 (p. 23–4):

jīvo akkho atthavvāvaṇa-bhoyaṇa-guṇaṇṇito jeṇaṁ /
taṁ pati vaṭṭi ṇāṇaṇ jaṁ paccakkhaṁ tayaṁ tividha //
akkhassa poggalakatā jaṁ davvindiyamaṇā parā teṇaṁ /
tehiṁto jaṁ ṇāṇaṁ parokkham iha tam aṇumāṇaṁ va //
kesiṁci indiyāïṁ akkhāïṁ tad-uvaladdhi-paccakkhaṁ /
taṁ ṇo tāïṁ jama-cetaṇāïṁ jāṇaṁti ṇa ghaḍo vva //

[‡] Is it *Gauḍa-kośa*? [§] VABh 95.

[124] This is the semi-etymological explication of the term 'perception': *pratyakṣa* = *akṣaṁ pratigataṁ*.

[125] For the formation of the word "*go*" see UṇādiS$_2$ 214, p. 80 (comm. to 2.68: ***gamer ḍoḥ***): *gamer dhātor ḍo-pratyayo bhavati. gacchatîti gauḥ catuṣpāt.*—'[The word *go*, or cow,] is formed by the suffix *ḍo* [applied] to the verbal root √*gam*, [meaning: "to walk",]: a cow, i.e. a quadruped, because it is walking.' Cf. also Pāṇ 3.3.1: ***uṇ-ādayo** bahulam*—'[the class of *kṛt* affixes] beginning with *uṇ* [can be] variously [applied to from names].'

[126] Devabhadra-sūri in his NAṬ explains: ***viparyayāt** puruṣâdau go-śabdasyâprasiddhatvāt.*—'"Because of the contrary" [means] because the speech element "*go*" is not known (*sc*. not used) with reference to people, etc.'

[127] The passage bears striking similarity to PVinṬ$_2$ 2.18–3.14 (p. 20.17–22.14) and to NBṬ$_2$ 1.3 (p. 38.1–6): *pratyakṣaṁ iti. pratigatam āśritam akṣam ...akṣâśritatvaṁ ca vyutpatti-nimittaṁ śabdasya. na tu pravṛtti-nimittam. anena tv akṣâśritatvenâikârtha-samavetam artha-sākṣāt-kāritvaṁ lakṣyate. tad eva śabdasya pravṛtti-nimittam. tataś ca yat kiñcid arthasya sākṣāt-kāri jñānaṁ tat pratyakṣam ucyate.*

[128] Compare a much later reference of Hemacandra in his *Pramāṇa-mīmāṁsā*, § 31 on 1.1.10, apparently to this locus: *aśnute akṣṇoti vā vyāpnoti sakala-dravya-kṣetra-kāla-bhāvān ity* ***akṣo jīvaḥ***; *aśnute viṣayam ity* ***akṣam indriyaṁ ca***. *pratiḥ pratigatârthaḥ.* ***akṣaṁ pratigataṁ*** *tad-āśritam; akṣāṇi cêndriyāṇi tāni pratigatam* ***indriyāṇi āśrityôjjihīte yaj jñānaṁ tat pratyakṣaṁ*** *vakṣyamāṇa-lakṣaṇam.* ***akṣebhyaḥ parato vartata*** *iti pareṇêndriyâdinā côkṣyata* ***iti parokṣaṁ*** *vakṣyamāṇa-lakṣaṇam eva.*—'That which seizes, or perceives, i.e. pervades all substances, all regions, all times and all states is the perceiving organ, i.e. the living element. And what seizes a [respective sensory] province is the perceiving organ, i.e. a sense. [The prefix] *prati*-° [means] "what has gone towards". What has gone towards the

perceiving organ [means] "depending on this [perceiving organ]". [The following is] the currently taught definition: the cognition which commences depending on the senses—i.e. which has gone towards these perceiving organs, or the senses—is perception. [The following is] the currently taught definition alone: indirect cognition is what operates aloof from the perceiving organs, viz., seizes [its objects] by something different than the senses, etc.' The bolded phrases of PMī bear striking correspondence to the following sections of our text and seem to be quotations: ... *akṣa-śabdo jīva-paryāyatayā prasiddhaḥ ...*; *akṣa-dhvanir indriya-vacano gṛhyate. tataś câkṣaṁ pratigataṁ pratyakṣaṁ. yad indriyam āśrityôjjihīte 'rtha-sākṣāt-kāri jñānaṁ tat pratyakṣam ity arthaḥ. ... akṣebhyaḥ parato vartata iti parokṣam*. Vide infra, NAV 27: *akṣa-śabdo jīva-paryāyas, tataś câkṣaṁ prati vartata iti pratyakṣaṁ, yatrâtmanaḥ sākṣād vyāpāraḥ. vyāvahārikaṁ punar indriya-vyavahitâtma-vyāpāra-sampādyatvāt paramârthataḥ parokṣam eva: dhūmād agni-jñānavat, tiro-dhānâviśeṣāt* (p. 80 of the English translation).

[129] The Sanskrit commentary has the dual form, *ca-śabdau*, since the original aphorism has *pratyakṣaṁ* ***ca*** *parokṣaṃ* ***ca***.

[130] Compare similar wording, which has additionally been bolded in the quotation, and further argumentation in PMī § 31 on 1.1.10: ***tena yad āhuḥ "sakala-pramāṇa-jyeṣṭhaṁ pratyakṣam" iti tad apāstam*** *pratyakṣa-pūrvakatvād itara-pramāṇānāṁ tasya jyeṣṭhatêti cen na, pratyakṣasyâpi pramāṇântara-pūrvakatvôpalabdheḥ, liṅgād āptôpadeśād vā vahṇy-ādikam avagamya pravṛttasya tad-viṣaya-pratyakṣôtpatteḥ.*—'Accordingly, it is controverted what has been promulgated, namely, that 'perception is superior to all cognitive criteria,' etc. If [you maintain that perception] is superior, because other cognitive criteria are preceded by perception, that is not [true], inasmuch as it is observed that also perception is [sometimes] preceded by other cognitive criteria, because in a person, who has [first] ascertained fire, etc., through the inferential sign or through an authoritative person's instruction, and has [afterwards] undertaken an action, [there may] originate perception the province of which is the very same [fire, etc.].'

[131] Cf. NA 22.

[132] Lit. 'by breaking the neck.'

[133] Alternatively: 'a forest temple, etc.,' I take the compound, however, as *dvandva* in view of the explanation *vana-viṣayaṁ deva-kulâdi-viṣayaṁ vā* in NAṬ below, cf. n.134. Comp. also a similar case on p.11 and n.95.

[134] Devabhadra-sūri further explains NAṬ 1 *ad loc.*: ***tathā smaraṇād ity-ādi***. *apūrvâpūrvârtha-darśana-viṣaye* ***kutūhalena ādi****-śabdāt prayojanâdinā kṛtvā hetunā vā vana-viṣayaṁ deva-kulâdi-viṣayaṁ vā parokṣa-pūrvam adhyakṣam īkṣitaṁ, kutūhalâdy api kuta ity āha—smaraṇāt; anubhūtam arthaṁ hi smṛtvôtpanna-kutūhalaḥ*[a] *pumān vartate iti.* ***tathā saṅketa-grahaṇāt****, gṛhīta-saṅketo hi saṅketite sthāne jāta-didṛkṣo draṣṭuṁ pravartate.*—'[We comment on the phrase]: "due to rec-

ollection ... as such", etc. Having set out with curiosity aiming at seeing objects not seen before, [or] with a purpose, etc., or with a reason—[both the purpose and the reason being expressed] by the speech element "etc."—perception, the domain of which is a forest, a temple, etc., is seen to be preceded by the indirect cognition. [In order to answer the question:] "Where does the curiosity likewise [come] from?," it is said: because due to recollection a man, in whom curiosity arose, having remembered an object experienced [before], undertakes an action. "Due to grasping the linguistic convention ... as such" [means that] a person who has indeed grasped the linguistic convention [relating the denotatum/object and its denoter] and is desirous of seeing [the object] proceeds to the locality alluded to in order to see [the described object].'

[a] A: °-*kuhalaḥ*.

[135] Cf. NAṬ 29: *sarvaṁ vākyaṁ sâvadhāraṇaṁ iti-nyāyāt* (p. 123 of the English translation). I failed to trace down the original source of the maxim. Perhaps, it was a very common saying; it is found, for instance, in NĀ 372 (p. 96): *sarvaṁ vākyaṁ sâvadhāraṇaṁ nyāyaḥ*, and in NUK (p. 95): *sarvaṁ vākyaṁ sâvadhāraṇaṁ iti-nyāyaḥ*. See also NAṬ *ad loc.*: ... *yad viniścayaḥ*:

ayogaṁ yogaṁ aparair atyantâyogam eva ca /
vyavachinatti dharmasya nipāto vyatirecakaḥ // iti

nipāta eva-kāraḥ, vyatirecako nivartakaḥ.

viśeṣaṇa-viśeṣyābhyāṁ kriyayā ca sahoditaḥ /
vivakṣāto 'prayoge 'pi tasyârtho 'yaṁ pratīyate //
vyavaccheda-phalaṁ vākyaṁ yataś caitro dhanur dharaḥ /
pārtho dhanu-dharo nīlaṁ sarojam iti vā yathā //

These verses are quotations from PVin II_1 9–11. They are quoted in subsequent Jaina and doxographic literature, e.g. in TRD § 71 on $ṢDSa_1$ 9 (p. 56.4–10) (the editor, Mahendra Kumar Jain, gives there wrong reference to PV 4.190–92).

[136] Cf. NAṬ 1 *ad loc.*: ***sa** hîty-ādi. sa pratyakṣâika-pramāṇa-vādī cārvākaḥ*.—'[The expression] "for he" [refers to] the materialist who claims that the only cognitive criterion is perception.'

[137] I.e., 'inasmuch as they do not make one reach a thing capable of being an object of an efficient action' (**artha-kriyā-samarthârthâprāpakatvena*).

[138] I.e., some acts of perception, being undeviating, are cognitive criteria, whereas some other acts of perception, being deviating, are not.

[139] Apparently the above paragraph—with minor alterations in wording, inclusive of the replacement of *jñāna-vyakti* for *pratyakṣa-vyakti* and *vyavasthāpaka* ('making one realise') for *pratyāyaka* ('making one know')—reappears in PMī § 33 on 1.1.11: *cārvāko hi kāścij jñāna-vyaktīḥ saṁvāditvenâvyabhicāriṇīr upalabhyānyāś ca visaṁvāditvena vyabhicāriṇīḥ, punaḥ kālântare api tādṛśītarāṇāṁ jñāna-vyaktīnām avaśyaṁ pramâṇetarate vyavasthāpayet. na ca sannihitârtha-balenôtpadyamānaṁ*

pūrvâpara-parāmarśa-śūnyaṁ pratyakṣaṁ pūrvâpara-kāla-bhāvinīnāṁ jñāna-vyaktīnāṁ prāmāṇyâprāmāṇya-vyavashtāpakaṁ nimittam upalakṣayituṁ kṣamate. na câyaṁ sva-pratīti-gocarāṇām api jñāna-vyaktīnāṁ prāmāṇyaṁ paraṁ prati prāmāṇyam aprāmāṇyaṁ vā vyavasthāpayituṁ prabhavati. tasmād yathâdṛṣṭa-jñāna-vyakti-sādharmya-dvāreṇêdānīntana-jñāna-vyaktīnāṁ prāmāṇyâprāmāṇya-vyavasthāpakaṁ para-paripādakaṁ ca parokṣântar-gatam anumāna-rūpaṁ pramāṇântaram upāsīta.

[140] *adṛṣṭa*, the 'invisible', viz., the well-known principle of future retribution for one's own deeds; Devabhadra-sūri explains it as *puṇya-pāpe*, i.e. the virtue and vice understood as morally qualified acts that will come to deserved fruition in future according to the accumulated *karman*.

[141] In other words, he does not meet expectations to prove in a consistent way his position as a Cārvāka, who is deemed by his antagonists to be a noisy, loquacious fool.

[142] The gist of the argument is as follows: 'perception, as you understand it, presupposes the recognition of positive and negative concomitance, the validity of which entails inferential reasoning, and the latter, on its part, comes within the scope of the indirect cognition. Thus, also the validity of the latter has to be accepted in order to maintain the validity of perception.'

[143] That is to say, when an entity has originated by the force of its causal complex and all the prerequisites for the occurrence of perception are fulfilled. This is an example of a positive concomitance: 'when perception of an entity takes place, the causal complex of the entity is complete.'

[144] This is an example of a negative concomitance: 'as long as the causal complex of an entity is not complete, the perception of the entity does not take place.'

[145] In other words, even though there might be a case of an indirect cognition, which proves to be fallacious due to the absence of an inferential sign (*liṅga*) related to the predicated object or due to the absence of some verbal statement following which we may infer the object, and, therefore, this particular instance of indirect cognition would be deemed the fallacy of the indirect cognition, nonetheless, that would not impair the validity of indirect cognition in general.

[146] What is noteworthy in the foregoing section is that the whole discussion of perception as well as the examples given above refer predominantly to the phenomenon of visual perception only.

[147] Or 'because [it has] no real thing [as its object],' in view of PMī 1.1.12: *bhāvâbhāvâtmakatvād vastuno nirviṣayo 'bhavaḥ.*—'Since a real thing has the nature of being and non-being, the absence [as negative proof] has no province.' For similar wording cf. PMī § 38 on 1.1.11: *yat tu pramāṇam eva na bhavati na tenântar-bhūtena bahir-bhūtena vā kiñcit prayojanam, yathâbhāvaḥ.*—'However, something that is no cognitive criterion at all brings nothing, be it included into [the two admitted cognitive criteria] or outside [of them], just like the absence [as negative proof].'

[148] *apakarṇanīya*; a doubtful word.

[149] I.e., someone who has seen a cow with his own eyes and who remembers the information that a *gayal* (*bos gavaeus*) resembles a cow. Cf. NAṬ *ad loc.*: *yathā gaur ity-ādi. yad uktam*:

> "*kīdṛg gavaya*" *ity evaṁ pṛṣṭo nāgarakair yadā*[a] /
> *bravīty āraṇyako vācyaṁ* "*yathā gaur gavayas tathā*" // *iti* /

— 'When the following [question] is asked by a townsmen: "What does a *gayal* look like?," a forest-dweller utters the statement: "*Gayal* is like a cow".'

[a] MŚV$_I$ 5.5(*Śabda-pariccheda*).1b: ... *yadi* /

[150] MŚV$_I$ 5.6.37 (*Upamāna-pariccheda*) p. 315 (ŚVVTT, p. 382) reads *smaryate*, instead of *dṛśyate*, and consequently 'Therefore, what is r e m e m b e r e d . '

[151] That is to say, they are free from conceptualisation (=*avikalpaka*).

[152] In other words, 'which is produced by the two objects, the one perceived previously and the one perceived subsequently'; cf. NAṬ *ad loc.*: ***tad-adhikaṁ*** *go-gavaya-pratyakṣa-grāhyāt utkalitam.*—'It sprung from the object to be grasped by perception of a cow and of a *gayal*.'

[153] That is, the province of analogy; cf. NAṬ *ad loc.*: ***tad-gocaraḥ*** *upamāna-viṣayaḥ*.

[154] Devabhadra-sūri leaves no doubt as regards the synonymy—as least, for the Jainas—of 'manifest particular entity' and 'individual thing'; cf. NAṬ *ad loc.*: ***vyaktiḥ*** *svalakṣaṇam*.

[155] Lit. 'advocacy of one of the two [alternatives] that unfold themselves [to the mind] should not be resorted to.'

[156] Cf. NAṬ *ad loc.*: ***etenêty*** *upamāna-prāmāṇya-vyavasthāpanena.*—'[The word] "through this" [means] "through establishing the cognitive validity of analogy".'

[157] Compare PMī 1.1.11 § 37: *yathā indriyaja-mānasâtma-saṁvedana-yogi-jñānānāṁ pratyakṣeṇa saṅgrahas tathā smṛti-pratyabhijñānôhânumānâgamānāṁ parokṣeṇa saṅgraho lakṣaṇasyâviśeṣāt*; as well as PMī 1.2.2: *smṛti-pratyabhijñānôhânumānâgamās tad-°(=parokṣa)°-vidhayaḥ.*—'Its (*sc.* of the indeterminate cognition) subvarieties are recollection, recognition, induction and the oral tradition.' Further, of relevance is the commentary in PMī 1.2 § 5: *yathâiva hi pratyakṣa-lakṣaṇa-saṅgṛhitānîndriya-jñāna-mānasa-svasaṁvedana-yogi-jñānāni saugatānāṁ na pratyakṣād atiricyante, tathâiva hi parokṣa-lakṣaṇâkṣiptāni smṛtyâdīni na mūla-pramāṇa-saṁkhyā-paripanthīnîti.*—'For exactly in the same way as cognition [acquired] through the senses, mental perception [of one's own thoughts], one's own [inward psychic] sensation [and supernatural] cognition of a *yogin*, comprised under the definition of perception of the Buddhists, do not differ from perception, in the very same way recollection and other [varieties] included in

the definition of the indirect cognition [do] not go counter the number of the main cognitive criteria.' Regarding the expression *yoga-kṣema*, cf. n.600.

[158] Or: 'establishes homogeneity', if we take the reading of H and V (°-*vyavasthāpakatvād*).

[159] These are uniquely Jaina notions of those times. Diachronic homogeneity (*ūrdhvatā-sāmānya*) expresses the self-identity of a substance in its temporal development, which undergoes several changes in the course of time, irrespective of the class-notion or of its actual form, whereas synchronic homogeneity (*tiraścīna-sāmānya*) subsumes a number of specimens possessed of the same property in the same point of time under the same class. The former concerns the temporal series of modifications of the same substance that, nonetheless, preserves its individual character, whereas the latter deals with the numeric arrangement within the same class in a given moment. In this place, worth pointing out is that the rendering of the terms *tiraścīna-sāmānya* (or *tiryak-sāmānya*) and *ūrdhvatā-sāmānya* as 'horizontal universality' and 'vertical universality', respectively (e.g. in SHASTRI (1990: 81ff.)), fails to express the basic idea and leads to misunderstanding. The concept of this two-fold homogeneity is explained, for instance, in PA 4.3–5: /3/ *sāmānyaṁ dvedhā tiryag-ūrdhvatā-bhedāt. /4/ sadṛśa-pariṇāmas tiryak, khaṇḍa-muṇḍâdiṣu gotva-vat. /5/ parâpara-vivarta-vyāpi-dravyam ūrdhvatā mṛd iva sthāsâdiṣu*[m].—'/3/ Homogeneity is two-fold, due to the division into synchronic (lit. the synchronic) and the diachronic (lit. diachronicity). /4/ The synchronic [homogeneity] is the permutation of the similar [property], like cowness in calves with half-grown horns, in young hornless [cows], etc. /5/ The [homogeneity based on] diachronicity is the substance pervading [all] its prior and subsequent manifestations, like clay in [different stages, say,] a lump of potter's clay[m], etc.' It is commented upon and elucidated further in PALV 4.3–5, p. 46: /4/ *prathama-bhedaṁ sôdāharaṇam āha. nityâika-rūpasya gotvādeḥ krama-yaugapadyābhyām artha-kriyā-virodhāt pratyekaṁ parisamāptyā vyaktiṣu vṛtty-ayogāc câneka-sadṛśa-pariṇāmâtmakam evêti tiryak-sāmānyam uktam. /5/ dvitīya-bhedam api sadṛṣṭāntam upadarśayati. sāmānyam iti vartate. tenâyam arthaḥ: ūrdhvatā-sāmānyaṁ bhavati. kiṁ tad dravyam? tad eva viśiṣyate. pūrvâpara-kāla-vṛtti tri-kālânuyāyîty arthaḥ. citra-jñānasyâikasya yugapad-bhāvy-aneka-svabhāva-nīlâdy-ākāra-vyāpti-vad ekasya krama-bhāvi-pariṇāma-vyāpitvam ity arthaḥ.*—/4/ [Māṇikyanandin] states the first division together with an example. The synchronic homogeneity is taught to be only of the nature of variation concerning many similar [specimens], because a single eternal property, like cowness, etc., taken [both] consecutively and simultaneously, would contradict purposeful activity and because it is improper to speak of its occurrence in individual things, [each] taken individually. /5/ [Māṇikyanandin] describes the second division together with an illustration, too. [As for "diachronicity" occurring in the *sūtra*,] "homogeneity" is [to be] supplied [from the preceding]. Hence such is the meaning: [it] proves to be the diachronic homogeneity (lit. the homogeneity of diachronicity). What is that substance [mentioned in the *sūtra* by Māṇikyanandin]? Exactly that is qualified [as

"something pervading all its prior and subsequent manifestations"]. The meaning is that it goes with three times (*sc.* the diachronic homogeneity encompasses past, present and future) [as something that] occurs in previous and subsequent points of time. The meaning is that, similarly, like pervasion—[in the case] of one knowledge of a [given] colour, [say, blue]—of [various] shades of blue, etc., that constitute the real nature of several [similar blue things] existing simultaneously [in the case of synchronic homogeneity]—one [knowledge] pervades the variations of one [substance] taking place in a [temporal] series.'

And this is what Devabhadra-sūri has to say in his gloss on NAṬ 1 *ad loc.*: ***tasyêty-ādi****. nanu kim iti saṁskāraḥ sa evâyaṁ taj-jātīyo vêti dvaidhaṁ pratyabhijñānaṁ*[a] *janayati? āha: tasya pratyabhijñā-jñānasya "parâpara-vivarta-vyāpi-dravyam ūrdhva-sāmānyaṁ mṛd iva sthāsa*[m]*-kośâdiṣu*[b]" [PA 4.5]; "*sadṛśa-pariṇāmas tiraścīna-sāmānyaṁ khaṇḍa-muṇḍâdiṣu gotvavad*" [PA 4.4] [*iti*] *tayor dvayor api nirṇāyakatvāt*[c]. *yadi punar dvaidhaṁ*[d] *pratyabhijñānaṁ*[e] *nôjjṛmbhate, tadôrdhva-tiraścīna-bheda-bhinna*[f]*-sāmānya-vyavasthā na syād iti. atha pūrvam artha-darśanaṁ, tataḥ saṁskāras, tatas*[g] *tasya prabodhas, tad-anu pratyabhijñānam*[h] *iti-paraṁparâśrayaṇa-nibandhanâbhāvāt prathamâkṣa-sannipāta eva pratyabhijñānaṁ*[i] *kiṁ nôtpadyata ity āha: na sañjātaṁ pūrvârtha-gocaraṁ darśanaṁ yasya tasya puṁsaḥ pratyabhijñānôdayâbhāvāt*[j]; *pratyabhijñānaṁ*[k] *hi tādṛśa-darśanataḥ saṁskāra-prabodhe, sa ca sati saṁskāre, saṁskāraś ca pūrvam artha-darśana*[l] *evêti.*—'[Now we comment upon the expression] commencing with [the word]: "its (= of recognition)". Well, [if one is in quandary as to the reason] why the subliminal impression produces two-fold recognition [of the form:] "This is the same [object]" or "it belongs to the same class," [then] it is said [by way of an explanation]: because this knowledge of recognition determines both these [homogeneities, which have been stated by Māṇikyanandin]: "The [homogeneity based on] diachronicity is the substance pervading [all] its prior and subsequent manifestations, like clay in [different stages, say,] a lump of potter's clay[m], an earthware vessel, etc." [PA 4.5]; "The synchronic [homogeneity] is the permutation of the similar [property], like cowness in calves with half-grown horns, in young hornless [cows], etc." [PA 4.4]. If, however, the twofold recognition did not emerge, the homogeneity, divided into the varieties of diachronic and synchronic, would not be established. If [someone still does not comprehend] why recognition [can] not arise in the very first contact of eyes [with a particular object] because of the absence of the foundation dependent on the following sequence: "initially the perception of an object [takes place], then [comes the turn of] the subliminal impression, next its awakening [is brought about, only] thereafter [can occur] recognition," [then] it is said [by way of an explanation]: because recognition cannot arise in such a man, in whom the perception the domain of which is the former object has not [yet] appeared; for recognition [takes place] on the awakening of the subliminal impression due to the perception of [an object] of [specifically] this sort; and that [awakening is possible] when the subliminal impression is there; and the subliminal impression [is possible] only when previously the perception of the object [took place].'

Two aspects of the above-mentioned essential feature of recognition represented by the following description: 'This is the same [object] or it belongs to the same class' accord with two divisions of homogeneity. In other words, the recognition of the type 'this is the same object' corresponds to diachronic homogeneity, whereas the recognition through description 'this object belongs to the same class' expresses the idea of synchronic homogeneity. These two notions reappear in the context of universal and particular objects (*viṣaya*) of cognition in BTBh 1.7.1.2 (SINGH: p. 26.10–13 in *pramāṇa-phala-vyavasthā*): *tac ca sāmānyaṁ dvividham: ūrdhvatā-lakṣaṇam tiryag-lakṣaṇaṁ cêti. tatrâikasyām eva ghaṭâdi-vyaktau sajātīya-vyāvṛttāyām aneka-kṣaṇa-samudāyaḥ sāmānyaṁ ūrdhvatā-lakṣaṇaṁ sādhana-pratyakṣasya viṣayaḥ. vijātīya-vyāvṛttās tv aneka-vyaktayaḥ tiryak-sāmānyaṁ vyāpti-grāhaka-pratyakṣasya viṣayaḥ.*—'And this homogeneity is two-fold: characterised by synchronicity (lit. characterised by the verticality) and characterised by diachronicity (lit. characterised by the horizontal). Among these [two varieties], the homogeneity characterised by diachronicity is the accumulation of several moments of one individual thing, e.g. a pot, etc., [which is] distinguished from [all other things] that belong to the same class, and [this homogeneity is] the object of perception establishing [a particular object]. The synchronic homogeneity, however, is [constituted by] several individual things [of one class] that are distinguished from [all other things] that belong to a different class; [this homogeneity is] the object of perception grasping the invariable concomitance.' The idea of diachronic homogeneity (*ūrdhvatā-sāmānya*) and synchronic homogeneity (*tiryak-sāmānya*) is referred to in NAV 29 by the notions of *saha-vartin* and *krama-vartin*, p. 88 of the English translation.

The notions of diachronic and synchronic homogeneities as well as their historical development and their question of likely influence onto the Buddhist thought is discussed in detail in BALCEROWICZ 1998 and BALCEROWICZ 1999/b.

[a] H,V: *pratyabhijñā-jñānaṁ*. [b] C: °-*kośâdiṣa*.
[c] A,C: *nirnāyakatvāt*. [d] C: *dvedhaṁ*.
[e] H,V: *pratyabhijñā-jñānaṁ*. [f] C: °-*bhinnaḥ* .
[g] A omits *tatas*. [h] H,V: *pratyabhijñā-jñānam*.
[i] H,V: *pratyabhijñā-jñānaṁ*. [j] H,V: *pratyabhijñā-jñānôdayâbhāvāt*.
[k] H,V: *pratyabhijñā-jñānaṁ*. [l] C: °-*darśina*; A, H,V: °-*darśane*.

[m] The obscure expression *sthāsa* (rendered by 'a lump of potter's clay') is nowhere to be found in any of available Sanskrit dictionaries—with the exception of the entry '*sthāsakaḥ* ... **1** Perfuming or smearing the body with fragrant unguents. **-2** A bubble of water or any fluid' in the Apte's *Practical Sanskrit-English Dictionary*, p. 1008. However, we encounter two more passages with a similar locution, viz., in AJP 2 Vol. I, p. 113.5–6: *tathā hi: mṛt-piṇḍa-śivaka-sthāsaka-ghaṭa-kapālâdiṣu viśeṣeṇa sarvatrânuvṛtto mṛd-anvayaḥ saṁvedyate*; and in AJPṬ 2, Vol. I, p. 104.27–29: ***tat-tat-kṛtau tat-tad-avasthā-bhāva-graha*** *iti. tasya tasya sthāsa-kośa-kuśūlâdeḥ kāryasya kṛtau karaṇe tasyās tasyās tat-tat-kārya-karaṇâṇkūlāyā avasthāyāḥ kumbha-kārâdeḥ kārya-kartuḥ sambandhinyā bhāva-grahaḥ sattâṅgī-kāraḥ.* Also Siddhasena-gaṇin refers to various stages of a pot, including 'a lump of potter's clay'

(*sthāsaka*) in TṬ 5.31, p. 398.2–3: *mṛt-piṇḍa-śivaka-sthāsaka-kośaka-kuśūla-ghaṭa-kapāla-śarkarā-pāṁśu-truṭi-paramâṇavaḥ*. In his note on p. 268 Vol. 2 *ad* p. 19.16–17 of AJP, H. R. KĀPADĪĀ provides us with the following explanation, to which I have nothing more to add: 'The words "mṛt-piṇḍa" and "śivaka" occur on p. 123. ll. 6–7, and these two along with "sthāsaka" and "kapāla" on p. 113, ll. 5–6. "Śivaka" occurs also on p. 114.3, too. In Koṭyācārya's comm. (p. 181) on *Viśeṣa* (v. 482) [= *Visesâvassaya-bhāsa*—PB] we come across "*mṛt-piṇḍa-śivaka-sthāsaka-kośa-kuśūlâdi-mṛt-paryāyaḥ*." So it follows that the word "ādi" occurring in *mṛt-piṇḍa-śivakâdi* stands for *sthāsaka, kośa, kuśūla*, etc. This is borne out by *sthāsa, kośa* and *kuśūla* occurring on p. 104.27 of Municandra's comm. on AJP. In Siddhasena Gaṇi's comm. (p. 308) on TS (V, 31) we have: "*mṛt-piṇḍa-śivaka-sthāsaka-kośa-kuśūla-ghaṭa-kapāla-śakala-śarkarā-pāṁśutruṭi-paramâṇavaḥ*." In *Durga-pada-prakāśa* (p. 23b), a comm. by Prabhānanda on *Vītarāgastotra* (VII, 1) we have "*sthāsa-kośa-kuśūlâdi*." In its avacūrṇi (p. 74b) by a pupil of Viśālarāja we have "*sthāsa-kośa-kuśūla-budhnôdara-karṇâdi*." A lump of clay assumes different forms before a pot, a jar, or the like is made out of it. These forms are given names according to the shapes they assume. Thus a ball of clay is called "mṛt-piṇḍa"; a lump of clay which has a shape of a *liṅga* of Śiva "śivaka"; "sthāsaka" is the name given to a lump of clay having the shape of a mirror; "kośa" to that resembling a bucket; and "kuśūla" to that resembling a granary.'

[160] Cf. NAṬ *ad loc.*: ***ābhogaḥ*** *praṇidhānam avadhānam iti yāvat* ...—'Afterthought is tantamount to reflection, or attention ...'

[161] I.e., 'retention in memory of the [previously] experienced thing,' or perhaps—in view of the facts mentioned beneath—to be more precise: 'non-deprivation [of recollection] of the [previously] experienced thing.' The expression *anubhūta-viṣayâsampramoṣa-lakṣaṇaṁ smaraṇam*, and the term *sampramoṣa* in particular, are reminiscent of the definition of reminiscence, or recollection, formulated by Prabhākara in Bṛ, p. 53.8–9: *śuktikāyāṁ rajata-jñānaṁ smarāmîti pramoṣāt smṛti-jñānam uktam*, which was later combated by Jayarāśi in TUS_1 1.c, p. 126.14–132.13, especially in the passage: *atha vipramuṣitatayânayā bhaṅgyôpajāyate, ko 'yaṁ vipramoṣo nāma?* up to *tasmād yathā yathā vicāryate smṛti-vipramoṣas tathā tathā nyāyaṁ na viṣahata iti* (p. 130.11–132.11). For details cf. FRANCO (1987: 370–375, n. 111).

[162] The Mīmāṁsakas, both of the Bhāṭṭa and Prābhākara schools, admitted unanimously the cognitive validity of recognition (*pratyabhijñāna*), while disavowing the status of cognitive criterion in the case of recollection (*smṛti*). The difference between these two lies in 'the immediate experience of an object ... produced by subliminal impressions accompanied by the senses' (*vide infra*), in the case of recognition (*pratyabhijñāna*), that is catalysed by the sensory apprehension of an object perceived previously, and, on the other hand, the deficiency of such a direct association between the information stored in memory as subliminal impression as well as and the factual present experience reviving it in the case of recollection (*smṛti*). Thus,

both Kumārila Bhaṭṭa and Prabhākara excluded recollection explicitly from the realm of valid cognitions already in theii definition of cognitive criterion; cf. respectively MŚV$_1$ 5 (*Autpattika-sūtra*) 11ab: *sarvasya'nupalabdhe 'rthe prāmāṇyam smṛtir anyathā* ('Every cognition is a cognitive criterion regarding an uncomprehended object; recollection [grasps] in a different manner [and, thus, is not cognitive criterion') and PP$_1$, p. 124.9–125.2 (= PP$_2$, p. 42.15–20): *pramāṇam anubhūtiḥ. na ca smṛteḥ prāmāṇyâpattir iti darśayati—sā smṛter anyêti. atha kā smṛtiḥ? smṛtiḥ punaḥ pūrva-vijñāna-saṁskāra-mātrajaṁ jñānam ucyate. na câivaṁ dhārā-vāhika-jñānānāṁ smṛtitvam, indriyârtha-sannikarṣa-jatvāt pūrvavat. mātra-grahaṇāc ca pratyabhijñānasya na smṛtitvam indriya-saciva-saṁskāra-jatvāt.*—'"Cognitive criterion is immediate experience". Accordingly, [Prabhākara] demonstrates the [idea] that recollection does not acquire cognitive validity, by [saying] that "this [immediate experience] is different from recollection." So, what is recollection? Recollection is, in its turn, said to be "a cognition which is produced solely by subliminal impressions of earlier contents of consciousness." And in this manner, [successive] acts of cognition that nourish (*sc.* partake of) [one and the same] stream [of mental representation of an object do] not [constitute] recollection, because [they are] produced by the contact of a [corresponding] sense organ with the object, just like the anterior [cognition of the same object]. And due to the use of [the speech element] "solely" [in the above definition] recognition [can] not [be] recollection, because [the former] is produced by subliminal impressions accompanied by a sense organ.' As regards the invalidity of recollection in the Mīmāṁsaka schools, cf. FRANCO (1987: 389–392, n. 135). Cf. also the standpoint expressed by Jayantabhaṭṭa in NMa$_2$ 1 in the section *smṛter aprāmāṇye hetu-vicāraḥ* (vol. I pp. 34.10–35.2), according to which the lack of cognitive validity in the case of recollection in due to its not being produced by an actual object:

na smṛter aprāmāṇyatvaṁ gṛhīta-grāhitā-kṛtam /
api tv anartha-janyatvaṁ tad-aprāmāṇya-kāraṇam //

nanu katham anarthajā smṛtiḥ? tad-ārūḍhasya vastunaḥ tadānīm asattvāt. kathaṁ tarhi bhūta-vṛṣṭy-anumānaṁ nânarthajam? tatra dharmiṇo 'numeyattvāt tasya ca jñāna-janakasya tatra bhāvāt. nady-ākhya eva dharmī vṛṣṭimad-uparitana-deśa-saṁsarga-lakṣaṇena dharmena tadvān anumīyate viśiṣṭa-salila-pūra-yogitvāt. sa cânumāna-grāhyo dharmī vidyata evêti nânarthajam anumānam. kathaṁ tarhi prātibham anāgatârtha-grāhi śvo me bhrātâgantêti pratyakṣam arthajam iṣyate bhavadbhiḥ? tatra deśântare vidyamānasya bhrātuḥ śvo bhāvyâgamana-viśeṣaḥ tasyâiva tathâiva grahaṇam, tena ca rūpeṇa gṛhyamāṇasya satas tasya jñāna-janakatvam ity arthajam eva prātibham. smaraṇaṁ tu nirdagdha-pitr-ādi-viṣayam anapekṣitârtham eva jāyamānaṁ dṛṣṭam ity anyatra deśântara-sthitârtha-smaraṇe tad-artha-sattvam akāraṇam eva.

tasmād anarthajatvena smṛti-prāmāṇya-vāraṇāt /
anagṛhītârtha-gantṛtvaṁ na pramāṇa-viśeṣaṇam //

[163] The term *ūha* is well attested in the Jinistic literature as well, e.g. TBh 1.15, where we find it, beside *tarka*, in the sequence of synonyms: *īhā*, *ūha*, *tarka*, *parīkṣā*, *vicāraṇā*, *jijñāsā*. Induction (*ūha*) occurs in the definition of *tarka* (reasoning) in NS 1.1.40: *avijñāta-tattve 'rthe kāraṇôpapattitas tattva-jñānârtham ūhas tarkaḥ.*—'Reasoning [consists in] induction in order to cognise the truth (*sc.* essence) [of an object]—in [the case of] an object the essence of which is unknown—by explicating [its] causes.' It is treated as synonymous to *tarka* in NBh 1.1.1: *tarko na pramāṇa-saṅgṛhītaḥ, tarko na pramāṇântaram, pramāṇānām anugrāhakas tattva-jñānāya kalpate. tasyôdāharaṇam—kim idaṁ janma kṛtakena hetunā nirvartyate āhosvid akṛtakena athâkasmikam iti? evam avijñāte 'rthe kāraṇôpapattyā ūhaḥ pravartate—'yadi kṛtakena hetunā nirvartyate, hetûcchedād upapanno 'yaṁ janmôcchedaḥ. athâkṛtakena hetunā, tato hetûcchedasyâśakyatvād anupapanno janmôcchedaḥ. athâkasmikam, ato 'kasmān nirvartyamānaṁ na punar nivartsyatîti nirvṛtti-kāraṇaṁ nôpapadyate, tena janânucchedaḥ' iti.*—'Reasoning is not reckoned among cognitive criteria, [because] reasoning is not another cognitive criterion; [it merely] assists cognitive criteria, as an ancillary, to [obtain] the cognition of the truth (*sc.* essence) [of an unknown object. So, here] is an illustration of that [reasoning]: is this birth (*sc.* mundane existence) brought about by a cause in force or by a [cause] not in force, or [is it] fortuitous? In such a manner proceeds induction with regard to an unknown matter by explicating [its] cause: "If [this birth (*sc.* mundane existence)] [were] brought about by a cause in force, then at the destruction of the cause the destruction of this birth (sc. mundane existence) [would] take place. If [this birth (sc. mundane existence)] is brought about by a [cause] not in force, then the destruction of this birth (sc. mundane existence) [could] not take place [at all], because the destruction of the cause is impotent. If [this birth (sc. mundane existence)] is fortuitous, then the cause of [its] termination does not take place, since [this birth (sc. mundane existence)], once being fortuitously brought about, will not terminate in its turn; hence [the result is] the non-destruction of this birth (sc. mundane existence)".' For another definition of *ūha*, cf. n. 174.

[164] Cf. NA 22.

[165] NAV 18: *anvaya-vyatireka-grāhi-pratyakṣânupalambhôttara-kāla-bhāvino 'vyabhicarita-tri-kāla-vyāpi-gocarasya mati-nibandhanasyôha-saṁjñitasya pramāṇântarasya* (p. 63 of the translation).

[166] I.e., fire must be possessed of the power of burning in order to be capable of causing blisters, burns, etc., that could, in their turn, not otherwise be accounted for. Cf. NAṬ *ad loc.* on the expression *sarveṣām ity-ādi* further below: ... *arthâpattau tu vahni-saṁyogāt kara-tala-gataṁ sphoṭa-lakṣaṇaṁ kāryaṁ pratyakṣeṇôpalakṣyamāṇam anyathā nôpapadyate, yadi vahneḥ kācid dāhikā śaktir na syāt.*—'In the case of presumption, the effect characterised by blisters that appeared on the palm of the hand as a result of the contact with fire would not be otherwise explicable for [people] observing [that] through perception, if fire did not possess the power of burning.'

[167] Instead of the usual way to render the term *arthâpatti* either as 'implication' or 'presupposition' (cf. PMĪ transl. by S. Mookerjee and N. Tatia, as well as TATIA (1951: 34), etc.), I translate it consistently 'presumption' for several reasons. Firstly, 'implication' is a well-known logical term that traditionally denotes one of two basic kinds of logical consequence, namely implication (the other being entailment; cf. BOCHEŃSKI (1954: 88ff.): 'Nun unterscheidet man in der heutigen klassichen mathematischen Logik wenigstens *zwei* Konsequenzbegriffe. Die Implikation und die Ableitbarkeit.'), of which there are two varieties: the formal implication and the material implication (cf. KOTARBIŃSKI (1929: 171ff)). The formal implication is a two-argument propositional functor represented variously as ⌜$\rightarrow$⌝, ⌜$\Rightarrow$⌝, ⌜$\supset$⌝, or ⌜$<$, consisting of an antecedent and the consequent, that forms propositional formulas of the form $\alpha\rightarrow\beta$, $p\Rightarrow q$, $p\supset q$ or $p<q$, respectively. It is true in case [1] when both the antecedent and the consequent are false (0,0), [2] when both the antecedent and the consequent are true 91,1) or [3] when the antecedent is false but the consequent is true (0,1); it is false if and only if the antecedent is true but the consequent is false (1,0). If we substitute names for the variables, and read *'if ...—then...'* we obtain the material implication, which has the form of a proposition, or a statement. Clearly, *arthâpatti* is n o t the implication in this sense and the rendering of the Sanskrit term as 'implication' would lead to unnecessary associations and misunderstandings.

Secondly, *arthâpatti* is not a form of inference limited to the use of the function of implication alone, even though the later is always involved in it, and the *arthâpatti* type of reasoning, be it not absolutely uniform, has a more complex structure. The *locus classicus* of *arthâpatti* is in found NBh 2.2.1: *arthād āpattir arthâpattiḥ. āpattiḥ prāptiḥ prasaṅgaḥ. yatrâbhidhīyamāne 'rthe yo 'nyo 'rthaḥ prasajyate so 'rthâpattiḥ, yathā megheṣv asatsu vṛṣṭir na bhavatiti. kim atra prasajyate? satsu bhavatîti.*—'Entailment due to circumstances is presumption. "Entailment" [means] "the [inferential] attainment of" [or] "(logical) consequence." This another thing that follows, as the consequence from the circumstances which are being stated, is presumption. For instance: "if there are no clouds, there is no rain." What consequence follows here? "If there are [clouds], there is [rain]".' If we represent the proposition 'there are clouds' with α, and 'there is rain' with β, we may represent the reasoning in the following way: $(\neg\alpha\rightarrow\neg\beta)\rightarrow(\alpha\rightarrow\beta)$. One remark is necessary, both here and in the next illustration of 'obese Devadatta' below, I avail myself of the propositional calculus notation only for the sake of brevity and simplicity, but it should be remembered that what those two instances represent is the predicate calculus. The form of the symbolised formula—which is false for $\alpha=1$ and $\beta=0$—shows, however, that what the author had in mind was not implication the way we understand it, and *arthâpatti* is more intricate. Granting the functor of implication was understood differently than we do, nonetheless, the whole reasoning is not valid, for there is another conceivable alternative, which everybody who has ever gone out with an umbrella unnecessarily, i.e. without having an occasion to make use of it, knows very well from his own experience, namely $\alpha\rightarrow\neg\beta$, and this predicament is observable occasionally also in India: despite the fact that clouds are being seen, not a rain drop is falling. Clearly, the consequent of the formula in question, viz., $\alpha\rightarrow\beta$, cannot be a formulation of the implication: 'if there are clouds, it will rain.'

Another current illustration of the *arthâpatti* type of reasoning is the following one, that stems from the Mīmāṁsā literature: *pīno devadatto divā na bhuṅkte pīnatva-viśiṣṭasya devadattasya rātri-bhojitva-rūpârthasya śabdânuktasyâpi āpattiḥ*.—'If obese Devadatta does not eat during the day, he eats at night, [then we have the] entailment of the unexpressed (*sc.* implicit) fact that Devadatta, qualified by obesity, eats at night.' The passage is quoted, e.g. in GBh *ad* SKā 4 (Mainkar: p. 48.4–5, Esnoul: p. 8.12–13) and in NMa$_2$ 1 in the section *ārutârthâpatti-khaṇḍanam*, vol. I, p. 67.15 ff.: *pīno devadatto divā na bhuṅkte*... If we symbolise 'Devadatta is obese' by α, 'Devadatta eats during the day' by β and 'Devadatta eats at night' by γ, the logical form of this inference is as follows: $[\alpha\rightarrow(\beta\vee\gamma)]\rightarrow(\neg\beta\rightarrow\gamma)$, the formula being false for α=1, β=0, γ=0. Incidentally, the formula would resemble $\ulcorner(\beta\vee\gamma)\rightarrow(\neg\beta\rightarrow\gamma)\urcorner$ which is involved in the definition of the functor of alternative $\ulcorner(\alpha\vee\beta)\equiv(\neg\alpha\rightarrow\beta)\urcorner$, except for the condition $\ulcorner\alpha\urcorner$ and one of unexpressed presuppositions, viz., 'the cause of overweight is (over)eating' (others being 'Devadatta eats regularly', 'Devadatta does not starve', etc.). As we can see, the structure of this statement, too, is more complex, although it is quite different from the clouds-and-rain case. This manner of quasi-inferential reasoning is, however, not absolutely binding for there may always be still some other possibilities: Devadatta—after years marked by gluttony and debauchery—sets on a fast, or Devadatta suffers from a disease (nowadays, we would refer to certain hormonal disorders or genetic factors, etc.). The above example was clad in an alternative wording in NK (entry *ārthāpatti* [*ṅa*], p. 79.5–10), preceded by a definition: *upapādya-jñānenôpādaka-kalpanam arthâpattiḥ. tatra upapādya-jñānaṁ karaṇam. upapādaka-jñānaṁ phalam. yena vinā yad anupapannaṁ tat tatrôpapādyam. yasyâbhāve yasyânupapattis tat tatrôpapādakam. yathā rātri-bhojanena vinā divā abhuñjānasya pīnatvam anupapannam iti tādṛśa-pīnatvam upapādyam. yathā vā rātri-bhojanasyâbhāve tādṛśa-pīnatvasyânupapattir iti rātri-bhojanam upapādakam.* [etc.]—'Presumption is the conjecture (*sc.* conclusion) of something-which-explicates [an event] through something-which-is-explicable. Regarding this [definition], the cognition of something-which-is-explicable is the instrument, [whereas] the cognition of something-which-explicates is the result; [e.g. if,] when *x* is absent, *y* is inexplicable, [then] *y* is something-which-explicates [an event], when *x* [is present]. For instance, obesity of [a person] who is not eating during the day is inexplicable without [presuming that] he eats at night; hence obesity of this sort is something-which-is-explicable, [or an instrument that allows to draw a conclusion with regard to something-which-explicates]. Or, alternatively, without [presuming that] he eats at night, obesity of this sort is inexplicable; hence [the fact that] he eats at night is something-which-explicates, [or is the result; etc.]' These explanations in NK hint at an unspoken condition: $\neg(\neg\beta\wedge\neg\gamma)$, viz., that under normal circumstances 'Devadatta must eat either during the day or at night' or 'Devadatta cannot but eat either during the day or at night', or 'it is impossible for Devadatta not to eat during the day and not to eat at night', whichever of these formulations be most appropriate. That being the case, we would be confronted with an instance of conversational implicature (*vide infra*) in the form of $[\alpha \rightarrow (\beta \vee \gamma) \wedge \neg(\neg\beta \wedge \neg\gamma)] \rightarrow (\neg\beta \rightarrow \gamma)$. Jayantabhaṭṭa, while recapitulating the position of the Bhāṭṭa-Mīmāṁsakas regarding the cognitive valid status of *arthâpatti* in NMa_2 1 in the section *arthâpatteḥ pramāṇântaram* (vol. I pp. 52.20–59.13), which in itself should deserve separate attention, avails himself of a similar instance of obesity clad in a verse form (NMa_2 1, vol. I pp. 56.3–4,13–14):

pīno divā ca nâttîti sākāṅkṣa-vacana-śruteḥ /
tad eka-deśa-vijñānaṁ śrutârthâpattir ucyate // ...
tasmād kalpâgama-kṛtaṁ naktam attîti vedanam /
tad-vākya-kalpanāyāṁ tu prāmāṇaṁ paricintyatām //

On the same page of *Nyāya-kośa* further on (the entry *arthâpatti* [*ṅa*], p. 79.10–25), we come across grammatical issues related to as well as typology and supplementary explanation of *arthâpatti*, that I shall only quote here by way of additional reference: *atra arthasya āpattir nāma kalpanêti ṣaṣṭhī-samāsena rātri-bhojana-kalpanā-rūpāyāṁ pramitāv arthâpatti-śabdo vartate. arthasya āpattir nāma kalpanā yasmād iti bahu-vrīhi-samāsena kalpanāyāḥ karaṇa-bhūte pīnatvād iti-jñāne 'pi vartate. evaṁ ca phala-karaṇayor ubhayor arthâpatti-pada-prayogo bhavati. sā cârthâpattir dvividhā: dṛṣṭârthâpattiḥ śrutârthâpattiś cêti. tatra dṛṣṭârthâpattir yathā idaṁ rajatam iti puro-vartini pratipannasya rajatasya nêdaṁ rajatam iti tatrâiva niṣidhyamānatvaṁ satyatve sati anupapannam iti rajatasya mithyātvaṁ kalpayati. śrutârthâpattir yathā yatra śrūyamāṇa-vākyasya svârthânupapatti-mukhenârthântara-kalpanaṁ sā. yathā tarati śokam ātmavid ity atra śrutasya śoka-śabda-vācya-bandha-jātasya jñāna-nivartyasyânupapattya bandhasya mithyātvaṁ kalpyate. śrutârthâpattiś ca dvividhā: abhidhānânupapattir abhihitânupapattiś ca. tatra yatra vākyâika-deśa-śravaṇe anvayâbhidhānânupapattyā anvayâbhidhānôpayogi padântaraṁ kalpyate tatrâbhidhānânupapattiḥ. yathā dvāram ity atra pidhehîty adhyāhāraḥ. abhihitârthânupapattis tu yatra vākyâvagato 'rthânupapannatvena jñātaḥ sann arthântaraṁ kalpayati tatra draṣṭavyā. yathā svarga-kāmo jyotiṣṭomena yajetêty atra kṣaṇikatayā avagata-jyotiṣṭomasya svarga-sādhanatvânupapattyā madhya-varty-apūrvaṁ kalpyate.* A similar typology following the Prābhākara-Mīmāṁsaka school is summed up by Jayantabhaṭṭa in NMa_2 1 in sections devoted to the discussion of Prabhākara's view on the question of *arthâpatti* (vol. I pp. 64.3–79.4), e.g. *prābhākarās tu dṛṣṭaḥ śruto vêti* ... (vol. I pp. 68.9). Likewise, the above typology—partly similar to the one found in NK and partly more elaborate, depending on various cognitive criteria that precede the *arthâpatti* form of reasoning—is found, e.g. in NMa_2 1 in the section *arthâpatteḥ pramāṇântaram* (vol. I pp. 52.20–59.13), already mentioned, as well as in the section *abhāva-pūrvikârthâpatti-khaṇḍanam* (vol. I pp. 63.3–64.2), wherein a handful of relevant instances of *arthâpatti* can be found as well. In the subsequent section *arthâpatteḥ pramāṇântaratā-nirāsaḥ* (vol. I, p. 60.1–12) of NMa_2 1, Jayantabhaṭṭa denies the status of a separate cognitive criterion to the *arthâpatti* type of reasoning.

Occasionally, presumption (*arthâpatti*) is juxtaposed with inference (*anumāna*) and classified as the reverse (*viparyaya*) of the latter, for instance by the followers of Prabhākara (cf. NMa_2 1 vol. I, p. 64.4–9): *prābhākarās tu prakārântareṇânumānād bhedam atrâcakṣate. anumāne gamaka-viśeṣaṇam anyathânupapannam analaṁ vinā dhūmo hi nôpapadyate. iha tu viparyayaḥ: gamyo gamakena vinā nôpapadyate. gamyo bahir-bhāvaḥ, sa jīvato gṛhâbhāvaṁ vinā nôpapadyate. gṛhān nirgato jīvan bahir bhavatîti bhāṣyam apy evaṁ yojayanti. dṛṣṭaḥ śruto vârtho 'rtha-kalpanā arthântaraṁ kalpayatîty arthaḥ. yataḥ sā kalpanā prameya-dvārikânyathā nôpapadyate, kalpyamāno 'rtho 'nyathā nôpapadyate sa ca gamya iti.*—'The followers of Prabhākara, however, argue for the difference from inference in this [case of presumption] in a different manner. In [the case of] inference, the distinctive feature that leads to the comprehension (*sc.* the probans) is inexplicable otherwise, [i.e. without the probandum], for without fire, smoke is not explicable. In this case [of presumption], the contrary [takes places]: something-to-be-comprehended (probandum) is not explicable without something that leads to the comprehension (probans). [For instance,] "being outside" is something-to-be-comprehended (probandum); it is not explicable without a living [person] who is not at home. Also in the *Śābara-bhāṣya* they reason in this manner: a living [person] who has left his house is outside. The meaning is that assumption of one object, either perceived or heard of, makes one assume another object, because this assumption, which is the means to [grasp] the cognoscible, is not explicable otherwise; the object which is being assumed is not explicable otherwise and it is something-to-be-comprehended (probandum).'

Thirdly, *arthâpatti* can hardly be deemed a valid and rigorous form of reasoning—unless it is either taken to be enthymematic this way or another or understood in terms of locutionary logic or logical pragmatics—despite the conviction of some Indian thinkers who reckoned it among cognitive criteria, as could be seen from the analysis of the instances quoted heretofore.

Furthermore, since there is always some expectancy of ideas involved in, or certain assumptions associated with the term 'presupposition', 'presumption' appears to be much more appropriate a rendering of *arthâpatti*, inasmuch as it seems to lack a standardised formulation in terms of modern logical analysis, unlike presupposition or implicature (*vide infra*), and it is not a valid form of inference either. Whereas the designation 'presupposition' is well-known to modern logicians since the critique of RUSSELL 1905 found, e.g. in STALNAKER 1970, 1973, 1974, well established through such works like STRAWSON 1950, VAN FRAASEN 1969 and formalised, e.g. in TOKARZ 1993, the notion 'presumption' is less rigid and should not be identified or confused with presupposition. By way of illustration, presupposition may be defined in the following manner: 'The sentence β, the truth of which is the necessary condition of the meaningfulness of a certain sentence α, is called the presupposition of the sentence α' (cf. TOKARZ (1993: 192 ff.)). In our example:

(1) *John's present wife is an industrious coal-miner.*

Let Wx stand for 'x is John's wife' and Cx represent 'x is an industrious coal-miner':

(2) $\exists x(Wx \wedge \forall y(Wx \rightarrow x{=}y) \wedge Cx)$.

The formula

(3) $\exists x(Wx \wedge \forall y(Wx \rightarrow x{=}y))$,

or 'John has a wife', is the presupposition of the sentence (1). The unique property of all presuppositions, which points to the fact that they cannot be considered simple logical consequences of a given sentence, is their inferrability even from the negated sentence; to wit, they preserve their validity and veracity whether a given sentence be preceded by negation or not. The presupposition (3) of the sentence (1), viz., the fact 'John has a wife', remains true even if we negate the sentence (1):

(4) *John's present wife is not an industrious coal-miner*.

We do not observe this property neither in the case of 'obese Devadatta' nor in the Naiyāyika example of 'clouds and rain' above, because the alleged presupposition: 'obese Devadatta eats at night', is by no means directly derivable from the sentence 'obese Devadatta eats during the day' and, similarly, the contention: 'if there are clouds, it rains', does not logically follow from the sentence 'if there are no clouds, it does not rain' preceded by the negation. Since the initial sentence, being negated as $\ulcorner(\neg(\neg\alpha\rightarrow\neg\beta)\rightarrow(\alpha\rightarrow\beta))\urcorner$, has the form of implication, there are four alternatives, according to the four laws of negating an implication, viz., [1] $\ulcorner\neg(\alpha\rightarrow\beta)\rightarrow(\beta\rightarrow\alpha)\urcorner$, [2] $\ulcorner\neg(\alpha\rightarrow\beta)\rightarrow(\alpha\rightarrow\neg\beta)\urcorner$, [3] $\ulcorner\neg(\alpha\rightarrow\beta)\rightarrow(\neg\alpha\rightarrow\beta)\urcorner$ and [4] $\ulcorner\neg(\alpha\rightarrow\beta)\rightarrow(\neg\alpha\rightarrow\neg\beta)\urcorner$. Let us, however, consider here only two entanglements: [2] the consequence of the conjunction of two statements: 'if there are no clouds, it does not rain' and 'if there are no clouds, it rains', would be 'clouds have nothing to do with rain'! [3] If 'if there are no clouds, it does not rain' and 'if there are clouds, it does not rain', then 'it never rains'! On the above ground, *arthâpatti* should not be therefore rendered as 'presupposition.'

And last but not least, the term 'presumption' is somehow, more historically and less genetically, related to the notion of 'implicature', 'pragmatic implicature' or 'conversational implicature' first analysis of which is associated with the lectures of H. P. GRICE in 1967. Some instances of *arthâpatti* may point to their implicatural character, whereas some other may not necessarily bear such affinity in a convincing way (e.g. the case of clouds-and-rain). The issue whether cases of *arthâpatti* should be subsumed under the common designation 'conversational implicature' was, on a limited scale though, positively resolved in OETKE 1992. To sum up, by rendering *arthâpatti* as 'presumption', a term which is quite comprehensive, not necessarily unequivocal and not strictly defined, I have decided to leave the question still open as regards the logical character of the idea underlying the *arthâpatti* type of reasoning, instead of confining the broad spectrum of instances of *arthâpatti* found in Indian text to the notion of pragmatic implicature or conversational implicature, despite my own personal leaning towards adopting the conviction that the notion of pragmatic implicature may indeed adequately reflect the reasoning involved in the case of *arthâpatti*.

There is no doubt left, in my opinion, that the issue of the logical status of *arthâpatti* needs further detailed research.

[168] I.e., presumption complies with the definition of cognitive criterion.

[169] I.e., there remains nothing (e.g. no doubt or uncertainty) left that might hinder accomplishing of the everyday practice.

[170] The spiritual advancement of an individual, that corresponds to various stages of the purity of his or her cognitive faculties, is dependent jointly on destruction-cum-subsidence (*kṣayôpaśama*) of the particular karmic matter veiling the faculties of the cognitive subject. The intensity of the obstruction coincides with infinite degrees of destruction-cum-subsidence of the *karman* veiling cognition and perception. The veiling (*āvaraṇa*) *karman* is described, e.g. in TS 8.5, where its two major varieties are therein enumerated; further subvarieties of *jñānâvaraṇa-°* and *darśanâvaraṇa-karman* are described in TS and TBh 8.7 and 8.8 respectively; cf. also SSi 8.22: *jñānâvaraṇasya phalaṁ jñānâbhavo, darśanâvaraṇasya phalaṁ darśana-śakty-uparodha ity eva ādi.*—'The effect of [the *karman*] veiling cognition is the absence of cognition, the effect of [the *karman*] veiling perception is the obstruction of the power of seeing.'

[171] *āhatya* < *ā√han*, an ambiguous term, lit. 'to gouge out, to single out', though NAṬ *ad loc.* explains the term: ***āhatyêti*** *pūrva-pakṣâdibhir niṣṭaṅkya.*—'to gouge out means to dissociate oneself from the initial thesis of the opponent.'

[172] This strictly pragmatic character of this argument is striking. Firstly, it goes counter the principle, expounded above, not to multiply cognitive criteria only on account of some insignificant distinction. Secondly, one wonders why then not to accord the status of a cognitive criterion in its own right to analogy or presumption, since scholars of various schools were not unanimous as to their independence, either?!

[173] Cf. NAV 4: *na câpṛthak-kṛtasya tad-viviktaṁ vaktuṁ śakyam, ato bhedenôpanyāsaḥ* (p. 38 of the translation). If verbal knowledge did not constitute a separate subvariety of the indirect cognition, nothing could be said about it.

[174] NAṬ *ad loc.*: *ūhâdīnāṁ lakṣaṇaṁ akārîti. yathā—"upalambhânupalambha-nimittaṁ vyāpti-jñānam ūhaḥ", yathêdam asmin saty eva bhavati, asati na bhavaty evêti ca. ādi-śabdāt saṁskārôdbodha-nibandhanā tad ity-ākārā smṛtir, yathā sa devadatta iti. darśana-smaraṇa-kāraṇakaṁ saṁkalanaṁ pratyabhijñānaṁ,* [H omits *yathā sa ... pratyabhijñānaṁ*] *yathā tad evêdam iti.*—'[Presently, I comment on the passage]: "the definition of induction, etc., formulated [by preceptors in other philosophic systems]," for instance: "Induction is the cognition of invariable concomitance by reason of comprehension or non-comprehension," e.g.: *y* occurs only when *x* is there, and [*y*] does not occur only when [*x*] is not there. Due to the expression "etc." reminiscence [is taken account of; it] is based on the awakening of subliminal impressions [and] has the form "that!", e.g. "That Devadatta [I saw some time ago]." Recognition is identification that has as its cause [jointly] seeing and recollection, e.g.

"This [here] is that very [thing I have seen before]!"' In view of the above illustration, the definition of induction based on the faulty invariable concomitance, rejected by Siddharṣi and Devabhadra on the grounds of its invalidity can be represented symbolically roughly as follows: **vyāpti* $=_{df}(x \rightarrow y) \wedge (\neg x \rightarrow \neg y)$, whereas the correct formulation of the rule of the invariable concomitance would, roughly speaking, be: *vyāpti* $=_{df}(x \rightarrow y) \wedge (\neg y \rightarrow \neg x)$ (the propositional variables x and y have existential connotation: 'x / y occurs'). Likewise, NBh 1.34–35 presents such an interpretation of the relation of invariable concomitance that stands in contradiction to the concept of *vyāpti* widely accepted by Indian logicians after Vasubandhu, Diṅnāga, etc., as I have pointed out in BALCEROWICZ (1996: 4–22; §§ II. Invariable concomitance, III. Some remarks on Indian 'syllogism'), cf. n. 393. Similar formulation of the notions of *anvaya* and *vyatireka* in the context of grammar occurs in Pr 2.78–9 ad 1.2.45: *sati śabde 'rthâvagamaḥ ... śabdâbhāve tad-arthânavagamaḥ.*—'The ascertainment of the meaning [takes place] when there is a word ...; when there is no word, no ascertainment of its meaning [takes place].' Cf. CARDONA 1967.

[175] I.e., *anvaya* and *vyatireka*; both terms usually refer to inference (*anumāna*) and mean positive and negative concomitance, cf. n. 174. However, in the above context referring to perception, which is, by definition, free of any reasoning, they must simply denote the affirmation of a property perceived (e.g. 'this is the ground') and the preclusion of properties not perceived at this time and place (e.g. 'there is no pot there'), respectively.

[176] Here the term *vastu*, lit. 'a real, really existing thing', refers to the whole situation and for this reason I render it as 'fact.' Otherwise, it would yield a seeming semantic nonsense: *the non-existence of a pot, etc., is a really existing thing*. A seeming nonsense, for the notion of *abhāva* in Mīmāṁsā (being a separate category) or in Navyanyāya (if it were non-existent it could not be negated, hence it must possess some reality or existence; on the problem of negation, the unnegatables and the existence of *abhāva* see MATILAL (1985: 76128)) possesses some kind of reality. Since the speaker is a Jaina realist (who does not grant any reality to non-existence) who recounts the position of a Mīmāṁsaka, I do not wish to predetermine what degree of reality a notion of 'non-existent pot' would have in this particular case. Besides, the circumstances that have been characterised as 'this is the surface of the ground, there is no pot, etc., [there],' can hardly be called 'a really existing thing.' Further below in this passage I generally translate *vastu*, where possible, as 'a real thing.'

[177] That this specific feature of every fact (a real thing), allegedly 'known to every creature', was not so obvious is evident from PMī 1.1.12, wherein Hemacandra considered it necessary to state it explicitly in the aphorism: *bhāvâbhāvâtmakatvād vastuno nirviṣayo 'bhāvaḥ.*—'Absence [as negative proof] has no province, because a real thing (fact) has the nature of existence and non-existence.' He appends the *sūtra* with a whole discussion in PMī 1.1 § 39, the major part of which forms the argumentation in support of this 'obvious' thesis that facts consists in both existence and non-existence: *nahi bhāvaika-rūpaṁ vastv asti viśvasya vaiśva-rūpa-prasaṅgāt. nâpy*

abhāvâika-rūpaṁ nīrūpatva-prasaṅgāt. kiṁ tu svarūpeṇa sattvāt para-rūpeṇa câsattvād bhāvâbhāva-rūpaṁ vastu, tathâiva pramāṇānāṁ pravṛtteḥ. tathā hi: pratyakṣaṁ tāvat "bhū-talam evêdaṁ, ghaṭâdir na bhavatîty" anvaya-vyatireka-dvāreṇa vastu paricchindat tad-adhikaṁ viṣayam abhāvâika-rūpaṁ nirācaṣṭa iti kiṁ viṣayam āśrityâbhāva-lakṣaṇaṁ pramāṇaṁ syāt? evaṁ parokṣāṇy api pramāṇāni bhāvâbhāva-rūpa-vastu-grahaṇa-pravaṇāny eva; anyathâsaṅkīrṇa-sva-sva-viṣaya-grahaṇâsiddheḥ, yad āha:

> *ayam evêti yo hy eṣa bhāve bhavati nirṇayaḥ /*
> *nâiṣa vastv-antarâbhāva-saṁvitty-anugamād ṛte //*
>
> (MŚV$_1$ 5.8.15 (*abhāva-pariccheda*), ŚVVTT, p. 416)

—'In no way does a real thing (fact) consists entirely of existence, because of the undesired consequence that all [things] would have all forms. Neither [does it] consist entirely of non-existence, because it would have no form. However, a real thing (fact) is constituted by [both] existence and non-existence, inasmuch as it is existent with regard to its own form and it is non-existent with regard to the form of some other [thing (fact)], because all cognitive criteria operate in such a way. For it is as follows: perception—to begin with—which determines the fact [like:] "this is the surface of the ground, there is no pot, etc., [there]," by affirmation and preclusion, rebuts the province consisting entirely of non-existence that is additional to this [existence]. Then with regard to what province would the [alleged] cognitive criterion defined as absence, [or negative proof, operate]? In the very same way, also other indirect cognitive criteria are only disposed to grasp facts constituted by both existence and non-existence. Otherwise they would incorrectly grasp their own [respective] provinces, [that are normally] unmingled. because it has been said [in *Śloka-vārttika*]: "For the following determination [of the form:] "there is only this [thing here]," which arises with respect to something existent, [is not possible] without the accompaniment of the awareness of the non-existence of another fact".' Again, it is needless to point out notable parallelism in wording and arguments between NAV and PMī. The concept of the reality as consisting in both existent and non-existent aspects, as described above—especially the formulation *svarūpeṇa sattvāt para-rūpeṇa câsattvād bhāvâbhāva-rūpaṁ vastu*—bears striking similarity to the first two propositions of the doctrine of *syād-vāda*: (1) *syād asti*—'in a certain sense, the object exists' and (2) *syān nâsti*: 'in a certain sense, the object does not exist.' Cf. p.113.

[178] I.e., 'the cognition that an object in question is not there in front of us'; *nāstitā*, lit. 'not-being there' (*das Nichtvorhandensein*), refers to the fact that some (existing) object cannot be seen in a given place. It should not be confused with absolute 'non-existence' connoting something unreal, a fictitious entity, void of existence.

[179] *pratiyogin*, viz., the locus of the negative property, sometimes is also translated as counterpositive (e.g. INGALLS 1951) or the absentee (e.g. MATILAL 1985, see esp. his note 1 on. p. 140 on the terms *pratiyogin* / *pratiyogitā*, and their rendering as

'absentee' and 'absenteehood'); e.g. the pot, etc., (*ghaṭâdi*) is the negatum of the absence of the pot, etc., (*ghaṭâdy-abhāva*). Cf. MATILAL (1980: 4ff).

[180] *utpādyate*, though MŚV$_{I}$ reads *utpadyate*—'does not arise.' Also PMī 1.1 § 40 reads *utpādyate*, though it may, in fact, quote NAṬ without referring directly to MŚV$_{I}$. The variation in reading brings in the question of the role of secondary sources in the transmission of the original texts, e.g. that of MŚV.

[181] MŚV$_{I}$ 5.8.18 (*abhāva-pariccheda*) p. 339–40 (ŚVVṬT, p. 414).

[182] I.e., having first perceived a real thing as present and existing with our senses.

[183] MŚV$_{I}$ 5.8.27 (*abhāva-pariccheda*) p. 342 (ŚVVTTvf, p. 416).

[184] Cf. NAṬ 1 *ad loc.*: ***vinirluṭhitam*** *rahitam*, and n.72.

[185] Cf. NAṬ 1 *ad loc.*: ***tad-abhāvêty-ādi***. *ghaṭâbhāvâparicchedasya ghaṭa-sadbhāva-jñāna-paratantratvāt.*—'[The expression] "[because non-grasping of] its absence," etc., [means] "because the lack of determination of the absence of the pot is invariant with the cognition of the presence of the pot".' The above formulations (NAV and NAṬ) are clearly an application of the law of double negation: $\ulcorner \neg\neg p = p \urcorner$.

[186] Especially in this paragraph we have to carefully distinguish two meanings of *abhāva*: either 'the absence [as negative proof],' which is a cognitive criterion, or 'absence', i.e. non-occurrence of an object in a given place. That *abhāva* in this locution means 'the absence [as negative proof]' is corroborated, beside the context itself, also by PMī 1.1 § 41: *tathā* ***câbhāva-pramāṇam*** *api paścāt pravṛttaṁ na tān utsārayitum paṭiṣṭhaḥ syāt, anyathâsaṅkīrṇasya saṅkīrṇatā-grahaṇāt pratyakṣam bhrāntaṁ syāt*. Also in this passage the similarity in wording is striking.

[187] NAṬ 1 *ad loc.* explains 'unmingled' as 'merely the surface of the ground,' and 'mingled' as 'accompanied by [the presence of] a pot, etc.': ***asaṅkīrṇasya*** *kevala-bhūtasya*. ***saṅkīrṇatā*** *ghaṭâdi-sāhityam*.

[188] I.e., perception (*pratyakṣa*), inference (*anumāna*), verbal testimony (*śabda*), analogy (*upamāna*) and presumption (*arthâpatti*).

[189] MŚV$_{I}$ 5.8.1 (*abhāva-pariccheda*) p. 335 (ŚVVTT, p. 409).

[190] In other words: 'it is only perception that possesses the capability to grasp the fact, established in each and every case, [in the following manner: "this is] the surface of the ground, [there is no pot there], etc.".'

[191] The comparison of this paragraph, too, with the corresponding succinct passage of PMī 1.1. § 42 quoted below—that actually seems but a recapitulation of the ideas expressed in NAV—confirms that Hemacandra, the author of the latter work, must have copiously availed himself of Siddharṣi-gaṇin's commentary: *api câyaṁ pramāṇa-pañcaka-nivṛtti-rūpatvāt tucchaḥ. tata evâjñāna-rūpaḥ kathaṁ pramāṇam bhavet? tasmād abhāvâṁśāt kathañcid abhinnaṁ bhāvâṁśaṁ paricchindatā pratyakṣâdinā pramāṇenâbhāvâṁśo gṛhīta evêti tad-atirikta-viṣayâbhāvān nirviṣayo*

'bhāvaḥ. tathā ca na pramāṇam iti sthitam.—'Furthermore, this [cognitive criterion] is hollow because it consists in the suspension of the quintuplet of cognitive criteria. For this very reason, how could [the absence as negative proof,] having the form of the absence of cognition, be a cognitive criterion? Therefore, the non-existent aspect is only grasped by a cognitive criterion, such as perception, etc., that determines the existent aspect somehow as not different from the non-existent aspect; so—because there is no province additional to this [existent aspect]—the absence [as negative proof] has no province. Therefore, it is proved that [the absence as negative proof] is not a cognitive criterion.' It is indubitably more plausible that Hemacandra—with his statement *pramāṇa-pañcaka-nivṛtti-rūpatvāt*—referred to the quotation of MŚV. occurring in NAṬ, and thus only indirectly to the *Śloka-vārttika*. For this very reason, the expression 'the quintuplet of cognitive criteria' (*pramāṇa-pañcaka*) occurring in PMĪ 1.1. § 42 should be understood as referring to the five other varieties of cognitive criteria, different from the absence [as negative proof] (*abhāva*), which were recognised by the Mīmāṁsaka, and not as a reference to the five subvarieties of *pramāṇa* maintained by the Jainas (*sc. mati, śruta, avadhi, manaḥ-paryāya* and *kevala*, cf. TS 1.9). Besides, the above argument, invalidating the absence [as negative proof], involves *petitio principii* hidden in the assumption that, since the absence [as negative proof] entails the suspension of all other cognitive criteria, it must necessarily undermine also its own validity as a cognitive criterion.

[192] Cf. PS Chapter II (*anumāna-pariccheda*): [1] *'bras bu*, [2] *raṅ bźin*, [3] *mi dmigs pa*.

[193] Cf. n. 5.

[194] In other words, having only perception and inference at his disposal, the Buddhist would not be able to prove that there is no other cognitive criterion, except these two.

[195] NAṬ 1 *ad loc.* exemplifies: ***tad yathêty-ādi***. [1] *viruddhôpalabdhir yathā—nâtra śita-sparśo 'gner iti.* [2] *viruddha-kāryôpalabdhir yathā—nâtra śita-sparśo dhūmād iti.* [3] *kāraṇânupalabdhir yathā—nâtra dhūmo 'gny-abhāvād iti.* [4] *svabhāvânupalabdhir yathā—nâtra dhūma upalabdhi-lakṣaṇa-prāptasyânupalabdher iti. śeṣās tu saptâpi. anupalabdhayo dharma-bindu-prabhṛti-śāstra-pratipāditā eṣv eva caturṣu bhedeṣv antar-bhavatîti. pratibheda-rūpatvān na pṛthag-abhihitāḥ.* The above is, of course, a reference to both 'Drops' of Dharmakīrti, viz., to the *Nyāya-bindu* and the *Hetu-bindu*. In the former work we find a systematic list of eleven varieties; NB_1 32–42: [1] *svabhāvânupalabhir yathā—nâtra dhūma upalabdhi-lakṣaṇa-prāptasyânupalabdher iti.* [2] *kāryânupalabdhir yathā—nêhâpratibaddha-sāmarthyāni dhūma-kāraṇāni santi dhūmâbhāvāt.* [3] *vyāpakânupalabdhir yathā—nâtra śiṁśapā vṛkṣâbhāvāt.* [4] *svabhāva-viruddhôpalabdhir yathā—nâtra śīta-sparśo 'gner iti.* [5] *viruddha-kāryôpalabdhir yathā—nâtra śīta-sparśo 'dhūmād iti.* [6] *viruddha-vyāptôpalabdhir yathā—"na dhruva-bhāvī bhūtasyâpi bhāvasya vināśo hetv-antarâpekṣaṇāt"*[†]. [7] *kārya-viruddhôpalabdhir yathā—nêhâpratibaddha-sāmarthyāni śīta-kāraṇāni santy agner iti.* [8] *vyāpaka-viruddhôpalabdhir yathā—nâtra tuṣāra-sparśo 'gner iti.*

[9] kāraṇânupalabdhir yathā—nâtra dhūmo 'gny-abhāvāt. [10] kāraṇa-viruddhôpalabdhir yathā—nâsya roma-harṣâdi-viśeṣāḥ sannihita-dahana-viśeṣatvād iti. [11] kāraṇa-viruddha-kāryôpalabdhir yathā—na roma-harṣâdi-viśeṣa-yukta-puruṣavān ayam pradeśo dhūmād iti. Except for the varieties [5] viruddha-kāryôpalabdhir and [6] viruddha-vyāptôpalabdhir, the above list is almost completely quoted, with hardly any alternation, in Tsop. 9, pp. 290–92, and appended with seven additional types: [12] svabhāva-viruddha-vyāptôppalabdhir yathā—nâtra vahnis tuṣāra-sparśād iti ... [13] kāraṇa-viruddha-vyāptôpalabdhir yathā—nâtra dhūmas tūṣara-sparśād iti ... [14] vyāpaka-viruddha-vyāptôpalabdhir yathā—nâyaṁ nityaḥ kadācit-kārya-kāritvād iti ... [15] kārya-viruddha-vyāptôpalabdhir yathā—nêhâpratibaddha-sāmarthyāni vahni-kāraṇāni santi tuṣāra-sparśād iti ... [16] svabhāva-viruddha-kāryôpalabdhir yathā—nâtra śīta-sparśo dhūmād iti ... [17] vyāpaka-viruddha-kāryôpalabdhir yathā—nâtra tuṣāra-sparśo dhūmād iti ... [18] kārya-viruddha-kāryôpalabdhir yathā—nêhâpratibaddha-sāmarthyāni śīta-kāraṇāni santi dhūmād iti ... In *Hetu-bindu*, esp. f. 248b–251b p. 70–27–84.29 (Tibetan text) = 4.30–4.311, p. 71.20–85.20 (Sanskrit text), however, varieties of non-comprehension are—instead of being simply systematically listed—discussed and minutely analysed with special reference to the validity of the logical reason.

† This passage, which is also quoted in *Dravyâlaṅkāra-svopajña-ṭīkā* p. 76, remains unidentified by JAMBŪVIJAYA (1981: 143.5).

[196] NAṬ 1 *ad loc.*: ***itarêti***. *pratiṣedhyasya śītâdeḥ.*

[197] NAṬ 1 *ad loc.*: ***dṛśyâtmana iti***. *dṛśya-svarūpasya viruddhasya vahnayâdeḥ.*

[198] Cf. KAJIYAMA (1966: n. 214).

[199] NAṬ 1 *ad loc.*: ***ekêty-ādi***. *ekasya cakṣur-ādi-jñānasya grāhyaṁ cakṣur-ādi-praṇidhānâbhimukhaṁ bhū-ghaṭâdi-vastu-dvayam anyonyâpekṣam eka-jñāna-saṁsargi kathyate, tayor hi sator*[a] *nâika-niyatā pratipattiḥ*[b] *syāt; pariccheda-yogyatayā*[c] *dvayor apy aviśeṣāt. jñāne vastu-dvaya-saṁsargaś ca tad-ākārayor ekasmin jñāne saṁsargād vastunor apy upacāreṇa saṁsarga-vyapadeśāt. tata ekasmin jñāne saṁsargaḥ sambandho*[d] *vidyayte yasya bhū-talâder ghaṭâdinêti prakaraṇāt svayam ūhyaṁ, sa câsau padârthaś ca tasyôpalambha*[e]*-paricchedo rūpaṁ yasyāḥ svabhāvânupalabdheḥ sā tathā; kevala-bhū-talôpalambha-rūpêti*[f] *yāvat.*

[a] C: *sato*. [b] C: *nâika-nipāta-pratiyatipattiḥ*.
[c] H,V: °*-yogyatāyā*. [d] C: *sambandhe*.
[e] A: °*-tasya upalambha-*°; C: °*-tasya upalambho* . [f] H,V: °*-rūpa iti*.

[200] Cf. n. 261.

[201] Lit. 'That exists on its back.'

[202] Cf. NAṬ 1 *ad loc.*: ***tat-svarūpam*** *pratyakṣânumāna-svarūpam.*—'Their intrinsic nature [means] the intrinsic nature of perception and inference.'

[203] Cf. n. 261.

[204] Cf. NAV 0 (introductory part): *apramāṇasyâkiñcit-karatvāt*—'because something which is [believed] not [to be] a cognitive criterion [must be] futile' (p. 2 of the translation).

[205] Cf. NAṬ 1 *ad loc.*: ***tat-prāmāṇyêti***. *tasya pratyakṣânumāna-prāmāṇya-nirṇāyakânumānasya*.

[206] Cf. NAV 1: *na tāvat pratyakṣāt, tasya nirvikalpakatayā sato 'py asat-kalpatvāt* ... (p. 24 ff. of the translation).

[207] Viz., 'Is this another inference is a cognitive criterion or not?' Cf. NAṬ 1 *ad loc.*: ***tad-avastham iti***. *tad apy anumānaṁ pramāṇam apramāṇaṁ cêti*.

[208] Cf. NAV 1 above: *tat-pṛṣṭha-bhāvī vikalpas* ...—'conceptualisation that immediately follows this [perception]' (p. 24 of the translation).

[209] The statement *anyad api yad evaṁ-vidham avisaṁvādi jñānaṁ tat pramāṇam astv* is apparently a pun on PV 1.3ab: *pramāṇam avisaṁvādi jñānaṁ*.

[210] *kākâkṣi-golaka-nyāya*—cf. Apte's PSED, p. 574: 'It takes its origin from the supposition that the crow has but one eye ..., and that it can move it, as occasion requires, from the socket on one side into that of the other; and the maxim is applied to a word or phrase which though used only once in a sentence, may, if occasion requires, serve two purposes.'

[211] Cf. Devabhadra-sūri's gloss: *vijātīyebhyo vyāvṛttatvān niyataḥ, sajātīyebhyaś câvyāvṛttatvāt sarva evâniyataḥ* ...—'Specific—inasmuch as it is distinguished from things that belong to a different class, and non-specific—inasmuch as it is not distinguished from things that belong to the same class ....'

[212] The words *sāmpratam* does not directly relate to the contents of the sentence; it apparently marks the beginning of the new paragraph. Cf. *adhunā* in the similar usage below, e.g. opening the commentary section on NA 3 and NA 4 (nn. 225 and 233, respectively).

[213] The use of *sūtra* not only in the sense of a short aphorism in prose but to denote also a versified *kārikā* is not unparalleled, cf. YDī$_1$ on SKā 1, p. 9.10/11: *tathā côttara-sūtreṇa* (=SKā 2) *pratiṣetsyaty ācāryaḥ*.—'And, accordingly, the preceptor will refute [them] in the subsequent *sūtra* (= *kārikā*).' Furthermore, Vacaspāti speaks occasionally of Īśvarakṛṣṇa, the author of the *kārikās*, as a *sūtra-kāra*, e.g. YDī$_1$ on SKā 15, p. 73.5: *dharmavat pradhāna-padârthasya vā prāg anupadeśād akuśalaḥ sūtra-kāra ity etad āpadyate. na câitad iṣṭam ubhayam*.

[214] Lit. 'so that no expectancy is left,' i.e. so that no further explanation is needed.

[215] I.e., 'Whether the utterance leaves any trace in the hearer's memory, whether it has any effect upon that person,' for *saṁskāras* are residual forces that are responsible for remembrance/memory and affect or determine future actions.

[216] The following argumentation is based on the fact that the first aphorism speaks of cognitive criterion in singular while the second one uses the plural: 'cognitive criteria.'

[217] It is apparently a reference to the Jaina theory of multiplexity of reality (*anekânta-vāda*).

[218] The verb *vi√ṭhap* is probably a prakritised word derivable from Skt. *vi√sthā* C. However, Devabhadra-sūri takes it 'in the sense of "derivation (acquisition)" (*upārjana*)', cf. NAṬ *ad loc.*: ***viṭhapitatvād iti****. upārjane vi-pūrvaṣ*[a] *ṭhap sautro dhātuḥ*.

[a] H,V: °*-pūrvaḥ*.

[219] In Jaina philosophic literature, the term *bhaṅga* is well attested to mean also 'one of many possible ways of predication; a conceivable partial statement.' It is not only related to the famous *sapta-bhaṅgī*, but we come across it in an analysis of the four varieties of standpoints (*nikṣepa*, *nyāsa*) in Umāsvāti's TBh 1.5 (p. 8.6–8): *dravya-jīva iti guṇa-paryāya-viyuktaḥ prajñā-sthāpito 'nādi-pāriṇāmika-bhāva-yukto jīva ucyate. anyathā śūnyo 'yaṁ* ***bhaṅgaḥ****...* In NAV, however, we come across three occurrences of the term °*-bhaṅga*, that cannot but mean 'invalidation, defeat, destruction,' and it is conjoined with either *vadana-*° or *vaktra*°-:

S1 *anyathā bhinnam eva rūpaṁ svābhāvikam itarat tu kalpanā-buddhi-darśitam ity api vadatāṁ na vadana-bhaṅgaḥ syāt* (above),

S2 *anyathâpramāṇakaṁ sarvaṁ sarvatra vidyata iti parasyâpi vadato na vadana-bhaṅgaḥ syāt* (p. 90, n. 617),

S3 *sāmānyam evânādy avidyā-darśitaṁ, viśeṣāḥ punaḥ pāramārthikā iti viśeṣa-vādino 'pi vadato vaktra-bhaṅgâbhāvāt* (p.113, n. 773).

Thus, the usage of the term *bhaṅga* is in accord with the Indian, not specifically Jaina, epistemic tradition, for we find the term in a rather similar context also in Udayana's ĀTV$_1$, p. 57: *jalpa-vitaṇḍayos tu pakṣâdiṣu pramāṇa-prāśna-mātra-pravṛttasya na sva-vacana-virodhaḥ. tatra pramāṇenôttaram aniṣṭam aśakyaṁ ca, apramāṇenâiva tûttare sva-vacanenâiva bhaṅgaḥ, mad-ukteṣu pakṣâdiṣu pramāṇaṁ nâstîti svayam eva svī-kārāt, anuttare tv apratibhâivêti*. Conspicuously, Udayana speaks of a self-defeating statement, and *bhaṅgaḥ* is construed with the instrumental case *sva-vacanena*. Moreover, *bhaṅga* is elucidated as 'annihilation' in NAVV 55 § 2, p. 113.7: *bhaṅgo vyayaḥ*.

It is still problematical how exactly the three statements S1–S3 should be understood. We would naturally construe:

S1' *vadatāṁ vadanasya bhaṅgaḥ*,

S2' *vadato vadanasya bhaṅgaḥ*,

S3' *vadato vaktrasya bhaṅgâbhāvāt*.

However, in view of Udayana's passage quoted from ĀTV$_1$. it would not be impossible, though less plausible in my opinion, to read:

S1" *vadatāṁ vadanena bhaṅgaḥ*,
S2" *vadato vadanena bhaṅgaḥ*,
S3" *vadato vaktrena bhaṅgâbhāvāt*.

This interpretation—which explains S1 and S2 (*vadana* = 'words')—is not absolutely satisfactory, inasmuch as highly problematic remains *vaktra* in S3. In S1 and S2, the term is conjoined with *vadana*-°. Therefore, one would expect *vaktra* to mean here 'speech, words', though this meaning in not attested by dictionaries or other reference works available to me, where it is unanimously taken to mean 'mouth, face, organ of speech.' On the other hand, *vadana* is taken to be synonymous with *vaktra* in the sense of 'mouth, face', cf., e.g. AmK 2.6.89ab (I, p. 418): *vaktrâsye vadanaṁ tuṇḍam ānanaṁ mukham* // Would it mean that *vadana* in the two previous cases would also mean 'mouth, organ of speech'?

In case we assume *vadana* and *vaktra* to be synonyms and mean 'face; mouth, organ of speech'—which is much less plausible though—*bhaṅga* would have to assume a meaning similar to *vadana-capeṭā*, 'a slap on the face.' This idea is, in fact, epitomised in the title of a Jaina critical anthology ascribed to Hemacandra, *Dvija-vacana-capeṭā Vedâṅkuśaḥ* (*saṁpūrṇaḥ*), or 'A slap on the face of the Brahmins: a goad [in the form] of Vedic [utterances]', examined and evaluated in WEZLER 1993. However, *bhaṅga* conveys an idea—much more violent than *capeṭā*—of 'blow, hit, stroke, split.'

Optionally, to pursue this s o m a t i c path, we know (see PW vol. V, p. 176, col. II, ll.13–15) of °-*bhaṅga* to mean 'weakening, wane, decrease' in such expressions as '*kaṇṭha-bhaṅga*: Entstellung –, Schwachwerden der Stimme, Gestammel', *vāg-bhaṅga*, *svara-bhaṅga*, etc., viz. 'stammering, stuttering, becoming silent.' Thus, we could consistently render the expressions S1, S2 and S3 as 'becoming silent.' Accordingly, the phrase above, *anyathā ... na vadana-bhaṅgaḥ syāt*, would mean 'Otherwise, there would be no speechlessness of people who express...', i.e. 'Otherwise, nothing would prevent them from saying....' This interpretation would come rather close to my initial suggestion of 'invalidation, defeat.'

[220] Cf. NAV 29 (on *ṛjusūtra-durnaya*) p. 120. The characteristic of the real thing is *utpāda-vyaya-dhrauvya* ([a] continued existence–rise–termination), discussed here at length on pp. 127–131 (§§ 31.3–31.6).

[221] 'Of this' refers to 'for stating the definition of cognitive criterion' below.

[222] For the refutation of the succeeding argumentation cf. p. 30.

[223] In other words: to formulate a definition embracing all cognitive criteria we need avail ourselves of a cognitive criterion that does not fall under this very definition.

[224] To sum up, the dialectical structure of the argument is as follows:

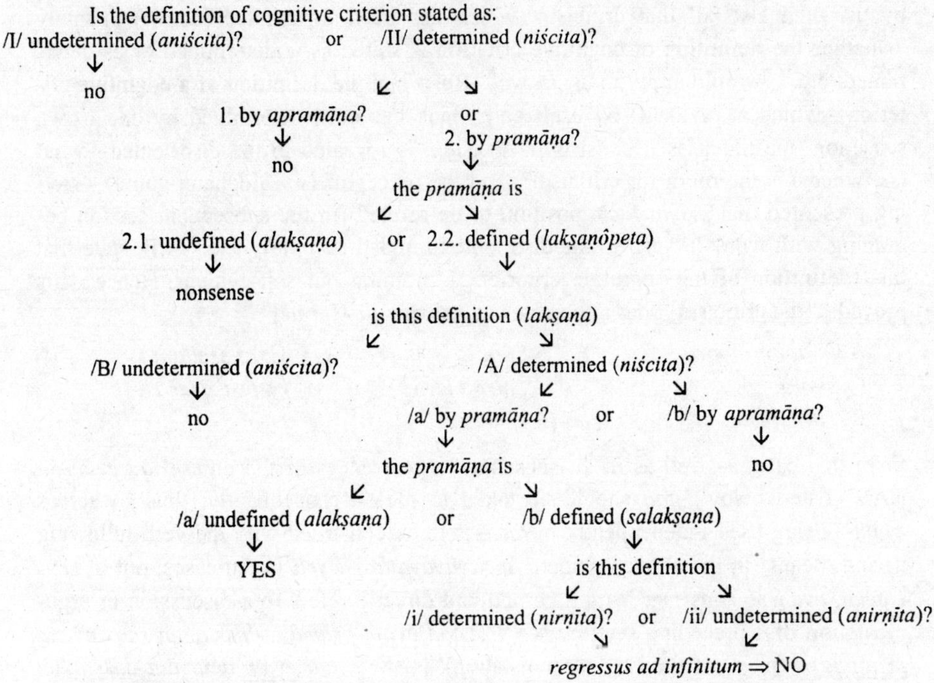

For the refutation of the above argumentation cf. NAV 3, especially the conclusion: *nirṇītaṁ tal-lakṣaṇam adhyakṣeṇa, tasya vyavasāya-rūpatvād, vacanaṁ punar viparītâropa-nirākaraṇe vyāpriyata iti sthitam.* (p. 30 of the translation)

225 Cf. n. 212 on *sāmpratam* opening the commentary section on NA 2.

226 Lit. 'with compassion the province of which are they.'

227 Lit. 'which is not contrary' (*aviparīta*).

228 Cf. p. 28 ff.

229 Lit. 'based in the middle of.'

230 Viz., in his criticism the opponent assumes the definition of cognitive criterion as something that should be first proved, although it is in fact already proved. Cf. NAṬ *ad loc.*: ***siddha-sādhyatā-madhya-pratibaddhatvād*** *iti. ayam abhiprāyaḥ:*[a] *yadi navaṁ*[b] *pramāṇa-lakṣaṇam abhidhīyate 'smābhis tadā yad uktaṁ "pramāṇa-lakṣaṇam aniścitaṁ*[c] *niścitaṁ vâbhidhīyata" ity-ādi tat samastam api dūṣaṇam asmākaṁ laged api; yadā tu svataḥ sato*[d] *vyavasāya-rūpatvāt sva-saṁvedanena nirṇītasya*[e] *ca pramāṇa-lakṣaṇasya vyāmūḍhān prati prakāśaḥ, kas*[f] *tadā doṣâvakāśaḥ? etac ca* ***vyāmūḍha-manaso 'pi pratîty-ādi*** *pūrva-pakṣam utthāpya svata evâtispaṣṭam ācāryo 'bhidhāsyati, tataḥ sthitam etan:*[g] *na* ***bādhâvidhāyî****ti.*— '[A Gloss on the phrase:] "[an argument] in which that to-be-proved is [already] proved". Such is the intention: if a new definition of a cognitive criterion were stated

by us, then also all that criticism, which has been formulated [above]—namely "whether the definition of cognitive criterion is stated as undetermined or as determined, etc."—would apply to us, as well. But when the definition of a cognitive criterion—which is [evident] by itself and which has been determined by one's own sensation, inasmuch as it consists in decision, is revealed to the disoriented—what (*sc.* where) is the room for criticism? And the preceptor (*sc.* Siddharṣi-gaṇin)—having presented that *prima facie* position to be refuted [in the subsequent section beginning with words]: "also to the disoriented-minded [people]," etc.—will state that this [definition of the cognitive criterion] is nothing but self-evident. Hence, it is proved: "[the criticism] does not create any subversion [for us]".'

[a] A,C: *abhiprāyo.* [b] V: *na.* [c] C: *anaścitaṁ.*
[d] C: *svato.* [e] A: *nirnītasya.* [f] C: *prakāśakas.*
[g] C: *sthitam en.*

[231] In this case, as well as in all subsequent occurrences of the phrase *tad evaṁ* in NAV (listed below), *tad* should be taken to mean 'consequently; thus'; whereas *evaṁ*—being used independently of *tad*—is to be construed with the verb following it, and means 'in the above manner.' In *Nyāyâvatāra-vivṛti* in ten cases, out of seventeen, *evaṁ* is construed with a gerund and directly refers to a discussion or argumentation of a preceding section: NAV 3: *tad evaṁ pramāṇa-lakṣaṇaṁ sāmānyena pratipādya* (p. 30 of the English translation), NAV 5: *tad evam anumāna-lakṣaṇaṁ pratipādya* (p. 42 of the English translation), NAV 8: *tad evaṁ svârthânumāna-lakṣaṇaṁ pratipādya* (p. 48 of the English translation), NAV 12: *tad evaṁ dvayor api parârthatāṁ pratipādya* (p. 55 of the English translation), NAV 14: *tad evam arthataḥ pakṣâdīn prastutya* (p. 59 of the English translation), NAV 24: *tad evaṁ hetv-ābhāsān pratipādya* (p. 71 of the English translation), NAV 25: *tad evaṁ sādharmyeṇa dṛṣṭântâbhāsān pratipādya* (p. 74 of the English translation), NAV 27: *tad evaṁ vyāvahārika-pramāṇasya pratyakṣa-parokṣa-svârtha-parârhâdi-bheda-bhinnasya lakṣaṇaṁ pratipādya* (p. 79 of the English translation), NAV 28: *tad evaṁ pramāṇa-viṣaye lakṣaṇa-saṁkhyā-vipratipattī nirākṛtya* (p. 82 of the English translation), NAV 31: *tad evaṁ naya-pramāṇa-svarūpaṁ pratipādya* (p. 126 of the English translation). At least in one case, in a similar context, *evaṁ* is combined with a gerund in its typical role—i.e. as an indicator pointing out to the manner, in which an action has been accomplished—however, without *tad*—that normally indicates a consequence drawn from the previous passage (*sc.* 'consequently; thus'), which also proves the independent use of *tad* and *evaṁ*—i.e. in NAV 21: *evaṁ pakṣâdi-lakṣaṇaṁ pratipādyêdānīṁ ... vaktavyāḥ* (p. 65 of the English translation). In the passage in question there is no place for the use of *tad*, inasmuch as a new section on fallacies is thereby started. In two cases *evaṁ* is construed with a past participle and likewise refers to a conclusion resulting from the preceding section: NAV 29: *tad evaṁ na sa kaścana vikalpo 'sti vastu-gocaro yo 'tra naya-saptake nântar-yātîti sarvâbhiprāya-saṅgrāhakā ete iti sthitam* (p. 98 of the English translation) and in NAV 29: *tad evaṁ pratyakṣe vivikta-vastu-grāhiṇi sakala-pramāṇa-praṣṭhe prasādhite* (p. 115 of the English translation). In a similar role—viz., that of

qualifying an action—*evaṁ* is used, though not directly, with verbs or participles, in NAV 26: *tad evaṁ parârthânumānaṁ vyācakṣaṇena yad uktam ... tat pakṣa-hetu-dṛṣṭântānāṁ sâbhāsānāṁ pratipādanāt prāyaḥ paryantitam* (p. 78 of the English translation), in NAV 29: *tad evaṁ bahir antaś caîkâneka-rūpatve pramāṇataḥ sthiteḥ svalakṣaṇasya* (p. 89 of the English translation) and in NAV 29: *tad evaṁ pramāṇa-prasiddhârthâpalāpitvād vyavahāro durnayaḥ* (p. 117 of the English translation). Besides, in the following cases, which may at first appear to constitute exceptions, *evaṁ* refers directly to foregoing argumentation. Accordingly, in NAV 23: *tad evam ekânta-dvaye 'pi ye ye hetavas te te yukteḥ samānatayā viruddhaṁ na vyabhicaranti* (p. 70 of the English translation), *evam* refers to two inconclusive ways of reasoning demonstrated just before; in NAV 29: *tad evam aneka-dharma-parītârtha-grāhikā buddhiḥ pramāṇam, tad-dvārâyātaḥ punar ... nayaḥ* (p. 107 of the English translation), *evam* relates directly the two conclusive definitions of *pramāṇa* and *naya* to former paragraphs that offer their respective expositions. These peculiarities of the phrase *tad evaṁ* are not observed in the case of single occurrences of *tad*. The use of *tad* as an indicator of a consequence or of a conclusion (in the sense of *tasmāt*) is widely attested, cf. the way Durveka Miśra explicates *tad* occurring in NBṬ$_1$ 2.20 (*tad ayam arthaḥ*—p. 110.12) in his DhPr 2.20: ***ayam artha iti***. *yata evam uktam* ***tat*** *tasmād ayaṁ tātparyârthaḥ* (p. 111.18).

[232] Thus, the criticism produced in NAV 2—ending with the conclusion: *tan na pramāṇa-lakṣaṇâbhidhānôpāyo 'sti, tasmāt prasiddhāni pramāṇānîty aṅgī-kartavyam iti* (p. 29 of the translation)—is rejected.

[233] Cf. n. 212.

[234] Lit. 'regarding the number, the province of which is only cognitive criterion [in general].'

[235] The verse is incorporated into ṢDSa as verse no. 56.

[236] This is how I render the Sanskrit solution of the compound: *tat-bhāvas tattā tayā*; the author follows here Pāṇ 5.1.119.

[237] For the derivation of *artha* from √*ṛ* see UṇādiS$_1$ 2.4 (=164): *uṣi-kuṣi-gârtibhyas thaN*.—'[The affix] *than* is added to [the roots] √*uṣ* (*sc. auṣṭha*), √*kuṣ* (*sc. koṣṭha*), √*gai* (*sc. gāyā*) and √*ṛ* (*sc. artha*).'

[238] The phrase *iti hṛdayam* is apparently used here in the sense of *iti arthaḥ*, in order to avoid plethoric mention (in two different meanings!) of *artha* in the short sentence. The phrase itself is not so unusual; I can think of at least one more occurrence of it: SVM 7.38 (p. 33.1): *idam atra hṛdayam. yathā tvan-mate pṛthivītvâbhisambandhāt pṛthivī tatra ...*

[239] See YDī$_2$ *ad* SKā 5, p. 76: "*śrotr-ādi-vṛttiḥ*" *iti vārṣagaṇaḥ*. as well as YDī$_2$ *ad* SKā 1ab, p. 5.11: *śrotr-ādi-vṛttiḥ pratyakṣam*. WEZLER–MOTEGI refer to PS: Peking. Ce.3B1, Derge Ce.3a3; NV and NVTṬ on NS 1.1.5.

The above formulation, slightly extended, occurs also, e.g. in. PMī 1.1 § 114 as is described there as the position of the early Sāṁkhya: *śrotr-ādi-vṛttir avikalpikā pratyakṣam iti vṛddha-sāṁkhyāḥ*.

[240] The propounders of *vijñapti-matratā*, e.g. the Yogācāra school of Buddhism, are meant, cf. NAṬ *ad loc.*: ***ye iti***—*yogâcārâdayaḥ*. But see also Diṅnāga in ĀPVṛ 1: *jñānena svarūpa[m eva] nirdhāryate, tad-ākāratayā jāyamānatvāt*.—'Cognition (*sc.* consciousness) ascertains only its intrinsic nature, because it arises in the form of that [object].' Also Sthiramati in TVBh, p. 17: *evaṁ bāhyârthâbhāvād vijñānam evârthâkāram utpadyate*.—'In this way only consciousness originates in the form of an object, without any external object.'

[241] Devabhadra-sūri explains in NAṬ *ad loc.*: *santāno jñāna-pravāhaḥ* ...—'Personal series is a stream of cognition ...' It should be borne in mind, however, that the term *santāna*, 'chain, series, sequence,' is a Buddhist term denoting 'series of moments constituting an illusory personality,' as well. Hence the expression *jñāna-santāna* refers not only to a train of thoughts, or a series of momentary ideas responsible for the continuous flow of cognition / psychic occurrences, but also points to the phenomenon of illusory personality. For this reason I render this phrase as above in order to comprise these two ideas.

[242] Cf. NAṬ *ad loc.*: ***itarathêty-ādi***. *santāno jñāna-pravāhaḥ, tasmād vivakṣitād anye santânāntarāṇi*. ***tad-anumānasya*** *santānântara-sādhakânumānasya, tathā hi: vivakṣita-devadattâder anyatra yajñadattâdau vyāpāra-vyāhārau buddhi-pūrvakau, vyāpāra-vyāhāratvāt, sampratipanna-vyāpāra-vyāhāravad iti santānântara-sādhakam anumānam*[a], *svasmin*[b] *vyāpāra-vyāhārayor jñāna-kāryatvena pratibandha-niścayāt. etasya cânumānasya svapna-dṛṣṭântenôpaplavo bhrāntatvam. tathā hi: yathā sarve pratyayā nirālambanāḥ, pratyayatvāt, svapna-pratyayavad*[c] *iti*[d] *bhavad-abhiprāyeṇa bahir-artha-sādhanasya nirālambanatayā bāhyârthâbhāvāḥ, tathā santānântara-sādhanasyâpi nirālambanatayā santānântarâbhāvaḥ*.—'[A gloss on]: "In the opposite case," etc. "Personal series" [means] "a stream of cognition". [Personal series that are] different from this [particular personal series] in question are "other personal series". "Their inference" [means] the inference proving [the existence of] other personal series; For it is as follows: "[The thesis:] In someone else than Devadatta, etc., in question, say, in Yajñadatta and in other [people] the activity and utterances are preceded by understanding, [the logical reason:] because they are activity and utterances, [the example:] just like [any] performed activities and utterances [are preceded by understanding]"—so [operates] the inference proving [the existence of] other personal series, because activity and declarations are determined [to possess] the invariable connection as being the effects of cognition in [the case of the agent] himself. And this inference is falsified, [i.e.] erroneous, by the example of dream. For it is as follows: just like there is no external object in conformity with your intention—namely: "all instances of cognition have no objective substratum, because [they are a sort of] cognition, like cognition in [the state] of dreaming"—inasmuch as the proof [of the existence] of external objects has no objective substra-

tum, in the same way there are no other personal series, because also the proof [of the existence] of other personal series has no objective substratum.'

[a] H,V: °-*sādhakànumānam*. [b] H,V: *tasmin*. [c] H,V: °-*pratyavad*.

[c] The proof formula (*sarve pratyayā nirālambanāḥ, pratyayatvāt, svapna-pratyayavat*) occurs below in NAṬ 7, n. 334. Cf. also NAV 24 (p.72 of the English translation).

[243] The criticism underscores a serious drawback of the Yogācāra: solipsism.

[244] NB_1 1.4: *tatra pratyakṣaṁ kalpanâpoḍham abhrāntam*. See also PVin I_1 4 (p. 40, n. 1). Cf. also Diṅnāga's formulation in PS 1.C,k3cd: *pratyakṣaṁ kalpanâpoḍhaṁ nāma-jāty-ādy-asaṁyuktam*.—'Perception is free from conceptual construction disconnected from name, class, etc.'
Tibetan translations evince minor variance from the original, viz., Vasudhararakṣita & Seṅ-rgyal, 14a.4: མངོན་སུམ་རྟོག་དང་བྲལ་བའོ་མིང་དང་རིགས་སོགས་སུ་སྦྱོར་བའོ། ('Perception is free from conceptual construction, which is [in its turn] connected with name, class, etc.') and Kanakavarman and Dad-paḥi śes-rab, 94b.3: མངོན་སུམ་རྟོག་པ་དང་བྲལ་བ་མིང་དང་རིགས་སོགས་བསྲེས་པའོ། ('Perception is free from conceptual construction, which is [in its turn] associated with name, class, etc.')
Comp. also the definition found in *Nyāya-praveśa* (p. 7.12–3), bearing striking similarity to the one formulated by Diṅnāga, which fact was initially one of the reasons responsible for the wrong attribution of Śaṅkarasvāmin's manual to Diṅnāga: *tatra pratyakṣaṁ kalpanâpoḍhaṁ. yaj jñānam arthe rūpâdau nāma-jāty-ādi-kalpanā-rahitam tad*.

[245] *kheṭayanti*, a doubtful word, cf. MW: '***kheṭana***—n. chase, hunting' and '***ākheṭa***—n. chase, hunting.'

[246] For the refutation see p. 33 ff.

[247] Cf. n. 675.

[248] Cf. Dharmakīrti in NB_1 5–6: /5/ *abhilāpa-saṁsarga-yogya-pratibhāsa-pratītiḥ kalpanā; /6/ tayā rahitaṁ … pratyakṣam*.—'/5/ Conceptual construction is awareness [in the form] of representation [of an object,] which is capable of being associated with speech designation. /6/ Perception … is devoid of that [association with speech designation].'

[249] See PVin I_1 263b, p. 48.21–30: | *gal te raṅ gi rjod par byed pa'i khyad par la ltos pa'i don ñid śes pas ṅes par bya ba yin no źes bya ba de ltar ṅes pa yin na | da ni dbaṅ po'i śes pa'i brjod pa yaṅ ldog par 'gyur te | rjod par byed pa'i khyad par dran par mi rigs pa'i phyir ro || gaṅ gi phyir don mthoṅ ba yod na ni de las don gyi khyad par ñe ba la mthoṅ ba'i sgra dran par 'gyur ba yin te* <|> *me daṅ du ba bźin no || 'dis sgra med par don mi mthoṅ źiṅ ma mthoṅ na yaṅ sgra'i khyad par mi dran la ma dran na sbyor bar mi byed do || ma sbyar na rtogs par mi 'gyur ba'i phyir 'gro ba ma lus pa loṅ ba ñid du 'gyur ro || = nanu evaṁ svâbhidhāna-viśeṣaṇâpekṣā evârthā*

vijñānair vyavasīyanta iti [prāptam], nivṛttêdānīm indriya-jñāna-vārttā, abhidhāna-viśeṣa-smṛter ayogāt. sati hy artha-darśane 'rtha-<viśeṣa>-saṁnidhau dṛṣṭe śabde tataḥ smṛtiḥ syād, agni-dhūmavat. na câyam aśabdam artham paśyati, apaśyan na śabda-viśeṣam anusmarati, ananusmaran na yojayati; ayojayan na pratyetîti āyātam āndhyam aśeṣasya jagataḥ. (Vetter after AJP, p. 139.11–140.7)

250 *dhāndhya*, a doubtful word; it must have occurred as such also to Devabhadra-sūri who considered it necessary not only to provide his own elucidation, but also to cite at least one more instance, when the word is used, as well as to give different readings, NAṬ *ad loc.*: ***dhāndhyād iti*** *dhandhyo jaḍas*[a] *tasya bhāvo dhāndhyaṁ jāḍyam, yad*[b] *viniścaya-ṭīkāyām dharmottaraḥ*[c]: *'dhandhyo jaḍa'*[g] *iti. kvacit tu*[d] *dhyāndhyād iti pāṭhas; tadâivaṁ vyākhyā—dhiyo buddher āndhyaṁ dhyāndhyaṁ*[e], *paraṁ*[f] *nâyaṁ paurāṇikaḥ.*—'"Foolish" means "inane"; the state of being such is foolishness, i.e. inanity; like Dharmottara [said] in [*Pramāṇa-*]*viniścaya-ṭīkā*: "foolish means inane."[g] But, occasionally, there is a various reading: *dhyāndhyād* [instead of *dhāndhyād*]; it is explained in the following way: "the blindness of understanding, i.e. of reason, is foolishness, [i.e. inanity]"; but this [reading] is not canonical.'

[a] A,H,V: *jaḍaḥ*. [b] H,V omit *yad*. [c] H,V omit *dharmottaraḥ*.
[d] H,V omit *tu*. [e] H,V add: *jāḍyam*. [f] C: *para*.

[g] I was unable to localise the exact source of the quotation in Dharmottara's *Pramāna-viniścaya-ṭīkā*.

251 Cf. PVin I_1 263ab, p. 48.30–50.11: *don ñe ba ñid kyis naṅ gi 'du byed sad par ḥyas pa des dran par 'gyur gyi don mthoṅ bas ni ma yin no že na | ... || de'i phyir mthoṅ bas na 'di sgra ma sbyar ba'i don ñid mthoṅ ba yin no* | = AJP, p. 140.7–142.2.

252 This is a recapitulation of the Buddhist position above: *artha-sāmarthyenôdīyate, ... na cârthe dhvanayaḥ santi* (p. 32 ff. of the translation). The qualification of *artha* above, i.e. *aśabdaka*, which is a *bahū-vṛhi* compound, corresponds to the phrase *na cârthe dhvanayaḥ santi*.

253 *vibhrama* is explained as *bhrāntatva* in DhPr, pp. 55 and as *vyāmoha* in NBṬ 66.

254 The text needs to be emended here by inserting—into position (2) below—another negative particle *na* on account of the context itself, for the sentence seems to be by no means constructed untypically, and its structure apparently is as follows: (1) the opponent's hypothetical thesis: *vibhramād iti cet*, (2) its general rejection: ***na***, (3) the ground for the rejection of the form: "not only—but also", i.e. "***na*** ... ***eva*** *pratibhāti*—... ***api*** ...". Cf. also Devabhadra-gaṇin's commentary, NAṬ *ad loc.*: ***tatrâsato 'pîti***[a] *paramâṇu-lakṣaṇe 'rthe 'vidyamānasyâpi pratibhāsanād*[b] *iti*[c] *śeṣaḥ.*—'[A gloss on]: "even though it is not there." It remains [to be supplemented]: because a l s o what does not exist in the object that consists in infinitesimal atoms, [that are invisible by their nature], is represented [in cognition].'

[a] C: *tatrâsītopati*. [b] A,C,H,V: *pratibhāsanāt*; [b] H,V add *jñāne iti*.

[255] This is a paraphrase rather than a word-for-word citation of the original: *smaraṇa-sampāditaṁ tad-abhidhāyaka-dhvani-saṁyojanaṁ pratīkṣyamāṇam tāvad āsīta* (cf. p. 32 of the translation).

[256] Cf. p. 33 of the translation.

[257] Alternatively, instead of Causative form of √*nud*—'to resolve', we may read *nôdayate* (*na* + *udayate*): 'as long as the subsequent pair of conceptualisations arises.' However, Devabhadra does take it to be a Causative of √*nud*, cf. NAṬ 4 *ad loc.*: *nodayata iti aya-vayêty-ādi-daṇḍaka-dhātuḥ, nodayaîti pāṭhe tu 'a-ṭa-paṭa-iṭa-kaṭa-i-ga.av' ity asya prayogaḥ.* I failed to track down the source of the derivation explicated here; perhaps it was borrowed from the manual on grammar by Hemacandra or a work of some other Jaina grammarian, which was not within my reach. Formation of any derivatives of √*nud* seems to absent in *Uṇādi-sūtras* (AuṇP, UṇādiK, $UṇādiS_2$ / $UṇādiS_1$). We find it, however, in DhP 6.2,132: *ṇuda preraṇe* (in the sense 'to incite').

[258] I have failed to identify the source of the quotation.

[259] Cf. n. 261.

[260] Cf. NAṬ 4 *ad loc.*: ***ayam iti***. *indriyajaḥ*.

[261] Cf. NAṬ 4 *ad loc.*: ***vikalpa-kalpo***[a] *vikalpa-sadṛśaḥ,*[b] *kalpa-śabdasyôpamârthatvāt*[c].[d] *yad āha:*[e]

sāmarthya-varṇanāyāṁ ca chedane karaṇe tathā /
aupamye câdhivāse ca kalpa-śabdaṁ vidur budhāḥ // [†]

—'[The expression] "resembling a conceptualisation" [means] "similar to a conceptualisation," because the speech element "resembling" [has the meaning] of similitude. Accordingly, it has been said:

> "The learned recognise the speech element "resembling" in [the meaning of] description of efficacy and in [the sense of] medical treatment, likewise in [the sense of] procedure, as well as in [the sense of] resemblance and in [the sense of] abode".'

[a] H,V: °-*kalpaḥ*. [b] A: °-*sadṛśaḥ //* .
[c] H,V: °-*śabdasya upamârthatvāt*. [d] A: // . [e] A: // .
[†] I have failed to identify the source of the quotation.

[262] Cf. NAṬ 4 *ad loc.*: ***eṣa*** *indriyajo vikalpaḥ*.

[263] Cf. Devabhadra-gaṇin's gloss on the formation of the verb, NAṬ 4 *ad loc.*: ***udagrāhîti*** *upanyastam*[a], *ut-pūrva iN-anto grahi-rūpa-nyāse vartate*; *yad ajayaḥ: udgrāhitam upanyaste baddhâgny-āhitayor*[b] *apîti.*—'"Has been given an account of" means "has been brought forward"; the ending "iN", preceded by [the prefix] "ut", operates with regard to forming the verb-from "grahi"; just as Ajaya [said]: "has been given an account of—has been brought forward—of both: the one who has put off

and who has laid down fire".' Devabhadra refers in all probability to the lexicographical work by Ajayapāla, who flourished at beginning of twelfth century, cf. VOGEL (1979: 325–6), viz., *Ajaya-koṣa* (AKo = *Nānârtha-saṁgraha* of Ajayapāla, ed. by T.R. Chintamani, MUSS 10, Madras, 1937). Alas, this publication was not available to me.

[a] C: *upanyasta*. [b] A: *baddhâgnâhitayor* / *baddhâgrâhitayor*?;
C: *baddhâśahitayor* / *baddhaśehitayor*?

[264] Now the author presents the genuine position of the Jainas.

[265] Cf. an unidentified quotation in *Dravyâlaṅkāra-svopajña-ṭīkā* p. 140, see Muni JAMBŪVIJAYA (1981: 139.1–2): *yat pratyakṣaṁ tan nâbhilāpa-saṁsarga-yogya-pratibhāsaṁ yathā nirvikalpakam. yad abhilāpa-saṁsarga-yogya-pratibhāsaṁ na tat pratyakṣaṁ yathā śābda-laiṅgika-vikalpau*.

[266] I.e., on account of both leaving subliminal impression of a thing in the mind and awakening a memory of it, cf. Devabhadra-gaṇin's gloss: ***yata iti*** *smṛti-bījâdhāna-tat-pratibhodhanābhyām*.—'"On account of which" [means] "due to leaving the seed of recollection and due to its awakening".'

[267] In other words: perception that is free from any conceptual construction could never be experienced by any cogniser.

[268] Cf. the definition, p. 32.

[269] Cf. p. 32.

[270] Lit.: 'because now in this case [non-erroneousness] does not take place together with this …'

[271] Cf. NAṬ *ad loc*.: ***anyathêty-ādi*** *nirṇayena grahāṇâbhāve* …

[272] I.e., neither what is directly perceived nor what is not perceived could be cognised. Cf. NAṬ *ad loc*.: *dṛṣṭasyâpi kṣaṇika-svalakṣaṇasya adṛṣṭād anatiśāyanaṁ aviśeṣo, adṛṣṭânatiśāyanaṁ tasmāt*.—'Momentary individual thing, even though it is experienced, does not go beyond what is not [directly] experienced; [i.e.] is not different [from it]; [since] it does not go beyond what is not experienced—therefore [everyday practice would not proceed].'

[273] Granting the reading of Mss. A and B is genuine, viz., *tasyâsākṣāt-kāritayā artha-grahaṇa-rūpatvād*, the passage should be rendered differently: 'because this [indirect cognition] consists in grasping an object, [only] inasmuch as [it] perceives [the object] indirectly.' Such an interpretation, however, would convey a meaning that would be incongruous with the idea of perception that is said to grasp directly.

[274] NAV 1: *sarvaṁ vākyaṁ sâvadhāraṇaṁ pravartate* (p. 17 of the English translation); cf. also NAṬ 29: *sarvaṁ vākyaṁ sâvadhāraṇam iti-nyāyāt* (p. 123 of the English translation).

[275] NS 1.1.4.

[276] MS_1 1.1.4. Devabhadra-sūri construes *puruṣa* with *buddhi-janma*, cf. NAṬ *ad loc.*: ***sat-samprayogêty-ādi***. *satā vidyamānena vastunā indriyāṇāṁ samprayoge sambandhe sati puruṣasya yo jñānôtpādas tat pratyakṣam. ādi-śabdāt sākṣāt-kāri-pramā-sādhanaṁ pratyakṣam ity-ādi gr̥hyate.*

[277] Cf. a similar idea in the context of the Mīmāṁsaka definition of perception (MS_1 1.1.4)—criticised by Jayarāśi, though—in TUS_1 5.3b, p. 278.17–19: *vidyamānôpalambhanatvāt kila pratyakṣaṁ vijñānaṁ vidyamānam avabodhayati.* Like E. FRANCO (n. 349), I was unable to identify that quotation, either.

[278] Cf. a similar idea in the context of the Naiyāyika definition of perception (NS 1.1.4) in TUS_1 1.42 (p. 140.19–20): [*indriyôtpādya-pratyakṣaṁ*] *vijñānaṁ svabhāvatayâiva vedyate, nâkārântareṇa.*

[279] Cf. n. 102.

[280] Cf. PS 1.7ab: *kalpanâpi sva-saṁvittāv*[a] *iṣṭā nârthe vikalpanāt.*—'Also conceptual construction is accepted [as a perception] with regard to its self-cognition[a]; [it is not accepted, however, as perception] with regard to an [external] object because [the conceptual construction] conceptualises [the object],' and the subsequent commentary of PSV on PS 1.7cd: *anumāna-tat-phalâdi-jñānaṁ pūrvânubhūta-kalpanayêti na pratyakṣam.*—'The cognition [consisting in] inference and its result, etc., is not perception, inasmuch as it is a conceptual construction of what has been previously experienced.' Cf. also PV 3.287:

śabdârtha-grāhi yad yatra taj jñānaṁ tatra kalpanā /
svarūpaṁ ca na śabdârthas tatrâdhyakṣam ato 'khilam //—

—'Whenever a cognition grasps the meaning of a speech-unit [that denotes an object] with reference to [that] particular [object], it is a conceptual construction with reference to that particular [object]; and [whenever] the intrinsic nature [is grasped], not a the meaning of a speech-unit, [this cognition] is a perception in its own right.'

[a] The term *sva-saṁvitti*, and similar ones, connotes the self-illuminatory character of cognition, which renders another second-level cognition-cognising cognition to cognise the first-level object-cognising cognition unnecessary. In such a way, one avoids *regressus ad infinitum*, viz., the situation when the second-level cognition-cognising cognition would necessitate the existence of a third-level cognition cognising the second-level cognition, etc. The idea is expressed, e.g. in TSa_1 2012:

svarūpa-vedanāyânyad vedakaṁ na vyapekṣate /
na câviditam astîdam ity artho 'yaṁ sva-saṁvidaḥ //

—'[Such a cognition which] neither requires another [cognition] cognising its own form nor [itself] remains uncognised—such is the meaning of self-cognition.'

[281] See NAV 1: *na câpṛthag-bhūtasya tad-viviktaṁ vaktuṁ śakyam iti, ataḥ pārthakyenôpanyāsaḥ* (p. 21 of the translation).

[282] Cf. VāVi: *tādṛg-avinâbhāvi-dharmôpadarśanaṁ hetuḥ*; cf. also FRAUWALLNER (1957/a: 118): 'Der Grund ist die Mitteilung einer Eigenschaft, welche mit einem solchen (zu Beweisenden) untrennbar verbunden ist.'

[283] 'Too' (*api*) links the NA 4 and 5, i.e. '***also here*** [in NA 5] the syntax is similar to that of the aphorism 4.' The definition is composed of the element expressing the definiendum (*lakṣya-nirdeśa*), or the thing to be indicated and delineated, as well as of the element expressing the definiens (*lakṣaṇa-nirdeśa*), or indicating the thing to be understood. On the idea of *lakṣaṇa* being the indicator and *lakṣya*––the indicated entity, also in the grammatical context, see MATILAL (1985: 177).

[284] I.e., analogically to the grammatical elucidation of the word '*pramāṇa*' in the portion of NAV 0, beginning with *adhunâkṣarâtho vivriyate* ... (§ 0.6, p. 7 of the translation).

[285] The idea to render *anumeya*, lit. 'what is to be inferred' or 'what is aimed at in the process of inference', by *inferendum* was suggested to me by STAAL 1973.

[286] For similar wording and explanation see (1) PVinṬ$_2$ 3,15–16 and NBṬ$_1$ 39.9: *liṅga-grahaṇa-sambandha-smaraṇasya paścān mānam anumānam.*—'The cognition subsequent to the reminiscence of the relation and to grasping the inferential sign is inference'; cf. STEINKELLNER–KRASSER (1989: 73): 'Wodurch sich nach (*paścāt*) dem Erfassen des Anzeichens und der Erinnering an die Verbindung ein sicheres Erkennen (*māna*) ergibt, das ist eine Schlußfolgerung (*anu-māna*)'; (2) NBh 1.1.3: *mitena liṅgena liṅgino 'rthasya paścān mānam anumānam.*—'The subsequent cognition of an object, which is probandum, on account of cognised inferential sign is inference'; (3) NBh 1.1.5: *liṅga-liṅgino sambandha-darśanaṁ liṅga-darśanaṁ câbhisambandhyate, liṅga-liṅgino sambaddhayor darśanena liṅga-smṛtir abhisambadhyate, smṛtyā liṅga-darśanena câpratyakṣo 'numīyate.*—'The perception of the connection of the inferential sign and the probandum is related to the perception of inferential sign; the reminiscence of inferential sign is related to the perception of the interrelated inferential sign and the probandum; and having remembered [that connection], something imperceptible is inferred on account of the perception of the inferential sign.'

[287] According to Pān.3.3.169: *arhé kṛ́tya-tṛ́C-aś ca.*—'[The *kṛt*-affixes, denoted by] *kṛ́tya* and *tṛ́c* [are introduced to express that *x*] deserves an action.'

[288] According to Pān.3.3.172: *śak-i lIṄ ca.*—'[The *kṛt*-affixes, denoted by *kṛ́tya*] and *lIṄ* are introduced to express that that *x*] is capable of [accomplishing an action].'

[289] Cf. NB$_1$ 2.5–7,11–12: (5) *trairūpyaṁ punar liṅgasyânumeye sattvam eva*; (6) *sapakṣa eva sattvam*; (7) *asapakṣe câsattvam eva niścitam*, (11) *trīṇy eva ca liṅgāni*; (12) *anupalabdhiḥ svabhāva-kārye cêti.*—'(5) Next, the triple-formed criterion [of

the logical reason is discussed]; the presence of the inferential sign in the inferendum only, (6) the presence [of the property] in the homologue only, (7) the absence [of a property] in the heterologue only ... (11) There are only three [kinds of] inferential sign, [namely] (12) non-comprehension, [essential] identity and effect.' One of the earliest passages available to the modern reader—beside *Shun Zhong Lun* attributed to Asaṅga and *Vāda-vidhāna* of Vasubandhu (cf. FRANCO 1990: 200–201)—which presents the theory of the triple-formed criterion of valid logical reason (*trairūpya*) is TŚ 2.1, p. 13.16–17: *asmābhis tri-lakṣaṇo hetuḥ sthāpitaḥ. tad yathā: pakṣa-dharmaḥ sapakṣatvaṁ vipakṣa-vyāvṛttiś ca.* The theory of *trairūpya* is dealt with in the second chapter (*anumāna-pariccheda*) of Diṅnāga's PS and stated in NM 2 (as quoted in NVTṬ 1.1.35.6, p. 289.16–17):

sapakṣe sann asan dvedhā pakṣa-dharmaḥ punas tridhā /
pratyekam asapakṣe ca sad-asad dvividhatvataḥ //

It is also dealt with in NP_1, p. 1.5–6: *hetus tri-rūpaḥ. kiṁ punas trairūpyam? pakṣa-dharmatvaṁ sapakṣe sattvaṁ vipakṣe câsattvam iti.*—'The logical reason has triple form. What is the triple-formed criterion like then? The inherence of a property in the locus, the presence [of a property] in the homologue, and the absence [of a property] in the heterologue.' Cf. also $NBṬ_1$ 2.5, p. 19.4–5: *anvyaya-vyatireka-pakṣa-dharmatva-niścayo liṅga-vyāpārâtmakatvād avaśya-kartavya iti sarveṣu rūpeṣu niścita-grahaṇam apekṣaṇīyam.*—'The grasping of the determined [element] in all three forms should be observed, so that the determination of positive concomitance, of negative concomitance and of the inherence of a property in the locus—inasmuch as [this determination] consists in the activity concerning the inferential sign—should be made necessary.' On the theory of *trairupya* see FRANCO 1990, OETKE 1994/b.

290 The first hemistich is beyond doubt taken from PS 2.5cd, which corresponds to PS Ce 4b.1–2: རྗེས་དཔག་བྱ་དང་དེ་མཚུངས་ལ། །ཡོད་དང་མེད་ལ་མེད་པའི། (= folio 111a.6 [Kanakavarman / Dad-paḥi śes-rab] and folio 30a.1 [Vasudhararakṣita / Seṅ-rgyal]) of the Peking edition PSV.

It is quoted by Uddyotakara in *Nyāya-vārttika* with a mistake (or misprint?): *anumāne 'tha tat-tulye sadbhāvo nâstivâsati* / (cf. HAYES (1980: 270, n. 60) and OETKE (1994/b: 59, n. 14). There may be some considerable amount of doubt whether the authorship of the second hemistich can be ascribed to Diṅnāga and whether its source is PS at all.

The Tibetan translation of the second half of the *kārikā*—viz., PS 2.6ab—reads: །འདིར་ནི་ཤེས་པ་འང་འཕངས་པ་ཡིན། །གང་ཕྱིར་ཤེས་བྱེད་དབང་བྱས་ཕྱིར།

Clearly, the meaning of PS 2.6ab as we have it from the Tibetan sources in no way corresponds to *niścitânupalambhâtma-kāryâkhyā hetavas traya*; cf. folio 111b.1 [Kanakavarman / Dad-paḥi śes-rab] and folio 30a.5 [Vasudhararakṣita / Seṅ-rgyal] of PSV in Hayes' translation: 'Q: In that case, should one not also mention the knowledge (of the indicator as a factor in inference)?[a] A: That is not necessary to mention, because [6a] *it is taken for granted here that there is also knowledge* (of the indicator). Q: How can what is not explicitly mentioned to be taken for granted? A: *Because (the indicator) is the principal one of the factors that produced knowledge* (of the indicator)' (1980: 253). [a Hayes, n. 64: *ji ltar rtags kyi yul can gyi shes pa (=liṅgaviṣayaṁ jñānam).*]

This much discussed passage of PS 2.5cd posits certain interpretational difficulties and I shall refrain myself here from further comments, and merely draw the attention of the reader to some secondary literature on the subject, e.g. RANDLE (1926: 22–25), HAYES (1980: 252–4), KATSURA (1983: 15/544) as well as OETKE (1994/b: 56 ff.). Diṅnāga's verse is quoted by Dharmakīrti in PVin II_1 5,1–2 (up to *niścita-*), partly altered though, cf. E. Steinkellner in PVin II_2, pp. 31–32, n. 57.

[291] VS_1 9.18; in fact the original text of VSU_1 reads: *asyêdaṁ kāryaṁ kāraṇaṁ sambandhi ekârtha-samavāyi virodhi cêti laiṅgikam.* Cf. the translation in HATTORI (1977: 219): '"This is the effect of *x*", "...the cause of *x*", "...the conjunct of *x*", "...something co-inhering with *x* in the same thing" or "...contradictory to *x*"—these are types of judgements based on an inferential mark.'

[292] Both editions H (p. 54.22/23) and V (p. 36.29/30) insert two following *pratīka*s of NAṬ referring to NAV 5 (H: p. 54.1 and V: p. 35.4) that read continuously as follows: |1| ***tat-putrâdīnām*** *iti. sa śyāmaḥ tat-putratvāt, paridṛśyamāna-putravad iti.* |2| ***ādîti****. ādi-śabdān nirupādhi-sambandha-bodha-samuttha-sādhya-pramā-sādhanam anumānam ity-ādi grahaḥ.* |3| *ādi-śabdāt pakvāny etāni āmra-phalāni, eka-śākhā-prabhavatvāt, upabhujyamānâmra-phalavad ity-ādi parigrahaḥ.* Both the editors, however, replaced three sections of two *pratīkas*. For the sake f convenience, I have preceded the three sections with |1|, |2|, |3|. The section |2| is, in fact, a reference to *ādi* of NAV above: "*pūrvavac cheṣavat sāmānyato-dṛṣṭam*" *ity-****ādi***. Mss. A and C read NAṬ *ad loc.* correctly: ***ādîti****. ādi-śabdān nirupādhi-sambandha-bodha-samuttha-sādhya-pramā-sādhanam anumānam ity-ādi grahaḥ. // Ø //*.—'By the word "etc." a reference [is made to] inference which [serves as] a proof for a valid cognition of probandum produced by the consciousness of the relation free from [any] extraneous condition [that could invalidate the inference].' This section is followed in both Mss. A and C by sections |1| and |3|, that belong to one *pratīka*, see n. 294 below.

The notion of *upādhi* is discussed, likewise, in note 294 below.

[293] NS 1.1.5. The complete *sūtra* runs as follows: *atha tat-pūrvakaṁ trividham anumānaṁ pūrvavac cheṣavat sāmānyato-dṛṣṭāntaṁ ca.* There is, however, much controversy about both the correct reading of the *sūtra* (*varia lectio* is: *sāmānyato 'dṛṣṭāntaṁ ca*) as well as the interpretation of the exact meaning these three obscure terms. Highly significant is the fact that Pakṣilasvāmin Vātsyāyana himself offers two parallel possible interpretations of these terms. The first of them is as follows: *pūrvavad iti yatra kāraṇena kāryam anumīyate, yathā meghônnatyā "bhaviṣyati vṛṣṭir" iti. śeṣavat tat yatra kāryeṇa kāraṇam anumīyate, pūrvôdaka-viparītam udakaṁ nadyāḥ pūrṇatvaṁ śīghratvaṁ ca dṛṣṭvā srotaso 'numīyate "bhūtā vṛṣṭir" iti. sāmānyato-dṛṣṭam vrajyā-pūrvakam anyatra dṛṣṭasyânyatra darśanam iti, tathā*

câdityasya, tasmād asty apratyakṣâpy ādityasya vrajyêti.—'The á priori [inference takes places] when the effect is inferred from the cause, for instance from the accumulation of clouds, [it is inferred] that "it will rain." The ā posteriori [inference takes places] when the cause is inferred from the effect; for instance, having seen the water[-level] of a river that is contrary to previous water[-level as well as its] overflow and velocity, one infers from the torrent that "it has rained." Commonly seen [means] the perception of [something] seen in one place that has been seen in another place after it has moved, and so is the sun, therefore, there must a movement of the sun, even though [the movement] is unperceived.' Pakṣilasvāmin explains subsequently the same terms in an alternative manner: *athavā: pūrvavad iti yatra yathā-pūrvaṁ pratyakṣa-bhūtayor anyatara-darśanenânyatarasyâpratyasyânumānam, yathā dhūmenâgnir iti. śeṣavan nāma: pariśeṣaḥ, sa ca prasakta-pratiṣedhe 'nyatrâprasaṅgācchiṣyamāṇe sampratyayaḥ, yathā "sad anityam" evam-ādinā dravya-guṇa-karmaṇām aviśeṣeṇa sāmānya-viśeṣa-samavāyebhyo vibhaktasya śabdasya tasmin dravya-guṇa-karma-guṇa-saṁśāye "na dravyam eka-dravyatvāt; na karma śabdântara-hetutvātyas tu viṣyate so 'yam" iti śabdasya guṇatva-pratipattiḥ. sāmānyato-dṛṣṭaṁ nāma: yatrâpratyakṣe liṅga-liṅginoḥ sambandhe kenacid arthena liṅgasya sāmānyād apratyakṣo liṅgī gamyate, yathêcchâdibhir ātmā, 'icchâdayo guṇāḥ, guṇāś ca dravya-saṁsthānāḥ, tadyadeṣāṁ sthānaṁ sa ātmā iti.* See also GBh$_1$, p. 51.29 *ad* SKā 5 (=GBh$_2$, p. 10.7–8): ***trividham anumānam ākhyātam.*** *pūrvavac cheṣavat sāmānyato-dṛṣṭāntaṁ cêti.*

The original meaning of these three terms, however, came into oblivion, and Vātsyāyana as well as other commentator like Uddyotakara, Jayantabhaṭṭa or Bhāsarvajña make guesses as to the true meaning of the terms in question. The problem is discussed in RUBEN (1928: 3, 158–161, nn. 15,16) and scrutinised further on in WEZLER 1969/a and WEZLER 1969/b, OBERHAMMER 1966 as well as offered a thorough analysis by MATILAL (1985: 29–42).

[294] Cf. NAṬ *ad loc.*: ***tat-putrâdīnām*** *iti. atrânumānaṁ.*[a] *sa śyāmaḥ tat-putratvāt, paridṛśyamāna-putravad iti. ādi-śabdāt pakvāny etāni āmra-phalāni, eka-śākhā-prabhavatvāt, upabhujyamānâmra-phalavad ity-ādi parigrahaḥ.*—'[A gloss on the phrase]: "being his son," etc. Here the inference [is as follows]: "He is dark-complexioned because he is his son, just like the son who is just being seen". By the word "etc." a reference [is made to the erroneous following reasoning]: "these mangoes are ripe, because they grow on the same branch, like the mango which is just being eaten".'

On the correct contents of this *pratīka* and the correct sequence of its fragments see note 292 above.

Malliṣeṇa furnishes an explicit explanation why the logical reason in question is thought to be invalid (cf. SVM 12.83, p. 76): *sādhanâvyāpakaḥ sādhyena samavyāptiś ca khalûpādhir abhidhīyate. tat-putratvâdinā śyāmatve sādhye śākâdy-āhāra-pariṇāmavat.*—'The extraneous condition, as one should realise, is called [such a property] which does not pervade the probans [completely] and which is co-extensive with the probandum; like a transformation [depending] on consumption of [a particular kind of] vegetable food, [while still within the mother's womb], in [the case of the proof formula] when being dark-complexioned is to be proved by the reason of being his son.' In order to vitiate the inference deemed to be invalid, Malliṣeṇa avails himself of the formal procedure and points out the extraneous condition, technically called *upādhi*, the very mention of which proves that the invariable connection between the probandum and probans is not natural or unconditional (*svābhāvika*), but adventitious or conditional (*aupādhika*), hence the whole inference is invalidated. Thus a mere occurrence of an extraneous condition (*upādhi*) in an inference renders it ineffective and invalid. It should be borne in mind that only the former variety of the invariable connection makes the inferential statement valid, cf. $\bar{A}TV_2$, p. 863: *kaḥ punar ayaṁ pratibandhaḥ? svābhāvikaḥ sambandhaḥ. kaḥ svabhāvârthaḥ? nirupādhitvam.* The definition of the extraneous condition, also rendered as 'associate condition' (cf. MATILAL (1985: 142)), formulated by Malliṣeṇa above (*sādhanâvyāpakaḥ sādhyena samavyāptiś ca khalûpādhir*) was one of two current formulations, a less known one, and we encounter it even in such late works like BhP 138 (BhP_1, p. 123–4; BhP_2 772):

sādhyasya vyāpako yas tu hetor avyāpakas tathā /
sa upādhir bhavet tasya niṣkarṣo 'yaṁ pradarśyate //

and in SMA thereon (*sādhyatvâbhimata-vyāpakatve sati sādhanatvâbhimatâvyāpakatvam upādhir ity arthaḥ*) or SDS_1 1.śl.9.ab (*Cārvāka-darśana*) p. 9 [SDS_2 1.97 (*Cārvāka-darśana*) p. 11]: *avyāpta-sādhane yaḥ sādhya-samavyāptir ucyate sa upādhiḥ.* The formulation of another, more prevalent definition, less restrictive, of the extraneous condition is to be found for instance in BhP_2 138: *sādhya-vyāpakatve sati sādhanâvyāpakatvam.* For a detailed discussion of the term *upādhi* cf. GANGOPADHYAY 1971 and MATILAL (1985: 142–145).

In other words, the invariable concomitance (*vyāpti*, cf. n. 174) in our case would be: *yatra yatra śākâdy-āhāratvaṁ tatra tatra śyāmatvaṁ* ('whenever one consumes [a particular kind of] vegetable food, [while still within mother's womb], in all those cases one becomes dark-complexioned'), not the invalid invariable concomitance underlying the fallacious logical reason under discussion: *yatra yatra tat-putratvaṁ tatra tatra śyāmatvaṁ* ('whenever one is his son, in all those cases one is dark-complexioned'). Hence the above logical reason (*tat-putratvāt*) is based on the concept of a particular condition, instead of invariable concomitance. Malliṣeṇa's definition of a particular condition R can be symbolised extensionally[b] in the following manner for S—probandum / *sādhya*, H—probans /*sādhana*):

T1 $upādhi =_{df} (x)[(x{\in}R{\rightarrow}x{\in}S.x{\in}S{\rightarrow}x{\in}R).(\exists x)(x{\in}R{\rightarrow}x{\notin}H)]$,

or intensionally[b]:

T1' $upādhi =_{df} (x)[(Rx{\supset}Sx.Sx{\supset}Rx).(\exists y)(Ry{\supset}{\sim}Py)]$.

In a typical schema of the reasoning based on the proof formula: $(h{\supset}s.p{\supset}h).{\supset}.p{\supset}s$, the premiss and necessary condition of valid inference $h{\supset}s$ (viz., the probans is encompassed by the extension of the probandum, cf. NAV 24, n. 474) cannot, therefore, be fulfilled. Cf. n. 426.

[a] H,V omit *atrânumānaṁ*.

[b] On the question of intensionality and extensionality of Indian logic cf. MATILAL (1985: 169 ff., esp. n. 1, p. 169).

[295] The purport of the argument is that, whereas *trairūpya*-variants formulate stronger—than the relation of *avinâbhāva*—requirements of inferential validity, and only under special circumstances, as well as they are not exhaustive, since they leave aside several valid inferences, the relation of *avinâbhāva* lays down the restriction that circumscribes all allowable valid types of inference and excludes invalid forms of inference (e.g. *tat-putratvâdi*). In other words, *avinâbhāva* is the necessary and sufficient condition that allows a valid conclusion regarding the inferendum and, that being the case, the notion of *trairūpya* is not only redundant, but also too narrow, as well. See also NB$_2$ 2.18–20: /18/ *atra dvau vastu-sādhanau. ekaḥ pratiṣedha-hetuḥ.* /19/ *svabhāva-pratibandhe hi saty artho 'rthaṁ gamayet.* /20/ *tad-apratibaddhasya tad-avyabhicāra-niyamâbhāvāt*; and NBṬ$_1$ 20: *na hi yo yatra svabhāvena na pratibaddhaḥ, sa tam apratibandha-viṣayam avaśyam eva na vyabhicaratîti nâsti tayor avyabhicāra-niyamaḥ—avinâbhāva-niyamaḥ. avyabhicāra-niyamāc ca gamya-gamaka-bhāvaḥ.* On the historical and epistemic relationship between the theory of *trairūpya* and *avinâbhāva* cf. OETKE (1994/b: 108–117).

[296] Flowers of this species are said to open at the moon-rise.

[297] The positive concomitance should assume the form: 'Whatever is audible is impermanent' (*yac chrāvaṇam tad anityam*) and the homologue instantiating the property of audibility should be an entity different from the locus (*śabda*) itself. There is, however, no other audible thing, save *śabda* (speech element / sound), and it is impossible to instantiate the relation of positive concomitance (*anvaya*) in this case.

[298] I.e., the heterologue should stand in contradiction to the property (viz., impermanence) of the locus and, consequently, be characterised by permanence.

[299] Compare a similar train of thought as well as the corresponding argumentation, save the wording, in PALV 3.10 (p. 26.19 ff.): *nanu trairūpyam eva hetor lakṣaṇam tasmin saty eva hetor asiddhâdi-doṣa-parihārôpapattiḥ. tathā hi. pakṣa-dharmatvam asiddhatva-vyavacchedârtham abhidhīyate. sapakṣe sattvan tu viruddhatvâpanodârtham. vipakṣe câsattvam evânaikāntika-vyudāsârtham iti. tad uktam*:

hetos triṣv api rūpeṣu nirṇayas tena varṇitaḥ /
asiddha-viparītârtha-vyabhicāri-vyapekṣataḥ //

iti. tad ayuktam. avinâbhāva-niyama-niścayād eva doṣa-traya-parihārôpapattiḥ. avinâbhāvo hy anyathânupapannatvam. tac câsiddhasya na sambhavaty eva. anyathânupapannatvam asiddhasya na siddhyati ity abhidhānāt. nâpi viruddhasya tal-lakṣaṇatvôpapattir viparīta-niścitâvinâbhāvini yathôkta-sādhyâvinâbhāva-niyama-

lakṣaṇasyânupapatter virodhāt vyabhicāriṇy api na prakṛta-lakṣaṇâvakāśas tata eva tato 'nyathânupapattir eva śreyasī na tri-rūpatā. tasyāṁ satyām api yathôkta-lakṣaṇâbhāve hetor gamakatvâdarśanāt. tathā hi sa śyāmas tat-putratvād itara-tat-putravad ity atra trairūpya-sambhave 'pi na gamakatvam upalakṣyate.

atha vipakṣād vyāvṛttir niyamavatī tatra na dṛśyate. tato na gamakatvam iti. tad api mugdha-vilasitam eva tasyā evâvinâbhāva-rūpatvāt. itara-rūpa-sadbhāve 'pi tad-abhāve hetoḥ sambhāvya-siddhiṁ prati gamakatvâniṣṭau sâiva pradhānaṁ lakṣaṇam upalakṣaṇīyam iti. tat-sadbhāve cêtara-rūpa-dvaya-nirapekṣatayā gamakatvaôpapattiś ca. yathā santy advaita-vādino 'pi pramāṇānîṣṭâniṣṭa-sādhana-dūṣaṇânya-thânupapattiḥ. na câtra pakṣa-dharmatvaṁ sapakṣânvayo vâsti. kevalam avinâbhāva-mātreṇa gamakatva-pratītiḥ.

yad apy aparam uktaṁ paraiḥ pakṣa-dharmatâbhāve 'pi kākasya kārṣṇyād dhavalaḥ prāsāda ity asyâpi gamakatvâpattir iti. tad apy anena nirastam. anyathânupapatti-balenâivâpakṣa-dharmasyâpi sādhutvâbhyupagamāt. na cêha sâsti. tato 'vinâbhāva eva hetoḥ pradhānaṁ lakṣaṇam abhyupagantavyam. tasmin saty asati vilakṣaṇatve 'pi hetor gamakatva-darśanād iti. na trairūpyaṁ hetu-lakṣaṇaṁ avyāpakatvāt. sarveṣāṁ kṣaṇikatve sādhye sattâdeḥ sadhānasya sapakṣe sato 'pi svayaṁ saugatair gamakatvâbhyupagamāt.

[300] The relation of essential identity (*tādātmya*) and the relation of causality (*tad-utpatti*), that correspond to the passage *asyêdaṁ kāryaṁ kāraṇaṁ* ('this is its effect, this is its cause ...') of VSU$_{I}$ 9.18 quoted above, are maintained to replace, or reduce, the three varieties of the logical reason conceived by Buddhist thinkers. For both these relations cf. n. 5.

[301] The verb *varteta* may be a play on words alluding to *vṛtti*, synonymous with *samavāya*.

[302] Cf. NAṬ 5 *ad loc.*: **virodhina ity-ādi**. *virodhī vāhniḥ*[a] *sva-viruddhasya śītasyâsattvaṁ*[b] *bodhayati. viruddhâbhāva-gamakatvam ity upalakṣaṇaṁ, viruddha-sadbhāva-gamakatvasyâpi darśanāt. ata eva pūrvam ahir visphūrjita-viśiṣṭo nakulâdi-liṅgam ity uktam.*[c] *tasya ca sāmānyasya tad-rūpatayā ca tena tasyâdhyavasāyād iti, svalakṣaṇa*[d]*-rūpatayā cânumānena sāmānyasya vikalpanāt. atasminn asvalakṣaṇe tad-grahasya svalakṣaṇatayā paricchedasya, bhrāntir api sambandhataḥ pramêti*[e]. *amum evârthaṁ dṛṣṭânta-pūrvakaṁ viniścaye dharmakīrtir akīrtayat, yathā*:

[1] *maṇi-pradīpa-prabhayor maṇi-buddhyâbhidhāvatoḥ /*
mithyā-jñānâviśeṣe 'pi viśeṣo 'rtha-kriyāṁ prati //

[2] *yathā tathā yathârthatve*[g] *'py anumāna-tadābhayoḥ /*
artha-kriyânurodhena pramāṇatvaṁ vyavasthitam // iti.[h]

[a] A: *vāhniḥ /*.
[b] H,V: *śītasya asattvaṁ*.
[c] A marks the end of a section here: // Ø //. Likewise C: //.
[d] C: *lakṣaṇa-°*.
[e] PVin II$_{1}$ 2,6–7. C: *sambandhata-pramêti*.
[f] C: *buddhyâbhidhāvitoḥ*.
[g] A marks an ellision: *tathā 'yathârthatve*.

[h] Both verse come from PVin II$_1$ 2,24–3,8 (verse 5–6), and are quoted in PV 2.57–58 (PV$_1$, p. 76–7). They are also quoted in TRD § 81 on ṢDSa 9 (p. 66.3–6).

[303] Cf. n. 231.

[304] For the criteria that differentiate *svalakṣaṇa* from *sāmānya* see PV 1.1–2:

mānaṁ dvividhaṁ viṣaya-dvaividhyāc chakty-aśaktitaḥ /
artha-kriyāyāṁ keśâdir nârtho 'narthâdhimokṣataḥ //
sadṛśâsadṛśatvāc ca viṣayâviṣayatvataḥ /
śabdasyânya-nimittānāṁ bhāve dhī-sad-asattvataḥ //

See also PVin II$_1$ 4,14–17 (verse 8):

atad-rūpa-parāvṛtta-vastu-mātra-prasādhanāt /
sāmānya-viṣayaṁ proktaṁ liṅgaṁ bhedâpratiṣṭhiteḥ //

and PV$_1$ 2.53d–54:

...meyaṁ tv ekaṁ svalakṣaṇam //
tasmād artha-kriyā-siddheḥ sad-asattā-vicāraṇāt /
tasya sva-para-rūpabhyāṁ gater meya-dvayaṁ matam //

See E. Steinkellner's note 51 in PVin II$_2$ (p. 29–30), who mentions several relevant passages, e.g. PS 1.2b: *laksana-dvayaṁ prameyam*, PSV *ad loc.*: *na hi sva-sāmānya-lakṣaṇābhyām aparam prameyam asti. sva-lakṣaṇa-viṣayaṁ hi pratyakṣam, sāmānya-lakṣaṇa-viṣayam anumānam iti pratipādayiṣyāmaḥ.* Cf. also E. Steinkellner's note 44 in PVin II$_2$, p. 28.

[305] Cf. n. 5.

[306] Clearly, Siddharṣi-gaṇin alludes to the opening section of Dharmakīrti's *svârthânumāna* section, PVin II$_1$ 1.23–2.31.

[307] PVin II$_1$ 2.6–7, p. 24.6–7:

དེ་མ་ཡིན་ལ་དེར་འཛིན་ཕྱིར།
འཁྲུལ་ཀྱང་འབྲེལ་ཕྱིར་ཚད་མ་ཉིད།།

= (*ibid.*, p. 25) *atasmiṁs tad-graho bhrāntir api sambandhataḥ pramā //* Regarding the quotation see also TUS$_1$, n. 179, as well as the criticism in TUS$_1$ 176.1–3: *na ca sat-sāmānya-viṣayatve bhrāntatôpapadyate. bhrāntir apy artha-sambandhataḥ premêti na vaktavyam.* Cf. also NBṬ$_2$ 1.5: *bhrāntaṁ hy anumānaṁ sva-pratibhāse 'narthe 'rthâdhyavasāyena pravṛttatvāt.*

[308] This is how I render the Sanskrit solution of the compound, which in fact cannot be translated into English: *tat-bhāvas tattvaṁ tasmāt*; *tattvaṁ* is a reference to *pramāṇatva* in the aphorism, *tasmāt* refers to the ablative case of the compound; the author follows here Pāṇ 5.1.119.

[309] Cf. note 91.

[310] This quotation from a Yogācāra-Sautrāntika work is found in Vinītadeva's commentary on NB_1 4, viz., $NBṬṬ_1$, p. 19.2–4 ($NBṬṬ_2$, p. 22.31): *tathā câha: 'sarvam ālambane bhrāntam' ity yogācāra-mate*. It is worth mentioning at this occasion that the comparison of the original passage with the reconstruction of the Sanskrit text in $NBṬṬ_3$, p. 7.21–22: *yogācārā hi sarvam ālambana-jñānaṁ bhrāntaṁ manyante*, shows how defective such reconstruction can be, especially when done absolutely uncritically, i.e. without taking into account extant excerpts and quotations of the reconstructed text, on the one hand, and, on the other, the main commented text (in our case, the *Nyāyabindu*). Cf. DhPr 1.4 (p. 44.8 ff.), where Durveka Miśra further specifies the proponents of this view: *nanv evam abhrāntatve yogācāra-matam asaṅgṛhītaṁ syāt. grāhya-grāhakâkāratayā pravṛtteḥ sarvasyâivâsarva-jña-vijñānasyâlambane bhrāntatvāt. tat kathaṁ pūrva-vyākhyānâvajñā na kriyata iti cet. ucyate. na yogācāra-naye lakṣaṇam idam, kintu sautrāntika-naya eva.*

[311] Cf. n. 7.

[312] NAV: ***bhrāntaṁ*** *viparyastam*, cf. $NBṬ_1$ 3.2 (p. 41.5–142.2): ***abhrāntam*** *artha-kriyā-kṣame vastu-rūpe 'viparyastam ucyate*.

[313] Cf. NAṬ 6 *ad loc.*: ***saṁvṛtim iti***. *kalpanām*[a]. *yad āhuḥ*:

anirūpita-tattvârthā pratītiḥ saṁvṛtir matā /[b]—

—'"The empirical truth" is conceptual construction. As they said: "Awareness, the object of which is imperceptibility, is known as the empirical truth".'

[a] A: *kalpenāṁ*. [b] This hemistich is also quoted in NAṬ 23 below, n. 456.

[314] The idea of two levels of truth (*saṁvṛti-satya* and *paramârtha-satya*) goes back to the Pāli tradition, cf. KVuA, p. 34:

duve saccāni akkhāsi sambuddho vadataṁ varo /
sammutiṁ paramatthaṁ ca tatiyaṁ n 'ūpalabbhati //
saṁketa-vacânaṁ saccaṁ loka-sammuti-kāraṇaṁ /
paramattha-vacanaṁ saccaṁ dhammānaṁ tathalakkhanaṁ // —

—'The Perfectly Enlightened One, the best of preceptors, spoke of two truths: the empirical reality and the ultimate reality, and no third is conceivable. A conventionally [true] statement is true by reason of people's convention, an ultimately [true] statement is true, having the nature corresponding to the constituents of reality.' Cf. ANK 1.95 reading *bhūtalakkhanaṁ*, instead of *tathalakkhanaṁ*.

[315] Cf. PVin II_1 7, p. 26.10–14:

de ñid kyi phyir mṅon sum daṅ rjes su dpag pa[c]*i tshad ma gñi ga dṅos po yi |*
| yul can
yin te | dpyod pa ni don byed par ruṅ ba[c]*i yul can yin pa*[c]*i phhyir ro ||*

[316] Cf. NS 4.2.11: *ekasmin bhedâbhāvād bheda-śabda-prayogânupapatter apraśnaḥ*; and NBh *ad loc.*: *kiṁ praty-avayavaṁ kṛtsno 'vayavī vartate athâika-deśenêti*

nôpapadyate praśnaḥ, kasmāt ekasmin bhedâbhāvād bheda-śabda-prayogânupapatteḥ. kṛtsnam ity anekasyâśeṣâbhidhānam, eka-deśa iti nānātve kasyacid abhidhānam, tāv imau kṛtsnâika-deśa-śabdau bheda-viṣayau nâikasminn avayaviny upapadyate bhedâbhāvād iti, anyâvayavâbhāvān nâika-deśena vartate ity ahetuḥ.

317 Seeing but a fringe of a piece of cloth, that is flapping and is red, would necessarily be followed by an act of erroneously perceiving that the entire cloth is read and is flapping.

318 Maybe we should take *tad-unmukho grāhyâkāraḥ* ... *grāhakâkāraḥ* as a *bahū-vṛhi* compound referring to *bahiḥ prabibhāsasya* above? In that case we would have: 'since [the representation concerning the external object] is deprived of a [real] object, [the representation] which anticipates this [object] and assumes a form of something-to-be-grasped is false; since it is false, [the representation]—even though [it assumes] a form of something-which-grasps—does not reproduce the [real] situation, because it is unjustified to assume something-which-grasps, if there is nothing-to-be-grasped,' etc.

319 Cf. Viṁś_1 11–15 and ViṁśV_1 *ad loc.* The argument against the whole and its parts was frequently used, on the one hand, by the Buddhist epistemologists in order to refute the possibly of the universal residing in particulars, the theory that was upheld by the Naiyāyikas, and, on the other, by Jayarāśi against the Buddhist logicians themselves in his criticism directed against the idea of production of one indivisible cognition. Cf. TUS_1 4.25bc (p. 230.11–232.14): *yat tad rūpôtpādyaṁ vijñānaṁ, tat kim eka-deśena rūpôtpādyatvena sthitaṁ sarvâtmanā vôtpādyatvena paryavasitam? tad yady eka-deśena sthitaṁ, tad ayuktam, akhaṇḍasyâika-deśa-virahāt. atha sarvâtmanā rūpôtpādyatvena paryavasitaṁ, tadā vijñānôtpādyaṁ na prāpnoti, yathâika-kāraka-samūhôtpādyatvena paryavasitasya kāryasya saṅghātântarôtpādyatvaṁ na dṛṣṭam. tataś ca vijñāna-saṅghātânupapattiḥ. tathā rūpam api jñānam eka-deśena kuryāt sarvâtmanā karaṇa-paryavasitaṁ vā. tad yady eka-deśena karoti, tad ayuktam, akhaṇḍasyâika-deśâyogāt. atha sarvātmanā karoti, tadā rūpaṁ sarvâtmanā vijñāna-karaṇe paryavasitaṁ na rūpântara-karaṇe pravartate. yathâika-kāraka-sāmagry eka-kāryôtpādana-paryavasitā kāryântara-savitrī na bhavati, tathā rūpam api rūpântarôtpādakaṁ na bhavati. tataś ca rūpântarasyâkasmikatvam. tadâkasmikatve kāryânumānaṁ vilupyate saugatānām. athâneka-kāryôtpādakatvena paryavasitaṁ rūpa-svarūpaṁ, tadā ghaṭa-saṅkhyā-sāmānyâder apy anekâdhikaraṇâśritâtmakaṁ rūpaṁ, vṛtti-vikalpa-doṣânupapattiḥ.* See also FRANCO's respective notes in 274 (TUS_1, p. 475 ff.) and 276 (TUS_1, p. 479 f.). Compare a similar *pūrva-pakṣa* argument, encountered as early as in NS 4.2.6–10: */6/ vṛtty-anupapatter api tarhi na saṁśayaḥ. /7/ kṛtsnâika-deśâvṛttitvād avayavānām avayavy-abhāvaḥ. /8/ teṣu câvṛtter avayavy-abhāvaḥ. /9/ pṛthak câvayavebhyo 'vtteḥ. /10/ na câvayavy-avayavāḥ.*—'There is no suspicion [that the whole is non-existent] also because [its] occurrence is inexplicable. Since the parts do not occur (*sc.* reside) in the entire [whole] nor in a piece [of the whole], the whole does not exist. And since [the whole] does not occur

(*sc.* reside) in [its] parts, the whole does not exist. And since the whole and the part [can] not occur separately, there are neither wholes nor parts.'

320 In other words: nobody ever experiences such a cognition which does not have the form of a cognoscible and a cogniser.

321 I was unable to grasp the import of the metaphor: *bhakta-madhya-niṣṭhyūta-darśinaḥ purato vipratāraṇa-pravaṇa-kuṭṭinī-śapatha-prāyam*.

322 Devabhadra-sūri explicates (NAṬ *ad loc.*): ***ekasyêti.*** *citra*[a]*-jñānasya, jñāne hy ekasminn eva nīla-pītâdayo bahavo ākārāḥ*[b] *pratibhānti, tatas teṣu nīla-pītâdy-ākāreṣu katham ekaṁ jñānaṁ vartata iti vicāraḥ pravartata eva.*—'"One" [means] "a cognition [grasping] a colour"; for various forms (colours), like blue, yellow, etc., occur in only one cognition; therefore, how can one cognition operate with regard to these [manifold] forms (colours), like blue, yellow, etc.?—thus proceeds this very examination.'

[a] C: *vicitra-°*. [b] H: *ākārā*.

323 I.e., is related to the past and the future.

324 Devabhadra-sūri comments (NAṬ *ad loc.*): ***bhinna-pravṛtti-nimittatvād iti.*** *paryāya-rūpatayā hi ekatva-pariṇāma-rūpasyâvayavinas*[a] *tantubhyo bhedaḥ, dravya-rūpatayā tv abhedaḥ*[b]*. evam utpādâdi-dharmāṇām api virodhâbhāvo bodhavyaḥ, uttara-paryāyasya hy udayaḥ pūrva-paryāyasya vyayaḥ. dravyasya tv anuyāyino*[c] *dhrauvyam iti.*—'[A gloss on]: "[Exist] by reason of [their] different occurrences, etc." [The means is follows:] there is a difference between threads and the whole [piece of cloth], consisting in the transformation [amounting to] the oneness, inasmuch as [the occurrence of the whole and the threads] consist in modes. But there is no difference [between the whole and the threads], inasmuch as [their occurrence] consist in [the same] substance. In this way, it should be understood that there is no contradiction between [apparently different] properties like the rise, etc., for the production of a subsequent mode is the annihilation of a previous mode; only the attendant substance is permanent.'

[a] C: *°-rūpasyâvayaṁvinas*. [b] C,H,V: *°-rūpatayâbhedaḥ*. [c] A: *anuyayino*.

325 How differently—reasoning on purely semantic premisses—one may proceed in order to refute the Buddhist critique of the whole-and-part complex is instantiated by Jayarāśi in TUS_2, p. 94.2–15: *yâpi yuktir apadiṣṭā vijñāna-mātra-sthitāv avayavi-nirākaraṇa-parā vṛtty-anupapatty-ādi-rūpā "na kilâvayavy eka-deśena vartate, nâpi sarvâtmanā, eka-deśa-vṛtty-abhyupagame hy avayavino bheda-prasaṅgaḥ. atha sarvâtmanā vartate, tarhy anyatrâvṛtti-prasaṅga" ity-ādikā; sâpi na yukti-yuktā. katham? kim eka-deśa-śabdenâvayavy abhidhīyate, 'vayavo vā? yady avayavy abhidhīyate, tadâika-deśenâiva sarvatra vartata iti brūmaḥ, sva-kāraṇān niyamitasya tathā-bhūtasyôtpatteḥ. athâvayavo 'bhidhīyate tad-eka-deśa-śabdena; tadā nâika-deśenâvayavī vartate, 'vaya[va]syâvayave vṛtty-ayogāt. bhavatu vâvyaveṣu vṛtter abhāvo 'vayavinas, tathâpy asattvaṁ na sidhyati, tad-dehôpalambhasya tad-astitva-*

vidhāna-paratvāt. yathā "anudakaḥ kamaṇḍalur" ity ukte saty udaka-kamaṇḍalu-sambandhâbhāvaḥ pratīyate, na tu kamaṇḍalor abhāvas, tad-udakasya vā. For the English transl. of the passage see TUS$_1$, pp. 478.14–479.3.

[326] cf. NAṬ *ad loc.*: ***tad-artha-prāpty-ādikam iti****. tatra pratibhāsamānasya jalâder arthasya prāptiḥ, ādi-śabdāt pānâvagāhanâdy-artha-kriyā-parigrahaḥ.*

[327] Ms. B as well as H,V are equivocal: *ārekânirākaraṇa-°* or *ārekā-nirākaraṇa-°* (?). Whereas Ms. A inserts, as a rule, an *avagraha* in the subscript in order to note the *sandhi*: *ă + ă*, we have no *avagraha* in the subscript in this particular compound, which can mean that either (1) its omission might have been due to carelessness of the scribe, who overlooked its insertion, or (2) the lack of an *avagraha* in the subscript is intended to be meaningful and points to the reading: *ārekā-nirākaraṇa-°*, which would imply that *ārekā* is feminine in this case. In all available lexicographic sources, however, I find *āreka* instead of *ārekā*, barring a single reference to *rekā* in PW VI 429 and the note (entry *reka*): 'ÇKDR. und WILSON angeblich nach H. auch *rekā*; es is aber 1375 *āreka* gemeint.' Nonetheless, there could hardly by any doubt that the statement *na ca tad-artha-prāpty-ādikam ārek**ă**-nirākaraṇa-kāraṇaṁ kalpanīyaṁ* is a direct continuation of the previous thought as well as the extension of the suspicion regarding the credibility of cognition onto purposeful activities, which might be regarded by the opponent to prove the reality of external objects. Thus, in view of the context and of the argumentative structure, wherein any efficient action is also rejected by the proponent as a possible means both of clearing away the doubt concerning the real status of the cognoscible and of establishing the object of cognition as really existent, we should (1) either take *ārekā* as feminine and split the compound *ārekā-nirākaraṇa-°*, or (2) take *āreka* as masculine and emend the text: *āreka-nirākaraṇa-°*.

[328] After NAṬ *ad loc.*: ***tasyêti****. svapna-jñānasya.*

[329] After NAṬ *ad loc.*: ***tasya*** *bādhaka-pratyayasya.*

[330] I.e., all representations are equally valid; cf. NAṬ *ad loc.*: ***samānatêti****. na kaścit pratibhāso*[a] *bādhyo nâpi kaścana*[b] *bādhakaḥ.*—'No representation can be subverted [by another representation,] nor there is any [representation] subverting [other representations].'

[a] A: *pratibhāse.* [b] H,V instead: *ca.*

[331] Cf. NAṬ *ad loc.*: ***vivekâbhāvenêti****. viveko bhrāntāt svapna-jñānâder abhrāntasya pārthakyena vyavasthāpanam.*—'Discrimination establishes a non-erroneous cognition as separate from an erroneous cognition in dream.'

[332] NAṬ *ad loc.*: *yo 'pîti. yogācārâdhiḥ.*

[333] NAṬ *ad loc.*: ***bhrāntatām iti****. 'sarvam ālambane bhrāntam' iti vacanāt.*—'Following the utterance: "every [cognition] is erroneous with regard to the objective

substratum",' Cf. NAV 6, n.310. The *pratīka* we find in the H.-edition of NAṬ, namely *bhrāntānām iti*, has to be emended as follows: *bhrāntatām iti*.

[334] Cf. NAṬ *ad loc.*: *tat-sādhakasya samasta-saṁvedana-bhrāntatā-sādhakasya, nirālambanāḥ sarve pratyayāḥ, pratyayatvāt, svapna-pratyayavad ity*[a] *anumānasya.*—'"Proving that" [means the reasoning] proving that all sensations are erroneous. The inference is as follows: "every cognition is devoid of objective substratum, because it is a cognition, just like a cognition in [the state of] dream".'

[a] The proof formula (*sarve pratyayā nirālambanāḥ, pratyayatvāt, svapna-pratyayavat*) occurs above in NAṬ 4, see n. 242. It is discussed by Siddharṣi-gaṇin in NAV 24, see p. 72 of the English translation as well as note 476.

[335] Cf. NAṬ *ad loc.*: ***tad-bhrāntatve***[a] *nirālambanatā-sādhakânumānâlīkatve*—'"If [that] were erroneous" [means] if the inference proving the absence of any objective substratum were erroneous.'

This is a case of a well-know paradox entailed by a self-referential statement with a universal quantifier stating the falsity of all members of a class it belongs to; it resembles, but is not identical with, the Epimenides paradox: 'If all cognition is erroneous and the cognition that "all cognition is erroneous" is true, then not all cognition is erroneous.'

[a] A,C: *bhrāntatve*.

[336] Cf. n. 231.

[337] The question of *parârthânumāna* is discussed at length in NA 10 and NAV *ad loc.* As a matter of fact, the first mention of the inference for others is to be found (at least, according to Siddharṣi-gaṇin in the introductory part to NA 10: *adhunā parârthânumāna-lakṣaṇaṁ vaktavyam, tac ca pratyakṣe 'pi paśyan*, p. 52 of the English translation) in the context of perception: NAV 1: *tasmād avaśyantayā yathâdṛṣṭa-pratyakṣa-vyakti-sādharmya-dvāreṇâdhunātana-pratyakṣa-vyaktīnāṁ prāmāṇya-pratyāyakaṁ para-paripādakaṁ ca parokṣântar-gatam anumāna-rūpaṁ pramāṇântaram urarī-kartavyam*. (p.17 ff. of the English translation).

[338] Three meanings of *tattva*, i.e. 'truth', 'reality' and 'ontological category', are inseparably interwoven in Jainism. I have already enumerated some instances of equivocal usage of the term *tattva* in the context of the expression *tattvârtha*, cf. note 61. The ambiguity of the term is also reflected in Siddharṣi's elucidation of the term *tattva* below, NAV 9 (p. 51 of the English translation). Here, I wish to draw the reader's attention to further examples where the term *tattva* does not leave any doubt regarding its meaning:

1. 'Righteousness is the predilection for <u>truth</u>'—TSṬ 2.3: *<u>tattva</u>-rucih samyaktvam*;
2. '<u>Reality</u> is, as a matter of fact, endowed with infinite properties ...':

ananta-dharmâtmakam eva <u>tattvam</u> ato 'nyathā sattvam asūpapādam /
iti pramāṇāny api te kuvādi-kuraṅga-saṁtrāsana-siṁha-nādāḥ // (AYVD 22)

See also the commentary of SVM 22,5/6, p. 136: *tattvaṁ paramârtha-bhūtaṁ vastu jīvâjīva-lakṣaṇam ananta-dharmâtmakam eva.*—'Reality—i.e. the real thing, which is the ultimate object (truth) characterised by the living element and the lifeless element—is, as a matter of fact, endowed with infinite properties.' But cf. SVM 22,9/10, p. 137: *sattvaṁ vastu-tattvam.*—'Existence is the reality (*or* nature) of the real thing.'

3. '...ontological categories which should be avoided and which should be pursued ...':
parīkṣâmukham ādarśaṁ heyôpadeya-tattvayoḥ /
saṁvide mādṛśo bālaḥ parīkṣād akṣavad vyadhām // (PA concluding stanza)

Moreover, in the sense of 'truth', *tattva* should be distinguished from *satya.* Whereas the former is the truth in the ontological sense, the latter refers to truth in the epistemological and logical sense: 'truth is what is endowed with propriety (logical congruity)' (*satyam yukti-yuktam*, SVM 3.13/14, p. 9).

339 Cf. $SvSt_1$ 24.3 = $SvSt_2$ 138:
anavadyaḥ syād-vādas tava dṛṣṭêṣṭâvirodhataḥ syād-vādaḥ /

340 Cf. n.283.

341 The aphorism begins with these words in the original.

342 There are other possible solutions of the compound *dṛṣṭêṣṭâvyāhata*, cf. NAṬ *ad loc.*: ***dṛṣṭenêtyâdi***[a]. *ayaṁ bhinnâdhikaraṇas*[b] *tri-pado bahu-vrīhiḥ yadi vêṣṭo*[c] *'vyāhato 'rtho yatra tad iṣṭâvyāhataṁ vākyam, tadanu dṛṣṭena pramāṇa-nirṇītenêṣṭâvyāhatam*[d] *iti tat-puruṣaḥ.*—'This is either a *bahu-vrīhi* compound consisting of three words, which has a substance different [from its constituent elements]: "such a statement in which the meaning is accepted [and] not contradicted", or it [may be understood as] a *tat-puruṣa* compound: "what is accepted [and] not contradicted by what is experienced, [viz.,] by what is determined through a cognitive criterion".' The compound may also be solved as 'what is neither contradicted by what is accepted nor by what is experienced.'

[a] C: *dṛṣṭanêtyâdi.*

[b] For *bhinnâdhikaraṇa* see Pāṇ 2.2.23–24: /23/ *śeṣo bahu-vrīhiḥ*; /24/ *anyêkam anya-padârthe.*—/23/ 'The remaining [compounds are classified as] *bahu-vrīhi*'; /24/ 'Two or more [words within such a compound refer] to another entity.'

[c] C,H,V: *vā iṣṭo.*

[d] H,V: °*-nirṇītena iṣṭâvyāhatam.*

343 Thereby I attempt to render *tasmāt* that indicates the ablative case of the compound.

344 *artha*, or 'object, meaning'; it is the constituent part of the compound *paramârtha*, which is usually rendered by me as 'the ultimate truth', and which here might be translated as 'the ultimate meaning (object).' Due to the ambiguity of *artha* in *paramârtha*, the correspondence of the above dissolution of the compound in question with the meaning of its constituent elements has been lost and the consistency of the English rendering is not so apparent.

[345] Dharmakīrti in his auto-commentary to PV_1 3.124 says: *sambandho vākyānām ekârthôpasaṁharôpakāraḥ, na daśa-dāḍimâdi-vākyānām*[a] *ivânupasaṁhāra eva; anyathā vaktur vaiguṇyam udbhāvayet. aśakyôpāya-phalāni ca śāstrāni phalârthī nâdriyeta vicārayitum apuruṣârtha-phalāni ca, viṣa-śamanāya takṣaka-phaṇa-ratnâlaṅkārôpadeśavat*[b] *kāka-danta-parīkṣāvac*[a] *ca. tad-viparyayeṇôpasaṁhāravac chakyôpāyaṁ puruṣârthâbhidhāyi ca śāstraṁ parīkṣyetânyatrâvadhānasyâvâ-yuktatvāt* ...—'The coherence [means] the serviceability of [a number of] sentences in application to [numerically] one object. There is no application [to any object in the case] of [a sentences like] the [empty] statement about ten pomegranates,[a] etc. Otherwise, the impertinence [of such sentences] would be pointed out to the speaker [who would try to use meaningfully such a statement]. [A person] aiming at a [particular] result would care neither to examine authoritative treatises leading to results [that are] ineffective means nor [to examine] results that [constitute] objectives [meant] not for people, just like [he does not care about] instruction of a carpenter (on carpentry?), [instruction] about snake hoods, crest-jewels and ornaments [in order to] to counteract [the effects of] a poison, and just like [he does not care about] an investigation of a crow's teeth[b]. And by [way of] something contrary to these [ineffective authoritative treatises, only] an authoritative treatise, endowed with an application, [being] effective means and communicating objectives [meant] for people, should be examined, because any attention (care) whatsoever for something else [that is ineffective] is unjustified ...'

[a] For expressions *daśa-dāḍimâdi-vākya* and *kāka-danta-parīkṣā* see n. 19.

[b] The phrase *jvara-hara-takṣaka-cūḍā-ratnâlaṅkārôpadeśa*, or Dharmakīrti's version of it, *takṣaka-phaṇa-ratnâlaṅkārôpadeśa*, is not very clear to me. In above renderings, I take the compound *jvara-hara-takṣaka-cūḍā-ratnâlaṅkāra* (or Dharmakīrti's *takṣaka-phaṇa-ratnâlaṅkāra*) as *dvandva*. However, the expression in PV 3.124 alludes to the context of the snake world by the fact of applying the *upadeśa* (instruction) as an antidote against poison (*viṣa-śamanāya*) and by the use of the word *phaṇa* ('snake hood'). The word *takṣaka* is used to denote, beside its second meaning 'carpenter', also 'snake', cf. AmK 3.3.4cd (II, p. 225–6): *takṣako nāga-vardhakayor*, and AmKV *ad loc.*: ***takṣako nāga-vardhakayor*** *nāgaḥ sarpa-viśeṣaḥ takṣaka-namnā prasiddhaḥ. takṣnoti tvāg-ādikam iti takṣakaḥ. takṣū tvakṣū tanū-karaṇe.* Perhaps the whole expression of PV 3.124 *viṣa-śamanāya takṣaka-phaṇa-ratnâlaṅkārôpadeśa*, should be understood as 'instruction about the ornament [in form] of a jewel, viz., the hood of the snake [in order to] to counteract [the effects of] a poison' or 'instruction about the hood, the jewel and the ornament of the snake [in order to] to counteract [the effects of] a poison'? Analogously, the phrase *jvara-hara-takṣaka-cūḍā-ratnâlaṅkārôpadeśa* of NAV above could be taken to mean either 'instruction about the ornament [in form] of a jewel, viz., the hood, of the snake [in order to] remedy fever' (**jvarasya harârthaṁ takṣakasya cūḍā sā yasyāḥ ratnaṁ tat yasyâlaṅkāro sa yasôpadeśaḥ saḥ*) or 'instruction about the hood, the jewel and the ornament of the snake [in order to] remedy fever' (**jvara-harāya takṣakasya cūḍā ca ratnaṁ câlaṅkāraś ca takṣaka-cūḍā-ratnâlaṅkārāḥ teṣām upadeśaḥ saḥ*), other pos-

sible solutions of the compound not excluding. Due to lack of further textual evidence, I was unable to decide which possibility is the correct one.

[346] The above is a refutation of the idea that verbal testimony as a cognitive criterion may refer to worldly things, which is expressed in NS 1.1.7–8: *āptôpadeśaḥ śabdaḥ. sa dvividhaḥ dṛṣṭâdṛṣṭârthatvāt.*—'Verbal testimony is the instruction of an authoritative person. [It is] twofold, because there are perceived and unperceived objects.'

[347] I.e., the word *māna* contains the prefix *pra*, although it is not expressed explicitly, and thus *māna* = *pramāṇa*.

[348] Since the verbal knowledge is stated to be a prerequisite of the inference for others, the Buddhists are meant, not the Cārvākas, who reject the validity of inference as well.

[349] Cf. p. 39 ff.

[350] Cf. NAṬ *ad loc.*: ***tena*** *śābdena*[a], ***tasya*** *hetoḥ*. In other words, there would be no need of inference.

[a] A: *śābdena*; H,V: *śabdena*.

[351] Cf. p.32 and n.244.

[352] Cf. pp. 6-6.

[353] I.e., the author defines the characteristics of authoritative treatise that produces the verbal knowledge, which in its turn is a cognitive criterion.

[354] I.e., the ontological categories, cf. TS 1.4: *jīvâjīvâsrava-bandha-saṁvara-nirjarā-mokṣās tattvam.*

[355] *gaja-snāna-nyāya*; the maxim describes futile or aimless endeavours and alludes to elephants, that cover themselves with dust and dirt, having just taken a bath. It appears to be the Indian counterpart of Sisyphus' work. Devabhadra-sūri spells out the metaphor explicitly in NAṬ *ad loc.*: ***gaja***[a]***-snāna-nyāyêty-ādi****. yathā gajo 'mbhasā rajo-viyuktam ātmānaṁ vidhāya punar eva rajobhir ātmānaṁ*[b] *malinayati, tathā tvam api rāga-dveṣôpahata-puruṣa-praṇayana-samutthaṁ vedānāṁ kāluṣyam apauruṣeyatvâbhyupagamena nirākṛtya vyākhyānârthaṁ punar api tathā-bhūtaṁ puruṣam abhyupagacchaṁs*[c] *tad evâṅgī-kuruṣe iti.*—'Just like an elephant, [first] cleansed of dirt by water, throws [the dirt] onto itself just afterwards [and] sullies itself again with the dirt, in the same manner you, too, [first] have kept off the defilement of the *Vedas* occasioned by the composition [of these texts] by man, who is [by nature] overpowered with enmity and passion, by [your] acceptance of the idea of the divine origin [of the *Vedas* and,] then again you accept man, who is so disposed, in order to [account for their] conveyance [and] sanction this [defilement].'

[a] C: *jaga-°*. [b] A: *eva rātmānaṁ*.
[c] A: *abhyupagacchas*; H,V: *abhyupagacchan*.

[356] Devabhadra-sūri explicates in NAṬ *ad loc.*: ***sva-kāryasya*** *para-lokâdāv adṛṣṭe 'rthe pravṛtti-rūpasya.*—'Effects of [the authoritative treatise] itself consisting in activity with regard to [attainment of] invisible things, such as the next world, etc.'

[357] Cf. NAṬ *ad loc.*: ***siddhāv iti***. *abhyupagamānāyām iti śeṣaḥ*.

[358] Devabhadra-sūri explains the term in the following manner in NAṬ *ad loc.*: ***tad-anuṣṭhānād iti***. *anuṣṭhānaṁ vyākhyātur vyākhyāna-lakṣaṇo vyāpāras, tasmāt.*—'Carrying out is an activity characterised by the conveyance (*sc.* handing down) [of authoritative texts] by a conveyor; on its account.' The purport of the argument is as follows: why does the opponent not accept the human origin of authoritative texts, even though he accepts the human factor in handing down the works in the oral tradition?

[a] C omits *vyākhyātur*.

[359] I.e., there is no other valid proof of the existence of supermundane phenomena.

[360] Cf. n. 102.

[361] Cf. NAṬ *ad loc.*: ***tad-vācyasyêti***. *śāstrâbhidheyasya.*—'"What is to be taught by it" [means] the subject-matter of the authoritative treatise.'

[362] The compound *adṛṣṭêṣṭa-virodhaka* must have appeared ambiguous, since Siddharṣi-gaṇin offers in NAV two possible solutions of it. Devabhadra-sūri seems to have been entirely content with neither of them, and forwards his own grammatical analysis in NAṬ *ad loc.*: ***dṛṣṭenêty-ādi***. *idam artha-kathana-mātram, samāsa-vigrahas tv evaṁ*[a]: *iṣṭasya virodho, dṛṣṭenêṣṭa-virodho, na vidyate dṛṣṭêṣṭa-virodho yatra tat-tathā.*—'This [elucidation of the aphorism offered by Siddharṣi-gaṇin above] merely recounts the meaning [of the aphorism]. The dissolution of the compound, however, is as follows. [There is] the contradiction on the part of what is accepted. [There is] the contradiction on the part of what is accepted with what is experienced. That in which there is no contradiction on the part of what is accepted with what is experienced is such, [i.e. the character of an authoritative treatise].' In view of these three interpretations, which are at variance with each other, I feel entitled to present my proposal, being in parallel with the expression occurring previous aphorism of NA 8, viz., *dṛṣṭêṣṭâvyāhata* ('not contradicted by what is accepted or by what is experienced'), that seems most plausible to my mind: 'in which there is no contradiction with what is experienced and with what is accepted' (**dṛṣṭasya iṣṭasya ca virodho na vidyate yatra tat-tathā*), which is tantamount to 'which is not contradicted by what is experienced or what is accepted' (**dṛṣṭena iṣṭena câvyāhato artho yasmin vākye tat-tathā*).

[a] C: *vigrahasteva*. H,V: *vigrahas tv ayam*. [b] C: °-*virodhena* (°-*virodhe na*?).

[363] I.e., the fact that authoritative treatise successfully realises the purposes assigned to it and with reference to itself.

[364] Cf. nn. 61, 338.

[365] *vidhāna*—'means, performance, accomplishment'; hence, optionally: 'or [it may mean] the rendering their rescue.' In view of *prāṇi-rakṣaṇôpāya-°* (*infra*), however, I am inclined to subscribe to the first interpretation.

[366] Cf. NAṬ 9 *ad loc.*: ***tattvêti***. *paramârtham.*

[367] *tīrthântara*, cf. n. 84.

[368] Cf. p. 17 ff.

[369] Cf. n. 600.

[370] Cf. PMī 2.1–2: /1/ *yathôkta-sādhanâbhidhāna-jaḥ parârtham. /2/ vacanam upacārāt.*—'[The inference] for others is produced by stating [explicitly] the probans, [which has characteristics] as described before; /2/ [The inference for others] is an utterance in a metaphorical sense.'

[371] The *°-vat* element of the compound *sva-niścayavat* in the aphorism as well as in *tadvat* in the *Nyāyâvatāra-vivṛti* above is explained by the syntactical structure of the subsequent sentence: *yathā... tathā...*

[372] Cf. NAṬ *ad loc.*: ***para-prayojana-mātratvād iti***. *parasya prayojanaṁ para-prayojanam, tad eva para-prayojana-mātraṁ, 'mātraṁ kārtsnye 'vadhāraṇe' iti vacanād, avadhāraṇârtho 'tra mātra-dhvaniḥ. yady api kasyacit tathā-vidhâbhyāsād vacanam uccārayataḥ*[a] *svayam apy artha-pratipattir vākyasya prayojanatvaṁ, tathâpy alpatvān nêha tad*[b] *vivakṣitam iti.*—'[A gloss on]: "because its sole purpose is for others." "Purpose is for others" [means] "purpose is for another [person]". There is only that [purpose for others], i.e. "Its sole purpose is for others." On the basis of the utterance: "Only [is used] in [the sense of] complete restriction", the linguistic unit "only" has the meaning of restriction here. Even though the [inferential] statement has a purpose for somebody who expresses an [inferential] utterance [in agreement] with such a repeated practice, [that is] surely his own understanding of the meaning [of this inferential utterance], nevertheless due to its insignificance that is not intended here.'

[a] C: *uccārayātaḥ* (*uccārayateḥ*?). [b] H,V omit *tad*.

[373] I.e., not directly involved. In other words, the cognition of the cognitive subject is the initial cause of the inference of others; it expresses itself immediately via inferential statements. Cognition arising in another person is also the eventual purpose of statements. Cf. NAṬ *ad loc.*: ***vyavahitatvād iti***. *jñānântaraṁ hi vivakṣā, sthāna-karaṇâbhighātâdinā śabdôtpattau para-santāne jñānôtpādād*[a] *iti.*—'[A gloss on]: "is separated". For the intention is another cognition, because if a word originates (*sc.* if statements are uttered) on account of articulation through organs of speech in places of articulation, etc., then cognition arises in another personal series (*sc.* person).'

[a] C: *jñānôpādod.*

[374] Instead of *pratipadyante* ('they recognise') one would expect to read quite naturally *pratipadyate* ('is recognised'), viz.: 'Efficacy for others in the case of inference

is indeed accepted by opponents; [it] is not recognised in the case of perception.' Otherwise, one has to face an awkward construction, in which *pārārthya* is the subject in the first passive clause, whereas in the second clause—of elliptical and active character—both the subject and the object are unexpectedly interchanged, and, consequently, *pārārthya* becomes the object. See the corresponding footnote of the Sanskrit edition.

[375] I.e., a particular thing grasped by perception is beyond the pertinence of speech. The compound *śabda-praveśa-śūnya* could either be dissolved as *śabdena praveśena śūnya* (*sc.* 'not penetrated with words') or as *śabde praveśena śūnya* (*sc.* 'not penetrating words'). In either case, the idea eventually expressed by it is the non-verbal character of the domain of perception; cf. n. 244.

[376] Cf. NAṬ *ad loc.*: ***vikalpa-yonaya iti.***[a] *vikalpo yoniḥ kāraṇaṁ yeṣāṁ te*[b] *tathā.*—'Such, whose inception, [i.e.] whose cause, is conceptualisation.'

[a] C omits the *pratīka*: *vikalpa-yonaya iti*.

[b] H,V omit *te*.

[377] The authorship of the above verse could not be tracked down. Helmut Krasser, inquired about the identification of the verse, mentions in his letter the opinion of Prof. E. Steinkellner, according to whom a probable historical source of the idea might be the following verse of PV_3 3.286:

vikalpa-vāsanôdbhūtāḥ samāropita-gocarāḥ /
jāyante buddhayas tatra kevalaṁ na artha-gocarāḥ //

K. Kunjunni RAJA (1963: 93, n. 3) believes it is a quotation from Diṅnāga, but as a proof refers only to STCHERBATSKY (1930: II: 405 n.).

The first hemistich is also quoted by Haribhadra-sūri twice: in his AJP 4, vol. I, p. 334.10, and in AJPV, vol. I, 337.16–17, where he identifies the author as Diṅnāga (referred to as *bhadanta-dinnena*): *yathôktaṁ bhadanta-dinnena*—***vikalpa-yonayaḥ śabdā vikalpā***—*śabda-vikalpāḥ* ***śabda-yonaya*** *ity-ādi*. As for the identification, see also Muni Jambūvijayajī's note 5 in his edition of DNC, vol. I, p. 587.23–27, esp.: *bauddhâcārya-**diṅnāga**sâiva 'bhadanta-dinnena' iti nāma iti dhyeyam*.

It is also quoted by Siṁha-sūri-gaṇin in his commentary to DNCV three times, Vol. I, p. 243.8–9, Vol. I, p. 498.1–2, and Vol. II, p. 547.7–8, where the second hemistich is different:

vikalpa-yonayaḥ śabdā vikalpāḥ śabda-yonayaḥ /
teṣām atyanta-sambandho nârthaṁ śabdāḥ spṛśanty api //

[378] Cf. n. 675.

[379] 'And … alike': *pratyakṣeṇâpy anumānenêva prasiddhârtha-prakāśanāt* ...

[380] I.e., NAV 4: *tasmād vyavasāyâtmakam adhyakṣam ity etad eva cārv iti sthitam* (p. 36 of the English translation).

[381] To sum up, the above reasoning based on the proof formula assumes the following form:

1. thesis (*pratijñā*): there is fire here,
2. logical reason (*hetu*): because there is smoke;
3a. an example based on similarity (*sādharmya-dṛṣṭânta*): wherever there is smoke, there is also fire, like in the kitchen, etc.,
3b. an example based on dissimilarity (*vaidharmya-dṛṣṭânta*): wherever there is no fire, there no smoke at all, like in a water reservoir, etc.;
4. application (*upanaya*): so, there is smoke here;
5. conclusion (*nigamana*): therefore—on account of the smoke—there is fire here.

For symbolical formulations cf. n. 497.

[382] After this clause one would expect *iti*.

[383] Either the above passage is corrupt or the construction is awkward. The particle *ca*, attested by A, B, H (save V), never accompanies *āha* in Siddharṣi-gaṇin's work. Besides, I could not account for the use of *ca* in the above context, preceded by a sentence ending with *iti*, and that is why I leave it out in the main text of the edition. Furthermore, being normally a correlative of *yat*, *yasmāt*, *hi* or *yadi*, the adverb *atas* is never, as a rule, associated with *yataḥ*. The latter, however, can hardly by a correlative of the initial *tataḥ*, because the correlatives *tataḥ* ... *yataḥ* have nothing to correlate in the sentence in view of the simple object-subject-verb clause (*tataś ca vacanād dvividhād api samagra-sāmagrīkasya pratipādyasyânumeya-pratyakṣârtha-viṣayā yataḥ pratītir ullasati*), provided that we take *atas* to begin a new sentence, that is not correlated with the preceding one through any adverbs. The adverb *tatah* cannot refer directly to the quotation *paśya rāja gacchati*, because one should expect *iti* preceding *tataḥ*; even then, the construction *iti tataḥ* is nowhere attested in the Siddharṣi-gaṇin's work (we have instead *ity anena*, *ity amunā*, etc.). I take *tataḥ* not as a correlative, but as an indicator of the conclusion—which is a typical function of *tataś ca*—ensuing from two examples instantiating *parârthânumāna* and *parârtha-pratyakṣa*. Whatever the case may be, this is how I eventually construe the doubtful passage: 'And therefore' (*tataś ca*) … 'since' (*yataḥ*) … 'that is why' (*atas*) … 'hence' (*iti*) …

[384] Cf. NAṬ *ad loc.*: ***pratipādaka-sthêty-ādi***. *pratipādaka-sthaṁ*[a] *pratyakṣânumāna-nirṇitârthasya*[b] *prakāśyate 'rthaḥ parebhyo 'nenêti*[c] *prakāśanaṁ vacanaṁ kāraṇaṁ yasya parasya, tasya bhāvas tattvaṁ*[†] *tasmāt*.

[a] C: °-*stha*-°. [b] A: *nirnitârthasya*.
[c] A: *'nanêti*. [†] Cf. Pāṇ 5.1.119.

[385] Cf. NAṬ *ad loc.*: ***etenêti***. *para-pratītiṁ prati vacanasyôpāyatā-pradarśanena*. ***pūrva-kārikôktêti***. *vākyaṁ tad-upacārata iti*.—'"Thereby" [means] by demonstrating that an utterance is the means with regard to the awareness of another [person]. "Mentioned in the previous verse" [means mentioned in the following verse]: "A

sentence … because of the metaphorical transference of this [cognitive criterion onto the sentence]".'

[386] The *pratīka*: '***tasyêti***. *pratyakṣasya*' of the H.-edition of NAṬ printed on the page 69 belongs in fact to p. 70 and in no way does it refer to '*tasya vikalpa-janakatvāt*' of NAV, as its position on p. 69 might suggest. It clearly refers to '*tasya kathañcid eka-viṣayatayā*...' below.

[387] Somehow, neither Siddharṣi-gaṇin nor Devabhadra-sūri explain what exactly they mean by 'somehow.' What the latter says is merely the following: ***eka-viṣayatayêti***. *śabdena sahêti śeṣaḥ. ayam abhiprāyaḥ: sāmānya-viśeṣâtmakaṁ vastu śabdānām gocaraḥ, pratyakṣam api kathañcit sāmānya-viśeṣâtmaka*[a]*-vastu viṣayam. tataḥ sāmānya-viśeṣâtmako 'rthaḥ pratyakṣa-pratipannaḥ parasmai pratipādyamānaḥ parârtha-pratyakṣaṁ bhavati.*—'"Together with words" is what remains [to be supplemented]. The intention is as follows: a real thing, having [both] universal and particular nature, is the domain of words; also perception is somehow such the domain of which is a real thing, as [something] having [both] universal and particular nature. Therefore, an object, as having [both] universal and particular nature, which has been recognised through perception, becomes a perception for others, when it is demonstrated to others.'

[a] A: °- *viśeṣâtmakaṁ*.

[388] NAV 4: *tasmād vyavasāyâtmakam adhyakṣam ity etad eva cārv iti sthitam* (p. 36 of the English translation).

[389] I.e., both perception and the indirect cognition are for others and no difference is to be seen between them in this regard.

[390] Cf. n. 231.

[391] Cf. NAṬ *ad loc.*: **pratyakṣa-rūpam iti**. *paśya paśya*[a] *mṛgo yātîti pratyakṣa-rūpatayā pratipādakatvād vaco 'pi tathôcyate.*—'Also the utterance is called in this manner, [i.e. it is called perception], because it—inasmuch as it consists in perception—demonstrates [something perceptible, like in the following example]: "Look, a deer is running!".'

[a] H,V read *paśya* once only.

[392] Both the editions H and V have the following punctuation: *tac ca pratyakṣa-rūpam evôcyamānaṁ pratyakṣaṁ vipratipannaṁ prati punar anumāna-dvāreṇôcyamānam anumānam evêti. ca-śabdenânekārthatvād darśayati.—vacanaṁ kutaḥ pratyakṣam?* It is obvious, however, that the phrase *enânekārthatvād darśayati*, that elucidates the meaning of *ca*, is to be construed with the initial *tac ca*, and not with the question following it.

[393] The usage of the term *pakṣa* was not unequivocal, since the *pakṣa* might denote both [1] the locus, viz., the substratum of a well-known property, or [2] a thesis (*propositio*; genetically, though not semantically, equivalent to θέσις), viz., a propo-

sition, or thesis. At an earlier stage, but not only, the term was used occasionally in both meanings in one and the same treatise, e.g. in the opening sentence of *Nyāya-praveśa*, *pakṣa* is mentioned among three propositions that constitute the proof (*sādhana*): *tatra pakṣâdi-vacanāni sādhanam*, and to be subsequently exemplified by an affirmative and a negative proposition (NP_1, p. 1.8): *nityaḥ śabdo 'nityo vêti.* However, not infrequently it is defined clearly as the locus, or inferential subject (NP_1, p. 6–7): *pakṣaḥ prasiddho dharmī prasiddha-viśeṣaṇa-viśiṣṭatayā svayaṁ sādhyatvenêpsitaḥ*. In the course of development of logical ideas, the conviction seems to prevail to take *pakṣa* to denote a proposition, which finds its unambiguous expression in the commentary to *Nyāya-praveśa* approximately six centuries later: *pratijñā pakṣa ity anarthântaram* (NPV p. 22.13–14). The commentary attests that the ambiguity was not unknown to epistemologists of that time, and that was apparently the reason why Haribhadra ventures an attempt to unify both meanings of the term *pakṣa*: *tataś ca na dharma-mātraṁ na dharmī kevalaḥ na svatantram ubhayaṁ na ca tayoḥ sambandhaḥ kiṁ tu dharma-dharmiṇor viśeṣaṇa-viśeṣya-bhāva iti bhāvârthaḥ* (NPV, p. 15.23–24)—'And therefore, thesis/locus is not merely the property, it is not the property-possessor alone, it is not both of them [existing] independently of each other, it is not the relation between these two, but rather it is the relationship between the qualifier and the qualificandum [that is a relation] between the property and the property-possessor.' Also a comparison of two Vasubandhu's definitions of the first member of the proof formula (listed in n. 407)—an earlier one, *pakṣa-vacanaṁ pratijñā* [VāVa fr. AI5] ('the thesis is the mention of the locus'), and an later one, *sādhyâbhidhānaṁ pratijñā* [VāVi fr. B3] ('the thesis is the explicit statement the probandum')—demonstrates that for Vasubandhu *pakṣa* ≠ *pratijñā*, inasmuch as *pratijñā* (thesis) is used by him in both cases as *definiendum*, whereas *pakṣa* occurs only in the first definition as a part of the *definiens* (alongside with *pratijñā*), in the sense of 'locus', and is replaced in the second formulation by *sādhya*.

Traditionally, the locus (*pakṣa*; *p*) of a proof formula, being the property-possessor (*dharmin*), was understood to be related to its property to-be-proved (*sādhya*; *s*), by the force of the logical reason (*hetu*, *h*) pervading it (*vyāpaka*), through the relation of invariable concomitance (*vyāpti*, *R*), or the relation of pervasion. In a valid inference, the locus was supposed to meet the condition $p =_{df} R(h, p) \supset R(s, p)$ ['If the locus is pervaded by the property of the logical reason, then the locus is pervaded by the property to be proved']. Bearing in mind that the relation of invariable concomitance resembles the converse of the relation of inclusion (*vide infra*), the above dependence between the locus and the two other terms may be illustrated graphically, by way of *approximation* only—for $p \in P$, $h \in H$ and $s \in S$—in the following manner:

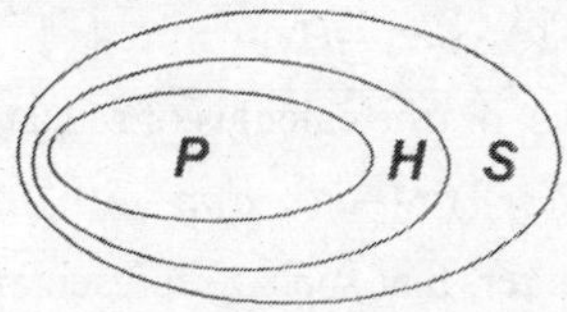

At any rate, in view of its ambiguous usage, it might be recommendable to render the term *pakṣa* as 'subject of inference', or 'inferential subject.' In the present context, however, there is no doubt that what Siddharṣi-gaṇin actually means—leaving aside the question whether Siddhasena understood the term *pakṣa* in the identical way—is proposition (thesis); cf. NAV 14: [*pakṣaḥ*] ***sādhyasyânumeyasyâbhyupagamo 'ṅgī-karaṇaṁ***, *prāśnikâdīnāṁ purataḥ pratijñā-svī-kāra ity arthaḥ*. Nevertheless, depending on the context, I render the term either as 'thesis' or 'locus.'

As it has been mentioned above in passing, the two-argument relation of invariable concomitance (*vyāpti*, R), viz., the dependence between the three terms of the proof formula, *pakṣa* (p), *hetu* (h) and *sādhya* (s), can be formulated as follows: $R(s, h)$ and $R(h, p)$; cf. STAAL (1973: 157–8). The term that has the broadest extension is s, whereas p is characterised by the narrowest extension. Certain affinity between the relation of invariable concomitance and the relation of inclusion can hardly escape our notion, but for the fact that that the dependence between these three terms is inverse in the case of invariable concomitance. Thus, the converse (symbolised by $\breve{R}$) of the relation of invariable concomitance R is the relation of inclusion such that for the pair of arranged set elements x, y the equivalence: $<x, y> \in R \equiv <y, x> \in \breve{R}$ is satisfied. In other words, the relation of invariable concomitance R is a relation that correlates two set elements x, y if and only if the inverted pair y, x is related by $\breve{R}$ (*sc.* inversion) and for $p \in P$, $h \in H$, $s \in S$ (i.e. elements p, h and s of the sets P, H and S, respectively) we observe the following relation $\breve{R}$: $P \subset H \subset S$. By availing ourselves, on the one hand, of two standard formulations of positive concomitance (*anvaya*) and negative concomitance (*vyatireka*)—found for instance in NP$_1$, p. 2.1,3–4, NBṬ$_1$ 3.5, etc.—by way of example:

(1) *anvaya*: *yat kṛtakaṁ tad anityam*, and
(2) *vyatireka*: *yan nityaṁ tad akṛtakam*,

and, on the other, by representing the property of 'being produced' (*kṛtakatva*) by H, and the property of 'being impermanent' (*anityatva*) by S, we can formulate the two definitions in the predicate calculus as follows:

T1 $anvaya =_{df} Hx \Rightarrow Sx$,
T2 $vyatireka =_{df} \neg Sx \Rightarrow \neg Hx$;

what corresponds to the following notation of the calculus of sets and relations:

T1' $anvaya =_{df} R(h, p) \Rightarrow R(s, p)$, and
T2' $vyatireka =_{df} \neg R(s, p) \Rightarrow \neg R(h, p)$.

The relation of invariable concomitance is thus the conjunction:

T3 $vy\bar{a}pti =_{df} (Hx \Rightarrow Sx) \wedge (\neg Sx \Rightarrow \neg Hx)$

notated in the predicate calculus, or (the calculus of sets and relations):

T3' $vy\bar{a}pti =_{df} (R(h, p) \Rightarrow R(s, p)) \wedge (\neg R(s, p) \Rightarrow \neg R(h, p))$.

We should remember, however, that such a representation is extensional, whereas the inference in India, what should be kept in mind throughout this discussion, was basically intensional (cf. n. 294). Intensionality of such inferences becomes conspicuous, for instance, in the fact that two conditions (viz., $Hx \Rightarrow Sx$ and $\neg Sx \Rightarrow \neg Hx$), even though they are extensionally equivalent (the law of simple transposition), have to be—in the opinion of most Indian logicians—mentioned jointly in any inference based on the proof formula.

A lucid formulation of both positive concomitance and negative concomitance understood in this manner is found even in a work as late as a Nyāya-Vaiśeṣika manual of Laugākṣi Bhāskara Śarmā (c. 1550), TK 58:

anvaye sādhanaṁ vyāpyaṁ sādhyaṁ vyāpakam iṣyate /
sādhyâbhāvo 'nyathā vyāpyo vyāpakaḥ sādhanâtyayaḥ //

—'In [the formulation] of positive concomitance, the probans is accepted as [a property] to-be-pervaded, [whereas] the probandum [is accepted] as the pervader. In the other case, [viz., in the formulation of positive concomitance], the absence of the probandum [is accepted] as [a property] to-be-pervaded, [whereas] the lack of probans [is accepted] as the pervader.'

Other formulations of the relation of invariable concomitance were considered faulty also by Siddharṣi and Devabhadra, cf. n. 174.

[394] Cf. NP_1, p. 1.4–5: *tatra pakṣâdi-vacanāni sādhanam. pakṣa-hetu-dṛṣṭânta-vacanair hi prāśnikānām apratīto 'rthaḥ pratipādyata iti.*

[395] Cf. NA & NAV 5, esp. p. 38.

[396] Cf. NAṬ 13 *ad loc.*: ***vāco yuktir iti***. *paśyad vāg-diśo hara-yukti-daṇḍe*[a] *iti ṣaṣṭhyā aluk-samāsaḥ.*

[a] SHŚ 3.2.32 (identification after Bhagavandas Harakhchand and P. L. Vaidya).

[397] For the lack of any illustration of the clearances (*śuddhi*), apart from the mention suggesting that each of the clearances applies to a respective member of the proof formula, it cannot be decided whether the ten-membered proof formula alluded to by Siddharṣi-gaṇin is the one described by Vātsyāyana or by Bhadrabāhu I. In NBh 1.1.32—in addition to the five members enumerated in the *sūtra*—we find [6] inquisitiveness (*jijñāsā*), [7] suspicion (*saṁśaya*), [8] confirmation of the demonstrative force (*śakya-prāpti*), [9] purpose (*prayojana*) and [10] rejection of suspicion (*saṁśaya-vyudāsa*).

VIDYĀBHŪṢAṆA (1920: 122, n. 1) expresses a suggestion that 'Here (viz., NBh 1.1.32—P.B.) Vātsyāyana refers perhaps to the Jaina "syllogism" of ten members as illustrated in the Daśavaikālika-niryukti of Bhadrabāhu I ...'

The ten members are [1] *pratijñā*, [2] *pratijñā-vibhakti*, [3] *hetu*, [4] *hetu-vibhakti*, [5] *vipakṣa*, [6] *vipakṣa-pratiṣedha*, [7] *dṛṣṭānta*, [8] *āśaṅkā*, [9] *āśaṅkā-pratiṣedha*, [10] *nigamana*, and the passage in question is found DN 142:

te u païnna vibhattī heü-vibhattī vivakkha-paḍiseho /
diḍḍhato āṁsako tappaḍiseho nigamanaṁ ca //

For a rough translation and an exposition of Bhadrabāhu's ten-membered proof formula see VIDYĀBHŪṢAṆA (1920: 165–7) and P. L. Vaidya's introduction to his edition of NV, pp. viii–ix.
See also DN 50 (p. 36):

katthaï pañcâvayavaṁ, dasahā vā savvahā na paṭi-siddhaṁ /
naya puṇa savvaṁ bhaṇṇaï, hondī sa-viyāram akkhāyaṁ //

What is striking, the fourth member of the proof formula, viz., application (*upanaya*), is entirely missing in Bhadrabāhu's enumeration, in the first place, unless we took the sixth member, or the negation of the counter-thesis (*vipakṣa-pratiṣedha*), to be a formulation of application. The members that overlap in formulations of Bhadrabāhu and Vātsyāyana are *pratijñā*, *hetu*, *dṛṣṭānta*, *āśaṅkā* / *saṁśaya*, *āśaṅkā-pratiṣedha* / *saṁśaya-vyudāsa*, *nigamana*. Yet, the argumentative structure of Bhadrabāhu's proof formula would still remain different in comparison with the standard five-membered formulation, where application (*upanaya*) necessarily follows example (*dṛṣṭânta*). Thus, the occurrence of ten members of the proof formula in the case of Bhadrabāhu and Vātsyāyana seems in my opinion rather coincidental and the latter could not have had Bhadrabāhu in mind.

It is likewise highly improbable that Siddharṣi refers to Bhadrabāhu, despite the fact that the latter was a prominent Jaina thinker, in view of the fact that the structure of Bhadrabāhu's ten-membered proof formula reveals a clear dialectical character of a proposition–counter-proposition scheme that stands in opposition to Siddharṣi's intention of a positive verification of five-membered proof formula by means of clearances (*śuddhi*). In other words, in the case of Bhadrabāhu, a group of four standard members of the proof formula, viz., *pratijñā*, *hetu*, *dṛṣṭānta* and *nigamana*, are correlated with members of the proof formula that negate them or demonstrate a contrary proposition by way of presenting a kind of *pūrva-pakṣa*. The structure betrays certain features that allow us to suppose that Bhadrabāhu's proof formula is directly—and, perhaps, even to a larger degree than it was the case with the traditional *pañcâvayava-vākya*—derived from the tradition of philosophical debate based precisely on such a method of presentation of one's own arguments. Certainly, such a scheme is worlds apart from the idea of clearances (*śuddhi*) expressed by Siddharṣi, that were supposed to render an additional justification to accept unconditionally each of the five standard members of the proof formula by means of cognitive criteria. In contradistinction to Bhadrabāhu's proof formula, the exposition of the early Nyāya ten-membered proof formula exhibits such a positive correlation of the five standard members of the proof formula and the remaining quintuplet (*jijñāsā*, *saṁśaya*, *śakya-prāpti*, *prayojana*, *saṁśaya-vyudāsa*), though too little evidence is at our disposal to conclude that what Siddharṣi had in mind was the tradition alluded to by Vātsyāyana.

[398] In other words: alone from the context, i.e. on account of the manner the opponent formulates his argument. Cf. VP Appendix V, p. 391: '*prakrama* II.399. Method of explaining the fundamental principles. Cf. *iha bhinnāny āgama-darśanāni laukikaiś*

cârvāg-darśibhiḥ tatrâbhiniviṣṭaiḥ parasparaṁ śāstrāṇāṁ pṛthag pṛthag prakramāḥ paripāṭhyo dṛśyante viruddhā iva paramârthatas tattvaṁ satyam eka-rūpam aviruddham eva sarvatra sthitam.' Alternatively, we could take *prakramād eva* literally: 'just by following the way of reasoning; in the course of debate.'

399 Cf. NAṬ 13 *ad loc.*: ***avismṛtêty-ādi***. *dṛṣṭântena smāryaḥ.*[a] *sa câsau pratibandho vyāptiś ca tasya grāhakaṁ ca*[b]. *tac ca tat-pramāṇaṁ ca. tato na vismṛtaṁ tad yasya sa tathā*. For the dissolution of the compound see also NAV 13 (*vide infra*, p.56 of the English translation): *(a)smaryamāne pratibandha-grāhiṇi pramāṇe* ...—'if the cognitive criterion grasping the invariable connection is (not) recollected ...'

[a] A,C insert number *2*: *smāryaḥ // 2*. [b] H,V omit *ca*: *grāhakaṁ*.

400 NAṬ *ad loc.*: ***parikarmita-matitvād iti***. *parikarma saṁjātam asyā*[a] *iti, tārakâder ākṛti-gaṇatvâdi-tac-pratyayaḥ*[b], *tataḥ parikarmitā matir yasyêti vigrahaḥ*.

[a] C: *saṁjātasyā*.

[b] A: °*-tac-pratyayo vā*. C repeats: *tat-pratyayo vā. tat-pratyayo vā*.

401 NAṬ *ad loc.*: ***akāṇḍe*** *aprastāve*, 'i.e. with no occasion (unexpectedly).'

402 Cf. n.600.

403 Cf. NAṬ 13 *ad loc.*: ***tat-sādhyêty-ādi***. *teṣāṁ pakṣâdīnāṁ sādhyaḥ pratipādyo yo 'rthas tasya pratīti-vikalatā, tayā kṛtvā hetu-bhūtayā vā,* ***tasya***[a] *pratipādyasya sākāṅkṣatvāt*.

[a] H,V read on and do not mark *tasya* as a separate *pratīka*.

404 *upasaṁharaṇa*, i.e. *upasaṁhāra* – *upanayana*, cf. PMī 2.1 § 30: *dṛṣṭânta-dharmiṇi visṛtasya sādhana-dharmasya sādhya-dharmiṇi yaḥ upasaṁhāraḥ sa upanaya, upasaṁhriyate 'nenôpanīyate 'nenêti vacana-rūpaḥ.*—'Such a use of a property [constituting] the probans, which extends itself onto the property-possessor in the example, in [the case of] the property-possessor [constituting] the probandum is application; that by which [something] is used [or] that by which [something] is applied [is application] that has a form of a proposition.'

405 Cf. NAṬ 13 *ad loc.*: ***paścāt tasyâiva pramāṇena samarthanam iti***. *yat yat tat sarvaṁ kṣaṇikam iti vyāpty-āliṅgita-hetûpanyāsânantaram*[a] *akṣaṇike krama-yaugapadyābhyām artha-kriyā-virodhād iti bādhaka-pramāṇena sattvâkhya-hetoḥ samarthanam.* ***punaḥ pakṣa-dharmiṇy-upasaṁharaṇam iti***. *kṛtakaś ca śabda ity-ādi-rūpam.*—'[The phrase] "the corroboration of this very [logical reason] by a cognitive criterion following immediately" [means] the corroboration of the logical reason called "existence"[b]—that immediately follows the specification of the logical reason embraced by the invariable concomitance in the form: "everything whatsoever is momentary, because it is existent"—by the subverting cognitive criterion in the form: "because [there would be] a contradiction [to execute] efficient action both consecutively and simultaneously with regard to a non-momentary [thing]". "Then the ap-

plication of a property-possessor to the thesis" consists in [propositions like] "and the speech element is [something] which has been produced, [hence is momentary]".'

[a] H,V: °-*hetûpanyāsântaraṁ*.

[b] The inference in question is: *sarvaṁ kṣaṇikaṁ sattvāt*; for the logical reason 'existence' cf. p. 70 and n. 465.

[406] Cf. n. 231.

[407] The above definition of the thesis (*sādhyâbhyupagamaḥ pakṣaḥ*) formulated by Siddhasena bears striking resemblance to the definition found in Vasubandhu's VāVi: *sādhyâbhidhānaṁ pratijñā* [fr. B3]. The following comparison of this definition with another definition of the thesis formulated by Vasubandhu (400–480) in his much earlier work VāVa [after FRAUWALLNER 1957/a and FRANCO (1990: 202)] points to an essential evolution of the term already within the life span of Vasubandhu himself, be it limited to the works of Vasubandhu alone (cf. also n. 393):

Vāda-vidhāna		*Vāda-vidhi*	
AI 5	*pakṣa-vacanaṁ pratijñā*	B 3	*sādhyâbhidhānaṁ pratijñā*
AI 7	*hetur vipakṣād viśeṣaḥ*	B 5	*tādṛg-avinâbhāvi-dharmôpadarśanaṁ hetuḥ*
AI 8	*tathā-siddho dṛṣṭântaḥ*	B 6	*udāharaṇaṁ tu yathā dhūmo 'gner iti*

[408] Cf. NP_1, p. 1.5–7: *tatra pakṣaḥ prasiddho dharmī prasiddha-viśeṣaṇa-viśiṣṭatayā svayaṁ sādhyatvenêpsitaḥ. pratyakṣâdy-aviruddha iti vākya-śeṣaḥ.*—'Out of these [members of the proof formula], the locus is a well-known subject; it is intended by [the propounder] himself to be proved as qualified by a well-known distinctive feature. The following annotation to the [above] statements [is tacitly implied: the locus] is not contradicted by perception, etc.' Cf. NM 1 (as restored by G. TUCCI):

pakṣâdi-vacanānîti sādhanam; tatra hi svayaṁ /
sādhyatvenêpsitaḥ pakṣo viruddhârthânirākṛtaḥ //

—'Proof [consists in] utterances [expressing] the locus, etc.. Among these very [utterances], locus is what is intended by [the propounder] himself as the probandum [and] which is not revoked by objects [that are] contrary [to it].'

[409] For possible formations of the word *pakṣa* comp. the following works: [a] *Uṇādi-kośa* of Mahādeva Vedāntin (2nd half of seventeenth century), [b] *Uṇādi-sūtra* of Śvetavanavāsin (between the tenth–sixteenth century) and [c] *Auṇādikapadārnava* of Peru-sūri (between 1350–1600, perhaps eighth century).

[1] *ḍupacaṣ pāke* (DhP 1.1045) + *asun* ($UṇādiS_2$ 4.219 [=$UṇādiS_1$ 662, p. 312]: *pacivacibhyāṁ suṭ ca*.—'The affix *asun* with the augment *suṭ* comes after √*pac* "to cook" and √*vac* "to speak"'); The affix *asun* itself is taken from $UṇādiS_2$ 4.188: *sarva-dhātubhyo 'suman*. See also:

[1.a] UṇādiK 695 (comm. to. 4.219: *pacivacibhyāṁ suṭ ca*), p. 108:

pakṣaḥ pakṣe patatre ca ktsarârdhe chadāv api //

Cf. also UṇādiK (Index, p. 189): '***pakṣas*** (*pac* + *asun* 4.219) *n.*—a fortnight; wing of a bird; a half year; the leaf of door 695.'

[1.b] UṇādiS$_2$ 651 (comm. to 4.225: *pacivacibhyāṁ suṭ ca*), p. 203: ... ***pakṣas*** *pati* [*pari*]*grahaḥ* //

[2] *patḷ gatau* (DhP 1.898) + *sa* (UṇādiS$_2$ 3.66 [=UṇādiS$_1$ 352, p. 237]: *gr̥dhipaṇyor dakau ca*.—'The affix *sa* comes after the roots *gr̥dh* "to covet" and *paṇ* "to purchase, to praise", the *dh* and *ṇ* of the roots are respectively changed to *d* and *k*.' The affix *sa* itself is taken from UṇādiS$_2$ 3.62: *vr̥tr̥̄vadihanikamikaśibhyaḥ saḥ*. Thus, we have: *paṇ* + *sa* → *pak* + *sa* → *pakṣa*.

[2.a] p. 61, UṇādiK 400 (comm. to. 3.69: *gr̥hipaṇyor dakau ca*):

smare gr̥tsaḥ, pakṣo māsârdha-parśvayoḥ /
grahe sādhye virodhe ca bale sakhi-sahāyayoḥ //
cullīrandhre patatre ca dehâṅge rāja-kuñjare /

Cf. also UṇādiK (Index, p. 188–9): '***pakṣa*** (*paṇ* + *saḥ* 3.69): *m.*—a fortnight; a side, flank; planet; a thesis, an argument to be maintained; contradiction; army; friend; ally; the ash-pit of the fire place; wing; a limb or part of the body; royal elephant 400–I.'

[2.b] UṇādiS$_2$ 337 (comm. to 3.66: *gr̥dhipaṇyor dakau ca*), p. 115: ... *patyata* [*varia lectio* B: *padyate*] *iti* ***pakṣaḥ*** *kāla-viśeṣaḥ* //

[2.c] AuṇP 202–3ab (comm. to 3.69: *gr̥dhiparṇo*[*ṇyo*]*r dakau ca*), p. 141:

pakṣo māsârdhake parsve gr̥he sādhya-virodhayoḥ /
keśādeḥ parato br̥nde bale sakhi-sahāyayoḥ //
cullīrandhre patatre ca rāja-kuñjara-pārśvayoḥ /

[2.c] p. 139 AuṇP 190 (comm. to 3.62: *vr̥tr̥̄vadihanikamikaśibhyaḥ saḥ*):

atra bāhulakād ardha-māse pakṣaḥ paceḥ sataḥ /
pakṣaḥ pārśva-garutsâdhya-sahāya-balabhittiṣu //

[3] *paṇa vyavahāre stutau ca* (DhP 1.466).

[410] Cf. PALV 3.17: *aniṣṭo mīmāṁsakasyânityaḥ śabdaḥ. pratyakṣâdi-bādhitaś câśrāvaṇatvâdiḥ. ādi-śabdenânumānâgama-loka-sva-vacana-bādhitātāṁ grahaṇam.* Here: *anirākr̥ta* = *abādhita*. Cf. also PMī 1.2.13–14: /13/ *sisādhayiṣitam asiddham abādhyaṁ sādhyaṁ pakṣaḥ.* /14/ *pratyakṣânumānâgama-loka-sva-vacana-pratītayo bādhāḥ.*—'/13/ The probandum, [i.e.] thesis, is what is intended to be proved, what is [yet] unproved, what cannot be subverted. /14/ Subversion [consists in cognitive criteria, viz.,] perception, inference, oral tradition, [as well as in] opinion prevalent among people, one's own utterances and [prevalent] understanding.' For the exemplification of these varieties of subversion see PMī 1.2. § 58: *tatra pratyakṣa-bādhā yathā anuṣṇo 'gniḥ, na madhu madhuram, na sugandhi vidalan-mālatī-mukulam, acākṣuṣo ghaṭaḥ, aśrāvaḥaḥ śabdaḥ, nâsti bahir-arthaḥ ity-ādi. anumāna-bādhā*

yathā sa-roma hasta-talam, nityaḥ śabda iti vā. atrânupalabhena kṛtakatvena cânumāna-bādhā. āgama-bādhā yathā pretyâsukha-prado dharma iti. para-loke sukha-pradatvaṁ dharmasya sarvâgama-siddham. loka-bādhā yathā śuci nara-śiraḥ-kapālam iti. loke hi nara-śiraḥ-kapālâdīnām aśucitvaṁ suprasiddham. sva-vacana-bādhā yathā mātā me bandhyêti. pratīti-bādhā yathā acandraḥ śaśīti. atra śaśinaś candra-śabda-vācyatvaṁ pratīti-siddhaṁ iti pratīti-bādhā.—'As for these [varieties of subversion], the subversion by perception [is represented by] such [examples]: "Fire is not hot," "Honey is not sweet," "A bursting bud of jasmine is not fragrant," "Pot is invisible," "Sound is not audible," "There is no external object," etc. The subversion by inference [is represented by] such [examples]: "The palm of the hand is overgrown with hair," or "Sound is permanent". In these [two] cases the subversion by inference [takes places], because [the palm of the hand is] not comprehended and because [sound] is produced. The subversion by oral tradition [is represented by] such [an example]: "Virtue results in unhappiness in the life hereafter." It is established in all oral traditions, [i.e. all scriptures], that virtue results in happiness in the other world. The subversion by opinion prevalent among people [is represented by] such [an example]: "Humans skulls are ritually clean," since it is very well-known among people that human skulls are ritually unclean. The subversion by one's own utterances (*contradictio in terminis*) [is represented by] such [an example]: "My mother is barren." The subversion by [prevalent] understanding [is represented by] such [an example]: "The moon is not a lunar planet." In this case it is established by [prevalent] understanding—hence the subversion by [prevalent] understanding—that the moon is a lunar planet.'

411 Cf. PV_3 3.27cd: *viduṣāṁ vācyo hetur eva hi kevalaḥ.*—'Since for scholars simply the logical reason alone is to be stated.' It is quoted in NAV 25 on p. 77 of the English translation. See also NB_1 3.36: *dvayor apy anayoḥ prayoge nâvaśyaṁ pakṣa-nirdeśaḥ.*—'If both of them together are pronounced, by no means there is any specific mention of the locus'; and $NBṬ_1$ 3.36 thereon: *yataś ca sādhanaṁ sādhya-dharma-pratibaddhaṁ tādātmya-tad-utpattibhyāṁ pratipattavyaṁ dvayor api prayogayos tasmāt pakṣo 'vaśyam eva na nirdeśyaḥ.*

412 NA 13 (p. 55 ff. of the translation).

413 I was unable to identify the source of the quotation.

414 These two reasons are supposed to account for two grammatical differences between *gocara-dīpakaḥ* of the aphorism and its explanation *viṣaya-sandarśakatvāt* of Siddharṣi-gaṇin's gloss. The first reason is to account for the transformation of the nominative case into the ablative. According to the second reason, the addition of °*tva*—in *viṣaya-sandarśakatvād*—is justified by *bhāva* or action (*sc.* the fundamental notion of a verb or *nomen actionis*, cf. n.50), and points out to the fact that the expressing element may play a role of a sentence, in contradistinction to a noun, the quintessence of which is *sattva* or existence.

415 Cf. n.398.

[416] Cf. NAṬ 14 *ad loc.*: ***na hîty-ādi***. *ayam abhiprāyaḥ: kvâpi nirṇīta-pakṣe prativādini hetuḥ prayujyate, kvâpy anirṇīta-pakṣe. tatra yadā nirṇīta-pakṣe prativādini hetuḥ prayujyate, tadā nirarthakatvāt pakṣôpanyāso 'smābhir na kriyate eva. dvitīye tu pakṣe viṣaya-darśakatvena saphalatvād avaśyaṁ kārya eva. kūrca-śobhāyāḥ puraḥ-saraṁ prathamam yasmin hetāv upanyaste kūrca-śobhā sampadyate, tattvato vailakṣyâbhāvaḥ, sāvaṣṭambhatā bhavatîti yāvat, athavā kūrca-śobhā puraḥ-saraṁ yatrêti, asmiṁś ca*[a] *pakṣe.*[b] *ayam abhiprāyo: yadā*[c] *samyag-bhūtaṁ kiñcid dvitvâdikaṁ*[d] *pratipādayitum ārabhyate tadā tat-pratipādanād arvāg api kūrca-śobhā*[e] *sāvaṣṭambhatā, śmaśru*[e]*-parāmarśanaṁ vā bhavatîti.*—'The intention [of the passage] beginning with "for not" is as follows: the logical reason is pronounced to the disputant in certain cases, when the thesis is determined, [and] in certain cases, when the thesis is not determined. Regarding these two [possibilities], when the logical reason is pronounced to the disputant with regard to a determined thesis, then the specification of the thesis is not done by us (*sc.* we do not follow this custom), inasmuch as it is purposeless, whereas with regard to the second [kind of] thesis (*sc.* undetermined) the specification of the thesis has to necessarily be carried out at all events, inasmuch as it is purposeful. Coming in front [in the case] of the elegance of the beard [means] to be foremost: in which specified logical reason the elegance of the beard occurs, viz., there is in fact no contrariety; which is tantamount to the fact that it has firm support. Alternatively, "[there] in which" the elegance of the beard comes in front [means]: in such a thesis. The intention is as follows: when one begins to demonstrate a particular [thesis] which is correct [but which] possesses ambivalence, etc., then—even before its demonstration—what is present is the elegance of the beard, viz., firm support, or pulling one's beard (potential defeat).'

This obscure expression *kūrca-śobhā* is explained by Devabhadra-sūri as 'absence of contrariety' (*vailakṣyâbhāva*), or 'possessing firm support' (*sāvaṣṭambhatā*), even b e f o r e the final demonstration of the proof. Its opposite is 'pulling one's beard' (*śmaśru-parāmarśana*). The word *kūrca* could also mean the middle point between the eyebrows, see AmK 2.6.92c (I, p. 421): *kūrcam astrī bruvor madhyam* ... and AmKV *ad loc.*: *kūrcam iti kocati brūromaṇi pratiṣṭabhnati kūrcam*, "*kuca samarcana-kauṭilya-pratiṣṭambha-vilekhaneṣu*". However, I do not think this is the case here. From NAṬ quoted above it is clear that *kūrca* is a synonym to *śmaśru*. Thus, would *kūrca-śobhā* be a kind of the subjective, intuitive *clair et distinct* conviction?

[a] H,V omit *ca*: *asmin*. [b] A,C: *pakṣe 'yam*; H,V: *pakṣe ayam*.
[c] C: *yad*<...>. [d] C: *dvetvâdikaṁ*. [e] A,C: *smaśru-°*; H,V: *śmaśrū-°*.

[417] *ārekita* < Pkt. *āreïā*, cf. PSM (*deśa*) = *mukulita*, *sakucita*, *bhrānta*, *mukta*, *romañcita*.

[418] And hence it is impossible to verify whether the archer is skilful or incompetent. The popular simile of an archer is found as early as in BĀU 3.8.2: *sā hôvācâhaṁ vai tvā yājñavalkya yathā pāśyo vā vaideho vôgraputra ujjyaṁ dhanur adhijyaṁ kṛtvā dvau bāṇavatau sapatnâtivyādhinau haste kṛtvôpottiṣṭha-devam evâhaṁ tvā*

dvyāmbhyāṁ praśnābhyām upodasthāṁ tau me brūhîti pṛccha gārgîti. Also Māgha in ŚPV 2.27 avails himself of the simile:

anirloḍita-kāryasya vāg-jālaṁ vāgmino vṛthā /
nimittād aparāddheṣor dhānuṣkasyêva valgitam //

Cf. MOOKERJEE (1971: 76, n. 1).

[419] Lit. 'viewers have curiosity.'

[420] The phrase 'Just the way … suspected of being contradictory …' is a quotation of NA 15.

[421] I.e. a universally valid definition (*nirviśeṣa* = *sāmānya*).

[422] NAṬ 5 (p. 38 of the translation).

[423] Devabhadra-sūri explains 'in certain cases' by 'with regard to a particular person to be taught': ***kvacid*** *iti. pratipādya-viśeṣe.*

[424] Siddharṣi-gaṇin apparently understands *upapatti*—at least here—merely in the ontological sense, viz., 'occurring, taking place.' The term however is not restricted to the physical occurrence of a phenomenon but entails also the logical possibility of such an occurrence. This is why I render it consistently as 'explicability' in order to render both the ontological and epistemological aspect.

[425] 'Otherwise', being a part (*avayava*), stands here for the expression '[its] inexplicability otherwise', which in its turn is the word aggregate (*samudāya*).

[426] The above passage refers, e.g. to the position of the Buddhists, cf. a quote from Diṅnāga in PVSV$_{\text{I}}$ 3.16ab: *yad āha—eṣa tāvan nyāyo yad ubhayaṁ vaktavyaṁ viruddhânaikāntika-pratipakṣeṇa iti*, which is further elucidated as follows: *sādharmya-vācanaṁ viruddha-pratipakṣeṇa, vaidharmya-vācanam anaikāntika-pratipakṣeṇa.* Cf. also NBṬ$_{\text{I}}$ 2.7: *nanu ca sapakṣa eva sattvam ity ukte vipakṣe 'sattvam evêti gamyata eva. tat kim arthaṁ punar ubhayor upādānam kṛtam. tad ucyate. anvayo vyatireko vā niyamavān eva prayoktavyo nânyathêti darśayituṁ dvayor apy upādānaṁ kṛtam. aniyame hi dvayor api prayoge 'yam arthaḥ syāt. sapakṣe yo 'sti vipakṣe ca nâsti sa hetur iti. tathā ca sati sa śyāmas tat-putratvāt, dṛśyamāna-putravad iti tat-putratva hetuḥ syāt. tasmān niyamavator evânvaya-vyatirekayoḥ prayogaḥ kartavyo yena pratibandho gamyeta sādhanasya sādhyena.*—'Now [an opponent may rise an objection]: "When one says that the occurrence [of the logical reason] is only in the homologue, then it is simply understood that in the heterologue there is nothing but non-occurrence [of the logical reason]. Therefore, for what purpose the mention of both has been made?" The following is said [by way of reply]. The mention of both of them together has been made to show that either positive concomitance or negative concomitance may be pronounced only as having a circumscription, [i.e. as being applicable within certain limits], not otherwise. For if the pronouncement of both of them were without any circumscription, that would be exactly the meaning. The logical reason is what exists in the homologue and what

does not exist in the heterologue. And if it were so, [i.e. if there were no circumscription,] then "being his son" could be the logical reason, [like in the following inference]: "He is dark-complexioned because he is his son, just like the son who is just being seen." Therefore, the pronouncement of both positive concomitance and negative concomitance only as having a circumscription has to be made, so that the invariable connection of the probans with the probandum could be understood.' For the faulty inference of "being his son" cf. n. 294. For definition of concomitance cf. n.174.

[427] Cf. the explication of the synonym *avinâbhāva* (the inseparable connection) in NAV 5: "***sādhyâvinâbhuna***" *iti*; *vinā bhavatîti vinâbhu, tato 'nyad avinâbhu, sādhyenâvinâbhu sādhyâvinâbhu.*

[428] The suffix *lyap* denotes a gerund form ending with °-*ya* and in certain cases (e.g. 'in a compound the first element of which is the negation *a*° ...') is substituted for the usual ending °-*tvā* following Pāṇ 7.1.32: *samāse 'nañ-pūrve ktvo lyap*. Besides, the suffix is mentioned in Pāṇ 2.4.36, 6.1.41 ff., 4.38.56 ff., etc. Thus, the idea is that the compound in the ablative case *sambandha-smaraṇād* ('because of the recollection of the relation') should stand for the locution *sambandhaṁ smarya* (= *sambandhaṁ smṛtvā*—'having recollected the relation'). Devabhadra-sūri, however, refers to the suffix *lyap* instead of the expected suffix *ktvā* (cf. Pāṇ 1.1.40: *ktvā-tosun-kasunaḥ*) instrumental in the formation of *smṛtvā*—apparently because of his own explication of the compound, viz., °-*sambandha-smaraṇam adhikṛtya*, in which the suffix *lyap* indeed is operative (the ending °-*ya*).

[429] Cf. PVin II$_1$ 63 (p. 91.23–26):

| *rgyu daṅ ᶜbras buᶜi dṅos po ᶜam* |
| *raṅ bźin ṅes par byed pa las* |
| *med na mi ᶜbyuṅ ṅes pa ste* |
| *ma mthoṅ las min mthoṅ las min* |

[430] I.e., how is it possible to ascertain that a particular relation holds invariably in all places and the three times? This problem was discussed by the Mīmāṁsaka, who emphasised a theoretical necessity to know all cases a relation of particular invariable concomitance could apply, e.g. to infer fire from smoke in a valid way, we would have to know all cases, past, present and future of smoke necessarily accompanied by fire, which is impossible, see NRĀ on MŚV$_1$ 5.4 (*Anumāna-pariccheda*).12 (p. 149.19–25): *satyam nâikena gamyate, bahubhis tu darśanair bahuṣu deśeṣu dhūmasyâgninā sāhityaṁ gamyate, tasmiṁs câvagate vyābhicāre cânavagate yathâdṛṣṭeṣu dhūmasyâgninā vyāpti avagatā bhavati. nanu nâdarśana-mātrād anagniṣu sarveṣu dhūmasyâbhāvaḥ sidhyati, ko vā brūte sidhyatîti, kintv adarśana-mātram evânagnau dhūmasya brūmaḥ, tāvatâiva bahuśo 'vagatâgni-sāhityasya paridṛṣṭeṣu deśa-kāleṣu vahni-niyamo 'vagato bhavati. tāvad evânumānâṅgam, tad-anantaraṁ tu 'yatra yatra dhūmḥ tatra tatrâgniḥ' iti yo 'vagamaḥ so 'py ānumānika eva, parkoṣa-rūpatvāt* ... Consequently, they postulated a pragmatic approach of re-

peated observation (*bhūyo-darśana*), which has so far not been invalidated by any exceptional case; see MŚV$_1$ 5.4.(*Anumāna-pariccheda*).12: *bhūyo-darśana-gamyā ca vyāptiḥ sāmānya-dharmayoḥ* / On the question of the validity of *vyāpti* and, *a fortiori* of *anumāna*, see TAKENAKA 1994.

[431] Here *abhāva* apparently does not occur in its usual meaning of 'absence' (cf. its next occurrence: *tatra parôpadeśâbhāvāt*!) but should be understood as a nominal paraphrase of a copula; Devabhadra-sūri supports this interpretation: ***tasyêty-ādi**. śabdasya parôpadeśa-rūpatayā kṛtvā śabda-janya-jñānasya svârthânumānatvaṁ bhavatîti.*

[432] I take the compound *avyabhicarita-tri-kāla-vyāpi-gocarasya* as *dvandva* in view of NAV 1: *tasmād anumānam abhilaṣatā gaty-antarâbhāvāt tat-sambandha-grahaṇa-pravaṇas tri-kāla-gocaro 'vyabhicārī vitarko 'bhyupagantavyaḥ* (p. 25 of the translation).

[433] For *mati-jñāna* see n. 629.

[434] For its description cf. NAV 1, p. 20 ff. of the translation and n. 174.

[435] The compound *dṛṣṭa-vyavahāra-°* has to be understood as a *dvandva*-compound (not *karma-dhāraya*: 'everyday practice [as it is] experienced') in view of a numerous passages; a few of them listed below (taken only from first sections of NAV) leave no doubt: *tathā dṛṣṭatvāt* (NAV 0; p. 5 of the translation), *nikhila-vyavahārôccheda-prasaṅgāt* (NAV 0; p. 29 of the translation), *atrâpi dṛṣṭa-hāner vyavahārôcchedasya samānatvāt* (NAV 0; p. 6 of the translation), *dṛṣṭa-hāny-adṛṣṭa-parikalpanā-prasaṅgāc ca* (NAV 1; p. 11 of the translation), *anyathā tat-kṛta-nikhila-vyavahārôccheda-prasaṅgāt, tad-ucchede ca dṛṣṭa-hāny-ādy-āpatteḥ* (NAV 3, p. 29 of the translation), *pratiniyata-vyavahārôccheda-prasaṅgāt* (NAV 1; p. 10 of the translation), *pramāṇa-paridṛṣṭa-sakala-vyavahārôcchedana-°* (NAV 4; p. 32 of the translation), *vikalpânutthānena sakala-vyavahārôccheda-prasaṅgaḥ* (NAV 4; p. 35 of the translation), *kṣaṇikatvâdy-aṁśavat sarvâṁśeṣu vyavahāraḥ pralīyeta* (NAV 4; p. 36 of the translation), *anyathā vyavahārâpravṛtter, dṛṣṭasyâpy adṛṣṭânatiśayanāt* (NAV 4; p. 36 of the translation), *iyatâiva dṛṣṭa-vyavahārôpapatteḥ* (NAV 31; p. 133 of the translation).

[436] Cf. n. 102.

[437] See A. B. Dhruva's note on *antar-vyāptâiva* in his edition of SVM, p. 236.8 ff.

[438] The above statement excludes the example (*dṛṣṭânta*) from the constituent members of a proof formula and thus explicitly limits the number of necessary members of the proof formula practically down to one, viz., the logical reason (*hetu*). Cf. MOOKERJEE (1935: 356–65) and SHAH (1967: 282–3). We find a similar tendency to limit also in NB$_2$ 3.121: *tri-rūpo hetur uktaḥ. tāvatā cârtha-pratītir iti na pṛthag-dṛṣṭânto nāma sādhanâvayavaḥ kaścit. tena nâsya lakṣaṇam pṛthag ucyate gatârthatvāt.*

[439] NAṬ 20 *ad loc.*: ***anyadā hîti***. *sambandha-vismaraṇâbhāve.*

[440] Cf. n. 474.

[441] The term *ābhāsa*, meaning 'semblance, false appearance, illusion, disguise,' occurs as early as MU 29–30 (p. 221):

yathā svapne dvayâbhāsaṁ spandate māyayā manaḥ /
tathā jāgrad dvayâbhāsaṁ spandate māyayā manaḥ //
advayaṁ ca dvayâbhāsaṁ manaḥ svapne na saṁśayaḥ /
advayaṁ ca dvayâbhāsaṁ tathā jāgran na saṁśayaḥ // —

—'Just like a thought in a dream becomes active in the disguise of duality due to illusion, similarly a thought in the waking state becomes active in the disguise of duality due to illusion. And [just like] there is no doubt that the thought in the disguise of duality is [in fact] non-dual in a dream, similarly there is no doubt that the thought in the disguise of duality is [in fact] non-dual in the waking state.'

[442] Cf. NAṬ 21 *ad loc.*: ***tad-vyudastā iti***. *pakṣâdi-lakṣaṇa-rahitāḥ.*—'"Opposed to them" [means] devoid of the characteristics of the thesis, etc.'

[443] In view of the reading adopted by Siddharṣi-gaṇin's commentary below (*tathā akṣa-lingato*) as well as on account of his further four-fold exemplification (*pratyakṣa-bādhito yathā*: ..., *anumāna-bādhito yathā*: ..., *loka-bādhito yathā*: ..., *sva-vacana-bādhito yathā*: ...), the *pāda* ***c*** of the *kārikā* text, as we have it in V. and H. editions, should be emended to *pakṣâbhāso 'kṣa-liṅgataḥ* (instead of *pakṣâbhāso 'sti liṅgataḥ*). Clearly, such an emended reading makes a much better sense, since a proposition may be revoked not only by inference (the exclusion of perception would be suggested by *'sti liṅgataḥ*) but also by perception. Moreover, we have already encountered a parallel reading in NAV 14 (*vide supra*): "*pratyakṣâdy-nirākṛta*" *iti*. "*pratyakṣaṁ*" ...; *ādi-śabdād anumāna-sva-vacana-lokā gṛhyate.*—'"Is not revoked by perception, etc.". "Perception" is [...]. On account of the speech element "etc." inference, one's own utterances and opinion prevalent among people are comprised.' The following parallel reading found in PALV 6.15,16: /15/ [*pakṣâbhāsaḥ*] *bādhitaḥ pratijñânumānâgama-loka-sva-vacanaiḥ.* /16/ *tatra pratyakṣa-bādhito yathâtuṣṇo 'gnir dravyatvāj jalavat*, corroborates an additional support for the suggested emendation. Also the editor P. L. Vaidya himself in the note on p. 108 corrects: 'Note the misprint *pakṣâbhāso 'sti liṅgataḥ* which should be read as *pakṣâbhāso 'kṣa-liṅgataḥ*. Thus we get five *pakṣâbhāsas*, viz., *pratipādya-siddha*, *akṣa-siddha*, i.e. *pratyakṣa-siddha*, *liṅga-siddha*, i.e. *anumāna-siddha*, *loka-siddha* and *sva-vacana-siddha*.' And last but not least, both Mss. A, B (which I received after I had formulated the above remarks) are in concord with my expectations and read: *pakṣâbhāso 'kṣa-liṅgataḥ*.

[444] Cf. NBṬ₁ 3.55: *pakṣavad ābhāsanta iti pakṣâbhāsāḥ.*

[445] What the opponent accepts stands in no need of further proof. If one were supposed to prove what is generally accepted to hold valid, all theses would be liable to

criticism and that would open the way to all-embracing scepticism, which is in no way a welcome attitude for the Jainas.

[446] The reading adopted by H,V, viz., *gamitam anekârthatvād dhātoḥ pratipāditaṁ*, in all probability misspells the ligature *anekârthatvād vā*. What is meant are not diverse meanings of a verbal root (√*hi*?), but a number of definitions of the logical reason presented in NAV 5.

[447] NA 5: *sādhyâvinâbhuno liṅgāt* and NAV 5: *evaṁ para-parikalpitam anyad api liṅga-lakṣaṇaṁ yad gamakatâṅgaṁ tad anyathânupapannatvaṁ na vyabhicarati, sādhyaṁ vinâpy upapadyamānasya gamakatā-vaikalyād iti; atrâiva vyāpake liṅga-lakṣaṇe antar-bhāvanīyam, viparītaṁ tu nirasanīyam iti sthitam* (p. 41 of the translation).

Actually, we could hardly assume that *īritam* of the aphorism NA 22 above referred initially to NA 5, as the commentator wants us to believe by saying: ***īritaṁ*** *gamitam anekârthatvād vā pratipāditaṁ svârthânumāna-prastāve*. In NA 5 we find actually no reference to the idea of the inexplicability otherwise (*anyathânupapannatva*) and the only definition of the *hetu* there is *sādhyâvinâbhuno liṅgāt*. Another possible passage might be NA 17: *hetos tathôpapattyā vā syāt prayogo 'nyathâpi vā*, see NAV *ad loc.*: ***anyathâpi vêty*** *anenâvayave samudāyôpacārād anyathânupapattiṁ lakṣayati*.

However, Siddhasena might have alluded to some earlier source, as well. In TSa_1 1364–1379 and TSaP thereon we come across an exposition of views held by Pātrasvāmin, especially his criticism directed against Dharmakīrti's idea of the triple-formed criterion of the logical reason (*trairūpya*) and his arguments corroborating the validity of the inexplicability otherwise (*anyathânupapannatva*) as the only criterion of the logical reason. The gist of the argument is formulated already in TSa_1 1364 (preceded by Kamalaśīla's *Pañjikā*): *anyathêty-ādinā pātrasvāmi-matam āśaṅkate*:

anyathânupapannatve nanu dṛṣṭā su-hetutā |
nâsati try-aṁśakasyâpi tasmāt klībās tri-lakṣaṇāḥ ||

Since, as a rule, Śāntarakṣita and Kamalaśīla are quite reliable and refer mostly to thinkers who were initiators of certain ideas, it is not improbable that Pātrasvāmin's lost work could be the source referred to in the first hemistich of NA 22, viz., *anyathānupapannatvaṁ hetor lakṣaṇam īritam*.

On the other hand, the idea of inexplicability otherwise is already know from $ŚBh_1$ 1.1.5 (p. 11.20–21) = $ŚBh_2$ 1.1.4a (p. 32.6–8): *arthâpattir api dṛṣṭaḥ śruto vā 'rtho 'nyathā nôpapadyata ity artha-kalpanā, yathā jīvato devadattasya gṛhâbhāva-darśanena bahir-bhāvasya adṛṣṭasya kalpanā*. However, Śabarasvāmin avails himself of the idea of inexplicability otherwise to explain one of the varieties of cognitive criteria (*pramāṇa*). For him *anyathânupapatti* is not a defining characteristic of logical reason (*hetu*).

[448] The nature of doubt is nicely explained in Devabhadra-gaṇin's gloss: ***dolāyamānêti.*** *dolo 'ndolakaḥ, ubhaya-pakṣa-gāmitvena tadvad ācaran sandeho 'pi*

dolāyamānas tasya bhāvaḥ tattā.—'"The fact of wobbling." wobbling [means] oscillating, inasmuch as one moves between two theses; proceeding in this way is also doubt, which is wobbling. Its state [means] the fact of being such.'

[449] Herein the position of Hemacandra deserves a separate mention, who considers the fallacies of the logical reason merely defective probantia. Cf. PMī 2.1 § 35: *ahetavo hetuvad ābhāsamānāḥ hetv-ābhāsā asiddhâdayaḥ. yady api sādhana-doṣā evâite 'duṣṭe sādhane tad-abhāvāt tathâpi sādhanâbhidhāyake hetāv upacārāt pūrvâcāryair abhihitās; tatas tat-prasiddhi-bādhām anāśrayadbhir asmābhir api hetu-doṣatvenâivôcyanta iti.*—'Those that are not logical reasons, [but] imitate logical reason, are fallacies of logical reason [subdivided into] unproved, etc. Even though they are nothing but defects of the probans, since they do not occur, if the probans is not defective, nevertheless, [these defects of the probans] have been transferred metaphorically, by former preceptors, onto the logical reason, which states [explicitly] the probans. Hence, [these defects of the probans] are said to be indeed the defects of the logical reason also by us, [who do] not [want to induce any] contravention with the traditional understanding of those [fallacies of the logical rea son].'

[450] Due to the fact that *tad* has two correlatives in the sentence, viz., *yena lakṣaṇena* and *yan-nāmā*, its hardly possible to render precisely such an intricate syntactical correlation in proper English. Lit.: 'Presently [the author] exposes what becomes a fallacy of the logical reason of which name on account of which characteristic.'

[451] Cf. PMī 2.1.13: *asiddha-viruddhânaikāntikās trayo hetv-ābhāsāḥ.*

[452] Cf. NAṬ 23 *ad loc.*: ***sattvād ity-ādi***. *yathā-sambhavaṁ nityânityatvayor amī hetavo yojyāḥ. tathā hi: sattvaṁ svâbhiprāyeṇānityatve nityatve ca*[a] *sādhye hetuḥ, utpattimattvaṁ kṛtakatvaṁ cânityatve eva, pratyabhijñāyamānatvaṁ tu nityatve evêti.*—'[A gloss on]: "Because it is existent", etc. These logical reasons are [equally] applicable to both permanence and impermanence as far as possible. For it is as follows: existence [constitutes] the logical reason, in accordance with the own intention [of a proponent], with regard to permanence as well as impermanence as the probandum. "Being endowed with origination" and "being produced" are [applicable] only to impermanence. "Being recognised" is [applicable] only to impermanence.'

[a] H,V: *svâbhiprāyeṇânityatve ca*. C: *abhiprāyeṇânityatve nityatve ca.*

[453] This is the Buddhist position.

[454] An exemplification of this fallacy of the logical reason is found, e.g. in PMī 2.1 § 38: *yathânityaḥ śabdaś câkṣuṣatvād iti.*

[455] According to Hemacandra, however, the non-occurrence of the logical reason within the locus is not a decisive factor responsible for the invalidity of a given logical reason. In other words, a particular property may not be present in the locus and may still offer justified grounds for a correct inference. Cf. PMī 2.1 § 38 (p. 60.30–61.5): *anyathânupapatti-rūpa-hetu-lakṣaṇa-virahād ayam asiddho nâpakṣa-*

dharmatvāt; nahi pakṣa-dharmatvaṁ hetor lakṣaṇaṁ, tad-abhāve 'py anyathânupapatti-balād dhetutvôpapatter ity ukta-prāyam. <u>*bhaṭṭo*</u> *'py āha*:

> *pitroś ca brāhmaṇatvena putra-brāhmaṇatânumā /*
> *sarva-loka-prasiddhā na pakṣa-dharmam apekṣate //*[a] *iti*—

—'It has been taught adequately enough that this [fallacious logical reason] is unproved because it is deprived of a characteristic of [correct] logical reason, that consists in the fact of being otherwise inexplicable, and not because it is not the property inherent in the locus; for the inherence of a property in the locus is not the characteristic of the logical reason, because—even if this [logical reason] is absent from this [locus]—it is [still] legitimate as logical reason by the force of being inexplicable otherwise. Also [Kumārila] Bhaṭṭa said:

> "The inference of the Brahminhood of the son from the fact that [his] father is a Brahmin is well known to all people; one does not require the inherence of a property in the locus".[a]'

[a] The verse does not occur in MŚV.

[456] Cf. NAṬ *ad loc.*: ***asad-ādîti***. *ādi-śabdād anutpannatvâdi-parigrahaḥ.*

> *anirūpita-tattvârthā pratītiḥ saṁvṛtir matā /*[a]

sā ca yady api sarvo 'py alīkâiva, tathâpi alīkêti svarūpa-viśeṣaṇam. yathâikânta-sukhadā muktir iti.

[a] This hemistich is also quoted in NAṬ 6 above, n. 313.

[457] NAṬ *ad loc.*: ***asāv*** *iti. acākṣuṣatva-vyavacchedaḥ.*

[458] I.e., 'In your criticism you want to split an indivisible phenomenon into parts, and that is impossible.'

[459] Cf. n. 675.

[460] The Jainas are well known to criticise two absolutist extreme positions: that of the Nyāya-Vaiśeṣika school, on the one hand, propounding the ultimate difference between properties and their substratum, and that of Advaita-vedānta, Yogâcāra, etc., on the other, according to which the properties were ultimately unreal. For the Jaina criticism directed against the Nyāya-Vaiśeṣika position cf. AYVD 7:

> *na dharma-dharmitvam atīva-bhede vṛttyâsti cen na tritayaṁ cakāsti /*
> *ihêdam ity asti matiś ca vṛttau na gauṇa-bhedo 'pi ca loka-bādhaḥ //*

'There [could be] no [relation between] the property and the subject, if there were an absolute difference [between them]. If [you say that this relation] is [possible] due to inherence (*vṛtti* = *samavāya*), [you are wrong, because] no triad [of entities] manifests itself (*sc.* is observable), [namely the property, the subject and the inherence, but only two, viz., the property and the subject]. The idea [of inherence that can be formulated as] "this is here" is [present] also (*ca* = *api*) in [the first] inherence [that leads eventually to *regressus ad infinitum*]. Neither there is any secondary difference[a]. And [the idea of inherence] is subverted by the opinion prevalent among people.'

[a] Malliṣeṇa further explains the nature of the secondary difference (*gauṇa-bhedo*) that concerns the secondary inherence, as juxtaposed with the primary one, SVM *ad loc.*: *tasmād dharma-dharmiṇoḥ sambandhe mukhyaḥ samavāyaḥ samavāye ca samavāyatvâbhisambandhe gauṇa ity ayaṁ bhedo nānātvaṁ nâstîti bhāvârthaḥ.*—'The intended meaning is the following: therefore, there is no such difference, i.e. diversity, [between two kinds of inherence,] namely, that in the relation between the property and the subject there is the primary inherence, whereas in the [second-order] inherence, which is the higher relation concerning the [primary] inherence condition, there is the secondary [inherence].' In other words, the inherence that binds a property and its locus (the subject) is of primary character, whereas the meta-inherence inherent in that primary inherence is of a different kind. This distinction between primary and secondary inherence was supposed to safeguard the Nyāya-Vaiśeṣika position from *regressus as infinitum* consisting in a series of inherence.

Malliṣeṇa, in his SVM commentary on AYVD 13, advances also a criticism against the Advaita position, whose monistic position is formulated in the following quotation:

sarvaṁ vai khalv idaṁ brahma nêha nānâsti kiṁcana /
ārāmaṁ tasya paśyanti na tat paśyati kaścana //

Also Devabhadra-sūri confirms that the two positions criticised above in NAV refer to these two schools, cf. NAṬ 23 *ad loc.*: ***nityâikānte 'pi dharmiṇo 'tyanta-vyatiriktānām iti.***[†] *naiyāyika-vaiśeṣikâbhiprāyeṇa.* ***apāramârthikānāṁ vêti.*** *advaita-vādy-abhiprāyeṇa.*

[†] A, C, H, V read the *pratīka* apparently wrongly: *nityâikānta ity-ādi. dharmiṇo 'tyanta-vyatiriktānām iti.* Such a reading should be emended, as I have done it, since the assumed *pratīka*: *nityâikānta ity-ādi*, would not be followed by any explanation and could not be otherwise accounted for.

[461] This is the statement of the Jaina position that mediates the aforementioned extreme poles of Nyāya-Vaiśeṣika and Advaita-vedānta, Yogâcāra, etc.: both properties and their substratum have real existence; moreover, the former are inconceivable without the latter, although the relation between them is not that of identity. Cf. SVM 7.74–76: *tasmād dharma-dharmiṇor aviṣvag-bhāva-lakṣaṇa eva sambandhaḥ pratipattavyo nânyaḥ samavāyâdiḥ.*—'Therefore, the relation between the property and the subject should be understood as characterised by nothing else but the state of being inseparable from each other; [apart from that relation], there is no other inherence, etc.'

[462] Cf. below p. 70: *sarva-vastu-dharmāṇāṁ vastuto 'nekânta-pratibaddhatvād iti*, as well as NA 29 and NAV 29 on *anekântâtmakaṁ vastu.*

[463] The text is apparently corrupt here. Despite the reading in both editions *paraspara-viruddhâvyabhicāritatvāt*, we should rather read *paraspara-viruddhâvyabhicāritvāt*, since the form *avyabhicārita* is not attested by any dictionary, lexicon or any other available textual source. Moreover, this compound is dissolved several lines later as *viruddhaṁ na vyabhicarantîti* as well as *virudhâvyabhicāriṇo 'naikāntikāḥ* wherein we does have the anticipated form *avyabhicārin* (instead of *avyabhicārita*). Mss. A and B confirm my suggestion. Also Dharmakīrti—referring to the fourth division of a fallacious logical reason formulated by Diṅnāga—has in NB_2 3.110: *viruddhâvyabhicāry api saṁśaya-hetur uktaḥ. sa iha kasmān nôktaḥ.*

[464] I.e., the same logical reason may be applied both to the homologue as well as to the heterologue with the same result. Similar idea in the same context is expressed later, for instance, by Hemacandra in AYVD 26:

> *ya eva doṣāḥ kila nitya-vāde vināśa-vāde 'pi samās ta eva /*
> *paraspara-dhvaṁsiṣu kaṇṭakeṣu*[a] *jayanty adhṛṣyaṁ jina-śāsanaṁ te //*

—'Those defects, with no exception, that are [found], as they say, in the theory of permanence, are all equal[ly operative] also in [the case of] the theory of [momentary] extinction (*sc.* momentariness = *kṣaṇika-vāda*). Among extremes[a] that annihilate each other, the unconquerable teaching of the Jina of yours conquers.'

[a] Malliṣeṇa, however, notices in the verse a military parable and accordingly explains *kaṇṭakeṣu* by *kṣudra-śastruṣu* (among petty enemies), by *parâbhibhāvuka* (destroyers of others, soldiers) in a battle-field.

[465] This whole argumentation is quoted later *in extenso* in SVM 7, p. 153–154.16–32: *anitya-vādī nitya-vādinaṁ prati pramāṇayati. sarvaṁ kṣaṇikaṁ sattvāt. akṣaṇike krama-yaugapadyābhyām artha-kriyā-virodhāt, artha-kriyā-kāritvasya ca bhāva-lakṣaṇatvāt, tato 'rtha-kriyā vyāvartamānā svakroḍī-kṛtāṁ sattvāṁ vyāvartayet iti kṣaṇika-siddhiḥ. nahi nityo 'rtho 'rtha-kriyāṁ krameṇa pravartayitum utsahate. pūrvârtha-kriyā-karaṇa-svabhāvôpamarda-dvāreṇôttara-kriyāyāṁ krameṇa pravṛtteḥ. anyathā pūrva-kriyā-karaṇâvirāma-prasaṅgāt. tat-svabhāva-pracyave ca nityatā prayāti*[a]*, atādavasthyasyânityatā-lakṣaṇatvāt. atha*[b] *nityo 'pi krama-vartinaṁ saha-kāri-kāraṇam artham udīkṣamāṇas tāvad asīt, paścāt tam āsādya krameṇa kāryaṁ kuryād iti cet, na. saha-kāri-kāraṇasya nitye 'rthe*[c] *'kiñcit-karatvād, akiñcit-karasyâpi pratīkṣaṇe 'navasthā -prasaṅgāt. nâpi yaugapadyena nityo 'rtho 'rtha-kriyāṁ kurute, adhyakṣa-virodhāt. nahy eka-kālaṁ sakalāḥ kriyāḥ prārabhamāṇaḥ kaścid upalabhate, karotu vā. tathâpy ādya-kṣaṇa eva sakala-kriyā-parisamāpter dvitīyâdi-kṣaṇeṣv akurvāṇasyânityatā balād āḍhaukate, karaṇâkaraṇayor ekasmin virodhād iti.*

[a] NAV: *apayāti.* [b] NAV omits *atha.* [c] NAV omits *'rthe.*

[466] A very similar argument, this time applied by the Buddhist against the existence of the universal, is first quoted and then rejected by Jayarāśi in TUS_1, d.7 (p. 248.17 ff.):

yad apy anyad uktaṁ nityasya kramêtarābhyām artha-kriyā-karaṇa-sāmarthyaṁ nāstîty asat sāmānyaṁ, tad etad ayuktam, ubhayathâpy artha-kriyā-sampādanam upapadyate yugapad krameṇa ca ... Comp. also TUS$_I$, n. 303. We come across a very similar, if not identical, argument in PVin II$_I$, p. 78.14–24: *skad cig ma ma yin pa ni de ltar ma yin te | rnam pa thams cad du mi srid pa^ci phyir ro || skad cig ma ma yin pa de ni don byed par srid pa ma yin te | rim daṅ cig car ^cgal ba^ci phyir ro || rim gyis ni ma yin te | ltos pa med par raṅ yod tsam gyis byed pa por gyur pa ni sdod par mi rigs pa^ci phyir ro || sṅar byed pa po ma yin pa ni phyis kyaṅ mi ^cgyur te | raṅ gi ṅo bor ^cgyur ba med pa^ci phyir ro || ltos pa yin na yaṅ bśad zin to || cig car byed pa yaṅ ma yin te | de^ci raṅ gi ṅo bo ni phyis kyaṅ mi byed par mi ^ctshad pa^ci phyir ro || des na nus pa thams cad ldog pa de ni yod pa^ci mtshan ñid las ^cdas pa yin no ||* Some formulations as well as the structure of the argument are identical, though Dharmakīrti is less elaborate.

[467] The idiomatic expression *avasthāṁ* √*bandh* is not entirely clear to me, and I have failed to find any parallel. From the context, however, two conceivable meanings may be conjectured, viz., (1) 'to hold on to the circumstances' (*sc*. 'to correspond to the state of affairs') and (2) 'to secure real foundation' (*sc*. 'to prove / become real').

[468] Cf. similar argumentation above, NAV 0: *tathā hi: kṣaṇa-naśvaro 'rthaḥ sva-kṣaṇe pūrvaṁ paścād vā kāryaṁ kuryād iti trayī gatiḥ* ... (p.2 ff. of the translation).

[469] Also this portion, like the previous argumentation of a propounder of *kṣaṇika-vāda*, occurs later in SVM 27, p. 153.8–16: *tathā hi nitya-vādī pramāṇayati. sarvaṁ nityaṁ sattvāt. kṣaṇike sad-asat-kālayor artha-kriyā-virodhāt tal-lakṣaṇaṁ sattvaṁ nâvasthāṁ badhnātîti tato nivartamānam ananya-śaraṇatayā nityatve 'vatiṣṭhate*[a]. *tathā hi kṣaṇiko 'rthaḥ san vā kāryaṁ kuryāt, asan vā, gaty-antarâbhāvāt. na tāvad ādyaḥ pakṣaḥ. sama-samaya-vartini vyāpārâyogāt, sakāla-bhāvānāṁ parasparaṁ kārya-kāraṇa-bhāva-prāptyâtiprasaṅgāc ca. nâpi dvitīyaḥ pakṣaḥ kṣodaṁ kṣamate. asataḥ kārya-karaṇa-śakti-vikalatvāt. anyathā śaśa-viṣāṇâdayo 'pi kārya-karaṇāyôtsaheran, viśeṣâbhāvād iti.*

[a] NAV has: *nityatvaṁ sādhayati*.

[470] Cf. n. 231.

[471] The V. and H. editions of NAV as well as A. B. Dhruva's edition of SVM (cf. n. 472) edit *virudhā vyabhicāriṇo'naikāntikāḥ*; this reading has to be emended (viz., *virudhâvyabhicāriṇo 'naikāntikāḥ*), since *virudhâvyabhicāriṇo* is an attribute of the fallacious logical reason of the *anaikāntikā*-type. The reading *virudhā vyabhicāriṇo 'naikāntikāḥ* might suggest three varieties of fallacious logical reasons. Indeed, there are three varieties of the fallacies of the logical reason, but they are enumerated differently, viz., *asiddha*, *viruddha* and *anaikāntika*; the sequence *virudhā vyabhicāriṇo 'naikāntikāḥ* corresponds neither to the original order of the *kārikā* nor to the initial part of the commentary. Besides, Siddharṣi-gaṇin speaks of each of the three divisions of the fallacious logical reason always in singular, whereas here they would be mentioned in plural (*virudhā vyabhicāriṇo 'naikāntikāḥ*).

[472] Malliṣeṇa (in SVM 7, p. 154.32–34) borrows the above conclusion, too: *tad evam ekânta-dvaye 'pi ye*[a] *hetavas te*[b] *yukti-sāmyād*[c] *viruddhaṁ na vyabhicarantîty*[d] *avicārita-ramaṇīyatayā mugdha-janasya dhy-āndhyaṁ*[e] *côtpādayantîti virudhâvyabhicāriṇo 'naikāntikā*[f] *iti.*

[a] NAV repeats *ye.* [b] NAV repeats *te.* [c] NAV: *yukteḥ samānatayā.*
[d] NAV omits *iti.* [e] NAV compounds: *mugdha-jana-dhy-āndhyaṁ.*
[f] A. B. Dhruva's edition reads *virudhā vyabhicāriṇo 'naikāntikā*, but the text should be emended as above for the reasons already specified (cf. n. 471).

[473] Cf. n. 231.

[474] In other words: the probans (*sādhana*, *hetu*) H is encompassed by the extension of the probandum (*sādhya*) S: $H \subset S$. Cf. n. 517.

[475] Since the theory of sets may—at least, for the sake of convenience—suit the purpose of demonstrating the relation of *ākrāntatā* ('being under the sway of'), viz., the relation of inclusion, or *nivṛtti* ('non-exclusion'), I shall avail myself of its symbolic expressions in order to show various forms of proof formulae and fallacious examples in the subsequent section. We can represent the above proof formula as well as subsequent ones, that are assumed to be correct by an opponent, in the following manner: $[(P \subset H) \cap (H \subset S)] \rightarrow (P \subset S)$, in which P represents the locus (*pakṣa*), viz., 'inference' (*anumāna*), S—the probandum (*sādhya*), viz., 'is erroneous' (*bhrānta*), H—the probans (*sādhana*, *hetu*), viz., 'is a cognitive criterion' (*pramāṇa*), D—the subject of the example (*dṛṣṭânta*) viz., perception (*pratyakṣa*); Besides,

(1) the thesis (*pratijñā*) is *bhrāntam anumānam* $(P \subset S)$;
(2) the logical reason (*hetu*) is *pramāṇatvāt*, that in fact consists of a conjunction of two assumptions: $P \subset H$ and $H \subset S$, the latter, being of enthymematic character, is not expressly stated in the proof formula but is taken for granted, on grounds of the principle: *sādhanaṁ sādhyâkrāntam* ('the probans is under the sway of the probandum');
(3) the example (*dṛṣṭânta*) is supposed to possess properties of both the probans and the probandum: $(D \subset H) \cap (D \subset S)$.

The refutation of the above example carried out by Siddharṣi-gaṇin is based on the assumption that $[(P \subset H) \cap (H \subset S')] \rightarrow (P \subset S')$. Subsequently, if one substitutes *pratyakṣa* (D) for *anumāna* (P) the result is the following proof formula: $[(D \subset H) \cap (H \subset S')] \rightarrow (D \subset S')$. The conclusion (= the thesis to be proved) of such a proof formula referring to the example $(D \subset S')$ clearly contradicts the well known that D is not included into S $(D \subset S')$. Hence, the example is *sādhya-vikala*, despite *sādhana-vṛtti* (the presence of the property of the example in the probans). To recapitulate, the example portrays, in fact, the following situation: $(D \subset H) \cap (D \subset S')$.

[476] This is instance of the so so-called 'Dreaming Argument', that—as it has been shown in TABER (1994: 28–31)—has never been expressed by the Buddhist thinkers in the form it appears in anti-Buddhist works. "The sensation in the waking state is

erroneous, because it is a cognitive criterion, like the sensation in a dream" (*jāgrat-saṁvedanaṁ bhrāntaṁ, pratyayatvāt, svapna-saṁvedanavat*) is an altered formulation—Siddharṣi-gaṇin has *pramāṇa* in place of the usual *pratyaya*—of a argument based on the proof formula, commonly ascribed to the Buddhist, the references to which can be found in non-Jinistic sources. In its usual formulation (with *pratyaya* or *khyāti* as the logical reason), the "Dreaming Argument" is refuted, for instance, by (1) Kumārila in $\acute{S}V_I$ 5.2. (*Nirālambana-vāda-adhikaraṇa*).23 (p. 159.7–8): *stambhâdi-pratyayo mithyā pratyayatvāt tathā hi yaḥ / pratyayaḥ sa mṛṣā dṛṣṭaḥ svapnâdipratyayo yathā //*; (2) by Uddyotakara in NV on NBh 4.2.33: *ayam jāgrad-avasthôpalabdhānāṁ viṣayāṇāṁ citta-vyatirekiṇām asattve hetuḥ khyātiḥ svapnavad iti*; (3) by Śaṅkara in BSŚBh 2.2.5.29 (p. 476.2–3): *yad uktaṁ bāhyârthâpalāpinā svapnâdivaj jāgarita-gocarā api stambhâdi-pratyayā vinâiva bāhyenârthena bhaveyuḥ pratyayatvâviśeṣād iti tad prativaktavyam*; and (4) and by Siddharṣi-gaṇin himself later on in NAV 29 (the *Śūnya-vāda* section): *nirālambanāḥ sarve pratyayāḥ, pratyayatvāt, svapna-pratyayavad* (p. 95 of the English translation). The proof formula occurs also in NAṬ 4 (see n. 242) and NAṬ 7 (see n. 334). Worth mentioning is that, while pointing to the 'Dreaming argument', Kumārila refers to his predecessor in this regard (in M$\acute{S}V_I$ .5.2. (*Nirālambana-vāda-adhikaraṇa*) 16cd–17) to ŚBh_I 1.1.5 (p. 10.6–13): *nanu sarva eva nirālambanaḥ svapnavat pratyayaḥ. pratyayasya hi nirālambanatā-svabhāva upalakṣitaḥ svapne ... yadi pratyayatvāt svapna-pratyayasya mithyā-bhāvaḥ, jāgrat-pratyayasyâpi tathā bhavitum arhati*. It is clear that *nirālambana* = *mithyā*, for both the terms are used by Śabara interchangeably.

Thus, Siddharṣi-gaṇin joints the party of critics of the idealist standpoint and refers, by availing himself of this illustration, to the 'Dreaming Argument' either directly or indirectly. It is not so absurd as it might appear at first sight to contend that Siddharṣi-gaṇin may have seen no qualitative difference *in this particular case* (*sc.* the refutation of the 'Dreaming Argument') between *saṁvedana*, *pramāṇa* and *pratyaya*, and used them interchangeably to describe cognitive states in the subsequent lines (e.g. *svapna-saṁvedanasya pramāṇatā-vaikalyāt tat-pratyanīka-jāgrat-pratyayôpanipāta-bādhitatvād iti*). Moreover, the term *pratyaya* in any standard formulation of the 'Dreaming Argument' (**mithyā stambhâdi-pratyayaḥ pratyayatvāt, yathā svapnâdipratyayaḥ*) is used in the sense of a cognition that is taken by ordinary people—erroneously, according to the Buddhist—to be factual and reliable, and therefore, in this manner, *in this particular sense* not very remote from the *pramāṇa*. Such being the case, Siddharṣi-gaṇin's illustration would be a *direct* criticism of the 'Dreaming Argument.'

[477] Similarly, the proof formula, believed by an opponent to be correct, as well as the refutation of the faulty example, assume their symbolic forms, as in the previous instance: $[(P\subset H)\cap(H\subset S)]\rightarrow(P\subset S)$ and $[(P\subset H)\cap(H\subset S')]\rightarrow(P\subset S')$, respectively. The necessary condition for the validity of the example, namely $(D\subset H)\cap(D\subset S)$, is revoked by the fact that cognition in dream (D) is not a cognitive criterion (H), hence the real situation is this: $(D\subset H')\cap(D\subset S)$, where D is not included into H, that is to say, the example is *sādhana-vikala*.

[478] In the above example D is neither included into H nor S: $(D\subset H')\cap(D\subset S')$, viz., it is *sādhya-sādhana-vikala*.

[479] For the first three 'lacking' (°*-vikala*) varieties cf. NB_1 3.125: *yathā nityaḥ śabdo 'mūrtatvāt. karmavat paramâṇuvad ghaṭavad iti sādhya-sādhana-dharmôbhya-vikalāḥ.*—'For instance: sound is permanent, because it is formless, (1) like effort, (2) like infinitesimal atom, (3) like a pot—such are [divisions of fallacious examples that] lack the probandum, the probans and both [respectively].' The reasons are enumerated in full form in NBṬ: (1) *sādhya-vikalaṁ karma tasyânityatvāt.* (2) *sādhana-vikalaḥ paramâṇur mūrtatvāt paramâṇūnām* ... (3) *ghaṭas tûbhaya-vikalaḥ, anityatvān mūrtitvāc ca ghaṭasya.*—'(1) Effort lacks the probandum, because it is impermanent. (2) Infinitesimal atom lacks the probans, because it has a form. (3) But a pot lacks them both, because a pot is impermanent as well as has a form.' The comparison of the sequence in which the examples are listed as well as the contents of all the almost identical examples enumerated in NAV 24–25 and NB_1 3.127–136 prove that both Siddharṣi-gaṇin and Hemacandra (cf. PMī 2.1.23 and n. 502) are indebted to Dharmakīrti in this regard. This question is discussed in detail in BALCEROWICZ 1999/a.

[480] Cf. NAṬ *ad loc.*: ***vyāhārâdîti***. *ādi-śabdāc ceṣṭâkāra-parigrahaḥ.*—'By the word "etc." [various] forms of gestures are included.' Cf. NAV 1: *pratyakṣeṇa para-ceto-vṛtti-sâkṣāt-karaṇâbhāvād vyāpāra-vyāhāra-ceṣṭā-viśeṣa-darśanād bodha-viśeṣâvagatau* ...—'... because a particular consciousness is ascertained by seeing particular acts, utterances and gestures, inasmuch as it is not possible to perceive directly other people's mental activities with [the help] of perception.' (p. 18 of the English translation).

[481] The invalid example, in which there is no certainty whether D is S or S', has the form: $(D\subset H)\cap[(D\subset S)\cup(D\subset S')]$.

[482] The invalid example, in which there is no certainty whether D is H or H', has the form: $[(D\subset H)\cup(D\subset H')]\cap(D\subset S)$.

[483] The faulty example, in which there is no certainty whether D is H or H' and whether D is S or S', is represented as $[(D\subset H)\cup(D\subset H')]\cap[(D\subset S)\cup(D\subset S')]$.

[484] For the latter three 'doubtful' (*sandigdha*-°) varieties cf. NB_2 3.125 (=NB_1 3.126): *yathā sandigdha-sādhya-dharmâdayaś ca. yathā rāgâdimān ayaṁ vacanād rathyā-puruṣavat. maraṇa-dharmâyaṁ* (NB_1 3.126: *maraṇa-dharmo 'yaṁ*) *puruṣo rāgâdimattvād rathyā-puruṣavat. asarva-jño 'yaṁ rāgâdimattvād rathyā-puruṣavad iti.*—'And as well as there are [three other types of example] in which the properties of the probandum, etc., are doubtful. For instance, (1) "He is passionate, because he speaks, just like a man in the street", (2) "This person is mortal, because it is endowed with passions, etc., like a man in the street", (3) "he is not omniscient, because he is endowed with passions, etc., [and] is like a man in the street".' Likewise, in the

case of typology of 'doubtful' examples, Siddharṣi-gaṇin is indebted to Dharmakīrti in this regard. This question is discussed in detail in BALCEROWICZ 1999/a.

[485] Cf. NB_1 3.127–128: /127/ *ananvayo 'pradarśitânvayaś ca* ... /128/ *tathā viparītânvayaḥ* ...

[486] Dharmottara explains in $NBṬ_1$ 1.127: ***iṣṭa-puruṣavad*** *iti. iṣṭa-grahaṇena prativādy api gṛhyate vādy api.*—'By the mention of "any selected" both the opponent and the proponent are referred to.' Durveka Miśra glosses on DhPr 3.126 referring to the same meaning: *yato dvayor api vādi-prativādinor dṛṣṭântatvena saṅgrahaḥ*... The expression *iṣṭa-puruṣa*, however, is used in NB almost synonymically to *rathyā-puruṣa*, inasmuch as it is used interchangeably with the latter and in the same context. Thus, it comes close to mean 'any arbitrarily selected person,' both the proponent and the opponent would agree upon. In this way, the semantic transformation of the past participle *iṣṭa* ('any arbitrarily selected') derived from the verbal root √*iṣ* ('to want, to accept') would resemble, to a certain degree, the German 'lieben/belieben > beliebig.'

[487] Cf. NB_1 3.127: ... *yathā yo vaktā sa rāgâdimān iṣṭa-puruṣavat* ...

[488] Cf. NB_1 3.127: ... *anityaḥ śabdaḥ kṛtakatvād ghaṭavad iti*.

[489] Cf. NB_1 3.128: *tathā viparītânvayaḥ. yad anityaṁ tat kṛtakatvam iti*.

[490] In the following reasoning it should be borne in mind that the recognition of the invariable concomitance (*vyāpti*) is a prerequisite to prove positive concomitance (*anvaya*); cf. n. 174.

[491] I.e., if also the speaker's inaccuracy could constitute a defective logical reason, the limited number of fallacious examples and their limited domain could prove infinite due to infinite number of potential mistakes on the part of the speaker.

[492] Cf. n. 102.

[493] Cf. n. 231.

[494] I face some difficulty to interpret the expression *iti dattârtham*, though its role—resembling the locution *ity arthaḥ*—and meaning seems to be more or less clear in the present context: 'such is the imparted sense [taken from the previous section on NA 24]' or 'such is the meaning given already [in the previous section on NA 24].' Since *artha* is exclusively masculine in the classical Sanskrit, the expression in question is probably used predicatively of *vaidharmyam*. The difficulty, however, lies in the fact that *vaidharmyam* is already directly related to the clause *atra dṛṣṭânta-doṣā nyāya-vid-īritā* by *tena* standing for *vaidharmyeṇa*. I have failed to find any parallels.

[495] What is meant is the following: the *kārikā* places *ca* untypically—due to metrical reasons—after the first element *anivṛtteś ca saṁśayāt* instead of usual *anivṛtteḥ saṁśayāc ca*.

[496] For further explanation of negative concomitance see NBṬ$_{I}$ 1.130: *teṣām (=sādhya-sādhanôbhayānām) avyatireko nivṛtty-abhāvaḥ*.—'Lack of negative concomitance with them (with the probandum with the probans or with both the probandum and the probans) [means] the absence of their exclusion.' Cf. n. 174.

[497] The quoted example is an instance of the negative inference, i.e. the inference based on dissimilarity (*vaidharmyeṇa = vaidharmyavat*), which follows the principle: *sādhyâbhāve sādhanâbhavaḥ, vahny-abhāve dhūmâbhāvaḥ*.—'In absence of the probandum there is absence of the probans, in absence of fire there is absence of smoke.' It can be illustrated by the following proof formula: *yatra yatra vahnir (S) nâsti tatra tatra dhūmo (H) nâsti, yathā jalâśayâdau* ('Wherever there is no fire, there is not smoke, like in a water reservoir, [in which there is neither fire nor smoke'), symbolically:

1. $\forall x\,(\neg Sx \rightarrow \neg Hx)$ ['for every *x*, if *x* is not fiery, then *x* is not smoky'],
2. $\neg Sa \wedge \neg Ha$ ['a water reservoir is neither fiery nor smoky'].

In the NAV-example above, *H* stands for 'is a cognitive criterion' and *S*—for 'is erroneous', respectively. The example of the negative inference is derived by the law of simple transposition $(p \rightarrow q) = (\neg q \rightarrow \neg p)$ from the positive inference, i.e. the inference based on similarity (*sādharmyeṇa = sādharmyavat*), e.g.: *yatra yatra dhūmas (H) tatra tatra vahniḥ (S), yathā mahānasâdau*, symbolically:

1. $\forall x\,(Hx \rightarrow Sx)$,
2. $Ha \wedge Sa$.

Cf. NAV 11 and n. 381.

[498] Let us represent the locus (*pakṣa*) with *P*, the probandum (*sādhya*) with *S*, the probans (*sādhana*) with *H* and the subject of the example (*dṛṣṭânta*) with *D*. The positive proof formula based on similarity (viz., 'inference is erroneous, because it is a cognitive criterion') assumes, like in all previous instances, the following form: $[(P \subset H) \cap (H \subset S)] \rightarrow (P \subset S)$. We can represent the inference underlying the fallacious example in the following manner: $[(S' \subset H') \cap (D \subset S')] \rightarrow (D \subset H')$; in other words:

1. *yad bhrāntam na bhavati na tat pramāṇam* $(S' \subset H')$, and
2. *yathā svapna-jñānam*, viz., *abhrāntaṁ svapna-jñānam* $(D \subset S')$,

hence: *apramāṇaṁ svapna-jñānam* $(D \subset H')$.
The subject of the negative example should be demonstrated as separated from both the probandum and the probans: $(D \subset H') \cap (D \subset S')$. The second assumption in our case, however, $D \subset S'$ ('cognition in dream is not erroneous') is false, because in fact $D \subset S$ ('cognition in dream is erroneous'), what is tantamount to *sādhyâvyatirekitva* $(D \subset H') \cap (D \subset S)$.

[499] This reasoning is based on the Buddhist position expressed and criticised in NAV 4.

500 The structures the positive proof formula based on similarity (viz., ‘perception is non-conceptual, because it is a cognitive criterion’) and of the fallacious example are the same, like in the preceding example: $[(P\subset H)\cap(H\subset S)]\rightarrow(P\subset S)$ and $[(S'\subset H')\cap(D\subset S')]\rightarrow(D\subset H')$, respectively. The condition $D\subset S'$ is not fulfilled, since the opposite is the case $D\subset S$ (‘inference is a cognitive criterion’), and that is tantamount to *sādhanâvyatirekitva* $(D\subset H)\cap(D\subset S')$, instead of the correct negative example: $(D\subset H')\cap(D\subset S')$.

501 The above proof formula based on similarity has the following form:

1. since *the sound is existent* $(P\subset H)$, and
2. *whatever is existent is* [*both*] *permanent and impermanent* $(H\subset S)$,

hence: *the sound is both permanent and impermanent* $(P\subset S)$.

The predicate (S) ‘being both permanent and impermanent’ is a particularly Jinistic ontological assumption derived from the Jaina doctrine of multiplexity of reality (*anekânta-vāda*). Both conditions of the negative example are not fulfilled, for—instead of $(D\subset H')\cap(D\subset S')$—we have $(D\subset H)\cap(D\subset S)$ (‘a pot is both permanent and impermanent as well as existent’), which is tantamount to the example being *sādhya-sādhanâvyatirekin*.

502 Cf. the three *avyatireka*-varieties mentioned in NB$_{\mathrm{I}}$ 3.130: *vaidharmyeṇâpi. paramâṇuvat karmavad ākāśavad iti sādhyâdy-avyatirekiṇaḥ*, and explicated in NBṬ$_{\mathrm{I}}$ 1.130: *nityatve śabdasya sādhye hetāv amūrtatve paramâṇuvad vaidharmya-dṛṣṭântaḥ sādhyâvyatirekī. nityatvāt paramâṇūnām. karma sādhanâvyatireki amūrtatvāt karmaṇaḥ. ākāśam ubhayâvyatireki nityatvād amūrtatvāc ca.*—‘If the sound is to be proved permanent, when the logical reason is [that the sound is] form less, then the example based on dissimilarity, that lacks negative concomitance with the probandum, is: “like infinitesimal atoms”, [namely:] “because infinitesimal atoms are permanent”. “Effort” is [the example] lacking negative concomitance with the probans, [namely:] “because effort is formless”. “Sky” is [the example] lacking negative concomitance with both [the probandum and the probans, namely:] “because sky is both permanent and formless”.’ Comp. striking similarities with PMī 2.1.23: *amūrtatvena nitye śabde sādhye karma-paramâṇu-ghaṭāḥ sādhya-sādhanôbhaya-vikalāḥ.*—‘If the sound is to be proved permanent, because it is formless, [then the examples:] effort, infinitesimal atom and a pot lack the probandum, the probans and both [respectively].’ Cf. and n. 479.

503 In other words, the subject of the negative example is supposed to be bereft from the properties of the probandum and of the probans, viz., $(D\subset H')\cap(D\subset S')$:

1. *ārya-satya-catuṣṭaya-pratipādakaḥ* (H') *buddhaḥ* (D), and
2. *sarva-jña āpto vā* (S') *buddhaḥ* (D).

Cf. the similar proof formula in NB$_{\mathrm{I}}$ 3.131, with the only difference that the subject of the negative example are in this case are Jinas instead of the Buddha: *tathā sandigdha-sādhya-vyatirekâdayaḥ, yathâsarva-jñāḥ*[a] *kapilâdayo 'nāptā vā, avidyamāna-sarva-jñatâptatā-liṅga-bhūta-pramāṇâtiśaya-śāsanatvād iti. atra vaidharmyôdaharaṇaṁ yaḥ sarva-jña āpto vā sa jyotir-jñānâdikam upadiṣṭavān, yatharṣabha-vardhamānâdir iti. tatrâsarva-jñatânaptatayoḥ sādhya-dharmayoḥ sandigdho vyatirekaḥ.*—'Similarly [fallacious is the fourth variety, namely the example] in which negative concomitance with the probandum is doubtful, for instance [in the proof formula]: "Kapila and other [thinkers of his kind] are neither omniscient nor authoritative persons, because [their] teaching is the best cognitive criterion which is the proof that they have no omniscience or authority." Here the exemplification based on dissimilarity [can be formulated in the following manner]: "Whoever is either an omniscient or an authoritative person, he teaches astrology, etc., like Ṛṣabha, Vardhamāna and other [Jinas]." In this [negative example] negative concomitance [of the subject of the example] with both properties of the probandum, namely non-omniscience and lack of authority, is doubtful.'

[a] Surprisingly, STCHERBATSKY's edition wrongly reads *yathā sarva-jñāḥ*, despite the explanation of $NBṬ_1$ of the same edition: *asarva-jñā ity ekaṁ sādhyam*, etc. It is corrected in MALVANIA's edition of DhPr.

[504] Strangely, the typical sequence of the four noble truths is here disturbed; the third and fourth noble truths are interchanged, instead of the usual: (1) *duḥkha* (Pāli, *dukkha*), (2) *duḥkha-samudaya* (Pāli, *dukkha-samudaya*), (3) *duḥkha-nirodha* (Pāli, *dukkha-nirodha*) and (4) *duḥkha-nirodha-gāminī pratipad* (Pāli, *dukkha-nirodha-gāminī paṭipadā*) = *mārga*. Regarding falsity of the widespread conviction about either historical or structural priority of the quadruple of the Indian medical sciences—namely disease (*roga*), cause of disease (*roga-hetu*), health (*ārogya*) and remedy against the disease (*bhaiṣajya*)—over the Buddhist four noble truths, see: WEZLER 1984.

[505] I.e., $(D \subset H') \cap (D \subset S)$: *ārya-satya-catuṣṭaya-pratipādakaś* (H') *ca asarva-jña anāpto vā* (S) *ca buddhaḥ* (D), because *asarva-jña anāpto vā* (S) *ārya-satya-catuṣṭaya-pratipādakaś* (H')—$H' \subset S$.

[506] I.e., to those who do not recognise that $H' \subset S$.

[507] I.e., it is not proved that teaching of the four noble truths must be accompanied by omniscience and authority.

[508] This seems to be an argument of a more pragmatic nature acknowledging the state of affairs, namely the variance of opinions regarding the Buddha's omniscience, and less that of logical character based merely on the internal structure of the proof formula and the example. To sum up, this instance can either be analysed as *sādhyâvyatirekin*, for someone who rejects Buddha's authority, or it can be an instance of *sandigdha-sādhya-vyatireka-dṛṣṭântâbhāsa*: $(D \subset H') \cap [(D \subset S) \cup (D \subset S')]$, provided one takes into account that indeed there are some people who recognise the Buddha's authority. Namely, the following situation is the case:

(1) *ārya-satya-catuṣṭaya-pratipādakaś* (H') *buddhaḥ* (D) and

(2a) *sarva-jña āpto vā* (*S*') *buddha* (*D*) *ity bauddhāḥ*, but
(2b) *asarva-jña anāpto vā* (*S*) *buddha* (*D*) *ity apare*.

[509] In other words, even though Buddha seems trustworthy to the Buddhist, nevertheless, it is doubtful whether the Buddha is free from passions.

[510] The proof formula has the structure:

(1) *rāgâdimān* (*H*) *asau* (*P*): $P \subset H$, and
(2) *anādeya-vākyo* (*S*) *rāgâdimān* (*H*): $H \subset S$,
hence: *anādeya-vākyo* (*S*) *'sau* (*P*): $P \subset S$.

Instead of the correct negative example: $(D \subset H') \cap (D \subset S')$, the fallacious example assumes the form $[(D \subset H) \cup (D \subset H')] \cap (D \subset S')$ on account of the alternative: *rāgâdimān* (*H*) *vā vīta-rāgo* (*H*') *vā sugataḥ* (*D*). One wonders, though, why Siddharṣi-gaṇin regards this example merely *sandigdha-sādhana-vyatireka*, not *sandigdha-sādhya-sādhana-vyatireka*, i.e. the fallacious example in which negative concomitance with b o t h the probandum and the probans is doubtful? In all probability he did not but distrust the Buddha's words and would have certainly classified him as *anādeya-vākya*, as well. Consequently one could have expressed the following doubt: *ādeya-vākyo* (*S*') *vânādeya-vākyo* (*S*') *vā sugataḥ* (*D*). The answer is provided by the fact that Siddharṣi-gaṇin not closely follows Dharmakīrti's classification, but also tried to rephrase the latter's examples in order to refute some Buddhist tenets. Thus, he followed a methodological procedure to attack one's own opponents via arguments clad in—at first sight—harmless illustrations of faulty proof formulae, that, in fact, expressed basic doubts concerning the veracity of some fundamental doctrines upheld by the rival school. This issue is discussed in detail in BALCEROWICZ 1999/a.

Thanks to NB_1 3.132 we can even know specifically who should not trust t h e u n t r u s t w o r t h y p a r t i c u l a r p e r s o n i n q u e s t i o n of the above proof formula! Cf. *sandigdha-sādhana-vyatireko yathā: na trayīvidā brāhmaṇena grāhya-vacanaḥ kaścit puruṣo rāgâdimattvād iti. atra vaidharmyôdāharaṇaṁ: ye grāhya-vacanā na te rāgâdimantaḥ, tad yathā gautamâdayo dharma-śastrāṇāṁ praṇetāra iti. gautamâdibhyo rāgâdimattvasya sādhana-dharmasya vyāvṛttiḥ sandigdhā.*—'[The fallacious example] in which negative concomitance with the probans is doubtful is, for instance, [the following]: "A particular person is not such whose statements could be trusted by a Brahmin learned in the three Vedas, because he is endowed with passion, etc." Here the exemplification based on dissimilarity [can be formulated in the following manner]: "Those who are [such people] whose statements can be trusted, are not endowed with passion, etc., like Gotama and others, who are promulgators of *Dharma-śāstra*." It is doubtful [here] whether the property of the probans, namely "being endowed with passion, etc.", does not occur in (is excluded from) Gautama and others.'

[511] The structure of the above positive proof formula is as follows:

(1) *adatta-nijaka-māṁsa-śakalāḥ* (H) *kapilâdayaḥ* (P): $P \subset H$, and
(2) *rāgâdimān* (S) *adatta-nijaka-māṁsa-śakalāḥ* (H): $H \subset S$,
hence, *rāgâdimantaḥ* (S) *kapilâdayaḥ* (P) : $P \subset S$.

On account of the assumption that *datta-nijaka-māṁsa-śakalaḥ* (H') *vīta-rāgaḥ* (S'): $S' \subset H'$, the subject of the negative example is believed to be: *datta-nijaka-māṁsa-śakalāś* (H') *ca vīta-rāgāś* (S') *ca boddhisattvāḥ* (D), viz., $(D \subset H') \cap (D \subset S')$. In this case, however, both qualities of D are undecided: $[(D \subset H) \cup (D \subset H')] \cap [(D \subset S') \cup (D \subset S'')]$. This whole reasoning obviously presupposes the equation: *vīta-raga* = *karuṇā-parīta-citta*.

Cf. similar proof formula in NB_I 3.133, in which the Buddhists and the Jainas unanimously pick out Kapila for the scapegoat and once again doubt his virtuous character. This time, however, it is a Jina who plays the role of the negative example: *sandigdhôbhaya-vyatireko yathā: avīta-rāgāḥ kapilâdayaḥ, parigrahâgraha-yogād iti. atra vaidharmyôdāharaṇaṁ: yo vīta-rago na tasya parigrahâgraho yatharṣabhâder iti. ṛṣabhâder avīta-rāgatva-parigrahâgraha-yogayoḥ sādhya-sādhana-dharmayoḥ sandigdho vyatirekaḥ.*—'[The fallacious example] in which negative concomitance with both [the probandum and the probans] is doubtful is for instance [the following]: "Kapila and other [thinkers of his kind] are not dispassionate, because they are possessed of covetousness and greed." Here the exemplification based on dissimilarity [can be formulated in the following manner]: "Whoever is dispassionate, he does not have covetousness and greed, like Ṛṣabha [the Jina]". [Here] negative concomitance with the properties of [both] the probandum and the probans—namely being not dispassionate and being possessed of covetousness and greed—is doubtful in the case of Ṛṣabha.'

[512] I am inclined—what Ms. B confirms—to read: *trayo 'vimṛśya-bhāṣitayā*, despite the reading of A, H and V: *trayo vimṛśya-bhāṣitayā* ('inasmuch as they are [people] who speak after deliberation'). It would be conceivable, however, that some irony directed against the Buddhists was intended, in which case the latter reading should be considered the original one.

[513] Cf. NB_I 3.134: *avyatireko yathā: avīta-rāgo vaktṛtvāt. vaidhārmyôdāharaṇam: yatra vīta-rāgatvaṁ nâsti sa vaktā. yathôpala-khaṇḍa iti. yady apy upala-khaṇḍād ubhayaṁ vyāvṛttaṁ tathâpi sarvo vīta-rāgo na vaktêti vyāptyā vyatirekāsiddher avyatirekaḥ.*—'[The fallacious example] lacking negative concomitance is like this: "[This person] is not dispassionate, because he is a speaker (*sc.* talks)". The exemplification based on dissimilarity [can be formulated in the following manner]: "[Such a person], in which there is no dispassionateness, is a speaker (*sc.* talks), like a bit of stone." Even though both [the probandum and the probans] do not occur in (are excluded from) a bit of stone, nevertheless there is no negative concomitance, inasmuch as negative concomitance is not proved by the invariable concomitance [of the form:] "every dispassionate [person] is not a speaker (*sc.* does not talk)".'

[514] In view of the reading of NB$_{I}$ 3.135—what is confirmed by Mss. A and B—we should read here *yathânityaḥ śabdaḥ*, instead of *yathā nityaḥ śabdaḥ*.

[515] Cf. NB$_{I}$ 3.135: *apradarśita-vyatireko yathā: anityaḥ śabdaḥ, kṛtakatvād; ākāśavad iti vaidharmyeṇa.*—'[The fallacious example] with unindicated negative concomitance looks is as follows: "Sound is impermanent, because it is produced, like space." [The example] based on dissimilarity is the following: "like the space".'

[516] Cf. NB$_{I}$ 3.136: *viparīta-vyatireko yathā yad akṛtakaṁ tan nityaṁ bhavatîti.*—'[The fallacious example] with inverted negative concomitance [is] as follows: "Whatever is not produced is permanent".'

[517] In other words: absence of the probandum (*sādhyâbhāva*) H' is encompassed by the extension of the absence of the probans (*sādhanâbhāva*) S': $S' \subset H$.' Cf. n. 474. This interdependence between the examples based on similarity and on dissimilarity—$(H \subset S) \equiv (S' \subset H')$—lays down the rule of simple transposition: $(p \rightarrow q) = (\neg q \rightarrow \neg p)$.

[518] The positive proof formula has the following structure:

(1) *kṛtakaḥ* (H) *śabdaḥ* (P): $P \subset H$, and
(2) *anityaḥ* (S) *kṛtakaḥ* (H): $H \subset S$,
hence: *anityaḥ* (S) *śabdaḥ* (P) : $P \subset S$.

The assumption of the negative example has the form: *yad akṛtakaṁ* (H') *tan nityaṁ* (S') *bhavati* ($H' \subset S'$), instead of *yad anityaṁ* (S') *tan akṛtakaṁ* (H') *bhavati* ($S' \subset H'$). Therefore, the first condition necessary for the validity of the negative example $(D \subset H') \cap (D \subset S')$ cannot be proved.

Cf. NBṬ$_{I}$ 3.136: *ihânvaya-vyatirekābhyāṁ sādhya-niyato hetur darśayitavyaṁ. yadā ca sādhya-niyato hetur darśayitavyas tadā vyatireka-vākye sādhyâbhāvaḥ sādhanâbhāve niyato darśayitavyaḥ. evaṁ hi hetuḥ sādhya-niyato darśitaḥ syāt. yadi tu sādhyâbhāvaḥ sādhanâbhāve niyato nâkhyāyate sādhana-sattāyām api sādhyâbhāvaḥ sambhāvyeta. tathā ca sādhanaṁ sādhya-niyataṁ na pratīyeta. tasmāt sādhyâbhāvaḥ sādhanâbhāve niyato vaktavyaḥ. viparīta-vyatireke ca sādhanâbhāvaḥ sādhyâbhāve niyata ucyate. na sādhyâbhāvaḥ sādhanâbhāve. tathā hi: yad akṛtakam iti sādhanâbhāvam anūdya tan nityam iti sādhyâbhāva-vidhiḥ.*—'Here the logical reason (H) should be shown as contained in the probandum (S) by the positive and negative concomitance (*sc.* $H \subset S$). And if the logical reason should be shown as contained in the probandum, then—in the statement of negative concomitance—the absence of the probandum should be shown as contained in the absence of the probans (*sc.* $S' \subset H'$), so that in this way the logical reason would be shown as contained in the probandum. But if the absence of the probandum is not announced as contained in the absence of the probans (*sc.* $S' \subset H'$), then the absence of the probandum would be possible also when the probans were there (*sc.* $S' \subset H$). And in this manner, the probans could not be cognised as contained in the probandum. Hence, the absence of the probandum, which is contained in the probans, has to be stated. But in [the example] of an inverted negative concomitance the absence of the probans is stated as contained in the absence of the probandum (*sc.* $H' \subset S'$), [and] not the absence of the probandum [contained] in the absence of probans (*sc.* $S' \subset H'$). For it is as follows: after the absence of the probans [in the form] "what is not produced" has been communicated, the confirmation of the absence of the probandum [in the form:] "that is permanent" [is expressed] (*sc.* $(x \in H') \rightarrow (x \in S')$ instead of the reverse: $(x \in S') \rightarrow (x \in H')$).'

519 See NAV 13: *tatra yadā pratipādyaḥ prakramād eva nirṇīta-pakṣo 'vismṛta-dṛṣṭânta-smārya-pratibandha-grāhaka-pramāṇo vyutpanna-matitvāc cheṣâvayavâbhyūhana-samarthaś ca bhavati, yad vâtyantâbhyāsena parikarmita-matitvāt tāvatâiva prastuta-prameyam avabudhyate, tadā hetu-pratipādanam eva kriyate, śeṣâbhidhānasya śrotṛ-saṁskārâkāritayā nairarthakyāt* ... (p.56 of the translation), as well as NAV 18: *gṛhīte ca pratibandhe smaryamāṇe kevalaṁ hetur darśanīyaḥ, tāvatâiva bubhutsitârtha-siddher dṛṣṭânto na vācyo, vaiyarthyāt* (p.63 of the translation).

520 PV_{I} 3.27cd and PVSV, p. 186.19 (Gnoli: 18.11) thereon. Cf. n. 411.

521 Alternatively, the phrase *sādhanâvayava* might be taken to mean: 'the member of the proof formula.' However, since it is explicitly attested in several places that example is indeed a part of the proof, in the present context *sādhana* cannot but mean the probans, and not the proof formula; see, e.g. NAV 13: *pakṣo vakṣyamāṇa-lakṣaṇaḥ sa ādir yeṣāṁ hetu-dṛṣṭântôpanaya-nigamanâdīnāṁ tāni tathā, teṣāṁ vacanāni pratipādakā dhvanayaḥ; tāny evâtmā svarūpaṁ yasya tat pakṣâdi-vacanâtmakam* (p.55 of the translation), NAV 13: *nâikaḥ prakāraḥ parârthânumānasya, kiṁ tarhi yathā parasya sukhena prameya-pratītir bhavati tathā yatnataḥ pratyāyanīyaḥ. tatra daśâvayavaṁ sādhanaṁ pratipādanôpāyaḥ. tad yathā—pakṣâdayaḥ pañca, tac-chuddhayaś ca* (p.56 of the translation), NA 13: *tasmād dhetuvat pakṣâdayo 'pi sādhanaṁ, hetor api kvacit pratipādye tad-apekṣatayā nirapekṣatâsiddher iti* (p.58 of the translation), or a few lines further below in NAV 26: *sādhyate ... anumeyaṁ yena tat sādhanam, ... tad yathā: ... kvacit pakṣa-hetu-dṛṣṭântāḥ* (p. 78 of the translation). Thus, in view of the above quotations, Siddharṣi-gaṇin's assertion *dṛṣṭântaḥ sādhanâvayavo nâbhyupagamyate*, in the sense of 'example is not accepted as a member of the proof formula,' would only manifest Siddharṣi-gaṇin's 'aptitude for formulations in which antecedent and subsequent statements are contradicted by each other' (**pūrvâpara-vyāhata-vacana-racanā-cāturya*). Another conceivable interpretation of the phrase: *dṛṣṭântasya sādhanâvayavatvenânabhyupagamāt*, could be to supplement it with a qualifier 'necessary': 'because the example is not accepted as a [necessary] member of the proof formula.'

522 See n. 231.

523 NA 13.

524 Surprisingly, in all consulted editions and MSS. the first hemistich of NA 26 has only 15 syllables and, apparently, one syllable is missing in *pāda* b to complete the

śloka! The only exception is the reading in VIDYĀBHŪṢAṆA (1909: 20): *vādy-ukte sādhane prokta-doṣāṇām udabhāvanam*, but *udabhāvanam* is clearly a missprint. Strangely enough, there is hardly any indication to be found NAV that would enable us to restore the correct reading of NA 26. The text should somehow be emended, most probably, by addition of one more syllable to *pāda* B, e.g.: (1) ***prokta-doṣāṇām tatrôdbhāvanam** (cf. NAV *ad loc.*: *tatra* ***prokta-doṣāṇāṁ*** *pratyakṣâdi-nirākṛta-pakṣâsiddhâdi-hetu-sādhyâdi-vikala-dṛṣṭântâdy-upanyāsa-lakṣaṇānām* ***udbhāvanaṁ***). In such an interpretation *tatra* would be, however, redundant, inasmuch as it would refer to *vādy-ukte sādhane*, already mentioned in the same sentence. Optionally, we might have (2) ***prokta-doṣâdīnām udbhāvanam**, analogous to NB_2 3.137–8: /137/ *dūṣaṇā nyūnatâdy-uktiḥ.* /138/ *ye pūrvaṁ nyūnatâdayaḥ sādhana-doṣā uktās teṣām udbhāvanaṁ dūṣaṇaṁ. tena parêṣṭârtha-siddhi-pratibandhāt.* The same idea (without the °*-ādi-*° element though) is expressed also in NP_2 6: *sādhana-doṣôdbhāvanāni dūṣaṇāni // sādhana-doṣo nyūnatvam. pakṣa-doṣaḥ pratyakṣâdi-viruddhatvam. hetu-doṣo 'siddhânaikāntika-viruddhatvam. dṛṣṭānta-doṣaḥ sādhana-dharmâdy-asiddhatvam. tasyôdbhāvanaṁ prāśnika-pratyāyanaṁ dūṣaṇam //* In NP, the °*-ādi-*° element refers, logically enough, to subvarieties of *doṣa*, not to something else than the *doṣa*s. The question thus arises what would °*-ādi-*° in the compound **prokta-doṣâdīnām udbhāvanam* exactly refer to? (3) Another possibility would be to read ***parôkta-doṣāṇāṁ**. One seems to hastily subscribe to such an interpretation. However, the latter interpretation is problematic as well. It would separate *para-*° in a highly unnatural manner (viz., *pāda* A: *vādy-ukte sādhane pa-*° + *pāda* B: °*-rôkta-doṣāṇām udbhāvanam*), in the first place. Secondly, its interpretation would not be free of additional difficulties. What would the phrase **parôkta* ('expressed by the opponent') acutally refer to? Would it refer to the *vādin* (in *vādy-ukte*) or to the *prativādin*? (3a) Since what is at stake are the 'defects' in the proof, one would readily take **parôkta* to refer to such defects: 'the defects expressed/said (*ukta*) by the opponent'. That being the case, the first hemistich would be either redundant or contradictory. (3b) Optionally, **parôkta* might refer to 'defects pointed out (*ukta*) by the opponent', in which *para* = *prativādin*. But then, syntactically the *pāda* B would be rather an awkward formulation of the expected: **parenôktam vādy-uktānāṁ doṣāṇām udbhāvanam*. Furthermore, if we consult the reading of Siddharṣi's commentary, there we find two arguments if favour of the reading *prokta-doṣ*°. First, the particle *prāk* in the phrase *tac câneka-rūpaṁ prāk pratyapādi* can be taken as an explication of the prefix *pra*° in *prokta*. Secondly, the elucidation of the compound *prokta-doṣāṇāṁ* in the commentary (***prokta-doṣāṇāṁ*** *pratyakṣâdi-nirākṛta-pakṣâsiddhâdi-hetu-sādhyâdi-vikala-dṛṣṭântâdy-upanyāsa-lakṣaṇānām*) goes back to the varieties that have been discussed previously. (4) Personally, I would suggest to emend NA 26ab by inserting *para-*° as follows: **vādy-ukte sādhane prokta-doṣāṇām* ***parô****dbhāvanam*, that would translate as 'Criticism is [the act of] pointing out **by the opponent** the defects, taught previously, in a proof enunciated by the propounder'. As a hint favouring such and interpretation we may take NAV *ad loc.*: ***udbhāvanaṁ*** *prāśnikānāṁ purataḥ prakāśanaṁ*, in which *udbhāvanaṁ* is explained by *prakāśanaṁ*, and *prāśnikānāṁ purataḥ* might be taken to allude to *parôdbhāvanam* (=*pareṇôdbhāvanam*).

[525] Cf. NAV 13, p. 55, 56, n.521.

[526] This is a direct reference to NA 14; however, for varieties of the fallacious thesis see NA 21.

[527] For varieties of the fallacious logical reason see NA 23.

[528] For varieties of the fallacious example see NA 24–25.

[529] Cf. PMī 2.1.29: *abhūta-doṣôdhāvanāni dūṣaṇâbhāsā jāty-uttarāṇi*, and the respective gloss in PMī 2.1 § 63: *avidyamanānāṁ sādhana-doṣāṇāṁ pratipādanāny adūṣaṇāny api dūṣaṇavad ābhāsamānāni 'dūṣaṇâbhāsāḥ.'*

[530] It is a linguistic justification of the term *dūṣaṇâbhāsa*: *dūṣaṇavad ābhāsata iti dūṣaṇâbhāsam*.

[531] The proof formula that has been formulated in a coherent and logically correct manner and that has proved the probandum cannot be blamed to be fallacious, even though a corrupt word might occur in its formulation or a defective poetical ornament, or a rhetoric figure of speech, has been employed in it, inasmuch as corrupt words are a subject matter of grammar, whereas defective rhetoric figures belong to a category of defects dealt with in the science of poetics. It is only a logically faulty formulation of a proof formula that allows its invalidation, not a formulation which is defective on the level of its purely verbal formulation alone. That occasionally the cognitive validity of verbal statements in general, and of inferences formulated on the speech level in particular, has been rejected on the grounds of their liability to a number of flaws of purely verbal nature, is attested as early as in NS_2 2.1.56: *tad* [=*śabdam*] *aprāmāṇyam anṛta-vyāghāta-punar-ukta-doṣebhyaḥ*. There, by way of a *pūrva-pakṣa* argument, Akṣapāda Gautama refers to an objection denying that the verbal testimony has the status of a cognitive criterion, inasmuch as it is exposed to defects like falsehood (*anṛta*), self-abortiveness (*vyāghāta*) and redundancy (*punar-ukta*). What is striking is the fact that self-abortiveness (*vyāghāta*) and redundancy (*punar-ukta*) are enumerated as defect of ornamentation and classified as *alaṅkāra-doṣa* in works on rhetoric, such as Mammaṭa's *Kāvya-prakāśa* or Daṇḍin's *Kāvyâdarśa*. For details cf. RAGHAVAN (1963: 114–5, 226, 234, 245–6). See also MK VI, p. 3404: ***vadato vyāghāta-nyāyaḥ***. *yathā jihvā me nâsti, mama mātā vandhyêty-ādau prasaratîti sarva-darśana-saṅgrahe bauddha-naye 'bhihita iti.* [*Bhuvaneśa-laukika-nyāya-*] *sahasrī* 693.

[532] Cf. a similar use in NBh 2.2.68: *tu-śabdo viśeṣaṇârthaḥ. kiṁ viśiṣyate pradhānâṅga-bhāvasyâniyamena padârthatvam iti.*

[533] Cf. PMī 2.1.30: *tattva-saṁrakṣaṇârthaṁ prāśnikâdi-samakṣaṁ sādhana-dūṣaṇa-vadanaṁ vādaḥ.*—'Debate [consists in] expressing the proof and the criticism in the presence of questioners, etc., [viz., the president of the council, the proponent and the

opponent (i.e. *sabhā-pati-vādi-prativādi*)] with an objective of preservation of truth.' Here we come across a Jaina criticism apparently directed, on the one hand, against the Buddhist and the Naiyāyika position according to which a debate aims, in the first place, at one's own victory, the former being formulated as early as in Vasubandhu's *Vāda-vidhāna* (Fr. A I 3): *sva-para-pakṣayoḥ siddhy-asiddhy-arthaṁ vacanaṁ vādaḥ.*—'Debate is a discussion aiming at proving one's own thesis and at disproving the opponent's thesis'; the latter being stated in NS 1.2.1: *pramāṇa-tarka-sādhanôpālambhaḥ siddhântâviruddhaḥ pañcâvayavôpapannaḥ pakṣa-pratipakṣa-parigraho vādaḥ.*—'Debate [consists in] propounding a thesis and a counter-thesis, supported by five-membered proof formulae, not contradicted by one's doctrine, wherein a proof [of one's own thesis and a refutation of a counter-thesis] is achieved through cognitive criteria and reasoning.' On the other hand, it is a censure of the Naiyāyika view that the objective of both disputation and cavil is the preservation of truth, as well; cf. NS 4.2.50: *tattvâdhyavasāya-saṁrakṣaṇârthaṁ jalpa-vitaṇḍe, bīja-praroha-saṁrakṣaṇârthaṁ kaṇṭaka-śākhâvaraṇavat.*—'Disputation and cavil aim at the preservation of the apprehension of truth, just like a hedge of thorny branches aims at the protection of growth of a sprout.'

[534] Throughout the whole text of NAV the verb form *darśayati*, and similar ones, are invariably accompanied by an object, the construction being based on the pattern '[subject] + object + *darśayati*.' The only deviation (apart from the present case) from this model—viz., the pattern with inverted object and verb: '[subject] + *darśayati* + object'—is found in NAV 29: *tathā hy: alakṣita-paramâṇu-pārimāṇḍalya-pratikṣaṇa-vivartam api svalakṣaṇaṁ sthira-sthūrâdy-ātmanā darśayati svarūpam.* In our case, the punctuation adopted by both P. L. Vaidya and Bhagavandas Harakhchand (i.e. H: *tu śabdena viśeṣaṇârthena darśayati—vastu-siddhy-arthaṁ vāda-pravṛtteḥ tasya siddhatvād*; V: *tu-śabdena viśeṣaṇârthena darśayati—vastu-siddhy-arthaṁ vāda-pravṛtteḥ*, *tasya siddhatvād*) clearly disregards this syntactical construction. Precisely due to this reason, a tentative suggestion that the text is apparently corrupt here and one should read *vāda-pravṛttiḥ* instead—inasmuch as, otherwise, the subject of the sentence would be missing and the whole passage, beginning with *vastu-siddhy-arthaṁ*, would consist of a sequence of ablatives—is highly implausible.

[535] Cf. NAṬ *ad loc.*: ***tāvan-mātreṇâivêti***. *apaśabdâlaṅkārâdi-doṣôdbhāvana-mātreṇâiva.*—'By nothing else but only by pointing out of defects, like corrupt words, ornamentation, etc.'

[536] Cf. n. 231.

[537] Cf. TS 10.1: *moha-kṣayāj jñāna-darśanâvaraṇântarāya-kṣayāc ca kevalam*.

[538] Cf. TS 1.30: *sarva-dravya-paryāyeṣu kevalasya*. See also PMī 1.1.15: *tat* [=*pratyakṣaṁ*] *sarvathâvaraṇa-vilaye cetanasya svarūpâvir-bhāvo mukhyaṁ*[a] *kevalam.*—'That [perception] which is the manifestation of the intrinsic nature of

consciousness, when karmic veils have been completely annihilated, which is primary[a] is the absolute cognition.'

[a] PMĪ 1.1 § 48 explains: *sarva-jñānānāṁ pradhānaṁ "mukhyaṁ" pratyakṣam.*—'Perception that is the main [one] among all kinds of cognition, [i.e.] primary.'

[539] Surprisingly, in all consulted editions and MSS. the first hemistich of NA 27 has as many as seventeen syllables! Most probably *pāda* A (*sakalâvaraṇa-muktâtma*) is faulty (nine syllables). The expression *sakalâvaraṇa-muktâtma* is likely to have been contaminated by *sakalârthâtma* of *pāda* C. Additionally, the respective explanation of NAV (***sakalaṁ*** *samastam, āvṛṇoty āvriyate vânenêty* ***āvaraṇaṁ***, *tat-svarūpa-pracchādanaṁ karmêty arthaḥ, sakalaṁ ca tad avāraṇaṁ ca sakalâvaraṇaṁ, tena* ***mukto*** *rahita,* ***ātmā*** *svarūpaṁ yasya tat-tathā*) must have prompted a scribe to change the original text of the aphorism. Originally perhaps the gloss of NAV might have read *...rahitaḥ, svarūpaṁ yasya tat-tathā* (and *ātmā* was added later), or similarly, analogously to NAV 1: *tatra* ***pramāṇam*** *iti pūrvavat.* ***sva*** *ātmā svarūpaṁ,* ***paro*** *'rthas, tāv ābhāsayituṁ prakāśayituṁ śīlam yasya tat-tathā* that explicates NA 1: *pramāṇaṁ sva-parâbhāsi jñānaṁ.* Perhaps we should emend the text of NA 27ab: *sakalâvaraṇa-muktaṁ kevalaṁ yat prakāśate*? In that case, the phrase *sakalâvaraṇa-muktaṁ* would remain a *bahu-vrīhi* compound and the respective gloss would apply as well: *...rahita, ātmā svarūpaṁ yasya tat-tathā*, with the proviso that *ātmā* would not be treated as a separate *pratīka*. Thus, the translation of the *śloka* should run even more naturally: "That which is freed from all veils, which shines as [something] absolute is perception representing constantly the essences of all objects."

[540] The pronoun *tad-°*—that links the previous term (*sakala*) with the subsequent one (*āvaraṇa*) in the explanation of the aphorism—in *tat-svarūpa-pracchādanaṁ* cannot but refer to *sakalaṁ samastam*. That being the case, however, the compound *sakalâvaraṇa-°* in the aphorism should rather be understood as a typical *tad-puruṣa* compound (*sakalasyâvaraṇam*), not as a *karma-dhāraya* compound (*sakalam āvaraṇam*), as I am inclined to interpret it, and as it is eventually dissolved (*sakalaṁ ca tad avāraṇaṁ ca*) by Siddharṣi-gaṇin himself. In view of the above, the aphorism should be then reinterpreted as follows: 'that the essence of which is freed from veils of everything ...' Still another possibility—especially, in order to account for the double use of *ca* in *sakalaṁ ca tad avāraṇaṁ ca*—would be to read the passage as follows: ***sakalaṁ*** *samastam, āvṛṇoty āvriyate vânenêty* ***āvaraṇaṁ***, *tat-svarūpa-pracchādanaṁ karmêty arthaḥ,* ***sakalaṁ*** *ca tad-avāraṇaṁ ca sakalâvaraṇaṁ.* In such a case, *sakala* would be taken by Siddharṣi-gaṇin in two meanings at the same time: [1] 'of everything' (*sakalasya*) marked by *tad-°* in *tat-svarūpa-pracchādanaṁ* ('obfuscating the intrinsic nature of everything') and [2] 'all' (*sakalam*) in ***sakalaṁ*** *ca tad-avāraṇaṁ* ('all veils of everything'). Such an reading would force us to render the compound in the aphorism as 'that the essence of which is freed from all veils of everything.'

[541] Viz., without any extraneous condition (*upādhi*). For the meaning of the term cf. n. 294.

[542] Cf. n. 128.

[543] Cf. n. 675.

[544] Viz., both the conventional perception as well as inference are instances of indirect cognition, inasmuch as in both cases the cognised object is obscured (by the sense organs, mind, speech, etc.), i.e. not directly cognised.

[545] I.e., 'flower' is the definiens that is destitute of its domain, because 'sky lotus cluster' is a non-existent definiendum, inasmuch as sky lotuses do not exist. Similarly the absolute cognition (*kevala-jñāna*) is not well-known to opponents, hence the definition formulated in the aphorism is defective.

[546] I construe *avadhāraṇīyatām* with *kevala-jñāna*, referred to as *pāramārthika-pratyakṣa* in the previous paragraph and only alluded to by *adaḥ* in the first clause of the above sentence. The abstract form of the gerundive *avadhāraṇīyatām* can hardly be construed with the pronoun *teṣāṁ* as its object (e.g. *te avadhāraṇīyāḥ*) in view of the fact that the meaning of *ava√dhṛ* is incompatible with *teṣāṁ* denoting 'people.' The phrase should rather be supplemented with *amuṣya* (or linked directly to *adaḥ* in the preceding clause), wherein *teṣāṁ* should be taken in the dative sense, viz., **teṣām amuṣyâvadhāraṇīyatām*, that would correspond to: **tebhyā 'do 'vadhāraṇīyaḥ*.

[547] *samasta-vastu-vicāra-gocara* can be treated either as a qualifier (*supra*) or as a predicate, viz.: 'a clear perception is possible as such, the domain of which is the range of all real things.' I am unable to decide which is more appropriate.

[548] Cf. PASS 10:

> *davvaṁ sal-lakkhaṇiyaṁ uppāda-vvaya-dhuvatta-saṁjuttaṁ /*
> *guṇa-pajjayâsayaṁ vā jaṁ taṁ bhaṇṇaṁti savvaṇhū //*

—'The omniscient call [as] "substance" what is characterised by something existent (*sc.* by existence), what is connected (*sc.* endowed) with origination, annihilation and permanence and what is based on qualities and modes.' See also PSā 1.18:

> *uppādo ya viṇāso vijjadi savvassa aṭṭhajādassa /*
> *pajjāeṇa du keṇavi aṭṭho khalu hodi sabbhūdo //*

as well as PSā 2.3–4:

> *aparіccatta-sahāveṇuppāda-vvaya-dhuvatta-saṁjuttaṁ /*
> *guṇavaṁ ca sapajjāyaṁ jaṁ taṁ davvaṁ ti vuccaṁti //*
> *sabbhāvo hi sahāvo guṇehiṁ saha pajjaëhiṁ cittehiṁ /*
> *davvassa savva-kālaṁ uppāda-vvaya-dhuvattehiṁ //*

Cf. also several other verses: PSā 2.7–8,10,27, etc. See likewise TS 5.29: *utpāda-vyaya-dhrauvya-yuktaṁ sat.*—'That what is existent is furnished with origination, annihilation and permanence'; AYVD 21: *pratikṣaṇôtpāda-vināśa-yogi-sthihrâikam adhyakṣam apîkṣamāṇaḥ* ...; SVM 21, p. 135.34 ff.: *vastu-tattvaṁ côtpāda-vyaya-dhrauvyâtmakam.*—'Reality as a real thing, by its nature, [undergoes] origination, annihilation and permanence'; ĀA 171: *ekam eka-kṣaṇe siddhaṁ dhrauvyôtpatti-vyayâtmakam.*

[549] Thereby *ratna-traya*, viz., the correct cognition, correct conation and correct conduct (*samyag-darśana-jñāna-cāritra*), is alluded to. Cf. n.552.

[550] In other words: if there is a means to purify an object, that very object can be purified.

[551] The *puṭa-pāka* process is described in BOSE–SEN–SUBBARAYAPPA (1971: 325): 'The substance is subjected to a prolonged heating which is technically called *puṭa* ... The source of heat is the fire of cow-dung, and depending on the quantity of the cow-dung cakes used as also the way they are heaped, different degrees are sought to be given to the substance. The substance itself is placed in an earthen flat container and enclosed by another, and sealed with a mud plaster.' For the process of *puṭa-pāka* and its varieties cf. D. JOSHI (1986: 287 ff.). The process of calcination, or roasting a mineral (e.g. a metal or jewel) in a furnace, technically called *puṭa-pāka*, forms a part of a pulverisation process that aims at converting a particular substance into powder (Rṇv 6.83: *bhasmatāṁ gatam*), which in its turn is further used to prepare a medicine. Very often the substance to be calcinated is diamond; its pulverisation processes are described, e.g. in the *vajra-vidhi* section of Rṇv (6.65–122), and are referred to as 'killing of a diamond' (*vajra-māraṇa*, Rṇv 6.84); cf. similar expressions: *vajraṁ tu mriyate kṣaṇāt* (Rṇv 6.88). For the *māraṇa*-process, see D. JOSHI (1986: 10 ff.). Diamond is, in its turn, divided into three varieties depending on their 'sex', among which 'male' diamonds are regarded superior (Rṇv 6.68: *puruṣāś ca striyaś câiva napuṁsakam anukramāt*, cf. RRS 4.27: *vajraś ca trividhaṁ proktaṁ naro narī napuṁsakam / pūrvaṁ pūrvam iha śreṣṭham*), as well as into four subtypes according to colour-classes of each of the three gender-subdivisions (Rṇv 6.66: *brāhmaṇāḥ kṣatriyā vaiśyāḥ śūdrāś câivam anekadhā*; cf. RRS 4.31: *śvetâdi-varṇa-bhedena tad ekâikam catur-vidham / brahma-kṣatriya-viṭ-śudram sva-sva-varṇa-phala-pradam*). The colours—viz., white, red, yellow and dark-bluish—are enumerated in corresponding section of RRSṬ: *catur-vidha-jāti-bhedam āha*: "*śvetâdîti.*" *ādi-śabdena rakta-pīta-kṛṣṇa-varṇa-parigrahaḥ.* The purification (*śodhana*) process of substances other than diamond is further described in the tenth chapter of Rṇv, wherein it is mostly referred to as *jāraṇa* and other derivatives of √*jṝ* (e.g. Rṇv 11.35,96: *jārayet*) are generally used in the context, although the derivatives of √*mṛt* (Rṇv 11.94: *mārayet*) do occur, less frequently though, as synonymous with more frequent derivatives of √*jṝ*. Varieties of furnaces and other alchemic equipment are discussed at length by D. JOSHI (1986: fifth chapter).

Wilhelm RAU (1983: 13–19) cites a passage from the *Agastya-saṁhitā*[a] (AgS) describing a method of polishing a jewel to obtain a burning lens. The described procedure is, apparently, different from the process of calcination.

There are some striking points to be noted here that may justify the analogy between the soul and a gem as well as the juxtaposition of the process of inner purification of the soul and the process of purification of a gem.

(1) The four colours (*varṇa*) of diamond (RRSṬ 4.31) resemble the coloration (*leśyā*) of the soul: *śveta* / *śukla*, *rakta* / *tejas*, *pīta* / *padma*, *kṛṣṇa*. A full list of the traditional six colourings, that correspond to the grade of inner development of an individual, comprise black (*kṛṣṇa*; Pkt., *kaṇha*), blue (*nīla*), grey (*kāpota*; Pkt., *kāü*), red (*tejas*; Pkt., *teü*), pinkish yellow (*padma*; Pkt., *paṁha*), white (*śukla*; Pkt., *sukka*); see, e.g. SSi 2.6: *sā ṣad-vidhā*: *kṛṣṇa-leśyā nīla-leśyā kāpota-leśyā tejo-leśyā padma-leśyā śukla-leśyā cêti*, and TBh 2.6; cf. GLASENAPP (1942: 47).
(2) The use of derivatives of √*jṝ*, viz., of the term *jāraṇa* with regard to the purifying pulverisation processes of a diamond and *nirjarā* for the purification of the soul, i.e. the removal of karmic matter by ascetic practices.
(3) The purification of diamond by its pulverisation / calcination does not destroy diamond itself, the process removes only its material impurities.

A comparison of a pious mendicant to a jewel is a well-known motif from Jaina works, e.g. ĀA 176:

śāstrâgnau maṇivad bhavyo viśuddho bhāti nirvṛtaḥ /
aṅgāravat khalo dīpto malī vā bhasma vā bhavet //

'A [person] competent for liberation, purified [and] restrained, gleams like a jewel in the fire of authoritative treatises; a base man, as one should realise, who burns like charcoal, turns either into filth or into ashes'; cf. ĀA 263cd:

udāsīnas tasya pragalita-purāṇaṁ na hi navaṁ
samāskandaty eṣa spurati suvidagdho maṇir iva //

I do not, by any means, intend to maintain that Jaina salvific doctrine of purification of the soul and its terminology might have influenced in any way the terminology of alchemy, or *vice versa*. Moreover, personally I am convinced that not only such a relation would be extremely difficult to establish beyond doubt, but also that there was any such direct relation whatsoever. The point I have been trying to make is that certain parallelism that concerned both the terminology and processes was responsible for the deliberate choice of particular similes.

[a] Before 1334/5 AD; cf. RAU (1983: 12, n. 30): '*Agastya-proktā agastya-saṁhitā. Buddhabhaṭṭa-racitā ratna-parīkṣā ca. etat pustaka-dvayaṁ paṁ.* Buddhi-sāgara-śramaṇaḥ *adhyakṣatāyāṁ sarva-darśanâcārya paṁ.* Kṛṣṇaprasāda Bhaṭṭa Rā'ī *ity etaiḥ saṁpāditam. vīra-pustakâlaya-dvārā prakāśitam = purā-tattva-prakāśana-mālā 15.* [Kathmandu / Nepal] *vi. saṁ.* 2020 [1962/3], pp. 32,22–33.24/.'

[552] Cf. NAṬ *ad loc.*: *jñānâbhyāsāt jñānâvaraṇa-vilaye jñānâvaraṇa-vilaya-kāryo jñāna-viśeṣo dṛśyate. ādi-śabdāt darśanâbhyāsāt darśanâvaraṇa-vilaye darśanâvaraṇa-vilaya-kāryo darśana-viśeṣânubhavo gṛhyate. evaṁ cāritrâbhyāse 'pi.*—'When the [karmic] veils [obstructing] cognition have been annihilated due to repeated practice of cognition, a particular cognition is seen [to occur], which is the effect of the annihilation of the [karmic] veils [obstructing] cognition. By the speech element "etc." the experience of a particular conation is comprised, which is the effect of the annihilation of the [karmic] veils [obstructing] conation, when the

[karmic] veils [obstructing] conation have been annihilated. In a similar manner [things take place] also in the case of conduct.' For this triad, frequently referred to as the triad of gems (*ratna-traya*), cf. TS 1.1: *samyag-darśana-jñāna-cāritrāṇi mokṣa-mārgaḥ*. Cf. ĀA 166:

viśuddhyati durācāraḥ sarvo 'pi tapasā dhruvam /
karoti malinaṁ tac ca kila sarvâdharo 'paraḥ //

—'All ill conduct, without exception, is invariably purified by austerities; another [person, viz., a non-mendicant,] who sullies this [ideal of austerities] is, as they say, the [most] ignoble of all.'

[553] Regarding the use of *kathañcit* with negation, I am inclined to endorse the expected interpretation of the phrase 'not ... at all.' Such a traditional interpretation is corroborated, e.g. by Malliṣeṇa who—in his refutation of absolute difference between cogniser and cognition—expresses his objection (SVM 8.79, p. 38): *atyanta-bhede sati katham ātmanaḥ sambandhi jñānam?*—'If it were absolutely different, how could cognition be connected with the cognitive subject?' Further, he says (SVM 8.206–207, p. 43): *tataś ca jñānâtmanor ubhayor api saṁvitti-lakṣaṇâika-kārya-sādhakatvād abheda eva.*—'Therefore, both of these, viz., cognition and cogniser, are not at all different, inasmuch as they produce one effect characterised by sensation [of an object].' Cf. also the opinion found in NAV 31 (p. 131 of the English translation) referred to in n. 554. Furthermore, it is clear that *kathañcid* + *na* means 'not ... at all' from the comparison of a gloss found in NAṬ 29 below (***itarathêti***. *yadi kathañcid vyatirekiṇāv api sāmānya-viśeṣau na syātām*) on a respective portion of NAV 29 ([*sāmānya-viśeṣayor*] *vyatirekiṇor api tayor vastuni kathañcid bhāvād*, ***itarathā*** *vivakṣayâpi tathā darśayitum aśakyatvāt*), where the connective is *itarathā*. There, the conjunction of *kathañcid* + *na* expresses a straightforwardly opposite thesis. Correspondingly, the statement of NAṬ 29 '...if the universal and the particular were n o t d i f f e r e n t a t a l l whatsoever." must be antithetical (*itarathā*) to '...both of them, [viz. the universal and the particulars, are] d i f f e r e n t [from each other] ...' of NAV 29. See p. 112 and n. 767.

In Jaina literature, however, *kathañcit* frequently stands for *syāt*, e.g. in SVM 23, p. 144.132: *syāt kathañcin nâsty eva kumbhâdiḥ*, which means 'in a certain sense, [i.e.] s o m e h o w, a pitcher does not exist', and not 'a pitcher does n o t exist a t a l l.' Accordingly, it would not at all be so unjustified to endorse an alternative rendering of the above sentence in view of this specifically Jaina use of the qualifier *kathañcit*: 'because s o m e h o w there is no difference between cognition and cogniser.'

[554] Cf. NAV 31: ***svânya-nirbhāsîty*** *anena ... pratikṣipati, jñāna-jñāninoḥ kathañcid abhedena tad-ukta-nyāyâviśeṣād iti*. (p. 131 of the English translation).

[555] There has been some debate on the meaning of the term *pratipakṣa* and its correlate *vipakṣa* with reference to the realm of soteriological usage. SCHLINGHOFF (1964) translates throughout both of them indiscriminately as 'Hindernis.' RUEGG (1967: 158) cen-

sures Schlinghoff for confusing these two terms and in his criticism of their unselective rendering refers to PV 2.129 (*kṛpā na cet ... / vipakṣair bādhyate ...*), PV 215, 266, etc., where these two terms are clearly distinguished. Thus, he suggests 'counteragent, antidote against certain obstacle' for *pratipakṣa* and 'Hindernis, obstacle' for *vipakṣa*. VETTER (1984: 41, n. 2) takes up the issue again pointing out that a sharp differentiation between these two terms into a positive and a negative opposite ('das positive Gegenteil oder Mittel' versus 'das negative Gegenteil oder Hindernis'), respectively, is not always possible. He argues—in view of PV 1.134 (*... sādhyate tad-vipakṣo 'pi heto rūpâvabodhataḥ //*) for *vipakṣa* and PV 2.273 for *pratipakṣa*, etc., attesting the usage of both of these terms in the sense of 'Gegensatz, das Gegenstück, also Hindernis, zum Wissen', viz., antithesis, opposition, obstacle to knowledge—that such a distinction lacks sound justification and proposes a neutral rendering by opposite ('Gegenteil').

[556] Apparently the Buddhists are meant. Cf. RNA 1,16–21 (*sarva-jñā-siddhi* section): *yo yaḥ sâdara-nirantara-dīrgha-kālâbhyāsa-sahita-ceto-guṇaḥ sa sarvaḥ sphuṭībhāva-yogyaḥ, yathā yuvaty-ākāraḥ kāminaḥ puruṣasya; yathôktâbhyāsa-sahita-ceto-guṇāś câmī catur-ārya-satya-viṣayā ākāra iti svabhāvo hetuḥ.*—'Whatever quality of the mind is accompanied by a repeated practice (*sc.* meditation) [carried out] with zeal, incessantly and for a long time, every such [quality] is capable if being manifested patently, like [the beloved] girl's form (mental image) for a man in love. And those forms (mental images), the province of which are the four noble truths are the qualities of the mind accompanied by a repeated practice (*sc.* meditation), as described above. Such is the logical reason [being] an essential identity.' This passage is quoted *verbatim* in BTBh$_3$ § 29. For *samasta-vastu-sambaddha-tattvâbhyāsa* as the cause of omniscience (*sarva-jñatva*) cf. TSa$_1$ 3381–3390:

/3381/ *samasta-vastu-sambaddha-tattvâbhyāsa-balôdgatam /*
sārva-jñaṁ mānasaṁ jñānaṁ mānam ekaṁ prakalpyate //

/3382/ *na tu netrâdi-vijñānaṁ tataḥ kim idam ucyate /*
nūnaṁ sa cakṣuṣā sarvān rasâdīn pratipadyate //

/3383/ *siddhaṁ ca mānasaṁ jñānaṁ rūpâdy-anubhavâtmakam /*
avivādaḥ parasyâpi vastuny etāvati sphuṭaḥ //

/3384/ *varṇyate hi smṛtis tena rūpa-śabdâdi-gocarā /*
svapne ca mānasaṁ jñānaṁ sarvârthânubhāvâtmakam //

/3385/ *tataś câniyatârthena mānasena prakalpite /*
sarva-jñe cakṣuṣā kasmād rasâdīn pratipadyate //

/3386/ *cakṣuṣeṇâiva tat-kḷptāv ayaṁ doṣo bhaved api /*
mānasena tu cittena vetty eva sa rasâdikam //

/3387/ *yatrâpy atiśayo dṛṣṭaḥ sva-svârthān atilaṅghanāt /*
dūra-sūkṣmâdi-dṛṣṭau syān na rūpe śrotra-vṛttitaḥ //

/3388/ *ity-ādikam ato 'niṣṭaṁ parair uktaṁ na no yataḥ /*
svârthâvilaṅghanenâiva mānase 'tiśayo mataḥ //

/3389/ *yaj jātīyaiḥ pramāṇaiś ca yaj jātīyârtha-darśanam /*

dṛṣṭaṁ samprati lokasya tathā kālântare 'pi naḥ //
/3390/ *viśuddhaṁ vā bhavej jñānaṁ sarvaṁ sarvârtha-gocaram /*
hetoḥ sambhāvyate kaścit phale 'py atiśayaḥ kvacit //

For the translation of the passage comp. the respective portion of TSa₃.

[557] The Mīmāṁsaka are meant.

[558] That is to say, the Mīmāṁsaka maintains that the sixth cognitive criterion, absence as negative proof, has its specific domain that neither coincides nor overlaps with the domain of the remaining five cognitive criteria. Hence, if an object can be proved by one of the remaining five cognitive criteria, say by inference, it is automatically excluded from the domain of the negative proof. Cf. p. 22.

[559] Cf. n. 102.

[560] Cf. n. 231.

[561] They are discussed in NA 1.

[562] It is discussed in NA 29.

[563] Siddharṣi-gaṇin, in his exposition, follows the sequence first enumerated in NAV 0: *iha ca lakṣaṇa-saṁkhyā-gocara-phaleṣu pramāṇaṁ prati vipratipadyante pare.* (p. 9 of the translation). It is worth mentioning that the commentator does not restrict himself to merely annotating and elucidating the contents of the aphorisms, but also argues to justify the structure of *Nyāyâvatāra*.

[564] This verse is quoted, e.g. in PMī 1.38 § 143 (p. 34).

[565] I.e., an inner happiness beyond pleasures related to, or derived from, external objects. The expression *vaiṣayika-sukhâtīta-paramâhlādânubhava* evokes a well-known idea of a complete withdrawal from all external stimuli and of an engrossment within one's own self (cf. YS 1.2: *yogaś citta-vṛtti-nirodhaḥ*), that was expressed in a simile of a tortoise as early as in Sū 1.8.16 (426):

jahā kumme sa-aṁgāiṁ saë dehe samāhare /
evaṁ pāvāiṁ medhāvī ajjhappeṇa samāhare //

—'Just the way a tortoise withdraws its limbs into its own body, in the same manner a sage withdraws inauspicious karmic matter by means of meditation.' That motif remained a recurrent theme in Jaina soteriological literature, cf. ĀA 16:

viṣaya-viṣa-prāśanôtthita-moha-jvara-janita-tīvra-tṛṣṇasya /
niḥśaktikasya bhavataḥ prāyaḥ peyâdy-upakramaḥ śreyān //

—'For you—[who has become] powerless [and who experiences] acute thirst born of confusion, [which, in its turn, has been] generated by tasting the poison of the provinces [of sense-organs]—generally the best are liquid remedies, etc.' See also ĀA 24: ... *viṣaya-sukhāny anubhavanti ye mohāt ... te pāpāḥ*. As B. BHATT (1989: 158) pointed out, the simile of a tortoise is known from non-Jinistic sources, as well:

NPU 3, p. 149: *indriyāṇi samāhṛtya kūrmo 'ṅgāṇîva sarvaśaḥ*. We find the same parable in BhG 2.58:

yadā saṁharate câyaṁ kūrmo 'ṅgānîva sarvaśaḥ /
indriyāṇînindiyârthebhyas tasya prajñā pratiṣṭitā //

—'And when he withdraws [his] sense-organs from sense-objects—just like a tortoise draws in its limbs [into its own body]—on all sides, his acumen becomes stable'; as well as in SN 1.7(17):

kummo va aṅgāni sake kapāle, samodahaṁ bhikkhu mano-vitakke /
anissito aññam aheṭhayāno, parinibbuto nūpavadeyya kañcī ti//

and in MDP 187.42:

yathā kūrma ihâṅgāni prasārya viniyacchati /
evam evêndriya-grāmaṁ buddhiḥ sṛṣṭvā niyacchati //

[566] The word *ādi* apparently refers to two other 'gems', viz., *jñāna* and *cāritra*, cf. n. 552.

[567] I take *sarva-saṁvidām* to mean 'of all acts of awareness', as against VIDYĀBHŪṢAṆA (1909: 23): 'Since things have many characters (that is, may be conceived from many points of view), they are the objects of all-sided knowledge [emphasis—P.B.]...' and MATILAL (1981: 41): 'Since a thing has manifold character, it is comprehended (only) by the omniscient [emphasis—P.B.]...'. Both VIDYĀBHŪṢAṆA and MATILAL speak of omniscience or the omniscient. However, the argumentative structure of the verse, in my opinion, is not: 'on the one hand, the omniscient know the many-faceted object, whereas the *naya*s show only one aspect', but rather: 'all acts of cognition apprehend the object as many-faceted (even if they are illusory, like in a dream); whereas it is only *naya*s that cognise one aspect of it.' In other words, what is contrasted here is not omniscience *versus* the viewpoint or the omniscient (viz. living beings) *versus* the viewpoint (one of many ways of cognising that are at the disposal of living beings), which would be unusual and unnatural. Rather, we have here the juxtaposition of all cognitive acts, which in a natural manner reveal the multiplex nature of the world, and viewpoints that select one aspect of it. This interpretation is supported by Siddharṣi-gaṇin's commentary who, step by step in sections 29.1–29.10, attempts to demonstrate that the nature of all cognitive acts, including false ones (e.g. the nature of *bodha* along the lines of the theory of *vijñāna-vāda*, discussed in §§ 29.5, 29.5), is to manifest the multiplex nature of the world. This holds true especially of valid cognitive acts (*pramāṇa*), as is confirmed by the concluding lines of the lengthy section of NAV 29 *ad* NA 29ab: *tasmād asiddhatâdi-doṣa-vinā-kṛto 'yaṁ tathā-pratibhāsa-lakṣaṇo hetur anekânta-gocaratām pramāṇasya parān abhyupagamayatîty alam vistareṇa* (§ 29.9), as well as by the passage of NAV 29 (§ 29.10): *ayaṁ ca yathâvasthita-pramāṇa-vyāpāra-paryālocaka-pramātr-abhiprāyeṇa pramāṇa-gocaro darśitaḥ. nayas tarhi kiṁ-bhūtam taṁ manyata iti vacanâvakāśe saty āha*: ***ekêty-ādi***. Cf. MOOKERJEE (1971: 41): 'An entity possessed of infinite number of attributes as constitutive

factors of its essence is the common object o f a l l s o r t s o f c o g n i t i o n [emphasis—P.B.]...'.

[568] I.e., 'the author excludes a possibility that a process of cognitions might take place without a multiplex object.'

[569] We come across an analogue to the above proof formula in Malliṣeṇa's commentary on AYVD 22ab: *ananta-dharmâtmakam eva tattvam*[a], *ato 'nyathā sattvam asūpapādam*[b] /
—'Ontological category[a] (the reality) cannot but have the essence [that consists of] infinite properties; existence is not easily explicable otherwise than in this way.' The first part the hemistich is parallel to NA 29a; see SVM 22.11–13, p. 137.4–6: *anena sādhanaṁ darśitam, tahā hi: tattvam iti dharmi, ananta-dharmâtmakatvaṁ sādhyo dharmaḥ, sattvânyathânupapatter iti hetuḥ.*—'By this [part of the aphorism, viz., "existence is not easily explicable otherwise than in this way"] the probans is exposed, namely: (1) "ontological category" is the subject (*sc.* the locus); (2) "having the essence [consisting of] infinite properties" is the probandum, i.e. the property. The logical reason is: "existence is otherwise inexplicable".'

[a] The term *tattva* (ontological category / the reality) is explained as synonymous to *vastu* (a real thing) in SVM 22.5–6, p. 136.22–23 *ad loc.*: ***tattvaṁ*** *paramârtha-bhūtaṁ vastu jīvâjīva-lakṣaṇam ananta-dharmâtmakam eva.* The editor, A. B. Dhruva in his 'Introduction,' p. CXX.28–29, fails to understand the meaning of AYVD 22a and renders it wrongly: 'Truth has numberless aspects.'

[b] The meaning of *asūpapādam* is nicely explained in SVM 22.10–11, p. 1367.3–4: ***asūpapādam***. *sukhenôpapadyate ghaṭanā-koṭi-saṇṭaṅkam āropyata iti sūpapādam, na tathā asūpapādam durghaṭam ity arthaḥ.*

[570] The thesis may be slightly rephrased—to match the formulation of NA 29—as follows: **yat pramāṇaṁ tat anekântâtmaka-vastu-grāhakaṁ.*

[571] Since we deal here with a clear case of two clauses linked by the pair of correlatives: *yathā ... tathâiva*, and not with the typical phrase introducing the example, viz., *tad yathā*, the punctuation of both Mss. A and B and of both editions H,V should be correspondingly altered. The pronoun *tad* alone, however, is hardly ever used as a marker of an example that is being introduced. In order to account for the unusual single use of *tad* in this meaning, one may consider here a possibility of a minor emendation of the text: *tad yathā—yathā nirādīnava-°... tathâiva*, wherein one *yathā* was left out by the scribe due to the repetition (*yathā yathā*).

[572] See NAṬ *ad loc.*: ***nirādīnavêti***. *ādīnavo doṣaḥ.*

[573] I.e., the form of the object possesses several facets inseparable from each other.

[574] The subsequent elaborate exposition and discussion of various objections brought forward against the prove of the multiplex object concludes with words: *tasmāt tasyâiva tatra pratibhāsanāt "sarva-saṁvidām anekântâtmakaṁ vastu gocara" iti sthitam.* (p.96 of the translation).

[575] It is one of the fallacious logical reasons, see NA 23. Siddharṣi-gaṇin will attempt presently to demonstrate that the logical reason furnished above is free from the defects represented by the three fallacies of the logical reason, viz., the unproved logical reason, the contrary logical reason and the inconclusive logical reason.

[576] This is the reference to the proof formula demonstrated on p. 84; cf. also nn. 569, 657. If opponents could demonstrate that the above-quoted logical reason proving the thesis of the multiplexity of cognised object represents one of the fallacies of the logical reason enumerated in NA 23, the whole proof formula, *ergo* the Jaina theory of multiplexity of reality (*anekânta-vāda*), would be thereby invalidated.

[577] For the expression *viśakalita* see NAṬ *ad loc.*: ***itarêtarêty-ādi***. *vividhāni śakalāni yeṣāṁ tāni viśakalāni, tāni karotîti iNi*[a] *viśakalyante pṛthak-kriyante*[b] *smêti karmaṇi Ktaḥ*[c]. *vividhāni śakalāni sañjātāni yeṣām iti tārakâder ākṛti-gaṇatvād itaC*[d]*-pratyayo vā. tata itarêtaraṁ*[e] *viśakalitānîti*[f] *viśeṣaṇa-samāse teṣāṁ*[g] *dharma-dharmi-bhāvaṁ vadantîty evaṁ śīlās taiḥ.*—'[Now we gloss the phrase]: "mutually", etc. "Those that have disparate sections" are discrete, hence [the verb] "to make [something] discrete". After the *iN*-suffix [is added to it, we obtain the verbal form:] "they have become disconnected" [from each other], i.e. "they have been made separate". When [one wants to express] the direct object, then the *Kta*-suffix [is added][c]. Or, [one can explain the derivation with] the *itaC*-suffix[d] [taken] from the grammatical set of patterns of "star, etc." [meaning]: "those whose sections originated as disparate". Hence "they are mutually disconnected". Thus, the [people]—who propound the [relation] of these [mutually disconnected elements which is characterised by] the relationship between the properties and [their] subject whole qualified in the above manner—are those who are so characterised, [viz., "propounders of such a relation between the subject and its properties". This whole composite expression is used] in the instrumental case.'

[a] C omits *iNi*. [b] H: *pṛthakriyante*.

[c] C: *Ktaṁ*. See Pāṇ 3.4.70: *tayor eva kṛtya-Kta-khal-arthāḥ.*—'The *kṛtya*-suffixes [forming necessitativa], *Kta*-suffixes [expressing the direct object] and suffixes having the meaning [denoted] by *khal*-suffixes, express only these two [namely the direct object (*karman*) and abstract impersonal notion denoted by a verb (*bhāva*; cf. n. 51 and n. 52)].'

[d] See Pāṇ 5.2.38: *tad asya sañjātaṁ-tārakâdibhyaḥ itaC*. [e] H: *itarêtaraṁ*.

[f] H: *viśakalitāvîti*; V: *viśakalitāv iti*. [g] H omits *teṣāṁ*.

[578] The phrase °*-vastuno 'vasthānâbhāvāt* is the nominal rendering of °*-vastu nâvatiṣṭhet*.

[579] The expression *tad-vṛtti-prasaṅgāt* seems to be an allusion to the idea of inherence (*samavāya*), the synonym of which is *vṛtti*.

[580] We can construe it differently: 'the net of criticism [directed against] the idea of occurrence of [such substrata like] connection, inherence, quality-bearer, the whole, the universal (whole set), etc., with regard to [such attributes like] the connected [attribute],

an inherent [property], quality, a part, the particular, etc.—out of [the following pairs of attributes and their substrata]: the connected [attribute] and connection, inherent [property] and inherence, quality-bearer and quality, a part and the whole, an individual thing and the universal (whole set), etc.—[understood] as [absolutely] separate from each other…'

[581] Sometimes *yad uta* can, in a redundant way, be followed with *iti*, as above in NAV 2: *sāmpratam yad asmābhiḥ prāg vivṛṇvadbhir vyudapâdi, yad uta vipratipannâvyutpanna-vyāmohâpoha-saham ihêdaṁ pramāṇa-lakṣaṇam iti tat-sūtra-darśanād eva vimala-buddhayo 'vagaccheyuḥ*. (p. 26 of the English translation) or below in NAV 29: *etāvad dhi pramāṇa-pratiṣṭhitam, yad uta vidhi-mukhena "śabdo 'rthasya vācaka" iti*. (p. 122 of the English translation).

[582] NAṬ 29 *ad loc.*: *teṣām saṁyogâdīnām*.

[583] Viz., *dūṣaṇa*, cf. a analogous passage above: *tad* [=*codyam*] *evâvarteta*.

[584] The structure of 'the reasoning by alternatives' is as follows:

[1] *saṁyogy-ādibhyo bhinnāḥ saṁyogâdayaḥ*
↙ ↘
[1.1] *eka-deśena* ↔ [1.2] *sāmastyena*
↙ ↘ ↓
[1.1.1] *saṁyogâdīnām niravayavatva* ↔ [1.1.2] *saṁyogâdīnām sâvayavatva* — *saṁyogâdi-bahutva-prasaṅga*
↓ ↓
tathā — [2.1] *avayavebhyo 'bhinnāḥ* ↔ [2.2] *avayavebhyo bhinnāḥ*
↙ ↓ ↘
anekânta — [2.2.a] *eka-deśena* — [2.2.b] *sāmastyena*
↓ ↓
anavasthā — ?

[2] *saṁyogy-ādy-abhinnāḥ saṁyogâdayaḥ*
↓
na vikalpa-bhājo bhavanti

The rebuttal of one alternative in the above argumentation is missing; that is evident from the chart ('the missing link' marked with the question mark). The following solution: *atha sāmastyena, tad apy asādhīyaḥ, pratyekaṁ parisamāptatayā saṁyogâdi-bahutva-prasaṅgāt* of a *sāmastyena*-alternative [1.2] might, however, be applied to [1.2.2.a] and to [1.2] with equal right; nevertheless, *atha* in the beginning (*atha sāmastyena, tad apy asādhīyaḥ…*) may suggest that this is a reply to a main alternative, viz., to [1.2]. This suggestion is further corroborated by the immediately following solution of the [2]-alternative.

[585] The purport is as follows: the substrata and their attributes are not absolutely different from each other, but, nonetheless, one can attempt to draw a line of distinction between them, if one wishes to.

[586] Cf. NAṬ *ad loc.*: ***dṛṣṭêty-ādi***. *saṁyogy-ādibhyaḥ kathañcid bhinnāḥ saṁyogâdaya iti dṛṣṭaṁ, ghaṭa-paṭâdivad ekânta-bhedinaḥ saṁyogâdaya iti svapne 'py adṛṣṭaṁ, tayor hāni-parikalpane te eva*[a] *dvāraṁ tena.*—'[Now we comment on the expression] beginning with [words] "empirical fact". It is an empirical fact that [substrata like] connection, etc., are somehow different from the connected [attribute], etc. It is a fiction even in a dream that [substrata like] connection, etc., are characterised by absolute difference [from their attributes], say, like a pot and a piece of cloth; hence: "discarding and assuming these two [respectively]"; these two are the way; [the whole expression is used] in the instrumental case.'

[a] H,V: *ta eva*.

[587] One of the fallacies of the logical reasons that are enumerated in NA 23; see n. 576.

[588] In other words, substance preserves invariably its identity, inasmuch as its essence never alters in time or space, whereas modes intermittently replace one another, inasmuch as they fluctuate in time or space.

[589] The particle *iti* marks the end of the argumentation that commences with *tathā hi*: *antar ekaṁ saṁvedanam...* at the beginning of the paragraph.

[590] The notions of *saha vartin* and *krama-vartin* correspond to the ideas of diachronic homogeneity (*ūrdhvatā-sāmānya*) and synchronic homogeneity (*tiryak-sāmānya*); cf. n. 159.

[591] It is a slightly reformulated conclusion of the proof formula on p. 84: *atas tad eva teṣāṁ gocaraḥ*.

[592] Cf. NAṬ *ad loc.*: ***sautrāntika*** *iti*. "*sūtra avamocane*" *cur-ādāv ad-antaḥ, tataḥ sūtryate nirṇīyate tattvam anenêti svarântatvādali*[a] *sūtram āgamaḥ. tasyâyaṁ sautro 'ntaḥ*[b] *pariniṣṭhāḥ, yad āhus tad-vādinaḥ*: "*pratikṣaṇaṁ viśarâravo rūpa-rasa-gandha-sparśa-paramāṇavo jñānaṁ cêty eva tattvam*" *iti. tataḥ sūtraś câsau*[c] *antaś ca sautrāntaḥ; sa vidyate*[d] *yasya* "'*ato 'neka-svarād*'"[e] *iti ikaḥ. yad vā sūtrântaḥ prayojanaṁ pravartakaṁ yasya iti*[f] '*prayojanam*'[g] *itîkaṇ*[h].

[a] A: °*dali*/°*hali*? C: *svarântatvādavi*. [b] H,V: *sautraḥ, antaḥ*. [c] H,V: *sautraś cāso*.

[d] C breaks off with *vidya*° (at the end of a line), and several subsequent lines are missing, up to (faulty in part) °*manaṁ sa tathā. paramāṇūnāṁ parimāḍalyaṁ pratikṣaṇa...* (= H p. 105.3, V: 67.16).

[e] SHŚ 7.2.6 (identification after Bhagavandas Harakhchand and P. L. Vaidya).

[f] A: *pravartakam asyêti*.

[g] A: *prayojane*. SHŚ 5.4.117 (identification after Bhagavandas Harakhchand and P. L. Vaidya). [h] H: *ikaṇ*.

[593] I.e., *tasyâiva tatra pratibhāsamānatvāt* (= **anekântâtmaka-vastuna eva pramāṇeṣu pratibhāsamānatvāt*); cf. n. 569.

[594] Cf. NAṬ *ad loc.*: ***svôttarêty-ādi***. *sva ātmīyaḥ sa câsāv uttara-kṣaṇaś ca, yad vā svasmād uttaraḥ svôttaraḥ, sa câsau kṣaṇaś cêti. svasyôttara-kṣaṇaḥ svôttara-kṣaṇa iti vā. svam ātmānam avagāhate viṣayī-karotîty evaṁ sīlaṁ svâvagāhi; tac ca taj jñānaṁ cêti.*[a] *ādi-śabdāt saha-kāri-kāraṇa-bhāvena rasâlokâdi-kārya-janana-grahaḥ.*—'[Presently, we comment upon the expression] beginning with "posterior to own". [There are three ways of explicating the expression]: either (1) "own" means "its", and this posterior moment [is its] own; or (2) "posterior regarding it" means "posterior to itself", and this is that moment, [i.e. a moment posterior to it]; or (3) "a posterior moment belonging to it" means "its own posterior moment". [As regards the expression "cognition plunging in it"], to plunge in it, or in its self (*sc.* in the form), [means] to make [it a] province [of cognition] (*sc.* to cognise it); hence what has such a character is [something] "plunging in it". And that is such a cognition.[a] By the [expression] "etc." producing of taste, visible shape, etc., are included, inasmuch as [it is their] auxiliary cause.'

[a] In the rather awkward phrase *tac ca taj jñānaṁ cêti*, either (1) the second *ca* is redundant (**svâvagāhi; tac ca taj-jñānam iti*—'..."plunging in it". And that is the cognition of this [form]'), or (2) one *iti* is missing (**svâvagāhîti tac ca taj jñānaṁ cêti*—'..."plunging in it". Hence [there is] both that [form] as well as the cognition of this [form].').

[595] Cf. NAṬ *ad loc.*: ***nitya-pakṣôditam iti***. *ekasya bhinna-kālâneka-kārya-janaka-svabhāvatve viruddha-dharmâdhyāsād anekatvam iti.*—'[Now we comment upon the expression]: "[the Sautrāntika criticism] brought forward against the thesis about the permanence". When one [causal complex is endowed with] an essential nature which produces multiple effects in different points of time, [it turns out to be] multiple on account of the attribution of contrary properties.'

[596] Cf. NAṬ *ad loc.*: ***tathâivêti***. *yathâika-kālam ekam aneka-deśaṁ nānā-kāryaṁ kurvad apy ekam eva, tathā bhinna-kālâneka-kārya-vartane 'py ekam evêti sthāyitva-siddhiḥ.*—'[Now we comment upon the expression]: "in exactly the same manner". Exactly the way one [cause, existing] in one point of time, [remains] just one [and the same], although it brings about various effects in several places, in exactly the same manner— even if something brings about several effects in different points of time— it is the only one [cause]; hence the immutability (*sc.* permanence) [of the cause] is established.' (*vartana* = *nirvartana*).

[597] By 'new and old modes, etc.' are meant externally perceptible and changing facets of an object, whereas 'form, taste, smell, touch' refer to internal perception, cf. below *bahir-mukha* and *antar-mukha* (n. 598).

[598] Any sensation of, or cognitive act apprehending a thing is admitted by the Sautrāntika, on the one hand, be d i r e c t e d o u t w a r d s , viz., to represent the external object, and—inasmuch as it is accompanied by conceptualisation—it is erroneous. On the other hand, the same act of cognition is—on the level of the direct perception, or self-cognition, that is d i r e c t e d i n w a r d s — non-conceptual and

non-erroneous. Compare similar view expressed above in NAV 4: *etad api sva-saṁvedanâpekṣayā pratyakṣam eva, bahir-arthâpekṣayā tu parokṣa-vyapadeśam aśnuta iti darśayann āha:* ***grahanêkṣayêti****; iha grahaṇaṁ prakramād bahiḥ pravartanam ucyate, anyathā viśeṣaṇa-vaiyarthyaṁ syāt; tasyêkṣā apekṣā tayā; bahiḥ-pravṛtti-paryālocanayêti yāvat. tad ayam arthaḥ: yady api svayaṁ pratyakṣam, tathâpi liṅga-śabdâdi-dvāreṇa bahir-viṣaya-grahaṇe sākṣāt-kāritayā vyāpriyata iti parokṣam ity ucyate.* (p. 37 of the English translation) Cf. NAṬ 29 *ad loc.*: ***bahir-mukhêti****. bahir bāhya-vastu-viṣaye mukham ārambhaḥ prakāśana-pravṛttir yasya tat-tathā bāhya-vastv-abhimukham ity arthaḥ. evam* ***antar-mukhêty*** *apy uktânusārato*[a] *vyākhyeyam.* ***ādi-śabdād*** *pramāṇâpramāṇâdi parigrahaḥ.*—'[Now we gloss on the expression]: "directed outwards". "Outwards" means "with regard to the external real thing"; "direction (lit. entrance)" means "[having its] source"; that the revealing activity of which [has its source outwards] it is that [the nature] of which is such [viz., directed outwards], which means: "directed towards (lit. 'with entrance open to') an external real thing". Similarly, [the expression] "directed inwards" is to be explained by the said procedure, as well. [Such notions like] "cognitive criterion", "improper cognitive criterion", etc., are included owing to the expression "etc.".'

The expressions *bahir-mukha* and *antar-mukha* are basically Buddhist, they occur, e.g. in PV_1 2.428:

bahir-mukhañ ca taj-jñānaṁ bhāty artha-pratibhasavat /
buddheś ca grāhikā vittir[b] *nityam antar-mukhâtmani /*

[a] C: *uktyânusārato.* [b] PV_2: *buddhir.*

[599] Tinted with, viz., qualified by; cf. NAṬ *ad loc.*: ***nānā-deśêty-ādi***[a]. *uparaktaṁ viśeṣitaṁ; ekaṁ saṁvedanam iti sambandhaḥ.*

[a] C: *tathā* ***nānā-deśêty-ādi.***

[600] Viz., sensations of both external objects and of internal objects (*sc.* emotions) are not different with regard to their 'acquisition and maintenance.' The Buddhist *locus classicus* of the expressions *abhinna-yoga-kṣema, eka-yoga-kṣema, samāna-yoga-kṣema,* and similar ones, used in an epistemological context—whose literal meaning is 'having the same acquisition and maintenance', i.e. based on the same causal and supportive principle—is HB and HBṬ, In the reconstructed Sanskrit the source reads (p. 3*.14–19 = p. 35.14–19): ... *tato 'pi vikalpād vastuny eva tad-adhyavasāyena pravṛtteḥ, pravṛttau vikalpasya pratyakṣeṇâbhinna-yoga-kṣematvāt. pūrva-pratyakṣa-kṣaṇenôpayogâbhedād uttareṣu kasyacid aprāmāṇya-prasaṅga iti cet, na, kṣaṇa-viśeṣa-sādhyârtha-vañchāyāṁ nānā-yoga-kṣematvāt.* The phrases *abhinna-yoga-kṣema* (p. 3*.16) and *nānā-yoga-kṣema* (p. 3*.19) are rendered imprecisely by Steinkellner (HB II, p. 36–7) as 'gleicher Nutzen' and 'verschiedener Nutzen.' Bhaṭṭa Arcaṭa offers a lucid explanation of both the locutions in the context of the logical reason: [1] HBṬ, p. 36.7–14: ***abhinna-yoga-kṣematvāt****. yogaḥ aprāptasya viṣayasya pariccheda-lakṣaṇā prāptiḥ, kṣemaḥ tad-artha-kriyânuṣṭhāna-lakṣaṇaṁ paripālanam. abhinna-yoga-kṣemāv asyêti sa tathôktaḥ. tatra vikalpasya nirvikalpa-*

pratyakṣeṇâbhinno yogaḥ svalakṣaṇâdhyavasāyataḥ. abhinnaḥ kṣemaḥ ālocanā-vijñānād iva vikalpād api svalakṣaṇa eva pravṛtteḥ. ayam abhiprāyaḥ: yadi vikalpo nirvikalpa-cetasaḥ prameyântara-viṣayasya tadā tatrâiva puruṣaṁ pravartayatu tat-sādhyām artha-kriyām adhigantum ... ; and [2] HBṬ, p. 37.6 ff.: ***nānā-yoga-kṣematvāt****. tathā hi: pratikṣaṇaṁ viṣaya-pariccheda-lakṣaṇo yogaḥ, tad-artha-kriyânuṣṭhāna-lakṣaṇaś ca kṣemaḥ paripālana-rūpo bhidyate, tato vipakṣe vṛtty-abhāvāt na hetur anaikāntikaḥ* ...—[1] '[The phrase] "because they are [based on] the same productive-supportive principle" [is explained as follows]. Productive principle is acquisition characterised by determination of a not [yet] acquired province (*sc.* uncognised object); supportive principle is maintenance, characterised by carrying out efficient action with regard to this object. Such which has the same productive principle and supportive principle is the one in question. Among these two, productive principle of conceptualisation is the same with [the productive principle of] the non-conceptual perception on account of the apprehension of (*sc.* because both of them apprehend) the individual thing. Supportive principle [in the case of perception and conceptualisation] is the same, inasmuch [any] activity [is undertaken] with regard to an individual thing and nothing else [in the same manner] on account of the discernment [in the form of] sight (*sc.* perception) as well as on account of conceptualisation. The intention is following: if the non-conceptual cognitive faculty (*sc.* perception), which has another cognoscible (*sc.* object) [as its] province, [is endowed with] conceptualisation, then [the conceptualisation] must instigate a person to accomplish efficient action with regard to precisely that [object] which can be effected (cognised) by that very [perception].' And [2] '[The phrase] "because they are [based on] diverse productive-supportive principle" [is explained below]. For it is as follows. Productive principle is characterised by determination of a province (*sc.* object) in every moment, whereas supportive principle, characterised by carrying out efficient action with regard to this object, differs [from the former, inasmuch as it] consists in maintenance (*sc.* assures continuity) [of that object], hence the logical reason is not inconclusive, because there is no occurrence in the heterologue ...' We find the expression *eka-yoga-kṣema* also in TVBh 2 (19.17).

The phrase *yoga-kṣema* occurs, in a non-epistemological context though, as early as in BhG 2.45:

traiguṇya-viaṣayā vedā nistraiguṇyo bhavârjuna /
nirdvandvo nitya-sattva-stho niryoga-kṣema ātmavān //

[601] It is so, inasmuch as divergent emotions can take place only in different points of time, not simultaneously, as it is the case with visible forms; cf. NAṬ *ad loc.*: ***tad-viparyayād iti****. bhinna-kāla-bhāvitvāt.*

[602] NAṬ *ad loc.*: ***tat-sāmarthyâdîty-ādi***[a]. *teṣāṁ saṁvid-antar-niviṣṭâkārāṇāṁ*[b] *sita-pītâdīnāṁ sāmarthyaṁ, tena*[c] *vyavasthāpyo yo 'rthas tasyâivâikya*[d]*-prasaṅgāt.*— '[The phrase] "the efficacy of these [forms]" [means] the efficacy of these forms located within the awareness, such as something white, something yellow, etc. [This

part of the compound is to be construed in the instrumental case (*tena*). Hence:] because of the undesired consequence of the oneness of this particular object, which is to be established by that [efficacy].' The gerundive *vyavasthāpya* is to be understood in the epistemological sense.

[a] A,C,H,V read, apparently wrongly: ***tat-sāmarthyād-ity-ādi***, for NAV reads ***tat-sāmarthya****-vyavasthāpyârthâbheda-prasaṅgāt* (no ablative case after °*-sāmarthya-*°).
[b] C: *anta-nirviṣṭâkārāṇāṁ*. [c] A: *te*. [d] A,H,V: *tasyâikya*.

603 Cf. NAṬ *ad loc*.: ***tad-ekatayā*** *ākārāṇām ekatayā, sita-pītâdi-vastu-viṣayiṇo* ***jñānasya bodha-rūpeṇâivâviśiṣṭatvāt***[a]; *bodha-rūpatâiva*[b] *jñānasyôddharitā*[c], *na*[d] *punaḥ sita-pītâdayo bahir-artha-vyavasthāpakāḥ*[e] *kecid ākārāḥ. kvâpi bodha-rūpeṇêvâviśiṣṭatvāt*[f] *iti pāṭhaḥ. tadâivaṁ vyākhyā: yathā bahuṣv*[g] *api sita-pītâdiṣu vastuṣu*[h] *jñānasya bodha-rūpeṇâviśiṣṭatvaṁ samānatvam, tathā sita-pītâdy-ākārāṇām ekatayâpîty-arthaḥ. ayam*[i] *abhiprāyo: yadâika*[j]*-jñānântar-vartināṁ nānā-deśa-sthitârtha*[k]*-prabhavānāṁ bahūnām apy ākārāṇām ekatvaṁ, tadā tad-ekâkāra-jñāna-vyavasthāpyasya bahir-vastu-stomasyâpy ekatvaṁ syāt; eka-nīlâkāra-jñāna-vyavasthāpya*[l]*-bahir-nīla-svalakṣaṇa ekatvavat*[m].—'"Inasmuch as these would be one" [means] inasmuch as forms would be one, the cognition the province of which are real things like something white, something yellow, etc., "[the cognition] would be non-distinguished (*sc*. undifferentiated) because of having the form of nothing but cognitive awareness"; it is the fact of having the form of cognitive awareness itself that differentiates cognition [from external things], whereas these are not some white, yellow forms, etc., that establish external objects. In certain [manuscripts] there is a variant reading: "[the cognition] would be non-distinguished (*sc*. undifferentiated) as if being the form of cognitive awareness." The explanation runs as follows: just like [one] cognition concerning real things, like white, yellow, etc., although they are numerous, [remains] non-distinguished (*sc*. undifferentiated), [i.e.] the same, inasmuch as it consists in consciousness, in the same manner white, yellow forms, etc., [would remain non-distinguished (*sc*. undifferentiated), i.e. the same], inasmuch as [the cognition] is one. Such is the meaning. The intention is as follows: when forms that have their origin in objects abiding in several places, although these [forms] are numerous, were one, then also the multitude of external real things that can be established through cognition [grasping] these [forms], which [itself] has one form, would [also] be one, just like oneness with regard to an external blue individual thing that can be established through a cognition of one blue form.'

[a] H,V: °*-rūpeṇâiva vā viśiṣṭatvāt*. A marks specifically the *sandhi eva + avi*° with an *avagraha* in the subscript: °*-rūpeṇâivâ 'viśiṣṭatvāt*.
[b] H: *bodhasya rūpatâiva*; C: *bodha-svarūpatâiva*.
[c] H,V: °*ôdvaritā*; C: °*ôdvaritā*/°*ôddharitā*? [d] C: *tu*.
[e] A: °*-artha-vyavasthāpakā*; C marks the *sandhi* °*-artha + avya*° with an *avagraha*: °*- arthâ 'vyavasthāpakāḥ*.
[f] H,V: °*-rūpeṇâivâviśiṣṭatvāt*. [g] C: *yathā huṣv*. [h] C: *sita-pītâdi-vastuṣu*.
[i] C: °*-artha ayam*. [j] C: *yad eka-*°. [k] H,V: °*-vyavasthitârtha-*°.

[l] C: °-*jñāta-vyāvasthāpya*-° (°-*jñātavyâvasthāpya*-°?).
[m] C: °-*svalakṣaṇâikatvavat*.

[604] See n. 231.

[605] Cf. NAṬ *ad loc*.: ***bahir antaś cêty-ādi***. *pramāṇata ekâneka-rūpatve*[a] *svalakṣaṇasya vyavasthite iti sambandhaḥ. yathā ca vṛkṣâdi-vastūnāṁ sannihitâsannihitābhyāṁ*[b] *spaṣṭâspaṣṭa-pratibhāsa-janakatvena svalakṣaṇatvam. yasyârthasya*[c] *sannidhānâsannidhānābhyāṁ jñāna-pratibhāsa-bhedas tat svalakṣaṇam iti tal-lakṣaṇāt. tathântaḥ-saṁvedanasyâpi. tathā hi: smaryamāṇa-saṁvedanam asannihitatvād asphuṭaṁ pratibhāti. anubhūyamānaṁ tu sannihitatvāt sphuṭam. yad*[d] *vā para-santāna-varti saṁvedanam asannihitatvād*[e] *asphuṭam. sva-santāna-varti tu sannihitatvāt sphuṭaṁ*[f]. *tasmād antaḥ-saṁvedanasyâpi*[g] *tal-lakṣaṇa-lakṣitatvāt svalakṣaṇam iti*[h].
[a] C:°-*svarūpatve*. [b] C: *sannihitātvâsannihitātvābhyāṁ*.
[c] C: *ya svârthasya*. [d] C punctuates differently: *sannihitatvāt. sphuṭaṁ yad*...
[e] H,V: *saṁvedanaṁ sannihitatvād*.
[f] C punctuates differently: *sannihitatvāt. sphuṭaṁ*. [g] C: *saṁvedasyâpi*.
[h] C: *tal-lakṣaṇa-lakṣinati* (:°-*lakṣimati*?)!

[606] Cf. NAṬ *ad loc*.: ***yogâcārêti***. *yojanaṁ yogo, jñānâkārayoḥ sambandhaḥ, tam ācaranti vyavaharantîti*[a] "*karmaṇy aṇ*"[b] *iti aṇ, sākāra-jñāna-mātra-vādina ity-arthaḥ. yogaḥ samādhiḥ sākāra-jñāna-mātrâikāgratā, tam ācarantîti*[c] *vā, pūrvavad aṇ*.
[a] C: *vyaharantîti*. [b] Pāṇ 7.3.20. [c] A, H,V: *ācaranti iti*; C: *ācaranti*.

[607] See n. 600.

[608] For the idea of two concepts of truth, viz., conventional (based on the empirical reality) and ultimate, see n. 314.

[609] For the Buddhist idea of self-revealing cognition (*sva-saṁvedana, sva-saṁvitti*) cf. n. 280.

[610] Cf. NAṬ *ad loc*.: ***brahmêti***. *jñānâdvaitam iti*.

[611] Cf. NAṬ *ad loc*.: ***muktatâvāpter iti*** "*tattva-jñānôtpattir muktir*"[†] *iti mukti-lakṣaṇâbhidhānāt. tattvaṁ ca jñānâdvaitam evêti teṣām abhiprāyaḥ*.—'[All creatures] "would attain liberation," because it has been explicitly stated [by the opponent] that "liberation has [its] origination in [gaining] the cognition of truth"; and the truth is the non-duality of cognition—such is their intention.'
[†] I have failed to identify the source of the quotation.

[612] Instead of *tūṣṇīm āsīt* ('became silent', imperfect derived from *tūṣṇīm*√*as*), we should read *tūṣṇīm āsīta* (optative derived from *tūṣṇīm*√*ās*), for the sudden change of the present into the past tense can in no way be accounted for. After all, the interpretation concerns either reading of overlooking the final *virāma* in the case of the edi-

tions H,V. My conjecture has been positively corroborated by the reading of Mss. A and B. after I received their copies. The phrasing seems to be a kind of mockery, alluding to the Buddhist concept of *tūṣṇī-bhāva*, or the silence concerning the *paramârtha* status of the reality. For a similar pan on *tūṣṇī-bhāva*, likewise, in the context of a dispute with the Yogācāra / Vijñāna-vādin, see MŚV$_I$ 5.2. (*Nirālambana-vādâdhikaraṇa*).12:

> *na hi svapna-sukhâdy-arthaṁ dharme kaścit pravartate /*
> *yādṛcchikatvāt svapnasya tūṣṇīm āsyeta paṇḍitaiḥ //*

Furthermore, the phrase is reminiscent of opening lines of VāN, p. 1.6–9: *iṣṭastârthasya siddhiḥ sādhanaṁ, tasya nirvartakam aṅgaṁ, tasyâvacanaṁ tasyâṅgasyânuccāraṇaṁ vādino nigrahâdhikaraṇaṁ, tad abhyupagamyâpratibhayā tūṣṇiṁ-bhāvāt, sādhanâṅgasyâsamarthanād vā*. Thus, Siddharṣi would refer to the rule of debate, laid down by Dharmakīrti himself, defining two conditions when the opponent is compelled to admit his defeat, one of them being his silence when he finally admits his proponent's argumentation and remains silent.

[613] The subsequent section deals with a hypothetical objection stating that the logical reason forwarded by the Jainas to prove the multiplex character of reality is in fact a fallacious logical reason of the inconclusive variety, and, consequently, the conclusions drawn by the Jainas and presented in a form of the theory of the multiplexity of reality are invalid. For the inconclusive variety of the fallacious logical reason cf. NA 23 and the corresponding section of NAV 23 (pp. 69–70 of the translation).

[614] The construction seems slightly awkward: we can only with some difficulty construe Gen. Sing. *śūnya-vādinaḥ* with the main sentence.

[615] Cf. n. 618.

[616] Both H and V edit: *iti cet, na*[a], *tasyâpi pramāṇa-prameyâbhāvena sarvâbhāvâvedanaṁ samasti*. [[a] V: *cen na*.]

It is apparent from the context and argumentation that the justification *tasyâpi ... samasti* requires to be a negative clause, and in the reading of H and V the negation is missing. The particle *na* following *cet* in the reading of editions H and V cannot be construed with the verb *samasti*, for the structure of the argument complies with the usual line of dialectical argument, the three steps of which are as follows:

(1) the opponent's argument:		(2) the proponent's general refusal to accept the opponents standpoint:		(3) justification of the refusal:
iti cet,	⇒	*na,*	⇒	/1/ ablative, or /2/ indicative clause†, or /3/ optative clause‡

† The verb is in the indicative mood, e.g. (1) NAV 4. *cen na, nêdānīm arthe yad asti tad eva pratibhāti*. (2) NAV 1: *iti cen nanu tad api sambandha-pūrvakaṁ pravartate*.

‡ The verb is in the optative mood, e.g. NAV 6: *cen na, tatrâpy avayava-mātram avayavi-mātraṁ vā syāt*.

Besides, the instrumental °*-prameyâbhāvena* does not make any good sense in the present context. Therefore, the reading necessitates a slight emendation: *iti cen na, tasyâpi pramāṇa-prameyâbhāve na sarvâbhāvâvedanaṁ samasti*, which boils down merely to a different separation of the continuous series of letters of the manuscript. However, also Ms. A, that—as a rule, but not always—marks incisions in the continuous flow of text, does not separate the compound: **प्रमाणप्रमेयाभावेन** (instead of the expected **प्रमाणप्रमेयाभावे'न**).

[617] See n. 219 and comp. similar instances on pp.27 and 113.

[618] Both H and V edit the corresponding *pratīka* of NAṬ *ad loc.*: as ***tasyâpîti***. *śūnya-vādinaḥ parasyâpi sāṁkhyasya*. In fact, we have here two *pratīkas* and the text should be accordingly edited: ***tasyâpîti***. *śūnya-vādinaḥ*. ***parasyâpi***. *sāṁkhyasya*.

[619] The explanation of question why propounding of the 'nothing-exists' thesis entails one's impotence to negate the counter-position, viz., that everything exists everywhere, is indirectly provided by Malliṣeṇa (in the context of Vijñāna-vāda) in SVM 16, p. 113.295–299: *arthâbhāve ca niyata-deśâdhikaraṇā pratītiḥ kutaḥ. na hi tatra vivakṣita*[a]*-deśe 'yam āropayitavyo nânyatrêty niyame hetuḥ. vāsanā-niyamāt tad-āropa-niyama iti cen na, tasyā api tad-deśa-niyama-kāraṇâbhāvāt. sati hy artha-sad-bhāve yad-deśo 'rthas tad-deśo 'nubhavas, tad-deśā ca tat-pūrvikā vāsanā.*— 'And if objects did not exist, how [could] the cognition ascribing a specific place [to them be possible]? For there [would be] no reason for the circumscription: "this [particular object] is to be ascribed to this place in question, not to any other [place]." If [the Buddhist claimed that] the circumscription ascribing [an object] to that [particular place is possible] due to circumscribing a past impression [to this place], that would not [be proper], because also this [past impression] is not a reason for the circumscription [of an object] to that [particular] place. For when an object is present, then in such a place in which the object is [located], in the same place [occurs] an experience [of this object]. And past impression is related to this place [as well as] is preceded by it. [In other words, the idea of a past impression entails a former perception of a real object].'

[a] The edition reads, apparently wrongly: *vivajñita*.

[620] The gist of the argument is this: in order to be able to negate the existence of all entities, the Śūnya-vādin has to admit some cognitive criteria that would prove the non-existence of things, but then the admission of cognitive criteria undermines his initial thesis of the absolute non-existence of things. See NAṬ *ad loc.*: ***tad-abhyupagame*** *pramāṇa-prameyayor aṅgī-kāre*. At the same time, the admission of a cognitive criterion presupposes the existence of the cognoscible, cf. SVM 17, p. 116,21–22: *pramāṇaṁ prameyaṁ vinā na bhavati* ...—'A cognitive criterion [can] not exist without the cognoscible.'

[621] Cf. similar argumentation pointing out the self-abortive character of the Śūnya-vāda in SVM 17, p. 116,19–24: *kiṁ ca, svâgamôpadeśenâiva tena vādinā śūnya-vādaḥ prarūpyata iti svī-kṛtam āgamasya prāmāṇyam iti kutas tasya sva-pakṣa-siddhiḥ? pramāṇâṅgī-karaṇāt. kiṁ ca, pramāṇaṁ prameyaṁ vinā na bhavatîti pramāṇânaṅgī-karaṇe prameyam api viśīrṇam. tataś câsya mūkatâiva yuktā, na punaḥ śūnya-vādôpanyāsāya tuṇḍa-tāṇḍava-ḍambaram, śūnya-vādasyâpi prameyatvāt.*—'Moreover, the theory of the universal emptiness is expounded by [its] propounder, who in fact follows the instruction [from] his own oral tradition; that means that [his own] oral tradition has appropriated validity [in his eyes, viz., is accepted as a cognitive criterion by him; then the question is] wherefrom his own thesis [promulgating the universal non-existence of things acquires the ground] to become established? [The only possible reply he could give is this:] because it is admitted to be a cognitive criterion. Furthermore, a cognitive criterion [can] not exist without the cognoscible. Hence, if cognitive criteria are not admitted, then also the cognoscible is shattered. And consequently, dumbness is the only proper [thing] for him, certainly not the commotion produced by the trickery of his mouth, because also the theory of the universal emptiness is the cognoscible.'

[622] It is a hint to the fallacy of the logical reason termed the inconclusive variety; cf. NA 23, esp. p.69 ff.

[623] NAṬ *ad loc.*: ***tad-abhyupagati-hetur iti****. pratibhāsamānârtha-gocaratvâṅgī-kāra*[a]*-kāraṇam anumānam iti kṣaṇikatva-sādhakam.*

[a] C: °-*kāre.*

[624] Cf. NAṬ *ad loc.*: ***vihodha-bhīrutayêti***[a]. *nahy ekasya vastuno nīlatvâdi gṛhyate, na punaḥ kṣaṇikatvâdîti bhāvaḥ.*—'This is the intent: neither is blueness of one real thing grasped, nor its momentariness.'

[a] H misprints: *bhirutayêti.*

[625] Cf. NAṬ *ad loc.*: ***prāthamakalpikenâivêti****. kalpaḥ pakṣaḥ,*[a] *prathamaś câsau kalpaś ca,*[b] *tatra bhavaḥ prāthamakalpikas tena, prathama-pakṣâbhihitenêty-arthaḥ, 'adhyātmâder' iti ṭhañ.*

[a] C punctuates: *kalpaḥ. pakṣaḥ...* [b] A and C insert here the number *2.*

[626] H and V fail to notice the *pratīka* NAṬ: ***athêty-ādinā*** *prācya-vikalpam evâṅgī-kurvann āha.* A highlights it by punctuation: ... *iti sthitam // **athêty-ādinā** prācya-°.*

[627] Both H and V fail to edit the respective *pratīkas* of NAṬ correctly; instead of: ***taj-janakatve iti****. nirṇaya-janakatve sannikarṣâdivad iti. yathā* ..., we should read: ***taj-janakatva***[a] ***iti****. nirṇaya-janakatve.* ***sannikarṣâdivad iti****. yathā pramāṇa-bhūta*[b]*-jñāna-janako 'pi sannikarṣo na pramāṇaṁ, dehâdibhir atiprasaṅgāt, tathā nirvikalpakam apîty-arthaḥ.*—'[The expression beginning with] "[even though] it produces this" means "[even though] it produces the ascertainment". [The expression] "just like the [sense-object] contact, etc.," means the following: just the way the [sense-object] contact which produces cognition that becomes a cognitive criterion [itself] is not a

cognitive criterion, because that would have too far-reaching consequences, namely that also body and other [auxiliary causes would turn out to be cognitive criteria], in the same way non-conceptual [cognition could not be a cognitive criterion].'

[a] C clearly: *naj-janakatva*! [b] C: *pramāṇâbhūta-°*.

[628] The Buddhist formulation bears striking resemblance to the Mīmāṁsaka's definition of cognitive criterion, see n. 65. The definition in all probability dates back to Dharmakīrti; it is formulated in HB, p. 3*.8–9 and quoted in HBṬ, p. 28.8: *anadhigatârtha-viṣayaṁ pramāṇam*[†]. It is further quoted and critically examined in TUS_1 3.1, p. 162.1–2 (TUS_2, p. 27.8): *tathā tāthāgatānām apy anadhigatârtha-gantṛ-viśeṣaṇam apārthakam apohya-jñānâsambhavāt*. This definition is discussed at length in FRANCO (1987: 407–410, n. 152). Cf. also PVin I_1 158b p. 60.1719: | *'di tshad ma sṅa ma'i yul 'dzin pa yaṅ ma yin te | tshad ma ni ma rtogs pa'i yul can yin pa ñid kyi phyir te | gźan du na ha caṅ thal ba'i phyir ro ||*

[†] It is quoted in *Dravyâlaṅkāra-svopajña-ṭīkā* p. 49, see Muni JAMBŪVIJAYA (1981: 134.24–25): *yad uktam—"anadhigatârtha-viṣayaṁ pramāṇam iti «anadhigate svalakṣaṇe» iti viśeṣaṇīyam"*.

[629] In other words, when nothing false is projected, or superimposed, then the determining cognition derived from ascertainment does not operate. Cf. NAṬ *ad loc.*: ***asamāropa-viṣaye 'pravṛtter iti***. *yatrâiva kiñcid viparītam āropitaṁ bhavati, tatrâiva tad-apanoda*-dvāreṇa*[a] *nirṇayasyâpi pravṛttir ity arthaḥ. tathā câgame: 'kim ayam sthāṇuḥ*[b] *puruṣo vêti, īhânantaram*[c] *eva puruṣa evâyam ity-apāyâ*bhidhānāt.'* [†] *ata eva kṣamāśramaṇo*[‡] *'pi*:

abbhatthe avāü cciya[d] *katthaï lakkhijjaï*[e] *imo*[f] *puriso*[g] *tti /* [§]

pūrva-pakṣayitvā:

uppala-patta-saya-vehe vva[h] *duvvi-bhāva*[i]*-ttaṇeṇa paḍihāï /*
samayaṁ ca sukka-sakkuli-dasaṇe[j] *visayāṇam uvaladdhī //* [**]

iti parihṛtavān.—

—'The [intended] meaning is as follows: with regard to whichever [object] something contrary (false) has been superimposed, precisely with regard to that [contrary (false) object] also the ascertainment operates by means of obliterating* [it]. And accordingly, [the same idea was expressed] in the scriptures: "Because [the resolution that] immediately follows after the speculation: «Is this a pillar or a man?», [receives] the designation of the perceptual judgement* [in the form]: «This is nothing else but a man»."[†] For that very reason, also Kṣamā-śramaṇa[‡] [was of the same opinion,] having [first] stated by way showing the *prima facie* position in the following way:

"Regarding a repeatedly investigated [thing], it is perceptual judgement that expresses [and] characterises [the thing]: "This is a man,"[§]

[he] avoided [the misconception] as follows:

"Just like while piercing a hundred petals of the blue lotus, inasmuch as they are hardly comprehensible, [one has an impression of piercing all petals simultaneously, similarly] while biting a white large sesame cake at one instant an [illusory] comprehension of [all] provinces of [sense-organs, i.e. taste, smell, etc.,] occurs"**.'

Cf. Hemacandra's relevant commentary on the verses VAV 297–298, p. 175–6.

* The term *apāya* is treated as synonymical to *apanoda* in TBh 1.15. Both terms, viz., *īhā* and *apāya*, are mentioned in TS 1.15: *avagrahêhâpāya-dhāraṇāḥ*, as two links in the process of four-staged sensuous cognition (*mati-jñāna*). The four subsequent stages are exemplified in SSi 1.15:

1. *yathā cakṣuṣā śuklaṁ rūpam iti grahaṇam avagrahaḥ* ('Perceptual sensation is grasping, say, a white form with eyes');
2. *yathā śuklaṁ rūpaṁ kiṁ balākā patākā vêti* ('[Speculation questions:] "Is [this], say, white form a crane or a banner?"');
3. *utpatana-nipatana-pakṣa-vikṣepâdibhir balākā evâyaṁ na patākêti* ('[Perceptual judgement resolves:] "due to beating with wings, etc., this [white form] is nothing but a crane, not a banner, due to the upward and downward flight".');
4. *avetasya kālântare 'vismaraṇa-kāraṇaṁ dhāraṇā. yathā sâivâyaṁ balākā pūrvâhṇe yām aham adrākṣam iti* ('Retention is the cause of not forgetting, [even] when some time elapsed, for instance: "This is exactly that very crane I saw this morning".').

Cf. also PMī 1.1.26–29: 26. *akṣârtha-yoge darśanânantaram artha-grahaṇam avagrahaḥ*. 27. *avagṛhīta-viśeṣâkāṅkṣaṇam īhā*. 28. *īhita-viśeṣa-nirṇayo 'vāyaḥ*. 29. *smṛti-hetur dhāraṇā*.

† I have failed to identify the source of the quotation.

‡ This is a reference to the author of *Viśeṣâvaśyaka-bhāṣya*, Jinabhadra-gaṇin Kṣamā-śramaṇa, who flourished around 489–593 according to MALVANIA (1966: 1) or at the turn of the sixth and seventh centuries according to BALBIR (1993: 75).

§ The complete verse, taken from VABh 297, p. 66 reads as follows:

abbhatthe 'vāö cciya katthayi lakkhijjate imo puriso /
aṇṇattha dhāraṇa cciya purovaladdhe imaṁ taṁ ti //

—'Regarding a repeatedly investigated [thing], it is perceptual judgement that expresses [and] characterises [the thing]: "This is a man." In another case, with regard to a thing comprehended previously, it is retention [that determines]: "This [thing in front of me] is that [thing I saw before]".'

** The verse is, likewise, a quotation from VABh 298, p. 66 (with minor differences):

uppala-dala-sata-vedhe vva duvvibhāva-ttaṇeṇa paḍibhāti /
samayaṁ va sukka-sakkuli-ḍasaṇe visayāṇam uvaladdhī //

[a] C: °-*apanodvāreṇa*. [b] A: *sthāṇu*.
[c] C: *sthāṇuḥ paruṣo vêti īhânantaram*. [d] H: *'vāöcciya*; V: *'vāö cciya*.
[e] A: *lakkhijjhaī*; C: *likkhijjhāī*. [f] A: *īmā*. [g] A: *puristo*.

[h] C: *uppalada / saya-veho cca*; H: *uppala-patta-saya-veho va*; V: *uppala-dala-saya-veho vva*.
[i] C: *duccibhāva-°*. [j] H,V: °-*ḍasaṇe*.

[630] In other words, the opponent's assumption that—in order to prove the cognitive validity of inference—one has to avail oneself of the three marks of the logical reason, that can be, in their turn, perceived directly, one undermines the validity of any conceptual cognition, which is not derivable directly from perception.

[631] Cf. n. 261. Note still another instance of alliteration, being the means of expression the author is very found of, here based on the derivatives of √*kḷp* (°-*kalpa-nirvikalpaka-kalpanayā*). In consonance with Pāṇ 5.3.67 (*īṣad-asamāptau kalpaB-deśya-deśīyaRaḥ*.—'[The *tad-dhita* affixes, such as] *kalaP*, *deśya* and *deśīyaR* [are added to a nominal stem to denote] "slightly incomplete"') *kalpa* is treated as a *tad-dhita* affix.

[632] Cf. NAṬ *ad loc*.: ***pāṭavâpāṭavâdaya ity-ādi***. *samādhānârthas tu tarhi nirvikalpaka*[a]*-darśanasyâpi nīlâdi-vikalpaṁ*[b] *janayato*[c] *nīlâdi-vikalpa-janane*[c] *pāṭavaṁ, kṣaṇikatvâdi-vikalpaṁ câjanayatas tatrâpāṭavam. ādi-śabdāt tu*[e] *bodha-rūpatva-nirvikalpatvâbhrāntatvâdayo*[f] *dharmā gṛhyante. te ca pāṭavâdayaḥ paraspara-viruddhāḥ nâikatra-darśane sambhavantîti*[g] *darśanasyâpi*[h] *na vikalpa-janakatvam ity-abhiprāyaḥ*.—'[A gloss on the expression]: "the potential, the lack of potential, etc.". But then, the meaning of a defence from (*sc*. countering) a possible objection is as follows. The non-conceptual perception which produces a conceptualisation of [forms such as] blue, etc., [possesses] the potential of producing [forms such as] blue, etc., and [the non-perceptual perception] which does not produce a conceptualisation of momentariness, etc., [does] not [possess] the potential of producing respective [conceptualisation]. By the speech element "etc." such properties [of perception] like possessing a form of cognitive awareness, non-conceptual character, non-erroneousness, etc., are comprised. Further, these [properties like] the potential, etc., being mutually contradictory, are not possible in a single perception, hence also perception does not produce any conceptualisation. Such is the intention.'

[a] H,V: *nirvikalpa-°*. [b] C: *nīlâdinā vikalpaṁ*. [c] H: *janayanto*. [d] C: *jane*.
[e] C: °-*śabdāt vastutvaṁ*. [f] C: °-*rūpatvaṁ nirvikalpakatvâbhrāntatvâdayo*.
[g] H,V: °-*nti iti*. [h] A: *darśasyâpi*.

[633] Notice the repeated, alliterative use of derivatives of the verbal root √*lakṣ*: °-*paramâṇu-lakṣaṇa-svalakṣaṇa-lakṣakaṁ kvacit kadācid darśanaṁ lakṣayanti* ...

[634] NAṬ *ad loc*.: ***yad iti***. *saṁvedanam*.

[635] NAṬ *ad loc*.: ***apramāṇam iti***. *kṣaṇa-kṣayitvâdi-viṣaye vikalpôtthāpanâbhāvāt. tathā ca tat-siddhāntaḥ*:

yatrâiva janayed enāṁ[a] *tatrâivâsya pramāṇatā*† / *iti*.

[a] A: *enaṁ*.

[†] I have failed to identify the source of the quotation. It is also referred to, and left unidentified, by Muni JAMBŪVIJAYA (1981: 134). In all probability, we can exclude Dharmakīrti's authorship in this case.

[636] Viz., in the stage (*sthity-anyathātva*) which is intermediate between the moment of the origination (*utpāda / jāti*) and the moment of extinction (*vyaya / anityatā*), see: *Trilakṣaṇa-sūtra* (AN 1.152 = SN 3.36): *trīṇîmāni bhikṣavaḥ saṁskṛtasya saṁskṛta-lakṣaṇāni. katamāni trīṇi. saṁskṛtasya bhikṣavaḥ utpādo 'pi prajñāyate, vyayo 'pi prajñāyate, sthity-anyathātvam api*. Cf. its quotation in AKBh *ad* AK 2.46b, as well as AK 2.45cd: *lakṣaṇāni punar jātir jarā sthitir anityatā*, and AKBh thereon, e.g.: *sthitiṁ jarāṁ câbhisamasya sthity-anyathātvam ity ekaṁ lakṣaṇam uktaṁ sūtre*. As for the non-simultaneity of the data and its perception—i.e. delayed rise of an image of an object (as a mental entity, a product of conceptualisation) after the object has been grasped by non-conceptual perception—in the context of *kṣaṇika-vāda*, see AKBh, p. 145.17 (*tatrâpi pūrvam indriyârthau paścād vijñānam*), cf. also ROSPATT (1995: 131f., § 2.1.4).

[637] Cf. NAṬ *ad loc.*: ***svapnâdîti***. *ādi*[a]*-śabdāj jāgrad-deśa*[b]*-bhāvino marīcikâdau jalâdi*[c]*-jñānasya parigrahaḥ*.

[a] A,C: *svapnâdîty-ādi-°*. [b] C: *jāgrad-daśa-°*. [c] C omits *jalâdi-°*.

[638] Ms. A, H and V omit the following gloss of Ms. C (between the *pratīkas*. *svapnâdîti*, n. 637, and *ayam iti*, n. 639): NAṬ *ad loc.*: ***niyata-deśa-cāritâdāv iti***. *ādi*[a]*-śabdād vastutva-sattvâdi-parigrahaḥ*.

[a] C: *°-cāritâdāv ity-ādi-°*.

[639] Cf. NAṬ *ad loc.*: ***ayam iti***. *anekânta-prakaśaḥ*.

[640] NAV 4 (pp. 32–36 of the translation) concluding with *tasmāt vyavasāyâtmakam adhyakṣam ity etad eva cārv iti sthitam*.

[641] Cf. NAṬ *ad loc.*: ***katham adṛṣṭêty-ādi***. *tasyâdvaya-saṁvedanasya kāryaṁ tat-kāryam,*[a] *tasya bhāvaḥ*[b] *tat-kāryatvam,*[c†] *na dṛṣṭaṁ tat-kāryatvaṁ yasya sa tathā, ayam anekâkāro bodhaḥ. ayam abhiprāyaḥ:*[d] *bhavad-āśayenâyam anekâkāro bodhaḥ ekasyâneka*[e]*-dharmatvâyogād bādhita eva; param asau bādhito 'py anekâkāro*[f] *bodho 'dvayaṁ na bhavatîti*[g]*; advayam anumāpayed yady advayasya kāryaṁ syāt.*— '"Its effect" [means] "the effect of non-dualistic sensation"; the state of that is "[the fact of] being its effect"; that in which case [the fact of] being its effect is not visible is such [in the case of which the fact of being the effect is invisible, namely] the cognitive awareness the form of which is multiplex. The intention is as follows: according to the purport [intended by] you, "this"—[viz.,] the cognitive awareness the form of which is multiplex—is indeed subverted, because it is unjustified to assume that [numerically] one [cognitive awareness] possesses multiple properties; further, this cognitive awareness the form of which is multiplex, although it is subverted, is not non-dual; [the multiplex cognitive awareness] could make one infer non-duality if it were the effect of non-duality.'

[a] A,C: °-*kāryaṁ* / .
[b] A,C: *tasya bhāvaṁ*; H,V: *tat-svabhāvaḥ*.
[c] A: °-*kāryatvaṁ* / .
[d] A,C: *bodho 'ayam abhiprāyo*.
[e] H,V: *bodhaḥ, ekasyâneka*-°.
[f] H: *anekāro*.
[g] H,V: *bhavati*.
[†] Cf. Pāṇ 5.1.119.

[642] NAṬ: ***asyêti***. *anekâkāra-bodhasya*.

[643] Used in the sense discussed on p. 89 and in n. 598.

[644] At first appearance, one might be led to read: *ekasyânekatâvabhāsa-bhāvād* (instead of *ekasyânekatâvabhāsâbhāvād*, attested in Mss.: 'since [numerically] one [sensation] h a s the appearance of multiple [reality]'). However, the dialectical structure of the whole passage is based on the opponent's arguments that, step by step, closely mirror the structure of the Vijñāna-vādin's argumentation. Thus, the structure, in the crudest formulation, of '*jaḍasya prakāśâyogāt saṁvittiḥ satyā, nârthaḥ*' is this: '*a* (*jaḍa*) is not *b* (*prakāśa*) → ¬*a*.' Accordingly, the opponent's argument (*ekasyânekatâvabhāsâbhāvād anekântaḥ satyo, nâdvaityam*) has the identical structure: '*c* (*eka*[*saṁvedana*]) is not *d* (*anekatâvabhāsa*) → ¬*c*.'

[645] Cf. NA 22.

[646] Alternatively, we could read jointly *sādhayantam* (not *sādhayan tam*): *tathā ca sthira-sthūrâdy-upalakṣitârthâṁśa-vaśād viśakalita-paramâṇu-kṣaṇa-kṣayi-paryāya-tādātmyaṁ* ***sādhayantam*** *anekânta-vādinaṁ na pratikṣeptum arhati*...—'And consequently, he (*sc*. the Vijñāna-vādin) is not in a position to disprove the propounder of the theory of multiplexity of reality who proves—on account of [only] one aspect of an object cognised as persistent, gross, etc.—the essential identity of [a series of] momentary modes of disconnected infinitesimal atoms...' This, I think, is less plausible.

[647] PV_I 3.57bd.

[648] In other words, all entities would remain non-dualistic and the mundane world of manifold appearance, as we perceive it, could not arise, because nothing which is non-dualistic could be projected into the cognition.

[649] NAṬ *ad loc*.: ***parâbhiprāyêti***. *parôbhyupagatânumāno jainâdiḥ*.—'"The opponent's intention" means "inference accepted by the opponent [and drawn by] the Jainas, etc.".'

[650] For the variety of the fallacious example that lacks the probandum (*sādhya-vikala-dṛṣṭântâbhāsa*) cf. NA 24.

[651] A woman can either be young or old, not semi-senile. The purport is this: why does the opponent stops half-way and, having accepted the premisses, refuses to accept the consequence. For the meaning of the maxim *ardha-jaratīya-nyāya* see JACOB (1907–1911: 7–8).

[652] That is to say, the opponent's second reply is not conclusive and one is inevitably confronted with the initial question. By 'clinging to grass this way or another' I try to render the use of two names of grass species in the expression ***kuśa-kāśâ****valambanena* (lit. 'clinging to *kuśa*-grass (of mostly ritual use) and *kāśa*-grass (of mostly practical use, for mats, roofs, etc.)'). As regards the joint usage of *kuśa*-grass and *kāśa*-grass, see *Divyâvadana* (cf. Burnouf, *Introduction a l'histoire du Bouddhisme indien*, Paris 1844, p. 314), in which Śariputta answers the question whether there is any *śramaṇa* in his company: *Est-ce que tu crois que les Śramaṇas qui nous suivent, naissent pour nous des plantes Kāśa ou Kouśa? Ce sont les enfants qu'obtiennent tes pareils, qui deviennent des Śramaṇa faits pour nous suivre.* See also MBhā 2.343: *tasyāṁ (yama-sabhāyāṁ) śiṁśapa-pālāśās tathā kāśa-kuśâdayaḥ // upāsate dharma-rājaṁ mūrtimantaḥ...* and MBhā 2.336: *palāśānāṁ śataṁ jñeyaṁ śataṁ kāśa-kuśâdayaḥ...*

[653] On the following few lines Siddharṣi-gaṇin rejects the supposition that the logical reason under discussion (quoted on p. 84) is a fallacy of the *viruddha* type (contrary logical reason: *viruddha-hetv-ābhāsa*, see NA 23).

[654] Lit. 'is nothing but such the stream of which is cast off far away.'

[655] Cf. NAṬ *ad loc.*: ***anenêti****. pramāṇa-nirṇite 'visaṁvādena.*—'"By virtue of this" [means] due to the absence of erring (*sc.* compliance) with regard to what is determined by cognitive criteria.'

[656] I apparently fail to correlate the spirit of the above picturesque simile with the Jinistic attitude of non-violence.

[657] This is the repetition of the logical reason on p.84. Here ends the exposition, the justification and the defence of the proof formula proving the multiplexity of the perceived reality. Cf. also n.569.

[658] Now follows the exegesis of the second hemistich of NA 29: 'an object qualified by [only] one facet is known as the province of a viewpoint.'

[659] The preceding paragraph was the verbatim exposition of the aphorism; *athavā* opens a polemical section, which presents, at the same time, an alternative analysis of the aphorism.

[660] The definition and the number of cognitive criteria have been discussed in NA 1, the domain in NA 29 and the result in NA 28. Cf. p. 9.

[661] Cf. STP 3.69:

baddaṁ micchā-daṁsaṇa-samūha-maïyassa amaya-sārassa /
jiṇa-vayaṇassa bhagavaö saṁvigga-suhāhigammassa // —

—'[Let there be] prosperity to Jina's words that are made of an amassment of false views, that are conducive to immortality, that are venerable, and lead to the salvific happiness.'

[662] The above phrasing: *tan nâyam aprastuta iti*, is one of, at least, two cases noticed in NAV when double negation (*na* + a negated past participle) is used in the sense of a strong affirmation. The other case is NAV 31: *evâvyatireka-pakṣaḥ pratibhāsa-nirākṛtatvān nâśaṅkitaḥ* (p.133 of the translation).

[663] The number, domain and result of the viewpoint are meant. Cf. p. 9 and n. 63.

[664] *tal-lakṣaṇâdi-°* viz., *nayasya lakṣaṇa-saṁkhyā-phala-°*, i.e. definition, number and result of the viewpoint, for the domain is already mentioned *expressis verbis* in the aphorism. In other words, it is no shortcoming not to specify the definition, the number and the result of viewpoints.

[665] Alternatively, 'to the sphere of what is to be avoided.' In other words, the author equates viewpoints, as it will be later demonstrated, with inadmissible convictions and beliefs of rival philosophic schools.

[666] The asserted emphasis and explicitness seem here rather to be a matter of Siddharṣi-gaṇin's personal taste and subjective impression.

[667] Taken literally, *antaḥ-pātin* could likewise imply the idea of the opponents' 'falling into their own doctrine', as if into a pitfall.

[668] Apparently, *dharma* is used here in place of usual *guṇa*. For the distinction between *dharma* / *guṇa* and *paryāya* see SSi 5.38: *anvayino guṇā vyatirekiṇaḥ paryāyāḥ. ubhayair upetaṁ dravyam iti. uktaṁ ca*: '*guṇa idi davva-vihāṇaṁ davva-viyāro hi pajjavo bhaṇido. tehiṁ aṇūṇaṁ davvaṁ ajuda-pasiddhaṁ have niccam.*' *etad uktaṁ bhavati*: *dravyaṁ dravyântarād yena viśiṣyate sa guṇaḥ. tena hi tad dravyaṁ vidhīyate. asati tasmin dravya-saṅkara-prasaṅgaḥ syāt. tad yathā*: *jīvaḥ pudgalâdibhyo jñānâdibhir guṇair viśiṣyate pudgalâdayaś ca rūpâdibhiḥ. tataś câviśeṣe saṅkaraḥ syāt. tataḥ sāmānyâpekṣayā anvayino jñānâdayo jīvasya guṇāḥ pudgalâdīnāṁ ca rūpâdayaḥ. teṣāṁ vikārā viśeṣâtmanā bhidyamānāḥ paryāyāḥ. ghaṭa-jñānaṁ krodho māno gandho varṇas tīvro manda ity evam ādayaḥ.*— 'Qualities are concomitant, modes are separable. Substance is endowed with both of them; and it has been taught accordingly: "Quality is [said to be] the determinant of substance; mode, however, is said to be the modification of substance. Substance is complete with (*sc.* inseparable from) them, is known to be unseparated (*sc.* to compose a whole) and is permanent." It has been said to the effect that quality is that by which [a particular] substance is distinguished from [everything] else different from [this particular] substance, because, if quality were not there, that would lead to the undesired consequence that [various] substances would mingle. For it is as follows: the living element is distinguished from [other substances like] matter, etc., by virtue of qualities such as cognition, etc., and [other substances like] matter, etc., [are distinguished from the living element] by virtue of the [perceptible] form, etc., Hence, if there were no distinction [based on qualities, all substances] would mingle. Therefore, qualities of the living element, such as cognition, etc., [on the one hand], and qualities of [inanimate substances] like matter, etc., such as [perceptible] form, etc.,

[on the other], are concomitant with regard to [substance] as such. Their (*sc.* of substances) modifications, that are essentially distinct [and] are divided [from each other], are modes, viz., the cognition of a pot, anger, pride, smell, colour, pungency, sluggishness and similar.'

669 Cf. JTBh$_2$ § 1: *pramāṇa-paricchinnasyânanta-dharmâtmakasya vastuna eka-deśa-grāhiṇas tad-itaraṁ sâpratikṣepino 'dhyavasāya -viśeṣā nayāḥ.*

670 The following passage is quoted, with minor alterations, in SVM 28.59 ff., p. 161,14 ff.: *tathâpi cirantanâcāryair sarva-saṅgrāhi-saptâbhiprāya-parikalpanā-dvāreṇa sapta nayāḥ pratipāditāḥ. tad yathā: "naigama-saṅgraha-vyavahāra-rju*[a]*-sūtra-śabda-samabhirūḍhâivaṁ-bhūtā nayāḥ" iti. katham eṣāṁ sarva-saṅgrāhakatvam iti ced ucyate: abhiprāyas tāvad artha-dvāreṇa śabda-dvāreṇa vā pravartate, gaty-antarâbhāvāt. tatra ye kecanârtha-nirūpaṇa-pravaṇāḥ pramātr-abhiprāyās te sarve 'py*[b] *ādye naya-catuṣṭaye 'ntar-bhavanti*[c].

[a] Dhruva edits: °-*ṛju-*°. [b] Dhruva: *sarvepy.* [c] Dhruva: *catuṣṭayentar-*°.

671 Cf. the parallel wording in NAV 29 below: *sarva-saṅgrāhakâbhiprāya-parikalpa-mukhenâiva sapta-bhedo darśitaḥ* (p. 108 of the English translation).

672 This passage is quoted and elaborated in SVM 28.56–57 and SVM 28.56–61, p. 161.11–16: *nayāś cânantāḥ. ananta-dharmatvād vastunas tad-eka-dharma-paryavastitānāṁ vaktur abhiprayāṇāṁ ca nayatvāt tathā ca vṛddhāḥ. 'jāvaïyā vayaṇa-vaha tāvaïyā ceva hoṁti ṇaya-vāyā'* [STP 3.47ab] *iti. tathâpi cirantanâcāryaiḥ sarva-saṅgrāhi-saptâbhiprāya-parikalpanā-dvāreṇa sapta nayāḥ pratipāditāḥ. tad yathā – 'naigama-saṅgraha-vyavahāra-rjusūtra-śabda-samabhirūḍhâivambhūtā nayā' iti.* The *locus classicus* for the seven *nayas* is TS 1.33 in the reading offered by SSi 1.33: *naigama-saṅgraha-vyavahāra-rjusūtra-śabda-samabhirūḍhâivam-bhūtā nayāḥ.* However, TBh 1.34–35 offers a *varia lectio* of TS , viz., /34/ *naigama-saṁgraha-vyavahāra-rjusūtra-śabdā nayāḥ.* /35/ *ādya-śabdau dvi-tri-bhedau.*

673 A corresponding passage of SVM (cf. n. 670) has the indicative form: *pravartate* ('operates').

674 If the comprehensive viewpoint considered the universal and the particular as being connected with each other, it would possess, as it were, much affinity to a cognitive criterion.

675 The two gerundives of the following series, viz., *sampādya* and *sādhya*, should be interpreted in the sense similar to *janya* (predicated below of *vyavahāra-naya*), which, being a gerundive ('to be produced, producible'), is used in the sense of passive participle ('produced'). The gerundives are used synonymously with the past participle *ghaṭita* below. Such a meaning of the gerundive *janya* is frequently attested, to cite only a few examples from the Naiyāyika literature: Dī *ad* TCM (*upādhi*-section): *śuṣka-*° and *ārdrêndhana-janya-vahni*, SMA as BhP$_2$ 138: *śaka-pāka-janyatva*. Cf. n. 879.

[676] I interpret *avatarantaṁ* predicatively of *ghaṭâdikaṁ padârtham*, viz., 'entity ... that enters (*sc.* becomes an object of) the everyday practice', although one could construe it adjectivally with *abhipreyanti* in the sense: '[outlooks] that intend an entity ... complying with everyday practice among people.'

[677] Apparently *saugatāḥ* and *mīmāṁsakāḥ* of Mss. B, H, V—occurring in *ye saugatās tu kṣaṇa-kṣayiṇaḥ paramâṇu-lakṣaṇā viśeṣāḥ satyā iti manyante tat-saṅghāta-ghaṭita ṛjusūtra iti / tathā ye mīmāṁsakāḥ rūḍhitaḥ śabdānāṁ pravṛttiṁ vāñchanti tan-nivaha-sādhyaḥ śabda iti.*—is a later interpolation. The exposition of the five remaining viewpoints, bearing structural identity with definitions of the two viewpoints in question, is limited to a general description of main features of respective viewpoints, without a slightest allusion to a particular philosophical school, say, to the Cārvākas, Naiyāyikas, etc.

[678] In the above section, an exceptional care of Siddharṣi-gaṇin for phraseology should be taken notice of, who is meticulous in avoiding any repetition by making use of synonyms: *sampādya* = *janya* = *sādhya* = *ghaṭita* and √*iṣ* = √*vāñch* = *abhipra*√*i*, etc.

[679] Cf. n. 231.

[680] Or: 'there is not any other conceptualisation, the domain of which is ...'; the ambiguity is apparently intended here.

[681] In view of a similar phrase below, viz., *sāmpratam eteṣām eva pratyekam abhiprāyaḥ kathyate* (translated on p. 105), *pratyekaṁ* is to be understood adverbially.

[682] Cf. exposition of the comprehensive viewpoint, based on similarly structured argumentation, in SVM 14.74–89, p. 87.5–19: *naigama-nayânugāminas tv āhuḥ ... iti svatantra-sāmānya-viśeṣa-vādaḥ*.

[683] See *prajñâdi-gaṇa* no. 151 in Böhtlingk's ed. *ad* Pāṇ 5.4.38: *prajnâdibhyāś ca* ('The affix *aṇ* (cf. 5.4.36) is added also to *prajñā*, etc.'); Pāṇ 5.4.36: *tad-yuktāt karmaṇo 'ṇ*.—'An *karman* (Geschäft) tritt *a* an, wenn es zu einem mündlichen Auftrage in Beziehung steht.'

[684] Pāṇ 4.3.53: *tatra bhavaḥ*.

[685] The notion of the cognition of recurrent continuity (*apekṣā-buddhi*), i.e. the cognition of interrelation, or a distinguishing perception of duality, is meant here. We encounter it, for instance, in BhP_2 107–8:

nityeṣu nityam ekatvam anitye 'nityam iṣyate /
dvitvâdayaḥ parârdhatā apekṣā-buddhi-jā matāḥ //
anekâśraya-paryāptā ete tu parikīrtitāḥ /
apekṣā-buddhi-nāśāc ca nāśas teṣāṁ nirūpitaḥ //

—'Oneness is accepted to be permanent in permanent [substances and to be] impermanent in impermanent [substances]. High [numbers] larger than two [including two] are known to be produced by the cognition of recurrent continuity. But they are said to extend over numerous substrata and their extinction is described as following the extinction of the cognition of recurrent continuity.' See also VIDYĀBHŪṢAṆA (1920: 118–119).

Regarding the cognition of recurrent continuity correlated with the notion of the universal (*vide infra* n.686), admitted also by the Naiyāyika, a hypothetical criticism against that idea is expressed as a *pūrva-pakṣa* and thereupon refuted in NV 2.2.64: *atha manyase yad idam gotvaṁ goṣv anuvṛtti-pratyaya-kāraṇaṁ tat kiṁ gavi vartata āhosvid agavi? yadi tāvad gavi, prāg gotva-yogād gaur eva asāv iti vyarthaṁ gotvaṁ. athâgavi, nâśvâdy api gotva-yogād gauḥ prāpnoti. na cânyā gatir asti. tasmān na gotvād anuvṛtti-pratyaya iti. na, vikalpânabhyupagamāt: na gavi gotvaṁ nâgavi, prāg gotvān nâsau gaur nâpy agaur iti.*—'If you maintain the following—"Does [the universal] «cow-ness», which is the cause of the cognition of r e c u r - r e n t c o n t i n u i t y , occur (*sc.* inhere) [1] in a [particular] cow or [2] in a [particular] non-cow? [Ad 1] If [it inheres] in a [particular] cow, to begin with, then [the universal] «cow-ness» [proves] pointless, because that [substratum in which it inheres] is [already] nothing but a cow [even] before the link with [the universal] «cow-ness» [is established]. [Ad 2] If [you say that it inheres] in a [particular] non-cow, [that is] not [correct], because also a horse, etc., becomes a cow due to the link with [the universal] «cow-ness». And there is no other logical alternative. Therefore, the cognition of recurrent continuity is not [possible] on account of [the universal] «cow-ness»."—[so, if you argue as above, that is] not [correct], because we do not accept [these two] alternatives: [the universal] "cow-ness" [inheres] neither in a [particular] cow nor in a [particular] non-cow. Before [establishing the link with the universal] "cow-ness", that [substratum in which it is to inhere] is neither a cow nor a non-cow.'

[686] Regarding the ultimate and intermediate sub-divisions of the universal and the particular, see VSU_{I} 1.2.3–6: *sāmānyaṁ viśeṣa iti buddhy-apekṣam. bhāvaḥ sāmānyam eva. dravyatvaṁ guṇatvaṁ karmatvaṁ ca sāmānyāni viśeṣāś ca. anyatrântyebhyo viśeṣebhyaḥ.* In his commentary, Praśastapāda offers relevant explanation on the universal, cf. PBh_{I} [22], p. 41.2–4 ad VSU_{I} 1.2.3: *sāmānyaṁ dvividhaṁ param aparañ ca. anuvṛtti-pratyaya-kāraṇam. tatra paraṁ sattā mahā-viṣayatvāt. sā cânuvṛtter eva hetutvāt sāmānyam eva. dravyatvâdy aparam, alpa-viṣayatvāt. tac ca vyāvṛtter api hetutvāt sāmānyaṁ sad-viśeṣâkhyām api labhate.*—'The universal is two-fold: ultimate and non-ultimate. It is the cause of the cognition of recurrent continuity[a]. Out of these two [varieties], the ultimate [universal] is existence, because [it has] the largest province; and this [existence itself] is the universal alone, because it is the cause of nothing but recurrent continuity[a]. Substantiality, etc., is non-ultimate [universal], because [it has] smaller province; and this universal, inasmuch as it is a cause of distinction (non-occurrence) as well, [not only a cause of recurrent continuity[a]], receives also the designation the particular of the existent.' That is followed by a brief mention of the particular in PBh_{I} [26], p. 46.2: *nitya-dravya-vṛttayo 'ntyā viśeṣāḥ. te khalv atyanta-vyāvṛtti-hetutvvād viśeṣā eva.*—'Occurrences (*sc.* in-

dividual manifestations) in permanent substances are intermediate particulars. These, as one should realise, are particulars alone, because ultimate distinction (non-occurrence) is [their] ground.' Both these passages were subsequently commented by Śrīdhara, cf. NKa [26], p. 46.7–47.8 *ad loc.*: ***nitya-dravya-vṛttayo 'ntyā viśeṣā** iti. nitya-dravyeṣv eva vartanta eva ye te viśeṣā iti. nitya-dravyeṣv e[vê]ti dravya-guṇa-karma-sāmānyānāṁ vyavacchedaḥ. dravya-guṇa-karmāṇi dravyeṣv eva vartante, na nityeṣv evêti. sāmānyāni tu na dravyeṣv eva. na nityeṣv eva vartanta evêti buddhi-śabdâdīnāṁ vyavacchedaḥ, teṣāṁ samasta-nitya-dravya-prāpty-abhāvāt. nanu kiṁ viśeṣā viśeṣā eva kiṁ vā dravyatvâdivad ubhaya-rūpā iti. tatrâha—**te khalv** iti. khalu-śabdo niścaye, nitya-dravya-vṛttayo ye viśeṣās te viśeṣā eva niścitā, na tu sāmānyāny api bhavantîty arthaḥ. **atyantaṁ** sarvadā, **vyāvṛtter** eva svâśrayasyêtarasmād vyavacchedasyâiva, **hetutvāt** kāraṇatvād iti.*—'[A gloss on]: "occurrences in permanent substances are intermediate particulars." Those that indeed occur (*sc.* inhere) in permanent substances alone are particulars. [The phrase] "in permanent substances alone" [expresses] the exclusion of [the universals:] substantiality, qualitativeness and motion; [particular] substances, qualities and movements occur (*sc.* inhere) in substances alone, [they do] not [occur (*sc.* inhere)] in permanent [substances] whatsoever, whereas the universals do not occur (*sc.* inhere) in substances alone. [The phrase] "[they do] not [occur (*sc.* inhere)] in permanent [substances] alone" [expresses] the exclusion of knowledge and speech elements, because they do not reach whole permanent substances. Now, [a question is raised]: "Are the particulars particulars alone or do they consist in both, like [the universals] substantiality, etc.?" Regarding that, it is replied by [the phrase] "these, as one should realise ...". The speech element "as one should realise" [is used] in [the meaning of] "determination". The meaning is as follows: these particulars that are occurrences (*sc.* individual manifestations) of permanent substances are determined [to be] particulars, but they are not simultaneously the universals, because "ultimate", [i.e.] invariable, distinction (non-occurrence) alone—[i.e.] nothing but the exclusion of one's own substratum from [every]thing else, is [their] ground, [i.e.] is their cause.' In his commentary to the sixth chapter of *Praśastapāda-bhāṣya*, Śrīdhara describes the ultimate and intermediate particulars in detail; see PBh$_1$ [264], p. 684.3–687.5: *antyeṣu bhavā antyāḥ, svâśraya-viśeṣakatvād viśeṣāḥ. vināśârambha-rahiteṣu nitya-dravyeṣv aṇv-ākāśa-kāla-dig-ātmanasu prati-dravyam ekâikaśo atyanta-vyāvṛtti-buddhi-hetavaḥ. yathâsmad-ādīnāṁ gavâdiṣv aśvâdibhyas tulyâkṛti-guṇa-kriyâvayava-saṁyoga-nimittā pratyaya-vyāvṛttir dṛṣṭā gauḥ śuklaḥ śīghra-gatiḥ pīnaḥ kakudmān mahā-ghaṇṭa iti, tathâsmad-viśiṣṭānāṁ yogināṁ nityeṣu tulyâkṛti-guṇa-kriyeṣu paramâṇuṣu muktâtma-manasu cânya-nimittâsambhavād yebhyo nimittebhyaḥ pratyādhāraṁ vilakṣaṇo 'yaṁ vilakṣaṇo 'yam iti pratyaya-vyāvṛttiḥ, deśa-kāla-viprakarṣa-dṛṣṭe ca paramâṇau sa evâyam iti pratyabhijñānaṁ ca bhavati, te 'ntyā viśeṣāḥ.*—'[Such that] have their existence among extremes are intermediate; because they are factors distinguishing their own substrata [from everything else], they are particulars; [when inhering] one by one individually per substance in permanent substances, that are devoid of extinction and beginning—viz., in atom, ether, time, space and soul—they are causes of the cognition of ultimate distinction (non-occurrence). In analogy to people like us who experience the differentiation in cognition occasioned by equal shapes, qualities, actions, parts or relations, with reference to cows, etc. [as different] from horses, etc.—[e.g. in the form] "[this] cow is white, of swift pace, with a fat neck hump, with a large bell"—in a similar manner yogins, who are superior to us, [experience] the differentiation in cognition with reference to permanent [entities like] atoms and minds and souls of liberated people that have identical shapes, qualities and actions. Since there is no other factor [that would make such a differentiation between seemingly identical things possible], the factors thanks to which [the yogins are able to distinguish] each and every substratum [of qualities and actions in the form]: "this is different, that is different", and [thanks to which in those yogins] a recognition arises: "this is that [atom]" with regard to an atom in distant place and time, are ultimate individuators.' See also Śaṅkara Miśra's VSU$_{I}$ 1.2.3 quoted in n.740 below.

For the ideas of exclusion / distinction (non-occurrence) an recurrent continuity[a] connoted by the notions of the particular and the universal, respectively, see NRĀ on MŚV$_{I}$ 4 (*Pratyakṣa-sūtra*).113: *viśeṣaḥ = vyavacchedaḥ, vyāvṛttiḥ. sāmānyam = samānatvam, anuvṛttir it yāvat.*

[a] *Vide supra* n.685.

[687] The above passage is quoted in SVM 28.66–69, p. 161,21–24: *tatra naigamaḥ sattā-lakṣaṇaṁ mahā-sāmānyam avāntara-sāmānyāni ca dravyatva-guṇatva-karmatvâdīni tathântyān viśeṣān sakalâsādhāraṇa-rūpa-lakṣaṇān avāntara-viśeṣāṁś*[a] *câpekṣayā para-rūpa-vyāvartana-kṣamān sāmānyād atyanta-vinirluṭhita-svarūpān abhipraiti.*

[a] A. B. Dhruva misprints: *avāntara viśeṣāṁś.*

[688] *ātman = svabhāva*: see NB$_{I}$ 3.114,118: /114/ *na hi sambhavo 'sti kārya-svabhāvayor ukta-lakṣaṇayor anupalambhasya ca viruddhatāyāḥ* ... /118/ *na hy asya sambhavo yathâvasthita-vastu-sthitiṣv ātma-kāryânupalambheṣu.* See also (1) a similar occurrence in NAV 29: *arthâtmanām adhyakṣam avalokayati* (p. 103 of the English translation), (2) NBṬ$_{I}$ 2.23:... *sa sādhyo 'rtha ātmā svabhāvo yasya tat tad-ātma* ... (n. 5). Comp. likewise *ātman = svabhāva = bdag ñid* in PVin I$_{I}$ 254b p. 50 n.1: *skyes bu so so la don rnams bdag ñid that dad pa ni ma yin te* | = *na hi pratipuruṣam arthānām ātma-bhedaḥ*. (Vetter after AJP, p. 140.7–142.2).

[689] Although the original has singular: *dravyam*, plural is to be understood by virtue of the repetitive *yat yat ... tat tat.*

[690] The sequence of enumeration is significant: one cannot admit the particular and rule out the universal at the same time; similarly, it is not possible to accept the universal and disregard the particular.

[691] The following *śloka*s quoted in NAṬ at the completion of each *naya*-section (H. p. 118–128, V. p. 76–82) occur also jointly in SVM 28.142–155, pp. 164.22–165.10, and are introduced as summary aphorisms (*atra saṅgraha-ślokāḥ*), as well; they were,

however, not traced back by the editor of SVM, A. B. Dhruva (cf. p. 60.19–20 of the *Appendix B*):

[1] *anyad eva hi sāmānyam abhinna-jñāna-kāraṇam /*
viśeṣo 'py anya evêti manyate nâigamo nayaḥ //

[2] *sad-rūpatânatikrānta-sva-svabhāvam idaṁ jagat /*
sattā-rūpatayā sarvaṁ saṅgṛhṇan saṅgraho mataḥ //

[3] *vyavahāras tu tām eva prativastu-vyavasthitām /*
tathâiva dṛśyamānatvād vyavahārayati dehinaḥ //

[4] *tatra ṛjusūtra-nītiḥ syāc chuddha-paryāya-saṁśritāḥ /*
naśvarasyâiva bhāvasya bhāvāt sthiti-viyogataḥ //

[5] *virodhe liṅga*[a]*-saṁkhyâdi-bhedād bhinna-svabhāvatām /*
tasyâiva manyamāno 'yaṁ śabdaḥ pratyavatiṣṭhate //

[6] *tathā-vidhasya tasyâpi vastunaḥ kṣaṇa-vṛttinaḥ /*
brūte samabhirūḍhas tu saṁjñā-bhedena bhinnatām //

[7] *ekasyâpi dhvaner vācyaṁ sadā tan nôpapadyate /*
kriyā-bhedena bhinnatvād evaṁ-bhūo 'bhimanyate //

I have failed to identify the source of these aphorisms. It is highly implausible that their authorship be ascribed to Siddharṣi-gaṇin.

[a] SVM : *virodhi-liṅga-°*.

692 Cf. exposition of the collective viewpoint, based on similarly structured *prasaṅga*-argumentation, in SVM 14.25–53, p. 85.5—p. 85.8: *tathā hi saṅgraha-nayâvalambino vādinaḥ pratipādayanti. sāmānyam eva tattvam ... iti sāmānyâikānta-vādaḥ.*

693 In view of the foregoing passage explaining *naigama-naya*, viz., *ayaṁ hi sattā-lakṣaṇaṁ ... abhiprâiti* (H.: p. 117.4–8; V.: p. 75.7–10), *ayam* above and in following sections (e.g. *asyâbhiprāya*) has to be taken to mean *naya*, and not a propounder of a particular viewpoint.

694 Note the emphatic inversion, instead of usual: *śeṣa-pramāṇa-vargasya pratyakṣa-mūlakatvāt*. To mark off this emphasis, I add 'undeniably' in the translation.

695 As regards the *saṅgraha-śloka* at the end of the NAṬ portion cf. n. 691.

696 For the translation of *lokâbādhita*, see *loka-bādhita* in NAV 14, NA 21 and NAV thereupon.

697 I.e., the past and future manifestations of an object do not constitute the domain of cognitive criteria.

698 Note the emphatic inversion, instead of usual: *teṣām avastutvāc ca*.

699 As regards the *saṅgraha-śloka* at the end of the NAṬ portion cf. n. 691.

700 The whole passage is quoted with minor changes and additions in SVM 28.74–91, p. 162.4–21: *yathā loka-grāham eva vastv astu kim anayā adṛṣṭâvyavahriyamāna-vastu-parikalpana-kaṣṭa-piṣṭikayā. yad eva ca loka-vyavahāra-patham avatarati*

tasyânugrāhakaṁ pramāṇam upalabhyate nêtarasya. na hi sāmānyam anādi-nidhanam ekaṁ saṅgrāhâbhimataṁ pramāṇa-bhūmiḥ. tathânubhavâbhāvāt. sarvasya sarva-darśitva-prasaṅgāc ca. nâpi viśeṣāḥ paramâṇu-lakṣaṇāḥ kṣaṇa-kṣayiṇaḥ pramāṇa-gocaraḥ. tathā pravṛtter abhāvāt. tasmād idam eva nikhila-lokâbādhitaṁ pramāṇa-prasiddhaṁ kiyat-kāla-bhāvi-sthūlatām ābibhrāṇam udukâdy-āharaṇâdy-artha-kriyā-nirvartana-kṣamaṁ ghaṭâdikaṁ vastu-rūpaṁ pāramārthikam. pūrvôttara-kāla-bhāvi-tat-paryāya-paryālocanā punar ajyāyasī. tatra pramāṇa-prasarâbhāvāt. pramāṇam antareṇa ca vicārasya kartum aśakyatvāt. avastutvāc ca teṣāṁ kiṁ tad-gocara-paryālocanena. tathā hi pūrvôttara-kāla-bhāvino dravya-vivartāḥ kṣaṇa-kṣayi-paramâṇu-lakṣaṇā vā viśeṣā na kathañcana loka-vyavahāram uparacayanti. tan na te vastu-rūpāḥ. loka-vyavahārôpayogināṁ eva vastutvāt. ata eva panthā gacchanti kuṇḍikā sravati girir dahyate mañcāḥ krośantîty-ādi-vyavahārāṇāṁ prāmāṇyam. tathā ca vācaka-mukhyaḥ. laukika-sama upacāra-prāyo vistṛtârtho vyavahāraḥ iti.

701 I take *atītânagata-vakra-*° as parallel to *vartamāna-kṣaṇa-*°. However, the rendering: 'the bends of the past and of the future', would be justified in view of the subsequent phrase: *atītasya vinaṣṭatvāt anāgatasyâlabdhâtma-lābhatvāt.*

702 For the meaning of *ātman*, cf. n. 688.

703 NAṬ *ad loc.*: ***sva-pratibhāsinaḥ*** *sāmānyasya*; cf. NAV 5: *bhrāntam anumānam, sāmānya-pratibhāsitvāt* (p. 42 of the translation).

704 Cf. NAṬ 29 *ad loc.*: ***tat-pratiṣṭhāpana-dvāreṇa*** *adhyavasāya-vaśāt svalakṣaṇa-vyavasthāpana-dvāreṇa* ***tasya*** *anumāsya.*—'"By means of determining that" [i.e.] by means of establishing the individual thing on account of the apprehension [in the case] of "this," [i.e. in the case] of inference.' Apprehension refers apparently to perception, cf. NAV 5: *... nirṇayâtmakam api pratyakṣaṁ ... sannihite 'rthe viśadâdhyavasāyena pravṛtteḥ* (cf. p.63 of the translation).

705 What is meant in the above argument is this: the validity of inference may only be maintained when it is considered to pertain, eventually and indirectly, to a particular real thing, and not when it is taken to grasp the universal, for the latter is ultimately non-existent according to the Buddhist.

706 Cf. NAṬ *ad loc.*: ***viplava iti****. sadṛśâparâparôtpatti-darśana-kṛto vibhramaḥ.*—'"Blunder" [means] a confusion produced by perception [which has its] origination in various similar [objects].'

707 As regards the *saṅgraha-śloka* at the end of the NAṬ portion cf. n. 691.

708 Note the syntactical inversion in the original of emphatic character.

709 Note the syntactical inversion in the original of emphatic character.

710 Cf. Bhartṛhari's definition of *saṅketa* (linguistic convention) in *Vākya-padīya* (VP) as quoted in *Śabda-śakti-prakāśikā* (ŚŚP) (after RAJA (1963: 23, n. 5)):

ājānikaś câdhunikas saṅketo dvividho mataḥ
nitya ājānikas tatra yā śaktir iti gīyate
kadācitkas tv ādhunikaś śāstra-kārādibhiḥ kṛtaḥ.

On word-object relations, or linguistic convention (*saṅketa*) and usage (*rūḍhi*), cf. RAJA (1963: 22–4,59–69) and STAAL 1969.

[711] The above proof formula, beginning with the thesis: 'object is not, [by any means,] different from speech element, because that [object] is cognised...' (*na vyatirikto 'rthaḥ śabdāt...*), is meant.

[712] The term *artha* is—in the context of the verbal viewpoint and the two remaining ones—not absolutely unequivocal, for it refers on the one hand, to an individual external thing (*svalakṣaṇa*) denoted by an expression, hence to the denotatum of the expression. On the other hand, however, the denotatum of an expression constitutes also the meaning of the expression. Thus, in several occurrences in the subsequent paragraphs, *artha* may be taken to be 'an [external] object [denoted by a linguistic unit]' or 'denotatum [of a linguistic unit]', or 'the meaning [of a linguistic unit].'

[713] Cf. n.712.

[714] The epithets of the god Indra mean 'one possessed of sovereign authority', 'one possessed of might', 'destroyer of strongholds', respectively; *vide infra*.

[715] This is probably a reference to the idea expressed in $DhĀ_1$ 1.20, p. 273 (=$DhĀ_2$ 1.17):

mukhyāṁ vṛttim parityajya guṇa-vṛttyârtha-darśanam /
yad uddiśya phalaṁ tatra śabdo nâiva skhalad-gatiḥ //

—'Having put aside [its] primary operation (function), speech element is by no means fallible in its significatory approach towards the result, which [the speech element] has expressed [and] which is the demonstration of the meaning by [its] secondary operation (function).'

[716] As regards the *saṅgraha-śloka* at the end of the NAṬ portion cf. n. 691.

[717] In other words, according to Siddharṣi, *samabhirūḍha* is to be explained as a compound consisting of the prefix *sam-°* (= *ekī-bhāvena*) and of a derivative of the root *abhi√ruh* (= *vyutpatti-nimittam āskandati*).

[718] As regards the *saṅgraha-śloka* at the end of the NAṬ portion cf. n. 691.

[719] The correspondence of the elements occurring in the explanation of the grammatical formation of the term *evambhūta* can be depicted as follows: *evaṁ* = *prakāra°* = *yathā vyutpādita°* + *bhūta°* = *(taṁ prakāraṁ) prāpta°*.

[720] Cf. NAṬ 29 *ad loc.*: ***tad-viṣayatvād iti***. *sa evambhūtaḥ śabdo viṣayo yasyâbhiprāyasya tad-bhāvas tattvaṁ tasmāt*.

[721] Cf. n. 261 and NAṬ 29 *ad loc.*: ***śaśa-viṣāṇa-kalpatvād*** *iti. īṣad-aparisamāpte*[a] *śaśa-viṣāṇe*[b] *śaśa-viṣāṇa-kalpe*[c], *tayor bhāvas tattvaṁ tasmāt.*—'[The phrase] 'because they would resemble a hare's horns' [is to be explained] as follows: [they both are] almost complete two horns of a hare, [which means that they] both resemble a hare's horns; their state [means] the fact of being such; because of [that].'

[a] A,C: °-*aparisamāptaṁ*. [b] A,C: °-*viṣāṇaṁ*. [c] See Pāṇ 5.3.67.

[722] *tad-dvāreṇa = sāmānya-dvāreṇa = sāmānyena*.

[723] That is to say: since a speech element is accepted to denote either past or future occurrences, that are non-existent in the present moment, it may likewise be taken to denote anything, either existent or non-existent.

[724] The word *kapāla* may also denote a spherical base of which a pot is produced; see, e.g. $YDī_2$ ad SKā 15d, p. 150.24: *kapāla-pūrvako ghaṭaḥ*. However, in view that both past and future movements—or situations in which a pot either has already occurred or will occur—are explicitly mentioned in the phrase *atīta-vartsyac-ceṣṭâpekṣayā*, I take *mṛt-piṇḍa* and *kapāla* as correlatives of the former and of the latter, respectively, that are to exemplify both a past and a future manifestation. Hence, *kapāla* in the context of a future occurrence could not but refer to 'potsherd.'

[725] As regards the *saṅgraha-śloka* at the end of the NAṬ portion cf. n. 691.

[726] Cf. NA 29ab (*anekântâtmakaṁ vastu gocaraḥ sarva-saṁvidām*) as well as the proof formula in NAV 29: *yat pramāṇaṁ tat parasparâvinirluṭhitâneka-dharma-parikarita-vastuno grāhakam* … (p. 84 of the English translation).

[727] Cf. n. 231.

[728] Cf. NAV above: *ananta-dharmâdhyāsitaṁ vastu svâbhipretâika-dharma-viśiṣṭaṁ nayati prāpayati saṁvedanam ārohayatîti nayaḥ, pramāṇa-pravṛtter uttara-kāla-bhāvī parāmarśa ity arthaḥ* (p. 96 of the English translation).

[729] Cf. the parallel wording in NAV 29 above: *sarva-saṅgrāhi-saptâbhiprāya-parikalpanā-dvāreṇa sapta nayāḥ pratipāditāḥ* (p. 97 of the English translation).

[730] The passage is quoted, with minor changes, in SVM 28.155 ff., p. 165.11, and followed by an extensive citation from PNT: *eta eva ca parāmarśā abhipreta-dharmâvadhāraṇâtmakatayā śeṣa-dharma-tiras-kāreṇa pravartamāṇā durnaya-saṁjñām aśnuvate. tad-bala-prabhāvita-sattākā hi khalv ete para-pravādāḥ. tathā hi: naigama-naya-darśanânusāriṇau naiyāyika-vaiśeṣikau. saṅgrahâbhiprāya-pravṛttāḥ sarve 'py advaita-vādāḥ sāṁkhya-darśanaṁ ca. vyavahāra-nayânupāti prāyaś cārvāka-darśanam. ṛjusūtrâkūta-pravṛtta-buddhayas tāthāgatāḥ. śabdâdi-nayâvalambino vaiyākaraṇâdaya iti. uktaṁ ca sôdāharaṇaṁ naya-durnaya-svarūpaṁ śrī-deva-gaṇin-pādaiḥ*...

[731] Note the intended allusion to the Buddha in the expression: °-*buddhayas tāthāgatāḥ*.

[732] Cf. NAṬ *ad loc.*: *ādi-śabdād abhidhāna-kośa-kartāro gṛhyante.*—'On account of the speech element "etc.", authors of *Abhidhāna-kośa* are comprised (*sc.* intended).'

[733] Cf. NAV 29 above: *ananta-dharmâdhyāsitaṁ vastu svâbhipretâika-dharma-viśiṣṭaṁ nayati prāpayati saṁvedanam ārohayatîti nayaḥ, pramāṇa-pravṛtter uttara-kāla-bhāvī parāmarśa ity arthaḥ* (p. 96 of the English translation).

[734] It is worthwhile to note that the above remark refers not to the ontological status of a real thing, which might also be postulated to be of multiplex character, but merely to its multiplex representation in the cognition. Needless to say, the latter does not necessary entail the former.

[735] The multi-level argumentative structure is as follows: the main reason for the assertion *śeṣa-dharma-pratikṣepa-dvāreṇa tu pravṛttau na kiñcana nayati* is *tad-apahnava-kāriṇāṁ kadabhiprāyāṇāṁ pratibhāsa-bādhitatvenâlīkatvāt.* The latter, viz., the rejection of recognition of viewpoints that assume non-multiplexity of cognised objects, is further (viz., beside the insertion *pratibhāsa-bādhitatvena*) justified on the grounds that such non-multiple objects, that are believed to be represented by means of defective viewpoints, are simply impossible (at least in cognition): *eka-dharmâliṅgitasya tasya vastuno 'sambhavād.* The latter thesis is corroborated by the way a real thing appears in cognition: *bahir antaś câneka-dharma-parikarita-svabhāvasya tasya pratibhāsād.*

[736] Cf. the proof formula in NAV 29 above: *paraspara-viśliṣṭau sāmānya-viśeṣau, pārthakyenôpalabdheḥ, iha yad yat pārthakyenôpalabhyate tat tat paraspara-viśliṣṭaṁ dravyam, tad yathā—devadatta-yajñadattāv iti, pārthakyena côpalabhyete sāmānya-viśeṣau, ataḥ paraspara-bhinnāv iti* (cf. p. 99 of the English translation).

[737] Cf. NAV 29 above: *na ca sāmānya-grāhiṇi vijñāne viśeṣâvabhāso 'sti, anuvartamānâikâkāra-parāmarśena tad-grahaṇād ... nâpi viśeṣa-grahaṇa-dakṣe saṁvedane sāmānyaṁ cakāsti ...* (cf. p. 99 of the English translation).

[738] Cf. NAṬ *ad loc.*: ***tad-virahe*** *viśeṣāṇām*[a] *abhāve.*

[a] C: *viśeṣaṇām.*

[739] Cf. NAṬ *ad loc.*: ***śaśa-viṣāṇa-rūpatvād iti.***[a] *yad uktaṁ*:

nirviśeṣaṁ na sāmānyaṁ bhavec chaśa-viṣāṇavat /
viśeṣo 'pi[b] *ca nâivâsti*[c] *sāmānyena vinā-kṛtaḥ //*[†] *iti /*

—'[A gloss on:] "for ... a form of a hare's horn." As it has been taught:

"There cannot be the universal without the particular, like a hare's horn. And, likewise, there is no particular destitute of the universal."[†]'

[a] H does not take this as a separate *pratīka* (***tad-virahe*** *viśeṣāṇām abhāve* ***śaśa-viṣāṇa-rūpatvād iti.***).
[b] A clearly: *ṣi.* [c] C: *'pi na câivâsti.*
[†] I have failed to identify the source of the quotation.

[740] Apparently, *sattā* is used here as a synonym to *sāmānya*, which is justified inasmuch as *sattā* is claimed by the Naiyāyika-Vaiśeṣika to be the highest, ultimate universal, common to all entities, see Śaṅkara Miśra's *Upaskāra*, a commentary to VSU_1 1.2.3 (p. 32.14–24): *sāmānyaṁ dvividhaṁ param aparaṁ ca. tatra paraṁ sattā. aparaṁ sattā-vyāpyaṁ dravyatvâdi. tatra sāmānyasya tad-viśeṣasya ca lakṣaṇaṁ buddhir eva. anuvṛtta-buddhiḥ sāmānyasya vyāvṛtta-buddhir viśeṣasya ... param api sāmānyam aparam api tathā. paraṁ tu sāmānyaṁ viśeṣa-saṁjñām api labhate yathā dravyam idaṁ dravyam idam ity-anuvṛtta-pratyaye saty eva nâyaṁ guṇo nêdaṁ karmêti viśeṣa-pratyayaḥ. tathā ca dravyatvâdīnāṁ sāmānyānām eva viśeṣatvam.* Cf. NAV 29: *ayaṁ hi sattā-lakṣaṇaṁ mahā-sāmānyam...* (p. 112 of the English translation) and SVM 28.66–69, p. 161.21–24, as well as NPV, p. 29.7–8: *tatra paraṁ sattā bhāvo mahā-sāmānyam iti côcyate.* See also n.686.

[741] Viz., 'if there were not only separated from other particulars but also...'

[742] Cf. NAṬ 29 *ad loc.*: ***upasarjanîty-ādi***. *upasarjanī-kṛtaṁ gauṇī-kṛtaṁ vaiṣamyaṁ viśeṣa-rūpatā yena tat-tathā.*

[743] Cf. NAṬ 29 *ad loc.*: ***nyak-kṛta-samatvam iti***. *tiras-kṛta-sāmānyam.*

[744] The verb *ucyate* is an insertion into the two-clause statement, each of the two clauses being marked by a separate *iti*: (1) *tad eva saṁvedanam upasarjanī-kṛta-vaiṣamyaṁ pradhānī-kṛtâikâkāraṁ sāmānyaṁ gṛhṇāti iti*, and (2) *nyak-kṛta-samatvam utkalita-nānātvaṁ punar viśeṣa-grahîti*. The reasons that follow (viz., *samatva-nānātvayoḥ kathañcid bhedâbhedinoḥ parasparaṁ sarvârtheṣu bhāvāt, tad-abhāve tathā-vidha-pratibhāsânupapatteḥ*) refer to both clauses of the statement.

[745] Cf. p. 99 of the translation.

[746] The distinction between the universal cow-ness (*gotva*) and particular cows is meant here.

[747] Cf. SVM 14.70–71, p. 87.1–2: *na hi sāmānyena kādacid artha-kriyā kriyate. tasya niṣkriyatvāt. vāha-dohâdikāsv artha-kriyāsu viśeṣāṇām evôpayogāt.*

[748] The universals (e.g. cow-ness or tree-ness), to which particular objects are related respectively, are supposed to be responsible for the distinction between specimen (particular cows or trees) belonging to different classes.

[749] Lit. 'a person instigated in the following manner: "cut the tree!".'

[750] Lit. 'accomplishes cutting with regard to.'

[751] *tatra tasya samavāyād* = **viśeṣeṣu sāmānyasya samavāyād.*

[752] Cf. NAV 29: *sāmānya-vyāptasyêti cet...* (cf. p. 99 of the translation).

[753] I.e., the universal eventually makes up the contents of cognition.

[754] Cf. similar argumentative structure in NAV 5 (p. 40 ff. of the translation): *sa hi vikalpataḥ paryanuyojyaḥ: samavāyibhyaḥ samavāyo 'bhinno bhinno vā ...*

sāmastyenâhosvid eka-deśena?..., as well as in NAV 29 (p. 40 ff. of the translation): *paraspara-vibhakteṣu ... yad dūṣaṇa-jālam upanipatati, tad api ... ekânta-bheda eva ... ekânta-bheda eva tad-upapatteḥ, anekânte tad-utthānâbhāvāt. ... kim eka-deśena yad vā sāmastyena...*

755 Lit., 'because of the impairment of the acceptance of oneness [of the universal].'

756 Viz., the universal would have as many parts as there are particulars.

757 The correct reading of the Ms. A: *te 'bhinnā bhinnā*—as against the version of H & V editions: *te bhinnā abhinnā*—is further corroborated by the analysis of the two alternatives, beginning with the first one *yady abhinnā*.

758 Cf. NAṬ 29 *ad loc.*: ***tad-darśanam** iti. sarva-vyaktīnāṁ pratyakṣatā*[a].

[a] C: *pratyakṣatāṁ*.

759 The sentence presents some difficulty. I take it to be supplemented with *vyavasthita* from the preceding question, and *viśeṣântarebhyas* to mean *cirantana-viśeṣebhyas*. Optionally, however, if we took the reading *na tāvad viśeṣântarebhyas tad utpitsu viśeṣa-deśaṁ gantum arhati*, we might translate: 'This [universal] which is about to arise from other (*sc.* old) universals, to begin with, is not in a position to reach to the location of the particular (*sc.* the new particular).' I.e., the relation of the universal with the particular cannot be established.

760 Viz., the universal can neither perform nor be an object of an action; cf. n. 747 and SVM 14.91–92, p. 87.22–23: *vastuno hi lakṣaṇam artha-kriyā-kāritvam*.

761 *vyakti* = *viśeṣa* = *svalakṣaṇa*; for the synonymy, cf. n. 154.

762 I.e., they could neither constitute the contents of cognition any longer nor be spoken of as belonging the same class as the new particular does, because the universal constitutes the basis of both mental conceptualisation and verbal level.

763 *Vide supra*, the alternative 1.2, p. 110 (*sâvayavatve 'pi punas te 'bhinnā bhinnā vā...*).

764 Cf. NAṬ 29 *ad loc.*: *nūtana-viśeṣa-sambandhâdîty-ādi-śabda-sūcitaṁ dūṣaṇam abhidhātum-kāma āha*: ***anyac côty-ādi.***—'[The author] desirous of stating [explicitly] the criticism indicated by the speech element "etc." of [the phrase] "the relation with the new particular, etc.", says "And [there is still] something else," etc.'

765 I.e., the highest universal, cf. NAV 29 above: *ayaṁ hi sattā-lakṣaṇaṁ mahā-sāmānyam avāntara-sāmānyāni ca* ... (p. 98 of the translation).

766 Cf. n. 600.

767 Cf. NAṬ 29 *ad loc.*: ***itarathêti***. *yadi kathañcid vyatirekiṇāv api sāmānya-viśeṣau na syātām.*—'[The phrase] "in the opposite case" [means]: if the universal and the particular were not different at all whatsoever." As regards the use of *kathañcid ... na*, cf. n. 553 and p. 82.

[768] Cf. NAṬ 29 *ad loc.*: ***tathêti***. *vyatirekeṇa.*—'By way of difference (*sc.* as different).'

[769] NAṬ 29 *ad loc.*: ***tat-kāriṇyā iti.*** *bheda-vidhāyinyā.*—'"Asserting that" [means] "introducing (*sc.* teaching as something unknown) [their] difference".'

[770] NAV 29: *ayaṁ hi manyate*: *bhāva-lakṣaṇa-sāmānyād vyatiricyamāna-mūrtayo vā viśeṣāḥ parikalpyeran, avyatiricyamāna-mūrtayo vā...* (cf. p. 100 ff. of the English translation).

[771] This interesting argument that—in order to refute the thesis maintained by the propounder of the sole existence of the universal—takes recourse to the fact that also the opponent, viz., the propounder of a contrary thesis ('the sole existence of the particulars'), might as well adduce a similar proof in support of his thesis, seems to be based on the idea of *anaikāntika-hetv-ābhāsa* (Cf. NAV 23).

[772] See NAV 29: *vyavahārasyâpy anādy-avidyā-bala-pravartitatvāt, tena pāramārthika-pramāṇa-pratiṣṭhita-tattva-pratibandhâbhāvāt* (p. 100 of the English translation).

[773] Cf. n. 219, and see similar instances on pp. 27 and 90.

[774] Cf., e.g. NAV 29: *pratyakṣaṁ hi tāvad bhāva-sampādita-sattākaṁ tam eva sākṣat-kartuṁ yuktam, nâbhāvaṁ* (p. 100 of the translation).

[775] Cf. NAṬ 29 *ad loc.*: ***yukti-kalāpenêti***. *bhāvâṁśenâiva saṁyogo yogyatvād indriyasya hîty*[a]*-ādinā*[b].

[a] C: *yogyatvād iti yasya hîty-°*.
[b] H,V read on: *°-ādinā vyāpriyate iti bhāvâbhāvâtmakaṁ vastv iti śeṣaḥ*.

[776] As above, if we read *mugdha-vipratārito 'si*. However, if we take the sentence to be *mugdha vipratārito 'si*, we should render it as: 'Fool! You are deceived!'

[777] Cf. n. 177.

[778] Or: 'from forms of other [things].'

[779] Cf. NAṬ 29 *ad loc.*: ***vyāpriyata iti***.[a] *bhāvâbhāvâtmakaṁ vastv iti śeṣaḥ*.

[a] H,V do not take it as a separate *pratīka*, but a continuation of the gloss on *yukti-kalāpenêti*. See n. 775.

[780] Cf. NAṬ 29 *ad loc.*: ***tad-rūpam iti***. *bhāvâbhāvâtmaka-vastu-rūpam*.

[781] Or, if we separate differently, *sva-rūpa-°*: 'by its own form.'

[782] Cf. n. 778.

[783] Cf. NA 27.

[784] Thereby I render *iti* marking the end of the fore-going section, concluding with the phrase: *na kevalaṁ sāmānya-rūpa* *iti*.

785 Cf. n. 778.

786 Cf. n. 231.

787 Cf. NAṬ 29 *ad loc.*: ***anumānataḥ siddhir iti***. *dvy-aṇukâdi-skandho bhedyo, mūrtatve sati sāvayavatvāt, kumbhavat. sāvayavair ākāśâdibhir vyabhicāra-parihārârthaṁ mūrtatve satîti viśeṣaṇam. ye ca dvy-aṇukâdi-bhedād anantaram aṁśāḥ*[a] *samutpadyante 'vayavās te paramāṇavaḥ. athavânyathânumānayāmaḥ—aṇu-parimāṇa-tāratamyaṁ kvacid viśrāntaṁ, parimāṇa-tāratamyatvād, ākāśa-parimāṇa-tāratamyavat. yatra câṇu*[b]*-parimāṇa*[c]*-tāratamyaṁ viśrāntaṁ te*[d] *paramāṇavaḥ.*

[a] H,V: *aṁśā*. [b] H,V omit *ca*: *aṇu-°*.
[c] A: *°-parimāṇu-°*. [d] H,V: *ta eva*.

788 NAṬ 29 *ad loc.*: ***ādya-paryāyasyêti***.*vārtamānikasya*[a].

[a] A: *vārtimānikasya*.

789 *Vide supra* NAV 29: *yad idaṁ kiyat-kāla-bhāvi sthūratām ābibhrāṇaṁ loka-vyavahāra-kāri ghaṭâdikaṁ bhavatas tāttvikam abhipretaṁ tan nâkasmikaṁ ...* (p. 116 of the translation). Cf. NAṬ 29 *ad loc.*: ***tatra côkto doṣa iti***[a].

nityaṁ sattvam asattvaṁ vâhetor anyânapekṣaṇāt /
apekṣāto hi bhāvānāṁ kādācitkatva-sambhavaḥ //[†] *iti.*

[a] H,V do not mark it as *pratīka*: *tatra côkto doṣa iti*. C: *tatra côkto iti*.
[†] The verse comes from PV 3.35 (PV_1, p. 160; PV_3, p. 22.21).

790 Cf. NAV 29: *yad eva loka-vyavahāra-patham avatarati tasyânugrāhakaṁ pramāṇaṁ upalabhyate, nêtarasya*. (Cf. p. 101 of the English translation).

791 Cf. NAV 29: *pūrvôttara-kāla-bhāvi-tat-paryāya-paryalocanā punar ajyāyasī, tatra pramāṇa-prasarâbhāvāt, pramāṇam antareṇa ca vicārasya kartum aśakyatvāt. avastutvāc ca teṣām, kiṁ tad-gocara-paryalocanena? tathā hi: pūrvôttara-kāla-bhāvino dravya-vivartāḥ kṣaṇa-kṣayi-paramâṇu-lakṣaṇā vā viśeṣā na kañcana loka-vyavahāram uparacayanti, tan na te vastu-rūpāḥ, loka-vyavahārôpayogināṁ eva vastutvād ...* (Cf. p. 101 of the English translation).

792 The argument is this: the capacity of being conducive to, or serviceable in, everyday practice cannot be regard as a criterion of existence of an object, because no object can be in use all the time; in the moment when it is not used it would become non-existent.

793 Cf. n. 102.

794 Cf. n. 231.

795 The expression *kuyukti-vikalpa* may also mean: 'the alternatives [based on] defective reasoning,' and it has been used precisely in the latter meaning already twice in NAV 6 (pp. 46, 46 of the translation). Also in the present context, the expression

clearly refers to a previous passage of NAV 29, wherein we do find two alternatives: *pramāṇato 'rtha-vyavasthā, na ca pramāṇaṁ deśa-kāla-vyāpti-grahaṇe kiñcana pravartate, sarva-pramāṇānāṁ vartamāna-prakāśa-rūpatvāt. tathā hi: (1) pratyakṣaṁ tāvad ... (2) nâpy anumānāt sthira-sthūra-vastu-siddhiḥ* ... (p. 102 ff. of the translation). On the other hand, a few lines below, the term *vikalpa* is clearly equated with *parāmarśa* (cf. n. 797 and p. 118 of the translation).

796 Cf. NAV 29: *na ca te 'pi svâṁśa-vyāpinaḥ praibhānti, tad-avayavānām apîtarêtaraviśakalita-rūpāṇāṁ pratibhāsatā tāvat yāvat paramâṇava eva prathante, vyāpi-rūpasya vicārâkṣamatvād ity ukta-prāyam.* (Cf. p. 103 of the English translation).

797 In the above passage the terms *vikalpa* and *parāmarśa* are clearly used as synonyms to denote a mental process of reasoning.

798 Cf. n. 795.

799 Apparently, we have here a pun on *uttara*, meaning either 'reply' or 'subsequent' (= *pāścātya*), and *viplava*.

800 Cf. NAV 29: *atītasya vinaṣṭatvāt anāgatasyâlabdhâtma-lābhatvāt khara-viṣāṇâdibhyo 'viśiṣyamāṇatayā sakala-śakti-viraha-rūpatvān nârtha-kriyā-nirvartana-kṣamatvam, artha-kriyā kṣamaṁ ca vastu, tad abhāvān na tayor vastutvam iti. vartamāna-kṣaṇâliṅgitaṁ ca punar samastârtha-kriyāsu vyāpriyata iti tad eva pāramārthikam*. (Cf. p. 102 of the English translation).

801 Cf. NAV 0: *kṣaṇa-naśvaro 'rthaḥ sva-kṣaṇe pūrvaṁ paścād vā kāryaṁ kuryād iti trayī gatiḥ. tatra na tāvad ādyaḥ pakṣaḥ kakṣī-karaṇīyaḥ, sama-kāla-bhāvini vyāpārâbhāvāt, itarathâika-kṣaṇa-vartiṇāṁ samastârtha-kṣaṇānām itarêtaraṁ kārya-kāraṇa-bhāvaḥ prasajyeta, tathā ca tat-prayukto grāhya-grāhaka-bhāvaś cêty asamañjasam āpanīpadyeta. atha sva-kṣaṇāt pūrvam—acārv etad api, svayam asato bhaviṣyac chaṅkha-cakravarty-āder iva pūrva-kāla-vartini kārye vyāpārâbhāvāt. atha sva-kṣaṇād ūrdhvaṁ—kāryaṁ vidhatta iti manyethāḥ; etad apy asādhīyaḥ, vinaṣṭasya kārya-karaṇâkṣamatvāt, anyathā mṛtasya śikhinaḥ kekāyitaṁ syāt.* (Cf. p. 2 of the English translation).

802 The two above reasons in the ablative case, viz., *abhedasya dravyatvāt* and *bhedasya paryāya-rūpatvāt*, explicate the expression *anuvārtamāna-vyāvartamana-rūpa* a few lines before.

803 Cf. NAV 2, p.27. Cf. NAṬ *ad loc.*: ***na cârtha-kriyā vastu***[a]***-lakṣaṇam*** *iti. yad āha rāgândhâvasthāyām api* *dharmakīrtiḥ*:

gacchatu kvâpi te svântaḥ kānte[b] *kāryaṁ tvayâiva me*[c] */*
yad evârtha-kriyā-kāri tad eva paramârtha-sat // † *iti /*

[a] H: °*-kriyā-vastu-*°. [b] A: *svākānte*; C: *svāntaṁ kānte*.
[c] C: *kāryatvayâiva me*; H,V: *kāryaṁ tvayâiva ca*.

[†] I have failed to identify the source of the verse ascribed to Dharmakīrti. Vaidya (the editor of V., p. 103) believes the verse is taken from Dharmakīrti's *Pramāṇa-viniścaya*. However, it occurs neither in PVin I, PVin II, PV, VāN, nor in NB. In PVin II_1 we find a similar verse 56 (p. 78–79):

don byed nus pa gaṅ yin pa |
| de [c]dir [c]don dam yod pa yin |
| de la rim daṅ rim ma yin |
| [c]gal phyir skad cig ma yin med ||

which Steinkellner believes is:

artha-kriyā-samarthaṁ yat[a] *tad atra paramârtha-sat |*
asanto 'kṣaṇikās tasmāt kramâkrama-virodhataḥ ||

[a] In his note 1 (p. 79), however, he gives a *varia lectio* taken from NBhūṣ:[1] *yad evârtha-kriyā-kāri*. Thus the *pādas* cd of our verse (*yad evârtha-kriyā-kāri tad eva paramârtha-sat*) and the *pādas* ab of NBhūṣ are identical (barring *eva* for *atra*). Problematic are, nonetheless, the *pādas* ab: *gacchatu kvâpi te svāntāḥ kānte kāryaṁ tvayâiva me* /, for they are not, as one might expect, the *pādas* cd of the preceding verse 55 (p. 74/75), which reads:

des na [c]bras gnas med pa[c]i phyir |
| [c]jig pa rgyu ldan smra rnams kyi |
| [c]jig pa[c]i rgyu ni thams cad dag |
| [c]khrul pa ñid du bśad pa yin ||

which Steinkellner reconstructs as follows:

etena vyabhicāritvam uktaṁ kāryâvyavasthiteḥ |
sarveṣāṁ nāśa-hetūnāṁ hetuman-nāśa-vādināṁ ||

[804] Cf. NAV 27: *iha yad yad asti tat sarvaṁ sthity-udayâpavarga-saṁsargam anubhavati, vastutvāt* (p. 81 of the English translation), and n.548.

[805] Cf. NAV 29: *iha yady atra pratibhāsati, tad eva tad-gocaratayâbhyupagantavyam. tad yathā—nirādīnava-nayana-prabhava-darśane pratibhāsamānaṁ pāṭalatayā japā-kusumaṁ tathâiva tad-gocaratayâbhyupagamyate, parasparâvibhaktâneka-svabhāvâkrānta-mūrtikaṁ ca bahir antaś ca vastu sarva-pramāṇeṣu prathata iti, atas tad eva teṣāṁ gocaraḥ.* (p. 88 of the English translation).

[806] Cf. NAV 29: *pramāṇato 'rtha-vyavasthā, na ca pramāṇaṁ deśa-kāla-vyāpti-grahaṇe kiñcana pravartate, sarva-pramāṇānāṁ vartamāna-prakāśa-rūpatvāt* (p. 102 of the translation).

[807] Cf. NAV 29: *yadi punar vinaṣṭam api pūrva-kṣaṇa-varti-rūpam ākalayet, tadā vinaṣṭatvâviśeṣān niravadhiḥ kṣaṇa-paramparā tatra pratīyeta, tathā ca sati saṅkalikayânādi-janma-paramparā-grāhi pratyakṣam anuṣajyeta* (p. 102 of the translation).

[808] Cf. NAV 29: *sākṣāt-kurvāṇā api kṣaṇa-vinaśvaratāṁ sadṛśâparâparôtpatti-vipralabdha-buddhayo mandā nâdhyavasyanti, anādi-kāla-prarūḍha-vāsanā-prabodha-samupajanita-mithyā-vikalpa-sāmarthyāc ca viparyasta-sthiratā-vyavahāraṁ pravartayanti* ... (cf. p. 103 of the English translation).

[809] Cf. NAV 0: *na ca sādṛśyaṁ bhavatāṁ darśane tāttvikam asti, vivikta-kṣaṇa-kṣayi-paramâṇu-lakṣaṇa-svalakṣaṇānāṁ pāramārthikatvâbhyupagamāt.* (cf. p. 3 of the English translation).

[810] Cf. NAṬ 29 *ad loc.*: ***sarvathêti***. *evaṁ vadann idam āha*[a]: *kathañcic chabdād avyatireko 'rthasyâbhyupagamyata eva*[b] *jainaiḥ. ayaṁ cârthaḥ: 'abhihāṇaṁ abhiheyāü hoï bhinnaṁ abhinnaṁ ca' ity-ādinā prāg darśita evêti.*—'[A gloss on the phrase:] 'complete[ly],' etc. [The author]—expressing himself in this manner—says the following: the Jainas themselves accept that an object is somehow non-different from the speech element. This meaning was in fact exposed long ago by [the maxim]: "denoter is [both] different and not different from the denotatum", etc.'

[a] C: *vadann im āha.* [b] C: *'rthasyâbhyupagamyata / evaṁ.*

[811] Cf. the (fallacious) proof formula in NAV 29: *na vyatirikto 'rthaḥ śabdāt, tat-pratītau tasya pratīyamānatvād, iha yat-pratītau yat pratīyate tat tato 'vyatiriktaṁ bhavati, tad yathā—śabde pratīyamāne tasyâiva svarūpaṁ, pratīyate ca śabde pratīyamāne 'rtho, 'to 'sau tato 'vyatirikta iti* (p.104 of the translation).

[812] Cf. n. 712.

[813] The logical reason occurs above in the proof formula: *na vyatirikto 'rthaḥ śabdāt, tat-pratītau tasya pratīyamānatvād, iha yat-pratītau yat pratīyate tat tato 'vyatiriktaṁ bhavati...* (p.104 of the English translation). Cf. NAṬ 29 *ad loc.*: ***asmiṁś ca hetāv iti***. *śabda-pratītāv arthasya pratīyamānatvād ity evaṁ-rūpe.*—'[The phrase] "And when this logical reason," etc., [means] when it has the form: "because the object (denotatum) is cognised, when the speech element is cognised".'

[814] *Vide supra* NAV 29: *sarve 'rthā vidyamāna-sva-vācakā, 'rthatvād, ghaṭârthavad iti* (p.105 of the translation).

[815] Cf. NAṬ 29 *ad loc.*: ***alakṣya-dravya-vivartānām iti***. *bālānām apy atipratītatvād*[a] *alakṣyêty*[b] *uktaṁ. yāvatā sphuṭam anubhūyamānā api kecana vastūnāṁ paryāyā anabhilāpyā eva. yad uktam:*

ikṣu-kṣīra-guḍâdīnāṁ mādhur yasyântaraṁ mahat /
tathâpi na tad ākhyātuṁ sarasvatyâpi[c] *śakyate //*[†]

siddhânta-rahasyaṁ câtra:

pannavaṇijjā bhāvā aṇanta-bhāgo u aṇabhilappāṇaṁ[d] */*
pannavaṇijjāṇaṁ puṇa aṇanta-bhāgo[e] *suyanibaddho //*[‡]

—'[Now we comment on the phrase]: "momentary or non-characterisable transient occurrences of a substance." It has been said [of substance] "indescribable" because it is too well known even to children, inasmuch as some modes of real things, although they are patently experienced, are in no way expressible, as it has been [once] said:

"The difference in sweetness between sugar cane, *khir* (sweet milk dish), molasses, etc., is enormous; and yet it cannot be verbalised even by Sarasvatī."

Regarding this, in the *Compendium of the Canon* [it was said]:

"On the one hand, communicable entities [form but] an infinite fraction of inexpressible [things]; on the other, [just] an infinite fraction of the communicable [things] have been composed [and included in] the scriptures".'

[a] C: *abhipratītatvād*. [b] H,V: *alakṣye ity*. [c] C: *ākhyātusvatyâpi*.
[d] C: *aṇabhilappaṇaṁ*. [e] H: *bhāgo ya*.
[†] I have failed to identify the source of the quotation.
[‡] It is the quote of VABh 141.

[816] Cf. p. 117 ff.

[817] As regards the case when the phrase *yad uta* is—in a redundant manner, as it were—followed with *iti*, see above in NAV 29: *tathā hi*: *bhinnāḥ khalu saṁyogâdayaḥ saṁyogy-ādibhyo vikalpayituṁ pāryante—yad uta katham ete eteṣu vartanta iti? kim eka-deśena yad vā sāmastyena?* (p. 86 of the English translation).

[818] Cf. NAṬ 29 *ad loc.*: ***deśa-kālêti***. *deśa-kāla-puruṣeṣu saṅketa ādir yeṣāṁ prastāvâdīnāṁ te tathā. teṣāṁ vicitratā, tayā. tathā hi*: *karkaṭī-śabdo mālavakâdau phala-viśeṣe rūḍho, gurjarâdau tu yonyām iti. evaṁ kālâdāv api draṣṭavyam.*—'[The meaning of the phrase] "place, time, [etc.]," is as follows: because such [convention]s of speaking—the origin of which [lies in] the linguistic convention [depending on] place, time and people—are manifold. For instance the word *karkaṭī* has grown (*sc.* is traditionally used) in [the meaning of] a particular fruit in Malwa and other [regions], whereas in Gujarat and other [districts it is used] in [the sense of] vagina. In the same manner also [manifoldness depending on different] time, etc., can be demonstrated.'

[819] For the synonyms cf. NAṬ *ad loc.*: ***avigānenêti***. *vigānaṁ vacanīyatā vipratipattir iti yāvat*.

[820] Cf. NAṬ 29 *ad loc.*: ***tad-aniṣṭāv iti***. *tasya śabdānāṁ aparâparârthâbhidhāyakatvasya*, *arthānāṁ tv aparâpara-śabdâbhidheyatvasya.*—'[The phrase] "if these [facts] were not accepted" [has the following meaning]: this fact that [1] speech elements denote various objects, whereas [2] objects can be denoted by various speech elements.'

[821] Cf. NAṬ 29 *ad loc.*: *sarvaṁ vākyaṁ sâvadhāraṇaṁ iti-nyāyāt*; as well as NAV 1: *sarvaṁ vākyaṁ sâvadhāraṇaṁ pravartate* (p. 17 of the English translation) and NAṬ 29 *sarvaṁ vacanaṁ sâvadhāraṇaṁ* (p. 123 of the English translation).

[822] Cf. n. 821.

[823] The negated term *sambhava* as well as the verb *sam√bhū* seem to be used in this section in a qualified sense of 'existence' or 'exist', which I render by augmenting

them with the qualifiers 'possible' or 'possibly.' A property the presence of which in the property-possessor is either admitted or rejected is predicated of in a qualified manner, viz., as something which is both possible and existent among a set of other allowable properties. Thus, in this meaning, *sambhava* is reminiscent here of its another connotation, viz., equivalence, an additional cognitive criterion (*pramāṇa*). In other words, apart from the aspect of a possible existence of a property or of an object in particular circumstances, which is taken for granted, *sambhava* connotes the inclusion of the property or the object into a collection of other possible properties or objects as well.

[824] NAṬ 29 *ad loc.* mentions a *varia lectio*: ***aprayogād iti***[a] *tu pāṭhe kim ity-avadhāraṇam.* ***śeṣa-puruṣântarāṇi*** *para-rūpeṇa*[b] *nāstitvaṁ ca na vyavacchinatti*[c] *ity-āha* ***tad iti***. *teṣāṁ śeṣa-puruṣântarāṇāṁ para-rūpeṇa nāstitvasya ca*[d] *vyavacchedâbhiprāyeṇa prastuta-vākyânabhidhānāt.*

[a] This *pratīka* is preceded by the *pratīka* quoted by me below in n. 825.
[b] C: *para-rūpeṇa ca.* [c] C: *vyavachinati.* [d] H,V omits *ca.*

[825] Cf. NAṬ 29 *ad loc.*: ***tad-vyavacchedâbhiprāyeṇêti.***[a] *tasya devadattâder asambhava-mātrasya vyavacchedâbhiprāyeṇa, devadatto 'stîti vākyasyôccāraṇāt.*

[a] This *pratīka* precedes by the *pratīka* quoted by me above in n. 824.

[826] Cf. NAṬ 29 *ad loc.*: ***prayoktr-abhiprāyâdîti***. *ādi-śabdāt saṅketâdi*[a]*-grahaḥ.*—'... On account of the word 'etc.' the linguistic convention, etc., are included.'

[a] A: °*-śabdāc chaṅketâd-*°.

[827] See n. 823.

[828] See LT 62 and LTV ad loc. (*Pravacana-praveśa*), pp. 686.2–688.2:

upayogau śrutasya dvau syād-vāda-naya-saṁjñitau /
syād-vādaḥ sakalâdeśo nayo vikala-saṁkathā //

[*Vivṛtiḥ*] *anekântâtmakârtha-kathanaṁ syād-vādaḥ, yathā pudgalaḥ dharmo 'dharmaḥ ākāśaṁ kāla iti. tatra jīvo jñāna-darśana-vīrya-sukhaiḥ asādhāraṇaiḥ amūrtatvâsaṁkhyāta-pradeśatva-sūkṣmatvaiḥ sādhāraṇâsādhāraṇaiḥ sattva-prameyatvâgurulaghutva-dharmitva-guṇitvâdibhiḥ sādhāraṇaiḥ anekântaḥ. tasya jīvasyâdeśāt pramāṇaṁ syād-vādaḥ. tathā itare paramâgamato yojyāḥ. jño jīvaḥ sukha-duḥkhâdi-vedanād ity-ādi vikalâdeśo nayaḥ. sākalyam ananta-dharmâtmakatā. vaikalyam ekântaḥ dharmântarâvivakṣātaḥ. tatra jīva ity ukte jīva-śabdo yogyatâpekṣo 'nādi-saṅketaḥ svabhāva-bhūtânyâpoha-svârtha-pratipādanaḥ nyakṣeṇa pratipakṣaṁ nirasya jīva-mātram eva abhidadhyāt tataḥ syāt-pada-prayogāt sarvathâikânta-tyāgāt svarūpâdi-catuṣṭaya-viśeṣaṇa-viśiṣṭo jīvaḥ abhidhīyata iti svêṣṭa-siddhiḥ. nayo 'pi tathâiva samyag-ekântaḥ. "syāj jīva eva" ity ukte 'nekânta-viṣayaḥ syāc-chabdaḥ, "syād asty eva jīvaḥ" ity ukte ekânta-viṣayaḥ syāc-chabdaḥ.*—'[Verse] Testimony [rests on] two procedures[a] technically called the [method of the seven-fold] modal description and technically called the viewpoint.

The [method of the seven-fold] modal description is the complete account, [whereas] the viewpoint is the incomplete account. [Commentary:] The [method of the seven-fold] modal description is the predicating of (viz. describing) an object the nature of which is multiplex; for example the living element, the matter, the principle of motion, the principle of rest, space and time. Among them, the living element is multiplex (1) with [its] specific (*sc.* not common to all) properties [such as] cognition, belief, the potential and happiness, (2) with [its] both non-specific and specific [properties] such as non-material character (*sc.* being not amenable to senses), being composed of uncountable space units, subtlety, [and] (3) with [its] both non-specific [properties such as] being existent (or: existence), being cognisable, having the equal status[b], being property-possessor and being quality-possessor. Because of the account of this living element[c] the [method of the seven-fold] modal description is a cognitive criterion. In the same manner other [substances enumerated above such as the matter, the principle of motion, etc.] can be [described (predicated of)] from the standpoint of the ultimate[ly true (reliable)] scriptures. "The living element is the knower, because of sensation (viz. experience) of happiness, unhappiness etc."[d]—this and similar ones is (are) the incomplete account. Completeness [means] having the nature endowed with infinite properties. Incompleteness [means] one aspect, because there is no intention of other properties (*sc.* because other properties are not intended). In this case when "the living element" is uttered, the speech element "living being"—[which is governed by] the beginningless linguistic convention dependent on [its] capacity [to denote], [and which generally] denotes its object by the exclusion of that which is different from what is its essential nature[e]—might denote, having completely rejected the "counter-object" (viz. everything different from), only the essence of the living being. Therefore [the speech element "the living being"] denotes—thanks to the pronouncement of the word "somehow", which completely discards one-sided (i.e. simplistic) [perspective] (lit. discards one aspect)—the living being as qualified by the four qualifiers such as its intrinsic nature, etc.[f] In this way what is accepted by [the propounder] himself is proved. The viewpoint, in its turn, is precisely in the same manner correctly one-sided (simplistic). If one says: "somehow [this is] indeed the living element," the speech element has a multiplex province; If one says: "somehow the living element indeed exists," the speech element has a one-sided (simplistic) province.'

[a] This is a direct reference to the two cognitive faculties of the living element (see TS 2.8). Just the way the living element has two modes of operating (*vyāpāra*; on the ontological level), also its cognitive faculties (i.e. on the epistemological level) have two modes of operating (*vyāpāra*). See also NKC *ad loc.*:, *upayoga* = *vyāpāra*.

[b] Lit. 'being light or weightless'. The term occurs several times in TS and other Jaina texts. A useful explanation of the term can be found, e.g. in SUKHLAL (1974: 196 ff.).

[c] I.e., 'Because it describes the living element as being of this kind', viz. as being multiplex (*tasya* = *evaṁ-vidhasya* = *anekāntasya*), the character that has just been referred to.

[d] What is conspicuous in the description of *naya* method is its form of the thesis and the logical reason! This may show the real scope of the applicability of this method, i.e. it may have been supposed to comprise one perspective in an *argumentative* context, whereas *syād-vāda* was supposed to be applied in 'one's own context,' or in reference to one's own scriptures (see above *paramâgamatas*). Therefore, these two methods had perhaps different pertinence. The *syād-vāda* exposition above refers to *jīva* step by step taking the scriptural, viz. the *outside-of-debate* standpoint.

[e] The editors should place a *daṇḍa*, or full-stop, either here (viz. after °-*pratipādanaḥ*) or before *tataḥ*.

[f] *svarūpâdi* is explained in NKC *ad loc.* as *sva-dravya-kṣetrâdi*, and what is meant are not the four standpoints (*nikṣepa*, *nyāsa*). What is really meant are *dravya-kṣetra-kāla-bhāva* (cf. SVM 23.113, p. 143.12).

829 See NA 31.

830 This is the first out of seven admitted propositions, preceded by modal functor *syād*, that furnish the structure of the theory of the seven-fold modal description.

831 I have failed to identify the source of the quotation.

832 The *syād-vāda-śruta* (of NA 30d) is meant here (*vide infra*; cf. n. 835).

833 Or 'property' (*dharma*); cf. NAV *ad loc.*: *eka niṣṭhānām eka dharma grahaṇa paryavasitānāṁ*. However, *eka-niṣṭha* may as well be supplemented by °-*deśa*-° (facet), cf. NAṬ 30: *nayasya punar eka-deśa-niṣṭhatvena* (p. 97 of the English translation).

834 Cf. NAṬ 30 *ad loc.*: ***paḍuppaṇṇêti.*** *sāmpratam*[a] *utpannaṁ pratyutpannas tat-kālôtpanna*[b] *ity arthaḥ. nirayo durgatis tatra bhavo nairayiko nārakikaḥ sa naśyati. atha kathaṁ tat-kṣaṇôtpannasya tasya vināśo nārakikāṇāṁ*[c] *jaghanyato 'pi daśa-varṣa-sahasra-sthāyitvasyâgame 'bhidhānād? ity āha* ***ṛjusūtrêty-ādi.*** *ayam abhiprāyāḥ: yāvanto nayās tāvat-samudāya-rūpo 'rhad-āgamaḥ, "savva-naya-mayaṁ jina-mayam"*[d] *iti vacanāt. yato yathā yat samaya-viśiṣṭaḥ*[e] *sampūrṇa*[f]*-sva-sthiti-dharmā ca prathama-samaye nairayika āsīt, na tathā dvitīya-samaye iti ṛjusūtrâbhiprāyeṇa spaṣṭâiva kṣaṇikatêti.*—'[A gloss on the phrase]: "originated at [a given] moment." 'Arisen presently', i.e. 'originated at [a given] moment', [which means] 'arisen at a given [point of] time.' Hell [means] the doom; [the one] living there [is] hellish being, [viz.,] infernal being; he/she expires. If [one wonders:] "How is the extinction of this [hellish being], who has arisen in this very moment [possible], whereas hellish beings have been explicitly stated in the Scriptures to live at least ten thousand years?", [the author] says: "[according to] the direct [viewpoint]". This is [his] intention: the oral tradition of the venerable ones is constituted by as extensive aggregate as there are viewpoints, on account of the utterance: "The teaching of the Jinas is composed of all viewpoints."[d] Thereby, just as a hellish being was [characterised by (*sc.* born in)] a particular instant and [was] a bearer of his/her own complete continued existence in the first instant, similarly [he/she is] not [such any more] in the second

instant—in the same manner [his/her] momentariness is under any circumstances undeniable following (according to) the outlook of direct viewpoint.'

[a] C: ***pannati*** *sāmpratam*...; A: ***paḍuppannîti*** *sāmpratam*...; H,V: ***paḍuppaṇṇêti*** *sāmpratam*...

[b] C: *utpannam. pratyutpannas tat-kālôtpanna*; A,H,V: *utpannas tat-kālôtpanna.*

[c] A,C: *nārayikāṇāṁ.*

[d] I have failed to identify the quotation. Cf. STP 3.69 (n. 661 above).

[e] C: °*-viśaṣṭaḥ.* [f] A: *sampūrṇi-*°.

[835] The word *punaḥ* apparently marks here the opposition between testimony based on the doctrine of seven-fold modal description (*syād-vāda-śruta*) describing a particular thing as a whole and testimony based on a particular viewpoint (*naya-śruta*) that pertains only to a selected facet of a predicated object.

[836] Cf. n. 231.

[837] In the epistemological context of NA, there can hardly be any doubt that the subject of the aphorism is *pramātṛ*, and the remaining substantives are a series of predicates. Siddhasena describes cognitive processes step by step to culminate in stating and defining the subject of cognitive processes. Additionally, Siddharṣi-gaṇin plainly indicates the subject of the aphorism: *pramātāram abhidhātu-kāma āha.* If the subject were *jīva*, we would read: **jīvam abhidhātu-kāma āha*. The subject is evident, e.g. from the conclusion: *tathā sati jīvo 'pi ... pramātêti*, which cannot but mean 'the cogniser ... is likewise the living element', not 'also the living element is ... ... is the cogniser.' The latter interpretation could suggest that apart from the living element, there are other entities that are cognisers. Furthermore, Siddharṣi-gaṇin, while refuting his opponents (e.g. Nyāya-Vaiśeṣika), speaks of *pramātṛ*, not of *jīva*: ***vivṛttimān*** *ity-amunā tv ekânta-nityam apariṇāminaṁ naiyāyika-vaiśeṣikâdi-prakalpitaṁ pramātāraṁ nirasyati.* In the Jaina-Buddhist debate below (*tatra jīvaḥ pramātêty-anena ye pāramārthikaṁ pramātāraṁ nâbhyupagacchanty*...), the issue is primarily the existence of an ultimately real cogniser, i.e. a real substratum of cognitive processes, not a soul as a separate substance being the subject of transmigration, even though the notion of *pramātṛ* and *jīva* may coincide. To take *jīva*, however, to be the subject (cf. VIDYĀBHŪṢAṆA (1909: 26): 'The spirit (soul or *jīva*) is the knower...') could be justified by the fact that Siddharṣi-gaṇin commences his gloss with *jīva*: *tatra tri-kāla-jīvanāj* ***jīvaḥ****, prāṇa-dhāraka ātmêty arthaḥ, sa pramiṇotîti* ***pramātā*** *prameya-paricchedakaḥ.* In addition, the closing section of NAV 31 likewise suggests that the subject is taken by Siddharṣi-gaṇin to be *jīva*: *sva-para-prakāśakaḥ ... jīvaḥ sakala-naya-pramāṇa-vyāpakaḥ pramātêti sthitam* (p. 136 of the English translation). Perhaps, this shift of the subject was intended to synthesise the epistemological and soteriological aspect as well as to account for the clearly salvific bent of the closing stanza of NAV: *nityaṁ parârtha-karaṇôdyatam ā bhavântād* ....

[838] Comp. the idea of self-revealing cognition (*sva-saṁvedana*, *sva-saṁvitti*) in Buddhism, n. 280.

[839] See p. 117 ff.

[840] Cf. n. 675.

[841] Cf. NAṬ 31 *ad loc.*: ***kalpa-sthāyîti***. *'yugaṁ dvā-daśa-sāhasraṁ kalpam viddhi catur yugam' iti laukikāḥ kalpam āhuḥ.*—'This is [how] common people explain [one aeon]: "One epoch [equals] 12000 [years]. Know that one aeon [equals] four epochs".'

[842] In other words, the examined object proves to be incapable of preserving the continuity of its existence, which fact eventually point's to its momentary character, cf. NAV 23: *atādavasthyasyânitya-lakṣaṇatvāt* (p.69 of the translation).

[843] Cf. NAṬ 31 *ad loc.*: ***atrêti***. *bhāva-vināśayoḥ.*

[844] In other words, there can be no relation of causality between the entity to be destroyed and its destruction, that is, in fact, brought about by another cause (not by the entity in question). Cf. NAṬ 31 *ad loc.*: ***anyêty-ādi***. *mudgara-hetukasya vināśyôttara-kāla-bhāvino vināśasya ghaṭâder vināśyād*[a] *utpatty-abhāvāt.*—'Because the extinction effected by a cause like a hammer, occurring in the [point of] time posterior to the existence of the object] to be destroyed, does not [acquire its] origination from [the object] to be destroyed like a pot, etc.'

[a] H,V: *vināśyad.*

[845] Cf. Dharmottara's PVinṬ$_1$ 289ab and later quoted in *Dravyâlaṅkāra-svopajña-ṭīkā* p. 77–78, see: JAMBŪVIJAYA (1981: 135.21–136.4 and Tibetan: 145.17–26): *dharmottaras tv āha*: "*kiṁ tasya sato bhāvasya nivṛtti-dharmā svabhāvaḥ sva-hetubhyo niṣpanna āhosvid anivṛtti-dharmā. yadi pūrvaḥ pakṣaḥ, nivṛtti-dharmatayā svayam eva nivarteta. na ca vināśa-hetu-sāpekṣa-nivṛttika eva hetubhir janita iti vaktuṁ yuktam. tathā hi*: *yāvad vināśa-hetu-sannidhi-kālaḥ tāvat sthiti-dharmā bhāvaḥ, asthiti-dharmatve prāg eva nivṛtti-prasaṅgāt. vināśa-hetu-sannidhi-kāle ca sa eva kiyat-kālâvasthāyī svabhāvo yaḥ prathame kṣaṇe āsīt, tato nâiva nivarteta kiyat-kālâvasthāyitvāt. tasmān na vināśa-hetu-sāpekṣa-nivṛttikaḥ kaścid bhāvo hetubhir janyate. athânivṛtti-dharmā tasya svabhāvaḥ, tarhi vināśa-hetubhir api na nivartayituṁ śakyate*" *iti.*

[846] See PSā 2.50–51:

uppādo paddhaṁso vijjadi jadi jassa eka-samayamhi /
samayassa so vi samaö sabhāva-samavaṭṭhido havai //
egamhi saṁti samaye saṁbhava-ṭhidi-ṇāsa-saṇṇidā aṭṭhā /
samayassa savva-kālaṁ esa hi kālâṇu-sabbhāvo // —

—'[50] If an instant has (*sc.* undergoes) origination and annihilation in one instant, even then it remains firmly established in its essential nature as an instant. [51] All the time in one instant, an instant has (*sc.* functions in) circumstances, technically called production, continued existence and extinction, for this is the real existence of the unit of time.'

From Amṛtacandra (TDī *ad* PSā 2.50, p. 183.3 ff.) we learn that origination and annihilation occur neither absolutely simultaneously nor absolutely consecutively in one instant: [*utpāda-pradhvaṁsau*] *tau yadi vṛtty-aṁśasyâiva kiṁ yaugapadyena kiṁ krameṇa? yaugapadyena cet nâsti yaugapadyaṁ ... krameṇa cet nâsti kramaṁ ...* [*vṛttimān*] *sa ca samaya-padârtha eva. tasya khalv ekasminn api vṛtty-aṁśe samutpāda-pradhvaṁsau sambhavataḥ*. However, Amṛtacandra does not offer any precise explanation in what other way they could occur, if neither simultaneously nor consecutively. He points out, however, that to accept that destruction takes places incessantly in all instants, without acceptance of origination and continued existence at the same time, amount to momentariness, see TDī *ad* PSā 2.52, p. 186.7–8: *evaṁ sati naśyati traikalyaṁ, ullasati kṣaṇabhaṅguraḥ ...*

[847] I take *tad-*° to refer to *asthiti-*° from the preceding.

[848] Cf. NAṬ 31 *ad loc.*: ***nanu cêty-ādi***. *pūrvaṁ hi bauddhena vināśasya nirhetukatve 'bhihite parôpanyasta-yukti*[a]*-kalāpenâiva mat-pakṣaḥ setsyatîti manyamānenâcāryeṇôtpāda-sthitī api nirhetuke pratyapādiṣātām. taṭasthaḥ*[b] *punaḥ sarvatrâpi sahetukatvaṁ paśyann evaṁ pūrva-pakṣayati. samādhānâbhiprāyas*[c] *tu sakalam api tri-lokī-gataṁ mṛd-ādi*[d]*-dravyam ātmanâiva pratikṣaṇam udaya-vyaya-dhrauvyâtmakaṁ, kulāla-laguḍâdayas*[e] *tu ghaṭa-ghaṭī-kapālâdi-viśeṣa-karaṇa eva vyāpriyanta iti.*—'[Gloss on the passage:] "And now...". "When [the opinion] expressed previously by the Buddhist that extinction is without a cause [is] brought forward by the opponent, my thesis will be established purely by the totality of logical reasoning (*sc.* argumentation)," maintaining the above [opinion], the preceptor (*sc.* Siddharṣi) has likewise taught origination and continued existence to be without a cause. An impartial witness, however—seeing that [origination, annihilation and continued existence] have [their] causes in all cases—states the *prima facie* position as follows. But the intention of defending from (*sc.* counter) a possible objection is this: in every moment all substances, without exception, like clay, etc., accommodated in the three worlds, consist by their very nature in rise, annihilation [and] permanence, whereas potter, club and [other causes of origination, annihilation and continued existence] are engaged in nothing but effecting particular larger and smaller pots (*sc.* origination), [particular] potsherd (*sc.* annihilation), etc.'

[a] H, V: °*-parôpanyaste yukti-*°. [b] A,C: *taṭastha*.
[c] C: *samādhānâbhiprāyās*. [d] C: *mṛgâdi-*°. [e] C: *kulāla-guḍâdayas*.

[849] Viz., as experiencing either the existence of the presence (*sc.* emergence) of causes of extinction or the non-existence of the non-presence (*sc.* absence) of causes of extinction.

[850] Cf. n. 823.

[851] The passage should be read as two parallel arguments referring respectively to [1] logical congruity (*yukti*), based on the inferred material, and [2] cognition (*pratīti*), based on the perceived data, viz., [Ad 1] *tenâiva sârddhaṁ teṣām anvaya-vyatirekânukaraṇa-darśanād ... pratīti-vikalāṁ yuktiṁ ... 'sambhavad-artha-*

gocaratayā and [Ad 2] *dṛṣṭasya câpahnave 'smākam apravṛttatvāt ... yukti-vinākṛtāṁ vā pratītiṁ ... nirālambanatvāt tasyā.*

[852] Cf. n. 102.

[853] See NA 1.

[854] I.e., in the commentary on the phrase *sva-parâbhāsin* in NA 1, p. 10 ff. of the English translation.

[855] Cf. NAV 27: *sāmastya-śuddhaś câtmā jñāna-jñāninoḥ kathañcid abhedāt kevalam abhidhīyta iti.* (p. 82 of the English translation).

[856] I.e., the notion of the experiencing subject presupposes the idea of an agent who executes the action of experiencing of any sort of phenomena.

[857] Cf. NAṬ *ad loc.*: ***akartur apîti****. yad āhuḥ sāṁkhyāḥ: prakṛtiḥ karoti, puruṣa upabhuṅkta*[†] *iti.*

[†] I have failed to identify the source of the quotation.

[858] I have failed to identify the source of the quotation.

[859] Cf. also the quotations in NAṬ *ad loc.*: ***prakṛti-vikārêty-ādi***[a]. *sattva-rajas-tamasāṁ sāmyāvasthā prakṛtis, tasyā vikāro*[b] *vaisamyaṁ; sa câsau nirmalatvena pratibimbôtpatti-yogyatvād darpaṇâkārā câsau buddhiś ca tatra pratibimbitānāṁ sukha-duḥkhâdi-rūpāṇām arthānām ātmā prakṛti-sannidhānād*[c] *bhoktâbhidhīyate. ayam abhiprāyaḥ: arthās tāvat prakṛty-ātmake buddhi-darpaṇe pūrvaṁ pratibimbyante, prakṛty-abhinna-svabhāvârthapratibimbavati*[d] *buddhir, ātmanîty eṣa pratibimba-lakṣaṇo bhogaḥ. vada-mahârṇavo 'py asmin darśane sthitaḥ prāha: "buddhi-darpaṇa-saṅkrānta-samartha-pratibimbakaṁ*[e] *dvitīya-darpaṇa-kalpe puṁsy adhyārohati, tad eva*[f] *bhoktṛtvam asya, na tu vikārâpattir"*[g] *iti. tathā câhur āsuri-prabhṛtayaḥ:*

viviktêdṛk-pariṇatau[h] *buddhau bhogo 'sya kathyate /*
pratibimbôdayaḥ svacche yathā candra-maso 'mbhasi //[i]

asyârthaḥ: viviktā spaṣṭā īdṛg viṣayâkāra-pariṇatêndriyâkārā pariṇatir yasyā buddheḥ sā tathā, tasyāṁ satyām asyâtmano bhogaḥ kathyate. kiṁ-svarūpaḥ? pratibimbôdayo, na vāstavaḥ, pratibimba-mātre dṛṣṭântam āha: yathā candra-maso nirmale jale pratibimbanam, evaṁ viśiṣṭâkāra-pariṇatāyā[j] *buddher ātmanîti. vibhaktêty-ādi-paṭhântareṇa vyākhyānântaraṁ tu haribhadra-sūri-kṛtaṁ nêha prakāśyate, bahu-vyākhyāne vyāmoha-prasaṅgāt. anye tu vindhyavāsi-prabhṛtayaḥ:*

puruṣo 'vikṛtâtmâiva sva-nirbhāsam acetanam /
manaḥ karoti sānnidhyād upādhiḥ[k] *sphaṭikaṁ yathā //*[l]

iti bhogam ācakṣate. vyākhyā: yathôpādhir japā-puṣpa-padma-rāgâdir atad-rūpam api sphaṭikaṁ svâkārāṁ raktâdi[m]*-chāyāṁ karoty, evam ayam ātmā svarūpād*[n] *apracyavamānaḥ caitanyaṁ puruṣasya sva-rūpam*[o] *iti vacanād acetanam api mano* *buddhi-lakṣaṇam antaḥ-karaṇam sva-nirbhāsaṁ cetanam iva karoti, sānnidhyān, na punar vastuto manasaś caitanyaṁ*[p], *vikāritvāt. tathā hi: mano 'cetanam, vikāritvād, ghaṭavad iti.*

[a] C omits *prakṛti-°*: *°-vikārêty-ādi.* [b] C: *myāvasthā prakṛti-kāro.*

[c] C: *°-sannidhonād.*

[d] C: *°-abhinna-svabhāvârtha[ḥ] // pratibimbavatī.* H,V: *°-abhinnatva-bhāvârthapratibimbavatī.*

[e] SVM 15.69, p. 97.13: *°-saṅkrāntam artha-pratibimbakaṁ.* [f] H,V: *evaṁ.*

[g] I have failed to identify the source of the quotation. The statement is also quoted (and untraced) in SVM 15.69–70, p. 97.13–14.

[h] C: *vivikte īdṛk-pariṇatau.* Cf. SVM 15.72, p. 97.16: *vivikte dṛk-pariṇatau.*

[i] I have failed to identify the source of the quotation. The verse is also quoted (and untraced) in SVM 15.72–3, p. 97.16–17.

[j] A,C: *°-pariṇatayā.* [k] A: *upādhi*; C: *upādhiṁ.*

[l] I have failed to identify the source of the quotation. The verse is also quoted (and untraced) in SVM 15.75–6, p. 97.19–20. As a matter of fact, the whole preceding section (commencing with *vāda-mahârṇavo 'py asmin darśane*) is very similar to a passage found in SVM 15.69–76, p. 97.13–20:

> *vāda-mahârṇavo 'py aha*: "*buddhi-darpaṇa-saṅkrāntam artha-pratibimbakaṁ dvitīya-darpaṇa-kalpe puṁsy adhyārohati, tad eva bhoktṛtvam asya, na tu vikārâpattir*" *iti. tathā câsuriḥ*:
>
> *vivikte dṛk-pariṇatau buddhau bhogo 'sya kathyate /*
> *pratibimbôdayaḥ svacche yathā candra-maso 'mbhasi //*
>
> *vindhyavāsī tv evaṁ bhogam ācaṣṭe*:
>
> *puruṣo 'vikṛtâtmâiva sva-nirbhāsam acetanam /*
> *manaḥ karoti sānnidhyād upādhiḥ sphaṭikaṁ yathā //*

[m] A: *°-svâkārā-raktâdi-°.* [n] C: *sva svarūpād.*

[o] A: *puruṣasya svaṁ rūpam*; H,V: *svaṁ vacanam.* [p] C: *manasa-caitanyam.*

[860] Cf. NAṬ 31 *ad loc.*: ***andhêti.*** *andhôpalaḥ pratibimbôtpādanânarhaḥ khakkhaṭaḥ*[a] *pāṣāṇaḥ.*—'A non-translucent stone [means a stone] that is unable to bring about a mirrored reflection [like] a *khakkhaṭa* stone or a *pāṣāṇa* stone.'

[a] H,V: *khakhaṭaḥ.*

[861] The phrase *japā-kusumâdi-sannidhānād* is to be construed both with *andhôpalâdau ... anāvir-bhavantī* and with *tatra punar āvir-bhavantī.*

[862] The idea of inherence has been dealt critically with thrice in NAV. For the refutation of the concept of inherence in the 'syllogistic' context, cf. NAV 5: *mā bhūt tasya tādātmya-tad-utpattibhyāṁ gamakatvaṁ, samavāyād bhaviṣyati, tathâpi nânyathânupapannatvam eva hetor lakṣaṇam iti yadi vaiśeṣiko manyeta, so 'nyathā nirloṭhanīyaḥ. sa hi vikalpataḥ paryanuyojyaḥ: samavāyibhyaḥ samavāyo 'bhinno bhinno vā ... tan na samavāya-balāt gamakatāṁ praty āśā vidheyā, tasyâiva tatra*

duḥsthitatvāt. (p. 40 ff. of the English translation). For the refutation of the concept of inherence in the context of the multiplex nature of entities, cf. NAV 29: *tatrâiva teṣāṁ samavāyān nânyatra vartanta iti cet, nanu so 'pi samavāyo yady upakāryôpakāraka-bhāva-vyatirekeṇâpi bhavati, tataḥ sarvatrâviśeṣeṇa prasajyeta, tad-abhāvâviśeṣāt* ... (p. 85 ff. of the English translation). For the refutation of the concept of inherence in the context of the interrelation between the universal and the particular, cf. NAV 29: *kiṁ ca, atyanta-vyatireke sāmānya-viśeṣayoḥ vṛkṣaṁ chindhîti coditaḥ kim iti tad-viśeṣe palāśâdau chedaṁ vidhatte? tatra tasya samavāyād iti cen na, samavāya-grāhaka-pramāṇâbhāvāt* ... (p. 109 ff. of the English translation).

[863] See NA 22 as well as the discussion in NAV 5: *etena sâtmakaṁ jīvac-charīram, prāṇâdimattvāt, nirātmakatve tad-vaikalya-prasaṅgāt, ghaṭâdivad ity ayam api gamako vyākhyātaḥ, sādhyârthânyathânupapannatvasyâtrâpi sad-bhāvāt* ... *evaṁ para-parikalpitam anyad api liṅga-lakṣaṇaṁ yad gamakatâṅgaṁ tad anyathânupapannatvaṁ na vyabhicarati, sādhyaṁ vinâpy upapadyamānasya gamakatā-vaikalyād iti; atrâiva vyāpake liṅga-lakṣaṇe antar-bhāvanīyam, viparītaṁ tu nirasanīyam iti sthitam.* (pp. 40-41 of the English translation)

[864] Cf. NAṬ 31 *ad loc.*: ***tad-bādhakatvāt.*** *vyatireka-bādhakatvāt.*—'[The phrase] 'because ... subverts this' [means]: because ... subverts this difference [between the cogniser and acts of cognition].'

[865] An optional interpretation, that divides the sentence into two independent clauses, could be conceived as follows: *vijñānôdaya-samaye 'pi yādṛśaḥ prāg-avasthāyāṁ tādṛśa eva santiṣṭhamānaḥ, prāg apramātā paścāt pramātêti.*—'[The cognitive subject who] persists invariably is exactly of such a kind in the previous state as [he is] in the very instant of the rise of consciousness (*sc.* cognition); [being] previously a non-cogniser [becomes] subsequently the cogniser.'

[866] Cf. n. 102.

[867] Note the grammatically redundant use of the particle *hi* in the ablative clause indicating that such and similar clauses in the ablative were recognised as ordinary sentences.

[868] According to NAṬ 31 *ad loc.* the verb form *utkālayanti* means 'they give rise to [consciousness] as something additional': ***utkālayantîti.*** "*kala-pila-ḍipa-kṣepe*" *curādāva 'nadantaḥ*[a], *adhikī-kurvantîty*[b]*-arthaḥ.* See also a relevant note in SHRIYAN (1969: 318, § 1378): '**utkalitam** "boiled". [Gloss on *mūravia-* at MP.12 11 10; Cf. PSM ukkaliya- (D) = "*ublā huā*". Cf. M. *ukaḷ-ṇẽ*, *ukaḷ-vũ* = "to boil". In Skt. *ut+kal-* (*ud-* √*kal-*) is used in the sense of "to unbind, loosen". MW: *utkalita* = "unbound, loosened" (Bhāva Prakāśa), *utkālayati* = (L) = "drives out, expels" (Kātyāyani Sūtra) and *utkalita* (L) = "prosperous, rising, increasing" is different from the above. See ND: *uklanu* and *uklinu* = "to ascend, go up, climb". Turner connects it with **utkalati* and compares with Skt. *utkalita* "rising".].'

[a] H: *curādāvanadantaḥ*; V: *curādāvadantaḥ*; A marks with a stroke in the superscript (a typical separation mark of Ms. A) as two separate words, but marks no *avagraha*: *curādāva nadantaḥ*.

[b] C: °-*kurvantāty*-°.

[869] I take the compound *dṛṣṭa-vyavahāra*-° as *dvandva*; cf. n.435.

[870] If an event (e.g. the occurrence of consciousness in a physical body) can be explained without assuming hypothetical and often debatable entities (e.g. the alleged existence of a soul), by taking recourse to lesser number of assumptions and in the most economic way, there is not ground for assuming such hypothetical entities. The above dictum appears to be based on a principle akin to Occam's razor, *entia non sunt multiplicanda praeter necessitatem* ('entities are not to be multiplied without necessity'), a maxim ascribed to William of Ockham. As a matter of fact, an *expressis verbis* formulation of the maxim is absent from his extant works altogether. The idea, however, was already present in Duns Scotus' writings.

[871] For the expressions *bahir-mukha* and *antar-mukha*, cf. n.598.

[872] For the use of double negation implying strong affirmation, cf. n.662.

[873] Cf. NAṬ 31 *ad loc*.: ***taj-janêti***. *kāyâkāra-pariṇāma-janyā*.

[a] A: °-*janyāḥ*.

[874] Cf. NAṬ 31 *ad loc*.: ***tan-nirvartanêti***. *kāyâkāra-pariṇāmôtpādana-samarthā*.

[a] C: °- *samarthāḥ*.

[875] Cf. PSā 2.78:

te te kammatta-gadā poggala-kāyā puṇo vi jīvassa /
saṁjāyaṁte dehā dehaṁtara-saṁkamaṁ pappā //—

— 'All these material particles, that are transformed into *karman*, generate bodies of the living element, when [the living element] assumes a succession of other bodies (*sc*. when it transmigrates).'

See also PSā 2.94–95.

[876] Note the pun: *bhūtāni ... kiṁ-bhūtāni*.

[877] Cf. NAṬ 31 *ad loc*.: ***puruṣa***[a]***-śarīrêty-ādi***. *yathā puruṣa-śarīre yac caitanyaṁ tat svôtpattaye śarīra-janakeṣu bhūteṣu caitanyaṁ kalpayati tathā*. ***tatrāpîti***.[b] *teṣv api bhūteṣu tair bhūtaiḥ*[c] *saha vartate yac caitanyaṁ tad api sva-janakeṣu bhūteṣu tebhyo bhūtebhyo bhinnam ātma-hetum aparaṁ caitanyaṁ gamayatîti*.

[a] H: *puṣa*-°. [b] C,H,V: *kalpayati. tathā tatrāpîti*. [c] C: *tai bhūtai*.

[878] NAṬ *ad loc*.: ***tad-avasthêti***. *anavacchinna-caitanya-santānasya jīva-rūpatvād ity-abhiprāyaḥ*.—'The intention is as follows: because a personal series of uninterrupted consciousness consists in the living element.'

[879] The gerundive *sādhya* is used here in the sense of *janya* ('produced'), vide infra: *kāyâkāra-pariṇāma-janyaṁ* (p. 135). Cf. n.675.

[880] Siddharṣi-gaṇin quite consistently uses the expression *kiṁ ca* in the sense 'furthermore, moreover' and I have found no cases of the phrase in question when, hypothetically, *kim* would mark a question, whereas the particle *ca*—being used, as it were, separately of *kim*—would link a given sentence to a preceding one. Besides, in Siddharṣi-gaṇin's commentary, I have failed to notice any single instance where the interrogative pronoun *kiṁ* would initiate a sentence. Due to these reasons, the above sentence cannot be analysed syntactically as a question, as both the editors Bh. Harakhchand and P. L. Vaidya seem to have done by positioning a question mark at the end of the sentence, although the interrogative character of the sentence is clearly implied.

[881] Instead of interpreting the three clauses above as two correlatives related by *ca* and followed by a conclusion introduced by *tena* (in the sense of *tasmāt*), as I do above, we might—to my mind with much lesser plausibility, though, inasmuch as the participle *dr̥ṣṭāni* actually implies the act of perception—take *tena* to be a pronoun standing for *pratyakṣeṇa*, and the third clause would not be then related to the two preceding ones by any particle or pronoun: 'Gross elements, precisely as they are perceived by this [perception], has to be assumed as the cause of this [consciousness].'

[882] Cf. n.167.

[883] The purport of the argument is clear: since no desire is unprecedented, in order to account for the very first and singular desire of a suckling just after his birth, which is the impulse to be breast-fed, we have to assume, as Siddharṣi wants us to believe, a previous existence of the infant, which offers the ground for the continuity of the cause-and-effect chain of desires.

[884] Cf. n.102.

[885] In the original the singular is used ('this foundation…').

[886] It is a reference to the definition, number, domain and result of cognitive criteria mentioned on p.63.

[887] In the original the singular is used ('this foundation…').